MCAT®

Biology Review

The Staff of The Princeton Review

Random House, Inc. New York

The Princeton Review, Inc.
2315 Broadway
New York, NY 10024
E-mail: editorialsupport@review.com

ISBN: 978-0-375-42792-3
ISSN: 2150-8828

Editor: Selena Coppock
Production Coordinator: Mary Kinzel
Production Editor: Jennifer Graham

Printed in the United States of America

10   9   8   7

Editorial

Rob Franek, VP Test Prep Books, Publisher
Seamus Mullarkey, Editorial Director
Laura Braswell, Senior Editor
Rebecca Lessem, Senior Editor
Heather Brady, Editor
Selena Coppock, Editor

Production Services

Scott Harris, Executive Director, Production Services
Kim Howie, Senior Graphic Designer
Ryan Tozzi, Production Manager

Production Editorial

Meave Shelton, Production Editor
Jennifer Graham, Production Editor
Kristen O'Toole, Production Editor

Random House Publishing Group

Tom Russell, Publisher
Nicole Benhabib, Publishing Manager
Ellen L. Reed, Production Manager
Alison Stoltzfus, Associate Managing Editor
Elham Shabahat, Publishing Assistant

CONTRIBUTORS

Daniel J. Pallin, M.D.
 Senior Author
Judene Wright, M.S., M.A.Ed.
 Senior Author

TPR MCAT Biology Development Team:
Jessica Adams, M.S.
John Bahling, M.D.
Kristen Brunson, Ph.D.
Joshua Dilworth, M.D., Ph.D.
Chris Fortenbach, B.S.
Judene Wright, M.S., M.A.Ed., Senior Editor, Lead Developer
Sarah Woodruff, B.S., B.A.

Edited for Production by:
Judene Wright, M.S., M.A.Ed.
 National Content Director, MCAT Program, The Princeton Review

The TPR MCAT BiologyTeam and Judene would like to thank the following people for their contributions to this book :
Kashif Anwar, M.D., M.M.S., Phil Carpenter, Ph.D., Khawar Chaudry, B.S., Nita Chauhan, H.BSc, MSc, Dan Cho, M.P.H., Glenn E. Croston, Ph.D., Nathan Deal, M.D., Ian Denham, B.Sc., B.Ed., Annie Dude, Rob Fong, M.D., Ph.D., Kirsten Frank, Ph.D., Isabel L. Jackson, B.S., Erik Kildebeck, George Kyriazis, Ph.D., Ben Lee, Travis MacKoy, B.S., Joey Mancuso, M.S., D.O., Evan Martow, BMSc, Brian Mikolasko, M.D., M.BA, Abhisehk Mohapatra, B.A., Christopher Moriates, M.D., Stephen L. Nelson, Jr., Ph.D., Rupal Patel, B.S., Mary Qiu, Ina C. Roy, M.D., Jayson Sack, M.D., M.S., Will Sanderson, Jeanine Seitz-Partridge, M.S., Preston Swirnoff, Ph.D., M.S., Rhead Uddin, Jia Wang.

Periodic Table of the Elements

1 H 1.0																	2 He 4.0
3 Li 6.9	4 Be 9.0											5 B 10.8	6 C 12.0	7 N 14.0	8 O 16.0	9 F 19.0	10 Ne 20.2
11 Na 23.0	12 Mg 24.3											13 Al 27.0	14 Si 28.1	15 P 31.0	16 S 32.1	17 Cl 35.5	18 Ar 39.9
19 K 39.1	20 Ca 40.1	21 Sc 45.0	22 Ti 47.9	23 V 50.9	24 Cr 52.0	25 Mn 54.9	26 Fe 55.8	27 Co 58.9	28 Ni 58.7	29 Cu 63.5	30 Zn 65.4	31 Ga 69.7	32 Ge 72.6	33 As 74.9	34 Se 79.0	35 Br 79.9	36 Kr 83.8
37 Rb 85.5	38 Sr 87.6	39 Y 88.9	40 Zr 91.2	41 Nb 92.9	42 Mo 95.9	43 Tc (98)	44 Ru 101.1	45 Rh 102.9	46 Pd 106.4	47 Ag 107.9	48 Cd 112.4	49 In 114.8	50 Sn 118.7	51 Sb 121.8	52 Te 127.6	53 I 126.9	54 Xe 131.3
55 Cs 132.9	56 Ba 137.3	57 *La 138.9	72 Hf 178.5	73 Ta 180.9	74 W 183.9	75 Re 186.2	76 Os 190.2	77 Ir 192.2	78 Pt 195.1	79 Au 197.0	80 Hg 200.6	81 Tl 204.4	82 Pb 207.2	83 Bi 209.0	84 Po (209)	85 At (210)	86 Rn (222)
87 Fr (223)	88 Ra 226.0	89 †Ac 227.0	104 Rf (261)	105 Db (262)	106 Sg (266)	107 Bh (264)	108 Hs (277)	109 Mt (268)	110 Ds (281)	111 Rg (272)	112 Cn (285)		114 Uuq (289)		116 Uuh (289)		

	58 Ce 140.1	59 Pr 140.9	60 Nd 144.2	61 Pm (145)	62 Sm 150.4	63 Eu 152.0	64 Gd 157.3	65 Tb 158.9	66 Dy 162.5	67 Ho 164.9	68 Er 167.3	69 Tm 168.9	70 Yb 173.0	71 Lu 175.0
*Lanthanide Series:														
†Actinide Series:	90 Th 232.0	91 Pa (231)	92 U 238.0	93 Np (237)	94 Pu (244)	95 Am (243)	96 Cm (247)	97 Bk (247)	98 Cf (251)	99 Es (252)	100 Fm (257)	101 Md (258)	102 No (259)	103 Lr (260)

MCAT BIOLOGY CONTENTS

Chapter 1
MCAT Basics

SO YOU WANT TO BE A DOCTOR

So...you want to be a doctor. If you're like most premeds, you've wanted to be a doctor since you were pretty young. When people asked you what you wanted to be when you grew up, you always answered "a doctor." You had toy medical kits, bandaged up your dog or cat, and played "hospital." You probably read your parents' home medical guides for fun.

When you got to high school you took the honors and AP classes. You studied hard, got straight As (or at least really good grades!), and participated in extracurricular activities so you could get into a good college. And you succeeded!

At college you knew exactly what to do. You took your classes seriously, studied hard, and got a great GPA. You talked to your professors and hung out at office hours to get good letters of recommendation. You were a member of the premed society on campus, volunteered at hospitals, and shadowed doctors. All that's left to do now is get a good MCAT score.

Just the MCAT.

Just the most confidence-shattering, most demoralizing, longest, most brutal entrance exam for any graduate program. At 5 hours (including breaks), the MCAT tops the list... even the closest runners up, the LSAT and GMAT, are only about 4 hours long. The MCAT tests significant science content knowledge along with the ability to think quickly, reason logically, and read comprehensively, all under the pressure of a timed exam.

The path to a good MCAT score is not as easy to see as the path to a good GPA or the path to a good letter of recommendation. The MCAT is less about what you know, and more about how to apply what you know...and how to apply it quickly to new situations. Because the path might not be so clear, you might be worried. That's why you picked up this book.

We promise to demystify the MCAT for you, with clear descriptions of the different sections, how the test is scored, and what the test experience is like. We will help you understand general test-taking techniques as well as provide you with specific techniques for each section. We will review the science content you need to know as well as give you strategies for the Verbal Reasoning section. We'll show you the path to a good MCAT score and help you walk the path.

After all...you want to be a doctor. And we want you to succeed.

WHAT IS THE MCAT...REALLY?

Most test-takers approach the MCAT as though it were a typical college science test, one in which facts and knowledge simply need to be regurgitated in order to do well. They study for the MCAT the same way they did for their college tests, by memorizing facts and details, formulas and equations. And when they get to the MCAT they are surprised...and disappointed.

It's a myth that the MCAT is purely a content-knowledge test. If medical school admission committees want to see what you know, all they have to do is look at your transcripts. What they really want to see, though, is how you *think*. Especially, how you think under pressure. And *that's* what your MCAT score will tell them.

The MCAT is really a test of your ability to apply basic knowledge to different, possibly new, situations. It's a test of your ability to reason out and evaluate arguments. Do you still need to know your science content? Absolutely. But not at the level that most test-takers think they need to know it. Furthermore, your science knowledge won't help you on the Verbal Reasoning section. So how do you study for a test like this?

You study for the science sections by reviewing the basics and then applying them to MCAT practice questions. You study for the Verbal Reasoning section by learning how to adapt your existing reading and analytical skills to the nature of the test (more information about the Verbal Reasoning section can be found in the *MCAT Verbal Reasoning Review*).

The book you are holding will review all the relevant MCAT Biology content you will need for the test, and a little bit more. Plus, it includes hundreds of questions designed to make you think about the material in a deeper way, along with full explanations to clarify the logical thought process needed to get to the answer. It also comes with access to two full-length online practice exams and many more online practice passages to further hone your skills.

GO ONLINE!

In addition to the review material you'll find in this book, there is a wealth of practice content available online at **PrincetonReview.com/cracking**. There you'll find:

- 2 full-length practice MCATs
- Dozens of practice passages and questions covering every topic reviewed in this book
- Useful information about taking the MCAT and applying to medical school

To register your book, go to **PrincetonReview.com/cracking**. You'll see a welcome page where you can register your book by its ISBN number (found on the back cover above the barcode). Set up an account using this number and your email address, then you can access all of your online content.

MCAT NUTS AND BOLTS

Overview

The MCAT is a computer-based test (CBT) that is *not* adaptive. Adaptive tests base your next question on whether or not you've answered the current question correctly. The MCAT is *linear*, or *fixed-form*, meaning that the questions are in a predetermined order and do not change based on your answers. However, there are many versions of the test, so that on a given test day, different people will see different versions. The following table highlights the features of the MCAT exam.

Registration	Online via www.aamc.org. Begins as early as six months prior to test date; available up until week of test (subject to seat availability).
Testing Centers	Administered at small, secure, climate-controlled computer testing rooms.
Security	Photo ID with signature, electronic fingerprint, electronic signature verification, assigned seat.
Proctoring	None. Test administrator checks examinee in and assigns seat at computer. All testing instructions are given on the computer.
Frequency of Test	28 times per year distributed over January, March, April, May, June, July, August, and September.
Format	Exclusively computer-based. NOT an adaptive test.
Length of Test Day	5 hours.
Breaks	Optional 10-minute breaks between sections.
Number of Questions and Timing	52 Physical Sciences (PS), 70 minutes. 40 Verbal Reasoning (VR), 60 minutes. 52 Biological Sciences (BS), 70 minutes. 32 optional questions*, 45 minutes.
Scoring	Test is scaled. Several forms per administration. PS, VR, and BS receive scaled scores of 1–15.
Allowed/Not allowed	No timers/watches. No ear plugs. Noise reduction headphones available. Scratch paper and pencils given at start of test and taken at end of test. Locker or secure area provided for personal items.
Results: Timing and Delivery	Approximately 30 days. Electronic scores only, available online through AAMC login. Examinees can print official score reports.
Maximum Number of Retakes	Can be taken a maximum of three times per year, but an examinee can be registered for only one date at a time.

* Beginning in January 2013, the Writing Sample will be eliminated from the MCAT. Test takers will have the option of taking a voluntary unscored trial section including multiple-choice questions from introductory psychology, sociology, and biochemistry. The AAMC states that those who take the optional section and put forth a good faith effort will be compensated. This section will become required and scored in 2015.

Registration

Registration for the exam is completed online at www.aamc.org/students/mcat. The AAMC opens registration for a given test date at least two months in advance of the date, often earlier. It's a good idea to register well in advance of your desired test date to make sure that you get a seat.

Sections

There are four sections on the MCAT exam: Physical Sciences (PS), Verbal Reasoning (VR), Biological Sciences (BS), and an optional psychology/sociology and biochemistry section. All sections consist of multiple-choice questions.

Section	Concepts Tested	Number of Questions and Timing
Physical Sciences	Basic concepts in physics and general chemistry, data analysis, basic non-calculus math, critical reasoning skills.	52 questions, 70 minutes, approximately 50% physics and 50% general chemistry.
Verbal Reasoning	Reading comprehension and critical thinking.	40 questions, 60 minutes.
Biological Sciences	Basic concepts in biology and organic chemistry, data analysis, critical reasoning skills.	52 questions, 70 minutes, approximately 80% biology and 20% organic chemistry.
Voluntary Unscored Trial Section	Basic concepts in psychology, sociology, and biochemistry.	32 questions, 45 minutes.

Most questions on the MCAT (39 out of 52 on the science sections, all 40 in the VR section) are **passage-based**, and each section of the test will have a total of seven passages. A passage consists of a few paragraphs of information on which several following questions are based. In the science sections, passages often include equations or reactions, tables, graphs, figures, and experiments to analyze. Verbal Reasoning passages come from literature in the social sciences, humanities, and natural sciences and do not test content knowledge in any way.

Some questions in the science sections are *freestanding questions* (FSQs). These questions are independent of any passage information. These questions appear in three groups of between 3 and 5 questions, and are interspersed throughout the passages. There are 13 freestanding questions in each of the science sections and the remaining 39 questions are passage-based.

Each section on the MCAT is separated by a 10-minute break:

Section	Time
Test Center Check-In	Variable, can take up to 40 minutes if center is busy.
Tutorial	10 minutes
Physical Sciences	70 minutes
Break	10 minutes
Verbal Reasoning	60 minutes
Break	10 minutes
Biological Sciences	70 minutes
Break	10 minutes
Voluntary Unscored Trial Section	45 minutes
Void Option	5 minutes
Survey	10 minutes

The survey includes questions about your satisfaction with the overall MCAT experience, including registration, check-in, etc., as well as questions about how you prepared for the test.

Scoring

The MCAT is a scaled exam, meaning that your raw score will be converted into a scaled score that takes into account the difficulty of the questions. There is no guessing penalty. The PS, VR, and BS sections are scaled from 1–15. Because different versions of the test have varying levels of difficulty, the scale will be different from one exam to the next. Thus, there is no "magic number" of questions to get right in order to get a particular score. Plus, some of the questions on the test are considered "experimental" and do not count toward your score; they are just there to be evaluated for possible future inclusion in a test.

At the end of the test, you will be asked to choose one of the following two options, "I wish to have my MCAT exam scored" or "I wish to VOID my MCAT exam." You have five minutes to make a decision, and if you do not select one of the options in that time, the test will automatically be scored. If you choose the VOID option, your test will not be scored (you will not now, or ever, get a numerical score for this test), medical schools will not know you took the test, and no refunds will be granted. You cannot "unvoid" your scores at a later time.

Even though we can't tell you a specific number of questions to get right in order to receive a particular score, we can tell you the percentile numbers that the scores correspond with. The percentile numbers tell you what percent of examinees scored lower or higher than you. For example, if you are in the 90th percentile, then 90 percent of examinees scored lower than you did, and 10 percent scored higher.

Score	Physical Sciences Percentile*	Verbal Reasoning Percentile*	Biological Sciences Percentile*
14–15	100%	100%	100%
13	97%	99%	97%
12	91%	96%	92%
11	82%	91%	80%
10	69%	75%	64%
9	52%	53%	41%
8	37%	35%	23%
7	22%	22%	12%
6	11%	14%	7%
5	4%	7%	4%
4	2%	4%	2%
3	1%	2%	1%
2	0%	1%	0%
1	0%	0%	0%
	Avg score 9.3, std dev 2.3	Avg score 9.0, std dev 2.3	Avg score 9.8, std dev 2.1

*Data from *The Official Guide to the MCAT Exam*, 2009 ed., © 2009 Association of American Medical Colleges

So, what's a good score? Most people would agree that since the average total score on the MCAT is around 28, you want to at least hit that number. To be competitive, you really want scores in the low 30s, and for the top-ranked medical schools, you'll want scores in the high 30s to low 40s. If your GPA is on the low side, you'll need higher MCAT scores to compensate, and if you have a strong GPA, you can get away with lower MCAT scores. But the reality is that your chances of acceptance depend on a lot more than just your MCAT scores. It's a combination of your GPA, your MCAT scores, your undergraduate coursework, letters of recommendation, experience related to the medical field (such as volunteer work or research), extracurricular activities, your personal statement, etc. Medical schools are looking for a complete package, not just good scores and a good GPA.

GENERAL TEST-TAKING STRATEGIES

CBT Tools

There are a number of tools available on the test, including highlighting, strike-outs, the Mark button, the Review button, the Exhibit button, and of course, scratch paper. The following is a brief description of each tool.

1) **Highlighting:** This is done in passage text (including table entries and some equations, but excluding figures and molecular structures) by clicking and dragging the cursor over the desired text. To remove the highlighted portion, just click over the highlighted text. Note that highlights DO NOT persist once you leave the passage.

2) **Strike-outs:** This is done on the various answer choices by clicking over the answer choice that you wish to eliminate. As a result, the entire set of text associated with that answer choice is crossed out. The strike-out can be removed by clicking again. Note that you cannot strike-out figures or molecular structures, and strike-outs DO persist after leaving the passage.

3) **Mark button:** This is available for each question and allows you to flag the question as one you would like to review later if time permits. When clicked, the "Mark" button turns red and says "Marked."

4) **Review button:** This button is found near the bottom of the screen, and when clicked, brings up a new screen showing all questions and their status (either "answered," "unanswered," or "marked"). You can then choose one of three options: "review all," "review unanswered," or "review marked." You can only review questions in the section of the MCAT you are currently taking, but this button can be clicked at any time during the allotted time for that section; you do NOT have to wait until the end of the section to click it.

5) **Exhibit button:** Clicking this button will open a periodic table. Note that the periodic table is originally large, covering most of the screen. However, this window can be resized to see the questions and a portion of the periodic table at the same time. The table text will not decrease, but scroll bars will appear on the window so you can center the section of the table of interest in the window.

6) **Scratch paper:** You will be given four pages (8 faces) of scratch paper at the start of the test. While you may ask for more at any point during the test, your first set of paper will be collected before you receive fresh paper. Scratch paper is only useful if it is kept organized; do not give in to the tendency to write on the first available open space! Good organization will be very helpful when/if you wish to review a question. Indicate the passage number in a box near the top of your scratch work, and indicate which question you are working on in a circle to the left of the notes for that question. Draw a line under your scratch work when you change passages to keep the work separate. Do not erase or scribble over any previous work. If you do not think it is correct, draw one line through the work and start again. You may have already done some useful work without realizing it.

Pacing

Since the MCAT is a timed test, you must keep an eye on the timer and adjust your pacing as necessary. It would be terrible to run out of time at the end to discover that the last few questions could have been easily answered in just a few seconds each.

If you complete every question, in the science sections you will have about one minute and twenty seconds (1:20) per question, and in the Verbal Reasoning section you will have about one minute and 30 seconds per question (1:30).

Section	# of Questions in passage	Approximate time (including reading the passage)
Physical Sciences and Biological Sciences	5	6.5–7 minutes
	6	8 minutes
	7	9–9.5 minutes
Verbal Reasoning	5	7.5 minutes
	6	9 minutes
	7	10.5 minutes

When starting a passage in the science sections, make note of how much time you will allot for it, and the starting time on the timer. Jot down on your scratch paper what the timer should say at the end of the passage. Then just keep an eye on it as you work through the questions. If you are near the end of the time for that passage, guess on any remaining questions, make some notes on your scratch paper (remember that highlighting disappears), Mark the questions, and move on. Come back to those questions if you have time.

For Verbal Reasoning, one important thing to keep in mind is that most people will maximize their score by *not* trying to complete every question, or every passage, in the section. A good strategy for a majority of test takers is to complete six of the seven passages, randomly guessing on one passage. This allows you to have good accuracy on the passages you complete, and to maximize your total percent correct in the section as a whole. To complete six of the passages, you should spend about 8 minutes on a five-question passage, 9 minutes on a six-question passage, and 10 minutes on a seven-question passage. That is, a total of about 3 minutes plus 1 minute for each question ("# of Q + 3").

To help maximize your number of correct answer choices in any section, do the questions and passages within that section in the order *you* want to do them in. Skip over the more difficult questions (guess and Mark them), and answer the questions you feel most comfortable with first.

Process of Elimination

Process of elimination (POE) is probably the most useful technique you have to tackle MCAT questions. Since there is no guessing penalty, POE allows you to increase your probability of choosing the correct answer by eliminating those you are sure are wrong. If you are guessing between a couple of choices, use the CBT tools to your advantage:

1) Strike out any choices that you are sure are incorrect or do not answer the issue addressed in the question.
2) Jot down some notes on your scratch paper to help clarify your thoughts if you return to the question.
3) Use the "Mark" button to flag the question for review at a later time. (Note, however, that in the Verbal Reasoning section, you generally should not be returning to rethink questions once you have moved on to a new passage.)
4) Do not leave it blank! If you are not sure and you have already spent more than 60 seconds on that question, just pick one of the remaining choices. If you have time to review it at the end, you can always debate the remaining choices based on your previous notes.
5) Special Note: if three of the four answer choices have been eliminated, the remaining choice must be the correct answer. Don't waste time pondering *why* it is correct, just click it and move on. The MCAT doesn't care if you truly understand why it's the right answer, only that you have the right answer selected.

Guessing

Remember, there is NO guessing penalty on the MCAT. NEVER leave a question blank!

SECTION SPECIFICS

Question Types

In the science sections of the MCAT, the questions fall into one of three main categories.

1) Memory questions: These questions can be answered directly from prior knowledge and represent about 25 percent of the total number of questions.

2) Explicit questions: These questions are those for which the answer is explicitly stated in the passage. To answer them correctly, for example, may just require finding a definition, or reading a graph, or making a simple connection. Explicit questions represent about 35 percent of the total number of questions.

3) Implicit questions: These questions require you to apply knowledge to a new situation; the answer is typically implied by the information in the passage. These questions often start "if…. then…." (for example, "if we modify the experiment in the passage like this, then what result would we expect?"). Implicit style questions make up about 40 percent of the total number of questions.

In the Verbal Reasoning section, the questions also fall into three main categories:

1) Specific questions: These questions ask you for specific information from the passage, such as a fact (retrieval question), an inference ("which of the following is best supported by the passage?"), or a definition (vocabulary-in-context question).

2) General questions: These questions ask you to summarize themes (main idea and primary purpose questions) or evaluate an author's opinion (tone/attitude questions).

3) Complex questions: These are typically more difficult questions that can ask you to do a number of different things. Generally, Complex questions will ask you to do one of the following: consider how the author constructs his/her argument (structure questions), decide how or how well the author supports his/her argument (evaluate questions), decide which answer most supports or undermines the author's argument (strengthen/weaken questions), evaluate how new facts or scenarios relate to or affect the author's points (new information questions), or apply the author's argument to a new situation (analogy questions).

Remember that for all sections, you should do the questions in the order you want to. In the science sections, it's wise to do all the FSQs first since they are often quick memory questions, and then tackle the passages. Start with the subject you feel the most comfortable with, and then come back to the other subject. This helps keep your brain focused on a single subject at a time, instead of jumping, for example, between biology and organic chemistry randomly. Do the passages within a section in the order that you feel most comfortable with, and within the passages themselves, tackle the easier questions first, leaving the most time consuming ones for last.

In the Verbal Reasoning section, it is best to do the Specific questions within a passage first, then the General questions (after you have learned more about the passage by answering the Specific questions) and to leave the Complex questions (which tend to be more difficult) until the end of the set. For the section as a whole, answer the questions for the easier passages in your first "pass" through the section, and then come back for a second pass, completing some of the more difficult passages.

BIOLOGY ON THE MCAT

Biology is the most comprehensive of all the subjects on the MCAT. Not only is the amount of material you should know fairly extensive, the potential topics for passages are virtually limitless. It's often helpful to skim the passage first, highlighting a few facts and mapping out the general ideas, before moving to the questions.

How to Map the Passage and Use Scratch Paper

1) The passage should not be read like textbook material, with the intent of learning something from every sentence (science majors especially will be tempted to read this way). Passages should be read to get a feel for the type of questions that will follow, and to get a general idea of the location of information within the passage.

2) Highlighting—Use this tool sparingly, or you will end up with a passage that is completely covered in yellow highlighter! Keep in mind that highlighting does not persist as you move from passage to passage within the section. If you want to make more permanent notes, use the scratch paper. Highlighting in a Biology passage should be used to draw attention to a few words that demonstrate one of the following:
   - The main theme of a paragraph
   - An unusual or unfamiliar term that is defined specifically for that passage (e.g., something that is italicized)
   - Statements that either support the main theme or counteract the main theme
   - List topics (see below)

3) Pay brief attention to equations, figures, and experiments, noting only what information they deal with. Do not spend a lot of time analyzing at this point.

4) For each paragraph, note "P1," "P2," etc. on the scratch paper and jot down a few notes about that paragraph. Try to translate biology-speak into your own words using everyday language. Especially note down simple relationships (e.g., the relationship between two variables).

5) Lists—Whenever a list appears in paragraph form, jot down on the scratch paper the paragraph and the general topic of the list. It will make returning to the passage more efficient and help to organize your thoughts.

6) Scratch paper is only useful if it is kept organized! Make sure that your notes for each passage are clearly delineated and marked with the passage number. This will allow you to easily read your notes when you come back to a review a marked question. Resist the temptation to write in the first available blank space as this makes it much more difficult to refer back to your work.

Biology Question Strategies

1) Remember that Process of Elimination is paramount! The strikeout tool allows you to eliminate answer choices; this will improve your chances of guessing the correct answer if you are unable to narrow it down to one choice.

2) Answer the straightforward questions first. Leave questions that require analysis of experiments and graphs for later.

3) Make sure that the answer you choose actually answers the question, and isn't just a true statement.

4) Try to avoid answer choices with extreme words such as "always," "never," etc. In biology, there is almost always an exception and answers are rarely black-and-white.

5) I-II-III questions: always work between the I-II-III statements and the answer choices. Unfortunately, it is not possible to strike out the Roman numerals, but this is a great use for scratch paper notes. Once a statement is determined to be true (or false) strike out answer choices which do not contain (or do contain) that statement.

6) LEAST/EXCEPT/NOT questions: Don't get tricked by these questions that ask you to pick that answer that doesn't fit (the incorrect or false statement). It's often good to use your scratch paper and write a T or F next to answer choices A–D. The one that stands out as different is the correct answer!

7) Again, don't leave any question blank.

A Note About Flashcards

Contrary to popular belief, flashcards are NOT the best way to study for the MCAT. For most of the exams you've taken previously, flashcards were probably helpful. This was because those exams mostly required you to regurgitate information, and flashcards are pretty good at helping you memorize facts. Remember, however, that the most challenging aspect of the MCAT is not that it requires you to memorize the fine details of content-knowledge, but that it requires you to apply your basic scientific knowledge to unfamiliar situations. Flashcards won't help you do that.

There is only one situation in which flashcards can be beneficial, and that's if your basic content knowledge is deficient in some area. For example, if you don't know the hormones and their effects in the body, flashcards can help you memorize these facts. Or, maybe you are unsure of some of the organic chemistry functional groups you need to know; flashcards can help you solidify that knowledge. You might find it useful to make flashcards to help you learn and recognize the different question types or the common types of wrong answers for the Verbal Reasoning section. (And remember that part of what makes flashcards useful is the fact that *you make them yourself*. Not only are they then customized for your personal areas of weakness, the very act of writing information down on a flashcard helps stick that information in your brain.) But other than straight, basic fact-memorization in your personal weak areas, you are better off doing and analyzing practice passages than carrying around a stack of flashcards.

TEST DAY TIPS

On the day of the test, you'll want to arrive at the test center about ½ hour prior to the starting time of your test. Examinees will be checked in in the order they arrive at the center. You will be assigned a locker or secure area in which to put your personal items. Textbooks and study notes are not allowed, so there is no need to bring them with you to the test center. Nothing is allowed at the computer station except your photo identification, not even your watch. Your ID will be checked, a digital image of your fingerprint will be taken, and you will be asked to sign in. You will be given scratch paper and a couple of pencils, and the test center administrator will take you to the computer on which you will complete the test. (Note that if there is a white-board and erasable marker is provided, you can specifically request for scratch paper at the start of the test.) You may not choose a computer; you must use the computer assigned to you.

If you choose to leave the testing room at the breaks, you will have your fingerprint checked again, and you will have to sign in and out. You are allowed to access the items in your locker except for notes and cell phones. At the end of the test, the test administrator will collect your scratch paper and shred it.

General Test Day Tips

- Take a trip to the test center a day or two before your actual test date so that you can easily find the building and room on test day. This will also allow you to gauge traffic, and see if you need money for parking or anything like that. Knowing this type of information ahead of time will greatly reduce your stress on the day of your test.
- Don't do any heavy studying the day before the test. Try to get a good amount of sleep on the days leading up to the test.
- Eat well. Try to avoid excessive caffeine and sugar. Ideally, in the weeks leading up to the actual test you should experiment a little bit with foods and practice tests to see which foods give you the most endurance. Aim for steady blood sugar levels; sports drinks, peanut-butter crackers, trail mix, etc. make good snacks for your breaks.
- Definitely take the breaks! Get up and walk around. It's a good way to clear your head between sections and get the blood (and oxygen!) flowing to your brain.
- Ask for new scratch paper at the breaks if you use it all up.

Chapter 2
Biochemistry and Cellular Respiration

The notion of life refers to both the activities and the physical structures of living organisms. [Check out *MCAT Organic Chemistry Review* for a review of the fundamental molecules of life and how molecules are used to store energy and to form physical structures.] Both the storage/utilization of energy and the synthesis of structures depend on a large number of chemical reactions that occur within each cell. Fortunately, these reactions do not proceed on their own spontaneously, without regulation. If they did, each cell's energy would rapidly dissipate and total disorder would result. Most reactions are slowed by a large barrier known as the activation energy (E_a), discussed below. The E_a is a bottleneck in a reaction, like a nearly closed gate. The role of the enzyme is to open this chemical gate. In this sense, the enzyme is like a switch. When the enzyme is on, the gate is open (low E_a), and the reaction accelerates. When the enzyme is off, the gate closes and the reaction slows. Before we can see how enzymes work, we must digress a bit to review the basics of thermodynamics.

2.1 THERMODYNAMICS

Thermodynamics is the study of the energetics of chemical reactions. There are two relevant forms of energy in chemistry: heat energy (movement of molecules) and potential energy (energy stored in chemical bonds). [What is the most important potential energy storage molecule in all cells?[1]] The **first law of thermodynamics,** also known as the **law of conservation of energy,** states that the energy of the universe is constant. It implies that when the energy of a system *decreases,* the energy of the rest of the universe (the **surroundings**) must *increase,* and vice versa. The **second law of thermodynamics** states that the disorder, or **entropy,** of the universe tends to increase. Another way to state the second law is as follows: Spontaneous reactions tend to increase the disorder of the universe. The symbol for entropy is S, and "a change in entropy" is denoted ΔS, where $\Delta S = S_{after} - S_{before}$. [If the ΔS of a system is negative, has the disorder of that system increased or decreased?[2]]

A practical way to discuss thermodynamics is the mathematical notion of **free energy** (**Gibbs free energy**), defined by Josiah Gibbs as follows:[3]

$$\text{Eq. 1} \quad \Delta G = \Delta H - T\Delta S$$

T denotes temperature, and H denotes **enthalpy,** which is defined by another equation:

$$\text{Eq. 2} \quad \Delta H = \Delta E - P\Delta V$$

Here E represents the bond energy of products or reactants in a system, P is pressure, and V is volume. [Given that cellular reactions take place in the liquid phase, how is H related to E in a cell?[4]] ΔG increases with increasing ΔH (bond energy) and decreases with increasing entropy.

- Given the second law of thermodynamics and the mathematical definition of ΔG, which reaction will be favorable: one with a decrease in free energy ($\Delta G < 0$) or one with an increase in free energy ($\Delta G > 0$)?[5]

The change in the Gibbs free energy of a reaction determines whether the reaction is favorable (**spontaneous,** ΔG negative) or unfavorable (**nonspontaneous,** ΔG positive). In terms of the generic reaction

$$A + B \rightarrow C + D$$

the Gibbs free energy change determines whether the reactants (denoted A and B) will stay as they are or be converted to products (C and D).

---

[1] ATP, which stores energy in the ester bonds between its phosphate groups.

[2] If ΔS is negative, then the system lost entropy, which means that disorder decreased.

[3] As in ΔS, the Greek letter Δ (delta) indicates "the change in." For example, $\Delta G_{rxn} = G_{products} - G_{reactants}$.

[4] $H \approx E$, since the change in volume is negligible ($\Delta V \approx 0$).

[5] Favorable reactions have $\Delta G < 0$. We can deduce this from the second law and Equation 1 because the second law states that increasing entropy is favorable, and the equation has ΔG directly related to $-T\Delta S$.

Spontaneous reactions, ones that occur without a net addition of energy, have $\Delta G < 0$. They occur with energy to spare. Reactions with a negative ΔG are **exergonic** (energy *exits* the system); reactions with a positive ΔG are **endergonic**. Endergonic reactions only occur if energy is added. In the lab, energy is added in the form of heat; in the body, endergonic reactions are driven by reaction coupling to exergonic reactions (more on this later). Reactions with a negative ΔH are called **exothermic** and liberate heat. Most metabolic reactions are exothermic (which is how homeothermic organisms such as mammals maintain a constant body temperature). Reactions with a positive ΔH require an input of heat and are referred to as **endothermic**. (Thermodynamics will be discussed in more detail in *MCAT General Chemistry Review*.)

The signs of thermodynamic quantities are assigned from the point of view of *the system*, not the surroundings or the universe. Thus, a negative ΔG means that the system goes to a lower free energy state, and a system will always move in the direction of the lowest free energy. As an analogy, visualize a spinning top as the system. What happens to the top? Does it spin faster and faster? No. It moves towards the lowest energy state. Let's expand the analogy, using an equation:

$$\text{motionless top} \;\rightarrow\; \text{spinning top}$$

Here the "reactant" is the motionless top, and the "product" is the spinning top. Which is lower: the free energy of product or reactant? The reactant. Is the reaction "spontaneous" as written? No; in fact, the reverse reaction is spontaneous. Hence,

$$G_{\text{spinning}} > G_{\text{motionless}}$$

and thus,

$$G_{\text{reaction as written (motionless to spinning; left to right)}} > 0$$

So the reaction is nonspontaneous. In other words, *it requires energy input*, namely, energy from your muscles as you spin the top. [If the products in a reaction have more entropy than the reactants, and the enthalpy (H) of the reactants and the products are the same, can the reaction occur spontaneously?[6]]

The value of ΔG depends on the concentrations of reactants and products, which can be variable in the body. Therefore, to compare reactions, biochemists calculate a standard free energy change, denoted $\Delta G°$, with all reactants and products present at $1\ M$ concentration. Furthermore, the biochemist's standardized ΔG determined at pH 7 is denoted $\Delta G°'$.

$\Delta G°'$ is related to the equilibrium constant for a reaction by the following equation:

Eq. 3 $\quad \Delta G°' = -RT \ln K'_{eq}$

where R is the gas constant (which would be given on the MCAT, along with the entire equation), and K'_{eq} is the ratio of products to reactants at equilibrium:

$$K'_{eq} = \frac{[\text{C}]_{eq}[\text{D}]_{eq}}{[\text{A}]_{eq}[\text{B}]_{eq}}$$

---

[6] Yes. If $\Delta S > 0$ and $\Delta H = 0$, then according to the second law of thermodynamics, the reaction is spontaneous; see Equation 1.

K'_{eq} is the ratio of products to reactants when enough time has passed for equilibrium to be reached [When $K'_{eq} = 1$, what is $\Delta G^{o\prime}$?[7]]

But what if we wanted to calculate ΔG for a reaction in the body? In this case, we need one more equation:

$$\text{Eq. 4} \quad \Delta G = \Delta G^{o\prime} + RT \ln K, \text{ where } K = \frac{[C][D]}{[A][B]}$$

Here, K is calculated using the actual concentrations of A, B, C, and D (for example, the concentrations in the cell). Equation 4 is simply a conversion from $\Delta G^{o\prime}$ (the laboratory standard ΔG with initial concentrations at 1 M) to the real-life here-and-now ΔG. Note that if we put 1 M concentrations of A, B, C, and D into a beaker (at pH 7), we have recreated the laboratory standard initial set-up: $K = 1$, so $\ln K = 0$, which means $\Delta G = \Delta G^{o\prime}$.

- You are studying a particular reaction. You find the reaction in a book and read $\Delta G^{o\prime}$ from a table. Can you calculate ΔG for this reaction in a living human being without any more information?[8]

Remember that K and K_{eq} are not the same. K is the ratio of products to reactants in any given set-up; K_{eq} is the ratio *at equilibrium*. **Equilibrium** is defined as the point where the rate of reaction in one direction equals the rate of reaction in the other. At equilibrium, there is constant product and reactant turnover as reactants form products and vice versa, but overall concentrations stay the same. Theoretically (given enough time), all reactant/product systems will eventually reach this point.

- How can ΔG be negative if $\Delta G^{o\prime}$ is positive (which indicates that the reaction is unfavorable at standard conditions)?[9]
- Does K_{eq} indicate the rate at which a reaction will proceed?[10]
- When K_{eq} is large, which has lower free energy: products or reactants?[11]
- When K is large, which has lower free energy: products or reactants?[12]

---

[7] Equation 3 says that $\Delta G^{o\prime} = 0$ when $K'_{eq} = 1$ since $\ln 1 = 0$. Note: for more information about MCAT Math, see *MCAT Physics and Math Review*.

[8] No. You need to know the concentrations of A, B, C, and D in the human cell. For example $\Delta G^{o\prime}$ might be +14.8 kcal/mol, indicating that the reaction is very unfavorable under standard conditions. But, if the concentration of reactants is much higher than the concentration of products in the cell, the reaction may be favorable in the cell since $K < 1$ and ΔG may be less than zero. (Although ΔG could still be positive if $\Delta G^{o\prime}$ is very large.) The significance of K as an independent variable in Equation 4 is that it accounts for Le Châtelier's principle: A high concentration of reactants will drive a reaction forward and a high concentration of products will drive it backward, regardless of the intrinsic thermodynamics ($\Delta G^{o\prime}$) of the reaction.

[9] The reaction may be favorable ($\Delta G < 0$) if the ratio of the concentrations of reactants to products is sufficiently large to drive the reaction forward (that is, if RT $\ln K$ is more negative than $\Delta G^{o\prime}$ is positive, which would make their sum (which, by Equation 4, is ΔG) negative).

[10] K_{eq} indicates only the relative concentrations of reagents once equilibrium is reached, not the reaction rate (how fast equilibrium is reached).

[11] A large K_{eq} means that more products are present at equilibrium. Remember that equilibrium tends towards the lowest energy state. Hence, when K_{eq} is large, products have lower free energy than reactants.

[12] The size of K says nothing about the properties of the reactants and products. K is calculated from whatever the initial concentrations happen to be. It is K_{eq} that says something about the nature of reactants and products, since it describes their concentrations after equilibrium has been reached.

- Which direction, forward or backward, will be favored in a reaction if $\Delta G = 0$? (*Hint*: What does Equation 4 look like when $\Delta G = 0$?)[13]
- Radiolabeled chemicals are often used to trace constituents in biochemical reactions. The following reaction with $\Delta G = 0$ is in aqueous solution:

$$A \rightleftharpoons B + C, \quad K_{eq} = \frac{[B][C]}{[A]}$$

A small amount of radiolabeled B is added to the solution. After a period of time, where will the radiolabel most likely be found: in A, in B, or in both?[14]

In summary, then, there are two factors that determine whether a reaction will occur spontaneously (ΔG negative) in the cell:

1) The intrinsic properties of the reactants and products ($\Delta G^{\circ\prime}$)
2) The concentrations of reactants and products ($RT \ln K$)

(In the lab there is third factor: temperature. If $\ln K$ is negative and the temperature is high enough, ΔG will be negative, regardless of the value of $\Delta G^{\circ\prime}$.)

Thermodynamics vs. Reaction Rates

The term *spontaneous* is used to describe a reaction system with $\Delta G < 0$. This can be misleading, since the common usage of the word *spontaneous* has a connotation of *rapid rate*; this is not what spontaneous means in the context of chemical reactions. For example, many reactions have a negative ΔG, indicating that they are "spontaneous" from a thermodynamic point of view, but they do not necessarily occur at a significant rate. Spontaneous means that a reaction may proceed without additional energy input, *but it says nothing about the rate of reaction.*

Thermodynamics will tell you where a system starts and finishes but nothing about the path traveled to get there. The difference in free energy in a reaction is only a function of the nature of the reactants and products. Thus, ΔG does not depend on the pathway a reaction takes or the rate of reaction; it is only a measurement of the difference in free energy between reactants and products.

- How does the ΔG for a reaction burning (oxidizing) sugar in a furnace compare to the ΔG when sugar is broken down (oxidized) in a human?[15]

---

[13] If ΔG is 0, then neither the forward nor the reverse reaction is favored. Look at Equations 3 and 4. Note that when $\Delta G = 0$, Equation 4 reduces to Equation 3, and thus $K = K_{eq}$ (which means K at this moment is the same as K_{eq}, measured after the reaction system is allowed to reach equilibrium). When $K = K_{eq}$, we are by definition at equilibrium. Understand and memorize the following: When $\Delta G = 0$, you are at equilibrium; forward reaction equals back reaction, and the net concentrations of reactants and products do not change.

[14] The reaction is in dynamic equilibrium where reactions are occurring in both directions, but at an equal rate. Because $\Delta G = 0$, we know that the forward reaction and the reverse reaction proceed at equal rates, even though we don't know the actual value. Therefore, after a period of time, the radiolabel will be present in both A and B.

[15] The ΔG is the same in both cases. ΔG does not depend on the pathway, only on the different energies of the reactants and products.

2.2 KINETICS AND ACTIVATION ENERGY (E_A)

The reason some spontaneous (i.e., *themodynamically favorable*) reactions proceed very slowly or not at all is that a large amount of energy is required to get them going. For example, the burning of wood is spontaneous, but you can stare at a log all day and it won't burn. Some energy (heat) must be provided to kick-start the process.

The study of reaction rates is called **chemical kinetics**. All reactions proceed through a transient intermediate that is unstable and takes a great deal of energy to produce. The energy required to produce the transient intermediate is called the **activation energy** (E_a). This is the barrier that prevents many reactions from proceeding even though the ΔG for the reaction may be negative. The match you use to light your fireplace provides the activation energy for the reaction known as burning. It is the activation energy barrier that determines the kinetics of a reaction. [How would the rate of a spontaneous reaction be affected if the activation energy were lowered?[16]]

The concept of E_a is key to understanding the role of enzymes, so let's spend some time on it. To illustrate, take this reaction:

$$Bob_{without\ a\ job} + job \rightarrow Bob_{with\ a\ job}$$

Is this a favorable reaction, i.e., will the universe be better off, with less total (nervous) energy, if Bob gets the job? Will things settle down? Let's assume yes. However, between the two states (without/with) there is an intermediate state, namely, $Bob_{applying\ for\ job}$. So the reaction will look this way:

$$Bob_{without\ a\ job} + job \rightarrow [Bob_{applying\ for\ job}]\ddagger \rightarrow Bob_{with\ a\ job}$$

The middle term is the **transition state** (TS), traditionally written in square brackets with a double-cross symbol: [TS]‡. It exists for a very, very short time, either moving forward to form product or breaking back down into reactants. The energy required for Bob to be job hunting is much higher than the energy of Bob with a job *or* Bob without a job. As a result, he may not go job hunting, even though he'd be happier in the long run if he did. In this model, we can describe the E_a as the energy necessary to get Bob to apply for a job.

A **catalyst** lowers the E_a of a reaction *without changing the ΔG*. The catalyst lowers the E_a by *stabilizing the transition state*, making its existence less thermodynamically unfavorable. The second important characteristic of a catalyst is that it is not consumed in the reaction; it is *regenerated* with each reaction cycle.

In our model, an example of a catalyst would be a career planning service (CPS). Adding a CPS won't make $Bob_{without\ a\ job}$ any happier or sadder, nor will it make $Bob_{with\ a\ job}$ happier or sadder. But it will make it much easier for Bob to move between the two states: without a job vs. with a job. The traditional way to represent a reaction system like this is using a *reaction coordinate* graph, as shown in Figure 1. This is just a way to look at the energy of the reaction system as compared to the three possible states of the system: 1) reactants, 2) [TS]‡, and 3) products. The x axis plots the physical progress of the reaction system (the "reaction coordinate"), and the y axis plots energy.

---

[16] The rate would be increased, since lowering E_a is tantamount to reducing the energy required to achieve the transition state. The more transition state intermediates that are formed, the greater the amount of product produced, i.e., the more rapid the rate of reaction.

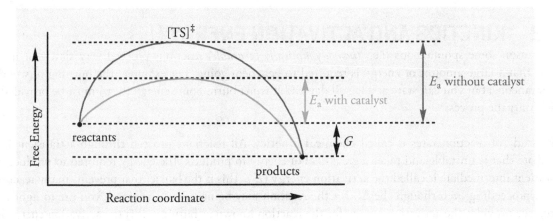

Figure 1 The Reaction Coordinate Graph

Enzymes are catalysts. They increase the rate of a reaction by lowering the reaction's activation energy, but they *do not affect* ΔG between reactants and products. As catalysts, enzymes have a kinetic role, *not* a thermodynamic one. [Will an enzyme alter the concentration of reagents at equilibrium?[17]] Enzymes may alter the rate of a reaction enormously: A reaction that would take a hundred years to reach equilibrium without an enzyme may occur in just seconds with an enzyme. (Contrast the kinetic role of enzymes with collision kinetics as discussed in *MCAT General Chemistry Review*.)

ATP as an Energy Source: Reaction Coupling

Enzymes increase the rate of reactions that have a negative ΔG. These reactions would occur on their own without an enzyme (they are spontaneous) but far more slowly than with one. However, there are many reactions in the body that occur which have a positive ΔG. The biosynthesis of macromolecules such as DNA and protein is not spontaneous ($\Delta G > 0$), but clearly these reactions *do* take place (or we wouldn't be here). How can this be? Thermodynamically unfavorable reactions in the cell can be driven forward by **reaction coupling**. In reaction coupling, one very favorable reaction is used to drive an unfavorable one. This is possible because *free energy changes are additive*. [What is the favorable reaction that the cell can use to drive unfavorable reactions?[18]] In the lab, the $\Delta G^{\circ\prime}$ for the hydrolysis of one phosphate group from ATP is –7.3 kcal/mol, so it is a very favorable reaction. In the cell, ΔG is about –12 kcal/mol, so in the cell it is even more favorable. [What's the difference between the situation *in vitro* (lab) and *in vivo* (cell)?[19]]

How does ATP hydrolysis drive unfavorable reactions? There are many ways. One example is by causing a conformational change in a protein; in this way ATP hydrolysis can be used to power energy-costly events like transmembrane transport. Another example is by transfer of a phosphate group from ATP to a substrate. Take the unfavorable reaction A + B → C. Let's say that Reactant A must proceed through an

---

[17] No. It will only affect the rate at which the reactants and products reach equilibrium.

[18] ATP hydrolysis!

[19] $K_{(cell)} \neq K_{eq}$. This means that the relative concentrations of ATP and ADP + P$_i$ are not at equilibrium levels in the cell. Actually, $K_{(cell)} \ll K_{eq}$ because the cell keeps a high concentration of ATP around.

intermediate, APO_4^{2-} in order to participate. Let's say $\Delta G = +7$ kcal/mol for the overall reaction. What if the two partial reactions have ΔGs as follows:

$$A + PO_4^{2-} \rightarrow APO_4^{2-} \qquad \Delta G = \quad +2 \text{ kcal/mol}$$

$$\underline{APO_4^{2-} + B \rightarrow C + PO_4^{2-} \qquad \Delta G = \quad +5 \text{ kcal/mol}}$$

$$Total \quad \Delta G = \quad +7 \text{ kcal/mol}$$

These reactions will not proceed, because the overall ΔG will be +7 kcal/mol. What will be the *overall* ΔG if we *couple* the reaction $A + B \rightarrow C$ to the hydrolysis of one ATP? All we have to do is add up all the ΔG values, as follows:

$$ATP \rightarrow ADP + PO_4^{2-} \qquad \Delta G = \quad -12 \text{ kcal/mol}$$

$$A + PO_4^{2-} \rightarrow APO_4^{2-} \qquad \Delta G = \quad +2 \text{ kcal/mol}$$

$$\underline{APO_4^{2-} + B \rightarrow C + PO_4^{2-} \qquad \Delta G = \quad +5 \text{ kcal/mol}}$$

$$Total \quad \Delta G = \quad -5 \text{ kcal/mol}$$

Now the overall reaction, shown below, is thermodynamically favorable. We have *coupled* the unfavorable reaction $A + B \rightarrow C$ to the highly favorable hydrolysis of ATP:

$$A + B + ATP \rightarrow C + ADP + PO_4^{2-} \quad \Delta G = -5 \text{ kcal/mol}$$

Note that we first stated that the enzyme has only a kinetic role (influencing rate only), not a thermodynamic one (determining favorability). Then we went on to discuss reaction coupling, which allows enzymes to promote otherwise unfavorable reactions. There is no contradiction, however. The only difference is viewing reactions in an isolated manner or in the complex series of linked reactions more commonly found in the body. The same rule applies in either case: ΔG must be negative for either a single reaction or a series of linked reactions to occur spontaneously. In summary:

- One reaction in a test tube: the enzyme is a catalyst with a kinetic role only. It influences the rate of the reaction, but not the outcome.
- Many "real life" reactions in the cell: enzyme controls outcomes by selectively promoting unfavorable reactions via reaction coupling.

2.3 ENMZYME STRUCTURE AND FUNCTION

2.3

Most enzymes are proteins that must fold into specific three-dimensional structures to act as catalysts. (Some enzymes are RNA or contain RNA sequences with catalytic activity. Most catalyze their own splicing, and the rRNA in ribosomes helps in peptide-bond formation.) An enzyme may consist of a single polypeptide chain or several polypeptide subunits held together in a __[20] (primary? secondary? etc.) structure. The reason for the importance of folding in enzyme function is the proper formation of the **active site**, the region in an enzyme's three-dimensional structure that is directly involved in catalysis. [What shape are enzymes more likely to have: fibrous/elongated or globular/spherical?[21]] The reactants in an enzyme-catalyzed reaction are called **substrates**. (Products have no special name; they're just "products.") What is the role of the active site, that is, how do enzymes work? The enzyme is like a career-planning service (CPS), and the active site is like the room where Bob can sit and do his job hunting. The CPS has counselors, books, and job lists, all of which make job hunting easier. The active site has amino acid residues that stabilize *the transition state* of a reaction. [For example, if a transition state intermediate possesses a transient negative charge, what amino acid residues might be found at the active site to stabilize the transition state?[22]] This lowers the activation energy barrier between reactants and products.

- Is it possible that amino acids located far apart from each other in the primary protein equence may play a role in the formation of the same active site?[23]
- If, during an enzyme-catalyzed reaction, an intermediate forms in which the substrate is covalently linked to the enzyme via a serine residue, can this occur at any serine residue or must it occur at a specific serine residue?[24]
- Compound A converts into Compound B in solution: $A \rightleftharpoons B$. The reaction has the following equilibrium constant: $K_{eq} = [B]_{eq}/[A]_{eq} = 1000$. If pure A is dissolved in water at 298 K, will ΔG for the reaction $A \rightleftharpoons B$ be positive or negative? Is it possible to answer this question without knowing $\Delta G^{\circ\prime}$?[25]

---

[20] quaternary

[21] Globular. Structural proteins such as collagen tend to be fibrous, but proteins that act as catalysts tend to be roughly spherical to form an active site in a cleft in the sphere.

[22] A positive charge would stabilize the negative charge in the intermediate. Such a charge might be contributed by His, Arg, or Lys. Alternatively, the hydrogen of the $-NH_2$ group in glutamine or asparagine could hydrogen bond with the negative charge.

[23] Yes, the amino acids at the active site may be distant from each other in a polypeptide's primary sequence but be near each other in the final folded protein. This is why protein folding is crucial for enzyme function.

[24] It must occur at a particular serine residue which sticks out into the active site.

[25] You don't need to calculate $\Delta G^{\circ\prime}$; all you need to know is that with a K_{eq} of 1000, there will be 1000 times more B than A in solution at equilibrium. If we create a solution with only A, the reaction must move spontaneously toward B.

- Regarding the reaction described in the previous question, if pure B is put into solution in the presence of an enzyme that catalyzes the reaction between A and B, which one of the following will be true?[26]
  - A. All the B will be converted into A, until there is 1000 times more A than B.
  - B. All of the B will remain as B, since B is favored at equilibrium.
  - C. The enzyme will have no effect, since enzymes act on the transition state and there is no transition state present.
  - D. The reaction that produces A will predominate until $\Delta G = 0$.

- The transition state intermediate for a reaction possesses a transient negative charge. The active site for an enzyme catalyzing this reaction contains a His residue to stabilize the intermediate. If the His residue at the active site is replaced by a glutamate which is negatively charged at pH 7.0, what effect will this have on the reaction, assuming that the reactants are present in excess compared to the enzyme?
  - A. The repulsion caused by the negative charge in the glutamate at the altered active site will increase the activation energy and make the reaction proceed more slowly than it would in solution without enzyme.
  - B. The rate of catalysis will be unaffected, but the equilibrium ratio of products and reactants will change, favoring reactants.
  - C. The transition state intermediate will not be stabilized as effectively by the altered enzyme, lowering the rate relative to the rate with catalysis by the normal enzyme.
  - D. The rate of catalysis will decrease, and the equilibrium constant will change.[27]

The active site for enzymes is generally highly specific in its substrate recognition, including stereospecificity (the ability to distinguish between stereoisomers). For example, enzymes which catalyze reactions involving amino acids are specific for D or L amino acids, and enzymes catalyzing reactions involving monosaccharides may distinguish between stereoisomers as well. [Which configurations are found in animals?[28]]

Many **proteases** (protein-cleaving enzymes) have an active site with a serine residue whose OH group can act as a nucleophile, attacking the carbonyl carbon of an amino acid residue in a polypeptide chain. Examples are trypsin, chymotrypsin, and elastase. These enzymes also usually have a **recognition pocket** near the active site. This is a pocket in the enzyme's structure which attracts certain residues on substrate polypeptides. The enzyme always cuts polypeptides at the same site, just to one side of the recognition residue. For example, chymotrypsin always cuts on the carboxyl side of one of the large hydrophobic residues Tyr, Trp, Phe, and Met. Enzymes that act on hydrophobic substrates have hydrophobic amino acids in their active sites, while hydrophilic/polar amino acids will comprise the active site of enzymes with hydrophilic substrates.

---

[26] If only B exists in solution, then the back-reaction producing A will predominate until equilibrium is reached ($\Delta G = 0$), regardless of the presence or absence of enzyme (choice **D** is correct and choice B is wrong). According to the K_{eq} given, at equilibrium there will be 1000 times more B than A, not the other way around (choice A is wrong). Note that enzymes do not act on the transition state, they act to produce the transition state (choice C is wrong).

[27] Beware of long, complex-sounding questions! They may not be as bad as they look; for instance, the phrase "assuming that the reactants are present in excess compared to the enzyme" adds nothing to the substance of this question. If His (which is positive or neutral at pH 7) is replaced by Glu (negatively charged at pH 7), this could decrease the effectiveness—or destroy altogether—the active site of the enzyme. This means the transition state would not be effectively stabilized, and the rate of the reaction would simply reduce to that of the uncatalyzed reaction (choice **C** is correct). The rate would not proceed more slowly than the uncatalyzed reaction (i.e., "in solution without enzyme," choice A is wrong), and remember that enzymes do not alter reaction equilibria (K_{eq} will be unaffected, choices B and D are wrong).

[28] L amino acids and D sugars. Remember the L in aLanine.

2.4 REGULATION OF ENZYME ACTIVITY

Metabolic pathways in the cell are not all continually on, but must be tightly regulated to maintain health. For example, if glycogen synthesis and breakdown occur in the same cell at the same time, a great deal of energy will be wasted without accomplishing anything. Therefore, the activity of key enzymes in metabolic pathways is usually regulated in one or more of the following ways:

1) **Covalent modification.** Proteins can have several different groups covalently attached to them, and this can regulate their activity, lifespan in the cell, and/or cellular location. The addition of a phosphoryl group from a molecule of ATP by a protein **kinase** to the hydroxyl of serine, threonine, or tyrosine residues is the most common example. Phosphorylation of these different sites on an enzyme can either activate or inactivate the enzyme. Protein **phosphorylases** also phosphorylate proteins, but use free-floating inorganic phosphate (P_i) in the cell instead of ATP. Protein phosphorylation can be reversed by protein **phosphatases**.

2) **Proteolytic cleavage.** Many enzymes (and other proteins) are synthesized in inactive forms (zymogens) that are activated by cleavage by a protease.

3) **Association with other polypeptides.** Some enzymes have catalytic activity in one polypeptide subunit that is regulated by association with a separate regulatory subunit. For example, there are some proteins that demonstrate continuous rapid catalysis if their regulatory subunit is removed; this is known as **constitutive activity** (*constitutive* means continuous or unregulated). There are other proteins that require association with another peptide in order to function. Still other proteins can bind many regulatory subunits. There are numerous examples of this in the cell, and many of them have diverse and complex regulatory mechanisms that all revolve around the theme of "associations with other polypeptides can affect enzyme activity."

4) **Allosteric regulation.** The modification of active-site activity through interactions of molecules with other specific sites on the enzyme (called **allosteric sites**). Let's look at this in a little more detail.

Allosteric Regulation

If the cell is to make use of the enzyme as a biochemical switch, there must be a way to turn the enzyme *on* or *off*. One mechanism of regulation is the binding of small molecules to particular sites on an enzyme that are distinct from the active site; this is allosteric regulation. This name comes from the fact that the particular spot on the enzyme which can bind the small molecule is *not* located close to the active site; *allo* means "other," and *steric* refers to a location in space (as in "steric hindrance"), so *allosteric* means "at another place." The binding of the allosteric regulator to the allosteric site is generally noncovalent and reversible. When bound, the allosteric regulator can alter the conformation of the enzyme to increase or decrease catalysis, even though it may be bound to the enzyme at a site distant from the active site or even on a separate polypeptide.

Feedback Inhibition

Enzymes usually act as part of pathways, not alone. Rather than regulate every enzyme in a pathway, usually there are one or two key enzymes that are regulated, such as the enzyme that catalyzes the first irreversible step in a pathway. The easiest way to explain this is with an example. Three enzymes (E1, E2, and E3) catalyze the three steps required to convert Substrate A to Product D. When plenty of D is around, it would be logical to shut off E1 so that excess B, C, and D are not made. This would conserve A and would also conserve energy. Commonly, an end-product such as D will shut off an enzyme early in the pathway, such as E1. This is called **negative feedback**, or **feedback inhibition**.

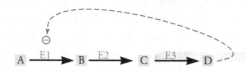

Figure 2   Feedback Inhibition

There are examples of positive feedback ("feedback *stimulation*"), but negative feedback is by far the most common example of feedback regulation. On the other hand, *feedforward stimulation* is common. This involves the stimulation of an enzyme by its substrate, or by a molecule used in the synthesis of the substrate. For example, in Figure 2, A might stimulate E3. This makes sense because when lots of A is around, we want the pathway for utilization of A to be active.

Allosteric regulation can be quite complex. It is possible for more than one small molecule to be capable of binding to an allosteric site. For example, imagine a reaction pathway from A through Z, where each step (A → B, B → C, etc.) is catalyzed by an enzyme. Let's say that an allosteric enzyme called E15 catalyzes the reaction O → P. It would be possible for A to allosterically activate E15 (feedforward stimulation) and for Z to allosterically inhibit E15 (feedback inhibition). This may sound complex, but it's quite logical. What it means is that when lots of A is around, E15 will be stimulated to use the molecules made from A (B, C, D, etc.) to make P, which could then be used to make Q, R, S, etc., all the way up to Z. On the other hand, if a lot of excess Z built up, it would inhibit E15, thereby conserving the supply of A, B, C, etc. and preventing more build-up of Z, Y, X, etc. Hence, in addition to acting as switches, enzymes act as *valves*, because they regulate the flow of substrates into products.

2.5 BASIC ENZYME KINETICS

Enzyme kinetics is the study of the rate of formation of products from substrates in the presence of an enzyme. The **reaction rate** (V, for velocity) is the amount of product formed per unit time, in moles per second (mol/s). It depends on the concentration of substrate, [S], and enzyme.[29] If there is only a little substrate, then the rate V is directly proportional to the amount of substrate added: double the amount of substrate and the reaction rate doubles, triple the substrate and the rate triples, and so forth. But eventually there is so much substrate that the active sites of the enzymes are occupied much of the time, and adding more substrate doesn't increase the reaction rate as much, that is, the slope of the V vs. [S] curve decreases. Finally, there is so much substrate that every active site is continuously occupied, and adding more substrate doesn't increase the reaction rate at all. At this point the enzyme is said to be **saturated**. The reaction rate when the enzyme is saturated is denoted V_{max}; see Figure 3. This is a property of each enzyme at a particular concentration of enzyme. You can look it up in a book for the common ones. [If a small amount of enzyme in a solution is acting at V_{max}, and the substrate concentration is doubled, what is the new reaction rate?[30]]

Another commonly used parameter on these enzyme kinetics graphs is the Michaelis constant K_m. K_m is the substrate concentration at which the reaction velocity is half its maximum. To find K_m on the enzyme kinetics graph, mark the V_{max} on the y-axis, then divide this distance in half to find $V_{max}/2$. K_m is found by drawing a horizontal line from $V_{max}/2$ to the curve, and then a vertical line down to the x-axis. K_m is unique for each enzyme-substrate pair and gives information on the affinity of the enzyme for its substrate. If an enzyme-substrate pair has a low K_m, it means that not very much substrate is required to get the reaction rate to half the maximum rate; thus the enzyme has a high affinity for this particular substrate.

low K_m → high affinity

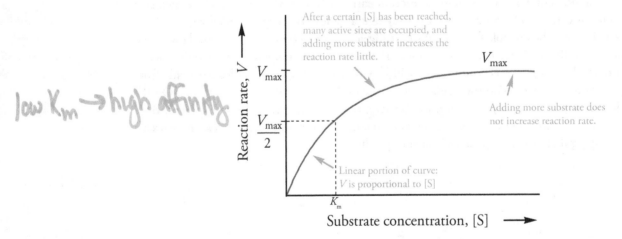

Figure 3 Saturation Kinetics

---

[29] Usually the concentration of enzyme is kept fixed, and [S] is taken as the only independent variable (the one the rate depends on). This is applicable to biological systems, where substrate concentrations change much more than enzyme concentrations.

[30] If the enzyme is acting at V_{max}, it is saturated with substrate; adding more substrate will not increase the reaction rate; the rate is still V_{max}.

Cooperativity

Many multi-subunit enzymes do not behave in the simple kinetic manner described above. In such enzymes, the binding of substrate to one subunit allosterically increases the affinity of other subunits for substrate. The conformation of the enzyme prior to substrate binding, with low substrate affinity, is sometimes termed "tense," and the conformation of enzyme with increased affinity is termed "relaxed."[31] Such enzymes are said to bind substrate *cooperatively* (Figure 4). This term just indicates that the substrates "cooperate" with each other. The binding of one substrate molecule to the enzyme complex enhances the binding of more substrate molecules to the same complex. Cooperative enzymes must have more than one active site. They are usually multisubunit complexes, composed of more than one protein chain held together in a quaternary structure. They may also be a single-subunit enzyme with two or more active sites.

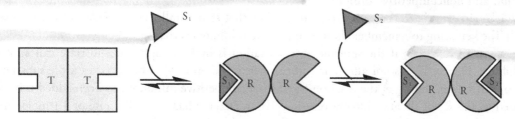

Figure 4   Enzyme Cooperativity

A sigmoidal curve results from cooperative binding. In Figure 5 below, the flat part at the bottom left (Region 1) is explained by the notion that at low [S] the enzyme complex has a low affinity for substrate (is in the tense state), and adding more substrate increases the rate little. The steep part in the middle of the curve (Region 2) represents the range of substrate concentrations where adding substrate greatly increases the reaction rate, because the enzyme complex is in the relaxed state. [The leveling off at the upper right part of the curve (Region 3) represents what?[32]]

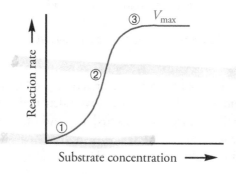

Figure 5   Sigmoidal Kinetics of Cooperativity

---

[31] Imagine a group of people who can't get any dates. They are all depressed about it, and they keep each other depressed, which makes it even less likely that any will get a date. They are tense, "turned off," and inactive. Then one of the depressed group gets a date and gets so excited about it that all the other friends in the group get so enthusiastic that they get dates too. They are "turned on," relaxed, hip, groovy, and active.

[32] Saturation, just as in the case of a noncooperative enzyme.

Cooperativity does not apply just to catalytic enzymes. For example, hemoglobin (Hb) is a protein complex made of four polypeptide subunits, each of which contains a heme prosthetic group with a single O_2-binding site. (So one Hb has four hemes and four binding sites.) Hb is a carrier (of oxygen), not a catalyst of any reaction (not an enzyme). It exhibits cooperative O_2 binding. This is why the Hb-O_2 dissociation curve is sigmoidal. [What is the relationship between the two notions *allosteric* and *cooperative*?[33]]

Inhibition of Enzyme Activity

Enzyme inhibitors can reduce enzyme activity by a few different mechanisms, including **competitive inhibition** and **noncompetitive inhibition**. **Competitive inhibitors** are molecules that *compete* with substrate for binding at the active site. [You can predict that structurally, competitive inhibitors resemble what?[34]] The key thing to remember about competitive inhibitors is that their inhibition can be overcome by adding more substrate; if the substrate concentration is high enough, the substrate can *outcompete* the inhibitor. Hence, V_{max} is not affected. You can get to the same V_{max}, but it takes more substrate (see Figure 6). Therefore, the K_m of the reaction to which a competitive inhibitor has been added is increased compared to the K_m of the uninhibited reaction. [If an enzyme has a reaction rate of 1 μmole/min at a substrate concentration of 50 μM and a rate of 10 μmole/min at a substrate concentration of 100 μM, does this indicate the presence of a competitive inhibitor?[35]]

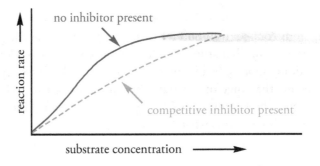

Figure 6   Competitive Inhibition

Noncompetitive inhibitors bind at an allosteric site, not at the active site. No matter how much substrate you add, the inhibitor will not be displaced from its site of action (see Figure 7). Hence, noncompetitive inhibition *does* diminish V_{max}. Remember that V_{max} is always calculated at the same enzyme concentration, since adding more enzyme will increase the measured V_{max}. Addition of a noncompetitive inhibitor changes the V_{max} and $V_{max}/2$ of the reaction, but typically does not alter K_m. This is because the substrate can still bind to the active site, but the inhibitor prevents the catalytic activity of the enzyme.

---

[33] Cooperativity is a special kind of allosteric interaction. One active site acts like an allosteric regulatory site for the other active sites. Secondly, cooperative enzyme complexes are often allosterically regulated also. Hb is an excellent example. Not only does O_2 binding to one subunit increase the other subunits' affinities, but also several other molecules can bind to various sites to change the affinity of the complex. For example, CO_2 stabilizes tense Hb, causing each of the four binding sites to have a lower affinity for oxygen. As a result, in the presence of CO_2, Hb tends to give up whatever O_2 it has bound. The most important thing to remember, though, is that the binding in cooperativity takes place at the active site, while the binding in allosteric regulation takes place at "other sites."

[34] Structurally, competitive inhibitors must at least resemble the substrate; however, the most effective competitive inhibitors resemble the transition state which the active site normally stabilizes.

[35] No. The rate increase is greater than linear, indicating that the effect is caused by cooperativity.

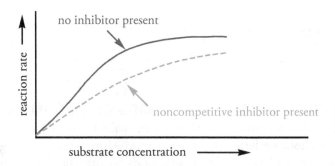

Figure 7 Noncompetitive Inhibition

- Carbon dioxide is an allosteric inhibitor of hemoglobin. It dissociates easily when Hb passes through the lungs, where the CO_2 can be exhaled. Carbon *mon*oxide, on the other hand, binds at the oxygen-binding site with an affinity 300 times greater than oxygen; it can be displaced by oxygen, but only when there is much more O_2 than CO in the environment. Which of the following is/are correct?[36]

    I. Carbon monoxide is an irreversible inhibitor.
    II. CO_2 is a reversible inhibitor.
    III. CO_2 is a noncompetitive inhibitor.

- In the figure below, the kinetics of an enzyme are plotted. In each case, an inhibitor may be present or absent. Which one of the following statements is true?[37]

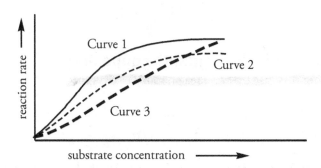

A. Curve 3 represents noncompetitive inhibition of the enzyme.
B. Curve 1 represents noncompetitive inhibition of the enzyme.
C. The V_{max} values of Curve 2 and Curve 3 are the same.
D. Curve 3 represents competitive inhibition of the enzyme, and the enzyme is uninhibited in Curve 1.

---

[36] Item I: False. The question states that CO can be displaced by oxygen. **Item II: True.** The question states that it dissociates easily. **Item III: True.** The question states it binds allosterically, which means "at another site" (not the active site).

[37] Since Curve 3 and Curve 1 have the same V_{max}, but Curve 3 has a reduced rate of product formation, it suggests that Curve 3 represents competitive inhibition of the enzyme in Curve 1 (choice **D** is correct). If Curve 3 represented noncompetitive inhibition, its V_{max} would be reduced compared to Curve 1 (choice **A** is wrong), and in no case would an inhibitor have a higher V_{max} than an uninhibited reaction (choice **B** is wrong). Lastly, it can be seen on the graph that Curve 2 has a reduced V_{max} compared to Curve 3 (choice **C** is wrong).

2.6   CELLULAR RESPIRATION

Energy Metabolism and the Definitions of Oxidation and Reduction

Where does the energy in foods come from? How do we make use of this energy? Why do we breathe? The answers begin with **photosynthesis**, the process by which plants store energy from the sun in the bond energy of carbohydrates. Plants are **photoautotrophs** because they use energy from light ("photo") to make their own ("auto") food. We are **chemoheterotrophs**, because we use the energy of chemicals ("chemo") produced by other ("hetero") living things, namely plants and other animals. Plants and animals store chemical energy in reduced molecules such as carbohydrates and fats. These reduced molecules are oxidized to produce CO_2 and ATP. The energy of ATP is used in turn to drive the energetically unfavorable reactions of the cell. That's the basic energetics of life; all the rest is detail.

In essence, the production and utilization of energy boil down to a series of oxidation/ reduction reactions. **Oxidize** is a chemical term meaning just what it sounds like: "bind to oxygen." **Reduce** means the opposite: "remove oxygen." In fact, there are three ways to "oxidize" (and "reduce") an atom. *Memorize them.*

The Three Meanings of Oxidize:
1) attach oxygen (or increase the number of bonds to oxygen)
2) remove hydrogen
3) remove electrons

The Three Meanings of Reduce (just the opposite):
1) remove oxygen (or decrease the number of bonds to oxygen)
2) add hydrogen
3) add electrons

Though you should memorize this, it is not a subject worthy of philosophizing. If you can answer questions like the following, you're set: Is changing CH_3CH_3 to $H_2C=CH_2$ an oxidation, a reduction, or neither?[38] What about changing Fe^{3+} to Fe^{2+}?[39] What about this: $O_2 \rightarrow H_2O$?[40]

When you reduce something, it's like compressing a spring; you store potential energy. The reduced substance "wants" to be oxidized back to where it started. Here is one other important fact about oxidation and reduction: When one atom gets reduced, another one *must* be oxidized; hence the term *redox pair*. As you study the process of glucose oxidation, you will see that each time an oxidation reaction occurs, a reduction reaction occurs too.

---

[38] It's an oxidation, because hydrogens have been removed.

[39] It's a reduction, because an electron has been added.

[40] It's a reduction, because bonds to oxygen have been replaced by bonds to hydrogen.

Catabolism is the process of breaking down molecules. The opposite is **anabolism**, which is "building-up" metabolism.[41] The way we extract energy from glucose is by **oxidative catabolism**. We break down the glucose by oxidizing it. The oxidative catabolism of glucose involves four steps: glycolysis, the pyruvate dehydrogenase complex (PDC), the Krebs cycle, and electron transport/oxidative phosphorylation. The stoichiometry of glucose oxidation looks like this:

$$C_6H_{12}O_6 + 6\,O_2 \rightarrow 6\,CO_2 + 6\,H_2O$$

- What are the two members of the redox pair in this reaction?[42]

As we oxidize foods, we release the stored energy plants got from the sun. But we don't make use of that energy right away. Instead, we store it in the form of ATP. Thus, cellular respiration is theoretically very simple: *It's just a big coupled reaction* (described in Section 2.2). We make the unfavorable synthesis of ATP happen by coupling it to the very favorable oxidation of glucose. ATP can then be used to drive other cellular processes.

Introduction to Cellular Respiration

When glucose is oxidized to release energy, very little ATP is generated directly. Instead, the oxidation of glucose is accompanied by the reduction of high-energy electron carriers, primarily the reduction of NAD^+ (nicotinamide adenine dinucleotide) to NADH. The energy in reduced NADH is then used to pump protons out of the interior of mitochondria and create a proton gradient. The proton gradient energy is then used to finally drive the production of ATP.

Glucose is oxidized to produce CO_2 and ATP in a four-step process: glycolysis, the pyruvate dehydrogenase complex (PDC), the Krebs cycle, and electron transport/oxidative phosphorylation. The first stage is **glycolysis** ("glucose splitting"). Here glucose is partially oxidized while it is split in half, into two identical **pyruvic acid** molecules. [How many carbon atoms does pyruvic acid have?[43]] Glycolysis produces a small quantity of ATP and a small quantity of NADH. Glycolysis occurs in the cytoplasm and does not require oxygen.

In the second stage (the **pyruvate dehydrogenase complex**), the pyruvate produced in glycolysis is decarboxylated to form an acetyl group. The acetyl group is then attached to **coenzyme A**, a carrier that can transfer the acetyl group into the Krebs cycle. A small amount of NADH is produced.

In the third stage, the **Krebs cycle** (also known as the **tricarboxylic acid cycle** or the **citric acid cycle**), the acetyl group from the PDC is added to oxaloacetate to form citric acid. The citric acid is then decarboxylated and isomerized to regenerate the original oxaloacetate. A modest amount of ATP, a large amount of NADH, and a small amount of $FADH_2$ are produced. Note that although the PDC and the Krebs cycle can only occur when oxygen is available to the cell, *neither uses oxygen directly*. Rather, oxygen is necessary

---

[41] The mnemonics are *cata* = breakdown, as in catastrophe, and *ana* = buildup, sounds like "add-a." (Think of anabolic steroids, which weightlifters use to bulk up.)

[42] The carbons in the sugar are oxidized (to CO_2), and oxygen is reduced (to H_2O).

[43] The text states that glucose is split in half in the formation of pyruvate. Since glucose has six carbons, pyruvate must have three.

2.6

for stage four, in which NADH and $FADH_2$ generated throughout cellular respiration are reconverted into NAD[+] and FAD. The PDC and the Krebs cycle occur in the innermost compartment of the mitochondria: the matrix.

In stage four of energy harvesting, **electron transport/oxidative phosphorylation**, the high-energy electrons carried by NADH and $FADH_2$ are oxidized by the **electron transport chain** in the inner mitochondrial membrane. The reduced electron carriers dump their electrons at the beginning of the chain, and oxygen is reduced to H_2O at the end. (The word *oxidative* in "oxidative phosphorylation" refers to the use of oxygen to oxidize the reduced electron carriers NADH and $FADH_2$.) The electron energy liberated by the transport chain is used to pump protons out of the innermost compartment of the mitochondrion. The protons are allowed to flow back into the mitochondrion, and the energy of this proton flow is used to produce the high-energy triphosphate group in ATP.

Glycolysis

Glycolysis is an extremely old pathway, having evolved several billion years ago. It is the universal first step in glucose metabolism, the extraction of energy from carbohydrates. All cells from *all domains* (a domain is the highest taxonomic category—see Chapter 6) possess the enzymes of this pathway. In glycolysis, a glucose molecule is oxidized and split into two pyruvate molecules, producing a net surplus of 2 ATP (from ADP + P_i) and producing 2 NADH (from NAD[+]+ H[+]):

$$\text{Glucose} + 2\,\text{ADP} + 2\,\text{P}_i + 2\,\text{NAD}^+ \rightarrow 2\,\text{Pyruvate} + 2\,\text{ATP} + 2\,\text{NADH} + 2\,\text{H}_2\text{O} + 2\,\text{H}^+$$

Of course it's not quite that simple. Glycolysis involves several reactions, each of which is catalyzed by a different enzyme (see Figure 8). The general strategy is to first phosphorylate glucose on both ends and then split it into two 3-carbon units which can go on to the PDC and Krebs cycle. In the first step of glycolysis, a phosphate is taken from ATP and used to phosphorylate glucose, producing glucose 6-phosphate (G6P). This is isomerized to fructose 6-phosphate (F6P), which is then phosphorylated on carbon #1 (with the phosphate again taken from ATP) to produce fructose-1,6-bisphosphate (F1,6bP). This is split into two 3-carbon units that are oxidized to pyruvate, producing 2 ATP and 1 NADH per pyruvate, or 4 ATP and 2 NADH per glucose (since we get two 3-carbon units from each glucose). Don't forget that *each* glucose gives rise to *two* 3-carbon units which pass through the second part of glycolysis and into the Krebs cycle.

- An extract of yeast contains all of the enzymes required for glycolysis, ADP, P_i, Mg^{2+}, NAD[+] and glucose, but when these are all combined, none of the glucose is consumed. Provided that there are no enzyme inhibitors present, why doesn't the reaction proceed?[44]

Hexokinase catalyzes the first step in glycolysis, the phosphorylation of glucose to G6P. G6P feedback-inhibits hexokinase.

---

[44] Although glycolysis results in a net ATP production, ATP is initially required to drive the reaction forward in the phosphorylation of glucose to glucose-6-phosphate and the phosphorylation of fructose-6-phosphate to fructose-1,6-bisphosphate. Without ATP to "prime the pump," there is no way to start the pathway. In case you're wondering about the Mg^{2+}, it's necessary for all reactions involving ATP.

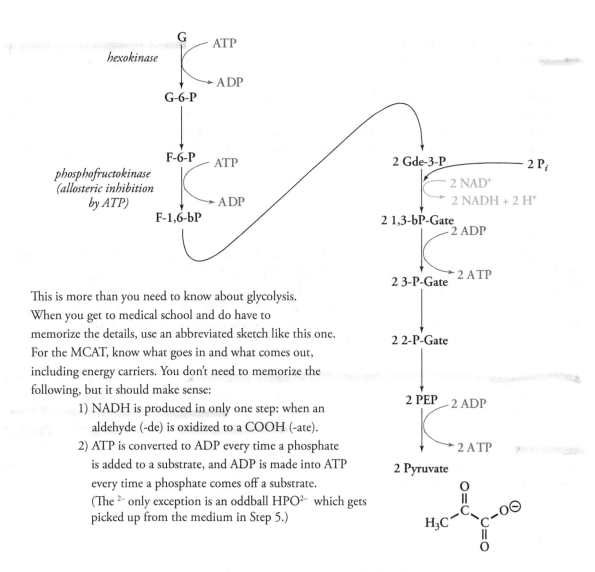

This is more than you need to know about glycolysis. When you get to medical school and do have to memorize the details, use an abbreviated sketch like this one. For the MCAT, know what goes in and what comes out, including energy carriers. You don't need to memorize the following, but it should make sense:

1) NADH is produced in only one step: when an aldehyde (-de) is oxidized to a COOH (-ate).

2) ATP is converted to ADP every time a phosphate is added to a substrate, and ADP is made into ATP every time a phosphate comes off a substrate. (The only exception is an oddball HPO_4^{2-} which gets picked up from the medium in Step 5.)

Figure 8   The 9 Reactions (Steps) of Glycolysis

Phosphofructokinase (PFK) catalyzes the third step: the transfer of a phosphate group from ATP to fructose-6-phosphate to form fructose-1,6-bisphosphate (F1,6bP). This is an important step because the reaction catalyzed by PFK is thermodynamically very favorable (like burning wood: $\Delta G \ll 0$), so it's practically irreversible. Also, G6P can be shunted to various pathways, but F1,6bP can only react in glycolysis. So once you light the PFK fire, you're committed to glycolysis. Hence PFK is the key biochemical valve controlling the flow of substrate to product in glycolysis, and the conversion of F6P to F1,6bP is known as a **committed step.** In the remainder of glycolysis, F1,6bP is split into two 3-carbon molecules that are converted to pyruvate, with the production of NADH and ATP. Very favorable steps in enzymatic pathways (those with a large negative ΔG) are practically irreversible (because the back-reaction is so unfavorable). These reactions are the ones that are usually subject to allosteric regulation. Another generalization about what steps get regulated is this: early steps in a long pathway tend to be regulated. This makes sense; if you're going from A to Z, it's more practical to regulate the A → B reaction than the W → X one.

For example, the enzyme PFK is a key regulatory point in glycolysis. PFK is allosterically regulated by ATP. [What effect would you think a high concentration of ATP would have on PFK activity?[45]]

Two molecules of NAD^+ are reduced in glycolysis per glucose catabolized, forming 2 NADH. As discussed above, NADH is an electron carrier, a molecule that is responsible for shuttling energy in the form of **reducing power** (i.e., reduction potential). Remember, these high energy electron carriers are not used directly as an energy source but are used later to generate ATP through electron transport and oxidative phosphorylation.

Fermentation

Under **aerobic** conditions (that is, in the presence of oxygen), the pyruvate produced in glycolysis enters the PDC and Krebs cycle to be oxidized completely to CO_2. The NADH produced in glycolysis and the PDC, as well as NADH and $FADH_2$ produced in the Krebs cycle, are all reoxidized in electron transport, where O_2 is the final electron acceptor. In **anaerobic** conditions (without oxygen), electron transport cannot function, and the limited supply of NAD^+ becomes entirely converted to NADH. [Would a limiting supply of NAD^+ stimulate or inhibit glycolysis?[46]]

Fermentation has evolved to regenerate NAD^+ in anaerobic conditions, therby allowing glycolysis to continue in the absence of oxygen. Fermentation uses pyruvate as the acceptor of the high energy electrons from NADH (see Figure 9). Two examples of this process are (1) the reduction of pyruvate to ethanol (yeast do this in the making of beer, wine, etc.) and (2) the reduction of pyruvate to lactate in human muscle cells. Lactate is thought to contribute to the "burn" that athletes encounter during anaerobic exertion, such as sprinting, when the cardiovascular system fails to deliver enough oxygen to keep the electron transport chain running in muscle cells.

---

[45] When energy (ATP) is abundant, the cell should slow glycolysis. High concentrations of ATP inhibit PFK activity by binding to an allosteric regulatory site. It is interesting to note that since ATP is a reactant in the reaction catalyzed by PFK, you would expect a high concentration of ATP to increase the rate of the reaction (Le Châtelier's principle). However the inhibitory allosteric effects of ATP on PFK outweigh this thermodynamic consideration. So lowering the concentration of ATP will increase the reaction rate, even though ATP is a reactant. Of course, if the ATP level went too low, the reaction could not proceed at all.

[46] If NAD^+ has all been converted to NADH, then the step in glycolysis that produces NADH (catalyzed by glyceraldehyde 3-phosphate dehydrogenase) cannot occur because it requires NAD^+ as a substrate. Thus, a lack of NAD^+ will *inhibit* glycolysis.

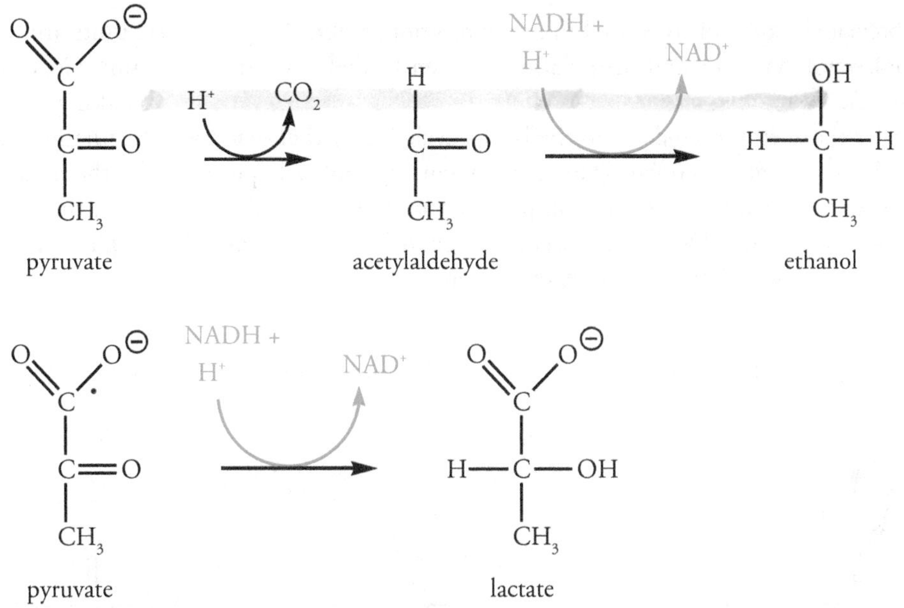

Figure 9   Anaerobic Pathways for Regeneration of NAD⁺ from NADH

The NAD⁺ produced by reducing pyruvate anaerobically is available for re-use in the glycolytic pathway, so more ATP can be produced. There is a limit to the use of anaerobic glycolysis as an energy source, however. The ethanol or lactate that is produced builds up, having no other use in the cell, and acts as a poison at high concentrations. Wine yeast die when the ethanol concentration reaches about 12 percent, and lactic acid is damaging at high concentrations in our tissues as well.

- What happens to the lactate in human muscle cells after a period of strenuous exercise?[47]

The Pyruvate Dehydrogenase Complex

The pyruvate produced in glycolysis in the cytoplasm is transported into the mitochondrial matrix, where it will be entirely oxidized to CO_2. Pyruvate does not enter the Krebs cycle directly, however. First it is oxidatively decarboxylated by the pyruvate dehydrogenase complex (PDC; Figure 10). **Oxidative decarboxylation** is a reaction repeated again in the Krebs cycle, in which a molecule is oxidized to release CO_2 and produce NADH. In oxidative decarboxylation, pyruvate is changed from a 3-carbon molecule to a __, while __ is given off and __ is produced.[48]   The PDC changes pyruvate into an activated acetyl unit. An acetyl unit is [(CH₃)(O=C–)], and *activated* means the acetyl is not floating around freely but rather is attached to a carrier, namely **coenzyme A.** This coenzyme is basically a long handle with a sulfur at

---

[47] The lactate is exported from the muscle cell to the liver. When oxygen becomes available, the liver cell will convert the lactate back to pyruvate, while making NADH from NAD⁺. Then the liver will utilize this excess NADH to make ATP in oxidative phosphorylation. This pyruvate can enter gluconeogenesis or the Krebs cycle in the liver, or it can be sent back to the muscle. (This cycle, whereby the liver deals with lactate from muscle, is known as the Cori Cycle.)

[48] Pyruvate is converted to a 2-carbon molecule, CO_2 is given off, and NADH is made from NAD⁺. You can figure all of this out based on your knowledge of oxidative decarboxylation. Also, note the name of the enzyme, "dehydrogenase." To remove a hydrogen (*dehydrogenate*) is to oxidize. So the name of the enzyme also tells us that pyruvate is oxidized.

the end, abbreviated CoA-SH. It is used in many reaction systems to pass acetyl units around (e.g., fatty acid and cholesterol synthesis and degradation). When loaded with an acetyl unit, CoA-SH is abbreviated acetyl-CoA. The bond between sulfur and the acetyl group is high energy, making it easy for acetyl-CoA to transfer the acetyl fragment into the Krebs cycle for further oxidation. Regulation of the PDC is crucial. [AMP (adenosine monophosphate) is a low-energy molecule produced by the hydrolysis of ATP during metabolism. What effect would you predict a high level of AMP to have on the activity of pyruvate dehydrogenase?[49] The PDC is composed of three different enzymes. Why might a complex of three enzymes be more efficient than three independent enzymes?[50]]

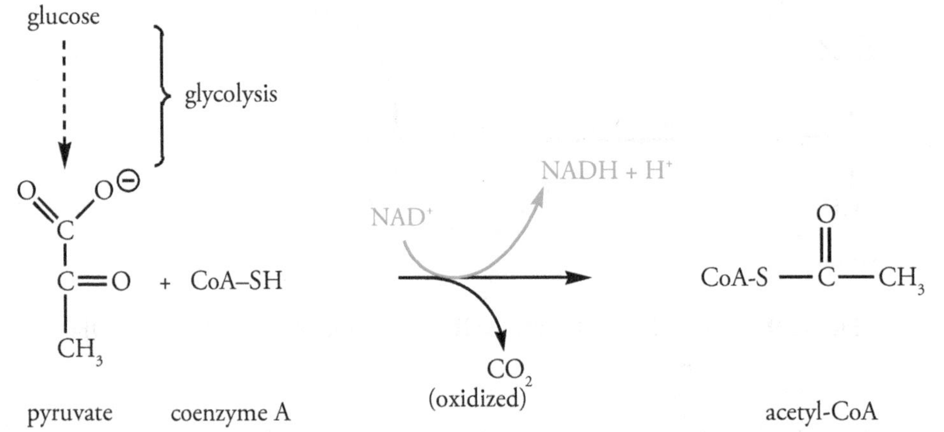

2.6

Figure 10 Oxidation of Pyruvate by Pyruvate Dehydrogenase

A **prosthetic group** is a nonprotein molecule covalently bound to an enzyme as part of the enzyme's active site. The PDC contains a thiamine pyrophosphate (TPP) prosthetic group at one of its active sites. The α-ketoglutarate dehydrogenase complex, which catalyzes the third step in the Krebs cycle, is very similar to the PDC; it has a TPP prosthetic group and catalyzes an oxidative decarboxylation. The **thiamine** in thiamine pyrophosphate is vitamin B_1. Vitamins often serve as prosthetic groups. Contrast this with NAD^+, which is a co-factor. **Co-factors** are various organic and inorganic substances necessary to the function of an enzyme but which never actually interact with the enzyme.

---

[49] A high ratio of AMP or ADP to ATP is described as low-energy charge. A low-energy charge will stimulate the PDC, increasing the rate of entry of pyruvate into the Krebs cycle.

[50] Simply because intermediates are passed directly from active site to active site, without having to diffuse.

- Beriberi is a disease caused by thiamine deficiency, which frequently results from a diet of white rice in underdeveloped nations. Which of the following would best describe the effect of thiamine deficiency on cellular metabolism in humans?[51]
  A. The rate of glycolysis would increase.
  B. Glycolysis would proceed anaerobically to maintain ATP production at normal levels.
  C. Glucose consumption would slow, and ATP production would increase.
  D. Acetyl-CoA would be provided by fatty acid metabolism, so the Krebs cycle would proceed uninhibited.

The Krebs Cycle

The **Krebs cycle** is a group of reactions which take the 2-carbon acetyl unit from acetyl-CoA, combine it with oxaloacetate, and release two CO_2 molecules. NADH and $FADH_2$ are generated in the process. The figure below shows an overview of the process; note that many of the names are not necessary to know and have intentionally been left out.

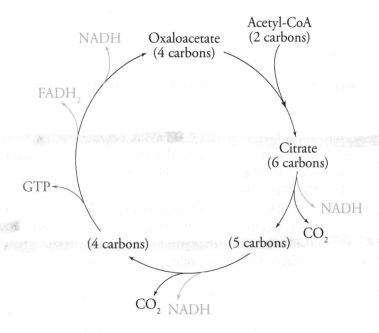

Figure 11   Overview of the Krebs Cycle

These reduced electron carriers (NADH and $FADH_2$) go on to generate ATP in electron transport and oxidative phosphorylation. Two other names for the Krebs cycle are the **tricarboxylic acid cycle (TCA cycle)** and the **citric acid cycle**. Citrate is the first intermediate produced in the cycle, as soon as the acetyl

---

[51] Thiamine deficiency would effectively shut down both the PDC and the Krebs cycle (choice D is wrong), since both of these processes require thiamine in their TPP prosthetic group. In the absence of PDC and Krebs, the amount of NADH and $FADH_2$ provided to the electron transport chain would be reduced, and ATP production would fall (choice C is wrong). In order to compensate and maintain ATP levels as close to normal as possible, the rate of glycolysis would increase (choice A is correct). Note that this would not happen anaerobically, as conditions are not anaerobic (choice B is wrong).

unit is supplied. Citrate possesses three carboxylic acid functional groups, hence the term "tricarboxylic acid." Note that a molecule with three carboxylic acids is ready to be oxidatively decarboxylated. We will now break the multistep cycle down into three general stages. The reactions are shown for conceptual understanding only; there is no need to memorize.

Krebs Stage 1: The two carbons in the acetate fragment of acetyl-CoA are condensed with the 4-carbon compound **oxaloacetate** (OAA; the name is worth remembering), producing **citrate**; see Figure 12. As you will see, the OAA is derived from the previous round of the Krebs cycle; it is recycled each time. [How many chiral carbons are present in citrate?[52] If pyruvate is radiolabeled on its number one (most oxidized) carbon, where will the labeled carbon end up in the Krebs cycle?[53]]

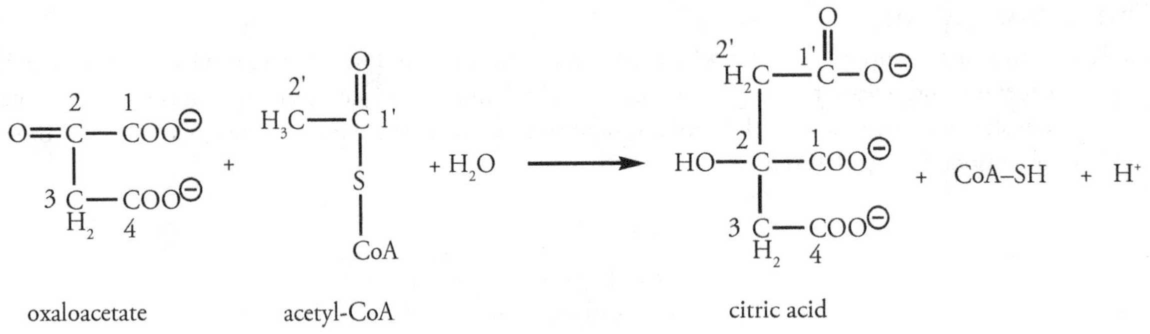

Figure 12   The Entry of Acetyl-CoA into the Krebs Cycle

Krebs Stage 2: Citrate is further oxidized to release CO_2 and to produce NADH from NAD^+ with each oxidative decarboxylation (Figure 13). If you're interested in the details, citrate is first isomerized to form isocitrate, which is then oxidatively decarboxylated to yield the 5-carbon compound α-ketoglutarate, one carbon dioxide, and one NADH. Then α-ketoglutarate is oxidatively decarboxylated to produce succinyl-CoA (four carbons), releasing another CO_2 and producing another NADH. The two carbons that leave as CO_2 during these reactions are not the same ones that entered the cycle as acetate. Thus the two original acetyl carbons remain within the Krebs cycle. They will be lost as CO_2 in later cycles. [How many carbons from the CoA component of acetyl-CoA enter into the Krebs cycle?[54]]

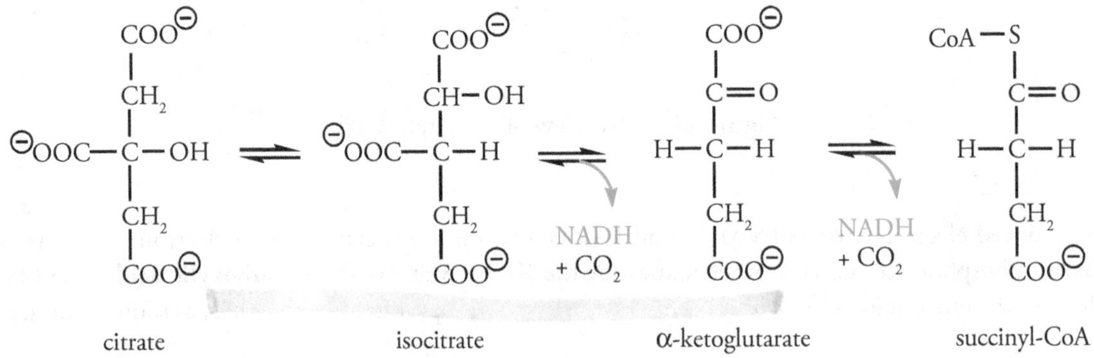

Figure 13   Oxidation of Citric Acid to Succinate

[52] None, since none of the six carbons has four unique substituents.

[53] In CO_2. Pyruvate's most oxidized carbon is a carboxylic acid which is removed by the PDC.

[54] None. CoA assists in catalysis, which means that it is not consumed in the reaction, but regenerated as CoA-SH.

Krebs Stage 3: OAA is regenerated so that the cycle can continue. In the process, reducing power is stored in 1 NADH and 1 $FADH_2$, and a high-energy phosphate bond is produced directly as GTP. Here GTP plays the role normally reserved for ATP. This GTP will eventually transfer its high-energy phosphate bond to ADP, converting it into ATP. $FADH_2$ is similar to NADH, but ultimately results in the production of less ATP.

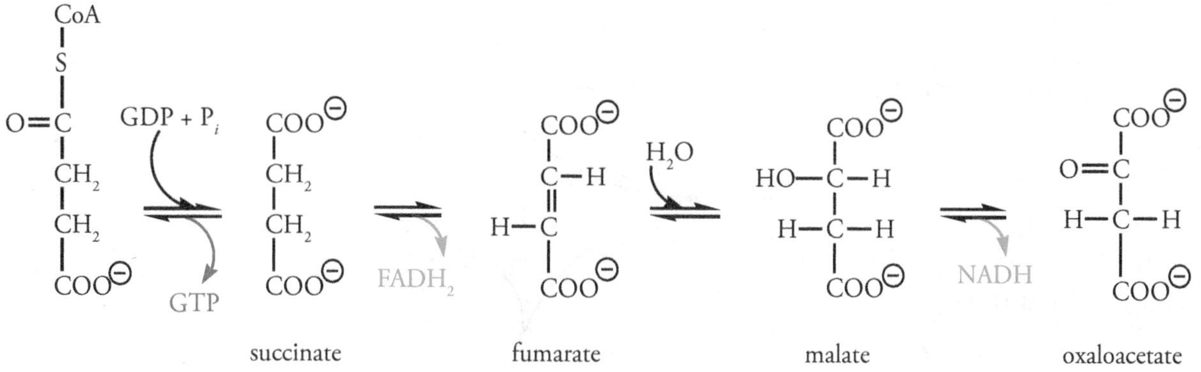

Figure 14 Succinyl CoA to OAA

To review, the oxidation of glucose has so far created:

1) 2 ATP and 2 NADH per glucose molecule in glycolysis
2) Pyruvate Dehydrogenase: 2 NADH per glucose (one per pyruvate)
3) Krebs cycle: 6 NADH, 2 $FADH_2$, and 2 GTP per glucose

Thus, most of the energy of glucose is not extracted directly as ATP (or GTP) but in high-energy electron carriers. We will see how ATP is generated from NADH and $FADH_2$ in electron transport/oxidative phosphorylation.

2.6

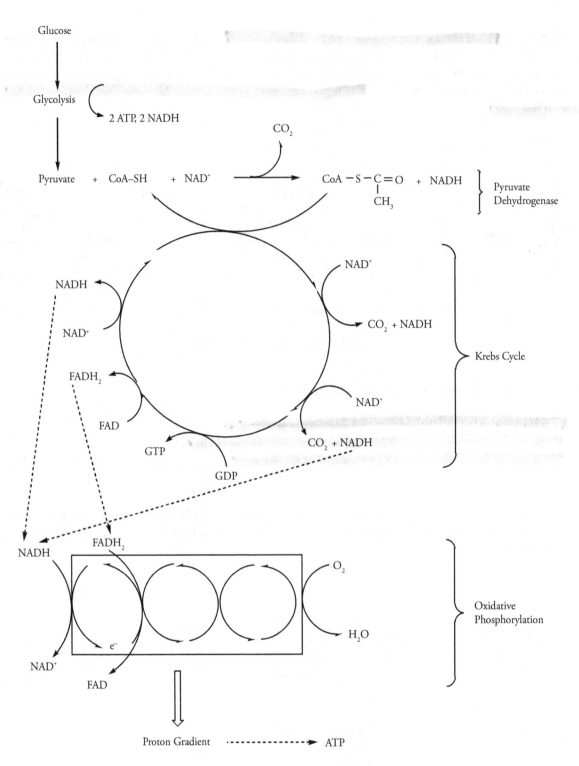

Figure 15 Cellular Respiration

Compartmentalization of Glucose Catabolism in Eukaryotes: The Mitochondria

To understand oxidative phosphorylation, you must know the structure of the mitochondrion (Figure 16). The mitochondrion contains two membranes, an **outer membrane** and an **inner membrane**, each composed of a lipid bilayer. The outer membrane is smooth and contains large pores formed by **porin** proteins. The inner membrane is impermeable, even to very small items like H^+, and is densely folded into structures termed **cristae**. The cristae extend into the **matrix**, which is the innermost space of the mitochondrion. The space between the two membranes, the **intermembrane space**, is continuous with the cytoplasm due to the large pores in the outer membrane. The enzymes of the Krebs cycle and the pyruvate dehydrogenase complex are located in the matrix, and those of the electron transport chain and ATP synthase involved in oxidative phosphorylation are bound to the inner mitochondrial membrane.

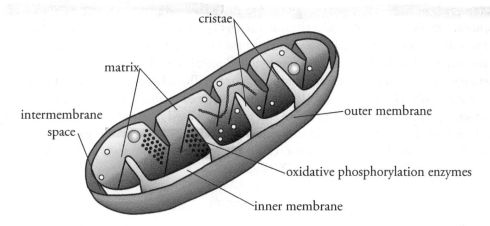

cristae

matrix

intermembrane space

outer membrane

oxidative phosphorylation enzymes

inner membrane

Figure 16 The Mitochondrion

The two goals of electron transport/oxidative phosphorylation are to:

1) reoxidize all the electron carriers reduced in glycolysis, PDC, and the Krebs cycle, and
2) store energy in the form of ATP in the process.

Where are all the reduced electron carriers located? Per each glucose catabolized, two NADH are created by glycolysis in the cytoplasm; the electrons from these NADH will have to be transported into the mitochondria before they can be passed along the electron transport chain. All the other NADHs and $FADH_2$s were produced inside the mitochondrial matrix, so they are in the right place to donate electrons to the electron transport chain.

The situation in prokaryotes is a bit different: All of the reduced electron carriers are located in the cytoplasm. In fact, everything is located in the cytoplasm, since there are *no membrane-bound organelles at all* in prokaryotes (no mitochondria, no nucleus, no lysosomes—everything just floats around in the cytoplasm). Since they have no mitochondria, can bacteria perform oxidative phosphorylation? *Yes, they can!* The way the process works is that a proton gradient must be created and then used to power ATP synthesis by the membrane-bound **ATP synthase**. So all that's required is a membrane impermeable to protons. Eukaryotes use the inner mitochondrial membrane; bacteria just use their cell membrane. The end result of this difference is that when eukaryotes perform aerobic respiration, they have to shuttle the electrons from cytosolic NADH into the mitochondrial matrix (at the cost of some energy) but bacteria do not. So, all things considered, prokaryotes get two more high-energy phosphate bonds from aerobic respiration than eukaryotes do (this will be discussed in more detail in just a bit). From this point forward, we will discuss the eukaryotic system. Remember that it's the same in prokaryotes except that they do it on the cell membrane instead of on the inner mitochondrial membrane (since they have no mitochondria!).

Electron Transport and Oxidative Phosphorylation

2.6

Oxidative phosphorylation is the oxidation of the high-energy electron carriers NADH and $FADH_2$ coupled to the phosphorylation of ADP to produce ATP. The energy released through oxidation of NADH and $FADH_2$ by the electron transport chain is used to pump protons out of the mitochondrial matrix. This proton gradient is the source of energy used to drive the phosphorylation of ADP to ATP. The **electron-transport chain** is a group of five electron carriers (Figure 17). Each member of the chain reduces the next member down the line. All five are named for their redox roles. Three of them are large protein complexes found embedded in the inner mitochondrial membrane. They contain heme prosthetic groups (as in hemoglobin) or iron-sulfur electron-transfer systems. The other two members of the electron transport chain are smaller electron carriers. The chain is organized so that the first large carrier receives electrons (reducing power) from NADH; the NADH is thus oxidized to NAD^+. Hence, the first large carrier in the e^- transport chain ("A" in the figure) is called **NADH dehydrogenase.** It passes its electrons to one of the small carriers in the transport chain, called **ubiquinone**, also known as **coenzyme Q**.[55] NADH dehydrogenase is also known as **coenzyme Q reductase**.

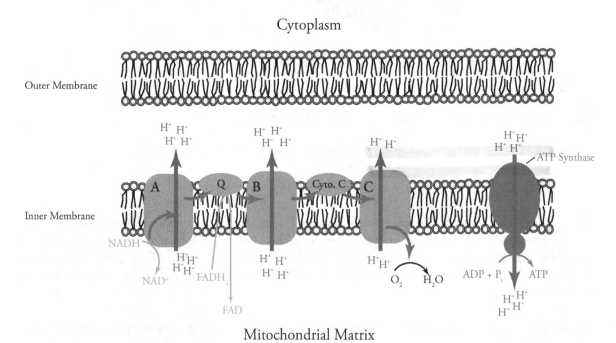

Cytoplasm

Outer Membrane

Inner Membrane

Mitochondrial Matrix

Figure 17 The Electron Transport Chain

---

[55] A quinone is a particular type of aromatic molecule, and the prefix "ubi" indicates that this molecule is ubiquitous, i.e., present in all cells.

Ubiquinone then passes its electrons to the second large membrane-bound complex in the chain ("B"), known as **cytochrome C reductase**. From this name, you can guess what the next carrier in the chain is called; it is **cytochrome C**, a small hydrophilic protein bound loosely to the inner mitochondrial membrane. The last member of the electron transport chain ("C") is simply called **cytochrome C oxidase**. [Where does it pass its electrons to?[56]]

Each of the three large membrane-bound proteins in the electron transport chain pumps protons across the inner mitochondrial membrane every time electrons flow past. Protons are pumped out of the matrix, into the intermembrane space. The inner mitochondrial membrane is highly impermeable to protons. As a result, the electron transport chain creates a large proton gradient, with the pH being much __[57] (higher/lower) inside the matrix than in the rest of the cell.

What does this have to do with ATP synthesis? Well, there is one more very important protein embedded in the inner mitochondrial membrane: **ATP synthase**. It is a large protein complex which contains a proton channel that spans the inner membrane. The passage of protons from the intermembrane space through the ATP synthase channel causes it to synthesize ATP from ADP + P_i. Thus, ATP production is dependent on a **proton gradient**. The overall process of electron transport and ATP production is said to be *coupled* by the proton gradient. Together, electron transport and ATP production are known as **oxidative phosphorylation**. Make sure you understand these questions:

- Dinitrophenol (DNP) is an uncoupler: It destroys the proton gradient by allowing protons to flow into the matrix. Which one of the following processes does it inhibit first?[58]
  - A. Pyruvate decarboxylation by the PDC
  - B. The TCA cycle
  - C. Electron transport
  - D. Muscular contraction

- Which one of the following processes has a positive ΔG under normal aerobic conditions in the cell?[59]
  - A. ATP hydrolysis
  - B. The pumping of protons to form a pH gradient
  - C. The oxidation of NADH by NADH dehydrogenase
  - D. The folding of a protein into its correct tertiary structure

---

[56] If it's the last member of the chain, it must pass its reducing power to O_2, reducing it to H_2O, an end product of electron transport. This is the only reason we breathe and the only reason we evolved with lungs, RBCs, etc.

[57] higher (remember, high pH = low [H^+])

[58] If the proton gradient is destroyed, the processes in A, B, and C will continue unabated, because NADH will be reoxidized to NAD^+ at a normal rate, or perhaps faster than normal. The problem will be that without a proton gradient no ATP will get made from all this glucose breakdown. The answer is **D** because this will be the first problem encountered from running out of ATP.

[59] A, C, and D are all thermodynamically favorable processes that occur spontaneously without any external energy input. Thus, all of these processes have a negative ΔG. However, the large positive ΔG of the process in **B** makes undoing it favorable enough for it to power ATP synthesis. Creation of the proton gradient is dependent upon the very negative ΔG of electron transport.

- The reason cyanide is a poison is that it inactivates cytochrome C oxidase by binding to its active site with high affinity. When a person is exposed to cyanide[60]
  - A. the difference in pH inside and outside the matrix is already as large as it can become, so no more electrons can be pumped against the gradient.
  - B. anaerobic glycolysis depletes pyruvate, thereby slowing the Krebs cycle and the electron transport chain and slowing the rate of proton pumping.
  - C. the electron transport chain ceases to transport electrons and therefore ceases to pump protons.
  - D. NADH becomes fully oxidized by the Krebs cycle and therefore cannot reduce NADH dehydrogenase, so no protons are pumped.

2.6

Energetics of Glucose Catabolism

How is electron transport quantitatively connected to ATP synthesis? For every NADH that is oxidized to NAD^+, the three large electron transport proteins pump about ten protons across the inner mitochondrial membrane, into the intermembrane space. The ATP synthase requires three protons to generate a molecule of ATP from ADP and P_i; however, an additional proton is required to bring P_i into the matrix. This brings the "cost" of ATP synthesis up to four protons per molecule of ATP. Since NADH is responsible for the pumping of 10 protons, each molecule of NADH provides the energy to produce approximately 2.5 ATP molecules.

Even though NADH and $FADH_2$ have similar functions, their fates are a little different. $FADH_2$ gives its electrons to ubiquinone instead of to NADH dehydrogenase. By bypassing the first proton pump, $FADH_2$ is only responsible for the pumping of six protons across the inner membrane.

- How many ATP are made every time an $FADH_2$ is reoxidized to FAD?[61]

As mentioned earlier, the PDC, the Krebs cycle and oxidative phosphorylation all occur in mitochondria in eukaryotes, while glycolysis occurs in the cytoplasm. The electrons from the NADH generated in glycolysis must be transported into the mitochondria before they can enter the electron transport chain. In most cells, they are transported by a pathway termed the **glycerol phosphate shuttle**. This shuttle delivers the electrons directly to ubiquinone (just like $FADH_2$ does), bypassing NADH dehydrogenase, and results in the production of only 1.5 molecules of ATP per cytosolic NADH, rather than the 2.5 normally formed from matrix NADH.[62] Bacteria, because they lack cellular organelles, do not need to transport cytosolic electrons across any membranes; hence the discrepancy in the table below in how much ATP is

---

[60] If the active site of cytochrome C oxidase is occupied with cyanide, then oxygen cannot bind there to be reduced to water; in other words, cytochrome C oxidase will be unable to get rid of its electrons and will remain reduced. Therefore it will be unable to accept electrons from cytochrome C, which will be unable to accept electrons from cytochrome C reductase, which will be unalbe to accept electrons from coenzyme Q, etc., etc., all the way back up the electron transport chain. The end result will be a cessation of all electron transport chain activity (choice C is correct). Note that protons, not electrons, are pumped against their gradient (choice A is wrong), and this will stop completely, not just be slowed down (choice B is wrong). Also, NAD^+ is reduced to NADH in the Krebs cycle, not the other way around (choice D is wrong).

[61] Only 1.5 ATP are made as a result of the reoxidation of $FADH_2$. Six protons divided by four protons per ATP equals 1.5 ATP.

[62] Some high energy-requiring tissues (such as liver and cardiac muscle cells) utilize a different shuttle (the malate-aspartate shuttle) to bring the electrons to NADH hydrogenase, thus getting the full 2.5 ATP from those electrons. But this is the exception, and generally the MCAT does not test exceptions.

yielded from each NADH from glycolysis in eukaryotes compared to prokaryotes. All values in the following table are per glucose molecule catabolized.

Process	Molecules Formed/Used	ATP Equivalents
Glycolysis	–2 ATP 4 ATP 2 NADH	–2 ATP 4 ATP 3 ATP (eukaryotes) 5 ATP (prokaryotes)
Pyruvate Dehydrogenase Complex	2 NADH	5 ATP
Krebs Cycle	6 NADH 2 FADH$_2$ 2 GTP	15 ATP 3 ATP 2 ATP
Total		**30 ATP (eukaryotes)** **32 ATP (prokaryotes)**

Table 1 Theoretical ATP Yield from Cellular Respiration

Notes:

1) These numbers are an estimate of the theoretical maximum amount of ATP that can be produced from a single molecule of glucose. As the proton gradient is used to transport other molecules into or out of the matrix, the actual yield may differ depending on the number of protons (i.e., the gradient) available for ATP synthesis.

2) These numbers reflect the most recent understanding of ATP synthesis, and as such, may not appear in some textbooks that still cling to the previously established counts of 36 ATP per glucose in eukaryotes and 38 ATP per glucose in prokaryotes.

Other Metabolic Pathways of the Cell

There are several other metabolic pathways that play important roles in maintaining sugar and energy levels.

Glycogenolysis vs. Gluconeogenesis

Glycogenolysis is the term for glycogen breakdown. Glycogen is a polymer of glucose that is found in muscle and liver cells, and is the main form of carbohydrate storage in animals. The synthesis of glycogen (glycogenesis) and glycogenolysis are opposing processes, controlled by hormones that regulate blood sugar levels and energy. Glycogenolysis occurs in response to glucagon, when blood sugar levels are low. It results in glucose being released into the blood.

Gluconeogenesis occurs when dietary sources of glucose are unavailable, and when the liver has depleted stores of glucose. This process occurs primarily in the liver (with a small amount occurring in the kidneys), and involves converting non-carbohydrate precursor molecules (such as lactate, pyruvate, Krebs cycle intermediates, and the carbon skeletons of most amino acids) into oxaloacetate and then glucose.

2.6

β-Oxidation

Fatty acids are made in the cytoplasm of hepatocytes (liver cells) via fatty acid biosynthetic pathways, and are stored in adipocytes (fat cells) as triglycerides (triacylglycerol or TAG). Fatty acids can be broken down in the hepatocyte mitochondria via fatty acid β-oxidation in response to metabolic need. This process involves removing two carbons at a time from the fatty acid and converting these carbons to acetyl-CoA. β-oxidation generates one NADH and one FADH$_2$ for each 2-carbon group removed. The acetyl-CoA can then enter the Krebs cycle. The glycerol backbone of the TAG can be converted into glucose and can enter cellular respiration at glycolysis.

Amino Acid Catabolism

Proteins in cells are constantly being made, kept for a certain period of time (minutes to weeks), and then degraded back into amino acids. In addition, humans absorb amino acids from dietary proteins. These free amino acids can be catabolized via several pathways. The amino group is removed and converted into urea for excretion. The remaining carbon skeleton (also called an α-keto acid) can either be broken down into water and CO$_2$, or can be converted to glucose or acetyl-CoA.

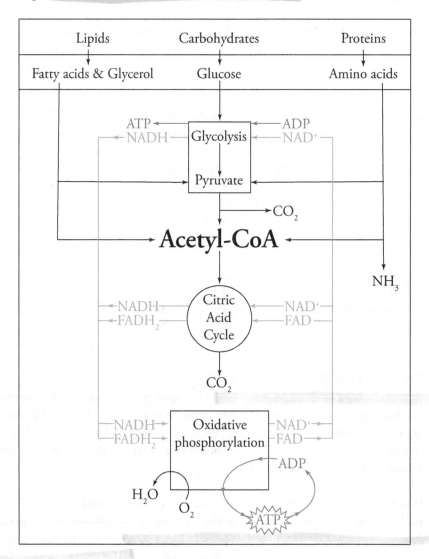

Figure 18   Metabolic Pathways

Summary

- Enzymes are biological catalysts which increase the rate of a reaction by lowering the activation energy.

- Unfavorable reactions in the cell are performed by coupling them to favorable reactions (such as ATP hydrolysis).

- Enzyme activity can be controlled via covalent modification, proteolytic cleavage, associations, or allosteric regulation.

- Competitive inhibitors bind at the active site of an enzyme, do not affect V_{max}, but increase K_m.

- Noncompetitive inhibitors bind at an allosteric site of an enzyme, decrease V_{max}, but do not change K_m.

- Cellular respiration is the oxidation of carbohydrates, reduction of electron carriers, and generation of ATP.

- Glycolysis occurs in the cytoplasm and generates two pyruvate molecules, two ATP, and two NADH per glucose.

- Under anaerobic conditions, the cell performs fermentation to regenerate NAD^+ so that glycolysis can continue.

- The pyruvate dehydrogenase complex (PDC) functions in the mitochondrial matrix, converts pyruvate into acetyl-CoA, and generates an NADH.

- The Krebs cycle in the mitochondrial matrix generates six NADH, two $FADH_2$, and two GTP per glucose.

- The electron transport chain in the inner mitochondrial membrane starts with the oxidation of the electron carriers NADH and $FADH_2$, and ends with the reduction of oxygen and the generation of a proton gradient across the inner mitochondrial membrane.

- ATP synthase in the inner mitochondrial membrane uses the proton gradient to generate ATP (2.5 ATP per NADH from the mitochondrial matrix, 1.5 ATP per NADH from the cytoplasm, and 1.5 ATP per $FADH_2$).

- Both eukaryotes and prokaryotes perform cellular respiration, but prokaryotes use their plasma membrane for the electron transport chain and generate two more ATP per glucose than eukaryotes.

- There are several other metabolic pathways in the cell and many of them converge on the Krebs cycle.

CHAPTER 2 FREESTANDING PRACTICE QUESTIONS

1. In eukaryotes, the ultimate yield of ATP from NADH is lower when the NADH is produced by:

   A) glycolysis.
   B) pyruvate dehydrogenase complex (PDC).
   C) Krebs cycle.
   D) electron transport and oxidative phosphorylation.

2. Some inhibitors bind irreversibly to enzymes by covalent attachment. Would the kinetics seen under these conditions (V vs. [S] curve) be similar to those seen with a reversible noncompetitive inhibitor?

   A) Yes, because it would reduce the K_m of the reaction.
   B) Yes, because the net effect would be a loss of active enzyme available for the reaction.
   C) No, because if enough substrate binds to the active site the reaction will reach V_{max}.
   D) No, because K_m will increase and V_{max} will stay the same, similar to competitive inhibition.

3. Some enzymes can modify their substrate, and by this means, regulate its activity. In many instances, these modifications are not permanent since other enzymes can reverse them. Which of the following category of enzymes will irreversibly modify their substrate?

   A) A kinase
   B) A protease
   C) A phosphatase
   D) An acetylase

4. A common cause of strep throat is a *Streptococcal pharyngitis* infection. When *S. pharyngitis* undergo aerobic cellular respiration, which of the following regions would have the lowest pH?

   A) Matrix of the mitochondria
   B) Intermembrane space of the mitochondria
   C) Cytoplasm
   D) Extracellular

5. Salicylic acid (aspirin) if taken in excess may act as an *uncoupling agent*. Uncoupling agents increase the permeability of the inner mitochondrial membrane, resulting in the dissipation of the proton gradient. Which of the following would most likely be true in the presence of an uncoupling agent?

A) Electron transport at the inner mitochondrial membrane would cease.
B) The energy from the proton-motive force would likely be dissipated as heat rather than in producing ATP from ADP.
C) H^+ ions would flow through the inner membrane into the intermembrane space.
D) There would be an increase in biosynthesis.

6. For a given enzyme concentration at a low substrate concentration, how does reaction rate change as the substrate concentration increases?

A) Logarithmically
B) Linearly
C) Exponentially
D) Indirectly

7. A new enzyme inhibitor for Enzyme X has been discovered. Keeping the enzyme concentration constant, experiments show that the addition of large amounts of substrate causes the enzyme-substrate-inhibitor reaction to occur at the same maximum reaction rate as an enzyme-substrate reaction. This is because:

A) the inhibitor binds at the active site and the addition of large amounts of substrate out-competed the enzyme inhibitor via noncompetitive inhibition.
B) the inhibitor binds at an allosteric site and the addition of large amounts of substrate out-competed the enzyme inhibitor via noncompetitive inhibition.
C) the inhibitor binds at the active site and the addition of large amounts of substrate out-competed the enzyme inhibitor via competitive inhibition.
D) the inhibitor binds at an allosteric site and the addition of large amounts of substrate out-competed the enzyme inhibitor via competitive inhibition.

CHAPTER 2 PRACTICE PASSAGE

Oxygen is a gas that is essential to life. Without it, human cells could not undergo cellular respiration. In order to get oxygen from the lungs to the tissues, the human body employs a complex metalloprotein called hemoglobin. Hemoglobin is an essential protein found in red blood cells of all humans and it consists of four separate units, each of which contains a globulin and a heme group.

There are various normal forms of hemoglobin found in the human body. By far the most abundant form in humans (95 percent of all hemoglobin) is Hemoglobin A, which consists of two α and two β subunits ($\alpha_2\beta_2$). The α subunits are encoded by the HBA1 and the HBA2 genes, while the β subunits are encoded by just one gene, the HBB gene. Hemoglobin A_2, on the other hand, is far less prevalent and consists of two α and two δ subunits ($\alpha_2\delta_2$). Finally, Hemoglobin F, which consists of two α subunits and two γ subunits ($\alpha_2\gamma_2$), is the dominant hemoglobin found in the developing fetus. After birth, Hemoglobin F is still present but in significantly reduced amounts. Figure 1 shows the oxygen dissociation curves for Hemoglobin A and Hemoglobin F.

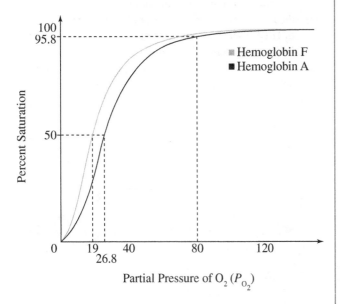

Figure 1 Oxygen Dissociation Curves for Hemoglobin

Alpha-thalassemia (from the Greek words *Thalassa* and *Haema*, which mean "sea" and "blood," respectively) is a blood disease found predominantly in the Mediterranean region. In this disease, a mutation of any of the four alleles that encode the α-globin subunit leads to decreased α-globin production. One mutation causes no symptoms, while two mutations cause mild symptoms (alpha-thalassemia trait). Three mutations will lead to severe symptoms and the presence of abnormal hemoglobins, such as Hemoglobin Barts (γ_4) and Hemoglobin H (β_4). Four mutations usually lead to a condition known as *hydrops fetalis*, which is incompatible with life.

1. Which of the following best describes Hemoglobin F as compared to Hemoglobin A?

    A) It has a higher affinity for oxygen, thus allowing oxygen to diffuse from the fetus to the mother.
    B) It has a lower affinity for oxygen, thus allowing oxygen to diffuse from the fetus to the mother.
    C) It has a higher affinity for oxygen, thus allowing oxygen to diffuse from the mother to the fetus.
    D) It has a lower affinity for oxygen, thus allowing oxygen to diffuse from the mother to the fetus.

2. Which of the following is NOT an example of feedback inhibition?

    A) The effect of estrogen on luteinizing hormone one week before ovulation
    B) The effect of high serum calcium on parathyroid hormone
    C) The effect of estrogen on luteinizing hormone one day before ovulation
    D) The effect of cortisol on ACTH

3. Carbon dioxide is an allosteric inhibitor of the formation of oxyhemoglobin. Which of the following best describes its effects on the binding of oxygen to hemoglobin?

A) It decreases the affinity of hemoglobin for oxygen and shifts the oxygen dissociation curve to the left.
B) It decreases the affinity of hemoglobin for oxygen and shifts the oxygen dissociation curve to the right.
C) It increases the affinity of hemoglobin for oxygen and shifts the oxygen dissociation curve to the left.
D) It increases the affinity of hemoglobin for oxygen and shifts the oxygen dissociation curve to the right.

4. Oxygen binding to the active site of one subunit of the hemoglobin tetramer causes the other subunits to have an increased affinity for oxygen. This phenomenon is known as:

A) allosteric regulation.
B) cooperativity.
C) feedforward stimulation.
D) covalent modification.

5. Protein phosphatases regulate the activity of metabolic pathways by:

A) proteolytic cleavage.
B) allosteric regulation.
C) constitutive activity.
D) covalent modification.

6. Carbon monoxide is a competitive inhibitor of the formation of oxyhemoglobin. Which of the following best describes its effects on the binding of oxygen with hemoglobin?

A) It binds to the active site and it decreases V_{max}.
B) It binds to an allosteric site and it decreases V_{max}.
C) It binds to the active site and it has no effect on V_{max}.
D) It binds to an allosteric site and it has no effect on V_{max}.

7. Which of the following best explains why Hemoglobin Barts causes significant symptoms?

A) It has a higher affinity for oxygen than Hemoglobin A, thus it is more difficult for oxygen to enter tissues.
B) It has a lower affinity for oxygen than Hemoglobin A, thus it is more difficult to bind oxygen in the lungs.
C) It has no affinity for oxygen because it has no α subunits.
D) The absence of β subunits causes a nonfunctioning form of hemoglobin.

SOLUTIONS TO CHAPTER 2 FREESTANDING PRACTICE QUESTIONS

1. **A** In order for the NADH produced during glycolysis to be utilized by the electron transport chain (ETC) in ATP formation, the electrons must be shuttled into the mitochondria (remember, glycolysis occurs in the cytosol and the ETC occurs along the inner mitochondrial membrane). When shuttled in, the electrons are typically used to reduce Coenzyme Q, and bypass NADH dehydrogenase. This results in the pumping of fewer protons out of the mitochondrial matrix, and thus, ultimately, in fewer ATP being formed. The NADH produced by the PDC or Krebs cycle is energetically equivalent because both occur in the mitochondrial matrix. Thus, this NADH is immediately accessible to the ETC (choices B and C are wrong). Finally, note that the ETC regenerates NAD$^+$ rather than producing NADH (choice D is wrong).

2. **B** An irreversible inhibitor (regardless of where it binds) will permanently deactivate some enzyme, reducing effective enzyme concentration. If the enzyme concentration is effectively lowered, V_{max} will be reduced (choices C and D are wrong). This is similar to what is seen in noncompetitive inhibition, where the inhibitor binds to an allosteric site and turns the enzyme off. Even if the noncompetitive inhibitor is reversible, because at any given time some enzyme is "off," the effective enzyme concentration is lowered and V_{max} is reduced. If K_m were affected, it would increase, not decrease; an increase in K_m indicates that the substrate-enzyme interaction has been compromised in some way (choice A is wrong).

3. **B** Proteases are enzymes that cleave their substrates at specific sites, permanently removing a part of the protein. This modification is practically irreversible—there are no enzymes that can reconnect proteins split by a protease. Answers A, C, and D are wrong because these categories of enzymes can reversibly modify their substrates. A kinase adds a phosphate to its substrate, but this modification can be reversed by a phosphatase that will remove the phosphate. An acetylase will add an acetyl group, while a deacetylase will remove it.

4. **D** *Streptococcal pharyngitis* are bacteria (prokaryotes). Unlike eukaryotes, prokaryotes do not have any membrane-bound organelles such as mitochondria (choices A and B can be eliminated). During cellular respiration, prokaryotes pump protons from the cytoplasm to the extracellular space between the plasma membrane and the cell wall. A gradient is established when protons accumulate in this space, thus lowering the pH of that region (choice D is correct and choice C is wrong). These protons return to the cytoplasm by flowing through the ATP synthase on the plasma membrane, thereby producing ATP.

5. **B** The proton gradient obtained by the electron transport chain (which pumps H$^+$ ions across the inner membrane into the intermembrane space) is necessary in order to create ATP at the ATP synthase. This enzyme allows the protons to move through its channel back into the matrix, and thus harnesses the energy created by the gradient to create ATP from ADP + P$_i$. If the inner membrane was made more permeable by uncoupling agents, then the H$^+$ ions would naturally move down their gradient, from the intermembrane space back to the mitochondrial matrix (choice C is wrong). This unharnessed energy would be dissipated as heat (known as non-exercise activity thermogenesis [NEAT]), and since the ions would not pass through the ATP synthase, less ATP would be created (choice B is correct). Although the utility of the electron transport chain would be compromised, the uncoupling agent

would not inhibit electron transport itself (choice A is wrong); in fact this would lead to the rapid oxidation of Krebs cycle substrates and would promote the mobilization of carbohydrates and fats. Since the energy is lost as heat, biosynthesis is not promoted (choice D is wrong), and weight loss can be dramatic. Experimental uncoupling agents have been used in the past as effective diet pills; however, their use is very dangerous and thankfully this practice has fallen out of use.

6. **B** At low substrate concentrations, the reaction rate increases linearly as the substrate concentration increases (see curve below). At or near saturation levels, the reaction rate begins to level off and does not change regardless of how much substrate it added. This is called the maximum velocity of reaction rate or V_{max}.

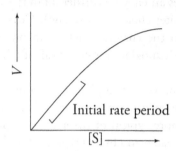

7. **C** This is a two-by-two question, where two decisions must be made to get to the correct answer. The question states that large amounts of added substrate can out-compete the inhibitor and result in the same V_{max} as the uninhibited reaction. This is only possible with competitive inhibition (choices A and B can be eliminated) where the inhibitor binds at the active site (choice D can be eliminated and choice C is correct). Noncompetitive inhibition occurs when an enzyme inhibitor binds to an allosteric site, a site on the enzyme that is distinct from the active site.

SOLUTIONS TO CHAPTER 2 PRACTICE PASSAGE

1. **C** This is an example of a two-by-two question, where two decisions are required to find the correct answer. In no case would we want oxygen to diffuse from the fetus to the mother; oxygen should always be delivered from mother to fetus (choices A and B can be eliminated). As shown in Figure 1, Hemoglobin F is more saturated at lower P_{O_2}s than Hemoglobin A, indicating that Hemoglobin F has a higher affinity for oxygen (choice D is wrong and C is correct).

2. **C** During the early stages of the menstrual/ovulatory cycle, lower levels of estrogen inhibit the release of luteinizing hormone (choice A is an example of feedback inhibition and can be eliminated). However, as ovulation approaches, high levels of estrogen stimulate the release of luteinizing hormone (positive feedback), thus choice C is the answer. Note that choices B and D are both examples of feedback inhibition and can be eliminated; high serum calcium inhibits parathyroid hormone release and cortisol inhibits the release of ACTH.

3. **B** This is another example of a two-by-two question, where two decisions are required to find the correct answer. An inhibitor of the formation of oxyhemoglobin would have to decrease the affinity of hemoglobin for oxygen (choices C and D can be eliminated). A decreased affinity for oxygen means that hemoglobin will be less saturated at the same P_{O_2}; this is represented by a right-shifted curve (choice A is wrong and choice B is correct). For confirmation, look at Figure 1; Hemoglobin A has a lower affinity for oxygen than Hemoglobin F and the curve for Hemoglobin A is shifted to the right with respect to the curve for Hemoglobin F.

4. **B** Cooperativity occurs when the binding of substrate to the active site of one subunit of an enzyme or protein causes an increase in substrate-affinity of the other active sites on that enzyme/protein. Allosteric regulation can be similar but does not occur at the active site (choice A is wrong). Feedforward stimulation occurs when substrate for one enzyme in a series of reactions stimulates an enzyme further on in the series (and most likely also involves binding at an allosteric site; choice C is wrong). Covalent modification requires covalent bonding of something to the enzyme, such as in phosphorylation or dephosphorylation. The binding of oxygen to hemoglobin is not covalent (choice D is wrong).

5. **D** A protein phosphatase removes a phosphate from a protein; this is a covalent modification. Proteolytic cleavage involves breaking peptide bonds between amino acids; phosphatases do not do this. This is more typical of the activation of digestive enzymes (such as when chymotrypsinogen is activated to chymotrypsin; choice A is wrong). Allosteric regulation occurs via the binding of a regulator molecule to an allosteric site of an enzyme and does not involve dephosphorylation (choice B is wrong). Constitutive activity occurs when the activity of an enzyme is continuously on; this can occur in response to association with an activating subunit, or dissociation from an inhibitory subunit (choice C is wrong).

6. **C** This is another example of a two-by-two question, where two decisions are required to find the correct answer. Competitive inhibitors bind to the active sites of enzymes (noncompetitive inhibitors bind to allosteric sites; choices B and D can be eliminated). Competitive inhibitors reduce V, but do not affect V_{max} (noncompetitive inhibitors decrease V_{max}; choice A can be eliminated and choice C is correct).

7. **A** The passage describes Hemoglobin Barts as having four γ subunits. As shown in Figure 1, Hemoglobin F (with two γ subunits) has a higher affinity for oxygen than Hemoglobin A (with two β subunits). Thus, γ subunits must have a higher affinity for oxygen, and hemoglobin made up exclusively of γ subunits would have a higher affinity for oxygen than even Hemoglobin F. Thus, it would not release oxygen to the tissues (choice A is correct and choices B and C are wrong). The absence of β subunits would not lead to a nonfunctioning form of hemoglobin; Hemoglobin F has no β subunits and functions just fine (choice D is wrong).

Chapter 3
Molecular Biology

It was once thought that simple living organisms were generated spontaneously from nonliving matter. When a steak went bad and became infested with larvae, it was because the decomposing meat actually became squirming worms. Most religions have traditional explanations for the origin of human life, too. Children are derived from adults due to the will of a deity; the original adults were placed on the earth by that deity. But as empiricism developed during the Enlightenment, rigorous experiments were used to explain life, resulting in "scientific" models that are gradually replacing more traditional explanations.

One early conclusion was that simple organisms were derived not from decomposing matter but from parental organisms. Subsequently, it was found that some organisms are too small to be seen with the naked eye. These "germs" were eventually implicated as the cause of most major diseases. Gradually the scientific community came to the conclusion that all life was derived from other life. The patterns of inheritance and evolution were elucidated by a chain of scientists, from Mendel through Darwin. But the mechanism remained a mystery. Finally, cellular biology advanced to the point that scientists were aware of two substances found in cells which seemed appropriate vehicles for the transmission of inherited information: DNA and protein. The extreme length and orderly arrangement of repeating units in DNA and protein made it seem very likely that they could contain information. Researchers had waded through a chemical ocean of alphabet soup and suddenly come upon long strings of what looked like letters.

This is where biology stood in the early 1940s. In the '40s and '50s, two monumental achievements in microbiology finally clarified the gears in the clock of evolution and how they turn. One was the elucidation of the structure of DNA by Watson and Crick. The other was the proof by Avery, Herriott, Hershey, Chase, and their coworkers that DNA was the fundamental unit of genetic inheritance in microorganisms. In the following discussion, we will summarize the wealth of information that has been built upon these two prescient cornerstones.

3.1   DNA STRUCTURE

General Overview

Understanding the structure of DNA provides great insight into its function, so let's start at the smallest level and work our way up. DNA is short for deoxyribonucleic acid. DNA and RNA (ribonucleic acid) are called **nucleic acids** because they are found in the nucleus and possess many acidic phosphate groups. The building block of DNA is the deoxyribonucleoside 5' triphosphate (dNTP, where N represents one of the four basic nucleosides). Deoxyadenosine 5' triphosphate (dATP) is shown in Figure 1. Deoxyribonucleotides are built from three components. The first is a simple monosaccharide, ribose. [What modification makes this ribose special?[1]] In a dNTP, carbons on the ribose are referred to as 1', 2', etc. The next component of the dNTP is an aromatic base, namely **adenine** (A), guanine (G), cytosine (C), or thymine (T); see Figure 2. (Don't mix up the DNA base thymine with vitamin B_1, thiamine.) These aromatic molecules are bases because they contain several nitrogens which have free electron pairs capable of accepting protons. G and A are derived from a precursor called purine, so they are referred to as **the purines**. C and T are **the pyrimidines**.[2] A nucleo*side* is ribose with a purine or pyrimidine linked to the 1' carbon in a β-N-glycosidic linkage. The nucleosides are named as follows: A-ribose = adenosine, G-ribose = guanosine, C-ribose = cytidine, T-ribose = thymidine, and U-ribose = uridine. [In the β-N-glycosidic linkage of a nucleoside, is the aromatic base above or is it below the plane of ribose in a Haworth projection?[3]] Both purines and pyrimidines have abundant hydrogen bonding potential. [Will adenine and thymine H-bond with each other in dilute aqueous solution (0.1 *M*, for example)?[4]]

The final component of the deoxyribonucleotide building block of DNA is a phosphate group. Nucleo*tides* are phosphate esters of nucleosides, with one, two, or three phosphate groups joined to the ribose ring by the 5' hydroxy group. When nucleotides contain three phosphate residues, they may also be referred to as **deoxynucleoside triphosphates**; they are abbreviated **dNTP**, where d is for deoxy and N is for nucleoside. In individual nucleotides, N is replaced by A, G, C, T, or U. Because they contain acidic phosphates, the nucleotides may also be referred to by a name ending in "ylate." For example, TTP is thymidylate. The ubiquitous energy molecule, ATP, is a nucleotide which may be called adenylate (it's not deoxy).

---

[1]   The 2' OH is missing, so it is *deoxy*ribose.

[2]   A mnemonic for this is: Pyramids (pyrimidines) have sharp edges, so they CUT. The U stands for *uracil*, which is a pyrimidine found in RNA instead of T. RNA will be discussed in Section 3.4.

[3]   A beta linkage indicates that the anomeric carbon has a configuration with the attached group (a nitrogen of the aromatic ring of a purine or pyrimidine base) drawn *above* the plane of the ribose ring. Remember, it's better to β up!

[4]   No. In dilute solution they will be H-bonded to water. However, H-bonds are the key determinant of the double-stranded structure of DNA; in DNA the bases do not interact with water because DNA coiling places them inside the tube-like structure of the double helix, where they interact with each other.

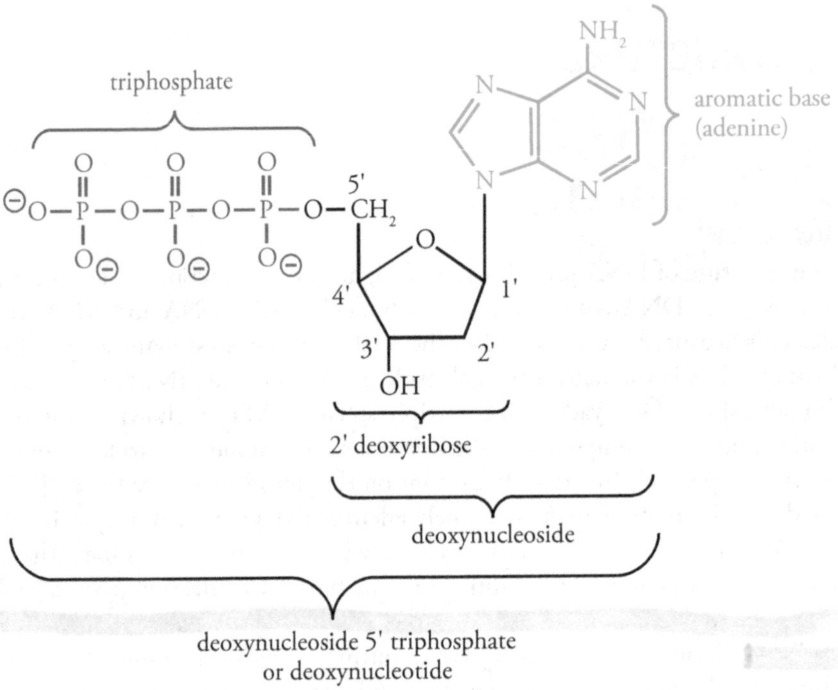

Figure 1   Deoxyadenosine Triphosphate (dATP)

The ribose + phosphate portion of the nucleotide is referred to as the **backbone** of DNA, because it is invariant. The base is the variable portion of the building block. Hence there are four different dNTPs, and they differ only in the aromatic base. [What is the backbone in protein, and what is the variable portion of the amino acid?[5] If an enzyme binds to a specific sequence of nucleotides in DNA, will the binding specificity be derived from interactions of portions of the polypeptide enzyme with the ribose and phosphate groups or with the purine and pyrimidine bases?[6]]

---

[5] Peptide bonds with a carbon between them are the backbone, and the R group attached to the α carbon is the variable portion.

[6] Since the backbone is the same regardless of the nucleotide sequence, the specificity in binding must be derived from interactions with bases.

PYRIMIDINE BASES

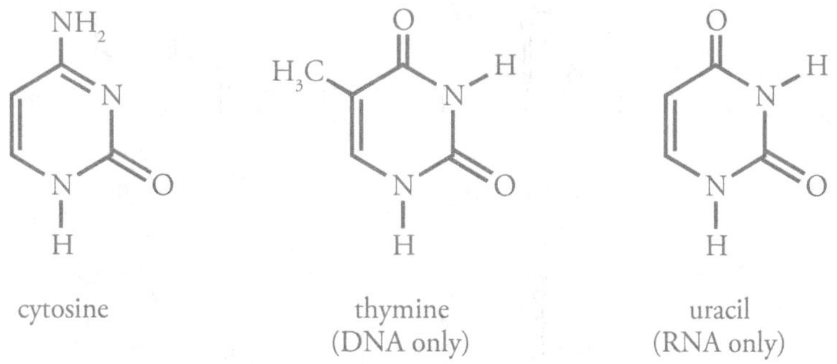

cytosine

thymine
(DNA only)

uracil
(RNA only)

PURINE BASES

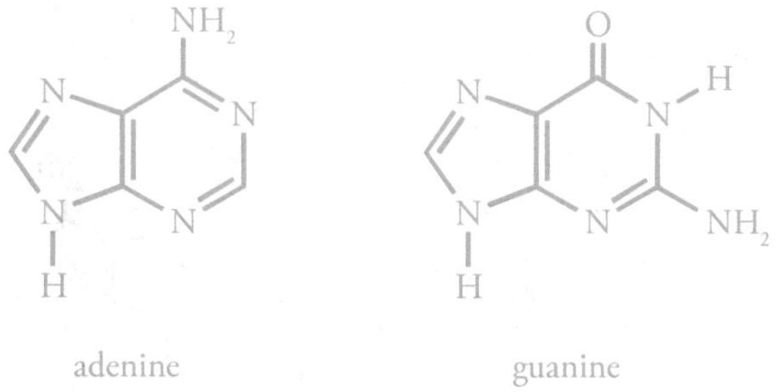

adenine

guanine

Figure 2   Aromatic Bases of DNA and RNA

Polynucleotides

Nucleotides in the DNA chain are covalently linked by **phosphodiester bonds** between the 3' hydroxy group of one deoxyribose and the 5' phosphate group of the next deoxyribose (Figure 3). [Which reaction is more thermodynamically favorable: the polymerization of nucleoside monophosphates, or the polymerization of nucleoside triphosphates?[7]] A polymer of several nucleotides linked together is termed an *oligo*nucleotide, and a polymer of many nucleotides is a *poly*nucleotide. Since the only unique part of the nucleotide is the base, the sequence of a polynucleotide can be abbreviated by simply listing the bases attached to each nucleotide in the chain. The end of the chain with a free 5' phosphate group is written first in a polynucleotide, with other nucleotides in the chain indicated in the 5' to 3' direction. [Which of the nucleotides in the oligonucleotide ACGT has a free 3' hydroxy group?[8]]

---

[7]   During polymerization of nucleoside triphosphates, pyrophosphate is released and hydrolyzed, driving the polymerization reaction forward. Hydrolysis of the high energy pyrophosphate molecule makes the polymerization of nucleoside triphosphates more energetically favorable.

[8]   The T is written last and is therefore the 3' nucleotide, or the nucleotide with the free 3' hydroxy group.

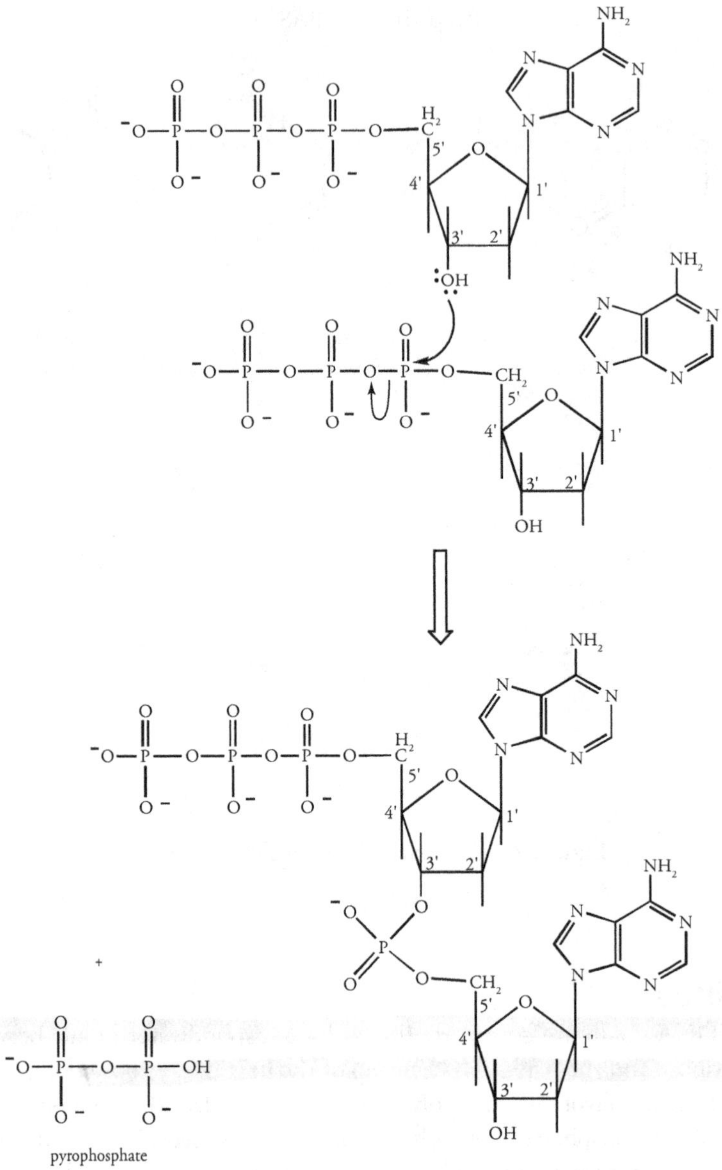

Figure 3 The Polymerization of Nucleotides

The Watson-Crick Model of DNA Structure

Watson and Crick developed a model of the structure of DNA in the cell. According to the **Watson-Crick model**, cellular DNA is a right-handed double helix held together by hydrogen bonds between bases. It is important to understand each facet of this model.

In the cell, DNA does not exist in the form of a single long polynucleotide. Instead, the DNA found in the nucleus is double-stranded (**ds**). In ds-DNA, two very long polynucleotide chains are hydrogen-bonded together in an **antiparallel** orientation. Antiparallel means the 5' end of one chain is paired with the 3' end of the other. [What common protein structure often depends on H-bonds between antiparallel chains?[9]] The H-bonds in ds-DNA are between the bases on adjacent chains. This H-bonding is very specific: A is always H-bonded to T, and G is always H-bonded to C (Figure 4). Note that this means an H-bonded pair always consists of a *purine plus a pyrimidine*.[10] Thus both types of base pair (AT or GC) take up the same amount of room in the DNA double helix. The GC pair is held together by three hydrogen bonds, the AT pair by two. Two chains of DNA are said to be complementary if the bases in each strand can hydrogen bond when the strands are oriented in an antiparallel fashion. If we are talking about ds-DNA 100 nucleotides long, we would say it is 100 base pairs (bp) long. A kbp (kilobase pair) is ds-DNA 1000 nucleotides long.

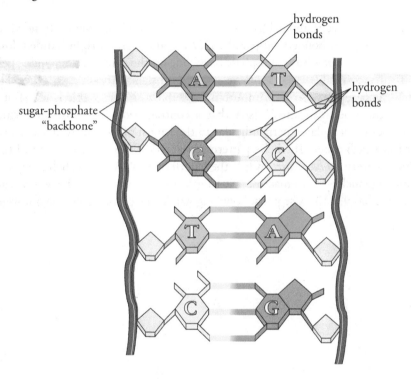

Figure 4   Base Pairing

The binding of two complementary strands of DNA into a double-stranded structure is termed **annealing**, or **hybridization**. The separation of strands is termed **melting**, or **denaturation**. The temperature at which a solution of DNA molecules is 50 percent melted is termed the T_m. [Would the T_m of ATTATCAT and its complementary strand be higher than, lower than, or equal to the melting temperature of AGTCGCAT and its complementary strand?[11] If you attached methyl groups to all the acidic phosphate oxygens along the length of a DNA double helix, would the chain have a higher or lower T_m than normal DNA?[12]]

---

[9] Antiparallel H-bonding is reminiscent of the β-pleated sheet, which is a common secondary structure (it can be quaternary, when two separate chains come together to form a sheet).

[10] This fact has a fringe benefit: We can calculate the number of purines if we know the number of pyrimidines. We can actually calculate several variables. Chargoff's rule states that [A] = [T] and [G] = [C]; and [A] + [G] = [T] + [C].

[11] The T_m of the first oligonucleotide pair would be lower because it contains more AT pairs. A and T only form two hydrogen bonds while G and C form three. Thus, it takes less kinetic energy to disrupt A-T rich ds-DNA than G-C rich ds-DNA.

[12] The charged phosphates electrostatically repel each other in normal DNA. Methyl esters will not be charged. The lack of electrostatic repulsion between the methyl ester backbones will increase the T_m, meaning that more kinetic energy will be required to melt the oligonucleotides.

- Which of the following is/are true about ds-DNA?
    I. If the amount of G in a double helix is known, the amount of C can be calculated.
    II. If the fraction of purine nucleotides and the total molecular weight of a double helix are known, the amount of cytosine can be calculated.
    III. The two chains in a piece of ds-DNA containing mostly purines will be bonded together more tightly than the two chains in a piece of ds-DNA containing mostly pyrimidines.
    IV. The oligonucleotide ATGTAT is complementary to the oligonucleotide ATACAT.[13]

There is another important detail about DNA structure: Not only is it double stranded, it is also *coiled*. In ds-DNA, the two hydrogen-bonded antiparallel DNA strands form a **right-handed double helix** with the bases on the interior and the ribose/phosphate backbone on the exterior. The double helix is stabilized by van der Waals interactions between the bases, which are stacked upon each other. Hydrophobic interactions between the bases are also very important in stabilizing the double helix. [But wait a minute. "Hydro*phobic* interactions between *bases*?" Isn't that a contradiction in terms? How can a *base* be hydro*phobic*?[14]] The bases lie in a plane, perpendicular to the length of the DNA molecule, stacked 3.4 angstroms (Å) apart from each other. The helix pattern repeats itself (i.e., completes a full turn) once every *34 angstroms*, which is every *10 base pairs*. While the length of a DNA double helix may vary enormously, from a few Å in an oligonucleotide to macroscopic lengths in a chromosome, the width is always 20 Å. [If a human chromosome has 9×10^7 base pairs, how long would the chromosome be if it were stretched out completely?[15]]

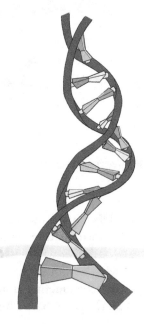

Figure 5   A Small Section of a DNA Double Helix

[13] **Item I: True.** For every G, there is a C; and for every A there is a T. **Item II: False.** The ratio of purines to pyrimidines is always the same (50:50) since each purine is paired with a pyrimidine. In order to calculate the amount of any one base, you have to know the ratio of AT to GC pairs. **Item III: False.** Again, the ratio of purines to pyrimidines is always the same; 50:50. However, two chains containing mostly GC pairs will bond more tightly than two chains containing mostly AT pairs, since GC pairs are held together by 3 H-bonds while AT pairs have only 2. **Item IV: True.** Remember: the strands are antiparallel, A and T pair, G and C pair, and the 5' end is always written first.

[14] Once a purine is H-bonded to a pyrimidine, most of the polar nature of the individual bases disappears because the charge dipoles are occupied in H-bonds.

[15] Since one angstrom is 10^{-10} meter, the length is (3.4×10^{-10} meters/base pair)(9×10^7 base pairs) = 30×10^{-3} meters = 30 millimeters.

The sum total of an organism's genetic information is called its **genome**. Eukaryotic genomes are composed of several large pieces of linear ds-*DNA*; each piece of ds-DNA is called a **chromosome**. Humans have 46 chromosomes, 23 of which are inherited from each parent. Prokaryotic (bacterial) genomes are composed of a **single circular chromosome**. Viral genomes may be linear or circular DNA or RNA. The human genome consists of over 10^9 base pairs while bacterial genomes contain only 10^6 base pairs. But there is no direct correlation between genome size and evolutionary sophistication, since the organisms with the largest known genomes are amphibians. Much of the size difference in higher eukaryotic genomes is the result of repetitive DNA that has no known function.

One final point: If the DNA remained as a simple double helix floating free in the cell, it would be very bulky and fragile. Prokaryotes have a distinctive mechanism for making their single circular chromosome more compact and sturdy. An enzyme called **DNA gyrase** uses the energy of ATP to twist the gigantic circular molecule. Gyrase functions by breaking the DNA and twisting the two sides of the circle around each other. The resulting structure is a twisted circle that is composed of ds-DNA. As discussed above, the two strands are already coiled, forming a helix. The twists created by DNA gyrase are called **supercoils**, since they are coils of a structure that is already coiled.

Since eukaryotes have even more DNA in their genome than prokaryotes, the eukaryotic genome requires denser packaging to fit within the cell (Figure 6). To accomplish this, eukaryotic DNA is wrapped around globular proteins called **histones**. After being wrapped around histones, but before being completely packed away, DNA has the microscopic appearance of beads on a string. The beads are called **nucleosomes**; they are composed of DNA wrapped around an octamer of (a group of 8) histones. The string between the beads is a length of double-helical DNA called linker DNA and is bound by a single linker histone. Fully packed DNA is called chromatin; it is composed of closely stacked nucleosomes. [Based on your knowledge of the interactions of macromolecules and the chemical composition of DNA, do you suppose that histones mostly basic or mostly acidic?[16]]

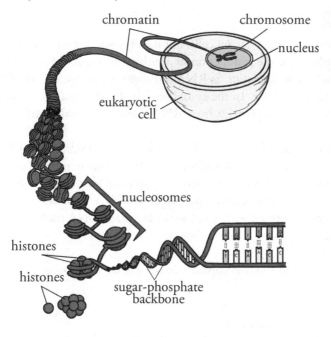

Figure 6   DNA Packaging

<hr>

[16] They're mostly basic, since they must be attracted to the acidic exterior of the DNA double helix. This basicity is supplied by the amino acids arginine and lysine, which are unusually abundant in histones.

The following flow equation summarizes the structure of DNA in the nucleus: **Deoxyribose** → *add base* → **nucleoside** → *add three phosphates* → **nucleotide** → *polymerize with loss of two phosphates* → **oligonucleotide** → *continue polymerization* → **single stranded polynucleotide** → *two complete chains H-bond in antiparallel orientation* → **ds DNA chain** → *coiling occurs* → **ds helix** → *wrap around histones* → **nucleosomes** → *complete packaging* → **chromatin**. Remember, each individual double-stranded piece of chromatin is condensed into a chromosome during mitosis and meiosis (see Chapter 6).

3.2   DNA'S JOB

The Role of DNA

DNA encodes and transmits the genetic information passed down from parents to offspring. Before 1944 it was generally believed that protein, rather than DNA, carried genetic information, since proteins have an "alphabet" of 20 letters (the amino acids), while DNA's "alphabet" has only 4 letters (the four nucleotides). But in that year, Oswald Avery showed that DNA was the active agent in bacterial transformation. In short, this means he proved that pure DNA from one type of *E. coli* bacteria could transform *E. coli* of another type, causing it to acquire the genetic nature of the first type. Later Hershey and Chase proved that DNA was the active chemical in the infection of *E. coli* bacteria by bacteriophage T2.[17]

The Genetic Code

DNA does not directly exert its influence on cells, but merely contains sequences of nucleotides known as **genes** that serve as **templates** for the production of another nucleic acid known as RNA. The process of reading DNA and writing the information as RNA is termed **transcription**. The RNA serves as a messenger from the nucleus to the cytoplasm. In the cytoplasm, the RNA is read, and the information is written down as protein. The production of proteins from RNA is termed **translation**.[18]

The overall process looks like this: DNA → RNA → protein. This unidirectional flow equation represents the **Central Dogma** (fundamental law) of molecular biology. This is the mechanism whereby inherited *information* is used to create actual *objects*, namely enzymes and structural proteins. An exception to the Central Dogma is that certain viruses (retroviruses) make DNA from RNA using the enzyme reverse transcriptase (see Chapter 4). Here we will examine the language DNA uses to orchestrate protein synthesis. The process goes like this:

1) Information contained in DNA is copied into a messenger, **messenger RNA (mRNA)**.

---

[17] Transformation and bacteriophage will be discussed in Chapter 4.

[18] To *transcribe* a letter is to listen to spoken words and write them down as printed text. The message doesn't change, and the language, English, doesn't change. To *translate* a letter is to change it from one language to another. Cellular transcription is the process whereby a code is read from a nucleic acid (DNA) and written in the language of another nucleic acid (RNA), so the language is the same. In cellular translation, nucleic acids are read and polypeptides are written, so here the language does change.

2) The mRNA travels to the cytoplasm, where it encounters the **ribosome** and other components of protein synthesis. The ribosome is a massive enzyme composed of many proteins and pieces of RNA (known as **ribosomal RNA** or **rRNA**).

3) The ribosome synthesizes polypeptides according to the DNA's original orders.

In this section, we will examine the command language used by DNA and mRNA to specify the building blocks of proteins. This language is known as the **Genetic Code**. The alphabet of the genetic code contains only four letters (A, T, G, C). How can four letters specify the ingredients of the multitude of proteins in every cell? [What is the smallest "word" size that would allow this four-letter alphabet to encode twenty different amino acids?[19]] A number of experiments confirmed that the genetic code is written in three-letter words, each of which codes for a particular amino acid. A nucleic acid word (3 nucleotide letters) is referred to as a **codon**.

The genetic code is represented in Figure 7. The first nucleotide in a codon is given at the left, the second on top, and the third on the right. At the intersection of these three nucleotides is the amino acid called for by that codon. [Why is uracil (U) shown in the chart, and why is thymine (T) absent?[20] The codon GTG in DNA is transcribed in RNA as __, which the ribosome translates into what amino acid?[21]]

1st Position (5' End)	2nd Position				3rd Position (3' End)
	U	**C**	**A**	**G**	
U	Phe	Ser	Tyr	Cys	U
	Phe	Ser	Tyr	Cys	C
	Leu	Ser	**Stop**	**Stop**	A
	Leu	Ser	**Stop**	Trp	G
C	Leu	Pro	His	Arg	U
	Leu	Pro	His	Arg	C
	Leu	Pro	Gln	Arg	A
	Leu	Pro	Gln	Arg	G
A	Ile	Thr	Asn	Ser	U
	Ile	Thr	Asn	Ser	C
	Ile	Thr	Lys	Arg	A
	Met	Thr	Lys	Arg	G
G	Val	Ala	Asp	Gly	U
	Val	Ala	Asp	Gly	C
	Val	Ala	Glu	Gly	A
	Val	Ala	Glu	Gly	G

Figure 7 The Genetic Code

---

[19] With four nucleotides, if a "word" (codon) is two nucleotides long, there are $4^2 = 16$ possible codons; too few to specify 20 unique amino acids. However, there are $4^3 = 64$ possible 3-letter "words," and 64 is more than enough different codons to specify 20 unique amino acids. Thus, three nucleotides is the minimum codon size.

[20] RNA is the nucleic acid that actually encodes protein during translation. RNA has U instead of T.

[21] The RNA codon transcribed from the DNA will be CAC, coding for histidine.

- The genetic code was studied by experimenters using a cell-free protein synthesis system. All of the materials necessary for protein synthesis (ribosomes, amino acids, tRNA, GTP, ATP) were purified and placed in a beaker. Then synthetic RNA was added, and protein was translated from this template. For example, when synthetic RNA containing only cytosine (CCCCC...) was added, polypeptides containing only proline (polyproline) resulted. What kind of synthetic RNA would give rise to a mixture of polyproline, polyhistidine, and polythreonine?[22]

There are 64 codons. Sixty-one of them specify amino acids; the remaining three are called **stop codons**. Their function is to notify the ribosome that the protein is complete and cause it to stop reading the mRNA (see Section 3.5). Stop codons are also called **nonsense codons**, since they don't code for any amino acid. Note that most of the twenty amino acids can be coded for by more than one codon. Often, all four of the codons with the same first two nucleotides (e.g., CU_) encode the same amino acid. [If the last nucleotide in the codon CUU is changed in a gene that codes for a protein, will the protein be affected?[23]] Two or more codons coding for the same amino acid are known as **synonyms**. Because it has such synonyms, the genetic code is said to be **degenerate**. However, it is very important to realize that though an amino acid may be specified by several codons, *each codon specifies only a single amino acid.* This means that each piece of DNA can be interpreted only one way: The code has no **ambiguity**.

Genetic Mutation

Genetic mutation refers to any alteration of the DNA sequence of an organism's genome. The causes of mutation include mistakes in replication of the genome during cell division, chance chemical malformations (such as spontaneous deamination, which means loss of a nitrogen group), and environmental agents such as chemicals and ultraviolet light. For example, compounds that look like purines and pyrimidines (with large flat aromatic ring structures) cause mutations by inserting themselves between base pairs, or **intercalating**, thereby causing errors in DNA replication. Any compound which can cause mutations is called a **mutagen**. There are three kinds of mutations:

1) point mutations
2) insertion mutations
3) deletion mutations

Point mutations are single base pair substitutions (A in place of G, for example). Point mutations can be **transitions** (substitution of a pyrimidine for another pyrimidine or substitution of a purine for another purine) or **transversions** (substitution of a purine for a pyrimidine or vice versa). There are three subclassifications of point mutations:

1) **missense mutations:** cause one amino acid to be replaced with a different amino acid
2) **nonsense mutations:** cause a stop codon to replace a regular codon
3) **silent mutations:** change a codon into a new codon for the same amino acid (no change in protein amino acid sequence)

---

[22] The RNA would have to be CCACCACCACCACCACCACCAC....This would yield polyproline if read as CCA, CCA, CCA. But if it were read as CAC, CAC, CAC, it would give rise to polyhistidine. If it were read ACC, ACC, ACC, it would encode polythreonine.

[23] No, since CUN codes for leucine, regardless of what N is. Notice that switching the 3rd nucleotide in the majority of codons will have no effect.

If a missense mutation leads to little change in the structure and function of the gene product (protein), it is referred to as a **conservative mutation**. [How can this occur?[24]]

Insertion refers to the addition of one or more extra nucleotides into the DNA sequence. **Deletion** is the removal of nucleotides from the sequence. Both of these mutations can cause a shift in the **reading frame**. For example, AAACCCACC can be read as AAA, CCC, ACC. It would code for lys-pro-thr. Inserting an extra G into the first codon could produce this: AGAACCCACC. This would be read AGA, ACC, CAC, C. It now codes for arg-thr-his (plus there's an extra C). Not only has the first codon changed; the whole piece of DNA will be read differently. Mutations causing a change in the reading frame are called **frameshift mutations**. Generally speaking, frameshift mutations are very serious. Note that a frameshift can lead to premature termination of translation (yielding an incomplete polypeptide) if it results in the presence of an abnormal stop codon. [Are all insertions and deletions frameshift mutations?[25] If the following oligonucleotide is mutated by inserting a G between the fifth and sixth codons, what effect will this have on the oligopeptide it encodes: AUG AAG GGG CCC UUU AAA UGA CCC?[26] For each type of mutation, does it involve a change in the genotype, the phenotype, or both?[27]]

- Sickle-cell anemia is a genetic disease caused by alteration of a single amino acid in the hemoglobin polypeptide. Which one of the following could cause such a mutation?[28]
    - A. An error in the translation of hemoglobin
    - B. Insertion of a single nucleotide into the DNA sequence of the gene encoding hemoglobin
    - C. A frameshift mutation
    - D. Alteration of a purine to a pyrimidine base

3.3 DNA REPLICATION

The DNA genome is the control center of the cell. When mitosis produces two identical daughter cells from one parental cell, each daughter must have the same genome as the parent. Hence, cell division requires duplication of the DNA, known as **replication**. This is an enzymatic process, just as the Krebs

---

[24] For example, substituting a small hydrophobe such as valine for another small hydrophobe like leucine will probably cause little disruption of protein structure. Another way of defining conservative mutations is that they cause changes in primary structure but do not affect secondary, tertiary, or quaternary structure.

[25] No. If you insert or delete one whole codon or several whole codons, you add or remove amino acids to the polypeptide without changing the reading frame.

[26] The original RNA codes for Met-Lys-Gly-Pro-Phe-Lys. After the insertion, the oligonucleotide will code for Met-Lys-Gly-Pro-Phe-Glu-Met-Thr. Note that this contains different amino acids and it's longer. The extra length is due to the fact that a stop codon, UGA, changed by the frameshift.

[27] By definition, all mutations involve a change in the genotype. Most mutations also cause a change in the phenotype, but in the case of conservative mutations it is a very subtle change that would be hard to detect.

[28] Alteration of a purine to a pyrimidine base is described in the text as a transversion mutation, which is classified as a point mutation. Point mutations could result in a single amino acid change (choice **D** is correct). An error in translation would temporarily result in defective hemoglobin, but the defect would not be genetic (it wouldn't be passed from parents to offspring; choice A is wrong). Insertion of a single nucleotide into the DNA sequence would cause a frameshift mutation. Frameshift mutations lead to massive changes in amino acid sequence and protein structure, since every codon after the mutation is changed. This could not produce the single amino acid change described in the question (choices B and C are wrong).

3.3

cycle and glycolysis are enzymatic processes. It occurs during S (synthesis) **phase** in interphase of the cell cycle (Chapter 5). Let's go through the process of replication, stopping to add essential facts to a list of things to memorize. But before we get bogged down with details, we should have a look at the big picture.

There is only one logical way to make a new piece of DNA that is identical to the old one: copy it. The old DNA is called **parental** DNA, and the new is called **daughter** DNA. What is the relationship between parental and daughter DNA after replication? There are several possibilities (Figure 8). In other words, where do the atoms from the parent go when the daughters are made? The way it works is that the individual strands of the double-stranded parent are pulled apart. Then a new daughter strand is synthesized using the parental DNA as a template to copy from.[29] [Each new daughter chain is perfectly __[30] to its template or parent.] After replication, one strand of the new double helix is parental (old), and one strand is newly synthesized daughter DNA, making DNA replication **semiconservative**.

Let's begin the list of things to memorize here:

1) **DNA replication is semiconservative.**

Experiments were done by two researchers, Messelson and Stahl, who studied DNA replication to determine whether it was semiconservative, conservative, or dispersive (Figure 8). In *conservative* replication, the parental ds-DNA would remain as-is while an entirely new double-stranded genome was created. The *dispersive* theory said that both copies of the genomes were composed of scattered pieces of new and old DNA. The results of the Messelson-Stahl experiments showed that replication is semiconservative.

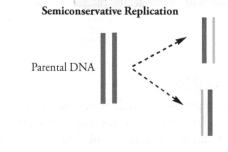

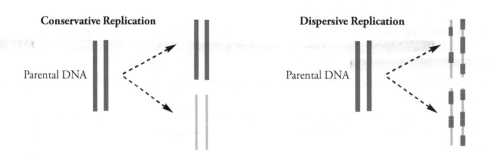

Figure 8 Messelson-Stahl Experiments

---

[29] A template is something that is copied. The metal plates used in printing presses are an example.

[30] complementary

Now we'll look at replication at the molecular level. Daughter DNA is created as a growing polymer. The enzyme that catalyzes the elongation of the daughter strand using the parental template is called **DNA polymerase (DNA pol)**. DNA polymerase checks each new nucleotide to make sure it forms a correct base-pair before it is incorporated in the growing polymer. The thermodynamic driving force for the polymerization reaction is the removal and hydrolysis of pyrophosphate ($P_2O_7^{4-}$) from each dNTP added to the chain. (This is an example of a coupled reaction, discussed in Chapter 2.) Here are some more replication rules to memorize:

2) **Polymerization occurs in the 5' to 3' direction, without exception.**
   This means the existing chain is always lengthened by the addition of a nucleotide to the 3' end of the chain. In fact, the 3' hydroxyl group acts as a nucleophile in the polymerization reaction to displace 5' pyrophosphate from the dNTP to be added. [The template strand is read in what direction?[31]]

3) **DNA pol requires a *template*.**
   It cannot make a DNA chain from scratch but must copy an old chain. This makes sense because it would be pretty useless if DNA pol just made a strand of DNA randomly, without copying a template.

4) **DNA pol requires a *primer*.**
   It cannot start a DNA chain but can only add nucleotides to an existing chain. If DNA pol is responsible for making new daughter DNA by copying parental DNA, but is incapable of synthesizing DNA without a primer, where does the primer come from? A special RNA polymerase called **primase** begins DNA replication by creating a small RNA primer that DNA pol can elongate by adding deoxyribonucleotides to the existing ribonucleotide primer. The RNA primer is later replaced by DNA.

• Can DNA polymerase make the following partially double-stranded structure completely double stranded in the presence of excess nucleotides, using the top strand as a primer?[32]

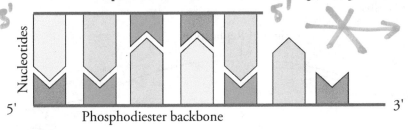

When it is not being replicated, DNA is tightly coiled. The replication process cannot begin unless the double helix is uncoiled and separated into two single strands. The enzyme that unwinds the double helix and separates the strands is called **helicase**. [Would you expect helicase to use the energy of ATP hydrolysis to do its job?[33]] The place where the helicase begins to unwind is not random. It is a specific location on the chromosome called the **origin of replication**. [How can the origin be found?[34]] When

---

[31] If the daughter is made 5' to 3', and the two strands have to end up antiparallel, *the template must be read 3' to 5'*. Add this important fact to #2 (write in the margin).

[32] No. The DNA strands are antiparallel, meaning that the upper strand would have to be extended in a 3' to 5' direction, which is impossible. Note that the phrase "in the presence of excess nucleotides" is extraneous. It just means there are plenty of building blocks around. Typical MCAT smokescreen.

[33] Yes. Separating the strands requires the breaking of many H-bonds.

[34] Remember that "a specific place on the chromosome" just means "a specific sequence of nucleotides." The origin is found by enzymes necessary for the beginning of replication. These enzymes have tertiary structures which specifically recognize a particular pattern of nucleotides. They scan along the chromosome (like a train on a track) until they find the right spot, then they call in helicase and other enzymes.

helicase unwinds the helix at the origin, the helix gets wound more tightly upstream and downstream from this point.[35] The chromosome would get tangled and eventually break except that enzymes called **topoisomerases** cut one or both of the strands and unwrap the helix, releasing the excess tension created by the helicases. Note that this is just the opposite of what DNA gyrase does; in fact, gyrase is considered a type of topoisomerase. Another potential problem is that single-stranded DNA is much less stable than ds-DNA. **Single-strand binding proteins** protect DNA which has been unpackaged in preparation for replication and help keep the strands separated. The separated strands are referred to as an **open complex**. Replication may now begin.

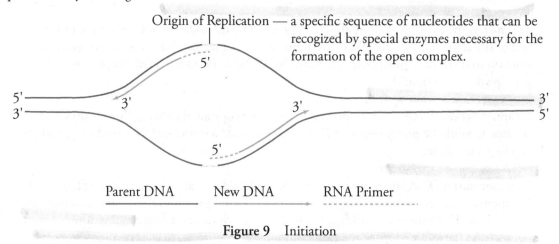

Figure 9   Initiation

The first step is the synthesis of an RNA primer on each template strand. Then DNA pol elongates the primer by adding dNTPs to its 3' end. Rapid elongation of the daughter strands follows. Since the two template strands are antiparallel, the two primers will elongate toward opposite ends of the chromosome. After a while it looks like this:

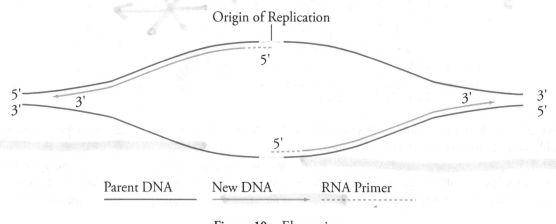

Figure 10   Elongation

---

[35] Imagine two long ropes wound around each other. What happens if you pull them apart in the middle?

Replication proceeds along in both directions away from the origin. Both template strands are read 3' to 5' while daughter strands are elongated 5' to 3'. The areas where the parental double helix continues to unwind are called the **replication forks**. Let's split the above picture and look at an enlargement of the right half.

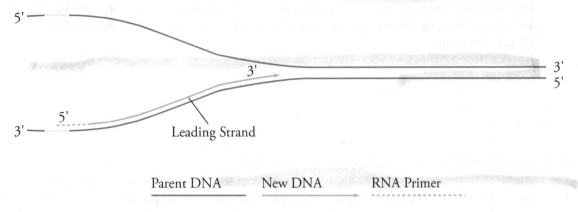

Figure 11   Leading Strand

See how it looks like a big fork? In examining these pictures, you have probably become aware of a problem. It seems like only half of each template strand will be replicated (in Figure 10, the right half of the bottom strand and the left half of the top strand). The problem is that chain elongation can only proceed in one direction, 5' to 3', but in order to replicate the right half of the top chain and the left half of the bottom one, we will have to go in the *opposite* direction. Here's the solution:

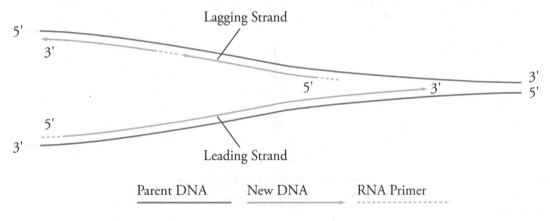

Figure 12   Leading and Lagging Strands

As the bottom chain is elongated continuously, the replication fork widens. After a good bit of the top template chain becomes exposed, primase comes in and lays down a primer, which DNA pol can elongate. Then when the replication fork widens again and more of the top template becomes exposed, these events are repeated. Because it elongates continuously right into the widening replication fork, the bottom daughter is called the **leading strand**. Because it must wait until the replication fork widens before beginning to polymerize, the top daughter is called the **lagging strand**. The small chunks of DNA comprising the lagging strand are called **Okazaki fragments**, after their discoverer. [As the replication forks grow, does helicase have to continue to unwind the double helix and separate the strands?[36]] Let's continue our memory-list:

5) **Replication forks grow away from the origin in both directions.**
Each replication fork contains a leading strand and a lagging strand. Replication of the leading strand is **continuous**; replication of the lagging strand is **discontinuous**, resulting in Okazaki fragments.

6) Eventually **all RNA primers are replaced by DNA**, and the **fragments are joined by an enzyme called DNA ligase**.

Eukaryotic vs. Prokaryotic Replication

In eukaryotic replication, each chromosome has several origins. This is necessary because eukaryotic chromosomes are so huge that replicating them from a single origin would be too slow. As the many replication forks continue to widen, they create an appearance of bubbles along the DNA strand, so they are referred to as "replication bubbles." Eventually the replication forks meet, and the many daughter strands are ligated together.

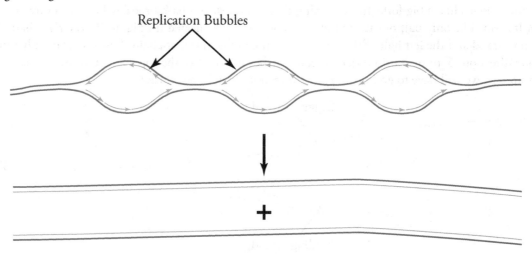

Figure 13 Eukaryotic Replication

Prokaryotes have only one chromosome, and this one chromosome has only one origin. Because the chromosome is circular, as replication proceeds the partially duplicated genome begins to look like the Greek letter θ (theta). Hence the replication of prokaryotes is said to proceed by the **theta mechanism** and is referred to as **theta replication** (see Figure 14).

---

[36] Yes

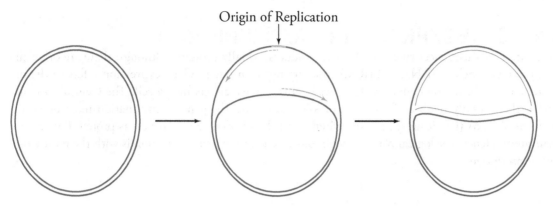

Origin of Replication

Figure 14   Theta (θ) Replication

The process of replication is actually more complex than we have described, mostly because there are many enzymes involved which haven't been mentioned. You do not need to worry about this complexity, with one exception. You should be aware of the three types of DNA pol in prokaryotes. You definitely don't need to know anything specific about eukaryotic DNA pol; this enzyme is very large and complex.

Prokaryotes have three types of DNA polymerase. They are simply called **DNA polymerase I, II, and III.**

1) DNA pol III is your basic polymerase enzyme. It is the one responsible for the super-fast, super-accurate elongation of the leading strand. This is a **5' to 3' polymerase activity.** Pol III can also correct mistakes by chopping off the nucleotide it just attached if it was incorrect (known as **proofreading**) using a **3' to 5' exonuclease activity.**[37]

2) The function of DNA pol II is very easy to remember: unknown (or at least, not very clear at all).

3) The main responsibility of DNA pol I is to remove the primer and replace it with DNA. Hence, it can do everything pol III can do, plus it has a **5' to 3' exonuclease activity,** which it uses to remove the RNA primer, while simultaneously leaving behind new DNA in a ___[38] activity. [If a bacterium possesses a mutation in the gene for DNA polymerase III, resulting in an enzyme without the 3' to 5' exonuclease activity, will mutations occur more often than in bacteria with a normal DNA polymerase gene?[39]]

Here is a summary of the activities of the three bacterial DNA polymerases. And remember: No matter what, *there can never be a 3' to 5' polymerase activity.*

DNA pol I: Same as III but slower, plus 5' to 3' exonuclease to remove RNA primers.
DNA pol II: Unknown
DNA pol III: 5' to 3' polymerase, 3' to 5' exonuclease. Fastest.

---

[37] **Exonuclease** means "cutting a nucleic acid chain at the end." An **endonuclease** will cut a polynucleotide acid chain in the middle of the chain, usually at a particular sequence. Two important types of endonucleases are: **repair enzymes** that remove chemically damaged DNA from the chain, and **restriction enzymes**, which are endonucleases found in bacteria. Their role is to destroy the DNA of infecting viruses, thus *restricting* the host range of the virus.

[38] 5' to 3' polymerase; remember, all polymerization is 5' to 3'.

[39] Yes. The 3' to 5' exonuclease activity is the polymerase's way of editing its work. Without this editing function, many more point mutations would occur due to the incorporation of wrong nucleotides. The normal polymerase is remarkably adept at sensing correct base pairing and removing bases that don't belong.

3.4 GENE EXPRESSION: TRANSCRIPTION

Genes are DNA sequences that encode gene products, usually proteins (although there are other mature gene products, such as tRNA and rRNA, that are not translated). **Gene expression** refers to the process whereby the information contained in genes begins to have effects in the cell. The Central Dogma tells us that there is only one way for gene expression to occur: The genetic information must be written in the form of RNA (i.e., it must be **transcribed**); and then it must be expressed as protein (i.e., it must be **translated**). Hence, the logical place to begin our discussion of gene expression is with the nature of RNA and transcription.

Types of RNA

RNA is chemically distinct from DNA in three important ways:

1) RNA is **single-stranded**, except in some viruses.
2) RNA contains **uracil** instead of thymine.
3) The pentose ring in RNA is **ribose** rather than 2' deoxyribose.

As a result of this last difference, the RNA polymer is less stable, because the 2' hydroxyl can nucleophilically attack the backbone phosphate group of an RNA chain, causing hydrolysis when the remainder of the chain acts as leaving group. This cannot occur in DNA, since there is no 2' hydroxyl. [Why is the stability of RNA relatively unimportant?[40] Anticancer drugs often seek to block growth of rapidly dividing cells by inhibiting production of thymine. Why is this an attractive target for cancer therapy?[41]]

There are several different types of RNA, each with a unique role: the three predominant types are **mRNA**, **rRNA**, and **tRNA**. You are already familiar with **messenger RNA** (mRNA). This is the molecule that *carries genetic information from the nucleus to the cytoplasm* where it can be translated into protein. Each unique polypeptide is created according to the sequence of codons on a particular piece of mRNA, which was transcribed from a particular gene. Eukaryotic mRNA is **monocistronic** and obeys the "one gene, one protein" principle; this means that each piece of mRNA encodes one and only one polypeptide. Hence, *there are as many different mRNAs as there are proteins*. Messenger RNA is constantly produced and degraded, according to the cell's need for the protein encoded by each piece of mRNA; in fact, this is the principal means whereby cells regulate the amount of each particular protein they synthesize. This is an important point which will be emphasized later. Note that prokaryotic mRNA often codes for *more* than one polypeptide and is termed **polycistronic**. The different genes on the same polycistronic mRNA are generally related in function.[42]

---

[40] Because a cell's DNA is necessary for the cell's entire life. RNA is a transient molecule which is transcribed, translated, and destroyed. As a matter of fact, the reason RNA contains uracil also has to do with the reduced need for fidelity in transcription as compared to replication. Without getting into the details, thymine is easier for DNA repair systems to work with, while uracil is much less energy-costly to make. So RNA has uracil, DNA has thymine.

[41] All cells require RNA production, even if they are not growing, in order to continually replenish degraded RNA. RNA contains the bases cytosine, guanine, uracil and adenine, but only DNA contains thymine. Thus, if thymine production is blocked, only DNA *replication* will be inhibited and only rapidly dividing cells such as cancer cells will be affected. Unfortunately, some normal cells in the body normally divide a lot (such as lining cells of the gut and hair follicles), explaining the side effects of chemotherapy.

[42] For instance, if five enzymes are necessary for the synthesis of a particular molecule, then all five enzymes might be encoded on a single piece of mRNA.

We have also mentioned **ribosomal RNA** (rRNA). *There are just a few different rRNAs.* They all have the same function: They serve as components of the ribosome, along with many polypeptide chains. The rRNAs seem to provide the catalytic function of the ribosome. Take note: This is a little odd. In general, cellular machines (enzymes) are made from only from polypeptides.

The last type of RNA is **transfer RNA** (tRNA); tRNA is responsible for translating the genetic code. Transfer RNA carries amino acids from the cytoplasm to the ribosome to be added to a growing protein. The structure of tRNA and how it does its job will be discussed later. [Estimate how many types of tRNA there are.[43]]

Replication vs. Transcription

Transcription is the synthesis of RNA (usually mRNA, tRNA, or rRNA) using DNA as the template. The word *transcription* indicates that in the process of reading and writing information, the language does not change. Information is transferred from one polynucleotide to another. This should lead you to expect transcription to be fairly similar to replication. And it is. Both replication and transcription involve **template-driven polymerization**. [Because of this, the RNA transcript produced in transcription is ___[44] to the DNA template, just as the daughter strand produced in replication was.] The *driving force* for both processes is the removal and subsequent hydrolysis of pyrophosphate from each nucleotide added to the chain, with the existing chain acting as nucleophile. [Transcription, like replication, can occur only in the ___[45] direction. Do the polymerase enzymes in both replication and transcription require a primer?[46]] Another important difference between transcription and DNA replication is that RNA polymerase has not been shown to possess the ability to remove mismatched nucleotides (it lacks exonuclease activity); in other words, it cannot correct its errors. Thus, transcription is a lower fidelity process than replication. [A virus possessing an RNA genome relies on RNA polymerase rather than DNA polymerase to replicate its genome. Will this virus have a higher or a lower rate of spontaneous mutation than organisms with ds-DNA genomes?[47]]

Another similarity is that transcription, like replication, begins at a specific spot on the chromosome. The name of the site where transcription starts (the **start site**) is different from the name of the place where replication begins, ___.[48] The sequence of nucleotides on a chromosome that activates RNA polymerase to begin the process of transcription is called the **promoter**, and the point where RNA polymerization actually *starts* is called the start site. In fact, from this point forward, just about every event in transcription is given a different name from the events in replication. You must be comfortable with the terminology in order to understand gene expression, because *transcription is the principle site of the regulation of gene expression in both eukaryotes and prokaryotes.* This means that the amount of each protein made in every cell is controlled by the amount of mRNA that gets transcribed.

---

[43] Each tRNA must recognize a codon on mRNA and respond by delivering the appropriate amino acid to the ribosome. There are 20 different amino acids, so there at least 20 different tRNAs. However, there are 61 possible codons, so there could be as many as 61 different tRNAs. The actual number is between 20 and 61, because the third nucleotide of the codon is often not needed for specificity of the amino acid.

[44] complementary

[45] 5' to 3'

[46] No, RNA pol does not require a primer. Remember, the primer in replication is a piece of RNA, made by an RNA polymerase.

[47] The virus will have a very high rate of mutation. It is a general law that most mutations are harmful. Hence, individual viruses will be far less likely to survive than organisms with DNA genomes. However, the high mutation rate will allow the entire species of virus to evolve very rapidly, making it very successful as a parasite (since it will evade host defense systems).

[48] the origin

Reference Points in Transcription

Before we discuss the mechanics of transcription, we need to clarify a few reference points (see Figure 15). We noted previously that the chromosome is referred to as the *template*, not *parent*. What about the individual strands of the chromosome? Are they both templates for the same mRNA? Let's answer with a thought experiment. Say there is a strand of DNA which has the sequence AAAAAAAAA. If we transcribe this strand, the resulting mRNA will look like: UUUUUUUUU. When it is translated, this mRNA will result in an oligopeptide with this primary structure: Phe-Phe-Phe. (Refer to the genetic code table in Section 3.2.) Now, what if we transcribe the other strand of the chromosome? What is its DNA sequence? What will the transcript look like? And the oligopeptide?[49] Our conclusion is that only one of the strands of the DNA template encodes a particular mRNA molecule. But it makes sense: paired DNA strands are *complementary*, not *identical*. The strand which is actually transcribed is called the **template**, **non-coding**, **transcribed**, or **antisense strand**; it is complementary to the transcript. The other DNA strand is called the **coding** or **sense strand**; it has the same sequence as the transcript (except it has T in place of U). It is customary to say that transcription starts at a point and proceeds **downstream**, which means toward the 3' end of the coding strand and transcript. **Upstream** means toward the 5' end of the coding strand, beyond the 5' end of the transcript. Upstream nucleotide sequences are referred to using negative numbers, and downstream sequences are referred to using positive numbers. The first nucleotide on the template strand which is actually transcribed is called the start site. The corresponding nucleotide on the coding strand is given the number +1. As we'll see below, regulatory sequences on the chromosome are referred to by where they occur on the coding strand.

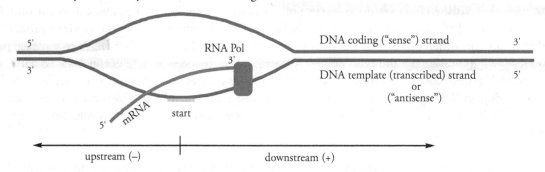

Figure 15   Reference Points in Transcription

- The figure above labels the transcript "mRNA." Is this accurate in all life forms? (Hint: In eukaryotes, is the initial transcript mature mRNA, ready to be translated?)[50]

---

[49] The DNA strand must be complementary to the first strand we discussed. So the sequence must be TTTTTTTTT. Hence the transcript will have to be AAAAAAAAA. Because AAA codes for lysine, the oligopeptide would be Lys-Lys-Lys.

[50] No, it is accurate for prokaryotes only. In eukaryotes, the RNA transcript must be processed (spliced) and transported out of the nucleus before it can be translated. We will discuss this in depth later in the chapter.

Prokaryotic Transcription

It is important to understand all the vocabulary and general principles presented above. In this section and the next, we will present some more detailed information. You don't need to memorize this material, but you should feel as comfortable reading it as if you were reading the newspaper, since you may see it in an MCAT passage.

In bacteria (prokaryotes), all types of RNA are made by the same RNA polymerase. Prokaryotic RNA polymerase is a large enzyme complex consisting of five subunits: two alpha subunits, a beta subunit, a beta' subunit, and an omega subunit ($\alpha_2\beta\beta'\omega$). This is the **core enzyme** responsible for rapid elongation of the transcript. However, the core enzyme alone cannot initiate transcription. An additional subunit termed the **sigma factor** (σ) is required to form what is sometimes referred to as the **holoenzyme** (*holo* = complete), which is responsible for initiation.

Transcription occurs in three stages: **initiation**, **elongation**, and **termination**. Initiation occurs when RNA polymerase holoenzyme binds to a promoter. The typical bacterial promoter contains two primary sequences: the **Pribnow box** at –10 and the **–35 sequence**. Holoenzyme scans along the chromosome like a train on a railroad track until it recognizes a promoter and then stops, forming a **closed complex**. The RNA polymerase must unwind a portion of the DNA double helix before it can begin to synthesize RNA. The RNA polymerase bound at the promoter with a region of single-stranded DNA is termed the **open complex**. Once the open complex has formed, transcription can begin.

The sigma factor plays two roles in helping the polymerase find promoters. The first is to greatly increase the ability of RNA polymerase to recognize promoters. The second is to decrease the nonspecific affinity of holoenzyme for DNA. Once the open complex and several phosphodiester bonds have been formed, the sigma factor is no longer necessary and leaves the RNA polymerase complex.

The core enzyme elongates the RNA chain *processively*, with one polymerase complex synthesizing an entire RNA molecule. As the core enzyme elongates the RNA, it moves along the DNA downstream in a **transcription bubble** in which a region of the DNA double helix is unwound to allow the polymerase to access the complementary DNA template. When a termination signal is detected, in some cases with the help of a protein called rho, the polymerase falls off of the DNA, releases the RNA, and the transcription bubble closes.

Regulation of Prokaryotic Transcription

Regulation of transcription is the primary method of regulation of gene expression. One simple mechanism of transcription regulation in bacteria is that some promoters are simply stronger than others. The problem with this mechanism of regulation is that it is "pre-set"; it does not respond to changing conditions within the cell. Bacteria also possess far more complex regulatory mechanisms, which activate or suppress transcription depending on current needs for specific gene products. For example, bacteria only produce the enzyme β-galactosidase and other proteins required for lactose catabolism when lactose is present. [Assuming these protein products do not have a harmful effect on the cell, what advantage might there be in turning off the genes when the protein products are not required?[51]]

---

[51] It takes a great deal of ATP to synthesize RNA and protein, so it's more energy efficient to transcribe and translate only the proteins that are needed.

- Are the terms *polypeptide enzyme* and *gene product* synonymous? Or are there gene products which are not polypeptide enzymes? Are there polypeptides which are not enzymes?[52]

Enzymes involved in anabolism (biosynthesis) should be produced when the item they help make (their product) is scarce. Enzymes involved in catabolism (degradative metabolism) should be produced when the item they help break down (their substrate) is abundant, such as food. Hence there are two basic ways we can imagine regulating transcription. The transcription of enzymes involved in biosynthetic pathways should be inhibited by their product. The transcription of enzymes involved in catabolic pathways should be automatically inhibited whenever the substrate is not around, and activated when it is. That is in fact just how it goes. Anabolic enzymes whose transcription is inhibited in the presence of excess amounts of product are **repressible**. Catabolic enzymes whose transcription can be stimulated by the abundance of a substrate are called **inducible enzymes**.[53]

As an example, let's look at the group of inducible enzymes encoded on the **lac operon**. An **operon** has two components:

1) coding sequence for enzymes, and
2) **upstream regulatory sequences** (control sites).

Operons may also include genes for regulatory proteins, such as repressors or activators, but don't have to. These genes can be located elsewhere in the genome.

The lac operon (short for lactose operon) is an operon which contains:

1) DNA encoding a piece of mRNA that codes for three enzymes necessary for lactose catabolism, and
2) two regulatory sequences: the promoter and the **lac operator.**

The three genes encoding enzymes are denoted Z, Y, and A, and the regulatory regions are denoted **P** for promoter and **O** for operator (see Figure 16). The system is really quite simple. The role of the repressor protein (encoded by a separate repressor gene) is to sit on the operator and prevent RNA pol from binding the promoter and transcribing the Z, Y, and A genes. So the lac operon automatically shuts itself off. But when lactose is around, it binds to the repressor protein, causing a conformational change in the tertiary structure such that repressor protein is no longer capable of binding to the operator (i.e., it falls off the DNA). Transcription of the Z, Y, and A genes then proceeds, and the new mRNA is translated to produce three enzymes that work together to catabolize lactose (see Figure 17). When the supply of lactose becomes very scarce, there isn't enough to bind to the repressors, and most of the repressor proteins return to their original structure. They now *rebind* to the operator, stopping the transcription of mRNA for the Z, Y, and A genes.

---

[52] They are not synonymous. All polypeptides are gene products, but some gene products are not polypeptides and some polypeptides are not enzymes. Transfer RNA and rRNA are gene products, but not polypeptides. Microfilaments and other elements of the cytoskeleton, as well as collagen and many other polypeptides, are not enzymes.

[53] So note: The default for repressible systems is "ON"; for inducible systems the default is "OFF."

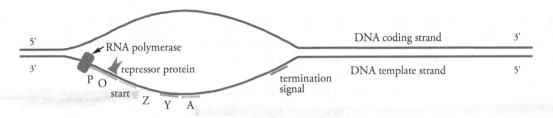

Figure 16 The lac Operon in the Absence of Lactose

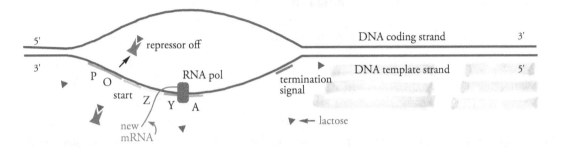

Figure 17 The lac Operon in the Presence of Lactose

- If the operator is mutated so that the lac repressor can no longer bind, what effect will this have on transcription?[54]
    - A. Transcription of Gene Z will be activated, and Genes Y and A will not be affected.
    - B. None of the genes will be transcribed, regardless of the presence or absence of lac repressor.
    - C. Transcription will still be activated by lactose.
    - D. All three genes will be expressed constitutively, regardless of the presence of lactose.

Comparing Prokaryotic and Eukaryotic Transcription

Eukaryotic and prokaryotic transcription are similar, but you need to be aware of differences in

1) the location of transcription (very important)
2) the primary transcript and the mRNA (very important)
3) the RNA polymerase(s) (worth noting)
4) regulation of transcription (worth noting)

Eukaryotic means "true-kernelled." Prokaryotic means "before-the-kernel." The **karyon** (kernel) is, of course, the nucleus. The fact that prokaryotes have no nucleus means transcription occurs free in the cytoplasm, in the same compartment where translation occurs, and transcription and translation can occur

---

[54] If the repressor cannot bind to the operator, nothing will prevent RNA polymerase from transcribing all the genes on the operon in an unregulated, constitutive (or continuous) fashion (choice **D** is true and choice **B** is false). All genes on the operon are expressed or repressed together (choice A is false), and lactose will no longer have any effect (the expression of the genes is unregulated, so choice C is false).

simultaneously. Eukaryotes must transcribe their mRNA in the nucleus, then modify it (see below), then transport it across the nuclear membrane to the cytoplasm where it can be translated. Transcription and translation in eukaryotes *does not* occur simultaneously.

In prokaryotes, all RNA is made by the $\alpha_2\beta\beta'\sigma\omega$ RNA polymerase complex. In eukaryotes, there is a different RNA polymerase for each of the three major types of RNA. The three RNA pols are denoted **RNA pol I**, **II**, and **III**. Please note: in our discussion of replication you had to memorize the three *pro*karyotic *DNA* polymerases, called DNA pol I, II, and III. Here you must learn the three *eu*karyotic *RNA* polymerases, also named I, II, and III. Don't get mixed up.

The roles of the three eukaryotic RNA polymerases are:

> RNA pol I: Transcribe rRNA
> RNA pol II: Transcribe mRNA
> RNA pol III: Transcribe tRNA

A more important difference between prokaryotic and eukaryotic gene expression is that the primary transcript in prokaryotes is mRNA. In other words, the product of transcription by prokaryotic RNA polymerase is ready to be translated. In fact, translation of prokaryotic mRNA begins before transcription is completed!

In contrast, the eukaryotic primary transcript (made by RNA pol II) is modified extensively before translation. The most important example is **splicing** (Figure 18). Eukaryotic DNA has non-coding sequences intervening between the segments that actually code for proteins. Sometimes these intervening sequences contain enhancers or other regulatory sequences. As a result, eukaryotic mRNA is made with sequences intervening between those that actually code for proteins. The *int*ervening sequences in the RNA are called **introns**. Protein-coding regions of the RNA are termed *ex*ons because they actually get *ex*pressed. Before the RNA can be translated, introns must be removed and exons joined together; *that's* splicing. There is a type of RNA found in the nucleus, called **heterogeneous nuclear RNA (hnRNA)**, thought to be the primary transcript made by RNA pol II, before splicing.

The other example of the modification of eukaryotic RNA before translation is the addition of two tags to the mRNA which "customize" it. The tags are called the **5' cap** and the **3' poly-A tail**. The 5' cap is a methylated guanine nucleotide stuck on the 5' end [which is the end made __ (first or last?)[55]]. The poly-A tail is a string of several hundred adenine nucleotides. The cap is essential for translation, while both the cap and the poly-A tail are important in preventing digestion of the mRNA by exonucleases that are free in the cell.

- Why would active exonucleases be floating free in the cell?[56]

---

[55] It is made first, since transcription proceeds from 5' to 3'.

[56] Two conceivable reasons: 1) *mRNA has a very short lifespan;* it is degraded rapidly, and more must be made if the protein is still needed. Note that this is consistent with the idea that regulation of gene expression occurs primarily at the transcriptional level since this is more efficient. 2) Viruses may inject RNA into the cell. If it does not have the correct cap and tail modifications, exonucleases will destroy it.

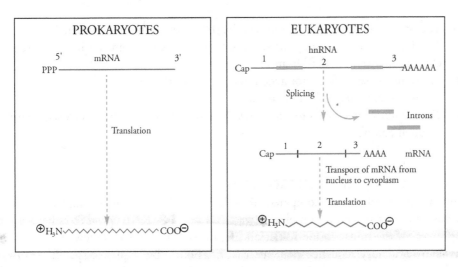

Figure 18 Eukaryotic Gene Expression

- One piece of RNA isolated from a human cell is found to produce two different polypeptides when added to a cell-free protein synthesis system containing all the enzymes necessary for eukaryotic gene expression. When the two polypeptides are separated and digested with trypsin, they produce fragments of the following molecular weights:

  Polypeptide 1: 5 kD, 8 kD, 12 kD, and 14 kD

  Polypeptide 2: 3 kD, 5 kD, 8 kD, 10 kD, 12 kD, and 14 kD

  How can we explain the synthesis of two different polypeptides from one piece of RNA?[57]

- Regulation of a gene is examined *in vitro* in the presence and absence of chromatin assembly, and in the presence and absence of a sequence-specific regulator of transcription. Transcription is quantitated after the experiment and the following results are obtained:

	Sequence Specific Factor	DNA	Relative Amount of Transcription
1.	None	unpackaged	.74
2.	None	packaged	.07
3.	Present	unpackaged	1.0
4.	Present	packaged	.59

---

[57] Here is an example of the use of splicing for the regulation of gene expression. The piece of RNA must have been hnRNA. In the cell-free system it underwent **differential splicing** to produce one of two different mRNA molecules. Apparently, Polypeptide 1 came from an mRNA which had more material spliced out than the mRNA coding for Polypeptide 2.

- Which one of the following conclusions can be drawn from this experiment?[58]
  - A. The degree of activation by the sequence-specific factor is greater in the presence of chromatin assembly than in its absence.
  - B. The sequence-specific factor acts to repress transcription.
  - C. The histones increase the rate of transcription.
  - D. The sequence-specific factor increases the rate of transition from a closed complex to an open complex.

Regulation of Eukaryotic Transcription

Given the complexity of eukaryotes compared to prokaryotes, it is not surprising that the regulation of eukaryotic transcription is also more complex. Most RNA pol II (mRNA) promoters have a **TATA box** at about −25 upstream of the transcription initiation site. Beyond that there are few clear rules. Eukaryotic promoters contain regulatory sequence elements that are bound by **sequence-specific transcription factors.** When these factors bind to DNA, transcription may increase or decrease. Another kind of regulatory DNA sequence in eukaryotes is the **enhancer.** The enhancer may be located many thousands of base pairs away from a promoter (either upstream or downstream) and still regulate transcription. Sequence-specific factors bind to enhancers as well as promoters to regulate transcription. The binding of many factors to DNA is regulated by extracellular signals. For example, steroid hormones bind to receptors in the cell to direct the receptors to bind DNA and regulate transcription. [If a mutation in a eukaryotic fat cell reduces the level of several proteins related to fat metabolism, does this mean the proteins are encoded by the same mRNA?[59]]

3.5   GENE EXPRESSION: TRANSLATION

Translation is the synthesis of polypeptides according to the amino acid sequence dictated by the sequence of codons in mRNA. During translation, an mRNA molecule attaches to a ribosome at a specific codon, and the appropriate amino acid is delivered by a tRNA molecule. Then the second amino acid is delivered by another tRNA. Then the ribosome binds the two amino acids together, creating a dipeptide. This process is repeated until the polypeptide is complete, at which point the ribosome drops the mRNA and the new polypeptide departs. It is very important to understand this basic outline, and you must keep in mind the differences between translation in eukaryotes and prokaryotes. In the following discussion, we will describe each of the players in translation and then go through the process step by step.

---

[58] A quick glance at the data indicates that transcription is increased in the presence of the sequence specific factor (compare lines 1 and 2 with lines 3 and 4, choice B is wrong), and that histones decrease the rate of transcription (packaged DNA has a lower rate of transcription than unpackaged, choice C is wrong). Looking closer, it appears that the sequence specific factor causes an approximate 8-fold increase in the transcription rate of packaged DNA (compare lines 2 and 4), but doesn't even double the rate of transcription of unpackaged DNA (compare lines 1 and 3). It might be that this occurs because the factor increases the rate of transition to an open complex, but there is no data to support this (choice **A** is a better answer than choice D). Don't confuse "open complex" (which means separated DNA strands) with "unpackaged" (which means not wrapped around histones).

[59] No, it does not. *Eukaryotic mRNA is monocistronic!* A more likely explanation is that a number of different genes located throughout the genome have related regulatory sequences that bind the same sequence-specific transcription factors. This is the means used by eukaryotes to achieve coordinated expression of genes. Related proteins are clumped together on the same piece of mRNA in prokaryotes only.

Transfer RNA [tRNA]

Each tRNA is composed of a single transcript produced by RNA polymerase III. The tertiary structure of every tRNA molecule is similar. tRNAs have a stem-and-loop structure stabilized by hydrogen bonds between bases on neighboring segments of the RNA chain (Figures 19 and 20). Several modified nucleotides are found in tRNA (e.g., dihydrouridine). One end of the structure is responsible for recognizing the mRNA codon to be translated. This is the **anticodon**, a sequence of three ribonucleotides which is complementary to the codon the tRNA translates. A key step in translation is *specific base pairing between the tRNA anticodon and the mRNA codon*. It is this specificity that dictates which amino acid of the twenty will be added to a growing polypeptide chain by the ribosome. [Is it likely that the three nucleotides of the anticodon contribute to the tertiary structure of tRNA by base-pairing with other nucleotides in the chain?[60]] The other end of the tRNA molecule has the **amino acid acceptor site**, which is where the amino acid is attached to the tRNA. [If you analyzed a thousand tRNA molecules, which region would you expect to vary the most?[61]] Since there is a tRNA for each codon, each tRNA is specific for one amino acid, while each amino acid may have several tRNAs. Each tRNA can be named according to the amino acid it's specific for. For example, a tRNA for valine would be written $tRNA_{Val}$. When the amino acid is attached, the tRNA is written this way: $Val\text{-}tRNA_{Val}$.

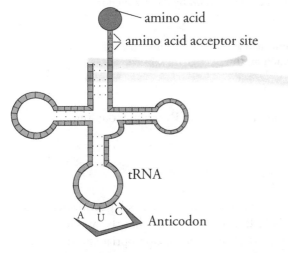

Figure 19   Cloverleaf (Two-Dimensional) Structure of tRNA

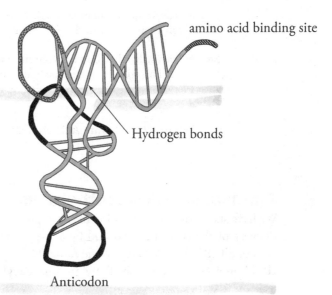

Figure 20   Three-Dimensional Structure of tRNA

Peptide bond formation during protein synthesis is a process that requires a lot of energy because the peptide bond has unfavorable thermodynamics ($\Delta G > 0$) and slow kinetics (high activation energy). Reaction coupling is used to power the process. The goal of the steps shown in Figure 21 is to attach an amino acid to its tRNA molecule, in a process called **tRNA loading** or **amino acid activation**. This is useful because breaking the aminoacyl-tRNA bond will drive peptide bond formation forward. In order to load the tRNA, reaction coupling is used: the amino acid is attached to AMP (adenosine monophosphate), and two high-energy phosphate bonds are hydrolyzed in the process.

---

[60] No. They must be available for base pairing with the codon.

[61] The anticodon is different for each of the different tRNA molecules. Part of the rest of the molecule varies from one tRNA to the next, but about 60 percent is constant. The amino acid binding site is always the same: CCA (at the 3' end of the tRNA molecule).

Step 1: An amino acid is attached to AMP to form *aminoacyl AMP*. In this reaction, the nucleophile is the acidic oxygen of the amino acid, and the leaving group is PP_i.

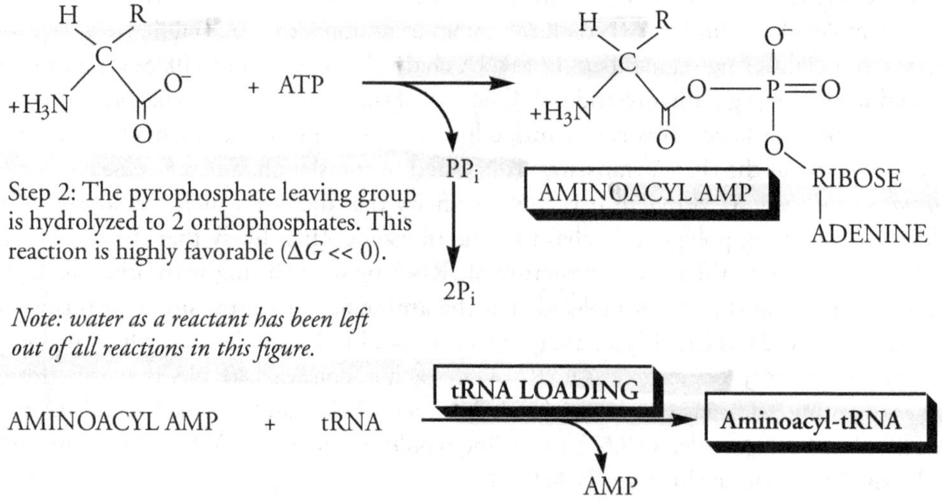

Step 2: The pyrophosphate leaving group is hydrolyzed to 2 orthophosphates. This reaction is highly favorable ($\Delta G \ll 0$).

Note: water as a reactant has been left out of all reactions in this figure.

AMINOACYL AMP + tRNA → [tRNA LOADING] → Aminoacyl-tRNA

Step 3: tRNA loading, an unfavorable reation, is driven forward by the destruction of the high-energy aminoacyl—AMP bond created in Step 1.

Step 4: Eventually, the bond between the amino acid and the tRNA molecule will be broken. This will power peptide bond formation: the nitrogen of another amino acid will nucleophilically attack the carbonyl carbon of this amino acid, and tRNA will be the leaving group.

Figure 21   Amino Acid Activation as an Example of Reaction Coupling

Aminoacyl-tRNA Synthetases

We have stated that incorporation of the appropriate amino acid in a growing polypeptide depends on the delivery of the correct amino acid by a specific tRNA. But we also noted that the amino acid acceptor sites of all tRNA molecules are the same. How is the attachment of the appropriate amino acid to each tRNA molecule accomplished? By an **aminoacyl-tRNA synthetase enzyme** specific to the amino acid. This enzyme must recognize *both* the tRNA and the amino acid based upon three-dimensional structure. There is at least one aminoacyl-tRNA synthetase for every amino acid. These enzymes must be *highly specific* because joining the wrong amino acid to a tRNA will result in the wrong amino acid being incorporated into a polypeptide. The specificity of these enzymes is amazing (some amino acids differ only by a *single methyl group*) and the error rate is very low. [If there is a 1/1000 error rate in amino acid incorporation, what percentage of polypeptides that are 500 amino acid residues long will not contain any errors?[62]]

Attachment of the amino acid to the tRNA is called **amino acid activation**. It serves two functions. One is specific amino acid delivery, as discussed above. The other is thermodynamic activation of the amino acid. The polymerization of amino acids is thermodynamically unfavorable because the formation of a

---

[62] The easiest way to calculate this is to figure out the probability of getting *all* amino acids in the protein correct, in other words, we must use the *non*-error rate for our calculation, not the error rate. If the error rate is 1/1000, then the non-error rate is 999/1000. The probability of having no errors is $.999^n$, where n = the number of amino acid residues. In other words, a single amino acid has .999 probability, or 99.9% probability of being correct. Two amino acids correct in a row have a .999 x .999 probability ($.999^2$), or .998, or 99.8% probability of happening. Continuing in this manner, a 500-amino acid protein has a $.999^{500}$ probability of being entirely correct, or .606, approximately a 60% probability. Longer proteins have a higher chance of containing errors.

peptide bond has $\Delta G > 0$. Hydrolysis of the high-energy bond between the amino acid and its tRNA helps drive protein synthesis. The N-terminus of the incoming amino acid attacks the terminal carboxyl group of the nascent chain, and the previous tRNA is the leaving group. The breaking of the bond between this tRNA molecule and its amino acid is very favorable; this is why the attachment of an amino acid to its tRNA may be called amino acid activation.

The reaction occurs in a multistep pathway in which amino acids are first activated by linkage to AMP and then transferred to the appropriate tRNA. Subsequent pyrophosphate hydrolysis drives the reaction forward. Note that two high-energy phosphate bonds (2 ATP equivalents) are used for the activation of each amino acid. (An ATP equivalent is a single high-energy phosphate bond. You can get 2 ATP equivalents by hydrolyzing 2 ATP to 2 ADP + 2 P_i or by hydrolyzing ATP to AMP + 2 P_i.)

- A bacterial strain with a point mutation in the gene for hexokinase is not able to metabolize glucose. The mutation causes a substitution of arginine for serine. These bacteria are used to test whether chemicals are mutagenic. The chemical is added to a culture of bacteria with glucose as the only carbon source. Any bacteria that grow must have undergone a mutation which remedied the problem (this is called *suppression* of the original mutation). When a particular hair spray ingredient is tested, several colonies grow on the glucose-only medium. Which one of the following might act as a suppressor of the first mutation?[63]
    - A. A point mutation during replication of a tRNA gene
    - B. A mutation in RNA polymerase that increases the rate of promoter recognition
    - C. A base pair deletion in the hexokinase gene
    - D. A point mutation during transcription of a tRNA molecule

The Ribosome

The ribosome is composed of many polypeptides and rRNA chains held together in a massive quaternary structure. The prokaryotic ribosome sediments in a gradient at a rate of 70S, so it is referred to as the **70S ribosome.** Eukaryotes have an **80S ribosome.**[64] Ribosomes float around in the cytoplasm in two subunits, large and small (**50S and 30S in prokaryotes, 60S and 40S in eukaryotes**); see Figure 22. The complete ribosome (both subunits together) has three special binding sites. The **A site** (*a*minoacyl-tRNA site) is where each new tRNA delivers its amino acid. The **P site** (*p*eptidyl-tRNA site) is where the growing polypeptide chain, still attached to a tRNA, is located during translation. The **E site** (*e*xit-tRNA site) is where a now-empty tRNA sits prior to its release from the ribosome. [During translation, the next codon to be translated is exposed in the __[65].] tRNAs move through the sites from $A \rightarrow P \rightarrow E$.

---

[63] A single base change in the anticodon of the tRNA for arginine could cause it to recognize the codon for serine. If that happened in the mutant bacteria, problems might ensue, but one good result would be that the correct amino acid would be incorporated at the mutated site in hexokinase (choice A is correct; note that point mutations in tRNA genes are actually a common means of suppression in bacteria). Increasing the rate at which RNA polymerase recognizes the promoter might increase the rate of transcription, but would not fix a mutant enzyme (choice B is wrong), and a base pair deletion in the hexokinase gene would cause a frameshift mutation and a serious significant change in protein structure and function (choice C is wrong). A point mutation during transcription of a tRNA molecule might have a temporary effect on a single bacterium, but would not be passed on to its progeny; remember than only DNA mutations have lasting effects and errors made during transcription are generally insignificant (choice D is wrong).

[64] S stands for "Svedbergs." Do not pay any attention to all this stuff about sedimentation, just remember the numbers. If you noticed that 50S + 30S ≠ 70S, you are correct, but it's not an error. Sedimentation rates are not arithmetically additive.

[65] A site, since this is where the next amino acid to be added must bind.

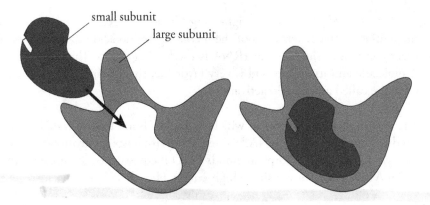

Figure 22   The Ribosome

Prokaryotic Translation

In prokaryotes, translation occurs in the same compartment and at the same time as transcription. In other words, *while the mRNA is being made* ribosomes attach and begin translating it. [That means that the first end of the mRNA to be translated is 5' or 3'?[66]] Note that it says ribosome**s** above. Several ribosomes attach to the mRNA and translate it simultaneously (you may hear the term *polyribosome* used to describe this arrangement; polyribosomes are seen in both prokaryotes and eukaryotes). [You figured out the direction of translation on the mRNA from what you already know. Do you have any previous knowledge that would help you answer this: Does translation always begin at the 5' end of the mRNA, or somewhere up the chain?[67]] As a matter of fact, it *never* begins right at the end, because an upstream regulatory sequence is essential for initiation, just as in transcription. Here, instead of a promoter, we have a **ribosome binding site**, also known as the **Shine-Dalgarno sequence**, located at −10 (ten ribonucleotides upstream, or on the 5' side of the start site). Like transcription, translation is discussed in three distinct stages: initiation, elongation, and termination. Many antibiotics function by inhibiting a particular stage.[68]

Initiation requires the formation of the **70S initiation complex.** Several initiation factors combine with the 30S subunit along with the mRNA and the first aminoacyl-tRNA, and finally, the 50S subunit completes the complex. This process is powered by the hydrolysis of one GTP molecule.[69] The first aminoacyl-tRNA is special; it is called the **initiator tRNA**, abbreviated **fMet-tRNA**$_{fMet}$. The "fMet" stands for *formylmethionine*, which is a modified methionine used as the first amino acid in all prokaryotic proteins.[70] The initiator tRNA sits in the P site of the 70S ribosome, hydrogen-bonded with the **start codon**. [What is the start codon? Does this codon initiate translation wherever it appears?[71]]

---

[66] 5' first, since the mRNA is made 5' end first. Transcription and translation go in the same direction on mRNA.

[67] It does not always occur at the very end. You can deduce this from the fact that mRNA is polycistronic. If there are more than one translation start site on the mRNA, they can't all be at the 5' end.

[68] For example, streptomycin and tetracycline bind to the 30S subunit of the prokaryotic ribosome. Chloramphenicol and erythromycin bind to the 50S subunit.

[69] This may seem odd, as ATP is normally the energy molecule. But a high energy phosphate is a high energy phosphate. Another example is the GTP produced in the Krebs cycle.

[70] In fact, cells of our immune system release cytotoxins when they sniff out fMet, because this chemical is a sure sign that bacteria are busily translating.

[71] Refer to the genetic code table. The codon for methionine is AUG; that's the start codon. It only initiates translation when it is preceded by a Shine-Dalgarno sequence (prokaryotes).

Elongation may now begin. It is a three-step cycle, involving the assistance of several elongation factors which will not be discussed. In the first step, the second aminoacyl-tRNA enters the A site and hydrogen bonds with the second codon. This process requires the hydrolysis of one phosphate from GTP. In the second step, the **peptidyl transferase** activity of the large ribosomal subunit catalyzes the formation of a peptide bond between fMet and the second amino acid. The amino group of amino acid #2 acts as nucleophile, and tRNA$_{fMet}$ is the leaving group; it dissociates from the ribosome. A new dipeptide is now attached to tRNA #2. Now you can figure out the direction of translation from the point of view of the polypeptide; you won't have to memorize it.[72] The third step is **translocation**, in which tRNA #1 (now empty) moves into the E site, tRNA #2 (holding the growing peptide) moves into the P site, and the next codon to be translated moves into the A site. Translocation costs one GTP. The new dipeptide is still attached to tRNA #2, and tRNA #2 is still H-bonded to codon #2. The presence of tRNA #1 in the E site (still H-bonded to codon #1), is thought to help maintain the reading frame of the mRNA (disruption of tRNA binding to the E site results in an increase in the number of frameshift mutations in the resulting protein). [Does the ribosome move relative to the mRNA during translocation?[73]] These three steps repeat over and over again, connecting amino acids in the order their codons appear along the mRNA strand (and thus appear in the A site).

Termination occurs when a stop codon appears in the A site. Instead of a tRNA, a **release factor** now enters the A site. This causes the peptidyl transferase to hydrolyze the bond between the last tRNA and the completed polypeptide. Now the ribosome separates into its subunits and releases both mRNA and polypeptide.

Let's focus for a moment on the energetics of translation. Why doesn't peptide bond formation require GTP hydrolysis, like the other steps in translation?[74] You should be able to answer questions like this: How many high energy phosphate bonds are required to make a 50 amino acid polypeptide chain, including the energy used to activate amino acids to aminoacyl-tRNAs?[75]

---

[72] The direction of synthesis is N → C, since the N of amino acid #2 binds to the C of #1. As the polypeptide elongates, its N terminus will come snaking out of the ribosome.

[73] It must, if the tRNA remains H-bonded to the mRNA while moving to another spot in the ribosome.

[74] Because the bond between each amino acid and its tRNA is a high energy bond whose hydrolysis drives peptide bond formation. Remember that the aminoacyl-tRNA bond was formed using the energy of two phosphate bonds from ATP.

[75] There are two phosphate bonds hydrolyzed per amino acid to make the aminoacyl-tRNAs, or 100 for the 50 amino acid polypeptide. Two phosphate bonds are required for each elongation step, one for the entrance of each new aminoacyl-tRNA into the ribosomal A site and the other for translocation. Since there are 49 elongation steps for a 50-amino acid protein, 98 high energy bonds are hydrolyzed during elongation. Finally, one GTP is hydrolyzed during initiation to position the first tRNA and mRNA on the ribosome. Thus, a total of 199 high-energy bonds are required for the translation of a 50-amino acid protein. In other words, it costs approximately $4n$ high-energy bonds to make a peptide chain, where n is the number of amino acids in the chain.

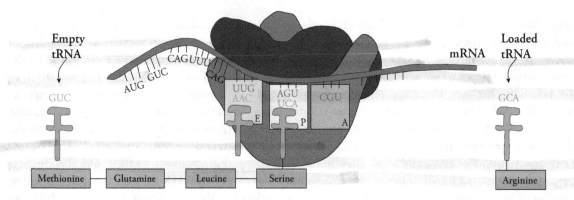

Figure 23 Translation Elongation

Eukaryotic Translation

Most of the important differences between eukaryotic and prokaryotic translation have already been noted. Remember what's different about eukaryotic translation: the ribosome is larger (80S), the mRNA must be processed before it can be translated (spliced, with cap and tail added), and the N-terminal amino acid is different (Met instead of fMet). Also remember that eukaryotic mRNA must not only be spliced, capped, and tailed, but it also requires transport from nucleus to cytoplasm, thus transcription and translation *cannot* proceed simultaneously. Note that eukaryotes do not use the Shine-Dalgarno sequence to initiate translation. There are sequences in eukaryotes that function in starting translation; a common one is the Kozak sequence, which is a consensus sequence typically located a few nucleotides before the start codon. Finally, the order in which the initiation complex is formed is different: the first tRNA binds to the small subunit, then the mRNA binds to the small subunit, and lastly the large subunit binds. [Are the nascent (newly formed) polypeptide chains emerging from a polyribosome in a eukaryote all the same?[76]]

- Which one of the following pairs of processes may occur simultaneously on the same RNA molecule in a eukaryotic cell?
  - A. Translation and transcription
  - B. Transcription and splicing
  - C. Splicing and translation
  - D. Messenger RNA degradation and transcription[77]

---

[76] In eukaryotes, the answer is: yes, always, because eukaryotic mRNA is monocistronic. In prokaryotes, however, different polypeptides may be translated from a single piece of mRNA, since prokaryotic mRNA is polycistronic.

[77] In order for processes in eukaryotes to occur simultaneously, they must occur in the same compartment. Transcription and splicing both occur in the nucleus and could therefore occur simultaneously (choice **B** is correct). Translation occurs in the cytoplasm while transcription and splicing occur in the nucleus, thus translation cannot occur at the same time as either of these processes (choices A and C are wrong). mRNA degradation and transcription cannot occur at the same time; if this were true no mRNA molecules would survive to be translated (choice D is wrong).

Summary

- DNA is the fundamental unit of inheritance in cells.

- DNA and RNA are polymers, made of nucleotide monomers. A nucleotide contains phosphate group(s), a sugar (either deoxyribose for DNA or ribose for RNA), and a nitrogenous base, either a purine (adenine or guanine) or a pyrimidine (thymine, cytosine, or uracil).

- Adenine always pairs with thymine via two hydrogen bonds, and cytosine always pairs with guanine via three hydrogen bonds.

- Uracil replaces thymine in RNA, and the ribose in RNA has an OH group on carbon 2.

- DNA is supercoiled in prokaryotes and packaged around histone proteins in eukaryotes.

- Point mutations are classified based on their effect on the DNA (transition/transversion) or their effect on the amino acid sequence (missense, nonsense, or silent).

- Frameshift mutations are caused by insertions or deletions in the DNA base sequence that affect the reading frame of a gene. These are generally very serious mutations because they affect every amino acid codon from the point of the mutation on.

- DNA replication occurs in the S-phase of the cell cycle and is semiconservative in nature.

- Several enzymes are involved in DNA replication. Helicases unwind the parental DNA at the origin of replication. Primases synthesize an RNA primer. DNA polymerase synthesizes new DNA, proofreads, and replaces the RNA primer. DNA ligase attaches the Okazaki fragments in the lagging strand.

- Transcription is the first part of protein synthesis; it is the creation of an RNA transcript by an RNA polymerase that reads the DNA template. Translation is the second part of protein synthesis; it is the creation of a polypeptide chain by ribosomes that read the mRNA transcript.

- All nucleotide synthesis (replication of DNA or transcription of RNA) occurs $5' \rightarrow 3'$.

- Key info about Prokaryotes: theta replication, genome is a single circular piece of DNA, three different DNA polymerases, one RNA polymerase, no mRNA processing, polycistronic mRNA, simultaneous transcription/translation, smaller ribosomes.

- Key info about Eukaryotes: replication bubbles, genome is several linear pieces of DNA, one DNA polymerase, three RNA polymerases, capping, tailing, and splicing of mRNA prior to translation, monocistronic mRNA, transcription in nucleus, translation in cytosol, larger ribosomes.

CHAPTER 3 FREESTANDING PRACTICE QUESTIONS

1. A competitive inhibitor of eukaryotic RNA polymerase III would have the greatest effect on:

    A) replication.
    B) reverse transcription.
    C) translation.
    D) mutation.

2. In the *lac operon*, transcription is regulated by a repressor protein and only takes place in the presence of lactose. Which of the following statements is correct?

    A) The repressor protein binds to the promoter site to inhibit transcription.
    B) Lactose binds to the promoter site to initiate transcription.
    C) Lactose binds to the repressor protein to inhibit transcription.
    D) The repressor protein binds the operator site to inhibit transcription.

3. Which of the following could not be caused by a single point mutation in the DNA?

    A) Ala-Gln-Cys-Asp-Leu → Ala-Gln
    B) Ala-Gln-Cys-Asp-Leu → Ala-Gln-Cys-Asp-Leu
    C) Ala-Gln-Cys-Asp-Leu → Ala-Gln-Cys-His-Lys
    D) Ala-Gln-Cys-Asp-Leu → Ala-Gln-Cys-His-Leu

4. Which of the following is/are true with respect to eukaryotic mRNA?

    I.   Monocistronic
    II. Transcription stops at the stop codon
    III. Has the same sequence as the template DNA that it was transcribed from

    A) I only
    B) I and II
    C) II and III
    D) I, II and III

5. Which DNA base pair requires the most energy to break?

    A) A-T
    B) C-A
    C) G-C
    D) U-A

6. Which of the following is NOT a similarity between replication and transcription?

    A) Both processes occur with the same fidelity.
    B) Polymerization in both processes is based on reading a template.
    C) A pyrophosphate is removed from every nucleotide as polymerization occurs.
    D) Both processes occur in the 5' to 3' direction.

7. Telomeres are guanine-rich caps on the ends of each chromosome. Which of the following is the most likely function of a telomere?

    A) High guanine content stabilizes parental strands to prevent excess tension during DNA unwinding.
    B) Protect the ends of the chromosomes from damage due to incomplete replication
    C) Provide a site for helicase attachment
    D) Seal the gaps left by Okazaki fragments in the lagging strand

CHAPTER 3 PRACTICE PASSAGE

Protein synthesis involves a number of complex steps, from transcription of the gene through to translation and post-translational modification. After mRNA is transcribed in eukaryotes, it must be processed (capped, poly-A tailed, and spliced) before it can be translated. Prokaryotes do not need to process their mRNA.

Due to the exonuclease activity of DNA polymerase, DNA replication is generally a high-fidelity process. Random errors occasionally occur and these mutations are classified as *frameshift mutations* (insertions or deletions in the base sequence) or *point mutations* (a single base pair change). Any mutation is subject to natural selection, with advantageous mutations preserved and the most deleterious mutations eliminated quickly. Thus, areas of the genome that appear to evolve very slowly (i.e., have a slower rate of mutation than other areas) do not actually have a slower rate; rather, that area is highly critical to normal functioning of the organism involved.

Point mutations can be further classified by their final effect on the mature protein. Because of the redundancy of the genetic code, some mutations do not alter the final amino acid sequence of the protein and are referred to as *silent mutations*. However, it was discovered that all redundant codons are not equal; some are used preferentially to enhance the speed or accuracy of protein translation. tRNAs corresponding to redundant codons are not found equally in the cell; some tRNAs are more common than others. Silent mutations can cause phenotypic changes by altering mRNA stem-and-loop folding, half-life, and splicing sites. Thus, mutations formerly considered "silent" have now been implicated in a number of different disorders, such as Marfan syndrome, phenylketonuria, Seckel syndrome, and increased pain sensitivity.

1st Position (5' End)	2nd Position				3rd Position (3' End)
	U	C	A	G	
U	Phe	Ser	Tyr	Cys	U
	Phe	Ser	Tyr	Cys	C
	Leu	Ser	**Stop**	**Stop**	A
	Leu	Ser	**Stop**	Trp	G
C	Leu	Pro	His	Arg	U
	Leu	Pro	His	Arg	C
	Leu	Pro	Gln	Arg	A
	Leu	Pro	Gln	Arg	G
A	Ile	Thr	Asn	Ser	U
	Ile	Thr	Asn	Ser	C
	Ile	Thr	Lys	Arg	A
	Met	Thr	Lys	Arg	G
G	Val	Ala	Asp	Gly	U
	Val	Ala	Asp	Gly	C
	Val	Ala	Glu	Gly	A
	Val	Ala	Glu	Gly	G

Figure 1 The Genetic Code

1. Based on information in the passage, genes coding for particularly abundant proteins in a cell would have all of the following EXCEPT:

A) codons corresponding to abundant tRNAs.
B) equal use of redundant codons.
C) greater use of preferential codons.
D) high-fidelity replication.

2. Which of following could account for the changes brought on by silent mutations in both eukaryotes and prokaryotes?

    I.   Decrease in mRNA half-life
    II. Disruption of splicing sites
    III. Changes in mRNA folding

A) I and II only
B) II and III only
C) I and III only
D) I, II, and III

3. Researchers studying a gene associated with breast cancer found that regions where silent mutations occur ("silent sites") in this gene evolve very slowly compared to other regions within this gene. Comparisons were made between mice and humans. Which of the following is most likely true about this gene?

A) Mutations at other sites are more detrimental to the health of the organism than mutations at the silent sites.
B) Mutations at the silent sites increase the accuracy of mRNA splicing.
C) Mutations within the silent sites often lead to the death of the organism.
D) The silent sites are less critical to overall function than the other sites.

4. Which of the following has 3' to 5' exonuclease activity but NOT 5' to 3' exonuclease activity?

A) DNA pol III
B) DNA pol I
C) RNA pol II
D) RNA pol III

5. Point mutations are found in three subclasses: nonsense mutations, missense mutations, and silent mutations. Which of the following represents a silent mutation?

A) UGC to UGA
B) UUA to CUA
C) CAC to CAA
D) CAU to CUU

6. How could changing the half-life of an mRNA lead to phenotypic changes?

A) A shorter mRNA half-life would lead to a truncated protein.
B) A longer mRNA half-life would increase the amount of time the mRNA stays bound to the template strand of DNA, and reduce the amount of protein translated.
C) Differences in mRNA folding could alter the rates of translation.
D) More or less of the protein encoded by that mRNA would be translated.

SOLUTIONS TO CHAPTER 3 FREESTANDING PRACTICE QUESTIONS

1. **C**   RNA polymerase III transcribes transfer RNA (tRNA), which then carries amino acids to ribosomes for use in translation. This polymerase plays no role in replication (choice A is wrong), and reverse transcription uses a DNA polymerase (in any case, it is not carried out by eukaryotes; choice B is wrong). Blocking the action of this enzyme would not alter the base sequence, so mutation would not be affected (choice D is wrong).

2. **D**   The lac operon includes an operator site to which a repressor protein binds (choice A is wrong). The operator site is located between the promoter region and the start transcription site. When the repressor is bound, RNA polymerase (which binds to the promoter site; choice B is wrong) cannot move forward to the start site, thus transcription is inhibited (choice D is correct). Lactose binds to the repressor protein at an allosteric site, causing a conformational change so that the repressor protein can no longer bind to the operator. When this happens, RNA polymerase can move forward to the start site and transcription will occur (choice C is wrong).

3. **C**   A point mutation is a single base pair substitution. There are few possibilities that can result if a single base is substituted. If the new codon is now a STOP codon, then the polypeptide will be truncated (choice A could result from a point mutation and can be eliminated). If the new codon codes for the same amino acid as before the mutation, then a silent point mutation has occurred and no change will be seen in the amino acid sequence (choice B could result from a point mutation and can be eliminated). If the mutation leads to a single new amino acid, then a missense point mutation has occurred (choice D could result from a point mutation and can be eliminated). However, if more than one base was changed, or bases were added/deleted (a frameshift mutation), this would lead to multiple new amino acids (choice C could not result from a point mutation and is the correct answer choice).

4. **A**   Item I is true: eukaryotic mRNA is monocistronic, meaning that only one protein is transcribed from each mRNA (choice C can be eliminated). Item II is false: Transcription does not stop at a STOP codon; *translation* stops at a STOP codon (choices B and D can be eliminated and choice A is the correct answer). Transcription stops when a termination signal is reached. Item III is also false: When mRNA is transcribed, it is complementary to the template strand, not identical to it.

5. **C**   Guanine and cytosine base pairing involves three hydrogen bonds, whereas adenine and thymine only involves two. Therefore, G-C bonds would require more energy to break (choice A is wrong). Cytosine does not base pair with adenine (choice B is wrong), and uracil is an RNA base, not DNA base pairing (choice D is wrong).

6. **A**   Fidelity refers to accuracy. Because RNA polymerases do not proofread, transcription is less accurate (i.e., a lower-fidelity process; choice A is not a similarity and is the correct answer choice). Both replication and transcription use DNA as a template (choice B is a similarity and can be eliminated). In both cases, the removal of pyrophosphate provides the energy for polymerization to occur (choice C is a similarity and can be eliminated). Lastly, although RNA polymerase (in transcription) and DNA polymerase (in replication) move along the parent chain in the 3' → 5' direction, the new chain is made in the 5' → 3' direction.

7. **B**   Because DNA polymerase can only elongate DNA from a primer (i.e., a free 3'-OH group), the ends of the lagging strands do not get replicated. Even if an RNA primer bound to the very end of the chromosome, it would not be possible to replace the primer with DNA because there is no free 3'-OH group ahead of the primer to elongate. Thus, with each round of replication, the chromosomes get shorter. Since it is only a telomere at the end and not a critical gene, this can continue for several rounds of cell division, with the telomere getting shorter each time (choice B is correct). Ultimately, however, the telomere will get "used up," and critical gene regions will begin to be shortened. At this point the cell enters senescence and is marked for destruction. Some cancer cells contain an enzyme (telomerase) that repairs the telomeres after replication, thus prolonging the cell's life span. Topoisomerases help prevent excess tension, and in any case, high guanine content might make it more difficult for the parental strands to separate, leading to increased tension (choice A is wrong). Helicase binds at the origin of replication (choice C is wrong), and DNA ligase seals the gaps between Okazaki fragments (choice D is wrong).

SOLUTIONS TO CHAPTER 3 PRACTICE PASSAGE

1. **B**   Proteins that are abundant require speed and accuracy during translation, and the passage states that this can be accomplished by using preferential codons (choice C is true and can be eliminated; choice B is false and the correct answer choice). Likewise, codons corresponding to abundant tRNAs would be used instead of those corresponding to the more rare tRNAs (choice A is true and can be eliminated). Choice D is true of all genes, abundant proteins or not (choice D can be eliminated).

2. **C**   The passage states that silent mutations can lead to all three of the Roman numeral items listed; however, prokaryotes do not undergo mRNA splicing. Thus Item I is true for both eukaryotes and prokaryotes (choice B can be eliminated), Item II is only true for eukaryotes (choices A and D can be eliminated), and Item III is true for both.

3. **C**   According to the passage, areas of the genome that appear to evolve very slowly are highly critical to normal functioning of the organism. Thus, mutations in these areas most likely disrupt function in a major way, leading to the death of the organism and thus the loss of the mutation (hence the reason it appears to evolve very slowly; choice C is correct and choice D is wrong). If other sites appear to evolve more quickly, mutations at those sites must be less detrimental (choice A is wrong). If mutations at the silent sites increase the accuracy of mRNA splicing, this would be beneficial, and thus preserved (choice B is wrong). Note that the information on breast cancer and humans vs. mice is not necessary to answer the question and is there solely to distract you. Focus on what the question is asking you.

4. **A**   Enzymes with exonuclease activity can remove base pairs from the ends of nucleic acid strands. This can happen in either the 3' to 5' direction, or the 5' to 3' direction. This removal of nucleotides is necessary, for example, to fix polymerization mistakes (3' to 5'), and also to remove the RNA primer during DNA replication (5' to 3'). RNA polymerases do not correct their errors, so they have no exonuclease activity in either direction (this is a 50/50 question and now choices C and D can be eliminated). DNA pol III has only 3' to 5' error

correction; as it is replicating DNA in the 5' to 3' direction, if it makes a mistake it can back up—3' to 5'—and correct its mistake (choice A is correct). DNA pol I has both exonuclease activities. If while synthesizing DNA it makes a mistake, it can back up and correct it (3' to 5' exonuclease activity), and it also has 5' to 3' exonuclease activity so that it can move in the 5' to 3' direction, remove the RNA primer, and replace it with DNA (choice B is wrong).

5. **B** Nonsense mutations convert a codon for an amino acid into a stop codon, missense mutations lead to amino acid substitutions, and silent mutations do not affect the amino acid sequence of a protein. To answer this question, you must use the genetic code in Figure 1. UGC codes for cysteine and UGA is a STOP codon, making this a nonsense mutation (choice A is wrong). The codons UUA and CUA both code for leucine, making this a silent mutation (choice B is correct). CAC codes for histidine and CAA codes for glutamine; this is a missense mutation (choice C is wrong). CAU codes for histidine and CUU codes for leucine; this is also a missense mutation (choice D is wrong).

6. **D** If the half-life of an mRNA is increased, it will stay in the cell longer and more of the protein would be translated. Likewise, if the mRNA's half-life is decreased, it will be eliminated from the cell more quickly and less of the protein would be translated. The mRNA half-life has nothing to do with the length of the protein; protein size is dictated by the length of the open reading frame on the mRNA molecule and the number of codons in the translated region (choice A is wrong). mRNA does not stay bound to the DNA template strand for any length of time, regardless of half-life. As mRNA is transcribed, the DNA helix reforms immediately behind it, releasing the mRNA from the transcription bubble as it is synthesized (choice B is wrong). Choice C is a true statement but does not address the question of half-life (choice C is wrong).

Chapter 4
Microbiology

A milestone in microbiology was the demonstration by Louis Pasteur in 1861 that microbes do not spontaneously arise in boiled broth; they must arrive there by contamination. This put the last nail in the coffin of the idea of spontaneous generation of life. Another major contribution to the golden age of microbiology was the isolation of the bacteria responsible for anthrax in 1876 by a physician named Robert Koch. This and other experiments led to the germ theory of disease, the idea that disease was not caused by bad air ("malaria"), but by microorganisms. In this chapter we will examine three major groups of disease-causing organisms, beginning with the smallest (viruses) and ending with the largest (fungi—which are often not microscopic at all but visible with the naked eye).

4.1 VIRUSES

With the identification of bacteria as the cause of anthrax and other diseases, medical science appeared in the late 1800s to be headed toward explanation of all infectious disease. Researchers soon found however that some infectious agents could not be trapped by passage through filters in the same manner as bacteria. These agents also proved invisible to the light microscope, unlike bacteria. With the advent of electron microscopy, the tiny infectious agents known as **viruses** were finally visualized. Today, molecular biology has shed great light onto viruses, down to the nucleotide sequence of entire viral genomes. However, viruses such as HIV still remain one of the most serious threats to health, indicating there is still much to learn.

Viruses infect all life forms on earth, including plants, animals, protists, and bacteria. A virus is an **obligate intracellular parasite**. As such, they are only able (*obligated*) to reproduce within (*intra*) cells. While within cells, viruses have some of the attributes of living organisms, such as the ability to reproduce; but outside cells, viruses are without activity. Viruses on their own are unable to perform any of the chemical reactions characteristic of life, such as synthesis of ATP and macromolecules.[1] *Viruses are not cells or even living organisms.* To reproduce, they commandeer the cellular machinery of the host they infect and use it to manufacture copies of themselves. In the final analysis, a virus is nothing more than a package of nucleic acid that says: "Pick me up and reproduce me." Remember this crucial definition: A virus is an obligate intracellular parasite which relies on host machinery whenever possible. In the following sections we will look at some of the variations on this basic theme.

- Cyanide (an inhibitor of the electron transport chain) is added to a culture of virus-infected mammalian cells. The virus has none of the components of electron transport nor any other proteins that are inhibited by cyanide. Which one of the following best describes the effect of cyanide?[2]
    - A. The mammalian cells will die, and all viruses will be destroyed as well, regardless of their stage of development.
    - B. Mammalian cells are killed, and viral replication halted, but the culture remains infectious.
    - C. Mammalian cells stop growing, and viral replication is unaffected.
    - D. Mammalian cells continue to grow, but viral replication is halted.

Viral Structure and Function

The structure of viruses reflects their life cycle. In general, all viruses possess a nucleic acid genome packaged in a protein shell. The exterior protein packaging helps to convey the genome from one cell to infect other cells. Once in a cell, the viral genome directs the production of new copies of the genome and of

---

[1] Note, however, that some viruses store some ATP in their capsids. They acquired this ATP from the previous host and typically use it to power penetration (see below).

[2] The mammalian cells are directly dependent on the ATP generated by the electron transport chain, so if cyanide inhibits the electron transport chain, the mammalian cells will die (choice D is wrong). The viruses are dependent on the mammalian cells for the ATP and enzymes needed for replication, so if the mammalian cells die, viral replication will stop (choice C is wrong). However, any viruses that had already completed the replication process when the cyanide was added will not be affected, and will remain infectious (choice **B** is correct and choice A is wrong).

the protein packaging needed to produce more virus. However, the nature of the genome, the protein packaging, and the viral life cycle vary tremendously between different viruses.

A viral genome may consist of either DNA *or* RNA that is either single- *or* double-stranded and is either linear *or* circular. Viruses utilize virtually every conceivable form of nucleic acid as their genome. However, a given type of virus can have only one type of nucleic acid as its genome, and mature virus does not contain nucleic acid other than its genome.[3] [If the ratio of adenine to thymine in a DNA virus is not one to one, what can be said about the genome of this virus?[4] A disease agent that is isolated from a human cannot reproduce on its own in cell-free broth but can reproduce in a culture of human cells. In its pure form it possesses both RNA and DNA. Is it possible that the disease agent is a virus?[5]]

A factor that influences all viral genomes, regardless of the form of the nucleic acid used as genome, is size as a limiting factor. Viruses are much smaller than the hosts they infect, both prokaryotic and eukaryotic. Figure 1 depicts the relative size of a **bacteriophage** (a virus that infects bacteria) and its host.

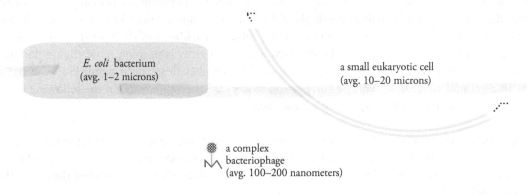

Figure 1   The Relative Size of a Virus

Not only are viruses small, but the exterior protein shell of a virus is typically a rigid structure of fixed size that cannot expand to accommodate a larger genome. [What is the likely result if a viral genome is tripled in size?[6]] To adapt to this size constraint, viral genomes have evolved to be extremely economical. One adaptation is for the viral genome to carry very few genes and for the virus to rely on host-encoded proteins for transcription, translation, and replication. [How do ribosomes used to translate viral proteins compare to host ribosomes?[7]] Another adaptation found in viral genomes is the ability to encode more than one protein in a given length of genome. A virus can accomplish this feat by utilizing more than one reading frame within a piece of DNA so that genes may overlap with each other.

---

[3] There are exceptions. For example, it has recently been discovered that the Hepatitis B virus has a circular DNA genome which is part single-stranded and part double-stranded. The take-home point here is that when a virus is not inside a host cell, it contains only its genome, which is always the same (except in special situations such as when a piece of host genome accidentally becomes incorporated in the viral genome). In contrast, a true cell contains not only its genome, but also mRNA, rRNA, and tRNA.

[4] Adenine base pairs with thymine in double-stranded DNA. Thus, for every A there should be one T for a one to one ratio of A to T. If the ratio differs from this, the genome must be single-stranded DNA, or RNA, which has no T.

[5] No, it cannot be a virus. Viruses possess only one kind of nucleic acid. The disease agent is another kind of obligate intracellular parasite (certain bacteria can only reproduce inside host cells, e.g., *Chlamydia*).

[6] The viral genome will probably no longer fit within the normal viral structure, and the genome will therefore not be packaged into infectious viral particles.

[7] Viruses use host ribosomes. Viral and host proteins are translated by the same ribosomes.

- A 1000 base pair region of viral genome is found to encode two polypeptides unrelated in amino acid sequence during infection of eukaryotic cells. If one of these polypeptides is 250 amino acids in length and the other is 300, what is the best explanation for this?[8]
  - A. A missense mutation
  - B. Viruses use a different genetic code than eukaryotes do
  - C. Overlapping multiple reading frames
  - D. The polypeptides are splicing variants

Surrounding the viral nucleic acid genome is a protein coat called the **capsid**. The capsid provides the external morphology that is used to classify viruses. It is made from a repeating pattern of only a few protein building blocks. *Helical* capsids are rod-shaped, while *polyhedral* capsids are multiple-sided geometric figures with regular surfaces. Complex viruses may contain a mixture of shapes. For example, the T4 bacteriophage has a helical sheath and a polyhedral head (Figure 2). This virus is commonly used in research; its host is the bacterium *E. coli*. The genome is located within the capsid **head**. Other parts of the capsid are used during infection of the host. The **tail fibers** attach to the surface of the host cell, as does the **base plate**. The **sheath** contracts using the energy of stored ATP, injecting the genome into the host. [Why might a bacteriophage inject its DNA, while animal viruses do not?[9]]

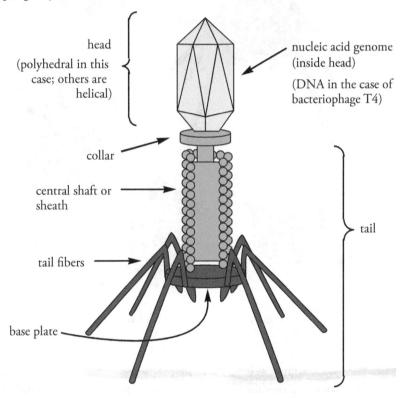

head
(polyhedral in this case; others are helical)

nucleic acid genome
(inside head)

(DNA in the case of bacteriophage T4)

collar

central shaft or sheath

tail

tail fibers

base plate

Figure 2 Bacteriophage T4

---

[8] The problem is that the virus must contain at least 750 bp (250 amino acids) and 900 bp (300 amino acids) of genetic information for unrelated polypeptides in 1000 bp of DNA. The only way to do this is overlapping multiple reading frames (choice C).

[9] Phage must puncture the bacteraial cell wall, while animal viruses can be internalized whole into animal cells (since they do not have a cell wall).

The most important thing to understand is that the entire viral capsid is composed of protein, while the viral genome is composed of nucleic acid (DNA or RNA). Most viruses are not as structurally complex as the bacteriophage shown in Figure 2. See Figure 3 for more examples.

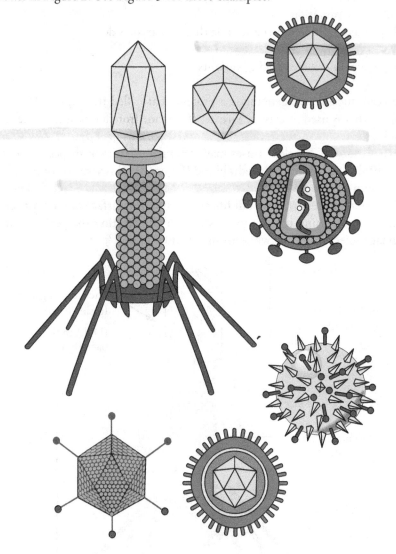

Figure 3   A Variety of Viruses

Many animal viruses also possess an **envelope** that surrounds the capsid. This is a membrane on the exterior of the virus derived from the membrane of the host cell. It contains phospholipids, proteins, and carbohydrates from the host membrane, in addition to proteins encoded by the viral genome. Enveloped viruses acquire this covering by **budding** through the host cell membrane. To infect a new host, some enveloped viruses fuse their envelope with the host's plasma membrane, which leaves the de-enveloped capsid inside the host cell. Viruses which do not have envelopes are called **naked viruses**. All phages and plant viruses are naked. [Can you imagine why this might be true?[10]]

---

[10] Remember: Viruses acquire envelopes by budding through host membranes. Phages and plant viruses infect hosts that possess cell walls. When viruses begin to exit the cell, the cell wall is destroyed, and host membranes rupture. Hence there is no membrane through which the remaining viruses must bud; they simply escape in a lytic explosion.

Whether enveloped or naked, the surface of a virus determines what host cells it can infect. Viral infection is not a random process, but highly specific. A virus binds to a specific receptor on the cell surface as the first step in infection. After binding, the virus will be internalized, either by fusion with the plasma membrane or by receptor-mediated endocytosis. Only cells with a receptor that matches the virus will become infected, explaining why only specific species or specific cell types are susceptible to infection. The viral surface is also important for recognition by our immune system. [If antibodies to a viral capsid protein are ineffective in blocking infection, what might this indicate about the virus?[11]]

Bacteriophage Life Cycles

Since viruses lack the ability to produce energy and replicate on their own, they use the machinery of the cell they infect to carry out these processes. The viral genome contains genes that redirect the infected cell to produce viral products. The first step is binding to the exterior of a bacterial cell in a process termed **attachment** or **adsorption**. The next step is injection of the viral genome into the host cell in a process termed **penetration** or **eclipse**. It is called "eclipse" because the capsid remains on the outer surface of the bacterium while the genome disappears into the cell, removing infectious virus from the media. From this point forward a phage follows one of two different paths: It enters either the **lytic cycle** or the **lysogenic cycle**.

The Lytic Cycle of Phages

As soon as the phage genome has entered the host cell, host polymerases and/or ribosomes begin to rapidly transcribe and translate it. One of the first viral gene products made is sometimes an enzyme called **hydrolase**, a hydrolytic enzyme that degrades the entire host genome. (Hydrolase is an example of an **early gene**; one of a group of genes that are expressed immediately after infection and which includes any special enzymes required to express viral genes.) Then multiple copies of the phage genome are produced (using the dNTPs resulting from degradation of the host genome), as well as an abundance of capsid proteins. Next, each new capsid automatically assembles itself around a new genome. Finally, an enzyme called **lysozyme** is produced. An example of a **late gene**, lysozyme is also present in human tears and saliva. It destroys the bacterial cell wall. Because osmotic pressure is no longer counteracted by the protection of the cell wall, the host bacterium bursts ("lyses," hence the name *lytic*), releasing about 100 progeny viruses, which can begin another round of the cycle (see Figure 4). [If lysozyme were an early gene, would this be advantageous to the virus?[12]]

---

[11] It suggests that the virus is enveloped, so the antibody cannot reach its epitope on the capsid surface in infectious virus.

[12] No. The host cell would lyse before the phage had time to replicate and assemble.

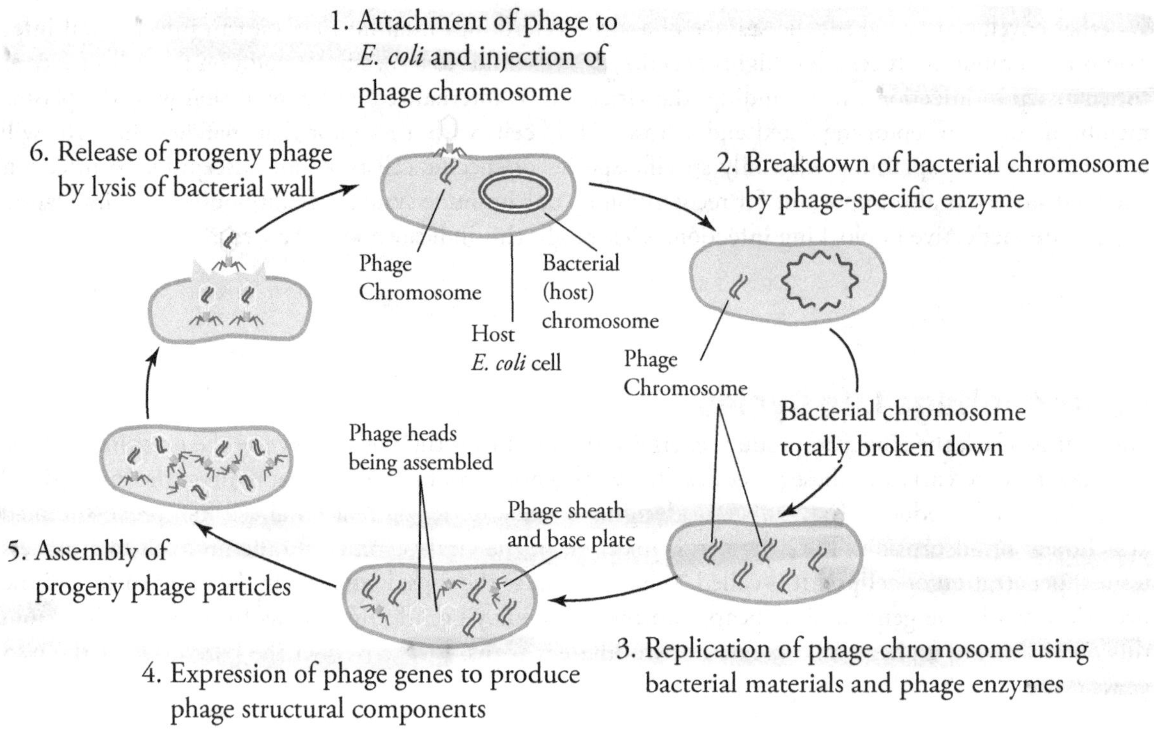

1. Attachment of phage to
E. coli and injection of
phage chromosome

6. Release of progeny phage
by lysis of bacterial wall

Phage
Chromosome

Bacterial
(host)
chromosome

Host
E. coli cell

Phage
Chromosome

2. Breakdown of bacterial chromosome
by phage-specific enzyme

Bacterial chromosome
totally broken down

Phage heads
being assembled

Phage sheath
and base plate

5. Assembly of
progeny phage particles

3. Replication of phage chromosome using
bacterial materials and phage enzymes

4. Expression of phage genes to produce
phage structural components

Figure 4   The Lytic Cycle

- When phage are first added to a bacterial culture, the number of infective viruses initially decreases before it later increases. Why does this occur?[13]
- Bacteria cultured in the presence of ^{35}S-labeled cysteine and ^{32}P-labeled phosphates are infected with phage T4. When phage from this culture are used to infect a new nonradiolabeled bacterial culture, which of the isotopes will be found in the interior of the newly-infected bacteria?[14]
- A bacteriophage with an important capsid gene deleted infects the same cell as another virus with a normal copy of the same gene. At the time of host-cell lysis:[15]
  - A. all released viruses will be capable of infecting new hosts, but only some of these new infections will give rise to phage capable of infecting new hosts.
  - B. no infective viruses will be released.
  - C. each individual virus that is released will produce a mixture of infective and noninfective viruses in subsequent infections.
  - D. only normal viruses will be released.

---

[13] The initial decrease is due to the simple fact that many phage have injected their genomes into hosts and are no longer infectious.

[14] The ^{35}S cysteine will be incorporated into viral coat proteins and the ^{32}P phosphate will be incorporated into the viral nucleic acid genome in newly released viral particles. (Proteins contain no P and nucleic acids contain no S.) When these viruses infect bacteria, their nucleic acids are injected into the bacteria while the capsid proteins remain on the exterior, which means that only the ^{32}P will be found in the interior of the newly infected cells.

[15] When two viruses infect the same cell, it is called co-infection. Some normal viruses will result, and some genomes from defective viruses will get packaged into capsids made from proteins encoded by the normal virus. The latter will be capable of infecting new hosts, but when they do their progeny will not survive due to the capsid abnormality. Choice **A** is correct and choices B and D are wrong. Think about it: where did the phage with the deleted capsid gene come from?! The deficient virus must have come from a co-infection such as this. The deficient phage can only infect host cells and reproduce with the help of normal viruses. Note that because a single virus carries only a single genome, it can produce only one type of progeny (choice C is wrong).

The Lysogenic Cycle of Phages

The lytic cycle is an efficient way for a virus to rapidly increase its numbers. It presents a problem though: All host cells are destroyed. This is an evolutionary disadvantage. Some viruses are cleverer: They enter the **lysogenic cycle**. Upon infection, the phage genome is incorporated into the bacterial genome and is now referred to as a **prophage**; the host is now called a **lysogen** (Figure 5). The prophage is silent; its genes are not expressed, and viral progeny are not produced. This dormancy is due to the fact that transcription of phage genes is blocked by a phage-encoded repressor protein that binds to specific DNA elements in phage promoters (operators). The cleverness of the lysogenic cycle lies in the fact that every time the host cell reproduces itself, the prophage is reproduced too. Eventually, the prophage becomes activated. It now removes itself from the host genome (in a process called **excision**) and enters the lytic cycle.

One potential consequence of the lysogenic cycle is that when the viral genome activates, excising itself from the host genome, it may take part of the host genome along with it. When the virus replicates, the small piece of host genome will be replicated and packaged with the viral genome. In subsequent infections, the virus will integrate the "stolen" host DNA along with its own genome into the new host's genome. The presence of the new DNA will become evident if it codes for a trait that the newly-infected host did not previously possess, such as the ability to metabolize galactose. This process is called **transduction**. [Why would a bacterial gene, carried with a virus and integrated with viral genes into a new bacterial genome, not be repressed along with the viral genes during lysogeny?[16]]

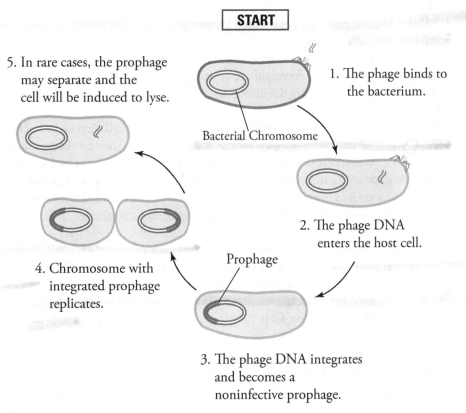

| START |

5. In rare cases, the prophage may separate and the cell will be induced to lyse.

1. The phage binds to the bacterium.

Bacterial Chromosome

2. The phage DNA enters the host cell.

Prophage

4. Chromosome with integrated prophage replicates.

3. The phage DNA integrates and becomes a noninfective prophage.

Figure 5   The Lysogenic Cycle

---

[16] Prophage latency results from a viral repressor protein binding to viral DNA in a sequence-specific manner. The specific DNA sequence to which the repressor binds is present in the viral genes but not in the bacterial genes, so the bacterial gene can be expressed while the viral genes are repressed.

Replication of Animal Viruses

There are a number of differences between phages and viruses which infect animal cells. (Animal viruses don't have a special name like "phage.") The general outline of the viral life cycle, however, remains the same. The virus must specifically bind to a proper host cell, release its genetic material into the host, take over host machinery, replicate its genome, synthesize capsid components, assemble itself, and finally escape to infect a new cell.

Animal cells have proteins on the surface of their plasma membranes that serve as specific receptors for viruses. These receptors play a role in normal cellular function; they do not exist simply for the benefit of the virus. Part of the tissue-specificity of animal viruses is due to the distribution of receptors necessary for adsorption. For example, the binding of the HIV virus protein gp120 to a T cell membrane protein termed CD4 is one of the first steps in HIV infection.

- Would treatment of an HIV-infected person with a soluble form of CD4 protein affect the infectivity of the virus?[17]
- Mutation of the cell-surface receptor that viruses attach to would be a means for an organism to become resistant to viral infection. Why is this mechanism not common?[18]
- Treatment of an enveloped animal virus with a mild detergent solubilizes several proteins from the virus, although the genome does not become accessible. Which one of the following is consistent with this scenario?[19]
    - A. Some of the proteins that are released by detergent may be encoded by the genome of the infected cell.
    - B. The infectivity of the virus is not affected by detergent treatment.
    - C. The proteins released by detergent are capsid proteins.
    - D. All the proteins released by the detergent are encoded by the viral genome.

The next step in the infection of an animal cell is penetration into the cell, just as in bacterial infection by a phage. Many animal viruses enter cells by **endocytosis** (a process whereby the host cell engulfs the virus and internalizes it). [Why don't phages enter their hosts by endocytosis?[20]] Once inside the host, the viral genome is *uncoated*, meaning it is released from the capsid. Alternatively, some viruses fuse with the plasma membrane to release virus into the cytoplasm. From this point, an animal virus may enter either a lytic cycle, a lytic-like cycle called the productive cycle, or a lysogenic cycle.

The lytic cycle in animal viruses is the same as in phages. The **productive cycle** is similar to the lytic cycle but does not destroy the host cell. It is possible because enveloped viruses exit the host cell by *budding through the host's cell membrane*, becoming coated with this membrane in the process. Budding does not necessarily destroy a cell since the lipid bilayer membrane can reseal as the virus leaves. Finally, in the animal virus lysogenic cycle the dormant form of the viral genome is called a **provirus** (analogous to a

---

[17] Yes, it would. The soluble CD4 protein would bind to the virus's CD4 receptor (gp120) and block attachment of the virus to the T cells.

[18] Two reasons: 1) The receptor has a specific role in the normal physiology of the host, which a mutation might compromise. 2) Viruses generally evolve so rapidly that they can keep up with any changes in the host, but this is not an absolute rule. Cells of our immune system keep us alive by keeping up with most microorganisms' tricks.

[19] The detergent solubilized the viral envelope (choice C is wrong). As stated in the text, some envelop proteins are encoded by the virus and some are derived from the host's membranes during budding (choice A is correct and choice D is wrong). Removal of envelope proteins will impair viral adsorption and reduce infectivity (choice B is wrong).

[20] Bacteria do not perform endocytosis, in part because they have a rigid cell wall which does not permit them to.

prophage). For example, Herpes simplex I is the virus that causes oral herpes. After infection, it may remain dormant as a provirus for an indefinite period of time. Then one day, usually when the host encounters stress (e.g., lack of sleep, upcoming professional school entrance exams, etc.), the virus reactivates.

Viral Genomes

Many factors determine the uniqueness of each virus. The type of genome, possession or lack of an envelope, nature of cell-surface proteins, and type of life cycle are examples. All of these parameters are used in the classification of viruses, and all are potential targets for therapeutic intervention. The nature of the genome is perhaps the most important of these and has important consequences for how infection by each virus proceeds. In the following discussion we will look at a few viral genomes with an eye to *what proteins the virus must encode or actually carry in its capsid based on its genome type.* Our purpose is not to provide new information, but rather to demonstrate what conclusions can be drawn from what you already know (typical MCAT passage material). Do not memorize, but rather read for comprehension. We will not discuss ds-RNA or ss-DNA genomes, but by the end of this section you should be able to imagine components they might require.

[+] RNA Viruses
—must *encode* RNA-dependent RNA pol (and do not have to carry it).

A (+) RNA virus, with a single-stranded RNA genome, is the simplest imaginable type of viral genome. (A piece of single-stranded viral RNA which serves as mRNA is called (+) RNA.) As soon as the (+) RNA genome is in the host cell, host ribosomes begin to translate it, creating viral proteins. The viral genome acts directly as mRNA. The technical way to describe this scenario is to say the genome is **infective**, meaning injecting an isolated genome into the host cell will result in virus production. In order for the virus to replicate itself, one of the proteins it encodes must be an **RNA-dependent RNA polymerase**, the role of which is __?[21] (+) RNA viruses cause the common cold, polio, and rubella. [Will infectious virus be produced if the genome of an enveloped (+) strand RNA virus is added to an extract prepared from the cytoplasm of eukaryotic cells that retains translational activity but lacks DNA replication or transcription of host genes?[22] If a viral genome is (+) strand RNA, what is used as a template by the RNA-dependent RNA polymerase?[23]]

---

[21] to copy the RNA genome for viral replication; the host never makes RNA from RNA.

[22] No. The (+) strand RNA virus will be able to produce viral genome and proteins, but progeny will not be able to acquire the envelope they need to be infectious.

[23] To make (+) strand copies of the genome, the virus needs the complementary strand as a template: the (−) strand RNA. Thus, the RNA-dependent RNA polymerase produces a (−) strand intermediate before generating new (+) strand genomes.

(–) RNA Viruses

—must *carry* RNA-dependent RNA pol (and, of course, encode it too).

The genome of a (–) RNA virus is *complementary* to the piece of RNA that encodes viral proteins. In other words, the genome of a (–) RNA virus is the template for viral mRNA production. If host ribosomes translate (–) RNA, useless polypeptides will be made. Hence, the virus must not only encode an RNA-dependent RNA polymerase, it must actually carry one with it in the capsid. When the virus enters the host cell, this enzyme will create a (+) strand from the (–) genome. Then the viral life cycle can proceed. (–) RNA viruses cause rabies, measles, mumps, and influenza. [Do (–) strand RNA viruses use host enzymes to catalyze RNA production in transcription or in replication of the genome?[24]]

Retroviruses

—must *encode* reverse transcriptase.

HIV, the virus that causes AIDS, and HTLV (Human T-cell Leukemia Virus) are examples of retroviruses. These are (+) RNA viruses which undergo lysogeny. In other words, they integrate into the host genome as proviruses. In order to integrate into our double-stranded DNA genome, a viral genome must also be composed of double-stranded DNA. Since these viral genomes enter the cell in an RNA form, they must undergo **reverse transcription** to make DNA from an RNA template. This snubbing of the central dogma is accomplished by an **RNA-dependent DNA polymerase** ("*reverse transcriptase*") encoded by the viral genome. Retroviruses are theoretically not required to carry this enzyme, only to encode it. [Why?[25]] The three main retroviral genes are gag (codes for viral capsid proteins), pol (polymerase codes for reverse transcriptase) and env (envelope codes for viral envelope proteins). [After integration of a retrovirus into the cellular genome, a reverse transcriptase inhibitor is added to the cell. Will the production of new viruses be blocked?[26]]

Double-stranded DNA Viruses

—often *encode* enzymes required for dNTP synthesis and DNA replication.

These viruses often have large genomes that include genes for enzymes involved in deoxyribonucleotide synthesis (which we do whenever we make DNA) and DNA replication. [Given the limited information that viruses may contain in their genomes, why carry around genes for an enzyme possessed by the host?[27]

---

[24] Neither. Viral RNA-dependent RNA polymerase first makes (+) strand as mRNA and then uses the (+) strand as the template to replicate new (–) strand genomes.

[25] Because the viral RNA genome can be translated by host ribosomes; thus reverse transcriptase may be made after the viral genome enters the host. It just so happens that HIV does carry its reverse transcriptase within its capsid. You should understand why this is not a theoretical necessity.

[26] No, it will not. Reverse transcriptase is required for only one phase of the retrovirus life cycle: the copying of the viral RNA genome into DNA so that it can integrate into the host genome and be transcribed. Once the viral genome has integrated, transcription to produce viral mRNA and new viral RNA genomes does not involve reverse transcriptase. It can proceed with the normal host-cell enzymes.

[27] The host cell will only make dNTPs in preparation for replication. If the virus wants to reproduce without waiting for the host to do so, it must encode its own enzymes for the synthesis of DNA building blocks.

Why don't RNA viruses do this?[28] What is a factor likely to limit the size of RNA genomes?[29] Some DNA viruses induce infected host cells to enter mitosis and may even override cellular inhibition of cell division so strongly that the cell becomes cancerous; what is the advantage to the virus of inducing host-cell division?[30]]

- Adenoviruses have a single linear ds-DNA genome, which contains a number of different promoters that are regulated during infection. Although transcription is carried out by cellular RNA polymerase, the viral E1A gene product is required for transcription of most viral genes. If the E1A gene is deleted from the virus or if the gene product is inactivated, viral infection is unable to proceed. Adenoviruses also encode much of their own replication machinery, including DNA polymerase. If two different adenoviruses infect the same cell, one with a deleted E1A gene and another with a deleted DNA polymerase gene, will successful infection of the cell result?[31]

[28] Transcription is always occurring in all cells, so NTPs (not dNTPs) are always present.

[29] The error rate in RNA synthesis is much higher than in DNA synthesis, in part because there are mechanisms to proofread and correct errors in DNA synthesis (but not in RNA synthesis). If an RNA genome were too large, every copy of the viral genome synthesized would suffer from so many errors that no infectious virus would be produced.

[30] To replicate, the DNA virus must either provide all of the necessary components (such as dNTPs) itself, infect a cell that is already dividing, or induce the cell it infects to enter mitosis and produce the ingredients for DNA synthesis.

[31] Yes, thanks to complementation. The mutant viruses will complement each other, one providing the E1A protein and the other providing DNA polymerase. Note that this had to have happened before; how else could a defective virus such as these exist? One virus which complements another is called a helper virus.

4.2 PROKARYOTES (DOMAIN BACTERIA)

All living organisms (which does not include viruses) can be classified as either **prokaryotes** or **eukaryotes**. The classification of organisms into these groups is based on examination of their internal cellular structure. Representatives from both groups are able to carry out the basic biochemical processes of photosynthesis, the Krebs cycle, and oxidative phosphorylation to produce ATP. The primary feature of prokaryotes that distinguishes them from eukaryotes is that they do not contain **membrane-bound organelles** (nucleus, mitochondria, lysosomes, etc.). *Prokaryote* means "before the nucleus," and the lack of a nucleus indicates that prokaryotes are evolutionarily the oldest kingdom. Unlike viruses however, prokaryotes possess all of the machinery required for life. They are true cells; true living organisms. The prokaryotes include **bacteria**, **archea** (extremophiles), and **blue-green algae** (cyanobacteria).

The classification of living organisms, **taxonomy**, is an important part of biology because it is used to determine the evolutionary relationship of organisms to one another. The largest taxonomic division is the **domain**. There are three recognized domains: Bacteria, Archea, and Eukarya. Domains Bacteria and Archea include prokaryotic organisms, and Domain Eukarya includes eukaryotic organisms. Each domain can be further subdivided into **kingdoms**. Currently there are three well-recognized eukaryotic kingdoms (Animalia, Plantae, and Fungi), and great debate over the number of kingdoms that should be present in the other prokaryotic domains and in the single-celled eukaryotes (protists).

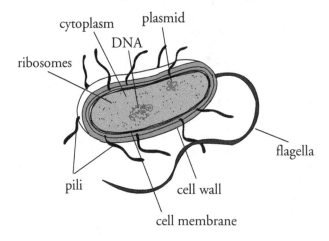

Figure 6   A Prokaryote

Bacterial Structure and Classification

Contents of the Cytoplasm

In this section we will tour the bacterial cell from the inside out. Unlike a eukaryotic cell, there are *no membrane-bound organelles* in prokaryotic cells (note that ribosomes, which are *not* membrane-bound, *are* found in bacteria). The prokaryotic genome is a single double-stranded circular DNA chromosome.[32] It is

---

[32]   There are a few exceptions to this (e.g., bacteria with more than one chromosome and/or linear chromosomes), but you do not have to know them for the MCAT.

not located in a nucleus and is not associated with histone proteins, as the eukaryotic genome is. In bacteria, transcription and translation occur in the same place, at the same time. Ribosomes begin to translate mRNA before it is completely transcribed. Many ribosomes translating a single piece of mRNA form a structure known as a polyribosome.

[In Figure 7 below, is the free end of the mRNA the 3' or the 5' end? Which end of the nascent polypeptides is the free end?[33]] Remember that the bacterial ribosome is structurally different from the eukaryotic ribosome, though both function the same way. The differences allow us to prescribe various antibiotics which interfere with bacterial translation without disrupting our own. (Examples are streptomycin and tetracycline, which only bind to bacterial ribosomes.)

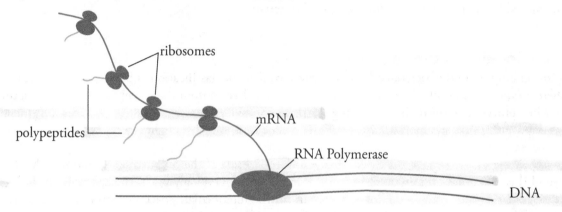

Figure 7   A Prokarytic Polyribosome

One last genetic element that can be found in prokaryotic cells is the **plasmid**. This is a circular piece of double-stranded DNA which is much smaller than the genome. Plasmids are referred to as **extrachromosomal genetic elements**. They often encode gene products which may confer an advantage upon a bacterium carrying the plasmid. For example, plasmids frequently carry antibiotic-resistance genes (genes that encode proteins which can break down antibiotics). Many plasmids are capable of autonomous replication, which means that a single plasmid molecule within a bacterial cell may cause itself to be replicated into many copies. Plasmids are important not only because they may encode advantageous gene products, but also because they orchestrate bacterial exchange of genetic information, or **conjugation**, which is discussed below.

Bacterial Shape

Bacteria are often classified according to their shape. The three shapes and their proper names are organized in the following table:

Shape	Proper name (plural)	Proper name (singular)
round	cocci	coccus
rod-shaped	bacilli	bacillus
spiral-shaped	spirochetes or spirilla	spirochete, spirillum

Table 1   Bacterial Classification by Shape

---

[33] The 5' end of the mRNA polymer is free, since elongation of mRNA proceeds 5' to 3'. Proteins are made N to C, so the free end of the polypeptides is the N terminus.

The Cell Membrane and the Cell Wall

The bacterial cytoplasm is bounded by a lipid bilayer which is similar to our own plasma membrane. Outside the lipid bilayer is a rigid cell wall. It provides support for the cell, preventing lysis due to osmotic pressure. (As we will discuss in Chapter 5, animal cells lack a cell wall. They deal with the problem of osmotic pressure by continuously pumping ions across the cell membrane.) The bacterial cell wall is composed of **peptidoglycan**, a complex polymer unique to prokaryotes. It contains cross-linked chains made of sugars and amino acids, including D-alanine, which is not found in animal cells (our amino acids have the L configuration). The bacterial cell wall is the target of many antibiotics, such as penicillin. The enzyme *lysozyme*, which is found in tears and saliva and made by lytic viruses, destroys the peptidoglycan in the bacterial cell wall, resulting in an osmotically fragile structure called a **protoplast**. [Would a protoplast moved from salt water to fresh water shrivel or burst?[34]]

Gram Staining of the Cell Wall

As part of our tour of the bacterial cell, we will say a word about classification of bacteria according to two different types of cell wall. The method of classification is derived from the extent to which bacteria turn color in a procedure termed **Gram staining**. The two groupings are **Gram-positive**, which stain strongly (a dark purple color) and **Gram-negative** bacteria, which stain weakly (a light pink color).

Gram-positive bacteria have a thick peptidoglycan layer outside of the cell membrane and no other layer beyond this. Gram-negative bacteria have a thinner layer of peptidoglycan in the cell wall but have an additional outer layer containing lipopolysaccharide. The intermediate space in Gram-negative bacteria between the cell membrane and the outer layer is termed the **periplasmic space**, in which are sometimes found enzymes that degrade antibiotics (see Figure 8). The increased protection of Gram-negative bacteria from the environment is reflected in their weak staining, as well as in their increased resistance to antibiotics. [Which bacteria would be more susceptible to lysis when treated with lysozyme: Gram-positive or Gram-negative?[35]]

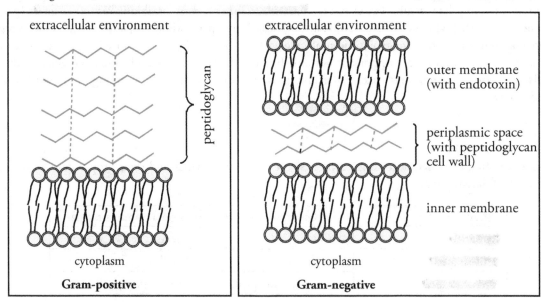

Figure 8 Gram-positive vs. Gram-negative Bacteria

---

[34] It would burst, since water would flow into the cell by osmosis.

[35] Lysozyme hydrolyzes linkages in peptidoglycan to weaken the cell wall. The peptidoglycan in Gram-positive cells is more accessible, since these cells do not possess an additional outer layer; therefore, Gram-positive cells will lyse more easily when treated with lysozyme.

Endotoxins vs. Exotoxins

Endotoxins are normal components of the outer membrane of Gram-negative bacteria that aren't inherently poisonous. However, they cause our immune system to have such an extreme reaction that we may die as a result. Endotoxins cause the most trouble when many bacteria die and their disintegrated outer membranes are released into the circulation. When this occurs, cells of the immune system release so many chemicals that the patient goes into what is called septic shock, in which much of the aqueous portion of the blood is leaked into the tissues causing a drop in blood pressure, and other problems, which may be fatal. Endotoxins can have various chemical structures including lipopolysaccharide, which contains sugars bound to lipids.

Exotoxins are very toxic substances secreted by both Gram-negative and Gram-positive bacteria into the surrounding medium. Exotoxins help the bacterium compete with other bacterial species, such as normal inhabitants of the mammalian gut. Some diseases that are caused by exotoxins are botulism, diptheria, tetanus, and toxic shock syndrome.

The Capsule

Another attribute which only some bacteria have is the **capsule** or **glycocalyx**. This is a sticky layer of polysaccharide "goo" surrounding the bacterial cell and often surrounding an entire colony of bacteria. It makes bacteria more difficult for immune system cells to eradicate. It also enables bacteria to adhere to smooth surfaces such as rocks in a stream or the lining of the human respiratory tract.

Flagella

Another item only some bacteria have are long, whip-like filaments known as **flagella**, which are involved in bacterial motility. [Can viruses move via flagellar propulsion to find host cells?[36]] A bacterium which possesses one or more flagella is said to be **motile**, because flagella are the only means of bacterial locomotion. Bacteria may be **monotrichous** (meaning they have a flagellum located at only one end), **amphitrichous** (meaning they have a flagellum located at both ends), or **peritrichous** (meaning that they have multiple flagella). The following is which?[37]

The structure of the flagellum is fairly complicated, with components encoded by over 35 genes, but it can be broken down into a few major components: the **filament**, the **hook**, and the **basal structure** (Figure 9). The basal structure contains a number of rings that anchor the flagellum to the inner and outer membrane (for a Gram-negative bacterium) and serve to rotate the **rod** and the rest of the attached flagellum in either a clockwise or counterclockwise manner. The most important thing to remember about the prokaryotic flagellum is that its structure is different from the eukaryotic one (which contains a "9 + 2" arrangement of microtubules, discussed in Chapter 5).

---

[36] No. Viruses lack any means of energy production on their own and any means of active movement. They rely on diffusion to find host cells.

[37] Monotrichous

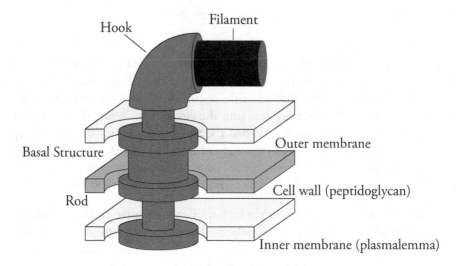

Figure 9 The Prokaryotic Flagellum

The rotation of the rod requires a large amount of energy (that is, ATP), which is supplied by the diffusion of H^+ down the proton gradient generated across the inner membrane by electron transport. Bacterial motion can be directed toward attractants, such as food, or away from toxins, such as acid, in a process termed **chemotaxis**. The connection between chemotaxis and flagellar propulsion is dependent upon **chemoreceptors** on the cell surface that bind attractants or repellents and transmit a signal which influences the direction of flagellar rotation. A good analogy would be the blind man's bluff game played by children, in which a person is blindfolded and moves randomly but selects among favorable or unfavorable movements toward the goal based on the responses "warmer" or "colder" (like chemoreceptors binding attractant or repellent and sending a signal to the bacteria to tumble or not to tumble). The response of flagellar rotation to chemical attractants (or repellents) is not dependent on an *absolute* concentration, but to a *change* in the concentration over time. Thus, as the bacterium moves through the solution it is able to detect whether it is moving toward or away from the highest concentration and respond accordingly.

Pili

Pili are long projections on the bacterial surface involved in attaching to different surfaces. The **sex pilus** is a special pilus attaching F^+ (male) and F^- (female) bacteria which facilitates the formation of **conjugation bridges** (discussed below). **Fimbriae** are smaller structures that are not involved in locomotion or conjugation but are involved in adhering to surfaces. [What other bacterial structure is involved in adhering to surfaces? Is it possible that the fimbriae play a role in infection by pathogenic organisms?[38]]

---

[38] The capsule, or glycocalyx is also involved in adherence. And yes, fimbriae do play a role in infection, by facilitating adhesion to cells so that the bacteria can colonize a tissue.

Bacterial Growth Requirements and Classification

Temperature

Another characteristic of bacteria used to categorize them is their ability to tolerate environmental variables, such as temperature. Though bacteria as a group can grow at a wide range of temperatures, each species has an optimal growth temperature. If the temperature is too high or too low, bacteria fail to grow and may be killed, hence the use of boiling to kill bacteria and refrigeration to slow bacterial growth and prevent food spoilage. Most bacteria favor mild temperatures similar to the ones that humans and other organisms favor (30°C); they are called **mesophiles** (moderate temperature lovers). **Thermophiles** (heat lovers) can survive at temperatures up to 100°C in boiling hot springs or near geothermal vents in the ocean floor. Bacteria that thrive at very low temperatures (near 0°C) are termed **psychrophiles** (cold lovers). [How might a decrease in temperature increase the bacterial growth rate?[39]]

Nutrition

Bacteria can be classified according to their *carbon source* and their *energy source*. "**Troph**" is a Latin root meaning "eat." **Autotrophs** utilize CO_2 as their carbon source. **Heterotrophs** rely on organic nutrients (glucose, for example) created by other organisms. **Chemotrophs** get their energy from chemicals. **Phototrophs** get their energy from light; not only plants but also some bacteria do this. Each bacterium is either a chemotroph or a phototroph and is either an autotroph or a heterotroph. There are thus four types of bacteria:

1) **Chemoautotrophs** build organic macromolecules from CO_2 using the energy of chemicals. They obtain energy by oxidizing inorganic molecules like H_2S.
2) **Chemoheterotrophs** require organic molecules such as glucose made by other organisms as their carbon source and for energy. (We are chemoheterotrophs.)
3) **Photoautotrophs** use only CO_2 as a carbon source and obtain their energy from the Sun. (Plants are photoautotrophs.)
4) **Photoheterotrophs** are odd in that the get their energy from the Sun, like plants, but require an organic molecule made by another organism as their carbon source.

- A bacterium that causes an infection in the bloodstream of humans is most likely to be classified as which one of the following?[40]
  - A. Chemoautotroph
  - B. Photoautotroph
  - C. Chemoheterotroph
  - D. Photoheterotroph

---

[39] Normally you expect decreasing temperature to decrease the rate of all chemical, biochemical, and biological processes, since reactions accelerate when kinetic energy increases. However, bacteria which have evolved to live at low temperature (psychrophiles) possess enzymes which may be optimally active at low temperature, leading to better growth.

[40] Since there's no sunlight in the bloodstream, B and D are out. If it's a parasite, it most likely uses some of our chemicals, so it must be a heterotroph, which eliminates A. The answer is C.

- Which one of the following categories best describes an organism which uses sunlight to drive ATP production but cannot incorporate carbon dioxide into sugars?[41]
  - A. Chemoautotroph
  - B. Photoautotroph
  - C. Chemoheterotroph
  - D. Photoheterotroph

Growth Media

The environment in which bacteria grow is the **medium** (plural: **media**). In the lab, the most common solid medium is agar, a firm transparent gel made from seaweed. Bacteria live in the agar but do not metabolize it. The agar is usually kept in a clear plastic plate called a **Petri dish**, and the process of putting bacteria on such a plate is called **plating**. When one bacterium is plated onto a dish, if it grows, it will eventually give rise to many progeny in an isolated spot called a **colony**. Minimal medium contains nothing but glucose (in addition to the agar). More key terms: A **wild-type** bacterium (or a wild-type strain) is one which possesses all the characteristics normal to that particular species. The dense growth of bacteria seen in laboratory Petri dishes is known as a bacterial **lawn**. A **plaque** is a clear area in the lawn. Plaques result from death of bacteria and are caused by lytic viruses or toxins.

Bacteria can reproduce very rapidly, provided that the conditions of their environment are favorable and nutrients are abundant. The **doubling time** is the amount of time required for a population of bacteria to double its number. It ranges from a minimum of 20 minutes for *E. coli* to a day or more for slow growers, such as the bacteria responsible for tuberculosis and leprosy. The doubling time of a bacterial species will vary, depending upon the availability of nutrients and other environmental factors.

One other important term in bacterial nutrition is **auxotroph** (don't confuse this term with *auto*troph). This is a bacterium which cannot survive on minimal medium because it can't synthesize a molecule it needs to live. Hence, it requires an *aux*iliary *troph*ic substance to live. For instance, a bacterium which is auxotrophic for arginine won't form a colony when plated onto minimal medium, but if the medium is supplemented with arginine, a colony will form. This arginine auxotrophy is denoted arg⁻. Auxotrophy results from a mutation in a gene coding for an enzyme in a synthetic pathway.

Bacteria can be differentiated not only by what substances they require, but also by what substances they are capable of metabolizing for energy. For instance, a strain of bacteria may be capable of surviving on minimal medium that has the disaccharide lactose as the only carbon source (no glucose). This would be denoted lac⁺. Mutation in a gene for the enzyme lactase would impair the bacterium's ability to survive on lactose-only medium. A bacterial strain incapable of growing with lactose as its only carbon source would be denoted lac⁻. Genetic exchange between bacteria by means of conjugation, transduction, or transformation (discussed below) can remedy these disabilities.

---

[41] The ability to use sunlight indicates that the organism is a phototroph, and the inability to use carbon dioxide as a carbon source indicates that it is a heterotroph—it must use organic molecules as a carbon source. The answer is **D**.

Oxygen Utilization and Tolerance

Oxygen metabolism is *aerobic* metabolism. Bacteria which require oxygen are called **obligate aerobes**. Bacteria which do not require oxygen are called **anaerobes**. There are three subcategories: **facultative anaerobes** will use oxygen when it's around, but don't need it. [How much more ATP can they make per glucose molecule when O_2 is present?[42]] **Tolerant anaerobes** can grow in the presence or absence of oxygen but do not use it in their metabolism. **Obligate anaerobes** are poisoned by oxygen. This is because they lack certain enzymes necessary for the detoxification of free radicals which form spontaneously whenever oxygen is around.[43] Obligate anaerobes commonly infect wounds.

- If a bacterium cannot use oxygen as an electron acceptor, is it an obligate anaerobe, a tolerant anaerobe, a facultative anaerobe, or is it not possible to distinguish based on the information given?[44]

- A sample of bacteria is evenly mixed into a cool liquid agar nutrient mix in the absence of oxygen and then poured into a glass-walled tube that is open to the atmosphere on top. When the agar mix cools, it solidifies, and bacterial growth is observed as shown below. How would you classify the bacteria in terms of oxygen utilization and tolerance? (*Note*: Agar is practically impermeable to oxygen.)[45]

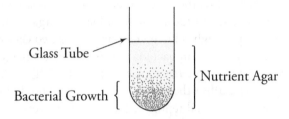

Glass Tube

Bacterial Growth {

} Nutrient Agar

Fermentation vs. Respiration

This was covered in Chapter 2. To briefly review, respiration is glucose catabolism with use of an inorganic electron acceptor such as oxygen. In contrast, fermentation is glucose catabolism which does not use an electron acceptor such as O_2; instead, a reduced by-product of glucose catabolism such as lactate or ethanol is given off as waste. [Why is fermentation necessary whenever an external electron acceptor is not used?[46]]

aerobic: 32 (16x)
anaerobic: 2

---

[42] Sixteen times as much (refer to Chapter 2).

[43] The enzymes include superoxide dismutase (converts O_2^- to H_2O_2) and catalase (converts H_2O_2 to $H_2O + O_2$). An example of a harmful O_2 by-product is superoxide anion, O_2^-.

[44] The bacterium cannot be a facultative anaerobe, since the question states it cannot use O_2. It could be either an obligate or a tolerant anaerobe depending on its ability to neutralize harmful oxygen free radicals.

[45] Since the bacteria grew only at the bottom of the tube, farthest away from any oxygen, this indicates that they could only grow in the absence of oxygen. Thus, they are obligate anaerobes.

[46] Because NAD^+ must be regenerated from NADH for glycolysis to continue. In fermentation, the electrons are passed from NADH to a molecule other than O_2, such as pyruvic acid.

Anaerobic Respiration

This is not a contradiction in terms! It refers to glucose metabolism with electron transport and oxidative phosphorylation relying on an external electron acceptor *other than* O_2. For example, instead of reducing O_2 to H_2O, some anaerobic bacteria reduce SO_4^{2-} to H_2S, or CO_2 to CH_4. Nitrate (NO_3^-) is another possible electron acceptor.

- In an experiment, facultative anaerobic bacteria that are growing on glucose in air are shifted to anaerobic conditions. If they continue to grow at the same rate while producing lactic acid, then the rate of glucose consumption will:[47]
    - A. increase 16 fold.
    - B. decrease 16 fold.
    - C. decrease 2 fold.
    - D. not change.

Bacterial Life Cycle

Bacteria reproduce asexually. In asexual reproduction, there is no meiosis, no meiotic generation of haploid gametes, and no fusion of gametes to form a new individual organism. Instead, each bacterium grows in size until it has synthesized enough cellular components for two cells rather than one, replicates its genome, then divides in two. This process in bacteria is also known as **binary fission** (fission means "to split"). [In prokaryotes, does reproduction increase genetic diversity?[48] If a eukaryote reproduces strictly by asexual reproduction, how will this affect the genetic diversity of a population?[49] How is asexual reproduction in a eukaryote different from asexual reproduction in a prokaryote?[50]] Although bacteria do not reproduce sexually, they do possess a mechanism, termed **conjugation**, for exchanging genetic information (more on this later).

Growth of bacterial populations is described in stages (see Figure 10). Under ideal conditions, bacterial population growth is exponential, meaning that the number of bacterial cells increases exponentially with time. This also means the log of the population size grows linearly with time, hence the name **log phase.** [If 10 bacteria in log phase are placed in ideal growth conditions and the doubling time is 20 minutes, how many bacteria will there be after four hours?[51]]

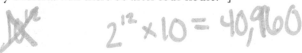

$2^{12} \times 10 = 40,960$

---

[47] Aerobic respiration produces 32 ATP per glucose in prokaryotes compared to only 2 ATP per glucose in fermentation. If the rate of growth is to remain the same, the rate of ATP production must remain the same to drive biosynthetic pathways forward. Since fermentation produces 1/16 the amount of ATP per glucose, the rate of glucose consumption must increase sixteen fold to maintain the rate of growth at the same level. The answer is **A**. (In reality the growth rate would probably decrease.)

[48] No. Each daughter cell is identical to the parent cell (assuming no mutation took place).

[49] Many eukaryotes reproduce asexually. Sexual reproduction allows for generation of new allelic combinations through meiotic recombination and random union of gametes. Without this, diversity will decrease over time.

[50] In eukaryotes, asexual reproduction occurs through mitosis. Prokarotes do not go through mitosis.

[51] Since four hours is equal to 240 minutes, the bacteria will divide twelve times. Therefore, one bacterium will produce $2^{12} = 4096$ bacteria after 12 divisions. Since there are 10 bacteria initially, the total after four hours will be $10 \times 2^{12} = 40,960$.

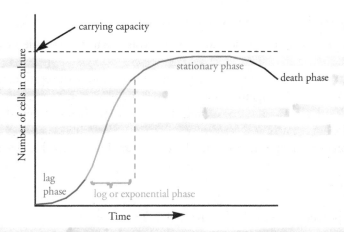

Figure 10 Bacterial Reproduction

Prior to achieving exponential growth, bacteria that were not previously growing undergo a **lag phase**, during which cell division does not occur even if the growth conditions are ideal.

- If growth conditions are ideal, why wouldn't cell division occur immediately?[52]
- Will bacteria that are transferred from a culture that is in log phase to a fresh new culture show a lag phase?[53]

As metabolites in the growth medium are depleted, and metabolic waste products accumulate, the bacterial population passes from log phase to **stationary phase**, in which cells cease to divide for lack of nutrients. The maximum population at the stationary phase is referred to as the **carrying capacity** for that environment. In the last stages of the stationary phase, cell death may occur as a result of the medium's inability to support growth. [If bacteria are grown in a medium with glucose as the main source of energy, when will the glycolytic pathway be more active: during the lag phase or during the stationary phase?[54]]

Endospore Formation

Some types of Gram-positive bacteria, such as the bacteria responsible for botulism, form **endospores** under unfavorable growth conditions. Endospores have tough, thick external shells comprised of peptidoglycan. Within the endospore are found the genome, ribosomes, and RNA which are required for the spore to become metabolically active when conditions become favorable. Endospores are able to survive temperatures above 100°C, which is why autoclaves or pressure cookers are required to completely sterilize liquids and substances that cannot be heated sufficiently in a dry oven. The metabolic reactivation of an endospore is termed **germination**. A single bacterium is able to form only one spore per cell. Thus, bacteria cannot increase their population through spore formation. [When are bacteria most likely to form endospores: during lag phase, log phase, or stationary phase? Is endospore formation a means for bacteria to reproduce?[55]]

---

[52] Cells that are not growing are not actively producing components that are needed for cell division, such as dNTPs. The lag period is a time when biosynthetic pathways are very actively producing new cellular components so that cells can then begin to divide.

[53] No, since they will have all the gear necessary for population growth at the ready.

[54] The bacteria will use glucose during the lag phase to produce ATP and cellular machinery. During this period, glucose is abundant, and the cell is actively performing biosynthesis, so glycolysis is very active. During the stationary phase, however, the glucose will be depleted, and the rate of metabolism will have slowed dramatically, so the rate of glycolysis will decrease as well.

[55] Stationary. Forming an endospore is like hibernating, not reproducing. Bacteria do it in order to sleep through the bad times.

Genetic Exchange Between Bacteria

Bacteria reproduce asexually, but genetic exchange is evolutionarily favorable because it fosters genetic diversity. Bacteria have three mechanisms of acquiring new genetic material: **transduction, transformation**, and **conjugation**. Note that none of these has anything to do with reproduction! Transduction was discussed in Section 4.1 under "lysogenic cycle"; it is the transfer of genomic DNA from one bacterium to another by a lysogenic phage. Transformation refers to a peculiar phenomenon: If pure DNA is added to a bacterial culture, the bacteria internalize the DNA in certain conditions and gain any genetic information in the DNA. Conjugation appears most likely to be related to normal bacterial function, however.

Conjugation

Although bacteria reproduce asexually, they have developed conjugation to exchange genetic information. In conjugation, bacteria make physical contact and form a bridge between the cells. One cell copies DNA, and this copy is transferred through the bridge to the other cell. A key to bacterial conjugation is an extrachromosomal element known as the **F (fertility) factor**. Bacteria that have the F factor are **male**, or **F⁺**, and will transfer the F factor to female cells. Bacteria that do not contain the F factor are **female**, **F⁻**, and will receive the F factor from male cells to become male. [If all cells in a population are F⁺, will conjugation occur?[56]]

The F factor is a single circular DNA molecule. Although much smaller than the bacterial chromosome, the F factor contains several genes, many of which are involved in conjugation itself. [Which cell will produce sex pili: the male cell or the female cell?[57]] After the male cell produces sex pili and the pili contact a female cell, a **conjugation bridge** forms. The F factor is replicated and transferred from the F⁺ to the F⁻ cell. DNA transfer between F⁺ and F⁻ cells is unidirectional; it occurs in one direction only (see Figure 11).

Although the F factor is an extrachromosomal element, it does sometimes become integrated into the bacterial chromosomes through recombination. A cell with the F factor integrated into its genome is called an **Hfr (high frequency of recombination) cell**. [Will an Hfr cell undergo conjugation with an F⁻ cell?[58]] When an Hfr cell performs conjugation, replication of the F factor DNA occurs as in F⁺ cells with the extra chromosomal F factor. Since the F factor DNA is integrated in the bacterial genome in Hfr cells, replication of F factor DNA continues into bacterial genes, and these too can be transferred into the F⁻ cell (see Figure 11).

- If bacteria contain only one copy of the bacterial genome, how can recombination occur?[59]

- If the F factor in an Hfr strain integrates near a gene required for lactose metabolism, is it likely that other genes involved in lactose metabolism will be transferred during conjugation at the same time?[60]

---

[56] No. Conjugation occurs only between F+ (male) and F⁻ (female).

[57] The male cell contains the F factor that encodes the genes for pili production and will produce pili.

[58] Yes. All of the genes of the F factor are still present and expressed normally in the Hfr cell.

[59] When an Hfr cell conjugates with an F⁻ cell and transfers a portion of the bacterial chromosomes, the F⁻ cell will have two copies of some genes, and recombination can occur between the two copies.

[60] Yes. Genes for proteins of related functions are often adjacent to each other in prokaryotes (in operons) and so will transfer to an F⁻ cell together.

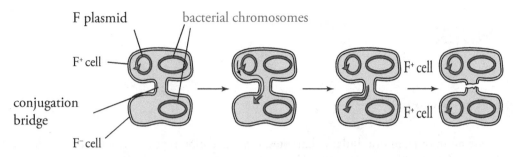

F plasmid   bacterial chromosomes

F⁺ cell

conjugation
bridge

F⁻ cell

a) Conjugation and transfer of an F plasmid from an F⁺ donor to an F⁻ recipient

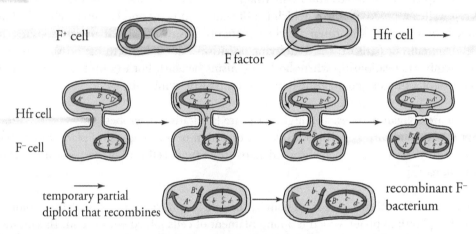

F⁺ cell

F factor

Hfr cell

Hfr cell

F⁻ cell

temporary partial
diploid that recombines

recombinant F⁻
bacterium

b) Conjugation and transfer of part of the bacterial chromosome from an
Hfr donor to an F⁻ recipient, resulting in recombination

Figure 11   Conjugation

Conjugation Mapping

Hfr bacteria provide a mechanism of mapping the bacterial genome. By allowing Hfr cells to conjugate in the lab and stopping the conjugation process after different time intervals, researchers can figure out the order of the genes on the bacterial chromosome by analyzing recipient cells to see what genes were transferred.

For example, you have two strains of *E. coli*. One is a normal Hfr bacterium. The other is F⁻ and auxotrophic for arginine, leucine, and histidine (F⁻ Arg⁻ Leu⁻ His⁻). You allow conjugation to begin and stop it after 2 minutes. You find that all the recipients are now F⁻ Arg⁻ Leu⁻ His⁺. Then you take another bunch of bacteria and allow conjugation to proceed for 5 minutes. Now all the recipients are F⁻ Arg⁺ Leu⁻ His⁺. You do the experiment a third and final time, allowing 8 minutes of conjugation, and find the recipients to be F⁻ Arg⁺ Leu⁺ His⁺.

- What is the arrangement on the genome of the enzymes responsible for synthesis of each amino acid, relative to the site of F plasmid integration?[61]

---

[61] The experiments showed that the ability to make histidine was transferred in a short time. After a slightly longer time, the ability to make both histidine and arginine was transferred. Lastly, the ability to make leucine were transferred. So the arrangement on the genome (the map) must be: His-Arg-Leu-plasmid integration site.

4.3

4.3 FUNGI

Fungal Structure

Most fungi are nonmotile, multicellular eukaryotes. One exception is yeast, which are unicellular. (Fungi possess all of the features that distinguish eukaryotes from prokaryotes, like nuclei, but for the moment we will focus on those features unique to fungi. The generalized structure of a eukaryotic cell will be discussed in Chapter 5.) The molds and fleshy fungi such as mushrooms are multicellular. All fungi possess a rigid cell wall composed of **chitin**, which is different from plant and bacterial cell walls but is found in the exoskeleton of insects. All fungi are chemoheterotrophs. Most are either **saprophytes** (feed off dead plants and animals) or **parasites** (feed off living organisms, doing harm to the host). Some are **mutualists** (live in a symbiotic relationship where both organisms benefit). For example, lichen are not plants, but rather consist of a fungus and an algae living in mutualistic symbiosis.

Most fungi are obligate aerobes, although yeasts are facultative anaerobes. The method of nutrition used by fungi is termed **absorptive**. This means that digestion of nutrients takes place *outside* the fungal cell. Simple organic molecules are then absorbed across the fungal cell wall. [Can yeast use carbon dioxide as a carbon source?[62]]

The fundamental fungal structure is, of course, the cell. The next level of structure in multicellular fungi is the **hypha** (plural: **hyphae**), which is a long filament of cells joined end-to-end. In **septate hyphae**, the cells are separated by walls called septae. **Aseptate hyphae** are composed of cells joined together in a long tube, in which the cytoplasmic contents and the nuclei are shared among the many cells making up the hypha. In other words, these fungi are multinucleate. Hyphae that are specialized to digest and absorb nutrients in a parasitic fashion are called **haustoria** (see Figure 12).

A meshwork of hyphae is called a **mycelium**. A large fungal structure which is visible to the naked eye is a **thallus**, meaning body (plural: **thalli**). The **vegetative** portion of the thallus is involved in obtaining nutrients, and the **fruiting body** functions in reproduction. The role of the fruiting body is to make spores. Mushrooms are fruiting bodies. The spores of fungi are distinct from bacterial endospores, both in structure and function. Each fungus may produce a great number of spores, while a bacterial cell can produce only a single endospore. [Which plays a role in reproduction, a bacterial endospore or a fungal spore?[63]]

---

[62] No. All fungi are chemoheterotrophs, so by definition require an organic (derived from another organism) carbon source.

[63] Only the fungal spore. Remember that the bacterial endospore just allows the bacterium to wait out the bad times.

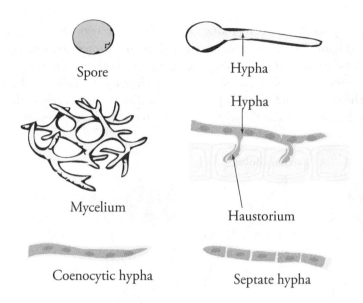

Figure 12   Some Fungal Structures

Fungal Life Cycles

Asexual Reproduction

Fungi reproduce both sexually and asexually. Asexual reproduction of fungi can occur either by budding, fragmentation, or spore production. In **budding**, a new smaller hypha (or single cell) grows outward from an existing one. In **fragmentation**, the mycelium can be broken into small pieces, each of which develops itself into a separate mycelium. **Asexual spore formation** in fungi occurs through mitosis to generate many spores from one cell. Spores are often produced in specialized structures, such as sporangia, found elevated on a stalk-like hypha (see Figure 13). The spores of fungi are in some cases surrounded by a tough wall resistant to environmental extremes. When environmental conditions are favorable, spores will germinate to form new hyphae. Whether budding, fragmentation, or spore production is used to reproduce asexually, the result is multiple identical genetic clones of the original fungi.

Fungal Sexual Reproduction

Every organism carries a distinct number of different (nonhomologous) chromosomes in each of its cells. Humans, for example, have 23 different chromosomes. A cell or species with only one copy of each chromosome is **haploid**, while those having two copies are **diploid**. Humans are diploid, with every somatic cell having two copies of each chromosome (leaving out sex chromosomes for the moment). There is a haploid stage in the human life cycle, however: the gamete (ova or sperm). Haploid gametes are produced from diploid cells through meiosis. Fusion of two human gametes results in a diploid zygote which then divides through mitosis to produce a diploid adult.

The life cycle of fungi is quite different. Fungal adults are haploid rather than diploid. Fungal sexual reproduction involves the fusion of haploid cells derived from haploid adults. Fusion of the haploid fungal gametes produces a diploid zygote, as in humans. In fungi, however, the diploid zygote quickly enters meiosis to produce haploid cells once again. These haploid cells produced by meiosis in fungi are not gametes but will repeatedly divide by mitosis to produce a new haploid adult.

Just as parts of fungi may specialize to reproduce asexually, some regions in fungal hyphae specialize to reproduce sexually (Figure 13). These specialized regions are termed **gametangia**. Gametangia can either produce and release gametes to fuse with other gametes, serve as a site for gamete fusion, or fuse with gametangia from other fungi of the same species. In some cases, fusion of the gamete nuclei does not occur right after the two haploid gametes join together. The result is a cell with two nuclei, called a **dikaryon**. As soon as the nuclei of the dikaryon *do* fuse, however, the cell enters meiosis and produces haploid cells.

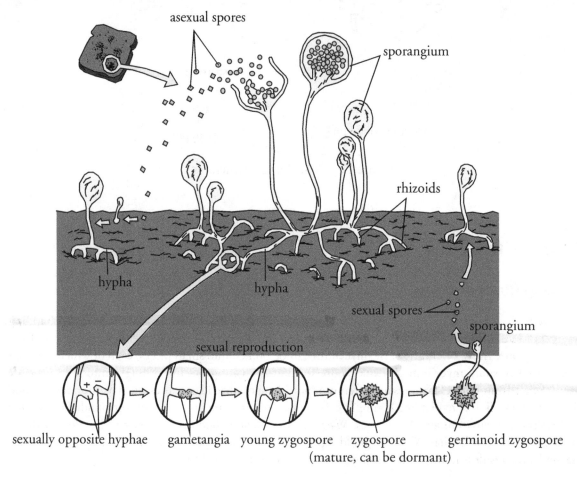

Figure 13 Fungal Reproduction

- For each item listed below, classify a disease agent which possesses the item as bacteria, virus, or fungi. (*Note*: More than one classification will apply in some cases.)[64]
    1) A nuclear envelope
    2) An RNA genome
    3) Genes with introns
    4) Ribsomes
    5) Meiotic cell division
    6) RNA-dependent DNA polymerase
    7) Krebs cycle
    8) DNA-dependent DNA polymerase

---

[64] 1: fungi. 2: virus. 3: virus, fungi. 4: bacteria, fungi. 5: fungi. 6: virus. 7: bacteria, fungi. 8: bacteria, virus, fungi.

Summary

- All viruses are made up of nucleic acids (either RNA or DNA) surrounded by a protein coat (capsid). They are obligate intracellular parasites and must rely on other cells to reproduce.

- Animal viruses may also have an envelope (lipid bilayer) surrounding the capsid. The envelope is derived from the host cell and is acquired by budding through the host cell membrane.

- Viral infection is specific; molecules on the viral surface determine which type of host cell it will infect.

- Viruses replicate via two major life cycles, the lytic cycle (in which more virus is made very quickly) and the lysogenic cycle (in which the virus goes dormant by integrating into the host cell genome). Viruses in the lysogenic cycle can excise from the genome and enter the lytic cycle.

- Animal viruses can also participate in a third life cycle, the productive cycle. This is very similar to the lytic cycle, but the new viruses escape by budding instead of by lysing the host.

- Lysogenic viruses can take pieces of the host DNA with them when they excise and transfer it to the next host. This is called transduction.

- RNA viruses require special virus-derived enzymes (RNA dependent RNA polymerases) in order to replicate their genomes.

- The primary difference between prokaryotes and eukaryotes is that prokaryotes have no membrane-bound organelles (e.g., nucleus, mitochondria, etc.), thus all cellular processes occur in the cytosol.

- Bacterial shape can be used to classify them (round = coccus, rod = bacillus, spiral = spirochete).

- Bacteria have cell walls made out of peptidoglycan that can bind crystal violet (a purple stain used in Gram stain). Gram positive bacteria have thick cell walls and stain a dark purple. Gram negative bacteria have thinner cell walls and an outer membrane; they stain a light pink.

- Some bacteria can be classified by the presence or absence of flagella. Bacterial flagella are used for motility and are distinct from eukaryotic flagella in structure.

- Preferred growth temperature, nutrition, and oxygen use/tolerance are means of characterizing bacteria and can be used to select for growth of a particular bacteria.

- Binary fission is a means of asexual bacterial reproduction that increases the population size exponentially, but does not increase the genetic diversity of the population.

- Conjugation is a means of increasing genetic diversity in a bacterial population by exchanging DNA (plasmid or genomic) via a conjugation bridge.

- Fungi are eukaryotic, have a cell wall made of chitin, and can reproduce both asexually and sexually. Yeast are unicellular fungi.

CHAPTER 4 FREESTANDING PRACTICE QUESTIONS

1. Which of the following statements is FALSE?

A) Both eukaryotes and prokaryotes contain the electron transport chain.
B) The ribosome of a prokaryote is 70S and the ribosome of a eukaryote is 80S.
C) Prokaryotes have one RNA polymerase and eukaryotes have three RNA polymerases.
D) Both eukaryotes and prokaryotes process mRNA between transcription and translation.

2. A researcher has an agar plate covered with a lawn of *E. coli*. She adds a drop of a substance, and the next day there is a clear spot on the plate where the substance was added. This substance could be:

I. a virus undergoing the lytic cycle.
II. a virus undergoing the productive cycle.
III. a chemical that is toxic to prokaryotes.

A) I only
B) III only
C) I and III
D) I, II and III

3. A lab technician grows a liquid bacterial culture overnight, in media without any antibiotics. The next morning, the culture is cloudy. She takes a small amount of this culture and puts it into new media containing tetracycline. The next day, she checks the culture and the media is not cloudy. What happened?

A) The bacterial culture grew the first night but not the second night.
B) The bacteria were resistant to the antibiotic tetracycline.
C) The bacteria were in the lag phase after the first night of growth.
D) The bacteria were in the stationary phase after the second night of growth.

4. Which of the following is associated with prokaryotes and does NOT introduce new genetic material?

A) Mitosis
B) Binary fission
C) Transformation
D) Transduction

5. Which of the following statements concerning viruses is true?

A) The productive cycle is the most efficient infective cycle for phages.
B) Viruses that infect human cells must have an envelope.
C) Genetic information can be transferred between hosts via transfection.
D) A virus with an RNA genome must code for an RNA-dependent RNA polymerase.

6. A researcher is trying to characterize a novel prokaryotic organism that has been found in the Indian Ocean. When Gram stained, the cells are a light pink color under the microscope. When exposed to antibiotics commonly used in the lab, the bacteria are able to enter the log growth phase in a manner similar to *E. coli* grown in media lacking ampicillin. A reasonable explanation is that:

A) this is a Gram-positive bacterium with an additional lipopolysaccharide layer that increases their resistance to antibiotics.
B) this is a Gram-positive bacterium with a cell membrane outside its peptidoglycan layer that increases their resistance to antibiotics.
C) this is a Gram-negative bacterium with an additional lipopolysaccharide layer that increases their resistance to antibiotics.
D) this is a Gram-negative bacterium with a peptidoglycan layer outside the cell membrane that increases their resistance to antibiotics.

7. Which of the following is true regarding prokaryotic flagella?

A) It is the predominant form of bacterial locomotion.
B) It is made of microtubules connected by dynein proteins.
C) It allows viruses to maneuver between host cells.
D) It can only be located on one end of a bacterium and this defines the polarity of the cell.

CHAPTER 4 PRACTICE PASSAGE

Laboratory tests are a useful diagnostic tool for determining the cause of illness. One such test is the complete blood count or, CBC, as it is commonly called. In an infected individual, the white blood cell count can increase from a normal range of 4000–10,000 cells/µL to 15,000 to 20,000 cells/µL. Circulating neutrophils have a short lifespan upon release from the bone marrow (generally about ten hours); however, the demand for phagocytic cells during an infection increases markedly. The result is the release of immature neutrophils called band cells. In a differential white blood cell count, the presence of band cells is referred to as a *shift to the left*. A decrease in the number of neutrophils (neutropenia) can also occur as a result of inflammation or severe infection, when the removal of the neutrophils from the circulation outpaces their production. Neutropenia is also seen in certain blood cancers, such as leukemia and lymphomas, as the neutrophil precursor cells are crowded out by the cancerous cells.

The type of microorganism responsible for an infection can often be determined by changes identified in the population of white blood cells. For example, an increase in neutrophils is commonly seen in bacterial infections. An increase in eosinophils frequently accompanies parasitic infections, as well as allergic responses. A decrease in neutrophils with an increase in lymphocytes (lymphocytosis) can signify a viral infection. All types of infections can result in inflammation (fever, swelling, redness, pain).

One busy spring Saturday evening in a hospital emergency room, several patients presented with respiratory complaints. The patients had either a productive (mucus-producing) or nonproductive cough. All patients presented with some form of fever, either mild or severe. A CBC was ordered on each patient. In addition, a blood sample was obtained from each patient for the purpose of culturing and identifying any infection-causing bacteria. Standard growth media (growth media that contains glucose, amino acids, and some vitamins) providing sufficient nutrients for a wide range of bacteria was used for this purpose. The following results were obtained:

Patient	Growth in culture
1	No
2	Yes
3	No
4	Yes

Table 1 Bacterial Culture Results in Four Different Patients

Patient	Elevated eosinophils	Elevated neutrophils	Elevated lymphocytes
1	Yes	No	No
2	No	No	Yes
3	No	No	Yes
4	No	Yes	No

Table 2 WBC Counts in Four Different Patients

1. If placed on a course of antibiotic therapy, which of the following patients would feel significantly improved after approximately 1–2 days?

A) Patient 1
B) Patient 2
C) Patient 3
D) Patient 4

2. Why did the culture performed on the sample obtained from Patient 3 not yield any growth?

A) The bacteria causing the infection in Patient 3 is a uracil auxotroph.
B) Patient 3 has a bacterial infection.
C) Patient 3 is suffering from allergic symptoms.
D) A different growth medium was required.

3. Patient 4 was prescribed a broad-spectrum antibiotic and released. The patient returned to the emergency room after a two-week period complaining of worsening symptoms. The patient admitted to discontinuing use of the antibiotic after four days of therapy because they felt much improved. Which of the following are possible explanations for the patient's symptoms?

   I. The susceptible bacterial population was not fully eradicated.
   II. The patient was resistant to the antibiotic.
   III. A resistant population of bacteria has begun to proliferate.

A) I only
B) II only
C) I and III only
D) I, II, and III

4. To determine the most appropriate type of antibiotic to prescribe, which of the following additional tests could be performed on a patient sample for classification purposes?

A) Phage-typing
B) Gram-staining
C) Fermentation
D) Transduction

5. Which of the following bacterial types are LEAST likely to cause a respiratory infection?

A) Tolerant anaerobe
B) Obligate aerobe
C) Facultative anaerobe
D) Obligate anaerobe

6. If a patient's symptoms included neutropenia and elevated lymphocyte counts, which of the following diagnoses could be possible?

    I.   Allergies
   II.   Leukemia/lymphoma
  III.   Viral infection

A) I only
B) II only
C) I and III only
D) II and III only

7. An experimental therapy to treat patients with multiple antibiotic-resistant bacteria involves introduction of a highly specific bacteriophage to the infected patient's bloodstream. Which of the following bacteriophage types would be the LEAST useful for this type of therapy?

A) A lytic bacteriophage
B) A lysogenic bacteriophage
C) An RNA virus
D) An enveloped virus

SOLUTIONS TO CHAPTER 4 FREESTANDING PRACTICE QUESTIONS

1. **D** Only eukaryotes process their mRNA between transcription and translation. (This, along with the fact that the processes occur in different locations, is why transcription and translation cannot occur simultaneously in eukaryotes; choice D is false and the correct answer choice.) Prokaryotes have an electron transport chain in the plasma membrane and eukaryotes have an electron transport chain in the inner mitochondrial membrane (choice A is true and can be eliminated). Prokaryotes have a 30S + 50S, total 70S ribosome and eukaryotes have a 40S + 60S, total 80S ribosome (choice B is true and can be eliminated). Prokaryotic cells use one RNA polymerase enzyme for transcription, while eukaryotes use three (one for rRNA, one for mRNA and a different one for tRNA; choice C is true and can be eliminated).

2. **C** A clear spot on a plate (known as a *plaque*) indicates that the *E. coli* are dead. This could be due to the addition of a lytic virus (Item I is true and choice B can be eliminated) or toxin (Item III is true and choice A can be eliminated). However, only animal viruses can go through the productive cycle because viruses cannot bud out of a cell with a cell wall, such as bacteria (Item II is false; choice D can be eliminated and choice C is correct).

3. **A** Cloudy cultures are usually in the stationary phase and clear cultures are either not growing or still in the lag phase. Since the culture was cloudy on the first morning, bacteria had grown overnight and were most likely in stationary phase (choice A is correct and choice C is wrong). The culture on the second morning was clear, indicating minimal growth (choice D is wrong). Since the first overnight culture did not contain tetracycline and the second overnight culture did, it is possible that the strain was sensitive to tetracycline, not resistant (choice B is wrong).

4. **B** Binary fission is the means by which bacteria divide and reproduce. It produces two progeny cells that are genetically identical to the parent; no new genetic information is introduced (choice B is correct). Although mitosis also does not introduce new genetic information, it is a process undergone by eukaryotic cells, not prokaryotes (choice A is wrong). Both transformation and transduction are associated with prokaryotes, but both involve the introduction of new genetic material. Transformation is the uptake of genetic material (plasmids or chromosomal DNA) from the extracellular environment (choice C is wrong) and transduction is the transfer of genetic information from one bacteria to another via a lysogenic phage (choice D is wrong).

5. **D** In order to replicate its genome, an RNA virus must code for an RNA-dependent RNA polymerase; this enzyme will create a new strand of RNA by reading a template strand of RNA. Viral host cells will not express these enzymes naturally; they have no need to make RNA by reading RNA. Host cells normally produce RNA using DNA as a template (choice D is correct). Phages only infect bacteria, and can only undergo the lytic and lysogenic cycles; the productive cycle involves budding through cell membrane and cannot occur in hosts with cell walls, such as bacteria (choice A is wrong). Although viruses with an envelope (lipid bilayer coating) are restricted to infecting animal cells, the outer membrane is not required (choice B is wrong). Genetic information can indeed be transferred between hosts, but this process is called *transduction*, not *transfection* (choice C is wrong).

6. **C** The answer options all start with Gram positive or Gram negative, and the light pink staining in the question stem indicates that this bacteria is Gram negative. Gram-positive bacteria have a peptidoglycan layer outside the cell membrane and therefore stain a dark purple (choices A and B are wrong). Gram-negative bacteria have a lipopolysaccharide layer outside the peptidoglycan layer. This additional outer layer prevents dark staining (hence the light pink color) and increases resistance to antibiotics (choice C is correct and choice D is wrong).

7. **A** Prokaryotic flagella are the predominant means of bacterial locomotion (choice A is correct). Only eukaryotic flagella are made of microtubules and dynein; bacterial flagella have a different structure and are made of the protein flagellin (choice B is wrong). Viruses rely on diffusion to maneuver between host cells, not flagella (choice C is wrong). Bacteria can have flagella on one end (monotrichous), both ends (amphitrichous), or in multiple places (peritrichous; choice D is wrong).

SOLUTIONS TO CHAPTER 4 PRACTICE PASSAGE

1. **D** Antibiotics only treat bacterial infections. Table 1 shows that Patients 2 and 4 have positive cultures, confirming a bacterial infection (choices A and C can be eliminated). However, from Table 2, only Patient 4 has elevated neutrophils, which the passage states is indicative of a bacterial infection, making this patient a candidate for antibiotic therapy. Patient 2 has elevated lymphocytes (not neutrophils), which indicates a concomitant viral infection; the lack of elevated neutrophils in this patient is most likely the result of overwhelming infection. While the bacterial infection of Patient 2 would begin to subside by 1–2 days, the viral infection would take longer to eradicate, and therefore this patient would still be feeling poorly at this point (choice D is better than choice B).

2. **D** From Table 2, Patient 3 has elevated lymphocytes, indicating a viral infection (choices A, B, and C can be eliminated); no growth would occur on standard growth media. Viruses are obligate intracellular parasites and require special growth media containing live cells for reproduction. According to the passage, standard growth media for bacterial culturing was used. Note that if the patient had elevated neutrophils and normal lymphocyte levels (indicating a bacterial infection), choice A would be the best answer, since uracil was not added to the culture media.

3. **C** Item I is true: If the symptoms return and/or worsen, it is possible that the infection was not completely eradicated (choice B can be eliminated). Item II is false: Bacteria are resistant, the patient is not (this is a common misconception; choices B and D can be eliminated). Item III is true: It is also possible that a strain resistant to the antibiotic being used remained alive and is now proliferating (choice C is correct).

4. **B** Determination of Gram status can aid in antibiotic selection. Phage typing applies to bacteriophage, not bacteria (choice A can be eliminated). Fermentation refers to metabolic activity (choice C can be eliminated). Transduction is not a classification method (choice D can be eliminated).

5. **D**   The lungs are a high oxygen environment that is unfavorable to obligate anaerobes. Tolerant anaerobes, obligate aerobes, and facultative anaerobes can all survive in the presence of oxygen (choices A, B, and C can be eliminated).

6. **D**   Item I is false: The passage states that elevated eosinophil counts (not lymphocytes) accompany allergic reactions (choices A and C can be eliminated). Note that both remaining answer choices include Item II, so it must be true: The passage states that neutropenia and elevated lymphocyte counts are seen in lymphoma and leukemia (blood cancers). Item III is true: neutropenia and lymphocytosis are seen in viral infections (choice B can be eliminated and choice D is correct).

7. **D**   Enveloped viruses infect only animal cells and would not be useful in eliminating bacteria from a human patient. The most useful type of virus would attack the infecting bacteria and cause the bacteria to lyse, eradicating the patient's infection (choice A would be useful and can be eliminated), and this virus could have either an RNA or a DNA genome (choice C could be useful and can be eliminated). A virus that incorporates itself into the bacterial genome and then goes dormant (a lysogenic virus) would not be as helpful as a lytic virus in eradicating an infection; however, it would still be more useful than a virus that cannot infect bacteria at all (choice B would be more useful than choice D).

Chapter 5
Eukaryotic Cells

The first cells were prokaryotes. They consisted of a cell membrane and a cell wall surrounding the cytoplasm or cell fluid. All the structures necessary for survival and reproduction floated in the cytoplasm, including the double-stranded circular DNA genome, ribosomes, the enzymes of aerobic and anaerobic metabolism, etc. As evolution proceeded, cell complexity increased. The greatest landmark in the evolution of the cell was the development of membrane-bound compartments within the cytoplasm known as organelles. These served to organize the cytoplasm, with each membrane acting to seal its compartment. The most important organelle is the control center of the cell: the nucleus. In fact, "eukaryotic" is from the Greek "karyon," meaning "kernel" or "nucleus," plus the prefix "eu," meaning "true." "Prokaryotic" means "before the nucleus" and also implies "before organelles." All true living organisms are either prokaryotes or eukaryotes. There are three well-defined eukaryotic kingdoms (Plantae, Animalia, and Fungi), and one group of organisms for whom the kingdom classifications are under debate (single-celled eukaryotes...the Protists).

5.1 INTRODUCTION

It would be impossible to understand medicine without sound knowledge of the eukaryotic cell. In this chapter we will examine each of the principal organelles, beginning with the nucleus. Next we will focus on the plasma membrane, then the cytoskeleton, and finally we will finish with a discussion of the cell cycle. You should be able to explain the function of each item labeled in Figure 1 below. Our discussion will be based on the animal cell. Fungi have already been discussed in the previous chapter, and neither plants nor protists (motile unicellular eukaryotes) are covered on the MCAT.

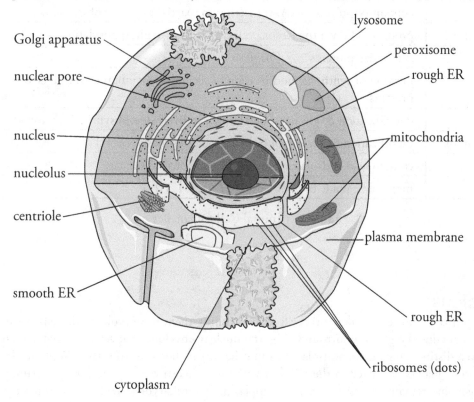

Figure 1 The Eukaryotic Cell

5.2 THE ORGANELLES

An **organelle** is a small structure within a cell that carries out specific cellular functions. Most organelles are bounded by their own lipid bilayer membrane. The membrane acts like a plastic bag to seal off the contents of the organelle from the rest of the cytoplasm and control what enters and exits. A summary of the major animal cell organelles is given in the table below:

Organelle	Function (number of membranes surrounding)
nucleus	contain & protect DNA, transcription, partial assembly of ribosomes (2)
mitochondria	produce ATP via the Krebs cycle and oxidative phosphorylation (2)
ribosomes	synthesize proteins (0)
RER	location of synthesis/modification of secretory, membrane-bound, & organelle proteins (1)
SER	detoxification & glycogen breakdown in liver; steroid synthesis in gonads (1)
Golgi apparatus	modification & sorting of protein, some synthesis (1)
lysosomes	contain acid hydrolases which digest various substances (1)
peroxisomes	metabolize lipids & toxins using H_2O_2 (1)

Table 1   Animal Cell Organelles

The Nucleus

One of the primary features of eukaryotic cells distinguishing them from prokaryotic cells is the **nucleus**. The nucleus contains the genome surrounded by the **nuclear envelope** that separates the contents of the nucleus into a distinct compartment, isolated from other organelles and from the cytoplasm. In prokaryotes the genome may be localized in the cell, but without a nuclear envelope to form a separate compartment, the genome remains accessible to the cytoplasm. In prokaryotes, replication, transcription and translation, and everything else all happens in the same compartment (the cytoplasm). In eukaryotes, replication, transcription, and splicing occur in the nucleus, while translation occurs in the cytoplasm.

- If an enzyme that degrades mRNA is injected into the cytoplasm of a cell and all translation ceases, is the cell prokaryotic or eukaryotic?[1]
- When an enzyme that degrades DNA (DNase) is incubated with intact DNA isolated from an organism, the DNA is degraded. But when DNase is injected into the cytoplasm of cells from the same organism, no effect on the genome is observed. Which one of the following is the best explanation for this?[2]
    - A.   The cell is a prokaryote; therefore, the genome is inaccessible to cytoplasmic enzymes.
    - B.   The cell is a prokaryote; therefore, the circular genome is resistant to DNase.
    - C.   The cell is a eukaryote; therefore, the genome is inaccessible to cytoplasmic enzymes.
    - D.   The cell is a eukaryote; therefore, the linear genome is resistant to DNase.

---

[1]   It could be either. mRNA and translation are found in the cytoplasm of both prokaryotes and eukaryotes, so the cell could be either.

[2]   The isolated genome and the genome in the cell respond differently, so the key is not the circular or linear nature of the genome (B and D are wrong). The key is that in prokaryotes the injected cytoplasmic DNase will have access to the genome to degrade since they are in the same compartment, while in eukaryotes the DNase will not have access to the genome unless it enters the nucleus (C is the best choice).

The Genome

The eukaryotic genome was introduced in Chapters 2 and 3, but we will touch on it again here, as well as in Chapter 6. Eukaryotic genomes are organized into linear molecules of double-stranded DNA, while the genome of prokaryotes is a single circular DNA molecule. The large size of the typical eukaryotic genome appears to make it necessary to split the genome into pieces, each a separate linear DNA molecule, termed a **chromosome**. Yeast have 4 different chromosomes, while there are 23 different human chromosomes. Since humans and most adult animals are diploid, they have two copies of each chromosome (except for the sex chromosomes; see Chapter 6). Chromosomes have a **centromere** near the middle to ensure that newly replicated chromosomes are sorted properly during cell division, one copy to each daughter cell (mitosis and meiosis, this chapter and Chapter 6). Each eukaryotic chromosome also has special structures at both ends termed **telomeres**. Telomeres have large numbers of repeats of a specific DNA sequence and, with the help of a special DNA polymerase termed *telomerase*, maintain the ends of the linear chromosomes during DNA replication. [What special problems are there in replicating the 5' ends of linear DNA chromosomes?[3]]

Within each chromosome is also a portion of the many thousands of genes in the genome as a whole. Genes can be mapped genetically and physically to the chromosome they reside on and to a specific location on that chromosome, a **locus**. The expression of eukaryotic genes is regulated by specific promoter and enhancer elements of that gene, but can also be affected by the position of the gene on the chromosome. Some regions of a chromosome are folded into densely packed chromatin, termed **heterochromatin**, within which genes tend to be inaccessible and turned off. Other regions known as **euchromatin** are more loosely packed (although still packaged into chromatin) and allow genes to be activated. [If a retrovirus inserts its genome into regions of heterochromatin and nowhere else, how is this likely to affect the infection process?[4]]

Finally, the nucleus is not a loose membrane bag with DNA floating inside. If nuclei are treated with DNase and with detergent, an insoluble mesh of protein, known as the **nuclear matrix** or **nuclear scaffold**, is left behind. The role of the nuclear matrix may be in part analogous to the role of the cytoskeleton in the cytoplasm: to support and provide overall structure. The matrix may also play a role in regulating gene expression. The DNA in chromosomes is attached to the matrix at specific sites, and these (in some cases) appear to be involved in regulating gene expression or in limiting the effects of promoters and enhancers to discrete chromosomal regions known as domains. The role of the nuclear matrix is an area of ongoing research.

---

[3] DNA polymerase cannot synthesize DNA without an RNA primer and cannot synthesize DNA in a 3' to 5' direction. It will replicate DNA from an RNA primer at (or very near to) the end of the chromosome, but the RNA primer cannot be replaced with DNA. With each round of replication, the chromosome grows shorter and shorter because of the inability to synthesize DNA at its very ends. Because of the large number of repeated sequences at the ends (the telomeres) the loss of a little bit of DNA is usually not critical. However, eventually all the telomere sequences are lost, and gene sequences start to be lost. If the lost gene sequence is critical for cell function, the cell will die at this point. Telomerase helps prevent this problem. This unique enzyme contains an RNA sequence and acts as a reverse transcriptase, utilizing this RNA sequence as a template to extend the DNA at the end of the chromosome. This provides a location where a normal primer can be synthesized and DNA replication can proceed along the very end of the chromosome, preserving it. Note that telomerase is turned off in most cells, and its inactivity is implicated in cell aging and death.

[4] The retroviral genes will not be expressed very frequently, and the virus will tend to remain as a provirus unless a change in the surrounding heterochromatin allows viral genes to be expressed.

The Nucleolus

The **nucleolus** ("little nucleus") is a region within the nucleus which functions as a ribosome factory. There is no membrane separating the nucleolus from the rest of the nucleus. It consists of loops of DNA, RNA polymerases, rRNA, and the protein components of the ribosome. [Would you expect the nucleolus to be larger in cells that are actively synthesizing protein, or in quiescent cells?[5] What role would the loops of DNA in the nucleolus play?[6]]

The nucleolus is the site of transcription of rRNA by RNA pol I. Transcription of mRNA and tRNA is performed by other polymerases in other areas of the nucleus. [Does a similar "division of labor" exist in the prokaryotic cell?[7]] The ribosome is partially assembled while still in the nucleolus. The protein components of the ribosome are not produced in the nucleolus; they are transported into the nucleus from the cytoplasm (remember that *all* translation takes place in the cytoplasm). After partial assembly, the ribosome is exported from the nucleus, remaining inactive until assembly is completed in the cytoplasm. This may serve to prevent translation of hnRNA.

The Nuclear Envelope

Surrounding the nucleus and separating it from the cytoplasm is the **nuclear envelope**, composed of two lipid bilayer membranes. The inner nuclear membrane is the surface of the envelope facing the nuclear interior, and the outer nuclear membrane faces the cytoplasm. The membrane of the endoplasmic reticulum is at points continuous with the outer nuclear membrane, making the interior of the ER (the **lumen** of the ER) contiguous with the space between the two nuclear membranes. [Is the space between the inner and outer membranes contiguous with the cytoplasm?[8]]

The nuclear envelope is punctuated with large **nuclear pores** that allow the passage of material into and out of the nucleus (see Figures 2 and 3). Molecules that are smaller than 60 kilodaltons, including small proteins, can freely diffuse from the cytoplasm into the nucleus through the nuclear pores. Larger proteins cannot pass freely through nuclear pores and are excluded from the nuclear interior unless they contain a sequence of basic amino acids called a **nuclear localization sequence**. Proteins with a nuclear localization sequence are translated on cytoplasmic ribosomes and then imported into the nucleus by specific transport mechanisms. It also appears likely that RNA is transported out of the nucleus by a specific transport system rather than freely diffusing into the cytoplasm. [If a 15 kD protein has a nuclear localization sequence that is then deleted from its gene, will the mutated protein still be found in the nucleus?[9]]

---

[5] The nucleolus is largest in cells that are producing large amounts of protein. The increased size reflects increased synthesis of ribosomes.

[6] The DNA will serve as template for ribosomal RNA production.

[7] No. Bacteria have only a single kind of RNA pol which is responsible for all transcription.

[8] No, it is not. The space between the nuclear membranes is contiguous with the ER lumen, which is isolated from the cytoplasm.

[9] Yes. The protein is small enough that it can still pass through the nuclear pores by diffusion even without a nuclear localization sequence.

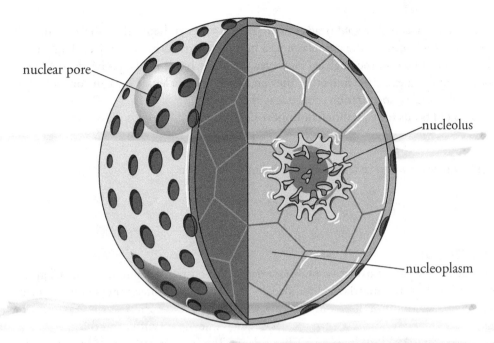

Figure 2 The Nucleus, Showing Pores

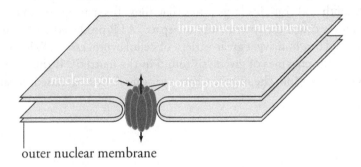

Figure 3 A Nuclear Pore Close-Up

- Which one of the following proteins would NOT be found within the nucleus?[10]
    - A. A protein component of the large ribosomal subunit
    - B. A factor required for splicing
    - C. A histone
    - D. An aminoacyl tRNA synthetase

---

[10] Aminoacyl tRNA synthetases are enzymes that function in the cytoplasm to attach amino acids to their respective tRNAs. They are never needed in the nucleus and would not be found there (choice **D** is correct). The protein components of ribosomes are synthesized in the cytoplasm and then imported into the nucleus to be assembled in the nucleolus (choice A would be found in the nucleus and can be eliminated). Splicing occurs in the nucleus, so anything involved in splicing would be found there (choice B can be eliminated). Histones are used for DNA packaging and would be found in the nucleus (choice C can be eliminated).

- A researcher injects tiny gold beads into a cell and waits an hour. Then she examines the cell and finds gold beads in the cytoplasm and in the nucleus. When she injects larger gold beads, they are not found in the nucleus. However, when she binds the larger beads to a nuclear localization sequence, she finds that they end up in the nucleus. One can conclude that:[11]
  - A. the nuclear localization sequence is lysine-rich.
  - B. gold beads have an inherent import signal.
  - C. the nuclear localization mechanism is nonspecific enough to confer nuclear import on gold beads.
  - D. nuclear import relies primarily on simple diffusion.

Mitochondria

Mitochondria are the site of oxidative phosphorylation (discussed in more detail in Chapter 2). The interior of mitochondria, the **matrix**, is bounded by the inner and outer mitochondrial membranes (see Figure 4). The matrix contains pyruvate dehydrogenase and the enzymes of the Krebs cycle. The inner membrane is the location of the electron transport chain and ATP synthase and is the site of the proton gradient used to drive ATP synthesis by ATP synthase. The inner membrane is impermeable to the free diffusion of polar substances, like protons, and is folded into the matrix in projections called **cristae**. The outer membrane is smooth and contains large pores that allow free passage of small molecules. The space between the membranes is called the intermembrane space. ATP produced within mitochondria is transported out into the cytoplasm to drive a great variety of cellular processes. [Why is the inner membrane folded into cristae?[12] Are the enzymes of glycolysis found in the matrix?[13] If the inner membrane is impermeable, how does pyruvate get into the matrix where pyruvate dehydrogenase is located?[14]]

---

[11] Gold beads are not normally found in cells, so there cannot be an existing mechanism for moving them. However, since the cell is capable of moving them when the localization signal is attached, the localization signal must be somewhat non-specific (choice C is correct). It is true that the nuclear localization signal is lysine-rich, but this cannot be concluded based on the given information (true, but doesn't answer the question, choice A is wrong). If gold beads had an inherent import signal, then they would be transported into the nucleus on their own, without the researcher having to bind them to the localization sequence (choice B is wrong). If simple diffusion were the primary means of moving things into the nucleus, no import signal would be needed (choice D is wrong).

[12] The folding of the membrane increases its surface area and allows for increased electron transport and ATP synthesis per mitochondrion. (Folding is used elsewhere to increase surface area, such as in the kidney tubules and the lining of the small intestine.)

[13] No, in the cytoplasm.

[14] Pyruvate is transported through the inner mitochondrial membrane by a specific protein in the membrane.

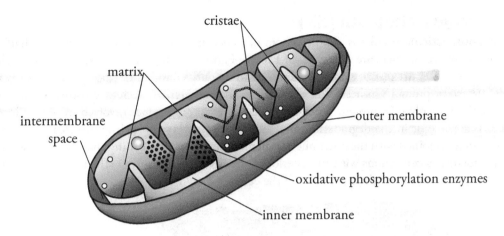

Figure 4   The Mitochondrion

Mitochondria possess their own genome which is far smaller than the cellular genome and consists of a single circular DNA molecule. (Sound familiar?) It encodes rRNA, tRNA, and several proteins, including some components of the electron transport chain and parts of the ATP synthase complex although most mitochondrial proteins are encoded by nuclear genes. Even more curious, mitochondria use a different system of transcription and translation than nuclear genes do. This includes a unique genetic code and unique RNA polymerases, DNA replication machinery, ribosomes, and aminoacyl-tRNA synthetases. In order to explain the fact that mitochondria possess a second system of inheritance, investigators have postulated that mitochondria originated as independent unicellular organisms living within larger cells. This is known as the **endosymbiotic theory** of mitochondrial evolution (*endo* = within; *symbiotic* = living together). In fact, if you compare a mitochondrion to a Gram-negative bacterium, you'll note that they look pretty similar. Pay attention to where the enzymes of electron transport are located and the genome shape.[15] Because many unique mitochondrial polypeptides are encoded by the cellular genome and not the mitochondrial genome, it has been suggested that the genes coding for these proteins may have been transferred to the nuclear genome over time. [What difficulty may be encountered in translation of a mitochondrial gene moved to the nucleus?[16]]

Mitochondria exhibit **maternal inheritance.** This means that mitochondria are inherited only from the mother, since the cytoplasm of the egg becomes the cytoplasm of the zygote. (The sperm contributes only genomic [nuclear] DNA.) Maternal inheritance departs from the rules of Mendelian genetics, which state that traits are inherited from both parents (Chapter 6). If a woman has a disease caused by an abnormality in her mitochondrial genome, what are the chances that her children will have the disease (assuming her mate does not have the disease)?[17]

---

[15]   Remember that bacterial electron transport depends on a proton gradient across the cell membrane. In a Gram-negative bacterium, this membrane would correspond to the mitochondrial inner membrane.

[16]   The coding system of the cellular genome is different from that of the mitochondrial genome. One might wonder how our transcription and translation machinery could sensibly produce mitochondrial gene products.

[17]   All of her children will have it, since they will inherit mitochondria exclusively from her. For a maternally inherited trait, it doesn't matter whether the father has it or not.

Endoplasmic Reticulum (ER)

The **endoplasmic reticulum** (ER) is a large system of folded membrane accounting for over half of the membrane of some cells. There are two types of ER (see Figure 5): **rough ER** and **smooth ER**, each with distinct functions. The rough ER is called rough due to the large number of ribosomes bound to its surface; it is the site of protein synthesis for proteins targeted to enter the secretory pathway. The smooth ER is not actively involved in protein processing but can contain enzymes involved in steroid hormone biosynthesis (gonads) or in the degradation of environmental toxins (liver). The membrane of the endoplasmic reticulum is joined with the outer nuclear membrane in places, meaning that the space within the nuclear membranes is continuous with the interior of the ER (the ER **lumen**). The rough ER plays a key role directing protein traffic to different parts of the cell.

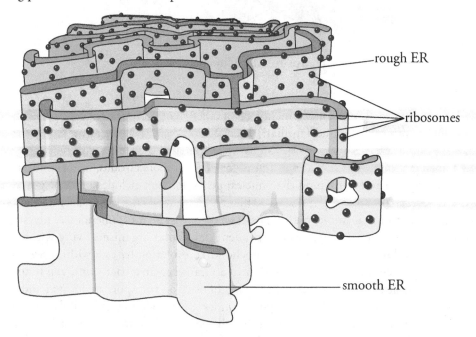

Figure 5   The ER

The Rough ER and the Secretory Pathway

There are two sites of protein synthesis in the eukaryotic cell: either on ribosomes free in the cytoplasm or on ribosomes bound to the surface of the rough ER. Proteins translated on free cytoplasmic ribosomes are headed toward peroxisomes, mitochondria, the nucleus, or will remain in the cytoplasm. Proteins synthesized on the rough ER will end up either 1) secreted into the extracellular environment, 2) as integral plasma membrane proteins, or 3) in the membrane or interior of the ER, Golgi apparatus, or lysosomes. Membrane-bound vesicles pass between these cellular compartments. Since the membranes of these organelles communicate through the traffic of vesicles, the interior of the ER, the Golgi apparatus, lysosomes, and the extracellular environment are in a sense contiguous. Proteins synthesized on the rough ER are transported in vesicles that bud from the ER to the Golgi apparatus, then to the plasma membrane or lysosome. A secreted protein that enters the ER lumen is separated by a membrane from the cytoplasm until the protein leaves the cell.

Whether a protein is translated on the rough ER is determined by the sequence of the protein itself. All proteins start translation in the cytoplasm; however, some proteins (secreted proteins and lysosomal proteins) have an amino acid sequence at their N-terminus called a **signal sequence**. The signal sequence of a nascent polypeptide is recognized by the **signal recognition particle (SRP)**, which binds to the ribosome. The rough ER has SRP receptors that dock the ribosome-SRP complex on the cytoplasmic surface (along with the nascent polypeptide and mRNA). Translation then pushes the polypeptide, signal peptide first, into the ER lumen. After translation is complete, the signal peptide is removed from the polypeptide by a signal peptidase in the ER lumen. For secreted proteins, once the signal sequence is removed, the protein is transported in the interior of vesicles through the Golgi apparatus to the plasma membrane, where it is released by exocytosis into the extracellular environment.

- The mRNA for a secreted protein encodes a longer protein than is actually observed in the cellular exterior. Why?[18]
    - A. The protein was cleaved by a cytoplasmic protease.
    - B. The mRNA was not spliced properly.
    - C. The gene encoding the protein contained a nonsense mutation.
    - D. The signal sequence of the protein was removed in the rough ER.

Integral membrane proteins are processed slightly differently. Integral membrane proteins have sections of hydrophobic amino acid residues called **transmembrane domains** that pass through lipid bilayer membranes. The transmembrane domains are essentially signal sequences that are found in the interior of the protein (that is, not at the N-terminus). They are *not* removed after translation. A single polypeptide can have several transmembrane domains passing back and forth through a membrane. During translation, the transmembrane domains are threaded through the ER membrane. The protein is then transported in vesicles to the Golgi apparatus and plasma membrane in the same manner as a secreted protein (see Figure 6). [For a protein in the plasma membrane, does the portion of the protein in the ER lumen end up facing the cytoplasm or the cellular exterior?[19]]

Additional functions of the rough ER include the initial post-translational modification of proteins. Although glycosylation (the addition of saccharides to proteins) is usually associated with the Golgi apparatus, some glycosylation occurs in the lumen of the ER. Disulfide bond formation also occurs in the ER lumen.

Two last notes about protein traffic throughout the cell: First, the default target for proteins that go through the secretory path is the plasma membrane. **Targeting signals** are needed if a protein going through that path needs to end up elsewhere (e.g., the Golgi, the ER, the lysosome). Second, proteins that are made in the cytoplasm but need to be sent to an organelle that is not part of the secretory path (e.g., the nucleus, mitochondria, or peroxisomes) require sequences called **localization signals**. The table below summarizes protein traffic.

---

[18] The only way a protein can be smaller than would be expected from its mRNA would be if some post-translational modification were to occur (choice **D** is correct). Choices B and C are pre-translational modifications and would not account for a size difference between mRNA and protein, and since secreted proteins are synthesized on the rough ER, they are inaccessible to cytoplasmic proteases (so A is wrong).

[19] The cellular exterior

Protein Final Destination	Signal Sequence?	Localization Signal?	Transmembrane Domains?	Targeting Signal?	Example
Secreted	Yes	No	No	No	Antibodies, Neurotransmitters, Peptide hormones
Plasma Membrane	Yes	No	Yes	No	Receptors, channels
Lysosome	Yes	No	No	Yes	Acid hydrolases
Rough ER	Yes	No	No	Yes	Enzymes required for protein modification
Smooth ER	Yes	No	No	Yes	Enzymes required for lipid synthesis
Golgi Apparatus	Yes	No	No	Yes	Enzymes required for protein modification
Cytoplasm	No	No	No	No	Glycolysis enzymes
Nucleus	No	Yes	No	No	Histones, DNA/RNA polymerase
Mitochondria	No	Yes	No	No	PDC/Krebs cycle enzymes
Peroxisome	No	Yes	No	No	Catalase

Table 2 Summary of Cellular Protein Traffic

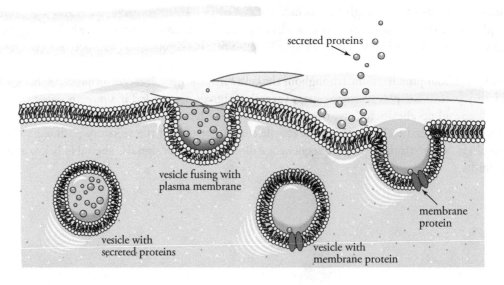

Figure 6 The Secretory Pathway—Secreted Proteins and Integral Membrane Proteins

- Disulfide bridges are found in extracellular proteins because the cytoplasm is a reducing environment that changes cystine to two cysteines. Given this fact, does it make sense that disulfide bridges are formed in the ER lumen?[20]
- Can mRNA coding for a protein destined to be embedded in the plasma membrane associate with rough ER prior to the initiation of translation?[21]

The Golgi Apparatus

The Golgi apparatus is a group of membranous sacs stacked together like collapsed basketballs (see Figure 7). It has the following functions: 1) Modification of proteins made in the RER; especially important is the modification of oligosaccharide chains. 2) Sorting and sending proteins to their correct destinations. 3) The Golgi also synthesizes certain macromolecules, such as polysaccharides to be secreted.

The vesicle traffic to and from the Golgi apparatus is mostly unidirectional; the membrane-bound or secreted proteins which are to be sorted and modified enter at one defined region and exit at another. (Traffic is said to be *mostly* unidirectional because on occasion, proteins that are supposed to reside in the ER accidentally escape, and must be returned to the ER from the Golgi. This is called "retrograde traffic.") Each region of the Golgi has different enzymes and a different microscopic appearance. The portion of the Golgi nearest the rough ER is called the *cis* stack, and the part farthest from the rough ER is the *trans* stack. The *medial* stack is in the middle.[22] Vesicles from the ER fuse with the *cis* stack. The proteins in these vesicles are then modified and transferred to the *medial* stack, where they are further modified before passing to the *trans* stack. Proteins leave the Golgi at the *trans* face in transport vesicles. [If vesicle fusion with the *cis* Golgi was inhibited, could plasma membrane proteins still reach the cell surface?[23]] The route taken by a protein is determined by signals within the protein that determine which vesicle a protein is sorted into in the *trans* Golgi.

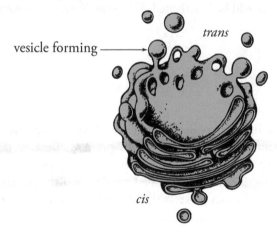

vesicle forming ⟶

trans

cis

Figure 7 The Golgi Apparatus

---

[20] Yes. Remember, the ER lumen is equivalent to (contiguous with) the extracellular space.

[21] No. It is the signal peptide in the nascent polypeptide that is recognized and bound by SRP and taken to receptors on the surface of the rough ER. The signal is an amino acid sequence on the nascent polypeptide, not a nucleotide sequence on mRNA.

[22] Note that *cis* means "near," as in a *cis* double bond. *Trans* means "far." *Medial* means "in the middle." Also note that the order is alphabetical: *cis-medial-trans*.

[23] No. Secretory proteins must proceed via a specific path: from the ER to the *cis* Golgi to the medial and *trans* Golgi and from there to the cell surface.

When a vesicle moves from the *trans* Golgi toward the cell surface, it fuses with the cell membrane. As a result, the contents of the vesicle are released into the extracellular environment in a process termed *exocytosis*. Alternatively, if the vesicle contains proteins anchored to its membrane, these proteins will remain attached to the cell as cell-surface proteins. Some proteins are sent in vesicles from the Golgi immediately to the cell surface, in the **constitutive secretory pathway**. *Constitutive* connotes *continuous* or *unregulated*. In contrast, specialized secretory cells (such as pancreatic cells, B-cells of the immune system, etc.) store secretory proteins in **secretory vesicles** and release them only at certain times, usually in response to a change in (or signal from) the extracellular environment. This is a **regulated secretory pathway**.

Lysosomes

Lyse means cut. The **lysosome** is a membrane-bound organelle that is responsible for the degradation of biological macromolecules by hydrolysis. Lysosome proteins are made in the RER, modified in the Golgi, and released in their final form from the *trans* face of the Golgi. Organelles such as mitochondria that have been damaged or are no longer functional may be degraded in lysosomes in a process termed **autophagy** (self-eating). Lysosomes also degrade large particulate matter engulfed by the cell by **phagocytosis** (cell eating). For example, **macrophages** of the immune system engulf bacteria and viruses. The particle or microorganism ends up in a **phagocytic vesicle**, which will fuse with a lysosome. Finally, **crinophagy** refers to lysosomal digestion of unneeded (excess) secretory products. After hydrolysis, the lysosome will release molecular building blocks into the cytoplasm for reuse.

The enzymes responsible for degradation in lysosomes are called **acid hydrolases**. This name reflects the fact that these enzymes only hydrolyze substrates when they are in an acidic environment. This is a safety mechanism. The pH of the lysosome is around 5, so the acid hydrolases are active. But the pH of the cytoplasm is 7.4. If a lysosome ruptures, its enzymes will not damage the cell because the acidic fluid will be diluted, and the acid hydrolases will be inactivated. However, if many lysosomes rupture at once, the cell may be destroyed.

Peroxisomes

Peroxisomes are small organelles that perform a variety of metabolic tasks. The peroxisome contains enzymes that produce hydrogen peroxide (H_2O_2) as a by-product. They are essential for lipid breakdown in many cell types. In the liver they assist in detoxification of drugs and chemicals. H_2O_2 is a dangerous chemical, but peroxisomes contain an enzyme called **catalase** which converts it to $H_2O + O_2$. Separating these activities into the peroxisomes protects the rest of the cell from damage by peroxides or oxygen radicals.

5.3 THE PLASMA MEMBRANE

The evolution of life most likely began with a separation of "inside" from "outside." Once this had occurred, processes in the cell could increase their orderliness despite the entropic chaos of the surroundings. An alternate hypothesis is that life began with self-replicating RNA floating free in the ocean. As it grew more complex, this early genome would require protection. In any case, the separation of the cytoplasm from the extracellular environment was a major milestone in evolution. Bacteria, plants, and fungi accomplish this by forming a cell membrane and a cell wall (made of peptidoglycan, cellulose, and chitin, respectively). Eukaryotic animal cells have no cell wall and thus rely on the cell membrane as the only boundary between inside and outside. And they must devise another means of structural support: just as chordates have a bony endoskeleton instead of the primitive exoskeleton arthropods have, animal cells rely on an internal cytoskeleton instead of an external cell wall. Further problems arise in multicellular eukaryotes. Not only must each cell maintain its structural integrity, but it must also interact with its neighbors in an organized fashion. In the following discussion, we will study how each of these goals is accomplished.

Membrane Structure

All of the membranes of the cell are composed of **lipid bilayer** membranes. The three most common lipids in eukaryotic membranes are **phospholipids**, **glycolipids**, and **cholesterol**, of which phospholipids are the most abundant. An example of a phospholipid is *phosphatidyl choline* (see Figure 8) with two long hydrophobic fatty acids esterified to glycerol, along with a charged phosphoryl choline group. Thus, phospholipids have portions that are distinctly hydrophilic and hydrophobic. Glycolipids, with fatty acids groups and carbohydrate side chains, also have hydrophilic and hydrophobic regions. When fatty acids or phospholipids are mixed with water, they spontaneously arrange themselves with the hydrophobic tails facing the interior to avoid contact with water and the hydrophilic regions facing outward toward water (see Figure 9). Fatty acids form small micelles, but, due to steric hindrance, phospholipids arrange themselves spontaneously into **lipid bilayer membranes**. Since the lipid bilayer is the lowest energy state for these molecules, the bilayer membrane can reseal and repair itself if a small portion of membrane is removed. [Does the formation of a lipid bilayer when phospholipids are mixed with water have a positive or a negative ΔG (change in free energy)?[24]]

The interior of the lipid bilayer membrane is very hydrophobic, with water largely excluded. Hydrophilic molecules such as ions, carbohydrates, and amino acids are not soluble in this environment, making the membrane a barrier to the passage of these molecules. Nonpolar molecules such as CO_2, O_2, and steroid hormones can cross the membrane easily. Water can also pass through the membrane but does so through specialized protein channels.

---

[24] Lipid bilayers form spontaneously, as the lowest energy state, without external energy input. This describes a process with a negative ΔG.

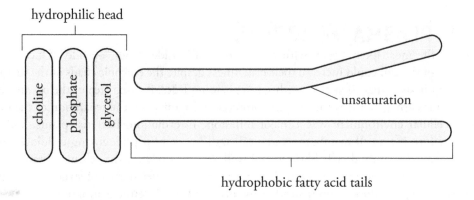

Figure 8 Phosphatidyl Choline, a Phospholipid

- Which one of the following statements best describes the physical characteristics of phospholipids?[25]
    - A. Negatively charged at pH 7 and therefore entirely hydrophilic
    - B. Hydrophobic
    - C. Partially hydrophilic and partially hydrophobic
    - D. Positively charged at pH 7 and therefore entirely hydrophilic

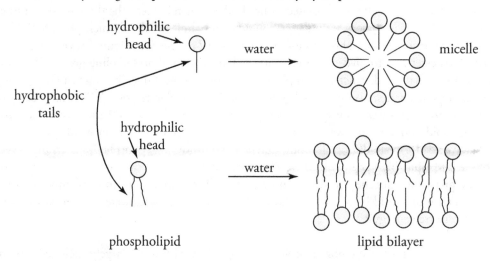

Figure 9 Lipid Behavior in an Aqueous Solvent

In addition to lipids, proteins are a major component of membranes. In some cases, such as the mitochondrial inner membrane, there is a higher protein than lipid concentration. Some proteins act to mediate interactions of the cell with other cells. Other proteins called **cell-surface receptors** bind extracellular signaling molecules such as hormones and relay these signals into the cell so that it can respond accordingly. **Channel proteins** selectively allow ions or molecules to cross the membrane. Each of these types of membrane protein is discussed below.

---

[25] **C.** Phospholipids have hydrophobic components (fatty acid acyl chains) and hydrophilic components (phosphate and choline, for example, in phosphatidyl choline).

In general, membrane proteins are classified as peripheral or integral (see Figure 10). **Integral membrane proteins** are actually embedded in the membrane, held there by hydrophobic interactions. Membrane-crossing regions are called **transmembrane domains** (see Figure 11). Integral membrane proteins may have a complex pattern of transmembrane domains and portions not within the membrane. [At which point in the secretory pathway would the insertion of transmembrane domains into the membrane occur?[26]] **Peripheral membrane proteins** are not embedded in the membrane at all, but rather are stuck to integral membrane proteins, held there by hydrogen bonding and electrostatic interactions.

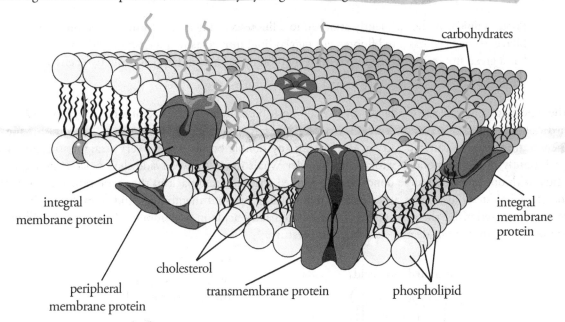

Figure 10   Membrane Proteins

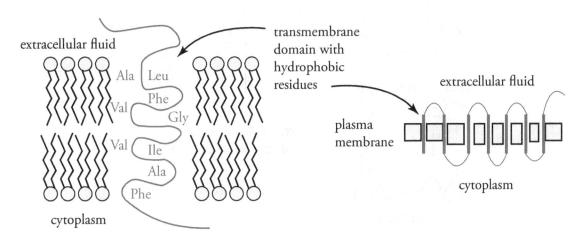

Figure 11   Transmembrane Domains

The current understanding of membrane dynamics is termed the **fluid mosaic model**, because the membrane is seen as a mosaic of lipids and proteins which are free to move back and forth fluidly. According to

---

[26] It occurs in the rough ER as the protein is translated and threaded across the ER membrane.

this model, lipids and proteins are free to diffuse laterally, in two-dimensions, but are **not free to flip-flop**. Phospholipid head groups and hydrophilic protein domains are restricted from entering the hydrophobic membrane interior just as hydrophilic molecules in the extracellular space are. Hence the membrane is said to have **polarity**. This just means that the inside face and the outside face remain different. We have already discussed one such difference: all glycosylations are found on the extracellular face. So the "fluid" in "fluid mosaic" means that things are free to move back and forth, but in two dimensions only. One exception is that some proteins are anchored to the cytoskeleton and thus cannot move in any direction.

- Phospholipids can be covalently attached to a fluorescent tag and then integrated into a lipid bilayer. If one cell has a red fluorescent tagged lipid in its plasma membrane and another cell has a green fluorescent tagged lipid in its membrane, what will happen if the two cells are fused together?[27]

The fluidity of a membrane is affected by the composition of lipids in the membrane (see Figure 12). The hydrophobic van der Waals interactions between the fatty acid side chains are a major determinant of membrane fluidity. Saturated fatty acids, lacking any double bonds, have a very straight structure and pack tightly in the membrane, with strong van der Waals forces between side chains. Unsaturated fatty acids, with one or more double bonds, have a kinked structure and pack in the membrane interior more loosely. Cholesterol also plays a key role in maintaining optimal membrane fluidity by fitting into the membrane interior. [If the percentage of unsaturated fatty acids in a membrane is increased, will membrane fluidity increase or decrease at body temperature?[28]]

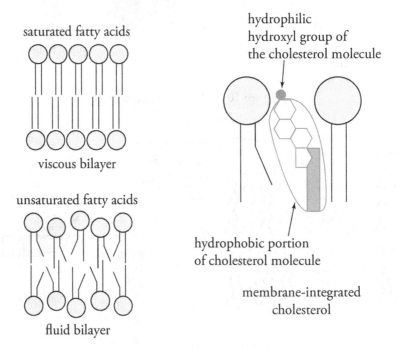

Figure 12 Factors Affecting Membrane Fluidity

---

[27] After a short period of time, the red and green tagged lipids will diffuse laterally and mix. An even distribution of the tags will be seen across the surface of the new hybrid cell.

[28] Unsaturated fatty acids, with a kinked structure, have fewer van der Waals interactions, and therefore allow a more fluid membrane structure. Increasing the unsaturated fatty acids will increase membrane fluidity.

Transmembrane Transport

The cell requires membranes to act as barriers to diffusion but also requires the transport of many different substances across membranes. Integral membrane proteins transport material through membranes that cannot diffuse on their own across membranes. Transport across a membrane can be either **passive** (does not require cellular energy) or **active** (requires cellular energy).

Review of Diffusion and Osmosis

Passive transport involves diffusion across a membrane. **Diffusion** is the tendency for liquids and gases to fully occupy the available volume (Figure 13). Particles in the liquid or gas phase are in constant motion, depending on temperature. If all particles are concentrated in one portion of a container, we have an orderly situation, which is unfavorable according to the second law of thermodynamics (law of entropy). The constant thermal motion of particles in the cell leads to their spreading out to occupy all available space, which maximizes entropy.[29] A solute will always diffuse *down its concentration gradient*, which means *from high to low concentration*. Diffusion continues until the solute is evenly distributed throughout the available volume. At this point, movement of solute back and forth continues, but no net movement occurs.

Osmosis is a special type of diffusion in which solvent diffuses rather than solute (Figure 13). For example, if a chamber containing water and a chamber containing a solution of sucrose are connected directly, sucrose will diffuse throughout the entire volume until a uniform concentration is reached. However, if the two chambers are separated by a **semipermeable membrane** that allows water but not sucrose to cross, then diffusion of sucrose between the chambers cannot occur. In this case, osmosis draws water into the sucrose chamber to reduce the sucrose concentration as well as the volume in the water chamber. Ignoring gravity, water will flow into the sucrose chamber until the concentration is the same across the membrane. The plasma membrane of the cell is a semipermeable membrane that allows water—but not most polar solutes—to cross by osmosis. [If a cell is placed in a hypotonic solution (solute concentration lower than in the cell), what will happen to the cell?[30]]

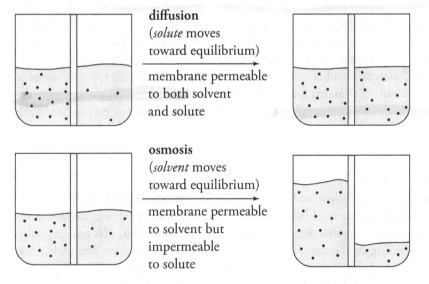

diffusion
(*solute* moves
toward equilibrium)

membrane permeable
to both solvent
and solute

osmosis
(*solvent* moves
toward equilibrium)

membrane permeable
to solvent but
impermeable
to solute

In both diffusion and osmosis, the final result is that solute concentrations are the same on both sides of the membrane. The only difference is that in diffusion the membrane is permeable to solute and in osmosis it is not.

Figure 13 Diffusion and Osmosis

---

[29] Remember, $\Delta G = \Delta H - T\Delta S$, so increasing ΔS decreases ΔG, indicating a thermodynamically favorable process.

[30] Water will flow into the cell through the plasma membrane until the cell volume increases to the point that the cell bursts.

The term **tonicity** is used to describe osmotic gradients. If the environment is **isotonic** to the cell, the solute concentration is the same inside and outside. A **hypertonic** solution has more total dissolved solutes than the cell, a **hypotonic** solution has less. You may also hear the terms **isoosmotic**, **hyperosmotic**, and **hypoosmotic**. The tendency of water to move down its concentration gradient can be a powerful force, able to cause cells to explode. This force is known as **osmotic pressure**. The greater the difference in tonicity across a semipermeable membrane, the greater the osmotic pressure. This is what accounts for the difference in fluid levels in the beaker at the bottom right-hand corner of Figure 13. The large difference in fluid levels may be a rather extreme example, but it is conceptually accurate: Just as osmotic forces can cause a cell to rupture, they can overcome gravity, as shown.

Passive Transport

Passive transport is a biochemical term that means diffusion. It refers to *any thermodynamically favorable movement of solute across a membrane*. Another way to phrase this is to say that passive transport is any movement of solute *down a gradient*. No energy is required since the concentration gradient drives movement of the solute. There are two types of passive transport: simple diffusion and facilitated diffusion.

Simple Diffusion

Simple diffusion is diffusion of a solute through a membrane without help from a protein. For example, steroid hormones are free to move back and forth across the membrane by simple diffusion as pushed by concentration gradients, thanks to their ___.[31]

However, lipid bilayer membranes are impermeable to most solutes; that is one of the main functions of membranes. The plasma membrane is a barrier to the free movement of all large and/or hydrophilic solutes. **Facilitated diffusion** is the movement of a solute across a membrane, down a gradient, when the membrane itself (the pure lipid bilayer) is intrinsically impermeable to that solute. Specific integral membrane proteins allow material to cross the plasma membrane down a gradient in facilitated diffusion. For example, red blood cells require glucose, which they get from the bloodstream. However, glucose is a bulky hydrophilic molecule that cannot cross the RBC lipid bilayer. Instead, it must be shuttled across by a particular protein in the RBC plasma membrane. There are two well-characterized types of proteins which serve this sort of function: **channel proteins** and **carrier proteins**. Channels and carriers give the membrane its essential feature of **selective permeability**; permeability to *some* things despite impermeability to *most* things.

Facilitated Diffusion: Channels

Channel proteins in the plasma membrane allow material that cannot pass through the membrane by simple diffusion to flow through the plasma membrane down a concentration gradient. Channels do this by forming a narrow opening in the membrane surrounded by the protein. Channels are very selective in what passes through the opening in the membrane. There are many kinds of ion channels, each of which allows the passage of only one type of ion through the channel down a gradient (see Figure 14). All cells have potassium ion channels, for example, that allow only potassium (and not sodium) to flow through the plasma membrane down a gradient. Ion channels are said to be **gated** if the channel is open

---

[31] hydrophobicity

in response to specific environmental stimuli. A channel that opens in response to a change in the electrical potential across the membrane is called a **voltage-gated** ion channel. One that opens in response to binding of a specific molecule like a neurotransmitter is called a **ligand-gated** ion channel. The regulation of membrane potential by gated ion channels plays a key role in the nervous system. [Can ion channels move ions against an electrochemical gradient?[32]]

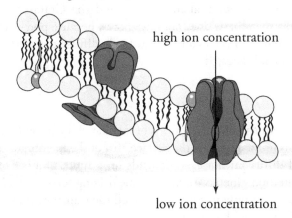

high ion concentration

low ion concentration

Figure 14 An Ion Channel

Facilitated Diffusion: Carriers

Carrier proteins also can transport molecules through membranes by facilitated diffusion, but they do so by a mechanism different from that of ion channels. Carrier proteins do not form a tunnel through membranes like ion channels do. Instead, carriers appear to bind the molecule to be transported at one side of the membrane and then undergo a conformational change to move the molecule to the other side of the membrane. Some carriers, called **uniports**, transport only one molecule across the membrane at a time (see Figure 15). Other carriers termed **symports** carry two substances across a membrane in the same direction. **Antiports**, on the other hand, carry two substances in opposite directions.

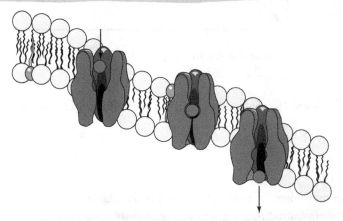

Figure 15 A Uniport

---

[32] No. Ion channels are only involved in facilitated diffusion, the movement of molecules down an elecrochemical gradient with the help of a protein.

Pores and Porins

A **pore** is a tube through the membrane which is so large that it is *not selective* for any particular molecule. Rather, all molecules below a certain size may pass. (Also, a molecule which is just barely small enough to cross may not cross if it has the wrong charge on its surface.) Pores are formed by polypeptides known as **porins**. You are already familiar with several examples of pores. We have studied pores in the double nuclear membrane, the outer mitochondrial membrane, and the Gram-negative bacterial outer membrane. The eukaryotic plasma membrane does not have pores, because pores destroy the barrier function of the membrane, allowing solutes in the cytoplasm to freely diffuse out of the cell. [Are porins and ion channels found in the same membranes?[33]]

Kinetic Concerns

Simple diffusion can be distinguished from all forms of facilitated diffusion by the kinetics of the process. The rate of simple diffusion is limited only by the surface area of the membrane and the size of the driving force (gradient). Facilitated diffusion, however, depends on a finite number of integral membrane proteins. Hence, it exhibits saturation kinetics. Increasing the driving force for facilitated diffusion increases the rate of diffusion (the **flux**), but only to a point. Then all the transport proteins become saturated, and no further increase in flux is possible (Figure 16).

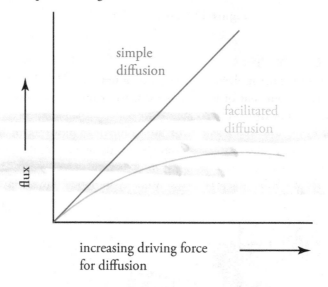

Figure 16   Saturation Kinetics of Facilitated Diffusion

Active Transport

Active transport is the movement of molecules through the plasma membrane against a gradient. Active transport requires energy input, since it is working against a gradient, and always involves a protein. Another way of saying that active transport requires energy input is to say that the transport process is coupled to a process which is thermodynamically favorable ($\Delta G < 0$). The gradient being pumped against is not necessarily just a concentration gradient, but for charged molecules, like ions, it can also involve

---

[33] No. Porins are large holes, and ion channels are small, usually regulated channels. If porins and ion channels were found in the same membrane, the ion channels would be useless, because ions would flow in an unregulated manner through the pores.

electric potentials that form a combined electrochemical gradient that must be pumped against. The form of energy input used to drive movement of molecules against an electrochemical gradient varies. In **primary active transport**, the transport of a molecule is coupled to ATP hydrolysis. In **secondary active transport**, the transport process is not coupled *directly* to ATP hydrolysis. Instead, ATP is first used to create a gradient, then the potential energy in that gradient is used to drive the transport of some other molecule across the membrane. Since ATP is not used in the actual transport of the "other" molecule, the ATP use is described as *indirect*. For example, the transport of glucose into some cells is driven *against the glucose* concentration gradient by the cotransport of sodium ions *down the sodium* electrochemical gradient, previously established by an ATPase pump (see below). A common mechanism driving secondary active transport of many different molecules involves coupling transport to the flow of sodium ions down a gradient.

- If a protein moves sodium ions across the plasma membrane down an electrochemical gradient, what form of transport is this?[34]
    - A. Simple diffusion
    - B. Facilitated diffusion
    - C. Primary active transport
    - D. Secondary active transport

The Na⁺/K⁺ ATPase and the Resting Membrane Potential

The Na^+/K^+ ATPase is a transmembrane protein in the plasma membrane of all cells in the body. The activity provided by this protein is to pump 3 Na^+ out of the cell, 2 K^+ into the cell, and to hydrolyze one ATP to drive the pumping of these ions against their gradients (Figure 17). [The pumping of sodium and potassium by the Na^+/K^+ ATPase is an example of what form of transport?[35]] The sodium which is pumped out of the cell stays outside, since the plasma membrane is impermeable to sodium ions. Some of the potassium ions which are pumped into the cell are able to leak back out, however, through **potassium leak channels**. Potassium flows down its concentration gradient out of the cell through leak channels. The movement of ions out of the cell helps the cell to maintain osmotic balance with its surroundings. As potassium leaves the cell through the leak channels, the movement of positive charge out of the cell creates an electric potential across the plasma membrane with a net negative charge on the interior of the cell. This potential created by the Na^+/K^+ ATPase is known as the **resting membrane potential**. (The resting membrane potential will be examined again in Chapter 7 in relation to action potentials in neurons). The concentration gradient of high sodium outside of the cell established by the Na^+/K^+ ATPase is the driving force behind **secondary active transport** of many different molecules, including sugars and amino acids. To summarize, the activity of the Na^+/K^+ ATPase is important in three ways:

1) to maintain osmotic balance between the cellular interior and exterior.
2) to establish the resting membrane potential.
3) to provide the sodium concentration gradient used to drive secondary active transport.

---

[34] Facilitated diffusion is the movement of molecules down a gradient with the help of a protein (choice **B** is correct). Membrane proteins are not required for simple diffusion (choice A is wrong), and active transport involves moving things *against* their gradients (choices C and D are wrong). Note also that in secondary active transport, the ion movement down its gradient must be coupled to the movement of some other molecule against *its* gradient.

[35] The pumping of ions against a gradient which is coupled to ATP hydrolysis is primary active transport.

- If an inhibitor of Na^+/K^+ ATPase is added to cells, which of the following may occur?[36]
  - A. The cell will shrink and lose water.
  - B. The interior of the cell will become less negatively charged.
  - C. Secondary active transport processes will compensate for the loss of primary active transport.
  - D. The cell will begin to proliferate.

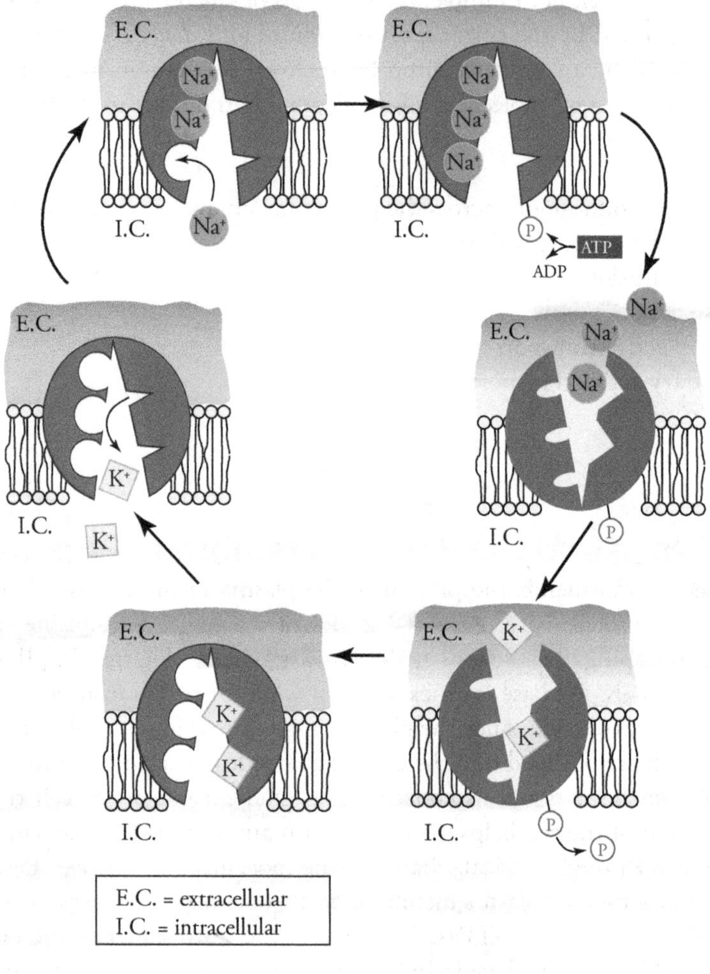

Figure 17 The Na^+/K^+ ATPase

How do we know exactly how the resting membrane potential is generated? For instance, how can we state with confidence that the electrogenicity of the Na^+/K^+ pump is far less important than the passive efflux of potassium in the generation of the RMP? The answer, given in the next two paragraphs, is not core MCAT material for memorization, but it is just the sort of thing that could show up in a passage.

---

[36] The Na^+/K^+ ATPase is required to establish the resting membrane potential in which the cellular interior has a negative charge. It pumps out one net positive ion. If this net positive ion stays inside the cell, the resting potential becomes less negative (choice **B** is correct). Since the interior of the cell is now more charged, the cell will have a tendency to take on water by osmosis, and will swell (choice A is wrong). Secondary active transport depends on the gradient established by primary active transport (the Na^+/K^+ pump). If the pump is shut down, the gradient won't be established, and secondary active transport will also stop (choice C is wrong). The Na^+/K^+ ATPase has nothing to do with cellular proliferation (choice D is wrong).

The answers were determined using experiments. An artificial cell with no pumps and no channels in its membrane would have identical concentrations and charges inside and outside. An artificial cell with potassium leak channels but no active transporters would also obviously have no gradients across its membrane.

What about an artificial cell with Na^+/K^+ ATPase pumps and normal cellular concentrations of ATP and $ADP + P_i$ but no potassium leak channels? Here is where experimentation was necessary. In this situation, the resting membrane potential is determined only by the electrogenicity of the Na^+/K^+ pump. The RMP in such a system turns out to be about –10 mV. [Why is it necessary to specify normal cellular concentrations of ATP and $ADP + P_i$? E.g., what would happen if there were much, much more $ADP + P_i$ than ATP, as well as very high extracellular Na^+ concentration and very high intracellular K^+ concentration, in the artificial cell?[37]]

When K^+ leak channels are added to the membrane (in addition to the Na^+/K^+ ATPase pumps and normal cellular concentrations of ATP and $ADP + P_i$), the RMP is measured at the normal cellular level, around –70 mV.

The following table gives the concentrations of Na^+, K^+, and Cl^- inside and outside the cell. (Know trends; don't memorize numbers.) You already know why the Na^+ and K^+ concentrations are as they are. [Why is chloride so concentrated outside the cell?[38]] A useful mnemonic is to remember that life evolved in the ocean, which has very high concentrations of NaCl; hence the concentrations of Na^+ and Cl^- are high outside the cell and low inside.

Ion	Intracellular Conc. (mM)	Extracellular Conc. (mM)
Na^+	10	142
K^+	140	4
Cl^-	4	110
Ca^{2+}	0.0001	2.4

Table 3   Concentrations of Ions Inside/Outside Cell

Endocytosis and Exocytosis

Another mechanism used to transport material through the plasma membrane is within membrane-bound vesicles that fuse with the membrane (see Figure 18). **Exocytosis** is a process to transport material outside of the cell in which a vesicle in the cytoplasm fuses with the plasma membrane, and the contents of the vesicle are expelled into the extracellular space. The materials released are products secreted by the cell, such as hormones and digestive enzymes.

---

[37] The pump would run backwards! Remember: All active transporters are reversible.

[38] The cell contains millions of negative charges on macromolecules (e.g., nucleic acids). For the charge to be "approximately" balanced on both sides of the membrane, some negatively-charged substance must be more concentrated outside. Chloride serves this role. Why did we say "approximately" balanced? Remember: The cell is a bit more negative on the inside; that's the RMP.

Endocytosis is the opposite of exocytosis: Generally, materials are taken into the cell by an invagination of a piece of the cell membrane to form a vesicle. Again, the cytoplasm is not allowed to mix with the extracellular environment. The new vesicle which is formed is called an **endosome**. There are three types of endocytosis:

1) phagocytosis,
2) pinocytosis, and
3) receptor-mediated endocytosis.

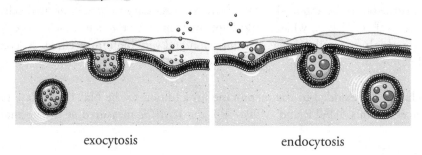

exocytosis   endocytosis

Figure 18   Endo- and Exocytosis

Phagocytosis means "cell eating." It refers to the nonspecific uptake of large particulate matter into a phagocytic vesicle, which later merges with a lysosome. Thus, the phagocytosed material will be broken down. The prime example of phagocytic human cells are macrophages ("big eaters") of the immune system, which engulf and destroy viruses and bacteria. (*Note*: This is *not* an invagination.)

Pinocytosis (cell drinking) is the nonspecific uptake of small molecules and extracellular fluid via invagination. Primitive eukaryotic cells obtain nutrition in this manner, but virtually all eukaryotic cells participate in pinocytosis.

Receptor-mediated endocytosis, on the other hand, is very specific. The site of endocytosis is marked by pits coated with the molecule **clathrin** (inside the cell) and with **receptors** that bind to a specific molecule (outside the cell). An important example is the uptake of cholesterol from the blood. Cholesterol is transported in the blood in large particles called lipoproteins. Cells obtain some of the cholesterol they require by receptor-mediated endocytosis of these lipoproteins. If they are not removed from the blood, cholesterol accumulates in the bloodstream, sticking to the inner walls of arteries. This results in **atherosclerosis** (a buildup of plaque on the walls of the arteries). [Does clathrin recognize and bind to lipoproteins?[39]] When the receptor-lipoprotein complex internalizes, it is taken into a vesicle that is termed an endosome. Lipoproteins are taken from the endosome to a lysosome where the cholesterol is released from the lipoprotein and the lipoprotein is degraded. The lipoprotein receptor is returned to the cell surface where it may again bind a lipoprotein. [How is receptor-mediated endocytosis similar to and different from active transport?[40]]

---

[39] No. Clathrin is a fibrous protein inside the cell that associates with the cytoplasmic portions of the cell-surface receptors that bind lipoproteins.

[40] Both import a particular substance. One difference is that in endocytosis the substance ends up sealed in an endosome, whereas in active transport the substance is just dumped into the cytoplasm.

5.4 OTHER STRUCTURAL ELEMENTS OF THE CELL

Cell-Surface Receptors

Receptors form an important class of integral membrane proteins that transmit signals from the extracellular space into the cytoplasm. Each receptor binds a particular molecule in a highly specific lock-and-key interaction. The molecule that serves as the key for a given receptor is termed the **ligand**. The ligand is generally a hormone or a neurotransmitter. The binding of a ligand to its receptor on the extracellular surface of the plasma membrane triggers a response within the cell, a process termed **signal transduction**. Many cancers result from mutant cell-surface receptors which constitutively relay their signal to the cytoplasm, whether ligand is present or absent. For example, a growth factor exerts its effects by binding to a cell-surface receptor, and constitutive activity of a receptor for the growth factor causes uncontrolled growth of the cell. There are three main types of signal-transducing cell-surface receptors: ligand-gated ion channels, catalytic receptors, and G-protein-linked receptors.

Ligand-gated ion channels in the plasma membrane open an ion channel upon binding a particular neurotransmitter. An example is the ligand-gated sodium channel on the surface of the muscle cell at the neuromuscular junction. When the neurotransmitter acetylcholine binds to this receptor, the receptor undergoes a conformational change and becomes an open Na$^+$ channel. The result is a massive influx of sodium down its electrochemical gradient, which depolarizes the muscle cell and causes it to contract.

Catalytic receptors have an enzymatic active site on the cytoplasmic side of the membrane. Enzyme activity is initiated by ligand binding at the extracellular surface. Generally, the catalytic role is that of a protein **kinase**, which is an enzyme that covalently attaches phosphate groups to proteins. Proteins can be modified with phosphate on the side chain hydroxyl of serine, threonine, or tyrosine. The insulin receptor is an example of a tyrosine kinase. Modification of proteins with phosphates regulates their activity.

A **G-protein-linked receptor** does not directly transduce its signal, but transmits it into the cell with the aid of a **second messenger**. This is a chemical signal that relays instructions from the cell surface to enzymes in the cytoplasm. The most important second messenger is **cyclic AMP (cAMP)**. It is known as a "universal hunger signal" because it is the second messenger of the hormones epinephrine and glucagon, which cause energy mobilization (glycogen and fat breakdown). Second messengers such as cAMP allow a much greater signal than receptor alone produces (see Figure 19). An epinephrine molecule activates one G-protein-linked receptor which activates many G-proteins, each G-protein activates many adenylyl cyclase enzymes, each adenylyl cyclase makes lots of cAMP from ATP, each cAMP activates many cAMP-dPK, and each cAMP-dPK phosphorylates many enzymes. Some of these enzymes will be activated, and others inactivated by phosphorylation, with the end result that the entire cell harmoniously works toward the same goal: energy mobilization.

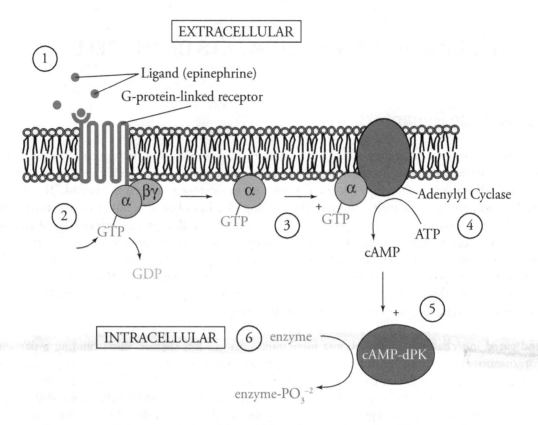

Figure 19 G-Protein Mediated Signal Transduction Stimulated by Epinephrine

1) Epinephrine arrives at the cell surface and binds to a specific G-protein-linked receptor.
2) The cytoplasmic portion of the receptor activates G-proteins, causing GDP to dissociate and GTP to bind in its place.
3) The activated G-proteins diffuse through the membrane and activate adenylyl cyclase.
4) Adenylyl cyclase makes cAMP from ATP.
5) cAMP activates cAMP-dependent protein kinases (cAMP-dPK) in the cytoplasm.
6) cAMP-dPK phosphorylates certain enzymes, with the end result being mobilization of energy. For example, enzymes necessary for glycogen breakdown will be activated, while enzymes necessary for glycogen synthesis will be inactivated, by cAMP-dPK phosphorylation.

There are different types of G-protein-linked receptors. The one depicted above is a stimulatory one. Its G-protein would be denoted G_s. Inhibitory G-protein-linked receptors activate inhibitory G-proteins (G_i) which serve to *inactivate* adenylyl cyclase instead of activating it. In this way different hormones can modulate each other's effects.

There are also G-protein-linked receptors which have nothing to do with cAMP. Instead, their G-proteins activate an enzyme called phospholipase C, initiating a different second messenger cascade, which results in an increase in cytoplasmic Ca^{2+} levels. The common theme shared by all G-protein-based signal transduction systems is their reliance on a G-protein, which is a signaling molecule that binds GTP. You should understand these key notions: cAMP as a second messenger, signal transduction, and signal amplification. The remaining details are not important for the MCAT; read for concepts, not memory.

The Cytoskeleton

The animal cell **cytoskeleton** provides the structural support supplied by the cell wall in bacteria, plants, and fungi. It also allows movement of the cell and its appendages (cilia and flagella) and transport of substances within the cell. Animal cells have an internal cytoskeleton composed of three types of proteins: **microtubules, intermediate filaments**, and **microfilaments** (see Figure 20). Microtubules are the thickest, microfilaments the thinnest. All three are composed of noncovalently polymerized proteins; in other words, they are a massive example of quaternary protein structure.

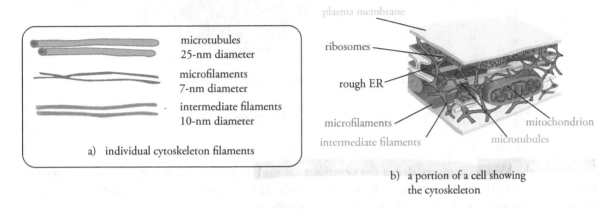

a)   individual cytoskeleton filaments

microtubules
25-nm diameter

microfilaments
7-nm diameter

intermediate filaments
10-nm diameter

plasma membrane

ribosomes

rough ER

microfilaments

intermediate filaments

mitochondrion

microtubules

b)   a portion of a cell showing
the cytoskeleton

Figure 20   Cytoskeleton

Microtubules

The **microtubule** is a hollow rod composed of two globular proteins: **α-tubulin** and **β-tubulin**, polymerized noncovalently. First, α-tubulin and β-tubulin form an αβ-tubulin dimer. Then many dimers stick to each other noncovalently to form a sheet, which rolls into a tube. Once formed, the microtubule can elongate by adding αβ-tubulin dimers to one end. The other end cannot elongate, because it is anchored to the **microtubule organizing center (MTOC)**, located near the nucleus. Microtubules are dynamic and can get longer or shorter by adding or removing tubulin monomers from the end.

Within the MTOC is a pair of **centrioles** (see Figure 21). Each centriole is composed of a ring of nine microtubule triplets. When cell division occurs, the centrioles duplicate themselves, and then one pair moves to each end of the cell. During mitosis, microtubules radiating out from the centrioles attach to the replicated chromosomes and pull them apart so that one copy of each chromosome (one chromatid) moves to each end of the cell. The resulting daughter cells each get a full copy of the genome plus a centriole pair. The microtubules that radiate out from the centrioles during mitosis are called the **aster**, because they are star-shaped. The microtubules connecting the chromosomes to the aster are **polar fibers**. The whole assembly is called the **mitotic spindle**. The centromere of each chromosome contains a **kinetochore** which is attached to the spindle by tiny microtubules called **kinetochore fibers**. Refer to the figure in the mitosis section on the following page.

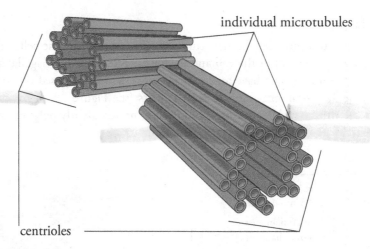

individual microtubules

centrioles

Figure 21   A Pair of Centrioles

In mitosis, the MTOC is essential, but the centrioles are not. There are two major pieces of evidence for this: 1) Plant cells lack centrioles but still undergo mitosis; 2) Experimenters have succeeded in removing the centrioles from animal cells, and the cells were still able to undergo mitosis.

Microtubules also mediate transport of substances within the cell. In nerve cells, materials are transported from the cell body to the axon terminus on a microtubule railroad. The transport process is driven by proteins that hydrolyze ATP and act as molecular motors along the microtubule.

Eukaryotic Cilia and Flagella

Cilia are small hairs on the cell surface which move fluids past the cell surface. For example, cilia on lining cells of the human respiratory tract continually sweep mucus toward the mouth in a mechanism termed the **mucociliary escalator**. A **flagellum** is a large tail which moves the cell by wiggling. The only human cell which has a flagellum is the ___.[41] Cilia are small and flagella are long, but they have the same structure, with a **"9 + 2"** arrangement of microtubules (see Figure 22). Nine pairs of microtubules form a ring around two lone microtubules in the center. Each microtubule is bound to its neighbor by a contractile protein called **dynein** which causes movement of the filaments past one another. The cilium or flagellum is anchored to the plasma membrane by a **basal body**, which has the same structure as a centriole (a ring of nine triplets of microtubules). Remember that the prokaryotic flagellum is different in structure, and its motion is driven by a different mechanism.

---

[41] sperm

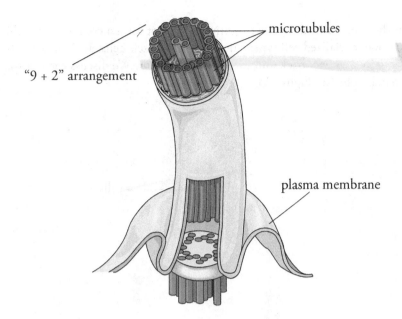

Figure 22 The Base of a Cilium or Flagellum

Microfilaments

Microfilaments are rods formed in the cytoplasm from polymerization of the globular protein **actin**. Actin monomers form a chain, and then two chains wrap around each other to form an actin filament. Microfilaments are dynamic and are responsible for gross movements of the entire cell, such as pinching the dividing parent cell into two daughters during cell division, and **amoeboid movement**. Amoeboid movement involves changes in the cytoplasmic structure which cause cytoplasm and the rest of the cell to flow in one direction.

Intermediate Filaments

Intermediate filaments are named for their thickness, which is between that of microtubules and microfilaments. Unlike microtubules and microfilaments, intermediate filaments are heterogeneous, composed of a wide range of polypeptides. Another difference is that intermediate filaments are more permanent, whereas microfilaments and microtubules are often disassembled and reassembled as needed by the cell. Intermediate filaments appear to be involved in providing strong cell structure, such as in resisting mechanical stress.

Cell Adhesion and Cell Junctions

In some tissues, cells are tightly bound to each other. For example, the intestinal wall is lined with a type of tissue called **epithelium**.[42] The layer of epithelial cells in the gut forms a tight seal, preventing items from moving freely between the intestinal lumen and the body; this is accomplished by **tight junctions**.

---

[42] An epithelial cell layer is a layer of cells which lies "upon nipples" of a type of extracellular connective tissue called *basement membrane* (*epi-* means "upon," and *-thele* means "nipple," in the sense of small bump). The basement membrane is a strong molecular sheet made of collagen. Under the microscope the basement membrane under epithelial cells has "bumps" which make epithelial cell layers easy to recognize.

5.4

Epithelial cells in the skin are held together tightly but do not form a complete seal; this is accomplished by **desmosomes.** Some specialized cell types, such as heart muscle cells, are connected by holes called **gap junctions** that allow ions to flow back and forth between them. We discuss each of the above structures in the following paragraphs (see Figure 23).

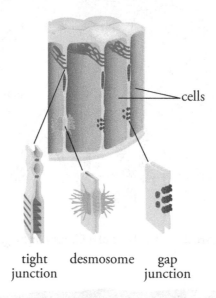

cells

tight desmosome gap
junction junction

Figure 23 Cell Junctions

Tight junctions are also termed *occluding junctions* because they do not just join cells at one point, but form a seal between the membranes of adjacent cells that blocks the flow of molecules across the entire cell layer. They are not spots where cells are stuck together, but rather bands running all the way around the cells. Intestinal epithelial cells are involved in the active transport of glucose and other molecules from one side of epithelium to the other. A tight seal between these cells is required to prevent the two compartments from mixing. Tight junctions also block the flow of molecules within the plane of the plasma membrane. For example, the surface of the plasma membrane facing the intestinal lumen, termed the **apical** surface, has different membrane proteins than the plasma membrane on the other side of the cell facing the tissues beneath, called the **basolateral** surface. [Will a transmembrane protein inserted into the apical surface of an intestinal epithelial cell diffuse in the plane of the plasma membrane to reach the basolateral surface of the cell?[43]]

Desmosomes do not form a seal, but merely hold cells together; they are also known as *spot desmosomes* because they are concise points, not bands all the way around the cell. The desmosome is composed of fibers that span the plasma membranes of two cells. Inside each cell, the desmosome is anchored to the plasma membrane by a plaque formed by the protein **keratin**. Intermediate filaments of the cytoplasm attach to the inside of the desmosome. Desmosomes do not freely diffuse in the plane of the plasma membrane, as suggested by the fluid mosaic model, because they are anchored in place by intermediate filaments of the cytoskeleton. As you can see, the fluid mosaic model is an idealization describing the plasma membrane in pure form. In the real cell membrane, things are highly organized.

Gap junctions form pore-like connections between adjacent cells, allowing the two cells' cytoplasms to mix. The connection is large enough to permit the exchange of solutes such as ions, amino acids, and carbohydrates, but not polypeptides and organelles. Gap junctions in smooth muscle and cardiac muscle allow the membrane depolarization of an action potential to pass directly from one cell to another.

---

[43] No. It is free to move around on the apical surface, but the tight junctions prevent it from diffusing to the basolateral surface.

5.5   THE CELL CYCLE AND MITOSIS

Our cells must reproduce themselves in order to replace lost or damaged cells and so that tissues can grow. Cells reproduce themselves by first doubling everything in the cytoplasm and the genome and then splitting in half. Some cells continually go through a cycle of growth and division, which is traditionally discussed in four phases (see Figure 24). **S (synthesis)** phase is when the cell actively replicates its genome, as described in Chapter 3. **M phase** includes **mitosis** and **cytokinesis**. Mitosis is the partitioning of cellular components (genes, organelles, etc.) into two halves. Cytokinesis is the physical process of cell division. Between M phase and S phase, there are two "gap" phases, G_1 and G_2. The gap phases plus S phase together form the part of the cell cycle between divisions, known as *interphase*.

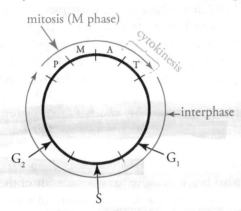

Figure 24   The Cell Cycle

The cell spends most of its time in interphase, busily metabolizing and synthesizing materials. Some cells are permanently stuck in interphase (G_0). In fact, the more specialized a cell becomes, the less likely it is to remain capable of reproducing itself. Examples are neurons, blood cells, and cells on the surface of the skin. They must be replenished by reproduction of less specialized precursor cells called **stem cells**. All the blood cells, for example, are derived from a single type of stem cell found in the bone marrow.

Inappropriate cell division can have disastrous consequences. A mutation in a protein that is normally involved in regulating progression through the cell cycle can result in unregulated cell division and cancer. Cancer means "**crab**," as in the zodiac sign. The name derives from the observation that malignant tumors grow into the surrounding tissue, embedding themselves like clawed crabs. Mutated genes that induce cancer are termed **oncogenes**. ("Onco-" is a prefix denoting cancer.) Normally, these genes are required for proper growth of the cell.

- In normal eukaryotic cells, mitosis will not begin until the entire genome is replicated. If this inhibition is removed so that mitosis begins during S-phase, which one of the following would occur?[44]
  - A. The cells would grow more quickly.
  - B. The genome would become fragmented and incomplete.
  - C. The cells would display unregulated, cancerous growth.
  - D. The genome would be temporarily incomplete in each daughter cell, but DNA repair will fill in missing gaps.

---

[44] If the genome is not completely replicated and condensed prior to mitosis, it will be torn during cell division. Each daughter cell will receive only pieces of the genome rather than the complete genome and will not be able to survive (choice **B** is correct and choice A and C are wrong). DNA repair systems can only repair sequence errors or minor structural problems; this problem would be too large to fix (choice D is wrong).

During interphase, the genome is spread out in a form that is not visible with a light microscope without special stains, and DNA is accessible to the enzymes of replication. By the end of S phase, the nucleus contains two complete copies of the genome. The cell now has twice the normal amount of DNA.

Mitosis is divided into four phases: **prophase, metaphase, anaphase,** and **telophase.**[45] The first sign of prophase is that the genome becomes visible upon condensing into densely-packed chromosomes, instead of diffuse chromatin. [Why do the chromosomes condense?[46]] Observing a human cell under the light microscope at the beginning of prophase, one can see 46 differently-shaped chromosomes. Upon closer observation, one notes that each chromosome actually consists of two identical particles joined at a centromere. These two particles are the two copies of a chromosome, known as **sister chromatids**. When mitosis is complete, each new daughter cell will have 46 chromosomes, each consisting of a single chromatid, separated from its sister. Spending a little more time staring at the nucleus, you might notice that the jumble of 46 chromatid pairs actually consists of 23 **homologous pairs** of identical-appearing sister chromatid pairs (23 pairs of pairs). Homologous chromosomes are different copies of the same chromosome, one from your mother and the other from your father. (Also refer to Chapter 6.) To repeat:

Sister chromatids are identical copies of a chromosome, attached to each other at the centromere. Homologous chromosomes are equivalent but nonidentical and do not come anywhere near each other during mitosis.

Other important events occur during prophase. The nucleolus disappears, the spindle and kinetochore fibers appear, and the centriole pairs begin to move to opposite ends of the cell. So now the cell has two MTOCs, called **asters** (stars) because of the star-like appearance of microtubules radiating out. Also at the end of prophase, the nuclear envelope converts itself into many tiny vesicles.[47]

Metaphase is simple: All the chromosomes line up at the center of the cell, forming the **metaphase plate**. The chromosomes line up in the center of the cell because the kinetochore of each sister chromatid is attached to spindle fibers that attach to MTOC at opposite ends of the cell. So each member of a pair of chromatids is pulled toward the opposite pole of the cell.

During anaphase, the spindle fibers shorten, and the centromeres of each sister chromatid pair are pulled apart. The cell elongates, and cytokinesis begins with the formation of a **cleavage furrow**, which is accomplished by __.[48]

In telophase (*telos* is Greek for "end"), a nuclear membrane forms around the bunch of chromosomes at each end of the cell, the chromosomes decondense, and a nucleolus becomes visible within each new daughter nucleus. Each daughter nucleus has $2n$ chromosomes. Cytokinesis is complete, and the cell is split in two (see Figure 25).

---

[45] A mnemonic is "I Pee on the MAT," where I is for interphase.

[46] Presumably so that they can be separated without tangling.

[47] This stage of prophase is also referred to as "**prometaphase.**" It is the last event in prophase and is rather dramatic; once the nuclear membrane is disintegrated into vesicles, the spindle fibers can attach to the centromeres of the chromosomes and the cell can enter metaphase.

[48] A ring of microfilaments encircling the cell and contracting

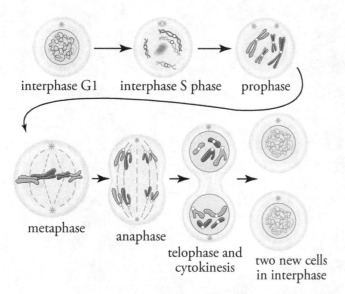

Figure 25   The Phases of Mitosis

The **karyotype** is a display of an organism's genome (see Figure 26). A cell is frozen during metaphase, its chromosomes are stained, and a photograph is taken. The micrograph is enlarged, and each chromosome is cut out of the picture with an artist's blade. Then all homologues are paired, and the entire genome is examined for abnormalities.

normal male karyotype

normal female karyotype

Figure 26   A Genetic Karyotype

- Eukaryotic chromosomes generally have only one of which of the following?[49]
    A. Reading frame
    B. Origins of replication
    C. Promoter
    D. Centromere

---

[49] If a chromosome had more than one centromere, it could be pulled toward different ends of the cell simultaneously and be torn (choice **D** is correct). Each eukaryotic gene has only one reading frame, but since there are many genes per chromosome there are different reading frames, too. Note that the total number of possible reading frames is only 3, since a codon is only 3 nucleotides long (choice **A** is wrong). Eukaryotic chromosomes are so large that they must have more than one origin of replication to finish replication of the genome in a reasonable time period (choice **B** is wrong), and each gene has its own promoter, and there are many genes per chromosome (choice **C** is wrong).

Summary

- For the MCAT, you should know the structures and functions of the following key eukaryotic organelles: nucleus, mitochondria, ribosomes, rough ER, smooth ER, Golgi apparatus, lysosomes, and peroxisomes.

- The rough ER is the site of translation of proteins to be either secreted from the cell, inserted into the membrane, or targeted to the lysosomes, ER, or Golgi apparatus.

- Signal sequences are specific amino acid sequences that direct proteins in translation to the rough ER and the secretory pathway (rough ER → Golgi apparatus → final location).

- Post-translational modification can occur in the rough ER or in the Golgi apparatus.

- All cellular membranes are composed of lipid bilayers with distinct hydrophobic and hydrophilic regions. The membranes act as selective barriers that regulate which molecules can cross.

- Molecules naturally want to move from regions of higher concentration to regions of lower concentration (with respect to that particular molecule). Diffusion is the movement of particles down their concentration gradient, and osmosis is the movement of water down *its* concentration gradient.

- Hydrophobic molecules (e.g., O_2, CO_2, and steroids) cross the membrane by simple diffusion, while hydrophilic, polar molecules (e.g., ions, glucose, and water) must cross the membrane with the help of a special membrane protein (a channel or a carrier). This is called facilitated diffusion.

- Active transport uses energy to move molecules against their concentration gradients (from low concentration areas to higher concentration areas). Primary active transport uses ATP directly, while secondary active transport relies on gradients previously established by a primary active transporter.

- The Na^+/K^+ ATPase is a primary active transporter that moves three Na^+ ions out of the cell for every two K^+ ions it moves into the cell. This helps establish the resting membrane potential of the cell, helps maintain osmotic balance in the cell, and sets up a Na^+ gradient that can be used for secondary active transport.

- G-proteins help transduce signals from extracellular ligands across the membrane. They change the level of cAMP or calcium (second messengers) in the cell, which changes the metabolic enzyme pathways active in the cell.

- Microtubules form centrioles, cilia, and eukaryotic flagella, while microfilaments participate in contractile activity.

- Tight junctions help form a seal between cells so that the flow of molecules across the entire cell layer is regulated. Desmosomes form general adhesions between cells. Gap junctions form connections between cells that allow the flow of cytoplasm from cell to cell.

- During the cell cycle, DNA replication occurs during the S-phase of interphase, and cell division occurs during mitosis (M-phase).

- Mitosis is comprised of four major phases (prophase, metaphase, anaphase, and telophase) and results in two daughter cells that are identical to each other and identical to the original parent cell.

CHAPTER 5 FREESTANDING PRACTICE QUESTIONS

1. *Kartegener's syndrome* is a rare genetic disorder that results in immotile cilia. The immotile cilia cause infertility, bronchiectasis (permanent dilation of the bronchi) and recurrent sinusitis (due to the inability to "push out" bacteria and particles from the sinuses). The genetic defect causes a deficiency of a protein primarily involved in which of the following structures?

A) Microfilament
B) Intermediate filament
C) Microtubule
D) Plasma membrane

2. Different proteins have been found to be involved in vesicular trafficking. Specific proteins are responsible for specific pathways; for instance, COP-I is responsible for retrograde transmission of vesicles, while COP-II is involved in anterograde transmission. Clathrin is involved in receptor-mediated endocytosis. Vesicles on which of the following pathways would be expected to have COP-I proteins on its surface?

A) RER → *cis* Golgi
B) RER → *trans* Golgi
C) *cis* Golgi → RER
D) Nucleus → RER

3. The steroid hormones produced by the smooth endoplasmic reticulum would be stored in which of the following organelles?

A) Secretory vesicles, so the hormones could be released when needed.
B) Peroxisomes, so the hormones could aid in lipid breakdown.
C) Lysosomes, so the hormones could aid in the destruction of excess secretory products.
D) Steroid hormones are not stored, as they are able to diffuse through lipid bilayers.

4. Which of the following gives the correct order for the signals leading to the formation of cyclic AMP? (GPCR = G-Protein Coupled Receptor)

A) Epinephrine → G-proteins → GPCR → adenylyl cyclase → cAMP
B) Epinephrine → GPCR → G-proteins → adenylyl cyclase → cAMP
C) Epinephrine → GPCR → adenylyl cyclase → G-proteins → cAMP
D) Epinephrine → adenylyl cyclase → cAMP → GPCR → G-proteins

5. The nuclear membrane is absent in which of the following phases of mitosis?

   I. Anaphase
   II. Telophase
   III. Metaphase

A) I
B) I and II
C) I and III
D) II and III

6. Both the Golgi complex and rough endoplasmic reticulum contribute to protein modification through all of the following EXCEPT:

A) phosphorylation.
B) creation of disulfide bridges.
C) glycosylation.
D) creation of peptide bonds.

7. Flow cytometry can be used to study the DNA content of cells. This could be used to study which of the following processes?

A) The level of cellular anabolism and catabolism
B) The proportion of cells in the phases of the eukaryotic cell cycle
C) The relative activities of transcription versus translation
D) Cellular stress response pathways

CHAPTER 5 PRACTICE PASSAGE

Apoptosis is the most studied form of programmed cell death. It is limited to multicellular organisms and is a process that involves cells being dismantled from within. When a cell is undergoing apoptosis, it has several characteristic morphological traits; for example, the cells retract and become rounded as they detach from the extracellular matrix and neighboring cells. In addition, the plasma membrane starts blebbing, and apoptotic bodies (similar to vesicles) are pinched off the plasma membrane.

There are several stimuli that could induce apoptotic pathways in a cell. For example, there are receptor-mediated or extrinsic signals that trigger a cell to initiate apoptosis (Figure 1). In this case, a death receptor ligand such as FasL or TNFα binds to a death receptor on the surface of the cell. This causes recruitment of adaptor proteins (such as FADD, or Fas-associated death domain protein) to the plasma membrane. The adaptor proteins serve as docking sites for other proteins, most commonly caspase 8, which is recruited to the plasma membrane, aggregated, auto-processed and ultimately activated. Active caspase 8 is a protease and cleaves other members of the caspase family (such as caspase 3, 6, or 7) and a protein called BID. The cleaved form of BID (tBID) promotes the release of cytochrome c from mitochondria, causing apoptosome assembly and downstream activation of other caspase family members. These proteins dismantle the cytoskeleton and cause nuclear fragmentation, detachment from the surrounding environment, genome degradation, and fragmentation of organelles such as the ER, Golgi, and mitochondria. After termination of the demolition phase, phagocytes are recruited to the apoptotic cell to clean up the cellular debris.

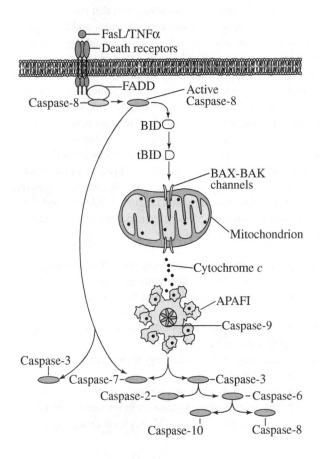

Figure 1   The Extrinsic Apoptosis Pathway

Autophagy is also a self-destructive process, but does not necessarily lead to cell death. When cells are under nutrient stress, reactive oxygen stress, or organelle stress, parts of the cytoplasm and intracellular organelles are sequestered in specialized double-membrane organelles called autophagosomes. These vacuoles ultimately fuse with lysosomes (to form autolysosomes) and the acid hydrolases in the lysosome degrade the contents, which are then recycled to the cell to provide the missing or limited nutrients.

In many situations, if the degradation of cellular material does not alleviate the stress that induced autophagy, the cell will switch to apoptosis. The signaling axis that controls the switch between these two pathways is complex and has been difficult to elucidate. It is now known that autophagy gene 5 (or Atg5) is an important and essential protein in autophagy induction and in the regulation of apoptosis. For example, Atg5 generally induces autophagy by promoting autophagosome and autolysosome formation. Atg5 also enhances the susceptibility of cancer cells to apoptosis. In cell culture experiments where Atg5 expression is decreased, autophagy is abolished and apoptosis incidence is reduced. It has been found that the full-length Atg5 protein induces autophagy. However, upon lethal stress, the full-length Atg5 is proteolytically cleaved to generate a 24 kDa pro-apoptotic protein. The truncated Atg5 translocates to the mitochondria and promotes cytochrome *c* release and mitochondrial permeabilization.

1. p53 is a tumor suppressor protein that is commonly mutated or deleted in aberrantly growing cancer cells. Which of the follow is the most likely function of p53?

   A) It is a transcription factor that induces expression of pro-apoptotic proteins.
   B) It indirectly induces autophagy to supply the cell with biomacromolecules.
   C) It stimulates phospholipid synthesis in the smooth ER.
   D) It induces cell cycle progression in response to genome stability, as part of the G2-M checkpoint pathway.

2. Which of the following are NOT examples of enzymes found in lysosomes?

   A) Phosphatases and nucleases
   B) Phospholipase C and adenylyl cyclase
   C) Proteases and peptidases
   D) Glucosidases and lipases

3. Which of the following would NOT induce autophagy?

   A) Increase in inner mitochondrial membrane permeability
   B) Accumulation of incorrectly folded proteins in the ER lumen
   C) Incomplete genome replication
   D) Decreased intracellular metabolite concentrations

4. Cytochrome *c*:

   I. is located in the inner mitochondrial membrane
   II. undergoes redox reactions
   III. functions in anaerobic respiration

   A) I only
   B) III only
   C) I and II
   D) I, II and III

5. A researcher adds the BAX channel inhibitor Bci1 to a plate of cells in the lab. Which of the following is observed?

   A) Retention of cytochrome c in the inner mitochondrial membrane
   B) Inhibition of BAX homodimer formation in the inner mitochondrial membrane
   C) Rounded cells and blebbing of the plasma membrane
   D) A rapid increase in the amount of cellular autophagy

6. Monophosphate Atg13 initiates autophagosome formation and mTOR phosphorylates three amino acids on Atg13 simultaneously. Which of the following is true?

   A) mTOR is anti-autophagic and functions as a kinase.
   B) mTOR activates Atg13 and functions as a phosphatase.
   C) Rapamycin, an mTOR inhibitor, represses autophagy.
   D) In cells that are undergoing autophagy, Atg13 is phosphorylated on three amino acids.

7. Which of the following is true of Atg5?

   A) Southern blot analysis of proteins from healthy cells would show a 24 kDa Atg5.
   B) Calpain, the protease that cleaves Atg5, is activated in cells that have bound FasL.
   C) Western blot analysis of proteins from cells undergoing autophagy would show a 19 kDa Atg5.
   D) Healthy cells and autophagic cells have alternative splicing of Atg5 to generate two different proteins.

SOLUTIONS TO CHAPTER 5 FREESTANDING PRACTICE QUESTIONS

1. **C** Cilia and flagella are both made up of microtubules; thus, a defect causing immotile cilia would likely involve a protein associated with microtubules (choice C is correct). In fact, *Kartegener's syndrome* is a defect in the dynein protein, which is an ATPase that links the peripheral 9 doublets of the cilium (remember that eukaryotic cilia and flagella both have a 9 + 2 arrangement of microtubules) and causes bending (motion) of the cilium by differential sliding of the doublets. Microfilaments are composed of the protein actin and are responsible for contractile motility and changing of cell shape, specifically, muscle contraction, leukocyte motility, and cytokinesis (choice A is wrong). Intermediate filaments are primarily responsible for the cytoskeletal structure of cells (choice B is wrong). The plasma membrane is composed of phospholipids and cholesterol, although it does include many different proteins. However, the proteins of the plasma membrane are not responsible for cilia motility (choice D is wrong).

2. **C** The question stem states that COP-I proteins are involved in retrograde, or "backward," vesicular trafficking. Therefore, these vesicles would be traveling in the reverse pathway. Choice C (*cis* Golgi to RER) is the only correct option listed. The anterograde, or "forward," pathway in cells involves vesicles traveling from the RER to the cis Golgi (choice A is wrong), the *medial* Golgi, the *trans* Golgi and then to the cell membrane or other target site within the cell. Vesicles do not normally travel from the RER to the *trans* Golgi (choice B is wrong). Also vesicles are not involved in transport from the nucleus (choice D is wrong).

3. **D** Because steroid hormones are made from cholesterol as lipid derivatives, they cannot be stored by lipid bilayers. Since secretory vesicles, peroxisomes, and lysosomes are membrane-bound, they cannot store steroids (choices A, B, and C are wrong). Note also that peptide hormones are stored in secretory vesicles (choice A would be true of a peptide hormone, but not of a steroid hormone). Be careful to differentiate between answer choices that are simply true versus answer choices that actually address the question. Though choices A, B, and C all describe the general function of their particular organelle, only choice D addresses the issue specific to steroids.

4. **B** Since the question is asking about the formation of cAMP, it should be the last step in the sequence (choice D can be eliminated). G-protein coupled receptors receive the signal from ligand binding (in this example, epinephrine), and affect G-proteins. Therefore, GPCR must come before G-protein in the sequence (choice A can be eliminated). GPCRs activate G-proteins, which then affect the enzyme adenylyl cyclase (choice B is correct and C is wrong). Remember also that some GPCRs activate adenylyl cyclase and others inhibit it. This depends on the cell, the ligand, and many other factors.

5. **C** Item I is true: the nuclear membrane is degraded by the end of prophase so that the chromosomes can be appropriately separated into the daughter cells. It is therefore absent in anaphase (choice D can be eliminated). Item II is false: The nuclear membrane reforms after cytokinesis in telophase (choice B can be eliminated). Item III is true: Since the membrane does not reform until telophase, it must be absent in metaphase (choice A can be eliminated).

6. **D** Phosphorylation, formation of disulfide bridges, and glycosylation are all types of protein modification and can occur in both the Golgi apparatus and the rough ER (choices A, B, and C can be eliminated). Peptide bond formation occurs during translation, prior to any protein modification (choice D is not a type of protein modification and is the correct answer choice).

7. **B** Since DNA content of the cell changes with the phases of the cell cycle, flow cytometry using DNA dyes (such as DAPI or propidium iodide) can be used to study cell cycle progression and/or arrest (choice B is the best answer). The other answer options describe processes that are independent of DNA content (choices A, C, and D are wrong).

SOLUTIONS TO CHAPTER 5 PRACTICE PASSAGE

1. **A** The key to answering this question is decoding the question stem: *If p53 is commonly defective in cancer cells, it must normally have some sort of protective role.* In other words, p53 loss is beneficial for cancer cells. If p53 normally induces apoptosis and becomes mutant or lost, then it would no longer cause cell death in aberrant conditions. This could be a benefit for cancer cells, and in fact could lead to the rapid cell proliferation and tumor growth that is typically seen in cancer (choice A is correct). The passage says that autophagy can help the cell deal with times of stress, including nutrient deprivation. Since cancer cells grow quickly, they have high metabolic demands, which are accommodated in part using autophagy to supply macromolecules. If p53 normally helped the cell supply macromolecules, p53 loss would not help the growth of cancer cells (choice B can be eliminated). Similarly, if cancer cells are growing quickly, they will need lots of phospholipids. If p53 normally stimulated phospholipid synthesis, its loss would not be beneficial for the cancer cell (choice C can be eliminated). Finally, if p53 normally pushed the cell cycle forward, its loss would arrest the cell cycle. This is clearly not the case in "aberrantly growing cancer cells" (choice D is wrong).

2. **B** The passage says that the lysosome contains acid hydrolases, which degrade the contents of the autophagosomes. Since the autophagosomes contain cellular and organelle material, it is possible that they would contain proteins (which would be broken down by proteases and peptidases; choice C can be eliminated), nucleic acids (which would be broken down by nucleases; choice A can be eliminated), carbohydrates (which would be broken down by glucosidases) and lipids (which would be broken down by lipases; choice D can be eliminated). However, phospholipase C and adenylyl cyclase are both involved in cell signaling pathways, downstream of ligands binding receptors. Neither of these would function in macromolecule degradation (choice B would not be found in lysosomes and is the correct answer choice). Note that phosphatases remove the phosphate group from molecules, and in many cases, this is part of degradation.

3. **C** The passage says that autophagy is induced when cells are under nutrient stress, reactive oxygen stress, or organelle stress. Decreased intracellular metabolite concentrations would be an example of nutrient stress (choice D would induce autophagy and can be eliminated). An increase in mitochondrial permeability and an accumulation of incorrectly folded proteins in the ER lumen are examples of organelle stress (autophagy degrades broken or sickly organelles; choices A and B could induce autophagy and can be eliminated). While incomplete genome replication in the S phase is a problem for cells, there is no information to indicate that this would induce autophagy. Also, the effects of autophagy as described in the passage (break down of cytoplasmic and organelle material) would not solve this problem since the genome cannot be degraded (there is only one, after all). In fact, incomplete genome replication is detected by cell cycle checkpoint pathways to halt cell cycle progression and allow time for DNA replication and repair (choice C would not induce autophagy and is the correct answer choice).

4. **C** Item I is true: Figure 1 shows that cytochrome c is normally located in the inner mitochondrial membrane (choice B can be eliminated). Item II is true: Cytochrome c is part of the electron transport chain and therefore undergoes redox reactions (choice A can be eliminated). Item III is false: The electron transport chain is a major component of aerobic respiration, not anaerobic respiration (choice D can be eliminated and choice C is correct).

5. **A** According to the figure, BAX proteins form channels in the mitochondrial membrane and this facilitates cytochrome c release. If Bci1 inhibits these BAX channels, it would cause cytochrome c to remain in the inner mitochondrial membrane (choice A is correct). This would prevent apoptosis (and thus rounded cells and blebbing; choice C is wrong). While choice B might be tempting, just because Bci1 inhibits BAX channels doesn't mean it has to inhibit homodimer formation (although this is certainly possible). We can be sure about the end result, though (retention of cytochrome c), even if we aren't sure of the mechanism (choice A is better than choice B). Note that BAX functions in apoptosis, not autophagy (choice D is wrong).

6. **A** Note that there is no information about Atg13 in the passage, so this question must be answered based entirely on information in the question. The question text states that when Atg13 is phosphorylated on one amino acid, it initiates autophagy by inducing autophagosome formation (choice D is wrong). If mTOR phosphorylates Atg13 on three amino acids, it is inhibiting Atg13 function and is inhibiting autophagy (choice A is correct and choice B is wrong). If rapamycin inhibits mTOR, it is inhibiting an inhibitor of autophagy. In other words, rapamycin would induce autophagy (choice C is wrong). A kinase phosphorylates molecules (using ATP as the source of the phosphate) and a phosphatase removes phosphate groups, although this information is not needed to answer the question.

7. **B** The passage says that Atg5 cleavage (from a longer precursor protein to a shorter 24 kDa protein) is involved in the switch from autophagy to apoptosis. If cells have bound FasL (a death receptor ligand), they are undergoing apoptosis, or will be soon. Since Atg5 cleavage induces apoptosis, choice B is very likely. Southern blot analysis is a lab technique used to study DNA, not proteins (choice A is wrong). While western blot analysis is the correct lab technique to study proteins, in cells undergoing autophagy (not apoptosis), Atg5 would be in the longer, nontruncated form (the 24 kDa protein, not the 19 kDa protein; choice C is wrong). The passage describes proteolytic cleavage as the mechanism for generating differently sized Atg5, not alternative splicing (choice D is wrong).

Chapter 6
Genetics and Evolution

The nature of the fundamental unit of inheritance, the gene, has been agreed upon by scientists only since the mid-nineteenth century. Aristotle believed that traits were passed on in the form of "pangenes," particles derived from all parts of the body and distilled into eggs and sperm. In the seventeenth century, different theorists believed that all genetic information was passed by either the father or the mother. Finally, early in the nineteenth century, people began to see that characteristics are passed from both parents; this led to the idea that parental characteristics were evenly mixed in offspring, in a process termed "blending." The notion that some characteristics were inherited in an either-or fashion, while others were in fact blended, remained unconceived.

The proponents of these early theories cannot be faulted for their lack of electron microscopes and other modern tools and techniques. But one is tempted to criticize their ideas for their obvious irrelevance to reality. One didn't need a Cray supercomputer to figure out that both parents contributed to a child's makeup. Why did researchers fail to arrive at this seemingly obvious hypothesis? Probably for two reasons: methods and dogma.

Their approach to discovery was not empirical, but rather *a priori*. They believed knowledge could be derived by speculation alone, and that to perform experiments in the physical world was to dirty one's hands. And the prevailing religious dogma strongly censored empirical exploration, since it threatened the metaphysical tenets of the church.

What is different today is the approach to discovery known as the scientific method. Modern scientists know that only through careful, sober consideration of a question, formulation of a tentative answer, and testing of that hypothesis can new knowledge be uncovered. In this chapter we will examine what is now considered to be the truth about genetics and evolution, all the way back to the origin of life.

We challenge you to attack this knowledge in the way its discoverers did. This is difficult material. Spend time thinking about the in-text questions before reading the answers. If you have trouble with a topic, stop and take out a fresh piece of paper. Write down all the facets of your current understanding, and look for internal inconsistencies and fallacies. Make up your own Punnett squares, pedigrees, and sketches of chromosomes during meiosis if the ones we present aren't sufficient. And finally, as you review, ask yourself which of the modern "truths" will one day be looked back on as preposterous ponderings of blindfolded pseudo-scientists.

6.1   INTRODUCTION TO GENETICS

Genes and Alleles

Genetics is the science that describes the inheritance of traits from one generation to another. At the origin of genetics, patterns of inheritance were observed to follow certain predictable patterns, as described by Mendel's laws. The reasons for these patterns of inheritance were to remain a mystery until the nature of DNA as the genetic material was known. Today we can use our knowledge of DNA and the cell to understand Mendel's laws at the molecular level.

One of the basic tenets of genetics is that children inherit traits from both parents. Humans have a life cycle in which life begins with a diploid cell, the zygote. Diploid organisms (or cells) have two copies of the genome in each cell, while haploid cells have one copy of the genome. In sexual reproduction, the diploid zygote is produced by fusion of two haploid gametes: a haploid ovum from the mother and a haploid spermatozoon from the father. The zygote then goes through many mitotic divisions to develop into an adult, with half of the genetic material in each cell from each parent. The adult, male or female, produces haploid gametes by meiotic cell division to repeat the life cycle once again.

The development of a zygote into an adult and the maintenance of adult cells and tissues requires many thousands of different gene products. All of these gene products are encoded in the genome and inherited from mother and father. The **gene**, a length of DNA coding for a particular gene product, is the fundamental unit of inheritance. [Are gene products always proteins?[1]] The genes are distributed among the chromosomes that compose the genome, and every gene can be pinpointed to a specific location called the **locus** (plural: **loci**) on a specific chromosome. [Can all physical traits of an organism be mapped to a single locus?[2]]

The human genome is split into 23 different chromosomes, of which every cell has two different copies (46 total chromosomes); one copy of each from the mother and one from the father. The two nonidentical copies of a chromosome are called **homologous chromosomes**. Although these two copies look the same when examined at the crudest level under a microscope, and although they contain the same genes, the copies of the genes in the two homologous chromosomes may differ in their DNA sequence. Different versions of a gene, called **alleles**, may carry out the gene's function differently. Since a person carries two copies of every gene, one on each homologous chromosome, a person can carry two different alleles. Individuals carrying different alleles of a gene will often have traits that allow the inheritance of alleles to be followed. [Is it possible for there to be more than two different alleles of a specific gene?[3]]

---

[1]   No. tRNA and rRNA genes, as well as other small nuclear RNA genes, do not encode polypeptides.

[2]   No. Every gene is located at a specific locus, but physical traits, particularly complex traits, like weight or height, can be controlled by many different genes and therefore do not map to a single locus, but to many.

[3]   Yes, there can be many versions (alleles) of a particular gene. Under normal circumstances, however, one individual cannot have more than two of those different alleles, since they have only two copies of a gene (one on each homologous chromosome). An exception is when an individual is polyploid for a certain chromosome (i.e., they have more than two homologous chromosomes, for example in Down syndrome and Klinefelter syndrome).

- Which one of the following is true if an individual has two different alleles at a given locus?[4]
    A. The individual has two phenotypes, e.g., one brown eye and one blue.
    B. There are two alleles in one place on one particular chromosome.
    C. Two siblings have different appearances.
    D. There is a different allele on each of the two members of a homologous pair.

Genotype vs. Phenotype

The **genotype** is the DNA sequence of the alleles a person carries. A person carrying two different alleles at a given locus is called a **heterozygote**, while an individual carrying two identical alleles is called a **homozygote**. The expression of alleles often is different in heterozygotes and homozygotes.

The **phenotype** is the physical expression of the genotype. For example, the phenotype of a gene involved in hair color may be brown or blond. Since there are many different kinds of alleles, there are different ways these alleles can be expressed in the phenotype. If an allele is the one expressed in the phenotype, regardless of what the second allele carried is, the expressed allele is referred to as **dominant**. An allele that is not expressed in the heterozygous state is referred to as **recessive**. For example, consider a heterozygous organism in which one allele encodes the functional version of an enzyme, while the second allele encodes an inactive version of that enzyme. Upon observation, it is noted that the organism's enzymes are all functional; then the functional-enzyme allele is *dominant* and the inactive-enzyme allele is *recessive*. Since recessive alleles are not expressed in heterozygotes, it is not always possible to tell the genotype of an individual based solely on the phenotype. [Can a haploid organism like an adult fungus have recessive alleles?[5]]

There are certain conventions used in denoting genotypes in genetics that are useful to know. The alleles of a gene are usually denoted by letters. For example, for a gene called "curly," a dominant allele may be denoted by the capital letter *C* and a recessive allele may be denoted by the lower case letter *c*. A heterozygote is referred to as *Cc*, while homozygotes would be either *CC* or *cc*. More complex situations require more complex conventions, but most questions probably only involve two alleles at a locus. [If the dominant allele for curly (*C*) results in curly hair and the recessive allele (*c*) causes straight hair, what are the phenotypes of *CC*, *Cc* and *cc* individuals?[6]]

Some alleles of genes display neither dominant nor recessive patterns of expression. If the phenotype of a heterozygote is a blended mix of both alleles, this is called **incomplete dominance**, and the alleles for that trait are given different, upper-case letters. For example, if a gene for flower color has two incompletely dominant alleles, *R* could be used to indicate the allele for red color and *W* to indicate the allele for white color. [If a gene for flower color has two alleles, *R* (red) and *r* (white), and *R* is dominant while *r* is

---

[4] An individual with two different alleles at a given locus has one allele on one chromosome and the other allele on its homologous partner (so D is correct and choice B is not possible). While choice A may be possible, it is an exceedingly complex phenomenon and not discernible from the information given. The question discusses a single individual, not a pair of siblings (eliminating choice C).

[5] No. If there is only one copy of a gene, then that is the copy which determines the phenotype.

[6] *CC* and *Cc* individuals have curly hair, and *cc* individuals have straight hair. Only homozygous recessive individuals express recessive traits. In the heterozygote, the presence of the recessive allele is masked by the dominant allele, so there are only two different phenotypes, although there are three different genotypes. This type of interaction between alleles is called **classical dominance**.

recessive, what is the phenotype of *Rr* heterozygotes?[7] If *R* and *W* display incomplete dominance, what is the phenotype of *RW* heterozygotes?[8] How many phenotypes are possible if *R* and *W* display incomplete dominance?[9]]

Codominance is a slightly different situation, in which two alleles are both expressed but are not blended. For example, the alleles of the gene for ABO blood group antigens that are found on the surface of red blood cells display codominance. Each of the alleles is expressed on red blood cells, regardless of the second allele in the cell. There are three alleles for the ABO blood group antigens: I^A, I^B, and *i*. The alleles I^A and I^B are codominant and will be expressed regardless of the second allele, while *i* is recessive to both I^A and I^B. The alleles I^A and I^B cause type A or type B antigens to be expressed, while *i* does not cause antigen expression.

- What is the phenotype of an individual heterozygous for the I^A and I^B alleles?[10]
- What is the phenotype of an individual heterozygous for I^B and *i*?[11]
- If a woman heterozygous for type A blood marries a man who is heterozygous for type B blood, what are the possible genotypes (and blood types) of their children?[12]

The other main antigen used in blood typing is the Rh (rhesus) factor. The expression of this antigen follows a classically dominant pattern; $Rh^D Rh^D$ and $Rh^D Rh^d$ (also seen as *RR* and *Rr*) genotypes lead to the expression of this protein on the surface of the red cell (Rh positive), and the $Rh^d Rh^d$ (or *rr*) genotype leads to the absence of the protein (Rh negative).

Although Mendel's peas all displayed very simple patterns of inheritance, there are often many complications in the inheritance of traits. For example:

Pleiotropism: Alteration of a gene is said to have pleiotropic effects if the result alters many different, seemingly unrelated aspects of the organism's total phenotype. Example: Mutation of a gene alters development of heart, bone, and inner ears.

Polygenism: Complex traits that are influenced by many different genes are called polygenic. Example: Height is polygenic since it will be influenced by genes for growth factors, receptors, hormones, bone deposition, muscle development, energy utilization, and so on.

---

[7] *Rr* heterozygotes will have the phenotype of the dominant allele: red.

[8] In this case, *RW* heterozygotes will be neither red nor white, but a blend of the two: pink.

[9] Three phenotypes and three genotypes: *RR* (red), *RW* (pink), and *WW* (white).

[10] The red blood cells will express both type A and type B antigens, so the blood type will be AB.

[11] The red blood cells will express type B antigen only, and the blood type will be B.

[12] Because they are both heterozygous, the woman's genotype is $I^A i$ and the man's genotype is $I^B i$. Thus, their children could be $I^A I^B$ (type AB), $I^A i$ (type A), $I^B i$ (type B), or *ii* (type O).

Penetrance: Penetrance describes the likelihood that a person with a given genotype will express the expected phenotype. While many traits are completely penetrant (all individuals with a given allele or mutation display the phenotype), there is a spectrum of options: alleles or mutations can also have high, incomplete, or low penetrance. The root cause of penetrance depends on the allele. Some have age-related penetrance, where the phenotype is displayed more frequently in mutation-carrying individuals as they age. The penetrance of other alleles depends on environmental and lifestyle modifiers. For example, women who carry a certain mutation that increases their risk of breast cancer display variable rates of breast cancer, depending on their diet, if they smoke, if they have had children and breast fed, etc. Finally, many alleles have genetic modifiers that affect penetrance; since several human traits are polygenic, alleles at different loci can affect penetrance.

Epistasis: Epistasis refers to a situation where expression of alleles for one gene is dependent on a different gene. Example: A gene for curly hair cannot be expressed if a different gene causes baldness.

- 100 people are homozygous for an allele that is implicated in cancer, but only 20 develop cancer. What are potential explanations for why only some people express a gene out of a broader population with the same genotype?[13]
- In one strain of mouse, homozygotes for an allele of a gene develop heart defects, while in another strain of mouse, homozygotes with the same allele develop normally. Heterozygotes develop normally in both strains. What is the most likely explanation for the difference between the two strains?[14]
  - A. The allele is recessive.
  - B. The development of the heart defect is influenced by more than one locus.
  - C. The allele has pleiotropic effects on development.
  - D. The allele is codominant.

The Sex Chromosomes

Early in the twentieth century it was observed that women have twenty-three pairs of chromosomes that are homologous, while men have only twenty-two pairs of chromosomes that match in appearance. The two chromosomes in men that did not match each other were termed the **X** and the **Y** chromosomes because of their appearance during mitosis (Figure 1). Males have an X and a Y, while females have two X chromosomes. The presence of a Y chromosome in humans (genotype XY) is a key factor in the determination of the sex of an embryo, and subsequent development into a male. The absence of a Y (genotype XX) results in a female as the default developmental pathway. During meiosis, females generate gametes that contain an X chromosome; males generate gametes with either an X or a Y chromosome, meaning that it is the *male* gamete that determines the gender of an embryo (Figure 2).

---

[13] The trait of cancer development is probably polygenic, so it does not display simple patterns of inheritance. Cancer development is also influenced by the environment, such as exposure to carcinogens, further complicating the penetrance of the genotype.

[14] The key variable must not lie within the allele itself, since this remains the same (so A and D are wrong). The genetic background of the two different strains of mice must affect whether or not the heart defect phenotype is expressed. Further, only one defect is observed (so it can't be pleitropic; choice C is wrong). Therefore, the heart defect phenotype must be influenced by some other locus that is different in the two strains of mice, making **B** the best choice.

This is an X chromosome during interphase.
(Note that it doesn't look like an "X" at all.)

This is a condensed X chromosome after S phase (replication). The X is formed by the two sister chromatids.

This is a Y chromosome after S phase.

Figure 1   The Sex Chromosomes

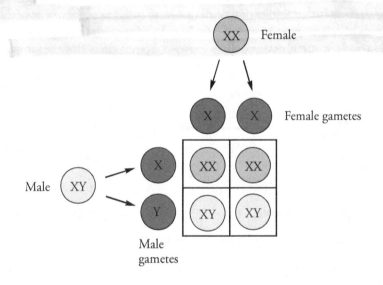

Figure 2   Determination of the Zygote's Sexual Genotype

The sex chromosomes also play a key role in the inheritance of other traits that are not directly involved in sexual development. Much of what has been discussed about inheritance was dependent on the assumption that there are two copies of every chromosome and therefore two copies of every gene in each cell. This is true for genes found on every pair of chromosomes except for one pair: the sex chromosomes. Genes that lie on the X chromosome will be present in two copies in females but only in one copy in males. [What pattern of expression will a recessive allele on the X chromosome display in males?[15]] Traits that are determined by genes on the X or Y chromosome are called **sex-linked traits** because of their unique patterns of expression and inheritance.

---

[15] In males, recessive alleles on the X chromosome are always expressed, since no other allele is present that can mask the recessive allele.

6.2 MEIOSIS

Mitotic cell division produces two daughter cells that are identical to the parent. However, the production of haploid cells such as gametes from a diploid cell requires a type of cell division that reduces the number of copies of each chromosome from two to one; this method of cell division is called **meiosis**. In males, meiosis occurs in the testes with haploid spermatozoa as the end result; in females, meiosis in the ovaries produces ova. (*Note*: This is not always the case, and while meiosis begins in the ovaries, it is completed only after fertilization; see Chapter 12 for a further discussion on oogenesis.) Specialized cells termed **spermatogonia** in males and **oogonia** in females undergo meiosis. Spermatogenesis and oogenesis share the same basic features of meiosis but differ in many of the specific features of gamete production. Meiosis itself will be discussed in this chapter, while the specifics of spermatogenesis and oogenesis will be discussed in Chapter 12.

Mitosis and meiosis are similar in many respects. Mitosis and meiosis are both preceded by one round of replication of the genome (S phase), leaving a diploid cell with four copies of the genome (Figure 3). The different phases in cell division are referred to by the same names (prophase, metaphase, anaphase, and telophase) in both meiosis and mitosis and are mechanistically very similar. The primary difference between meiosis and mitosis is that replication of the genome is followed by one round of cell division in mitosis and two rounds of cell division in meiosis, **meiosis I** and **meiosis II** (Figure 4). Another important difference is that in meiosis, recombination occurs between homologous chromosomes.

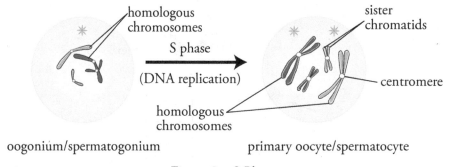

Figure 3 S-Phase

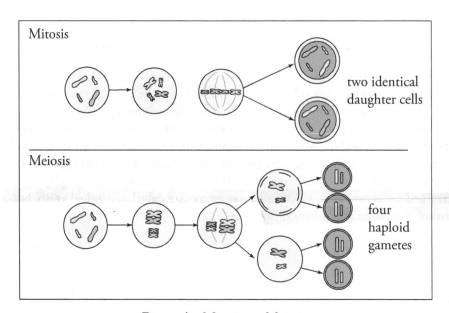

Figure 4 Mitosis vs. Meiosis

The first step in meiosis is **prophase I** (Figure 5). To depict meiosis, we will use a hypothetical model organism with a diploid genome with two different (nonhomologous) chromosomes (Figures 5–8).

- How many chromosomes are present in a cell from this organism during prophase I of meiosis?[16]

As in mitotic prophase, chromosomes condense in meiotic prophase I, and then the nuclear envelope breaks down. Unlike mitosis, however, homologous chromosomes pair with each other during meiotic prophase I in **synapsis**. Homologous chromosomes align themselves very precisely with each other in synapsis, with the two copies of each gene on two different chromosomes brought closely together. The paired homologous chromosomes are called a **bivalent** or **tetrad**. When the DNA is aligned properly, it can then be cut and then re-ligated with genes swapped between homologous chromosomes (Figure 5). This process is known as **crossing over** or **recombination** (Figure 6). Due to the extreme complexity of crossing over, meiotic prophase takes the most time in meiosis, days sometimes. Recombination during meiosis is an important source of genetic variation during sexual reproduction.

- Does crossing over change the number of genes on a chromosome?[17]
- Does recombination create combinations of alleles on a chromosome that are not found in the parent?[18]

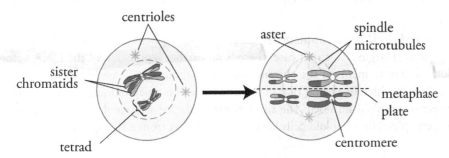

Figure 5   Prophase I and Metaphase I

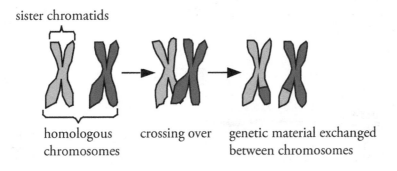

Figure 6   Crossing Over (Recombination)

---

[16] The organism is diploid normally, with two copies of two chromosomes, or four chromosomes total. After DNA synthesis, during prophase I, the cell still has four chromosomes; however, the chromosomes are replicated and held together at the centromere. Thus each chromosome consists of two sister chromatids, and the cell has a total of eight sister chromatids.

[17] Not if it is done correctly. Error free recombination involves a one-for-one swap of DNA between homologous chromosomes.

[18] Yes. Although each chromosome contains the same genes after crossing over, it may contain different alleles of some genes that were not present on the same chromosome previously.

After prophase I is **metaphase I**. In meiotic metaphase I, alignment along the metaphase plate occurs, as in mitosis. The difference is that in meiotic metaphase I, the *tetrads* are aligned at the center of the cell (the metaphase plate), whereas in mitosis, *sister chromatids* are aligned on the metaphase plate. In **anaphase I**, homologous chromosomes separate, and sister chromatids remain together (Figure 7). The cell then divides into two cells during **telophase I** (Figure 8). *It is important to note that at this point the cells are considered to be haploid.* Each cell has a single set of chromosomes. The chromosomes, however, are still replicated (still exist as a pair of sister chromatids). The whole point to the second set of meiotic divisions is to separate the sister chromatids so that each cell has a single set of unreplicated chromosomes.

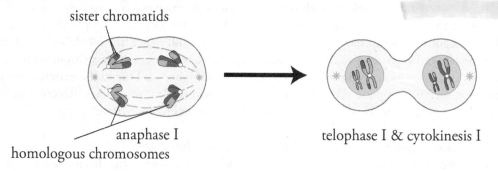

sister chromatids

anaphase I

homologous chromosomes

telophase I & cytokinesis I

Figure 7   Anaphase I, Telophase I, and Cytokinesis I

In some species, meiosis II begins immediately after telophase I, while in other species, there is a period of time before meiosis II begins. In either case, there is no further replication of the DNA before the second set of divisions. The movements of the chromosomes during meiosis II are identical to the movements in mitosis, with the sole difference being that in meiosis II there is a haploid number of chromosomes, while in mitosis there is a diploid number. The sister chromatids are separated during anaphase II, and after telophase II is complete, four haploid cells have been produced from a single diploid parent cell (Figure 8).

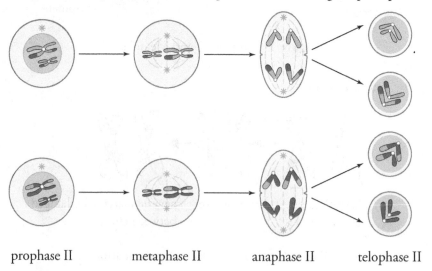

prophase II   metaphase II   anaphase II   telophase II

Figure 8   Meiosis II

- When homologous chromosomes separate, do all paternal and maternal chromosomes stay together in the daughter cells?[19]

- Are the sister chromatids that separate during meiotic anaphase II identical in their DNA sequence?[20]

- Which of the following occur in meiosis but NOT in mitosis?[21]
  - I.   Separation of sister chromatids on microtubules
  - II. Pairing of homologous chromosomes
  - III. Recombination between sister chromatids

  - A. I only
  - B. II only
  - C. I and II
  - D. II and III

- If cells are blocked in meiotic metaphase II and prevented from moving on in meiosis, which one of the following will be prevented?[22]
  - A. Crossing over
  - B. Separation of homologous chromosomes
  - C. Separation of sister chromatids
  - D. Breakdown of the nuclear envelope

Nondisjunction

Sometimes during meiosis I homologous chromosomes fail to separate, and sometimes during meiosis II sister chromatids fail to separate. Such a failure of chromosomes to separate correctly during meiosis is called **nondisjunction**. [A gamete normally contains how many copies of each chromosome?[23] If two homologous chromosomes of chromosome #12 fail to separate during meiosis I, how many copies of chromosome #12 will the resulting gametes have?[24]] Gametes resulting from nondisjunction will have two copies or no copies of a given chromosome. Such a gamete can fuse with a normal gamete to create a zygote with either three copies of a chromosome (**trisomy**) or one copy of a chromosome (**monosomy**).

---

[19] No. Homologous chromosome separate (segregate) randomly. This is one aspect of meiosis that increases genetic variation during sexual reproduction.

[20] The sister chromatids *would* be identical, except that recombination with homologous chromosomes occurred earlier in meiosis, during prophase I, altering the sister chromatids.

[21] Item I is false: The spindle separates sister chromatids during both (choices A and C can be eliminated.) Note that both remaining answer choices include Item II, so Item II must be true. **Item II is true**: Only meiosis involves pairing and recombination between homologous chromosomes. Item III is false: Meiotic recombination occurs between homologous chromosomes, not sister chromatids (choice D can be eliminated and choice **B** is correct).

[22] Crossing over occurs during prophase I, separation of homologous chromosomes occurs during anaphase I, and nuclear envelope breakdown occurs during prophase I and sometimes prophase II (choices A, B, and D are false). Only separation of sister chromatids occurs after metaphase II, in anaphase II. Answer: C.

[23] Normal gametes have one copy of each chromosome; this is the definition of haploid.

[24] If the homologous chromosomes do not separate in meiosis I, then one daughter cell from this division will have four copies of this chromosome and the other cell will have none. In meiosis II, sister chromatids will separate, leaving two gametes with two copies of the chromosome and two gametes with no copies of the chromosome.

6.3

The genetic defect caused when an entire chromosome is either added or removed is usually so great that a zygote with either trisomy or monosomy cannot develop into a normal individual. There are examples in which nondisjunction is not lethal in humans, although it results in significant developmental abnormalities. Trisomy of chromosome #21 results in Down syndrome, with mental retardation and abnormal growth. Nondisjunction of the sex chromosomes is also generally not lethal during development. Individuals who have only one X chromosome and no Y, for example, have Turner syndrome, with external female appearance but underdeveloped ovaries and sterility. Individuals with nondisjunction of the sex chromosomes will develop to have male appearance if they have at least one Y, no matter how many X chromosomes are present, and will have female genitalia if only X chromosomes are present. Most will be sterile, however, and many will suffer mental retardation. [In an individual with Down syndrome, are the defects in development caused by an absence of genetic information?[25] If not, why does trisomy of this chromosome or other chromosomes have such dramatic effects?[26]]

6.3 MENDELIAN GENETICS

Gregor Mendel described the statistical behavior of the inheritance of traits in pea plants long before the nature of DNA and chromosomes was known. Unlike Mendel, however, we are now familiar with the molecular basis of genetics in meiosis and genes, and the laws of genetics that Mendel formulated can now be presented with insight based on this knowledge. Although Mendelian genetics generally only involves the simplest patterns of inheritance, it forms the foundation for understanding more complicated situations.

Mendel observed that traits were governed by pairs of hereditary material (alleles). The first of Mendel's laws, the **law of segregation**, states that the two alleles of an individual are separated and passed on to the next generation singly. [At what stage during meiosis are different alleles of a gene separated?[27]] Mendel's second law, the **law of independent assortment**, states that the alleles of one gene will separate into gametes independently of alleles for another gene. We will illustrate these principles using the garden pea plant, but the principles apply equally well to humans.

A trait that can be studied in the pea plant is the color of the pea. We can call *G* the allele for green color, while *g* is the allele for yellow pea color. Mating between plants, a **cross**, is used as a tool in genetics to discern genotypes by looking at the phenotypes of progeny from a cross. A **pure-breeding strain** of yellow or green peas consistently yields progeny of the same color when mated within the strain. For example, if mating yellow plants with yellow plants always produces yellow progeny, yellow is a pure-breeding strain. [Can anything be deduced about the genotype of the pure-breeding strain of yellow peas?[28] If a pure-breeding yellow and pure-breeding green strain are crossed, and all of the progeny are green, what does

[25] There is no information missing in a person with trisomy. All of the chromosomes are present, and there is no reason to believe that any of the genes on these chromosomes are deleted or mutated to render them inactive.

[26] The problem with trisomy appears not to be that genetic information is missing, but that there is *too much* present. A mechanism involved might be gene dosage. Genes are regulated to produce the right amount of each gene product. In trisomy, many genes are present in one more copy than usual, resulting in greater quantities of the gene products encoded on this chromosome. The extra quantities of so many gene products, even if they are normal in sequence, can have dramatic consequences.

[27] During meiosis I, at the time when homologous chromosome separate.

[28] If a strain always produces the same trait when mated with itself, it is likely to be homozygous for the trait. The pure-breeding yellow pea is homozygous for the yellow allele *g* of the color gene.

this indicate about the expression of the yellow and green alleles?[29]] Let's assume that *G* is the dominant allele of the color gene, and *g* is the recessive allele. [Is it possible to deduce the genotype of a pea plant at the color gene if it is green?[30]] If a green plant is encountered, to deduce the genotype of the plant one can do a **testcross**. The progeny of a testcross are called the **F$_1$ generation**. [If a green plant is testcrossed with a pure-breeding yellow strain, and some of the F$_1$ generation are yellow while others are green, what is the genotype of the original green plant?[31]] The results of a testcross are dependent on statistics and follow Mendel's laws.

The principle of segregation can be illustrated with the color gene described above for the pea. If a pea is heterozygous *Gg*, its gametes will contain either the *G* allele or the *g* allele, but never both. [If a gamete contained both *G* and *g*, what occurred during meiosis?[32]] The probability that a gamete in the heterozygote will contain one allele or the other is 50%, completely random. [Would the principle of segregation apply to a gene on the X chromosome in a woman?[33]] To illustrate the law of independent assortment, we need to introduce a second gene, one that controls the shape of the pea. *W* is the dominant allele, resulting in wrinkled peas, while *w* is the recessive allele, resulting in smooth peas in homozygous *ww* plants. According to the law of independent assortment, the genes for the color of peas and the shape of peas are passed from one generation to another independently. [If the color gene and the shape gene are right next to each other on a chromosome, will they display independent assortment?[34]] The nature of the shape gene in a given gamete does not depend on and is not influenced by the color gene, if independent assortment is true. [If an individual is heterozygous at the color gene, *Gg*, and heterozygous at the shape gene, *Ww*, what are the chances that a gamete containing the *G* allele will also contain the *W* allele?[35]]

The Punnett Square

It is possible to predict the results of a cross between two individuals using the laws of segregation and independent assortment. Determining the result can be complex, however, so a visual tool called the **Punnett square** is often employed to make the process simpler. Let's use a simple square first, with only one trait involved (Figure 9); we will then tackle a more complicated problem with two different traits (Figure 10).

---

[29] The two strains were both pure-breeding and could only produce gametes containing one type of allele. All of the progeny would be the *Gg* genotype. If all progeny are green, then the green allele is dominant and the yellow allele is recessive.

[30] No. A green plant could either be heterozygous *Gg* or homozygous *GG*.

[31] The original pea is heterozygous *Gg*.

[32] The gamete must be the result of nondisjunction.

[33] Yes. The principles are the same for human genes as for pea genes, as long as an organism is diploid and goes through sexual reproduction.

[34] No, they would not. They would display an important exception to independent assortment, linkage, which is discussed later.

[35] According to independent assortment, the segregation of one gene does not depend on segregation of another. The chances of a gamete containing the *W* allele are 50%, regardless of the identity of the color allele.

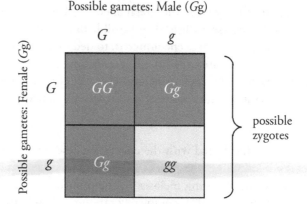

Figure 9 A Punnett Square Involving One Gene

In Figure 9, a Punnett square depicts a cross between two pea plants that are heterozygous for the color gene, with G the dominant green allele and g the recessive yellow allele. To draw a Punnett square, the following steps are involved:

Step 1: Determine the gametes that are possible from each parent in the cross.
Step 2: Draw a square with the possible gametes from each parent on two sides.
Step 3: Fill in the square with the zygote genotypes that would result from each possible combination of gamete.
Step 4: Determine the phenotype of each genotype.
Step 5: Find the probability of each genotype and each phenotype.

- In the situation shown in Figure 9, which one of the following will be true?[36]
    - A.   25% of the offspring will be green, and 75% will be yellow.
    - B.   50% of the offspring will be green, and 50% will be yellow.
    - C.   75% of the offspring will be green, and 25% will be yellow.
    - D.   100% of the offspring will be green.

A more complicated Punnett square is needed to look at two traits during a cross. In Figure 10, a cross is performed between Plant 1, heterozygous at the color gene (Gg), and Plant 2, also heterozygous at the color gene. Plant 1 is also homozygous for the dominant allele of the shape gene (wrinkled peas) while Plant 2 is homozygous for the recessive allele (smooth). [What are the phenotypes of the plants being crossed?[37]] The same steps are followed to construct the Punnett square in Figure 10 as the one in Figure 9. First, determine the possible gametes for each pea plant being crossed. (In this case, there are really two possible gamete types from each parent, so the box could be simplified to have only two gametes on a side). Then, determine the possible combinations of gametes that could join to form zygotes and the phenotypes and frequencies of the F_1 generation. [What percentage of the F_1 generation will have smooth peas?[38] What

---

[36] If G (green allele) is dominant, then both GG homozygotes and Gg heterozygotes will be green, while only gg homozygotes will be yellow. 25% of the offspring in Figure 9 will be GG homozygotes, and 50% will be Gg heterozygotes, so a total of 75% of the offspring will be green (choice **C**).

[37] Plant 1 has green wrinkled peas, while Plant 2 has green smooth peas.

[38] All peas receive one w allele and one W allele, so all are wrinkled Ww heterozygotes (i.e., 0% are smooth).

percentage of peas will be green and wrinkled?[39] Yellow and wrinkled?[40] The cross depicted in Figure 10 was performed and produced 77 green wrinkled plants and 20 yellow wrinkled plants; why do these results not agree exactly with the ratios predicted in the Punnett square?[41]] Independent assortment and the principle of segregation are assumptions built into this Punnett square.

Plant 1: *GgWW*

Plant 2: *Ggww*

Gametes	*GW*	*GW*	*gW*	*gW*
Gw	*GGWw*	*GGWw*	*GgWw*	*GgWw*
Gw	*GGWw*	*GGWw*	*GgWw*	*GgWw*
gw	*GgWw*	*GgWw*	*ggWw*	*ggWw*
gw	*GgWw*	*GgWw*	*ggWw*	*ggWw*

Figure 10 A Punnett Square Depicting a Cross with Two Traits Involved

- In the cross depicted in Figure 10, how does the shape gene affect inheritance of the alleles for the color gene?[42]
  A. The percentage of green peas is increased by the shape gene.
  B. The shape gene has no effect on the inheritance of the alleles for the color gene.
  C. The percentage of green peas is decreased by the shape gene.
  D. The shape gene prevents segregation of the alleles for the color gene.

[39] All F_1 peas are wrinkled and 75% are green, so 75% are green and wrinkled.

[40] All F_1 peas are wrinkled and 25% are yellow, so 25% are yellow and wrinkled.

[41] The results obtained in reality rarely agree exactly with the predicted result. If the results differ slightly from the prediction, the most likely explanation is statistical variability. The more progeny from the cross, the closer the result should be to the prediction.

[42] Independent assortment and the principle of segregation are inherent in the Punnett square. There is no reason to believe that these are not followed, making choice **B** the best response. Choices A, C, and D all assume that either independent assortment or segregation did not occur.

- If a green wrinkled plant from the F_1 generation in Figure 10 is crossed with a pure-breeding yellow smooth pea plant, what phenotypes are possible?[43]
- If any yellow smooth progeny are observed in this testcross, what does this indicate about the genotype of the F_1 plant?[44]

The Rules of Probability

Punnett squares are only one way to determine the probability of an outcome in a cross. Another way involves using statistical rules called the *rule of multiplication* and the *rule of addition*. The **rule of multiplication** states that the probability of both of two independent events happening can be found by multiplying the odds of either event alone. For example, if the probability of being struck by lightning is 1 in a million (10^{-6}) and the probability of winning the lottery is 10^{-7}, then the probability of both happening is the product: $10^{-6} \times 10^{-7} = 10^{-13}$.

The **rule of addition** can be used to calculate the chances of *either* of two events happening. The chance of either A or B happening is equal to the probability of A added to the probability of B, minus the probability of A and B occurring together. For example, the chance of either getting hit by lightning *or* winning the lottery is $10^{-6} + 10^{-7} = 1.1 \times 10^{-6}$. (*Note*: The product of 10^{-6} and 10^{-7} is so small that it can be neglected from the equation.) These rules can be a shortcut to using a Punnett square in some problems.

- A man that is homozygous for eye color, *bb*, is married to a woman who is heterozygous at the same gene: *Bb*. What are the chances that a child will have the *Bb* genotype and be a boy?[45]

---

[43] There are two different genotypes possible for the green wrinkled phenotype in the F_1 generation: *GGWw* or *GgWw*. The best way to determine all possible phenotypes in the cross is to draw a Punnett square for both of these potential genotypes:

If the F_1 plant is *GGWw*:

	GW	GW	Gw	Gw
gw	GgWw	GgWw	Ggww	Ggww

Two genotypes are produced in equal ratios:
50% *GgWw* = green wrinkled phenotype
50% *Ggww* = green smooth

If the F_1 plant is *GgWw*:

	GW	Gw	gW	gw
gw	GgWw	Ggww	ggWw	ggww

Four genotypes are produced:
25% *GgWw* = green wrinkled phenotype
25% *Ggww* = green smooth
25% *ggWw* = yellow wrinkled
25% *ggww* = yellow smooth

[44] If yellow smooth progeny are observed, the F_1 plant must be *GgWw*.

[45] Without drawing a Punnett square, it is possible to see that all children must receive at least one *b* allele (from the father), and that 50% of the children will receive the *B* allele from the mother; thus, 50% of the children will be *Bb*. The odds of a boy are 50%. Therefore, the odds a child is both a boy and has the *Bb* genotype are, by the rule of multiplication, $0.5 \times 0.5 = 0.25$, or 25%.

6.4 LINKAGE

The traits that Mendel studied and based the law of independent assortment on were located on separate chromosomes. Genes that are located on the *same* chromosome may not display independent assortment, however. The failure of genes to display independent assortment is called **linkage**.

- If eye color is controlled by a gene on chromosome #11 and the hair color locus is located on chromosome #14, do these genes assort independently?[46]
- If the portion of chromosome #14 containing the hair color gene is translocated onto chromosome #11, will these genes still assort independently?[47]

If genes are located very close to each other on the same chromosome, then they will probably *not* be inherited independently of each other. Let's illustrate this with a pea gene for height and two alleles of the height gene, tall (*T*) and short (*t*), with the *T* allele dominant and the *t* allele recessive. If the height gene and the color gene are very near each other on the same chromosome, then the alleles of these genes on a specific chromosome will probably assort together into gametes during meiosis (Figure 11). This limits the possible combinations of the alleles in the gametes.

*Tt*G*g* Individual: Independent Assortment

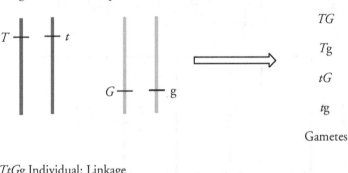

*Tt*G*g* Individual: Linkage

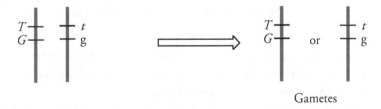

OR

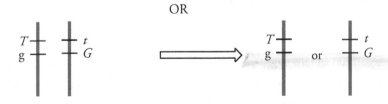

Figure 11   Linkage of Alleles during Meiosis

---

[46] Yes, they will. Assortment of nonhomologous chromosomes into gametes is random during meiosis.

[47] A translocation occurs when a piece of one chromosome is moved onto another chromosome. The two genes are then found on the same chromosome and may not assort independently.

- If the color gene and the height gene display linkage, is it possible to predict the possible gametes of a *TTgg* individual?[48] of a *TtGg* individual?[49]

To know how alleles that display linkage assort during meiosis, it may be necessary to know which alleles were on a chromosome together. As seen in Figure 11, there are two possible ways the height and color genes could be linked. The dominant alleles of two different genes can be linked together on the same chromosome (*TG*), the recessive alleles of two different genes can be linked (*tg*), or one dominant and one recessive allele can be linked (*Tg* and *tG*).

With genes that are found on the same chromosome, the design of a Punnett square is slightly different. The possible gametes are limited since they cannot assort independently. Consider a cross between a homozygous *ttgg* pea plant and a double-heterozygous plant with both dominant alleles on one chromosome and both recessive alleles located together on another chromosome. They can only make a limited number of different gametes, not the four possible combinations of alleles that would be found if the genes were on different chromosomes. A Punnett square will help to illustrate linkage in this example (Figure 12).

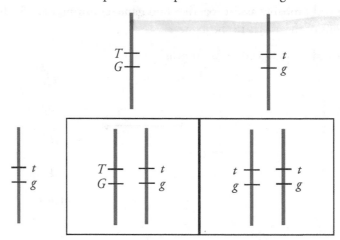

Figure 12   Assortment of Linked Genes

- What are the phenotypes of the F₁ progeny in the cross in Figure 12?[50]
- If a tall green pea from the F₁ progeny is crossed with a pure-breeding short yellow plant, what phenotypes will be observed and in what ratios?[51]
- If height and color genes were not linked, what ratios of phenotypes would be observed in a cross between a *TtGg* and a *ttgg* individual?[52]

---

[48] Yes. A *TTgg* individual can only make *Tg* gametes, regardless of whether the genes are on the same chromosome or not.

[49] No. To predict how these traits will assort, it is necessary to know which alleles are present together on the same chromosome.

[50] There are only two phenotypes: 50% tall green and 50% short yellow.

[51] The pure-breeding short yellow plant can only have *tg* gametes. The tall green plant can make only two types of alleles, the same gametes shown for its parent. The results of the backcross will be the same as for the original cross in Figure 11, with 50% tall green and 50% short yellow plants.

[52] The *ttgg* individual can make only *tg* gametes. The *TtGg* individual can make four different types of gametes if the genes are not linked: *TG*, *Tg*, *tG*, and *tg*. The genotypes and phenotypes of the cross will be 25% *TtGg* (tall green), 25% *Ttgg* (tall yellow), 25% *ttGg* (short green), and 25% *ttgg* (short yellow).

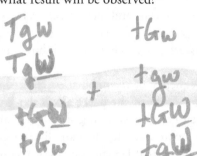

- Assume all of the characteristics already introduced for the height, color and shape pea genes that have been used as examples. The height and color genes are located near each other on the same chromosome and display complete linkage but the shape gene is located on a different chromosome. If an individual with a *TtGgWw* genotype and the *T* and *g* alleles on the same chromosome is crossed with a *ttGgWw* individual, what result will be observed?[53]
    - A. All tall peas will be wrinkled.
    - B. All wrinkled peas will be tall.
    - C. All yellow peas will be tall.
    - D. All tall peas will be yellow.

6.4

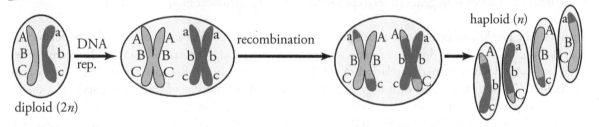

Linkage and Recombination

Linkage is the exception to the law of independent assortment. When genes are located on the same chromosome, they will display linkage and will not assort independently. Meiotic recombination provides the exception to linkage. During the formation of gametes, meiotic recombination between homologous chromosomes can separate alleles that were located on the same chromosome. In the example in Figure 13, three genes are located on the same chromosome. Prior to recombination, *ABC* were found on one chromosome and *abc* were found on the homologous chromosome. [What combinations of alleles will be found in gametes in the absence of recombination?[54]] Recombination produces new combinations of alleles not found in the parent and also allows genes located on the same chromosome to assort independently.

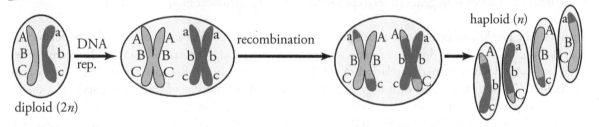

diploid (2n)   DNA rep.   recombination   haploid (n)

Figure 13   Recombination—Another Look

The example of the height and color genes in pea plants will help to illustrate linkage and the effects of recombination on patterns of inheritance. As before, the height and color genes are located on the same chromosome. There are two alleles of the height gene, dominant *T* (tall) and recessive *t* (short) and two alleles of the color gene, dominant *G* (green) and recessive *g* (yellow). The following cross is performed: A pure-breeding tall green plant is crossed with a pure-breeding short yellow plant. [What phenotypes are predicted in this cross if linkage is complete?[55]] A pea plant from this cross is then self-pollinated (crossed with itself) to produce an F$_2$ generation. [If linkage is complete, what genotypes and phenotypes will be

---

[53] The gene for shape (wrinkled vs. smooth) is on a different chromosome than the other two genes, so there is no correlation between the wrinkled trait and the other traits (eliminating choices A and B). To be yellow, a pea must be homozygous *gg*. One of the *g* alleles must come from the chromosome with *T* and *g* together, making all yellow plants tall (choice C is correct). Some of the *Tg* gametes will join with *tG* gametes from the *ttGg* individual, meaning that some plants are tall and green (choice D is wrong). Drawing a Punnett Square can help to solve this problem.

[54] *ABC* or *abc* genotypes

[55] Only one phenotype. The F$_1$ generation will all receive a *TG* chromosome from the pure-breeding tall green parent and a *tg* chromosome from the pure-breeding short yellow parent.

observed in the F₂ generation?[56] If the genes assort completely randomly, what genotypes and phenotypes will be observed in the F₂ generation?[57] The F₂ generation in this cross was observed to have the following plants: 30 tall green plants, 9 short yellow plants, 2 tall yellow plants, and 1 short green plant. [Which of these phenotypes are recombinant phenotypes?[58]] Often in a cross involving genes on the same chromosome, the result will be intermediate between independent assortment and complete linkage. The reason for this is that recombination occurs between the genes during meiosis of *some* of the gametes but not *all* of the gametes. [If it is known that two genes are located on the same chromosome but during a cross they assort completely randomly, how can this be?[59]]

The frequency of recombination between two genes on a chromosome is proportional to the physical distance between the genes along the linear length of the DNA molecule. [Does recombination occur between genes more frequently if they are near each other or far apart?[60]] The farther apart two genes are on a chromosome, the more likely recombination will occur between the genes during meiosis. If the genes are located far enough apart, recombination will occur so frequently between the genes that they will no longer display linkage and will assort as independently as if they were on separate chromosomes. The **frequency of recombination** is given as the *number of recombinant phenotypes* resulting from a cross *divided by the total number of progeny.*

$$\text{RF} = \text{recombination frequency} = \frac{\text{number of recombinants}}{\text{total number of offspring}}$$

Since the frequency of recombination is proportional to the physical distance of genes from each other, it can be used as a tool to map genes in relation to each other on chromosomes.

Example: The height and color gene in pea plants are on the same chromosome as a third gene for big or small flowers. The alleles of flower size are a dominant *B* (big) and a recessive *b* (small). The color gene (*G*, green or *g*, yellow) is studied in relation to the flower size gene. In the first cross, pure-breeding homozygous *BBGG* plants are crossed with *bbgg* plants. [What is the phenotype of the F₁ progeny?[61] If a small flower green plant is observed in the F₁ generation, was recombination responsible?[62]] An F₁ progeny is then crossed with a *bbgg* plant and the following phenotypes observed: 44 big flower green plants, 40 small flower yellow plants, 8 big flower yellow plants, and 8 small flower green plants.

---

[56] 75% tall green and 25% short yellow. Try a Punnett square to verify this result, remembering to assort alleles together into gametes.

[57] 9:3:3:1 of tall green, tall yellow, short green, and short yellow, respectively. This is a classical Mendelian ratio observed when heterozygotes at two alleles are crossed.

[58] The tall yellow and short green phenotypes would not be observed if linkage was complete (as in #56). The only way to produce these phenotypes is if a small number of gametes received chromosomes in which the *TG* and *tg* alleles were separated from each other by recombination, so these are the recombinant phenotypes.

[59] If the genes are on the same chromosome, but are far apart from one another, then recombination occurs frequently. The genes will assort randomly during meiosis and will not display any linkage even though they are on the same chromosome.

[60] The farther two genes are away from each other, the greater the odds that recombination will occur between them.

[61] The F₁ progeny are all *BbGg* genotype and therefore are big flower green plants.

[62] The small flower green phenotype could not be produced by recombination. These alleles do not exist together in either parent and so could not be recombined together in the gametes. This must be the result of mutation.

Handwritten notes: Parental: BbGg, bbgg (44), (40) — Recombinant: Bbgg, bbGg (8) (8) $\frac{16}{100}$ = 0.16

- Which of these are recombinant phenotypes?[63]
- What is the frequency of recombination between the genes?[64]
- What is the maximal frequency of recombination?[65] *50%*
- In another cross, the frequency of recombination between the flower size and height genes is examined and found to be 10 recombinant plants out of 100 progeny. Is the height gene or the color gene closer to the flower size gene?[66] *yes height*
- If the recombination frequencies are 0.16 between the height and color genes, 0.10 between the height and flower size genes, and 0.26 between the flower size and color genes, what is the order of the genes on the chromosome?[67] *B H G*
- Is it possible to map the distance between genes on the same chromosome even if they are so far apart that they assort independently?[68] *Yes!*
- Assume that hair color in humans is determined by a gene for which there are two alleles: *B* or brown, which is dominant, and *b* or blond, which is recessive. The hair color gene is located on the same chromosome as another gene that determines the strength of bones, and the two genes are very close together. The alleles of the bone strength gene are *S*, the dominant sturdy bone allele, and *s*, the recessive fragile bone allele. Jose and Tonya have dark hair and sturdy bones. One of their children has brown hair and fragile bones. One grandparent of Jose and one grandparent of Tonya had fragile bones and blond hair, while the remaining grandparents were homozygous for brown hair and sturdy bones. Which of the following is/ are true?[69]
  - I. The child of Jose and Tonya represents a recombinant phenotype. *True*
  - II. All of the children of Jose and Tonya must have fragile bones.
  - III. Jose and Tonya may have other children with blond hair and fragile bones.

  - A. I only
  - B. II only
  - C. I and III only
  - D. II and III only

6.4

Handwritten notes (right margin): $\frac{BS}{BS} \times \frac{bs}{bs}$; Jose + Tonya ⟹ BbSs × BbSs ; $\frac{BS}{bs} \times \frac{BS}{bs}$; $F_1 ⟹ \frac{3}{5}\frac{B}{B} + \frac{3}{5}\frac{B}{b} + \frac{b}{bs}$ (brown, sturdy) (blond, sturdy)

---

[63] Big flower yellow plants and small flower green plants can only be produced through recombination between the flower size and color genes.

[64] The frequency of recombination is 16 recombinant phenotypes out of 100 progeny = 16%.

[65] The maximal frequency of recombination would be when there as no linkage and the genes assorted independently. In this case there would be 25% big flower yellow plants and 25% small flower green plants, or 50% maximal frequency of recombination.

[66] There is less recombination between the height and flower size genes (10% frequency) than between the color and flower size genes (16%), so the height gene is closer to the flower size gene than the color gene is.

[67] The flower size and color genes have the most recombination between them, so they must be farthest apart, with the height gene in the middle.

[68] Yes, but it requires one or more genes located between the two genes. The distance between the two genes could not be mapped directly by measuring the frequency of recombination between them, but if the distance from both of them to a gene in the middle can be mapped, then the overall distance between the genes can be mapped. Whole chromosomes can be mapped this way.

[69] **Item I is true:** The simplest explanation is that the grandparent on each side passed on the fragile allele and the blond allele, but recombination occurred, so that the fragile and blond alleles assorted independently. **Item II is false:** Jose and Tonya both have the dominant sturdy bone gene in at least one copy, so some children are likely to have sturdy bones. **Item III is true:** Both Jose and Tonya may have one chromosome with the blond allele and the fragile bone allele linked. If so, a nonrecombinant phenotype would be blond/fragile. The answer is C.

6.5 INHERITANCE PATTERNS AND PEDIGREES

There are six inheritance patterns that you should be familiar with: autosomal recessive, autosomal domi-nant, mitochondrial, Y-linked, X-linked recessive and X-linked dominant. In this section, each will be described and then a summary table is presented.

Autosomal traits are caused by genetic variation on the autosomes (the 22 pairs of non-sex chromosomes in humans). These traits can be **autosomal dominant** (in which case a single copy of the allele will confer the trait or disease phenotype) or **autosomal recessive** (in which case two copies of the allele are required for the affected phenotype). Both tend to affect males and females equally; in other words, there is no sex bias for these traits.

There is a small, haploid DNA genome inside the mitochondria and humans inherit this genome from their mothers. This is because the sperm contributes only nuclear chromosomes to the zygote; the ovum contributes nuclear chromosomes and the rest of the cellular material including the organelles. There are some traits that are inherited via the mitochondrial genome, although these **mitochondrial traits** are rare. Luckily, they are fairly easy to spot because affected females have all affected offspring (sons and daugh-ters). Affected individuals must have an affected mother, and affected males cannot have any affected offspring. An individual cannot inherit mitochondrial traits from their father. Mitochondrial traits (like Y-linked traits and X-linked traits in human males) are an example of **hemizygosity**; the individual only has one copy of the chromosome in a diploid organism. Because of this, there is only one allele to keep track of for each individual. Genes encoded by the mitochondrial genome are usually given the prefix **mt** (for example, mt-*Atp6* is encoded in the mitochondrial genome and codes for a subunit of the ATP syn-thase). When working with inheritance patterns though, it is best to define the allele letters you are going to use and then use one letter per individual. For example, you could assign "*a*" as a normal individual and "*A*" as an affected individual. The assignment here is arbitrary since one allele is not dominant to the other (they are mutually exclusive since humans only have one mitochondrial genome). The key is to be consistent.

Traits that are determined by genes located on the X or Y chromosome are called **sex-linked traits** and display unusual patterns of inheritance. Traits encoded by genes on the Y chromosome (Y-linked traits) would only be passed from male parents to male children. [Would it be possible for a father to pass a Y-linked trait to female children?[70] Can males be carriers of recessive Y-linked traits without expressing them?[71]] Y-linked traits are quite rare, because the Y chromosome is small and contains a relatively small number of genes. Many of the genes on the Y-chromosome function in sex determination.

X-linked traits are observed quite frequently and can be X-linked recessive or X-linked dominant. There are several well-studied examples of X-linked recessive traits that are common in the human population; hemopilia is an example. Women are often carriers of X-linked recessive alleles but only express recessive X-linked traits when they are homozygous. Men are hemizygous for X-linked traits; they have only one copy of genes on the X chromosome. As a result, males *always* express recessive X-linked alleles. [From which parent do males receive X-linked traits?[72]] These traits tend to affect males more than females.

---

[70] No. Females never have a Y chromosome and so can never carry or express a Y-linked trait.

[71] No. Y-linked traits are carried in only one copy, since there is only one Y chromosome per cell. If a male carries a recessive Y-linked trait, he will express it.

[72] Since males receive their X chromosome from their mother (and their Y chromosome from their father), they receive X-linked traits from their mother.

Red-green colorblindness, an X-linked trait, is caused by a defect in a visual pigment gene on the X chromosome. The allele that is responsible for colorblindness is a pigment gene that does not produce functional protein. [Is the colorblindness allele recessive or dominant?[73]] The color-blindness allele, like many recessive traits carried in the population, is not expressed in heterozygotes. Colorblindness is unusual in women but fairly common in men. Females have two copies of the gene, so will not express the trait if they are heterozygotes, while males have only one X chromosome and so will always express the allele whenever they receive it. [A man is colorblind, and his wife is homozygous normal for genes encoding visual pigment proteins. What will be the phenotypes and genotypes of sons and of daughters of this couple?[74]]

X-linked dominant traits are harder to identify. A female will display an X-linked dominant phenotype if she has one or two copies of the allele on her X chromosomes. A male will express the phenotype if he inherited the affected allele from his mother. While these traits still tend to affect males more than females, this trend is less obvious than for X-linked recessive traits.

Table 1 on the following page summarizes the six inheritance patterns you should be familiar with, and lists some strategies you can use to distinguish between them.

---

[73] An allele that encodes inactive protein or no protein is generally recessive, since the gene's function can be compensated for by the remaining normal copy of the gene.

[74] Sons will have a normal phenotype and carry one copy of the normal gene. Daughters will carry one normal gene and one recessive color-blindness allele and will have the normal phenotype.

Inheritance Pattern	Identification Techniques	Unaffected Genotypes	Affected Genotypes
Autosomal recessive	• Can skip generations (affected individuals can have unaffected parents) • Number of affected males is usually equal to the number of affected females	AA Aa	aa
Autosomal dominant	• Does not skip generations (affected individuals must have an affected parent) • Number of affected males is usually equal to number of affected females • An affected parent passes the trait to either all or half of offspring	aa	AA Aa
Mitochondrial	• Maternal inheritance • Affected female has all affected children • Affected male cannot pass the trait onto his children • Unaffected female cannot have affected children	a	A
Y-linked	• Affects male only; females never have the trait • Affected father has all affected sons • Unaffected father cannot have an affected son	XY^a	XY^A
X-linked recessive	• Can skip generations (affected individuals can have unaffected parents) • Tend to affect males more than females • Unaffected females can have affected sons • Affected female has all affected sons, but can have both affected and unaffected daughters	X^AX^A X^AX^a X^AY	X^aX^a X^aY
X-linked dominant	• Hardest to identify • Does not skip generations (affected individuals must have an affected parent) • Usually affects males more than females • Affected fathers have all affected daughters • Affected mothers can have unaffected sons (and unaffected daughters), and pass the trait equally to sons and daughters	X^aX^a X^aY	X^AX^A X^AX^a X^AY

Table 1 Summary of Inheritance Patterns

- Two mouse genes located on the X chromosome are being studied. The alleles of the genes are:
  Fuzzy hair: F, dominant (normal hair) and f, recessive (fuzzy hair)
  Extra toes: E, dominant (extra toes), and e, recessive (normal toes)
  A female with normal hair and extra toes is crossed with a male with normal hair and extra toes. The progeny have the following phenotypes:

Phenotype	Male	Female
Normal hair, extra toes	46	100
Normal hair, normal toes	4	0
Fuzzy hair, extra toes	5	0
Fuzzy hair, normal toes	45	0

Which one of the following is true concerning this experiment?[75]
  A. Males have a higher rate of recombination than females do.
  B. In the absence of recombination, all males would have normal hair and extra toes.
  C. The rate of recombination on the X chromosome is the same in males and females.
  D. Both males and females have recombinant genotypes, but only males have recombinant phenotypes.

Often it is not possible to perform controlled genetic crosses to ascertain the nature of inheritance of a trait, particularly when people are involved. In these cases, families can be studied to determine the pattern of inheritance. Researchers organize the information learned from families into **pedigrees**, which are charts depicting inheritance of a trait (Figure 14). By studying the pedigree of families, researchers can determine the pattern of inheritance of a gene, whether it is linked to other genes, and whether an individual is likely to pass on a trait to their offspring. Pedigrees follow certain conventions in how they are drawn:

1) Males are represented by squares and females by circles.
2) A cross (mating) between a male and female is represented by a horizontal line connecting them.
3) Offspring from a cross are connected to their parents by a vertical line, and to each other by a horizontal line with vertical branches for each sibling.
4) Offspring of uknown gender (unborn children) are represented by a diamond shape.
5) Individuals afflicted with a trait being studied are shaded in; unaffected or normal individuals are not shaded in.

Many pedigrees make a common assumption: individuals mating into the family (i.e., individuals for which you have no information on their parents or grandparents) are assumed to be homozygous normal unless their phenotype tells you differently. The basis of this assumption is that the traits being studied

---

[75] The genotype of the male parent must be X^{FE} Y. The predominance of the normal hair-extra toes and fuzzy hair-normal toes phenotypes in the F_1 generation indicates that the female parent must have one X chromosome with both dominant alleles together, and one X chromosome with both recessive alleles together, in other words, her genotype must be $X^{FE} X^{fe}$. The fuzzy hair-extra toes and normal hair-normal toes phenotypes are much less common and must be the result of recombination in the female parent, producing X^{Fe} and X^{fE} chromosomes. Note that recombination between the X and Y chromosomes in males is not possible due to the fact that the X and Y carry different genes (choices A and C are wrong). If recombination had not occurred in the female parent, all F_1 males would have received either X^{FE} or X^{fe}, giving both normal hair-extra toes and fuzzy hair-normal toes phenotypes (choice B is wrong). Choice **D** is the correct answer: The F_1 females must also have recombinant genotypes on the X chromosomes they received from their mother, but every F_1 female also received both dominant alleles on the X chromosome they received from their father. Thus only the dominant phenotypes are seen in the F_1 females.

are usually relatively rare in the human population and therefore it is most likely that a non-family member is homozygous for the wild type allele.

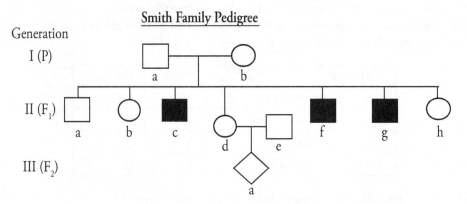

Figure 14   A Pedigree

Once drawn, a pedigree can be analyzed as follows:

STEP 1:

Is the allele that causes the trait dominant or is it recessive? Recessive traits commonly skip generations (affected individuals can have unaffected parents), but dominant traits do not (affected individuals must have at least one affected parent).

STEP 2:

Is the gene involved carried on a sex chromosome (sex-linked)? If so, there tends to be an unequal distribution of affected males (more) vs. affected females (fewer). If the numbers of affected males and females are approximately equal, the gene is most likely autosomal.

STEP 3:

If the disease is sex-linked, is it on the X or the Y chromosome? Diseases linked to the Y chromosome will show father-to-son transmission, while diseases linked to the X chromosome will not.

STEP 4:

Check for mitochondrial inheritance. Affected females will have all affected children, but affected males cannot pass the trait on.

STEP 5:

Figure out the genotypes and calculate the probabilities of inheritance where necessary. When writing genotypes for sex-linked traits, make sure to include the chromosomes (e.g., $X^A Y$, or $X^A X^a$, etc.). When writing genotypes for autosomal traits, make sure NOT to include the chromosomes (e.g., DD or Dd, etc.).

STEP 6:

If more than one trait is involved, go through Steps 1–5 for each.

- In the pedigree in Figure 14, the darkened squares represent individuals afflicted with a certain genetic disease. This disease is most likely caused by:[76]
    - A. a dominant allele.
    - B. an autosomal recessive allele.
    - C. an X-linked recessive allele.
    - D. a Y-linked allele.

- In the pedigree in Figure 14, what is the probability that IIIa will have the disease?[77]
    - A. If male, IIIa will have the disease.
    - B. Overall, there is a 1/8 chance that IIIa will have the disease.
    - C. Overall, there is a 1/4 chance that IIIa will have the disease.
    - D. IIIa will not have the disease.

Below there are example pedigrees for six modes of inheritance (X-linked recessive, X-linked dominant, autosomal recessive, autosomal dominant, mitochondrial, and Y-linked). For each pedigree, determine which mode of inheritance is displayed.

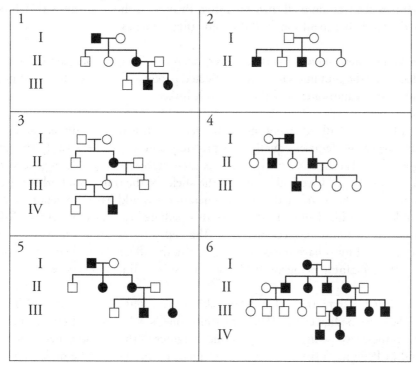

---

[76] Since the affected individuals have unaffected parents, the disease is most likely recessive (choice A is wrong), and since the affected individuals are all male, it is most likely sex-linked (choice B is wrong). There is no father-to-son transmission (all affected males have an unaffected father), so the disease is X-linked (choice C is correct and choice D is wrong).

[77] The disease is X-linked recessive, and IIe (IIIa's father) is not affected, so IIe cannot pass the allele on. Thus the probability of IIIa getting the disease depends on the genotype of IId (she would have to be a carrier) and what she passes on to IIIa. It also depends on the gender of IIIa; females would not be affected because they would have to receive the allele from both IId and IIe, and IIe does not carry the disease allele. Bottom line, in order for IIIa to get the disease, IId would have to be a carrier, would have to pass the disease allele on, and IIIa would have to be male. The probability of IId being a carrier is 1/2; we know she received a good X chromosome from her father Ia (all he has is a good X chromosome), and the probability she received the affected X chromosome from her mother (Ib) is 1/2. The probability she passes the bad X chromosome on to IIIa is 1/2; she has one good X and one bad X. The probability that IIIa is male is 1/2. Finally, we can use the rule of multiplication to determine the overall probability: 1/2 × 1/2 × 1/2 = 1/8 overall probability (choice B is correct and choices C and D are wrong). Note that choice A is wrong because being male does not guarantee the disease; IIIa could be male (get the Y chromosome from IIe) and still be unaffected (get the good X chromosome from IId).

Answers

1) autosomal dominant
2) X-linked recessive
3) autosomal recessive
4) Y-linked
5) X-linked dominant
6) mitochondrial inheritance

Explanations

The easiest inheritance patterns to spot are mitochondrial (passed from mothers to all offspring) and Y-linked (passed from fathers to sons, and females are never affected). Let's start by finding these two. Since Pedigree 6 shows a trait with maternal inheritance, this must be mitochondrial inheritance. The affected father in generation II does not pass the trait to any of his children, but the affected mothers in generations I, II and III pass the trait onto all their offspring. Pedigree 4 shows a trait with Y-linked inheritance. The trait is passed from father to all sons and does not affect females.

Next, Pedigrees 2 and 3 both show traits that skips generations. That is, there are individuals on the pedigree that are affected by the trait but who have unaffected parents. Therefore, these two pedigrees must be for recessive traits. One is autosomal and the other is X-linked.

Since the trait on Pedigree 2 affects males more than females, it is likely X-linked, and since the trait on Pedigree 3 affects males and females equally, it is probably autosomal. Let's verify this by looking more closely at Pedigree 3. If this trait is X-linked recessive, then the affected female in generation II must have the genotype $X^a X^a$, and would have had to receive the allele for the trait from both her parents. However, for an X-linked recessive, the unaffected male in generation I would have the genotype $X^A Y$, and would only have X^A to donate to his daughter. Therefore this pedigree cannot represent an X-linked recessive trait; it must represent an autosomal recessive trait. The male in generation I must have the genotype Aa, the female in generation I must have the genotype Aa, and the affected female in generation II must have the genotype aa. The remaining pedigree, Pedigree 2, must be X-linked recessive.

Finally, Pedigrees 1 and 5 show traits that do not skip generations. That is, affected individuals have affected parents. These are pedigrees for dominant traits; one is X-linked and one is autosomal. The only difference between these two pedigrees is the middle daughter in the second generation; in Pedigree 1 she is unaffected and in Pedigree 5 she is affected. Let's focus on her father (the male in generation I) since this is where she gets the allele for the trait. If the trait is X-linked dominant, the male in generation I would be $X^A Y$; thus all females in generation II would inherit X^A from their father, and all of them would be affected. Since the middle daughter in Pedigree I is not affected, Pedigree 1 must show autosomal dominance and the pedigree for the X-linked dominant trait must be Pedigree 5.

6.6 POPULATION GENETICS

Mendelian genetics describes the inheritance of traits in the progeny of specific individuals. For the purposes of large topics such as natural selection and evolution, however, the more relevant issue is not the inheritance of traits from individuals but in a whole population from one generation to another. **Population genetics** describes the inheritance of traits in populations over time. The word *population* has a specific meaning in this setting: *a population consists of members of a species that mate and reproduce with each other.* [If a group of sea turtles lives most of the year dispersed over a large area of ocean without contact with each other but congregate once a year to reproduce, is this group a population?[78]] To a population geneticist, each individual is merely a temporary carrier of the alleles in a population.

In population genetics, the units of genetic inheritance are alleles of genes, just as in Mendelian genetics. However, in population genetics alleles are examined across the entire population rather than in individuals. The sum total of all genetic information in a population is called the **gene pool.** [For an autosomal gene in a population of 2000 individuals, how many copies of the gene are present in the gene pool?[79]] The frequency of an allele in a population is a key variable used to describe the gene pool. [If there are 5000 hippos in a population, out of which there are 100 homozygotes of an autosomal allele *h* and 400 heterozygotes, what is the frequency of the *h* allele in the population?[80] If 20% of the population is heterozygous for an allele *Q* and 10% is homozygous, what will be the frequency of the allele in the population?[81]]

Hardy-Weinberg in Population Genetics

Population genetics does not simply describe the gene pool of a population but attempts to predict the gene pool of a population in the future. The **Hardy-Weinberg law** states that the *frequencies of alleles in the gene pool of a population will not change over time*, provided that a number of assumptions are true:

1) There is no mutation.
2) There is no migration.
3) There is no natural selection.
4) There is random mating.
5) The population is sufficiently large to prevent random drift in allele frequencies.

What Hardy-Weinberg means at the molecular level is that segregation of alleles, independent assortment, and recombination during meiosis can alter the combinations of alleles in gametes but cannot increase or decrease the frequency of an allele in the gametes of one individual or the gametes of the population as a whole.

---

[78] Yes. A population does not need to live with each other, only to reproduce sexually with each other.

[79] There are two copies of the gene in each of the 2000 individuals, for a total of 4000 copies in the gene pool.

[80] The allele frequency is the number of copies of a specific allele divided by the total number of copies of the gene in the population. If there are 5000 hippos, and each has 2 copies of the gene, there are 10,000 copies of the gene in the population. There are 100 homozygotes of the *h* allele, each with 2 copies of it, and 400 heterozygotes with one *h* allele, for a total of 600 *h* alleles in the population. Thus, the frequency of the *h* allele is 600/10000 = 0.06.

[81] In this case, the number of individuals in the population is not provided, but it is not needed. The total number of alleles is 100%. The frequency of the allele is 0.5 × (20% heterozygotes) + 10% homozygotes = 20%.

- If 100 homozygous green pea plants and 100 homozygous yellow pea plants are crossed, 1000 green pea plants are produced. Does this mean that the yellow alleles disappeared from the population?[82]
- What is the frequency of the yellow allele in the gene pool of the progeny?[83]
- If the green peas from the F$_1$ generation are allowed to mate randomly within the population, and there is no mutation, migration, natural selection, or random drift, what will be the frequency of the yellow allele in the population after four generations?[84]
- If two genes are closely linked on the same chromosome, will Hardy-Weinberg still apply to these genes?[85]
- According to Hardy-Weinberg, what will happen to the frequency of the yellow allele if predation occurs on yellow plants, but yellow plants attract bees more successfully?[86]

The Hardy-Weinberg law has also been translated into mathematical terms. Assuming that there are two alleles of a gene in a population, the letter p is used to represent the frequency of the dominant allele, and the letter q is used to represent the frequency of the recessive allele. Since there are only two alleles, the following fundamental equation must be true:

$$p + q = 1$$

Based on allele frequency, it is possible to calculate the proportion of genotypes in a population. Take a situation where the frequency of a dominant allele, G, equals p and the frequency of a recessive allele, g, equals q. If the equation above is squared on both sides, it becomes:

$$(p + q)^2 = 1$$

$$p^2 + 2pq + q^2 = 1$$

where

$$p^2 = \text{the frequency of the } GG \text{ genotype}$$

$$2pq = \text{the frequency of the } Gg \text{ genotype}$$

$$q^2 = \text{the frequency of the } gg \text{ genotype}$$

---

[82] The yellow alleles are still there (but in the heterozygous state) so they do not appear in the phenotype.

[83] The frequency of the yellow allele will be 50%, just as it was in the parents. None of the alleles in a population were destroyed, so the frequency is the same as in the parental generation.

[84] According to Hardy-Weinberg, there will be no change in the frequency of the allele. The frequency of the yellow allele will still be 50% after four generations.

[85] Yes. Independent assortment is not a requirement of Hardy-Weinberg. Allele frequencies for the genes will still remain constant, regardless of the extent of recombination between the genes, as long as the assumptions of Hardy-Weinberg hold true.

[86] Hardy-Weinberg says nothing about this situation. Once the assumptions no longer hold true, Hardy-Weinberg no longer applies.

- If the frequency of the G allele is 0.25 in a population of 1000 mice, determine the number of individuals who are Gg heterozygotes if there is random mating but no migration, mutation, random drift, or natural selection.[87]
- If allele frequencies in a population are constant, and genotype frequencies can be calculated from allele frequencies, how will genotype frequencies vary over time?[88]

After one generation, a population will reach **Hardy-Weinberg equilibrium**, in which allele frequencies no longer change. Since allele frequencies do not change, and genotype frequencies can be calculated from allele frequencies, it follows that genotype frequencies also do not change over time. [If 100 green peas (GG) and 100 yellow peas (gg) are allowed to mate randomly, will the genotype frequencies in the next generation (F_1) be the same?[89] If not, why not?[90] If the plants are allowed to mate randomly for another generation (F_2), will the genotype frequencies in the F_1 and F_2 generations be the same?[91]]

Hardy-Weinberg in the Real World

Hardy-Weinberg requires a number of assumptions in order to be true. The assumptions, as presented earlier, are that in a population there is random mating and no mutation, migration, natural selection, or random drift. Thus, Hardy-Weinberg describes a highly idealized set of conditions required to prevent alleles from being added or removed from a population. In reality, it is not possible for a population to meet all of the conditions required by Hardy-Weinberg.

1) **Mutation**: Mutation is inevitable in a population. Even if there are no chemical mutagens or radiation, inherent errors by DNA polymerase would over time cause mutations and introduce new alleles in a population.

2) **Migration**: If migration occurs, animals leaving or entering the population will carry alleles with them and disturb the Hardy-Weinberg equilibrium.

3) **Natural Selection**: For there to be no natural selection, there would have to be unlimited resources, no predation, no disease, and so on. This is not a set of conditions encountered in the real world.

4) **Non-random Mating**: If individuals pick their mates preferentially based on one or more traits, alleles that cause those traits will be passed on preferentially from one generation to another.

5) **Random Drift**: If a population becomes very small, it cannot contain as great a variety of alleles. In a very small population, random events can alter allele frequencies significantly and have a large influence on future generations.

---

[87] If the frequency of the G allele (p) is 0.25, then the frequency of the g allele (q) must be 0.75, since $p + q = 1$. The frequency of the heterozygotes in the population will be $2pq = 2(0.25)(0.75) = 0.375$. Therefore, the number of individuals in this population who are heterozygotes will be $0.375 \times 1000 = 375$.

[88] Genotype frequencies as well as allele frequencies will remain constant according to Hardy-Weinberg.

[89] No. The next generation will include GG, Gg, and gg genotypes.

[90] The population was not at Hardy-Weinberg equilibrium to start out.

[91] Yes. A population reaches Hardy-Weinberg equilibrium after one generation. The F_2 generation (and all generations after that) will have the same genotype frequencies as the F_1 generation.

6.7 EVOLUTION BY NATURAL SELECTION

At one time, life on Earth was generally viewed as static and unchanging, but we now know that this is not the case. Over the geologic span of Earth's history, many species have arisen, changed over millions of years, given rise to new species, and died out. These changes in life on Earth are called **evolution**. Although he did not arrive at his theory alone, Charles Darwin played an important role in shaping modern thought by proposing natural selection as the mechanism that drives evolution. **Natural selection** is an interaction between organisms and their environment that causes differential reproduction of different phenotypes and thereby alters the gene pool of a population. In essence the theory of evolution by natural selection is this:

1) In a population, there are heritable differences between individuals.
2) Heritable traits (alleles of genes) produce traits (phenotypes) that affect the ability of an organism to survive and have offspring.
3) Some individuals have phenotypes that allow them to survive longer, be healthier, and have more offspring than others.
4) Individuals with phenotypes that allow them to have more offspring will pass on their alleles more frequently than those with phenotypes that have fewer offspring.
5) Over time, those alleles that lead to more offspring are passed on more frequently and become more abundant, while other alleles become less abundant in the gene pool.
6) Changes in allele frequency are the basis of evolution in species and populations.

To put it simply, evolution occurs when natural selection acts on genetic variation to drive changes in the genetic composition of a population. A key term in evolution is **fitness**. In evolutionary terms, fitness is not how well an animal is physically adapted to a niche in the environment, or how well it can feed itself, but how successful it is in passing on its alleles to future generations. The way to have greater fitness is by having more offspring that pass on their alleles to future generations of the population. Some species achieve greater fitness through sheer numbers of progeny produced, who are then left to fend for themselves. Other species have fewer progeny, but protect and nurture the young to maturity.

- If an allele of a gene causes cancer in elderly polar bears after their reproductive years have passed, how will it affect the fitness of bears carrying the allele?[92]
- If a recessive allele causes sterility in homozygotes, how will it affect the fitness of heterozygotes?[93]
- A group of mice are infected with recombinant virus in bone marrow cells that allows the mice to live longer. The mice are then released into a wild population. Will natural selection act to increase the life span of the population?[94]
- Which of the following will have greater fitness: A fish that has two offspring and protects and nurtures its young to maturity, or a fish that has 10 offspring and abandons them, resulting in the death of 8 young fish before maturity?[95]

---

[92] The allele will not affect fitness. The bears will only be affected at a time when they can no longer have offspring, so it will not affect the ability of bears to transmit their alleles to future generations.

[93] If the allele is truly recessive, it will not affect fitness at all. Natural selection can act only on phenotypes, not genotypes.

[94] No. Natural selection only acts on heritable traits. Infected bone marrow cells will not be passed on in the germ line to the next generation and so the long life span of these mice is not a heritable trait.

[95] The fish will technically have the same fitness, since both will contribute to the gene pool of future generations equally.

- The recessive allele that causes cystic fibrosis is strongly selected against in modern society, since individuals with this disease often die before sexual maturity. However, the frequency of the allele takes many generations to decrease in the population. Why?[96]
- A certain genetic disease is caused by a recessive allele. In the absence of effective therapy, homozygous individuals with this allele generally die before reaching sexual maturity. The allele also protects heterozygous individuals against several life-threatening viral diseases. If a medicine is found that provides a complete remedy for the disease, allowing individuals with the disease to live an entirely normal life, which of the following statements describes what will happen to the frequency of the allele in the population after that time?[97]
  - A. The frequency of the allele will decrease.
  - B. The frequency of the allele will remain constant.
  - C. The frequency of the allele will increase.
  - D. It is not possible to predict the future frequency of the allele.

6.7

Sources of Genetic Diversity

Natural selection acts on the genetic diversity in a population to alter allele frequencies, causing evolution. Genetic diversity in a population is a requirement for natural selection to occur. [If a population of sea otters contains only one allele of a gene that protects against cold, can natural selection drive evolution of this trait?[98] Can natural selection cause new alleles to appear in the population?[99]] Natural selection does not introduce genetic diversity, however; it can act only on existing diversity to alter allele frequencies.

There are two sources of genetic variation in a population: *new alleles* and *new combinations of existing alleles*. New alleles are the result of mutations in the genome. New combinations of alleles are generated during sexual reproduction as a result of independent assortment, recombination and segregation during meiosis. By increasing and maintaining genetic variation in a population, sexual reproduction allows for greater capacity for adaptation of a population to changing environmental conditions.

- Do new alleles in a population generally confer greater or lesser fitness on an individual carrying them?[100]

---

[96] Natural selection acts on phenotypes, not genotypes. Even if the allele is lethal in homozygotes, heterozygotes will not be selected against if the allele is not expressed. It takes many generations for deleterious recessive alleles to decrease in frequency in a population.

[97] The correct answer is **C**. Homozygotes have low fitness in the absence of medicine, while heterozygotes have increased fitness due to their resistance to viral disease. In the absence of the medicine, natural selection tends to reduce the frequency of the allele by removing individuals who are homozygous but tends to increase the frequency of the allele through the higher fitness of heterozygotes. Over time these opposing selection pressures can be balanced to keep the allele at a relatively constant frequency. If medicine removes the selection against homozygotes, then the heterozygotes with the increased fitness cause to allele frequency to increase over time.

[98] If there is only one allele, then there is no variability that natural selection can act on, and no way that allele frequencies can change to cause evolution.

[99] No. Natural selection can only alter the frequency of existing alleles, not create new alleles.

[100] New alleles caused by mutation generally render gene products less active or even inactive. Animals have adapted over long periods of time to have most gene products function in the optimal manner, so most changes are harmful rather than beneficial.

- If a mutation occurs in a muscle cell of an individual who then has many progeny, does this mutation increase genetic variation in the population?[101]
- Does mitosis contribute to the genetic variation in a population?[102]
- If a population of flowers loses the ability to reproduce sexually and reproduces only asexually, how will this affect natural selection in the population?[103]
- Plants that are pollinated by insects sometimes have physical features of the flower that prevent self-pollination. What is the advantage to the plant of preventing self-pollination?[104]
- Which one of the following can create new alleles in a population?[105]
  - A. Non-random mating
  - B. Random drift
  - C. Recombination
  - D. Deletion

Modes of Natural Selection

Natural selection can occur in many different manners and have different effects in a population. The following are a few examples:

1) **Directional Selection:** Polygenic traits often follow a bell-shaped curve of expression, with most individuals clustered around the average and some members of a population trailing off in either direction away from the average. If natural selection removes those at one extreme, the population average over time will move in the other direction. Example: Giraffes get taller as all short giraffes die for lack of food.

2) **Divergent Selection:** Rather than removing the extreme members in the distribution of a trait in a population, natural selection removes the members near the average, leaving those at either end. Over time divergent selection will split the population in two and perhaps lead to a new species. Example: Small deer are selected for because they can hide, and large deer are selected because they can fight, but mid-sized deer are too big to hide and too small to fight.

3) **Stabilizing Selection:** Both extremes of a trait are selected against, driving the population closer to the average. Example: Birds that are too large or too small are eliminated from a population because they cannot mate.

---

[101] No. Mutation must occur in the germ line to introduce a new allele into a population. A mutation in a somatic cell cannot be passed on to the next generation.

[102] No. Mitosis can only copy a cell into an identical cell; it is not involved in creating new combinations of alleles in the same manner as meiosis.

[103] If the flowers can only reproduce asexually, then they have lost the ability of meiosis to generate new combinations of alleles and new genetic variation for natural selection to act on.

[104] Self-pollination reduces genetic variability. More variability is maintained in the population if different individuals mate, making new combinations of alleles.

[105] Nonrandom mating and random drift will alter allele frequencies but do not create new alleles (A and B are incorrect). Recombination will not alter allele frequencies or create new alleles, but create new combinations of alleles (C is wrong). The correct answer is **D**. Only mutation of the genome can create new alleles. A deletion can create a new allele, even if the new allele is a truncated gene product or does not express any gene product at all.

4) **Artificial Selection:** Humans intervene in the mating of many animals and plants, using artificial selection to achieve desired traits through controlled mating. Example: The pets and crop plants we have are the result of many generations of artificial selection.

5) **Sexual Selection:** Animals often do not choose mates randomly, but have evolved elaborate rituals and physical displays that play a key role in attracting and choosing a mate. Example: Some birds have bright plumage to attract a mate, even at the cost of increased predation.

6) **Kin Selection:** Natural selection does not always act on individuals. Animals that live socially often share alleles with other individuals and will sacrifice themselves for the sake of the alleles they share with another individual. Example: A female lion sacrifices herself to save her sister's children.

6.8   THE SPECIES CONCEPT AND SPECIATION

A **species** is a group of organisms which are capable of reproducing with each other sexually. (Other criteria, such as morphology, are used to classify species that only reproduce asexually.) [What's the difference between a population and a species?[106]] Two individuals are not members of the same biological species if they cannot mate and produce fit offspring. [When a horse mates with a donkey a mule is born. Mules are healthy animals with long life spans, but they are sterile. Are horses and donkeys members of the same species?[107]] **Reproductive isolation** keeps existing species separate. There are two types of reproductive isolation: **prezygotic** and **postzygotic**.

Prezygotic barriers prevent the formation of a hybrid zygote. Such barriers may be *ecological* (e.g., individuals who could otherwise mate are separated by a river), *temporal* (individuals mate at different times of the year), *mechanical* (e.g., Great Danes and Chihuahuas cannot mate), *behavioral* (some species require special rituals before mating can occur), or *gametic* (e.g., the sperm of a cat could not fertilize the egg of a dog due to incompatibilities in the sperm-egg recognition system, discussed in Chapter 11). *Postzygotic* barriers to hybridization prevent the development, survival, or reproduction of hybrid individuals (as in the example of the horse and donkey; the fact that the mule is sterile prevents continuation of the hybrid).

The creation of new species is known as **speciation**. An important premise in modern biology is that all species come from pre-existing species. *Cladogenesis* is branching speciation (*clado* is from the Greek for branch), where one species diversifies and becomes two or more new species. *Anagenesis* is when one biological species simply becomes another by changing so much that if an individual were to go back in time, it would be unable to reproduce sexually with its ancestors. One type of cladogenesis, *allopatric isolation*, is initiated by geographical isolation. Over time, geographical isolation leads to reproductive isolation. *Sympatric* speciation occurs when a species gives rise to a new species in the same geographical area, such as through divergent selection.

---

[106] Members of a species *can* mate and produce fit offspring. Members of a population *do*. Remember it this way: A population is a subset of a species.

[107] No, since their offspring are unfit (unable to reproduce).

Cladogenesis has left traces which taxonomists use to classify organisms. **Homologous structures** are physical features shared by two different species as a result of a common ancestor. For example, bird wings have five bony supports which resemble distorted human fingers, and dog paws also resemble distorted human hands. The explanation is that dogs, birds, and people all have a common ancestor which had five-toed feet. **Analogous structures** serve the same function in two different species, but *not* due to common ancestry. The flagellum of the human sperm and bacterial flagella are an example; they have entirely different structures from different organisms yet play the same role in motility. **Convergent evolution** is when two different species come to possess many analogous structures due to similar selective pressures. For example, bats and birds appear very similar even though bats are mammals. The opposite of convergent evolution is **divergent evolution**, in which divergent selection causes cladogenesis. **Parallel evolution** describes the situation in which two species go through similar evolutionary changes due to similar selective pressures. For example, in an ice age, all organisms would be selected for their ability to tolerate cold.

6.8

6.9 TAXONOMY

Taxonomy is the science of biological classification, originated by Carolus Linnaeus in the eighteenth century. He devised the **binomial classification** system we use today, in which each organism is given two names: genus and species. The binomial name of an organism is written in italics (or is underlined) with the genus capitalized and the species not, as in *Homo sapiens* (man the wise). There are 8 principal taxonomic categories: **domain, kingdom, phylum, class, order, family, genus, and species**.[108] You should know how humans are classified and the defining characteristics of each category. Table 1 on the following page provides a general summary. Table 2 summarizes human taxonomy. We will not discuss the characteristics of our genus and species.

Domain	Bacteria	Archaea	Eukarya			
Kingdom	(formerly Monera)		Protista	Fungi	Plantae	Animalia
Cell wall	peptidoglycan	polysaccharides and proteins, but no peptidoglycan	+/–, varied	chitin	cellulose	none
Organelles	none	none	all are eukaryotes			
Chromosomes	1 circular ds DNA	1 circular ds DNA	several linear ds DNA chromosomes			
Life cycle	asexual repro. (binary fission)	asexual repro. (binary fission)	varied (some sexual)	sexual repro., multicellular form haploid	sexual with *n* & *2n* multicellular forms	sexual w/ diploid multicellular form only
Cellular motility	flagella	flagella	amoeboid or flagellar	non-motile	some flagellated sperm	amoeboid or flagellar
Cilia/flagella	unique structure	unique structure	characteristic 9 + 2 arrangement of microtubules			
Nutrition	varied, absorptive	varied, absorptive	varied	chemo-hetero., absorptive	most photoauto. w/ chlorophyll	chemo-hetero., ingestive
Glycolysis/ATP	All living organisms perform glycolysis & use ATP. All kingdoms contain at least some members which perform oxidative phosphorylation.					
Examples	bacteria & blue-green algae	Archaea (extremophiles)	*Plasmodium* (causes malaria), plankton, algae	yeasts, molds, mushrooms	trees, flowers, mosses	mammals, birds, reptiles, worms, insects, sponges

Table 2 Taxonomic Characteristics

---

[108] A mnemonic goes: "Dumb King Philip Came Over From Greece Sunday" (or "Dumb King Phil Came Over For Great...").

Category	Human	Characteristics
Domain	**Eukarya**	See Table 1
Kingdom	**Animalia**	See Table 2
Phylum	**Chordata**	Possess notochord, dorsal hollow nerve cord, and pharyngeal gill slits at some time in embryonic development.
Subphylum	**Vertebrata**	bilateral symmetry, cephalization, endoskeleton w/ vertebral column, four limbs (or fins), 2 or 4-chambered heart & closed circulatory system, respiratory system, excretory system w/kidneys, mostly separate sexes
Class	**Mammalia**	hair, 4 limbs, 4-chambered heart, diaphragm for resp., mammary glands, internal fertilization, some have placental development
Order	**Primates**	well-developed cerebral cortex, opposable thumbs, omnivorous, forward-facing eyes
Family	**Hominidae**	erect posture, intelligence, long period of parental care, cooperation

Table 3   Human Taxonomy

6.9

Regarding subphylum Vertebrata: *Cephalization* refers to the development of a head region with a brain and sensory organs. Bilateral symmetry contrasts the radial symmetry of organisms such as starfish and the asymmetry of primitive animals such as sponges. Our bony endoskeleton contrasts the chitinous[109] exoskeleton of phylum Arthropoda (insects, spiders, crustaceans such as lobsters). The following table (Table 4) and Figure 15 will give you perspective on subphylum Vertebrata.

Class	Characteristics	Examples
Agnatha	jawless fishes, similar to ancestral vertebrates	lampreys
Chondrichthyes	cartilaginous fish; not our ancestors (side-branch from Agnatha)	sharks
Osteichthyes	bony fish, ancestors of amphibians	tuna, bass
Amphibia	water-dwelling larvae, land-dwelling adult, respiration: lungs and/or skin, ancestors of reptiles	salamanders, frogs
Reptilia	land-dwellers with 4 limbs, respiration: lungs, embryo surrounded by amnion, born in shelled egg or live, ancestors of birds and mammals	lizards, snakes
Aves	2 wings + 2 legs, respiration: lungs, endothermic, shelled amniotic eggs, descended from reptiles	birds
Mammalia	descended from reptiles in a separate branch from Aves, see Table 2	lawyers

Table 4   Characteristics of the Vertebrate Classes

---

[109] Note that the arthropods have an exoskeleton surrounding their entire bodies which is composed of the same chemical comprising the fungal cell wall.

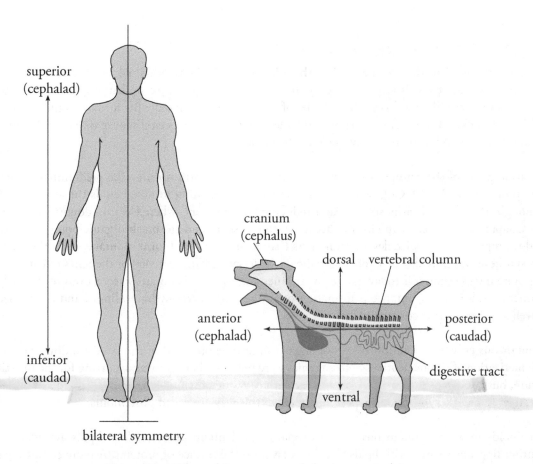

superior
(cephalad)

inferior
(caudad)

bilateral symmetry

cranium
(cephalus)

dorsal   vertebral column

anterior
(cephalad)

posterior
(caudad)

digestive tract

ventral

Figure 15   Bilateral Symmetry and the Anatomical Axes

Anatomists describe bodies with reference to axes such as the dorsal-ventral axis and the anterior-posterior axis (Figure 15). These are imaginary planes through the body. **Anterior** means "front-facing"; **posterior** is the opposite. **Dorsal** means "on top." A shark has a "dorsal fin," and the spines of dogs and humans are considered dorsal as well. **Ventral** is the opposite of dorsal. The bellybutton is a ventral structure in dogs and humans. In humans, **superior** is used to indicate "toward the head." **Inferior** means "toward the feet." Another way to say "toward the head" is **cephalad**. (Cephalus is Latin for head.) The opposite is **caudad**, meaning "toward the tail." [Does the axis of bilateral symmetry in vertebrates run parallel or perpendicular to the dorsal-ventral axis?[110]]

---

[110] The dorsal-ventral axis slices the body in half, separating front from back. The axis of symmetry separates left from right. So the two axes are perpendicular. Remember: The axes are planes, not lines.

6.9

6.10   THE ORIGIN OF LIFE

Based on radioisotope dating, the earth is thought to be 4.5 billion years old. All life evolved from pro-karyotes. The oldest fossils are 3.5 billion-year-old outlines of primitive prokaryotic cell walls found in stromatolites (layered mats formed by colonies of prokaryotes). Even older life forms certainly existed, but lacked cell walls and thus left no fossil record (at least none have yet been discovered). Hence life on Earth is older than 3.5 billion years, nearly as old as the planet itself.

The atmosphere of the young Earth was different from today's atmosphere. The predominant gases then were probably H_2O, CO, CO_2, and N_2. The most important thing to note here is the absence of O_2. It is thought that the early atmosphere was a **reducing environment**, where electron donors were prevalent (see Chapter 2). Oxygen is an electron acceptor, and as such tends to break organic bonds. In this early world, simple organic molecules, or monomers ("single units") could form spontaneously. The energy for this synthesis was provided by lightning, radioactive decay, volcanic activity, or the Sun's radiation, which was more intense than it is today due to the thinner atmosphere. Laboratory recreations of the early envi-ronment result in the spontaneous formation of amino acids, carbohydrates, lipids, and ribonucleotides, as well as other organic compounds.

Spontaneous polymerization of these monomers can also be observed in the lab (including spontaneous polymerization of ribonucleotides). No enzymes were present when this was occurring for the first time in nature, but it is thought that metal ions on the surface of rocks and especially clay acted as catalysts. This is known as **abiotic synthesis**. Polypeptides made in this way are called **proteinoids**.

Proteinoids in water spontaneously form droplets called **microspheres**. When lipids are added to the solution **liposomes** form, with lipids forming a layer on the surface of proteins. A more complex particle known as a **coacervate** includes polypeptides, nucleic acids, and polysaccharides. Coacervates made with pre-existing enzymes are capable of catalyzing reactions. Microspheres, liposomes, and coacervates are collectively referred to as **protobionts**.

Protobionts resemble cells in that they contain a protected inner environment and perform chemical reactions. They can also reproduce to a certain extent: when they grow too large they split in half. What is lacking, however, is an organized mechanism of heredity. This was first provided by RNA. As noted above, RNA chains form spontaneously in the appropriate solution. Even more interesting is the observa-tion that single-stranded RNA chains can be self-replicating. A daughter chain lines up on the parent by base pairing and then spontaneously polymerizes with a surprisingly low error rate. A nonspecific catalyst such as a metal ion can further increase the efficiency of RNA self-replication. Furthermore, it is now known that RNA has catalytic activity in modern cells. For example, in primitive eukaryotes, introns are spliced out of the mRNA by **ribozymes**, which are RNA enzymes.

Somehow a mechanism evolved for polypeptides to be copied from early RNA genes. You already know about the inherent tendency for phospholipids to form lipid bilayers. Given all this information, it's not too hard to imagine true cells evolving from a primordial soup at the dawn of time. The last step in the evolution of the earliest cells would have been the switch from RNA to DNA as the genetic material. DNA is more stable due to its 2'-deoxy structure and also due to the fact that it spontaneously forms a compact double-stranded helix.

6.10

Summary

- Organisms express phenotypes (physical characteristics) according to their genotypes (combinations of alleles).

- Classical dominance occurs when a phenotype or trait is determined by one gene with two alleles, and one allele is dominant (expressed) and the other is recessive (silent). There are several exceptions to classical dominance, including incomplete dominance, codominance, epistasis, pleiotropism, polygenism, and penetrance.

- Incomplete dominance occurs when two different alleles for a single trait result in a blended phenotype. Codominance occurs when two different alleles for a single trait are expressed simultaneously, but independently (no blending).

- Epistasis occurs when the expression of one gene depends on the expression of another.

- Pleitropic genes affect many different aspects of the overall phenotype, while polygenic traits are affected by many different genes.

- Penetrance refers to the likelihood that a particular genotype will result in a given phenotype. Penetrance can be affected by several factors including age, environment, and lifestyle.

- From a single diploid precursor cell, meiosis generates four haploid cells (gametes) with a random mix of alleles. This is due to crossing over in prophase I, and separation of homologous chromosomes in anaphase I. Nondisjunction is a failure to separate the DNA properly during meiosis, and can result in gametes with improper numbers of chromosomes.

- The Punnett square or the rules of probability can be used to determine the genotypes and phenotypes of offspring from given crosses, or the probability of having offspring with certain traits.

- The rule of multiplication states that the probability of A and B occurring is equal to the probability of A multiplied by the probability of B.

- The rule of addition states that the probability of A or B occurring is equal to the probability of A plus the probability of B, minus the probability of A and B together.

- Linkage occurs when two genes are close together on the same chromosome; it leads to alleles being inherited together (less recombination) instead of independently.

- Pedigrees can be used to analyze the patterns of inheritance of different traits. There are six primary modes of inheritance: autosomal recessive, autosomal dominant, mitochondrial, Y-linked, X-linked recessive, and X-linked dominant.

- The Hardy-Weinberg law can be used to study population genetics. It assumes classical dominance with only two alleles and unchanging allele frequencies. It is based on five assumptions: no mutation, no natural selection, no migration, large populations, and totally random mating.

- Natural selection drives evolution by allowing individuals with random, beneficial mutations to survive and pass those beneficial mutations on to their offspring.

- Homologous structures are the result of divergent evolution to form new species, and analogous structures are the result of convergent evolution, in which different start species must meet similar environmental challenges.

CHAPTER 6 FREESTANDING PRACTICE QUESTIONS

1. A woman is phenotypically normal but had a brother who had an autosomal recessive disorder that resulted in death during infancy. What is the probability that this woman is a carrier for the disorder that afflicted her brother?

A) 1/4
B) 1/3
C) 1/2
D) 2/3

2. A set of inherited traits show a phenotypic ratio of 9:3:3:1 among offspring of a given mating. A possible explanation for this observation is a two locus–two allele system where each locus exhibits:

A) independent assortment.
B) linkage.
C) epistasis.
D) incomplete dominance.

3. If a woman is a carrier for an X-linked recessive disorder and mates with a normal, unaffected male, what is the probability her grandson has the disorder? Assume she has a normal son and a daughter, and they both have homozygous normal partners.

A) 0
B) 1/4
C) 1/2
D) 3/4

4. A geneticist is analyzing a family tree, where mothers affected by the trait under study pass the trait on to 100% of their offspring, both sons and daughters. Fathers affected by the trait pass it on to 0% of their offspring. All affected individuals have an affected mother. What is the inheritance pattern of this trait?

A) Y-linked
B) Autosomal dominant
C) Autosomal recessive
D) Mitochondrial

5. A purebred long-tailed cat with long whiskers (*TTww*) is mated to a purebred short-tailed cat with short whiskers (*ttWW*). The kittens will be:

A) 100% long-tailed with long whiskers.
B) 100% long-tailed with short whiskers.
C) 100% short-tailed with short whiskers.
D) 50% long-tailed cat with long whiskers, 50% short-tailed cat with short whiskers.

6. A homozygous white bull is mated to a homozygous cow with a red coat. The offspring all have a roan coat color, which is composed of a mix of white hairs and red hairs. Which of the following is true?

A) Coat color in cattle is an example of codominance.
B) White hair is recessive to red hair.
C) Coat color in cattle is an example of incomplete dominance.
D) White hair is dominant over red hair.

7. If the genes for ear size (*E* or *e*) and aggressiveness (*A* or *a*) in mice are linked and 25 mu apart, what is the probability of getting a large-eared aggressive pup (*EeAa*) from a mating between a small-eared aggressive female (*eeAA*) and a large-eared nonaggressive male (*EEaa*)?

A) 12.5%
B) 25%
C) 75%
D) 100%

CHAPTER 6 PRACTICE PASSAGE

The fruit fly, *Drosophila melanogaster*, is an ideal organism on which to study genetic mechanisms. This organism has simple food requirements, occupies little space, and the reproductive live cycle is complete in about 12 days at room temperature, allowing for quick analysis of test crosses. In addition, fruit flies produce large numbers of offspring, which allows for sufficient data to be collected quickly. Many *Drosophila* genes are homologous to human genes, and are studied to gain a better understanding of what role these proteins have in humans.

To understand the inheritance patterns of certain genes in *Drosophila*, the following experiments were carried out. Assume that the alleles for red eyes, brown body, and normal wings are dominant and the alleles for white eyes, ebony body, and vestigial wings are recessive.

Experiment 1:

A red-eyed female and a white-eye male were crossed. The subsequent generation of flies was also crossed. The phenotypic results of both generations are shown below:

Generation	Red-eyed female	White-eyed female	Red-eyed male	White-eyed male
Parental	1	0	0	1
F_1	9	0	13	0
F_2	27	0	12	14

Experiment 2:

Five of the red-eyed female *Drosophila* from the F_1 generation of Experiment 1 were crossed with white-eyed males. The result of this cross is shown below:

Generation	Red-eyed female	White-eyed female	Red-eyed male	White-eyed male
F_1	5	0	0	10
F_2	8	8	9	8

Experiment 3:

The white-eyed females from Experiment 2 were crossed with red-eyed males. The result of this cross is shown below:

Generation	Red-eyed female	White-eyed female	Red-eyed male	White-eyed male
Parental	0	8	7	0
F_1	9	0	0	10

Experiment 4:

A male heterozygous for body color and wing type is crossed with an ebony, vestigial-winged female. The results of the cross are shown below:

Phenotype	Male	Female
Brown body, normal wings	32	30
Brown body, vestigial wings	2	1
Ebony body, normal wings	1	3
Ebony body, vesigial wings	28	33

1. What is the most likely mode of inheritance for white eye color?

A) X-linked recessive
B) X-linked dominant
C) Autosomal recessive
D) Autosomal dominant

2. What ratio of white-eyed to red-eyed females would be expected if the F_1 generation of Experiment 3 were crossed?

A) White-eyed females would not be present.
B) Red-eyed females would not be present.
C) 1:1
D) 1:2

3. Approximately how many of the red-eyed females of the F_2 generation of Experiment 2 are homozygous dominant?

A) 0
B) 2
C) 4
D) 8

4. Which of the following statements is/are true with regard to the results obtained from Experiment 4?

    I. The genes for body color and wing type are on the same chromosome.
    II. Recombination occurred.
    III. The heterozygous male had a dominant and recessive allele on each homologous chromosome.

A) I only
B) I and II
C) I and III
D) II only

5. What is the recombination frequency shown by the results of Experiment 4?

A) Recombination did not occur.
B) 5%
C) 50%
D) 95%

6. Assume that short legs are due to a recessive allele on a chromosome other than body color and that dominant alleles are considered wild-type. A white-eyed male is mated to an ebony colored, short-legged female and the F_1 males resulting are wild type. If these males are backcrossed to ebony-colored, short-legged females, what proportion of the F_2 offspring will be wild-type males?

A) 0
B) 1/2
C) 1/4
D) 1/8

7. If the frequency of vestigial wings in a population of *Drosophila* ($n = 1500$) is 4%, how many flies would be heterozygous with regard to wing type? Assume random mating, but no migration, mutation, random drift, or natural selection.

A) 60
B) 240
C) 480
D) 960

SOLUTIONS TO CHAPTER 6 FREESTANDING PRACTICE QUESTIONS

1. **D** If the woman's brother was affected with this autosomal recessive disorder, both of her parents must have been carriers for the trait. Since it is lethal in infancy, you know both parents must have been heterozygous. The mating between two heterozygotes produces the following genotypic ratio in their offspring: 25% homozygous recessive, 50% heterozygous, 25% homozygous dominant. Since the woman is phenotypically normal, she must not have the disorder, so she is not in the 25% homozygous recessive group. She is either in the 25% homozygous dominant group or the 50% heterozygous group, so the chance she is a carrier is 2/3 (choice D is correct).

2. **A** If two heterozygous parents are mated (for example, $AaBb \times AaBb$), the expected F_1 phenotype ratio if the two traits are assorting independently is 9:3:3:1 (choice A is correct). If linkage were occurring, this ratio would be skewed after the mating of two double heterozygotes, since alleles would be preferentially inherited together. Since the ratio is not skewed, linkage is not occurring (choice B can be eliminated). This is not a case where one gene is silencing another, or controlling the expression of the other, as this would also lead to a skewed ratio (choice C can be eliminated). Incomplete dominance of two alleles leads to a blended heterozygous phenotype; thus, if it occurs at a single locus, it produces three different phenotypes. If it were to occur at two different loci (as in this case), there would be nine possible phenotypes (3 possible phenotypes at the first locus times 3 possible phenotypes at the second locus = $3^2 = 9$). In this case there are only four different phenotypes (choice D can be eliminated).

3. **B** If we assign "A" as the normal allele and "a" as the affected allele, the woman is $X^A X^a$ and her mate is $X^A Y$. The question stem says that she has a normal son, who must have the genotype $X^A Y$; he received the X^A from his mother and his Y chromosome from his father. There is no probability associated with this that must be factored into the solution, because this is the only way the couple could have a normal son. If this son mates with a homozygous normal female, he will pass his Y chromosome onto his son(s), which means there is zero chance of having an affected son. In other words, an $X^A Y \times X^A X^A$ mating cannot generate $X^a Y$ sons. Next, let's work with the daughter of the woman in the question stem. The question says she has a normal phenotype. She must receive an X^A from her father. There is a 50% probability she will receive an X^a from her mother. If the daughter is $X^A X^a$ (remember there is a 50% chance of this) and her mate is $X^A Y$, there is a 50% chance their son will be affected. Overall, then, the probability that a grandson is affected is $0 + (1/2)(1/2)$, or 1/4. Therefore, choice B is correct.

4. **D** Females are not affected by Y-linked traits (choice A is wrong). If the trait was autosomal dominant, affected fathers would pass the trait to at least some of their offspring (choice B is wrong). Autosomal recessive traits do not demonstrate the sex bias that is described in the question stem (choice C is incorrect). By process of elimination, this trait must be inherited via the mitochondrial genome. All humans inherit their mitochondrial genome from their mothers; during fertilization, the sperm only contributes 23 chromosomes but the ovum contributes 23 chromosomes along with all other cellular organelles and cytoplasm (choice D is correct).

5.   B   The offspring will be 100% *TtWw* and will display the dominant phenotype for each trait. Since each parent has a dominant and a recessive phenotype, the kittens will not have the phenotype of either parent (choice B is correct and choices A, C, and D are wrong).

6.   A   Since the offspring are neither red nor white, this trait is not inherited via simple Mendelian genetics, and neither trait is dominant or recessive (choices B and D are wrong). The individual hairs on the F_1 cattle are either red or white, which means that both alleles are being expressed. This best matches the definition of codominance (choice A is correct). If the individual hairs were a blend of white and red, the best answer would have been incomplete dominance (choice C is wrong).

7.   D   The pups will get *eA* from their mom and *Ea* from their dad. All the pups will be *eA/Ea*, so the answer must be D. Note that the linkage information was not useful in answering this question.

SOLUTIONS TO CHAPTER 6 PRACTICE PASSAGE

1.   A   The passage states that the allele for red eyes is dominant and the allele for white eyes is recessive (choices B and D are wrong). The results from Experiments 1 suggest that the gene for eye color is X-linked. If it were autosomal, all F_1 flies from that experiment would be heterozygous, and there would be an equal distribution of both genders and colors in the F_2 generation. Remember that a gender bias in the phenotype of a trait usually indicates that you're working with a sex-linked trait.

2.   C   The passage states that the red allele is dominant and the white allele is recessive; further eye color is a sex-linked trait (see the explanation for Question 1). For Experiment 3, the female parental genotype must be homozygous recessive (X^cX^c), and the male parental genotype must be X^CY. Thus, the F_1 generation consists of heterozygous females (X^CX^c) and males with the recessive white-eyed allele (X^cY). If these two were mated with each other, the female progeny of this generation would consist of homozygous recessive (X^cX^c) and heterozygous (X^CX^c) females in an approximate 1:1 ratio (choice C is correct).

3.   A   Experiment 2 is a cross between an F_1 female and a white-eyed male. The genotype of the F_1 females from Experiment 1 is X^CX^c; they have red eyes, so they must have X^C, and they are female, so they inherited X^c from their white-eyed father. If these X^CX^c females are crossed with X^cY (white-eyed) males, the females generated in the F_2 must be 50% X^CX^c (red-eyed) and 50% X^cX^c (white-eyed). If the father has white eyes, it is impossible to generate homozygous red-eyed females in the F_2 (choice A is correct).

4. **B** There is no sex bias in the results from Experiment 4, so we can assume the alleles are autosomal. The passage states that the alleles for brown bodies and normal wings are dominant, and the alleles for ebony bodies and vestigial wings are recessive. Let's assign B = brown and b = ebony for body color, and W = normal and w = vestigial for wing phenotype. Thus the cross in Experiment 4 is $BbWw \times bbww$. Item I is true: If the genes for body color and wing type were on separate chromosomes, one would expect the law of independent assortment to hold true and the phenotypic ratio of the progeny would be expected to be 1:1:1:1. However, this is not the case. Two of the phenotypes predominate, indicating that the genes are close together on the same chromosome, or are linked (choice D can be eliminated). Item II is also true: The recombinant phenotypes, although rare, are nonetheless seen. Recombination between homologous chromosomes is the best explanation for this observation (choices A and C can be eliminated and choice B is correct). Note that Item III is false: The double heterozygous *Drosophila* must have both dominant alleles on one chromosome and both recessive alleles on the other to account for the results seen. In other words, the cross performed was $BW/bw \times bw/bw$. The parental combinations of alleles are BW and bw (more frequent), and the recombinant combinations of alleles (less frequent) are Bw and bW.

5. **B** Recombination did in fact occur (see explanation for Question 4; choice A is wrong). Recombination frequency = number of recombinants/total number of offspring. In this case, the total number of recombinants is 7 and the total number of offspring is 130. 7/130 = 0.05 or 5% recombination frequency (choice B is correct and choices C and D are wrong). Note that choice D is the frequency of non-recombination, and choice C would be correct if the genes were not linked.

6. **D** Similar to above, let's assign X^C = red eyes (dominant and wild type), X^c = white eyes, B = brown body color (dominant and wild type), b = ebony body color, and now S = long legs (dominant and wild-type), and s = short legs. The first cross in the question stem is: $X^CYBBSS \times X^CX^cbbss$. Note that if the phenotype is not listed, we can assume it is wild-type. Also, since all the male offspring from this cross are wild-type, then the male parent must have been homozygous for body color and leg length, and the female parent must have been homozygous for eye color. The male F_1 offspring will be X^CYBbSs. Next, this male was backcrossed to a female from the previous generation ($X^CYBbSs \times X^CX^cbbss$), and we are asked for the probability of a wild-type male. This is equal to the proportion that they are male (1/2), multiplied by the proportion that they will have brown body color (1/2), multiplied by the proportion that they will have long legs (1/2). Therefore, the proportion that are wild type = $1/2 \times 1/2 \times 1/2 = 1/8$ (choice D is correct). Notice that we do not have to factor in the probability of the *Drosophila* being red-eyed because this is guaranteed given the genotype of their mother.

7. **C** Using the Hardy-Weinberg equations for allele frequency and genotype, the frequency of the vestigial wing allele (q) must be equal to $\sqrt{0.04}$, or 0.20. Therefore, the frequency of the normal wing allele (p) is 0.80 and the frequency of the heterozygous genotype (pq and qp) is equal to $2 \times 0.2 \times 0.8$, or 0.32. The actual number of *Drosophila* that would have this genotype would be 480 (0.32×1500).

Chapter 7
The Nervous and Endocrine Systems

The nervous and endocrine systems are presented in the same chapter since their functions are related: They both provide communication, integrating and coordinating the activities of the tissues and organs of the body. The means of communication by the two systems are quite different (although complementary) in many ways. The nervous system communicates through electrochemical signals (action potentials), while the endocrine system uses chemical messengers carried in the blood (hormones). The nervous system in general regulates rapid responses such as those of skeletal muscle or smooth muscle, while the endocrine system takes longer to have an effect and regulates longer-term responses such as metabolism and homeostasis. The two systems are interconnected, with two of the primary endocrine glands—the pituitary and the adrenals—regulated by the nervous system, and with the endocrine system feeding back to modulate the nervous system.

7.1 NEURONAL STRUCTURE AND FUNCTION

Neurons are specialized cells that transmit and process information from one part of the body to another. This information takes the form of electrochemical impulses known as **action potentials.** The action potential is a localized area of depolarization of the plasma membrane that travels in a wave-like manner along an axon. When an action potential reaches the end of an axon at a synapse, the signal is transformed into a chemical signal with the release of neurotransmitter into the synaptic cleft, a process called **synaptic transmission** (Section 7.2). The information of many synapses feeding into a neuron is integrated to determine whether that neuron will in turn fire an action potential. In this way the action of many individual neurons is integrated to work together in the nervous system as a whole.

Structure of the Neuron

The basic functional and structural unit of the nervous system is the **neuron** (Figure 1). The structure of these cells is highly specialized to transmit and process **action potentials**, the electrochemical signals of the nervous system (Figure 3). Neurons have a central cell body, the **soma**, which contains the nucleus and is where most of the biosynthetic activity of the cell takes place. Slender projections, termed **axons** and **dendrites**, extend from the cell body. Neurons have only one axon (as long as a meter in some cases), but most possess many dendrites. Neurons with one dendrite are termed **bipolar**; those with many dendrites are **multipolar**. Neurons generally carry action potentials in one direction, with dendrites receiving signals and axons carrying action potentials away from the cell body. Axons can branch multiple times and terminate in **synaptic knobs** that form connections with target cells. When action potentials travel down an axon and reach the synaptic knob, chemical messengers are released and travel across a very small gap called the **synaptic cleft** to the target cell. The nature of the action potential and the transmission of signals across the synaptic cleft are key aspects of nervous system function. [In Figure 1, in what direction does an action potential travel in the axon shown?[1] What's the difference between a neuron and a nerve?[2]]

---

[1] Action potentials travel from the cell body down the axon, or from left to right in Figure 1.

[2] A neuron is a single cell. A nerve is a large bundle of many different axons from different neurons.

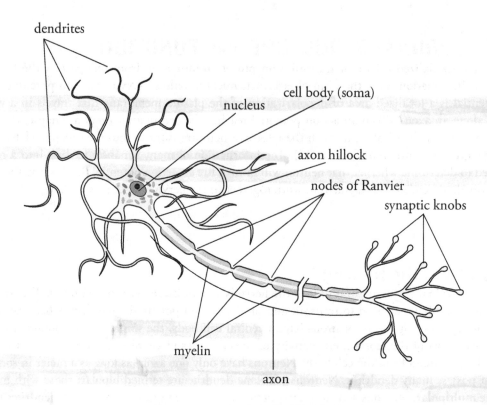

Figure 1   A Multipolar Neuron

- A protein motor called *kinesin* is one of several different proteins that drive movement of vesicles and organelles along microtubules in axons. Kinesin specifically drives anterograde movement (movement from the soma toward the axon terminus). If a kinesin inhibitor is added to neurons in culture, what is the likely result?[3]
    - A.   Spontaneous action potentials
    - B.   Cell division
    - C.   Accumulation of material in the synaptic knob
    - D.   Atrophy of axons

The Action Potential

The Resting Membrane Potential

The **resting membrane potential** was described briefly in Chapter 5. This is an electric potential across the plasma membrane of approximately –70 millivolts (mV), with the interior of the cell negatively charged

---

[3]   A large amount of biosynthetic activity takes place in the cell body, and materials are transported from the cell body down the axon to its end by kinesin. The correct answer is **D**. If material cannot be transported through the axon from the cell body, the axon will atrophy. Note that although this may not immediately be apparent, choices A, B, and C should have been easily eliminated; kinesin has nothing to do with action potentials, neurons in general do not divide (and inhibiting kinesin should not change this), and the inhibition of kinesin would prevent materials from accumulating at the synaptic knobs.

with respect to the exterior of the cell. Two primary membrane proteins are required to establish the resting membrane potential: the Na⁺/K⁺ ATPase and the potassium leak channels. The **Na⁺/K⁺ ATPase** pumps three sodium ions out of the cell and two potassium ions into the cell with the hydrolysis of one ATP molecule. [What form of transport is carried out by the Na⁺/K⁺ ATPase?[4]] The result is a sodium gradient with high sodium outside of the cell and a potassium gradient with high potassium inside the cell. **Leak channels** are channels that are open all the time, and that simply allow ions to "leak" across the membrane according to their gradient. Potassium leak channels allow potassium, but no other ions, to flow down their gradient out of the cell. The combined loss of many positive ions through Na⁺/K⁺ ATPases and the potassium leak channels leaves the interior of the cell with a net negative charge, approximately 70 mV more negative than the exterior of the cell; this difference is the resting membrane potential. Note that there are very few sodium leak channels in the membrane (the ratio of K⁺ leak channels to Na⁺ leak channels is about 100:1), so the cell membrane is virtually impermeable to sodium.

- Are neurons the only cells with a resting membrane potential?[5]
- If the potassium leak channels are blocked, what will happen to the membrane potential?[6]
- What would happen to the membrane potential if sodium ions were allowed to flow down their concentration gradient?[7]

The resting membrane potential establishes a negative charge along the interior of axons (along with the rest of the neuronal interior). Thus, the cells can be described as **polarized**; negative on the inside and positive on the outside. An action potential is a disturbance in this membrane potential, a wave of **depolarization** of the plasma membrane that travels along an axon. Depolarization is a change in the membrane potential from the resting membrane potential of approximately –70 mV to a less negative, or even positive, potential. After depolarization, **repolarization** returns the membrane potential to normal. The change in membrane potential during passage of an action potential is caused by movement of ions into and out of the neuron through ion channels. The action potential is therefore not strictly an electrical impulse, like electrons moving in a copper telephone wire, but an electro*chemical* impulse.

Depolarization

Key proteins in the propagation of action potentials are the **voltage-gated sodium channels** located in the plasma membrane of the axon. In response to a change in the membrane potential, these ion channels open to allow sodium ions to flow down their gradient into the cell and depolarize that section of membrane. [What is the effect of opening the voltage-gated sodium channels on the membrane potential?[8]] These channels are opened by depolarization of the membrane from the resting potential of –70 mV to a **threshold potential** of approximately –50 mV. Once this threshold is reached, the channels are opened fully, but below the threshold they are closed and do not allow the passage of any ions through the channel. When the channels open, sodium flows into the cell, down its concentration gradient, depolarizing that

---

[4] The Na⁺/K⁺ ATPase uses ATP to drive transport against a gradient; this is primary active transport.

[5] No. All cells have the resting membrane potential. Neurons and muscle tissue are unique in using the resting membrane potential to generate action potentials.

[6] The flow of potassium out of the cell makes the interior of the cell more negatively charged. Blocking the potassium leak channels would reduce the resting membrane potential, making the interior of the cell less negative.

[7] Sodium ions would flow into the cell and reduce the potential across the plasma membrane, making the interior of the cell less negative and even relatively positive if enough ions flow into the cell.

[8] Sodium (positively charged) flows into the cell, down its concentration gradient, making the interior of the cell less negatively charged, or even positively charged.

section of the membrane to about +35 mV before inactivating. Some of the sodium ions flow down the interior of the axon, slightly depolarizing the neighboring section of membrane. When the depolarization in the next section of membrane reaches threshold, those voltage-gated sodium channels open as well, passing the depolarization down the axon (Figure 2). [If an action potential starts at one end of an axon, can it run out of energy and not reach the other end?[9]]

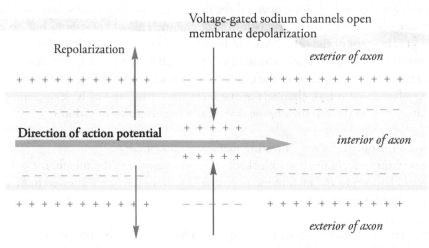

Figure 2 The Action Potential is a Wave of Membrane Depolarization

- Which one of the following can cause the interior of the neuron to have a momentary positive charge?[10]
  - A. Opening of potassium leak channels
  - B. Activity of the Na+/K+ ATPase
  - C. Opening of voltage-gated sodium channels
  - D. Opening of voltage-gated potassium channels

- Given the above description, which of the following best describes the response of voltage-gated sodium channels to a membrane depolarization from –70 mV to –60 mV?[11]
  - A. All of the channels open fully.
  - B. 50% of the channels open fully.
  - C. All of the channels open 50%.
  - D. None of the channels open.

---

[9] No, it cannot. Action potentials are continually renewed at each point in the axon as they travel. Once an action potential starts, it will propagate without a change in amplitude (size) until it reaches a synapse.

[10] Choices A, B, and D all make the interior of the cell more negative. **C** is the answer. Voltage-gated sodium channels can make the interior of the cell momentarily positive during passage of an action potential.

[11] Voltage-gated sodium channels require a threshold depolarization to open. A depolarization below the threshold will produce essentially no response, while a depolarization greater than or equal to the threshold will cause all of the channels to open fully. This is called an **all-or-none** response. The correct answer is **D**. The depolarization is less than the threshold, so there is no response.

Repolarization

With the opening of voltage-gated sodium channels, sodium flows into the cell and depolarizes the membrane to positive values. As the wave of depolarization passes through a region of membrane, however, the membrane does not remain depolarized (Figure 3).

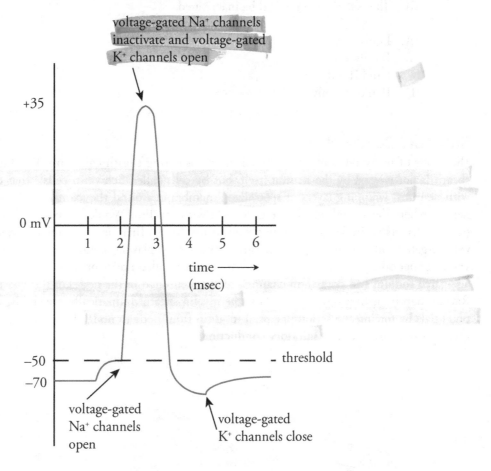

Figure 3 The Action Potential at a Single Location

After depolarization, the membrane is **repolarized**, re-establishing the original resting membrane potential. A number of factors combine to produce this effect:

1) Voltage-gated sodium channels inactivate very quickly after they open, shutting off the flow of sodium into the cell. The channels remain **inactivated** until the membrane potential nears resting values again.

2) Voltage-gated potassium channels open more slowly than the voltage-gated sodium channels and stay open longer. Voltage-gated potassium channels open in response to membrane depolarization. As potassium leaves the cell down its concentration gradient, the membrane potential returns to negative values, actually overshooting the resting potential by about 20 mV (to about −90 mV). At this point the voltage-gated potassium channels close.

3) Potassium leak channels and the Na^+/K^+ ATPase continue to function (as they always do) to bring the membrane back to resting potential. These factors alone would repolarize the membrane potential even without the voltage-gated potassium channels, but it would take a lot longer.

- If a toxin prevents voltage-gated sodium channels from closing, which of the following will occur?[12]
    I.   Voltage-gated potassium channels will open but not close.
    II.   The membrane will not repolarize to the normal resting membrane potential.
    III. The Na⁺/K⁺ ATPase will be inactivated.

    A.   I only
    B.   II only
    C.   I and II only
    D.   II and III only

Saltatory Conduction

The axons of many neurons are wrapped in an insulating sheath called **myelin** (Figure 4). The myelin sheath is not created by the neuron itself, but by cells called **Schwann cells**[13] that exist in conjunction with neurons, wrapping layers of specialized membrane around the axons. No ions can enter or exit a neuron where the axonal membrane is covered with myelin. [Would an axon be able to conduct action potentials if its entire length were wrapped in myelin?[14]] There is no membrane depolarization and no voltage-gated sodium channels in regions of the axonal plasma membrane that are wrapped in myelin. There are periodic gaps in the myelin sheath however, called **nodes of Ranvier** (Figures 1, 4, and 5). Voltage-gated sodium and potassium channels are concentrated in the nodes of Ranvier in myelinated axons. Rather than impeding action potentials, the myelin sheath dramatically speeds the movement of action potentials by forcing the action potential to jump from node to node. This rapid jumping conduction in myelinated axons is termed **saltatory conduction**.

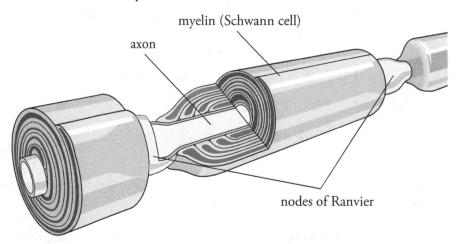

myelin (Schwann cell)

axon

nodes of Ranvier

Figure 4   A Schwann Cell Wrapping an Axon with Myelin

---

[12] **Item I is true:** Voltage-gated potassium channels are normally closed by the repolarization of the membrane, so if the membrane is not repolarized, they will not close. **Item II is true:** Sodium ions will continue to flow into the cell, even as the Na⁺/K⁺ ATPase works to pump them out. This will prevent the repolarization of the membrane. Item III is false: The Na⁺/K⁺ ATPase will work harder than ever. The answer is **C**.

[13] Schwann cells are found in the peripheral nervous system (PNS). In the central nervous system (CNS) myelination of axons is accomplished via similar cells called oligodendrocytes.

[14] No. The action potential requires the movement of ions across the plasma membrane to create a wave of depolarization.

- Which one of the following is true concerning myelinated and unmyelinated axons?[15]
  A. The amount of energy consumed by the Na$^+$/K$^+$ ATPase is much less in myelinated axons than in unmyelinated axons.
  B. Myelinated axons can conduct many more action potentials per second than can unmyelinated axons.
  C. The size of action potential depolarization is much greater in myelinated axons than in unmyelinated axons.
  D. Voltage-gated potassium channels do not play a role in repolarization in unmyelinated axons.

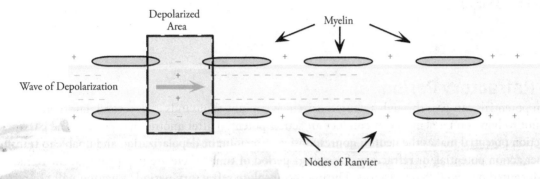

Figure 5   Propagation of the AP in a Myelinated Axon (cross section)

Equilibrium Potentials

During the action potential, the movement of Na$^+$ and K$^+$ ions across the membrane through the voltage-gated channels is *passive*; driven by gradients. The **equilibrium potential** is the membrane potential at which this driving force (the gradient) does not exist; in other words, there would be no net movement of ions across the membrane. Note that the equilibrium potential is specific for a particular ion. For example, the Na$^+$ equilibrium potential is *positive*, approximately +50 mV. Na$^+$ ions are driven inward by their concentration gradient. However, if the interior of the cell is too positive, the positively-charged ions are repelled; in other words, the *electrical* gradient would drive sodium *out*. These forces, the chemical gradient driving sodium in and the electrical gradient driving sodium out balance each other at about +50 mV, so this is the equilibrium potential for Na$^+$.

K$^+$, however, has a *negative* equilibrium potential. K$^+$ ions are driven outward by their concentration gradient. However if the interior of the cell is too negative, the positively-charged ions cannot escape the attraction; the electrical gradient drives potassium *in*. The chemical gradient driving potassium out and the electrical gradient driving potassium in balance each other at about −90 mV, so this is the equilibrium potential for K$^+$.

---

[15] Since the area of membrane that is conducting is much less in myelinated axons, Na$^+$/K$^+$ ATPase only works to maintain the resting potential in the nodes of Ranvier, whereas in unmyelinated axons the Na$^+$/K$^+$ ATPase hydrolyzes ATP to maintain the resting potential across the entire membrane (choice **A** is correct). The length of the refractory period (and hence the frequency of action potentials) is based on the characteristics of the voltage-gated sodium and potassium channels, which do not change (choice **B** is false). The size of depolarization in an action potential does not vary greatly; action potentials are an all-or-nothing response (choice **C** is false). Voltage-gated potassium channels are the same in both neurons (choice **D** is false).

Note that the fact that the resting membrane potential is –70 mV reflects both the differences in the equilibrium potentials for Na⁺ and K⁺, and also the relative numbers of leak channels for these two ions. If the cell were completely permeable to K⁺, the rest potential would be about –90 mV. The fact that the rest potential is *very close* to the K⁺ equilibrium potential indicates that there are a large number of K⁺ leak channels in the membrane; the cell at rest is almost completely permeable to potassium. However, the resting potential is slightly more positive than –90 mV, indicating that there are a few Na⁺ leak channels allowing Na⁺ in. Not very many Na⁺ leak channels, though, or the rest potential would be much more positive; closer to the Na⁺ equilibrium potential. (This is in fact what we see when the cell *does* become completely permeable to Na⁺ at the beginning of the action potential; the membrane potential shoots upward to +35 mV.)

The Refractory Period

Action potentials can pass through a neuron extremely rapidly, thousands each second, but there is an upper limit to how soon a neuron can conduct an action potential after another has passed. The passage of one action potential makes the neuron nonresponsive to membrane depolarization and unable to transmit another action potential, or **refractory**, for a short period of time. There are two phases of the refractory period, caused by two different factors. During the **absolute refractory period**, a neuron will not fire another action potential no matter how strong a membrane depolarization is induced. During this time, the voltage-gated sodium channels have been inactivated (not the same as *closed*) after depolarization. They will not be able to be opened again until the membrane potential reaches the resting potential and the Na⁺ channels have returned to their "closed" state. During the **relative refractory period**, a neuron can be induced to transmit an action potential, but the depolarization required is greater than normal because the membrane is **hyperpolarized**. When repolarization occurs, there is a brief period in which the membrane potential is more negative than the resting potential (Figure 3) caused by voltage-gated potassium channels that have not closed yet. Because it is further from threshold, a greater stimulus is required to open the voltage-gated sodium channels to start an action potential. [If a fruit fly mutant is found that has voltage-gated potassium channels that shut more quickly after repolarization, how would this affect the refractory period in the fly?[16]]

7.2 SYNAPTIC TRANSMISSION

A **synapse** is a junction between the axon terminus of a neuron and the dendrites, soma, or axon of a second neuron. It can also be a junction between the axon terminus of a neuron and an organ. There are two types of synapse: electrical and chemical. **Electrical synapses** occur when the cytoplasms of two cells are joined by gap junctions. If two cells are joined by an electrical synapse, an action potential will spread directly from one cell to the other. Electrical synapses are not common in the nervous system although they are quite important in propagating action potentials in smooth muscle and cardiac muscle. In the nervous system, **chemical synapses** are found at the ends of axons where they meet their target cell; here, an action potential is converted into a chemical signal. The following steps are involved in the transmission of a signal across a chemical synapse in the nervous system (Figure 6), as well as at the junctions of neurons with other cell types, such as skeletal muscle cells:

---

[16] The absolute refractory period would not be altered, since this is due to the inability of voltage-gated sodium channels to open. However, the relative refractory period would be decreased.

1) An action potential reaches the end of an axon, the synaptic knob.
2) Depolarization of the presynaptic membrane opens voltage-gated calcium channels.
3) Calcium influx into the presynaptic cell causes exocytosis of neurotransmitter stored in secretory vesicles.
4) Neurotransmitter molecules diffuse across the narrow synaptic cleft (small space between cells).
5) Neurotransmitter binds to receptor proteins in the postsynaptic membrane. These receptors are ligand-gated ion channels.
6) The opening of these ion channels in the postsynaptic cell alters the membrane polarization.
7) If the membrane depolarization of the postsynaptic cell reaches the threshold of voltage-gated sodium channels, an action potential is initiated.
8) Neurotransmitter in the synaptic cleft is degraded and/or removed to terminate the signal.

Presynaptic Neuron
1. Voltage-gated calcium channels open.
2. Influx of calcium
3. Exocytosis of secretory vesicle
4. Release of neurotransmitter into synaptic cleft

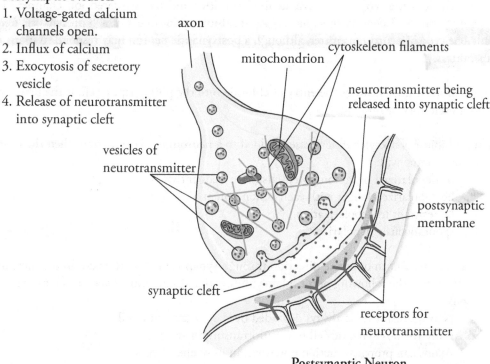

axon
mitochondrion
cytoskeleton filaments
neurotransmitter being released into synaptic cleft
vesicles of neurotransmitter
postsynaptic membrane
synaptic cleft
receptors for neurotransmitter

Postsynaptic Neuron
1. Neurotransmitter binds to ligand-gated ion channel.
2. Ions enter postsynaptic cell.
3. Membrane polarization is increased or decreased.

Figure 6   A Typical Synapse

An example of a chemical synapse that is commonly used is the **neuromuscular junction** between neurons and skeletal muscle. The neurotransmitter that is released at the neuromuscular junction is **acetylcholine (ACh)**. When an action potential reaches such a synapse, acetylcholine is released into the synaptic cleft. The acetylcholine binds to the acetylcholine receptor on the surface of the postsynaptic cell membrane. When acetylcholine binds to its receptor, the receptor opens its associated sodium channel, allowing sodium to flow down a gradient into the cell, depolarizing the postsynaptic cell membrane. Meanwhile, acetylcholine in the synaptic cleft is degraded by the enzyme **acetylcholinesterase (AChE)**.

There are several different neurotransmitters and neurotransmitter receptors. Some of the other neurotransmitters are **gamma-aminobutyric acid (GABA)**, **serotonin**, **dopamine**, and **norepinephrine**. If a neurotransmitter, such as acetylcholine, opens a channel that depolarizes the postsynaptic membrane, the neurotransmitter is termed **excitatory**. Other neurotransmitters, however, have the opposite effect, making the postsynaptic membrane potential more negative than the resting potential, or hyperpolarized. Neurotransmitters that induce hyperpolarization of the postsynaptic membrane are termed **inhibitory**. (Note, however, that ultimately it is not the *neurotransmitter* that determines the effect on the postsynaptic cell, it is the *receptor* for that neurotransmitter and its associated ion channel. The same neurotransmitter can be excitatory in some cases and inhibitory in others.) Each presynaptic neuron can release only one type of neurotransmitter, although a postsynaptic neuron may respond to many different neurotransmitters.

- If a neurotransmitter causes the entry of chloride into the postsynaptic cell, is the neurotransmitter excitatory or inhibitory?[17]

- If an inhibitor of acetylcholinesterase is added to a neuromuscular junction, then the postsynaptic membrane will:[18]
    - A. be depolarized by action potentials more frequently.
    - B. be depolarized longer with each action potential.
    - C. be resistant to depolarization.
    - D. spontaneously depolarize.

- Signals can be sent in only one direction through synapses such as the neuromuscular junction. Which of the following best explains undirectional signaling at synapses between neurons?[19]
    - A. Neurotransmitter is always degraded by the postsynaptic cell.
    - B. Only the postsynaptic cell has neurotransmitter receptors.
    - C. Axons can propagate action potentials in only one direction.
    - D. Only the postsynaptic cell has a resting membrane potential.

---

[17] Chloride ions are negatively charged. The entry of chloride ions into the cell will make the postsynaptic potential more negative, or hyperpolarized, so the neurotransmitter is inhibitory.

[18] **B is the correct answer.** If acetylcholinesterase is inhibited, acetylcholine will remain in the synaptic cleft longer, and acetylcholine-gated sodium channels will remain open longer with each action potential that reaches the synapse. If the sodium channels are open longer, the depolarization of the postsynaptic membrane will last longer.

[19] Signaling is unidirectional because only the presynaptic cell has vesicles of neurotransmitter that are released in response to action potentials, and only the postsynaptic neuron has receptors that bind neurotransmitter (choice B is correct). The degradation of neurotransmitter is irrelevant to the direction of signal propagation (choice A is wrong), axons are capable of propagating action potentials in both directions (even though this is not what they normally do; choice C is wrong), and all cells have a resting membrane potential (choice D is wrong).

Summation

Once an action potential is initiated in a neuron, it will propagate to the end of the axon at a speed and magnitude of depolarization that do not vary from one action potential to another. The action potential is an "**all-or-nothing**" event. The key regulated step in the nervous system is whether or not a neuron will fire an action potential. Action potentials are initiated when the postsynaptic membrane reaches the threshold depolarization (about −50 mV) required to open voltage-gated sodium channels. The postsynaptic depolarization caused by the release of neurotransmitter by one action potential at one synapse is not generally sufficient to induce this degree of depolarization. A postsynaptic neuron has many different neurons with synapses leading to it, however, and each of these synapses can release neurotransmitter many times per second. The "decision" by a postsynaptic neuron whether to fire an action potential is determined by adding the effect of all of the synapses impinging on a neuron, both excitatory and inhibitory. This addition of stimuli is termed **summation**.

Excitatory neurotransmitters cause postsynaptic depolarization, or **excitatory postsynaptic potentials** (**EPSPs**), while inhibitory neurotransmitters cause **inhibitory postsynaptic potentials** (**IPSPs**). One form of summation is **temporal summation**, in which a presynaptic neuron fires action potentials so rapidly that the EPSPs or IPSPs pile up on top of each other. If they are EPSPs, the additive effect might be enough to reach the threshold depolarization required to start a postsynaptic action potential. If they are IPSPs, the postsynaptic cell will hyperpolarize, moving further and further away from threshold, effectively becoming inhibited. The other form of summation is **spatial summation**, in which the EPSPs and IPSPs from all of the synapses on the postsynaptic membrane are summed at a given moment in time. If the total of all EPSPs and IPSPs causes the postsynaptic membrane to reach the threshold voltage, an action potential will be fired.

- In which one of the following ways can a presynaptic neuron increase the intensity of signal it transmits?[20]
  - A. Increase the size of presynaptic action potentials
  - B. Increase the frequency of action potentials
  - C. Change the type of neurotransmitter it releases
  - D. Change the speed of action potential propagation

---

[20] A neuron cannot change the size of action potentials it transmits, but it can increase the *number* of action potentials it transmits in a given amount of time (the *frequency* of action potentials). The increased frequency of action potentials will add up through temporal summation in the postsynaptic cell to produce an increased response (choice **B** is correct). Action potentials are all-or-nothing once they are started. The magnitude of membrane depolarization during propagation of the action potential does not change (choice A is wrong). A neuron can release only one type of neurotransmitter and does not change this (choice C is wrong), and the speed of propagation cannot be varied from one action potential to the next (choice D is wrong).

7.3 FUNCTIONAL ORGANIZATION OF THE HUMAN NERVOUS SYSTEM

The nervous system must receive information, decide what to do with it, and cause muscles or glands to act upon that decision. Receiving information is the **sensory** function of the nervous system (carried out by the peripheral nervous system, or **PNS**), processing the information is the **integrative** function (carried out by the central nervous system, or **CNS**), and acting on it is the **motor** function (also carried out by the PNS).[21] **Motor neurons** carry information from the nervous system toward organs which can act upon that information, known as **effectors**. [What are the two types of effectors?[22]] Notice that "motor" neurons do not lead only "to muscle." Motor neurons, which carry information away from the central nervous system and innervate effectors, are called **efferent** neurons (remember, efferents go to effectors). **Sensory neurons**, which carry information toward the central nervous system, are called **afferent** neurons.

Reflexes

The simplest example of nervous system activity is the **reflex**. This is a direct motor response to sensory input which occurs without conscious thought. In fact, it usually occurs without any involvement of the brain at all. In the simplest example, a sensory neuron transmits an action potential to a synapse with a motor neuron in the spinal cord, which causes an action to occur. For example, in the **muscle stretch reflex**, a sensory neuron detects stretching of a muscle (Figure 7). The sensory neuron has a long dendrite and a long axon, which transmits an impulse to a motor neuron cell body in the spinal cord. The motor neuron's long axon synapses with the muscle that was stretched and causes it to contract. That is why the quadriceps (thigh) muscle contracts when the patellar tendon is stretched by tapping with a reflex hammer. A reflex such as this one, involving only two neurons and one synapse, is known as a **monosynaptic reflex arc**.

Something else also happens when a physician taps the patellar tendon. Not only does the quadriceps *contract*, but the hamstring also *relaxes*. If it did not, the leg would not be able to extend (straighten). The sensory neuron (that detects stretch) synapses with not only a motor neuron for the quadriceps, but also with an **inhibitory interneuron**. This is a short neuron which forms an inhibitory synapse with a motor neuron innervating the hamstring muscle. When the sensory nerve is stimulated by stretch, it stimulates both the quadriceps motor neuron and the inhibitory interneuron to the hamstring motor neuron. As a result, the quadriceps contracts and the hamstring relaxes. An interneuron is the simplest example of the integrative role of the nervous system. Concurrent relaxation of the hamstring and contraction of the quadriceps is an example of **reciprocal inhibition**.

- If a reflex occurs without the involvement of the brain, how are we aware of the action?[23]

---

[21] More detailed information about the anatomy and functions of the CNS and PNS will be presented later in this chapter.

[22] Muscles and glands

[23] Two ways: First, the sensory neuron also branches to form a synapse with a neuron leading to the brain. Second, other sensory information is received after the action is taken.

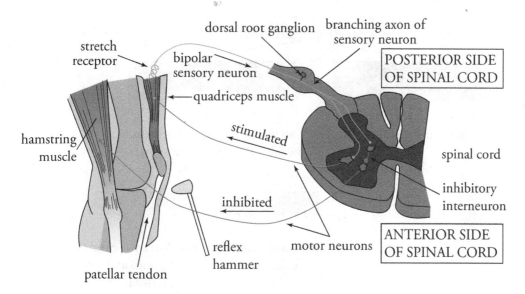

Figure 7   The Muscle Stretch Reflex

Large-Scale Functional Organization

The peripheral nervous system can be subdivided into several functional divisions (Figure 8). The portion of this system concerned with conscious sensation and deliberate, voluntary movement of skeletal muscle is the **somatic** division. The portion concerned with digestion, metabolism, circulation, perspiration, and other involuntary processes is the **autonomic** division. The somatic and autonomic divisions both include afferent and efferent functions, although the sources of sensory input and the target of efferent nerves are different. The efferent portion of the autonomic division is further split into two subdivisions: **sympathetic** and **parasympathetic**. When the sympathetic system is activated, the body is prepared for "fight or flight." When the parasympathetic system is activated, the body is prepared to "rest and digest." Table 1 summarizes the main effects of the autonomic system. Notice that many sympathetic effects result from release of epinephrine.[24] into the bloodstream by the adrenal medulla. The parasympathetic system prepares you to rest and digest food.

---

[24] In Greek, "epi" means upon or on top of, and "nephr" refers to the kidney (as in nephron, the microscopic functional unit of the kidney); hence epinephrine is "the hormone secreted by the gland on top of the kidney." Another name for epinephrine is adrenaline. In Latin, "ad" also means upon, and "renal" likewise refers to the kidney. The gland which secretes epinephrine is the adrenal gland.

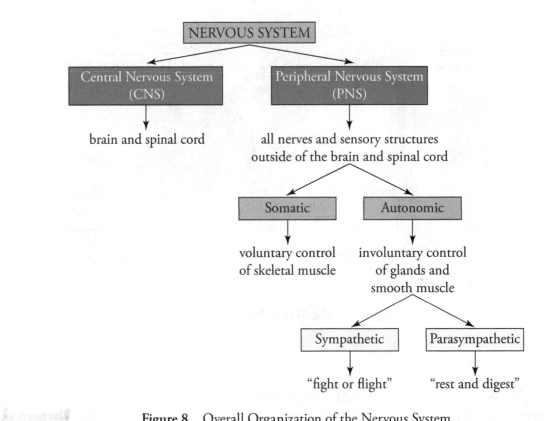

Figure 8   Overall Organization of the Nervous System

Organ or System	Parasympathetic: rest and digest	Sympathetic: fight or flight
digestive system: glands	stimulation	inhibition
motility	stimulation (stimulates digestion)	inhibition (inhibits digestion)
sphincters	relaxation	contraction
urinary system: bladder	contraction (stimulates urination)	relaxation (inhibits urination)
urethral sphincter	relaxation (stimulates urination)	contraction (inhibits urination)
bronchial smooth muscle	constriction (closes airways)	relaxation (opens airways)
cardiovascular system heart rate and contractility blood flow to skeletal muscle	 decreased —	 increased increased
skin	—	sweating and general vasoconstriction; emotional vasodilation (blushing)
eye: pupil	constriction	dilation
muscles controlling lens	near vision accommodation	accommodation for far vision
adrenal medulla	—	release of epinephrine
genitals	erection / lubrication	ejaculation / orgasm

Table 1   Effects of the Autonomic Nervous System

7.4 ANATOMICAL ORGANIZATION OF THE NERVOUS SYSTEM

The main anatomical division of the nervous system is between the **central nervous system** (CNS) and the **peripheral nervous system** (PNS). The central nervous system is the brain and spinal cord. The peripheral nervous system includes all other axons, dendrites, and cell bodies. The great majority of neuronal cell bodies are found within the central nervous system. Sometimes they are bunched together to form structures called **nuclei.** (Don't confuse this with the nucleic-acid-containing nuclei of cells.) Somas located outside the central nervous system are found in bunches known as **ganglia**. The anatomy of both the central and the peripheral system will be presented.

CNS Anatomical Organization

The CNS includes the **spinal cord** and the brain. The brain has three subdivisions: the **hindbrain** (or the rhombencephalon), the **midbrain** (or the mesencephalon), and the **forebrain** (or the prosencephalon). These four regions of the CNS (which will be discussed individually below) perform increasingly complex functions. The entire CNS (brain and spinal cord) floats in **cerebrospinal fluid (CSF)**, a clear liquid that serves various functions such as shock absorption and exchange of nutrients and waste with the CNS.

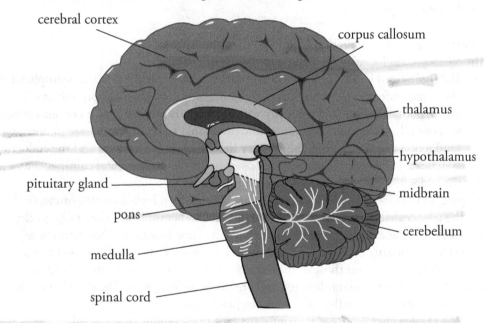

Figure 9 Organization of the CNS (cross-section of the brain)

1) The spinal cord is connected to the brain and is protected by the CSF and the vertebral column. It is a pathway for information to and from the brain. Most sensory data is relayed to the brain for integration, but the spinal cord is also a site for information integration and processing. The spinal cord is responsible for simple spinal reflexes (like the deep tendon reflex) and is also involved in primitive processes such as walking, urination, and sex organ function.

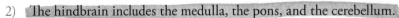

2) The hindbrain includes the medulla, the pons, and the cerebellum.
- **The medulla** (or medulla oblongata) is located below the pons and is the area of the brain that connects to the spinal cord. It functions in relaying information between other areas of the brain, and regulates vital autonomic functions such as blood pressure and digestive functions (including vomiting). Also, the respiratory rhythmicity centers are found here.
- **The pons** is located below the midbrain and above the medulla oblongata. It is the connection point between the brain stem and the cerebellum (see below). The pons controls some autonomic functions and coordinates movement; it plays a role in balance and antigravity posture.
- **The cerebellum** (or "little brain") is located behind the pons and below the cerebral hemispheres. It is an integrating center where complex movements are coordinated. An instruction for movement from the forebrain must be sent to the cerebellum, where the billions of decisions necessary for smooth execution of the movement are made. Damage to the cerebellum results in poor hand-eye coordination and balance. Both the cerebellum and the pons receive information from the vestibular apparatus in the inner ear, which monitors acceleration and position relative to gravity.

3) **The midbrain** is a relay for visual and auditory information and contains much of the reticular activating system (RAS), which is responsible for arousal or wakefulness.

Another term you should be familiar with is **brainstem**. Together, the medulla, pons and midbrain constitute the brainstem, which contains important processing centers and relays information to or from the cerebellum and cerebrum.

4) The forebrain includes the **diencephalon** and the **telencephalon**.
   a) The diencephalon includes the thalamus and hypothalamus:
   - **The thalamus** is located near the middle of the brain below the cerebral hemispheres and above the midbrain. It contains relay and processing centers for sensory information.
   - **The hypothalamus** interacts directly with many parts of the brain. It contains centers for controlling emotions and autonomic functions, and has a major role in hormone production and release. It is the primary link between the nervous and the endocrine systems, and by controlling the pituitary gland is the fundamental control center for the endocrine system (discussed later in this chapter).
   b) All parts of the CNS up to and including the diencephalon form a single symmetrical stalk, but the telencephalon consists of two separate cerebral hemispheres. Generally speaking, the areas of the left and right hemispheres have the same functions. However, the left hemisphere primarily controls the motor functions of the right side of the body, and the right hemisphere controls those of the left side. Also, in most people, the left side of the brain is said to be dominant. It is generally responsible for speech. The right hemisphere is more concerned with visual-spatial reasoning and music.
   - **The cerebral hemispheres** are connected by a thick bundle of axons called the **corpus callosum**. A person with a cut corpus callosum has two independent cerebral cortices and to a certain extent two independent minds![25]
   - **The cerebrum** is the largest region of the human brain and consists of the large, paired cerebral hemispheres. The hemispheres of the cerebrum consist of the **cerebral cortex** (an outer layer of gray matter) plus an inner core of white matter connecting the cortex to the diencephalon.[26] The gray matter is composed of trillions of somas; the

---

[25] Anyone interested in reading about jaw-dropping neurological cases should begin with Oliver Sack's *The Man Who Mistook His Wife for a Hat*. You will *not* be sorry if you buy this book.

[26] The word cortex means "outside layer"; for example, an orange peel may be called the cortex of the orange; the outside layer of a gland is also known as its cortex.

7.4

white matter is composed of myelinated axons. (Most axons in the CNS and PNS are myelinated.) The cerebral hemispheres are responsible for conscious thought processes and intellectual functions. They also play a role in processing somatic sensory and motor information. The cerebral cortex is divided into four pairs of lobes, each of which is devoted to specific functions:

i)   the **frontal lobes** initiate all voluntary movement and are involved in complex reasoning skills and problem solving.

ii) the **parietal lobes** are involved in general sensations (such as touch, temperature, pressure, vibration, etc.) and in gustation (taste).

iii) the **temporal lobes** process auditory and olfactory sensation and are involved in short-term memory.

iv) the **occipital lobes** process visual sensation.

Figure 10 shows some of the more important cortical areas.

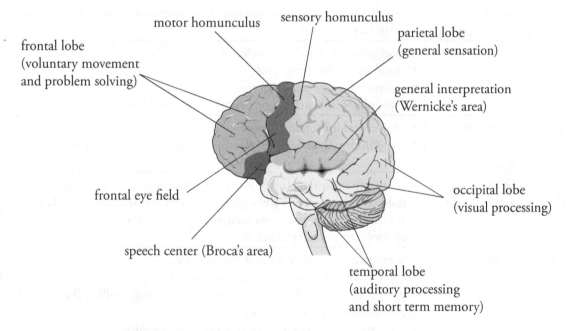

Figure 10   Principal Areas of the Cerebral Cortex

Two last regions of the brain deserve mention:

- The **basal nuclei** (cerebral nuclei) are composed of gray matter and are located deep within the cerebral hemispheres. They include several functional subdivisions, but broadly function in regulating body movement.

- The **limbic system** is located between the cerebrum and the diencephalon. It includes several substructures (such as the amygdala, the cingulate gyrus, and the hippocampus) and works closely with parts of the cerebrum, diencephalon, and midbrain. The limbic system is important in emotion and memory.

The information above describes the general functions of each region of the brain. Table 2 on the next page summarizes the brain functions and provides a little more specific detail for each region.

7.4

Structure	General Function	Specific Functions
Spinal cord	Simple reflexes	• controls simple stretch and tendon reflexes • controls primitive processes such as walking, urination, and sex organ function
Medulla	Involuntary functions	• controls autonomic processes such as blood pressure, blood flow, heart rate, respiratory rate, swallowing, vomiting • controls reflex reactions such as coughing or sneezing • relays sensory information to the cerebellum and the thalamus
Pons	Relay station and balance	• controls antigravity posture and balance • connects the spinal cord and medulla with upper regions of the brain • relays information to the cerebellum and thalamus
Cerebellum	Movement coordination	• integrating center • coordination of complex movement, balance and posture, muscle tone, spatial equilibrium
Midbrain	Eye movement	• integration of visual and auditory information • visual and auditory reflexes • wakefulness and consciousness • coordinates information on posture and muscle tone
Thalamus	Integrating center and relay station	• relay center for somatic (conscious) sensation • relays information between the spinal cord and the cerebral cortex
Hypothalamus	Homeostasis and behavior	• controls homeostatic functions (such as temperature regulation, fluid balance, appetite) through both neural and hormonal regulation • controls primitive emotions such as anger, rage, and sex drive • controls the pituitary gland
Basal nuclei	Movement	• regulate body movement and muscle tone • coordination of learned movement patterns • general pattern of rhythm movements (such as controlling the cycle of arm and leg movements when walking) • subconscious adjustments of conscious movements
Limbic system	Emotion, memory, and learning	• controls emotional states • links conscious and unconscious portions of the brain • helps with memory storage and retrieval
Cerebral cortex	Perception, skeletal muscle movement, integration center	• divided into four lobes (frontal, parietal, temporal, and occipital) with specialized subfunctions • conscious through processes and planning, awareness, and sensation • intellectual function (intelligence, learning, reading, communication) • abstract thought and reasoning • memory storage and retrieval • initiation and coordination of voluntary movement • complex motor patterns
Corpus callosum	Connection	• connects the left and right cerebral hemispheres

Table 2 Summary of Brain Functions

The motor and sensory regions of the cortex are organized such that a particular small area of cortex controls a particular body part. A larger area is devoted to a body part which requires more motor control or more sensation (Figure 11). For example, more cortex is devoted to the lips than to the entire leg. The body parts represented on the cortex can be sketched. The drawing looks like a distorted person, known as a **homunculus** (little man).

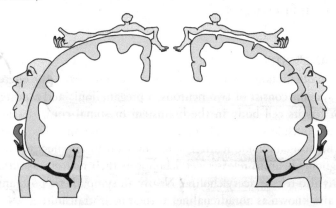

Figure 11   The Sensory Homunculus

PNS Anatomical Organization

All neurons entering and exiting the CNS are carried by 12 pairs of **cranial nerves** and 31 pairs of **spinal nerves.** Cranial nerves convey sensory and motor information to and from the brainstem. Spinal nerves convey sensory and motor information to and from the spinal cord. The different functional divisions of the nervous system have different anatomical organizations (Figure 12).

The **vagus nerve** is an important example of a cranial nerve, and one that you should be familiar with for the MCAT. The effects of this nerve upon the heart and GI tract are to decrease the heart rate and increase GI activity; as such is it part of the *parasympathetic division* of the autonomic nervous system. It is a bundle of axons that end in ganglia on the surface of the heart, stomach, and other visceral organs. The many axons constituting the vagus nerve are preganglionic and come from cell bodies located in the CNS. On the surface of the heart and stomach they synapse with postganglionic neurons. The detailed terminology in this paragraph will make more sense to you as you read through the next couple of sections.

Somatic PNS Anatomy

The somatic system has a simple organization:

- *All* somatic motor neurons innervate skeletal muscle cells, use ACh as their neurotransmitter, and have their cell bodies in the brain stem or the ventral (front) portion of the spinal cord.

- *All* somatic sensory neurons have a long dendrite extending from a sensory receptor toward the soma, which is located just outside the CNS in a **dorsal root ganglion.** The dorsal root ganglion is a bunch of somatic (and autonomic) sensory neuron cell bodies located just dorsal to (to the back of) the spinal cord. There is a pair of dorsal root ganglia for every segment of the spinal cord, and thus the dorsal root ganglia form a chain along the dorsal (back) aspect of the vertebral column. The dorsal root ganglia are protected within the vertebral column but are outside the **meninges** (protective sheath of the brain and cord) and thus outside the CNS. An axon extends from the somatic sensory neuron's soma into the spinal cord. In all somatic sensory neurons, the first synapse is in the CNS; depending on the type of sensory information conveyed, the axon either synapses in the cord, or stretches all the way up to the brain stem before its first synapse!

Autonomic PNS Anatomy

Anatomical organization of autonomic efferents is a bit more complex.[27] The efferents of the sympathetic and parasympathetic systems consist of two neurons: a preganglionic and a postganglionic neuron. The **preganglionic neuron** has its cell body in the brainstem or spinal cord. It sends an axon to an autonomic ganglion, located outside the spinal column. In the ganglion, this axon synapses with a **postganglionic neuron**. The postganglionic neuron sends an axon to an effector (smooth muscle or gland). *All* autonomic preganglionic neurons release acetylcholine as their neurotransmitter. *All* parasympathetic postganglionic neurons also release acetylcholine. Nearly all sympathetic postganglionic neurons release norepinephrine (NE, also known as noradrenaline) as their neurotransmitter.

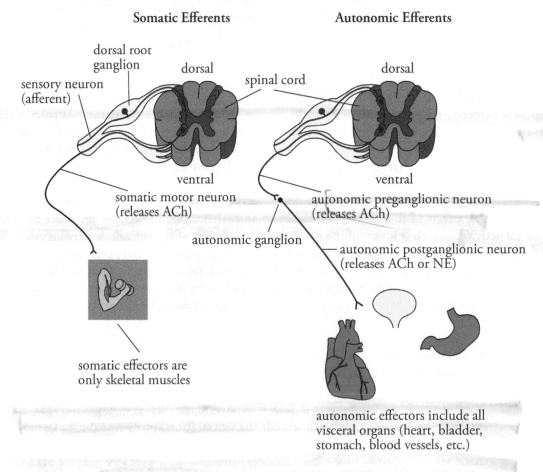

Figure 12 Anatomical Organization of PNS Efferents

[27] The anatomy of autonomic sensory neurons (afferents) is poorly defined and will not be on the MCAT.

All sympathetic preganglionic efferent neurons have their cell bodies in the thoracic (chest) or lumbar (lower back) regions of the spinal cord. Hence the sympathetic system is also referred to as the *thoracolumbar system*. The parasympathetic system is known as the *craniosacral system*, because all of its preganglionic neurons have cell bodies in the brainstem (which is in the head or cranium) or in the lowest portion of the spinal cord, the sacral portion. In the sympathetic system, the preganglionic axon is relatively short, and there are only a few ganglia; these sympathetic ganglia are quite large. The sympathetic postganglionic cell sends a long axon to the effector. In contrast, the parasympathetic preganglionic neuron sends a long axon to a small ganglion which is close to the effector. For example, parasympathetic ganglia controlling the intestines are located on the outer wall of the gut. The parasympathetic postganglionic neuron has a very short axon, since the cell body is close to the target.[28] Table 3 summarizes these differences.

The autonomic afferent (sensory) neurons are similar to the somatic afferent neurons with one exception: They can synapse in the PNS (at the autonomic ganglia) with autonomic efferent neurons in what is known as a "short reflex." (Recall that the first synapse of somatic afferent neurons is in the CNS.)

	Sympathetic	Parasympathetic
General function	fight or flight, mobilize energy	rest and digest, store energy
Location of preganglionic soma	thoracolumbar = thoracic and lumbar spinal cord	craniosacral = brainstem ("cranial") and sacral spinal cord
Preganglionic axon neurotransmitter = acetylcholine (ACh)	short	long
Ganglia	close to cord; far from target	far from cord, close to target
Postganglionic axon (usual neurotransmitter)	long (norepinephrine [NE])	short (ACh)

Table 3   Sympathetic vs. Parasympathetic

The Adrenal Medulla

The **adrenal gland** is named for its location: "Ad-" connotes "above," and "renal" refers to the kidney. There are two adrenal glands, one above each kidney. The adrenal has an inner portion known as the **medulla** and an outer portion known as the **cortex**. The cortex is an important endocrine gland, secreting **glucocorticoids** (the main one is cortisol), **mineralocorticoid** (the main one is aldosterone), and some sex hormones.

The adrenal medulla, however, is part of the sympathetic nervous system. It is embryologically derived from sympathetic postganglionic neurons and is directly innervated by sympathetic preganglionic neurons. Upon activation of the sympathetic system, the adrenal gland is stimulated to release **epinephrine**, also known as **adrenaline**. Epinephrine is a slightly modified version of *nor*epinephrine, the neurotransmitter released by sympathetic postganglionic neurons. Epinephrine is a hormone because it is released into the bloodstream by a ductless gland. But in many ways it behaves like a neurotransmitter. It elicits its effects very rapidly, and the effects are quite short-lived. Epinephrine release from the adrenal medulla is what causes the sudden flushing and sweating one experiences when severely startled. In general, epinephrine's effects are those listed in Table 1 for the sympathetic system. Stimulation of the heart is an especially important effect.

---

[28] The mnemonic "*para* long *pre*" will help you in med school.

7.5   SENSATION

Types of Sensory Receptors

Sensory receptors are designed to detect one type of stimulus from either the interior of the body or the external environment. Each sensory receptor receives only one kind of information and transmits that information to sensory neurons, which can in turn convey it to the central nervous system. [How does the brain know the difference between stimulation of visual receptors and olfactory receptors?[29]] Sensory receptors that detect stimuli from the outside world are **exteroceptors** and receptors that respond to internal stimuli are **interoceptors**. A more important distinction between sensory receptors is based on the type of stimulus they detect. The types of sensory receptors are listed below.

1) **Mechanoreceptors** respond to mechanical disturbances. For example, **Pacinian corpuscles** are pressure sensors located deep in the skin. The Pacinian corpuscle is shaped like an onion. It is composed of concentric layers of specialized membranes. When the corpuscular membranes are distorted by firm pressure on the skin, the nerve ending becomes depolarized and the signal travels up the dendrite (note that these are graded potential changes—*not* action potentials). Another important mechanoreceptor is the **auditory hair cell**. This is a specialized cell found in the cochlea of the inner ear. It detects vibrations caused by sound waves. **Vestibular hair cells** are located within special organs called semicircular canals, also found in the inner ear. Their role is to detect acceleration and position relative to gravity. An example of an autonomic mechanoreceptor would be a receptor detecting stretch of the intestinal wall.

2) **Chemoreceptors** respond to particular chemicals. For example, **olfactory receptors** detect airborne chemicals and allow us to smell things. Taste buds are **gustatory receptors**. Autonomic chemoreceptors in the walls of the carotid and aortic arteries respond to changes in arterial pH, PCO_2, and PO_2 levels.

3) **Nociceptors** are pain receptors.[30] They are stimulated by tissue injury. Nociceptors are the simplest type of sensory receptor, generally consisting of a free nerve ending that detects chemical signs of tissue damage. (In that sense the nociceptor is a simple chemoreceptor.) Nociceptors may be somatic or autonomic. Autonomic pain receptors do not provide the conscious mind with clear pain information, but they frequently give a sensation of dull, aching pain. They may also create the illusion of pain on the skin, when their nerves cross paths with somatic afferents from the skin. This phenomenon is known as **referred pain**.

4) **Thermoreceptors** are stimulated by changes in temperature. There are autonomic and somatic examples.

5) **Electromagnetic receptors** are stimulated by electromagnetic waves. In humans, the only examples are the rod and cone cells of the retina of the eye (also termed **photoreceptors**). Other animals can sense infrared radiation, and some creatures (e.g., certain whales) can even sense the earth's magnetic field.

---

[29] Both signals are received in the brain as action potentials from sensory neurons. The brain distinguishes the sensory stimuli based on which sensory neurons are signaling.

[30] *Noci-* is from the Latin *nocuus*, meaning harmful, as in *noxious*.

An interesting property of sensory receptors is their ability to adapt to a stimulus. Adaptation is a decrease in firing frequency when the intensity of a stimulus remains constant. For example, if you walk into a kitchen where someone is baking bread, the bread odor molecules stimulate your olfactory receptors to a great degree and you smell the bread baking. But if you remain in the kitchen for a few minutes, you stop smelling the bread; the continuous input to the olfactory receptors causes them to stop firing even though the odor molecules are still present. This is what allows us to "get used to" certain environments and situations, for example, cold pool water, loud background noise, etc. The receptors don't stop being *able* to respond; they can be retriggered if the stimulus intensity increases. For example, if you open up the oven door, you will smell the bread again. Likewise, if you are used to the background noise in a restaurant, but someone drops a plate, you'll hear it. In other words: the nervous system is programmed to respond to *changing stimuli* and not so much to constant stimuli, because for the most part, constant stimuli are not a threat whereas changing stimuli might need to be dealt with. (Note that nociceptors *do not adapt* under any circumstance. We can learn to ignore them, but pain is something that the nervous system wants us to *do* something about since it is an indication that something is wrong.)

Proprioceptors

This is a broad category including many different types of receptors. Proprioception refers to awareness of self (i.e., awareness of body part position).[31] An important example of a proprioceptor is the **muscle spindle**, a mechanoreceptor. This is a sensory organ specialized to detect muscle stretch. You are already familiar with it because it is the receptor that senses muscle stretch in the deep tendon reflex. By monitoring the activity of many muscle spindles, the proprioceptive component of the somatic sensory system allows us to know the positions of our body parts. This is most important during activity, when precise feedback is essential for coordinated motion. [What portion of the CNS would you expect to require input from proprioceptors?[32]]

Gustation and Olfaction

Taste and smell are senses that rely on chemoreceptors in the mouth and nasal passages. **Gustation** is taste, and **olfaction** is smell. Much of what is assumed to be taste is actually smell. (Try eating with a bad head cold.) In fact, taste receptors (known as **taste buds**) can only distinguish five flavors: sweet (glucose), salty (Na^+), bitter (basic), sour (acidic), and umami (amino acids and nucleotides). Each taste bud responds most strongly to one of these five stimuli. The taste bud is composed of a bunch of specialized epithelial cells, shaped roughly like an onion. In its center is a **taste pore**, with **taste hairs** that detect food chemicals. Information about taste is transmitted to the brain by cranial nerves.

Olfaction is accomplished by olfactory receptors in the roof of the **nasopharynx** (nasal cavity). The receptors detect airborne chemicals that dissolve in the mucus covering the nasal membrane. Humans can distinguish thousands of different smells. Olfactory nerves project directly to the **olfactory bulbs** of the brain. The olfactory bulbs are located near certain centers in the brain which are important for memory (which may explain why unexpected smells can bring back vivid memories).

---

[31] *Proprio-* means *of or pertaining to the self*, as in "proprietary."

[32] The cerebellum, which is responsible for motor coordination.

Hearing and the Vestibular System

Structure of the Ear

The **auricle** or **pinna** and the external **auditory canal** comprise the **outer ear**. The **middle ear** is divided from the outer ear by the **tympanic membrane** or eardrum. The middle ear consists of the **ossicles**, three small bones called the **malleus** (hammer), the **incus** (anvil), and the **stapes** (stirrup). The stapes attaches to the **oval window**, a membrane that divides the middle and **inner ear**. Structures of the inner ear include the **cochlea**, the **semicircular canals**, the **utricle**, and the **saccule**. The semicircular canals together with the utricle and saccule are important to the sense of balance. The **round window** is a membrane-covered hole in the cochlea near the oval window. It releases excess pressure. The **Eustachian tube** (also known as the **auditory tube**) is a passageway from the back of the throat to the middle ear. It functions to equalize the pressure on both sides of the eardrum and is the cause of the "ear popping" one experiences at high altitudes or underwater.

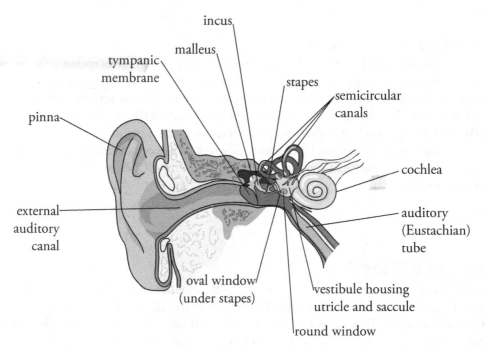

incus

malleus

tympanic
membrane

stapes

semicircular
canals

pinna

cochlea

external
auditory
canal

auditory
(Eustachian)
tube

oval window
(under stapes)

vestibule housing
utricle and saccule

round window

Figure 13 The Ear

Mechanism of Hearing

Sound waves enter the external ear to pass into the auditory canal, causing the eardrum to vibrate. The malleus attached to the eardrum receives the vibrations, which are passed on to the incus and then to the stapes. The bones of the middle ear are arranged in such a way that they amplify sound vibrations passing through the middle ear. The stapes is the innermost of the three middle-ear bones, contacting the oval window. Vibration of the oval window creates pressure waves in the **perilymph** and **endolymph**, the fluids in the cochlea. Note that sound vibrations are first conveyed through air, next through bone, and then through liquid before being sensed. The pressure waves in the endolymph cause vibration of the **basilar membrane**, a thin membrane extending throughout the coiled length of the cochlea. The basilar membrane is covered with the auditory receptor cells known as **hair cells**. These cells have **cilia** (hairs) projecting from their apical (top) surfaces (opposite the basilar membrane). The hairs contact the **tectorial**

7.5

membrane (tectorial means "roof"), and when the basilar membrane moves, the hairs are dragged across the tectorial membrane and they bend. This displacement opens ion channels in the hair cells, which results in neurotransmitter release. Dendrites from bipolar auditory afferent neurons are stimulated by this neurotransmitter, and thus sound vibrations are converted to nerve impulses. The basilar membrane, hair cells, and tectorial membrane together are known as the **organ of Corti**. The outer ear and middle ear convey sound waves to the cochlea, and the organ of Corti in the cochlea is the primary site at which auditory stimuli are detected.

Summary: From Sound to Hearing

sound waves → auricle → external auditory canal → tympanic membrane → malleus → incus → stapes → oval window → perilymph → endolymph → basilar membrane → auditory hair cells → tectorial membrane → neurotransmitters stimulate bipolar auditory neurons → brain → perception

---

Pitch (frequency) of sound is distinguished by which *regions* of the basilar membrane vibrate, stimulating different auditory neurons. The basilar membrane is thick and sturdy near the oval window and gradually becomes thin and floppy near the apex of the cochlea. Low frequency (long wavelength) sounds stimulate hair cells at the apex of the cochlear duct, farthest away from the oval window, while high-pitched sounds stimulate hair cells at the base of the cochlea, near the oval window. **Loudness of sound is distinguished by the *amplitude* of vibration.** Larger vibrations cause more frequent action potentials in auditory neurons.

- If a sensory neuron leading from the ear to the brain fires an action potential more rapidly, how will the brain perceive this change?[33]
- In some cases of deafness, sound can still be detected by conduction of vibration through the skull to the cochlea. If the auditory nerve is severed, can sound still be detected by conductance through bone?[34]
- If the bones of the middle ear are unable to move, would this impair the detection of sound by conductance through bone?[35]

Balance

The **semicircular canals** are three tubes filled with endolymph. Like the cochlea, they contain hair cells that detect motion. However, their function is to detect not sound, but rather rotational acceleration of the head. They are innervated by afferent neurons which send balance information to the pons, cerebellum, and other areas. The **utricle** and **saccule** are two other balance-monitoring organs located in the inner ear. They monitor static equilibrium and linear acceleration.

---

[33] More rapid firing of a cochlear neuron indicates an increase in volume of sound. If the pitch changed, a different set of neurons would fire action potentials.

[34] Conductance through bone allows some hearing by causing the cochlea to vibrate, which stimulates action potentials that pass through the auditory nerve to the brain. However, if the auditory nerve is severed, no hearing of any kind is possible.

[35] The bones of the middle ear serve to conduct vibration from the outer ear to the liquid within the cochlea but are not involved directly in detecting sound. Bone conductance can still stimulate the cochlea and result in hearing if the middle ear is nonfunctional.

Vision: Structure and Function

The eye is the structure designed to detect visual stimuli. The structures of the eye first form an image on the retina, which detects light and converts the stimuli into action potentials to send to the brain. Light enters the eye by passing through the **cornea**, the clear portion at the front of the eye. Light is bent or **refracted** as it passes through the cornea (which is highly curved and thus acts as a lens), since the refractive index of the cornea is higher than that of air. The cornea is continuous at its borders with the white of the eye, the **sclera**. Beneath the sclera is a layer called the **choroid**. It contains darkly-pigmented cells; this pigmentation absorbs excess light within the eye. Beneath the choroid is the **retina**, the surface upon which light is focused.

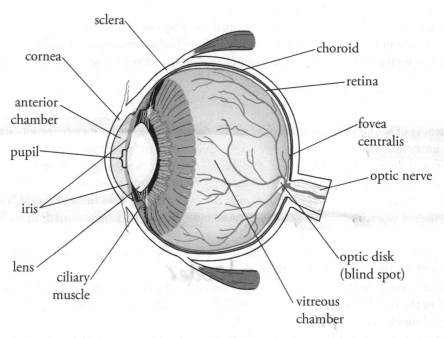

Figure 14   The Eye

Just inside the cornea is the **anterior chamber** (front chamber), which contains a fluid termed **aqueous humor**. At the back of the anterior chamber is a membrane called the **iris** with an opening called the **pupil**. The iris is the colored part of the eye, and muscles in the iris regulate the diameter of the pupil. Just behind the iris is the **posterior chamber**, also containing aqueous humor. In the back part of the posterior chamber is the **lens**. Its role is to fine-tune the angle of incoming light, so that the beams are perfectly focused upon the retina. The curvature of the lens (and thus its refractive power) is varied by the **ciliary muscle**.

Light passes through the **vitreous chamber** en route from the lens to the retina. This chamber contains a thick, jelly-like fluid called **vitreous humor**. The retina is located at the back of the eye. It contains electromagnetic receptor cells (photoreceptors) known as **rods** and **cones** which are responsible for detecting light. The rods and cones synapse with nerve cells called **bipolar cells**. In accordance with the name "bipolar," these cells have only one axon and one dendrite. The bipolar cells in turn synapse with **ganglion cells**, whose axons comprise the **optic nerve**, which travels from each eye toward the occipital lobe of the brain where complex analysis of a visual image occurs. In Figure 15, you may notice that light has to pass through two layers of neurons before it can reach the rods and cones. The neurons are fine enough to not significantly obstruct incoming rays.

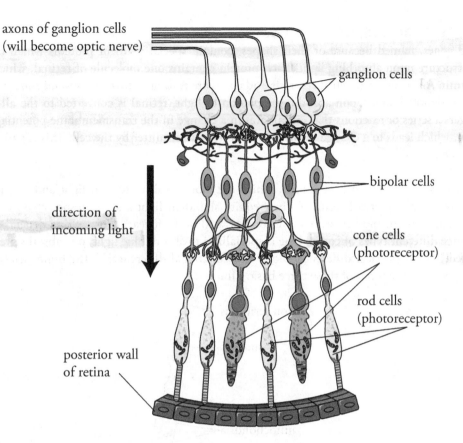

axons of ganglion cells
(will become optic nerve)

ganglion cells

bipolar cells

direction of
incoming light

cone cells
(photoreceptor)

rod cells
(photoreceptor)

posterior wall
of retina

Figure 15 Organization of the Retina

The point on the retina where many axons from ganglion cells converge to form the optic nerve is the **optic disk**. It is also known as the **blind spot** (Figure 16) because it contains no photoreceptors. Another special region of the retina is the **macula**. In the center of the macula is the **fovea centralis** (focal point), which contains only cones and is responsible for extreme visual acuity. When you stare directly at something, you focus its image on the fovea.

A   ●   ●   B

Cover your left eye and focus your right eye on dot A while holding the page about 5 inches
away from your face. Move the page forward and back. You will find that at a certain distance,
dot B becomes invisible. You are placing dot A on the fovea by focusing on it, and at the
correct distance, dot B becomes focused on the blind spot.

Figure 16 The Blind Spot

7.5

The Photoreceptors: Rods and Cones

Rods and cones, named because of their shapes, contain special pigment proteins which change their tertiary structure upon absorbing light. Each protein contains one molecule of **retinal**, which is derived from vitamin A. In the dark, when the rods and cones are resting, retinal has several *trans* double bonds and one *cis* double bond. Upon absorbing a photon of light, retinal is converted to the **all-trans form**. This triggers a series of reactions that culminates in a change in the transmembrane potential of the photoreceptor, which leads to a change in the release of neurotransmitter by the cell. This is passed on to the brain via the optic nerve.

Night vision is accomplished by the rods, which are more sensitive to dim light and are more concentrated in the periphery of the retina. Cones require abundant light and are responsible for color vision and high-acuity vision, and hence are more concentrated in the fovea.[36] Color vision depends on the presence of three different types of cones. One is specialized to absorb blue light, one absorbs green, and one absorbs red. [What physical difference allows this functional difference?[37]] The brain perceives hues by integrating the relative input of these three basic stimuli.

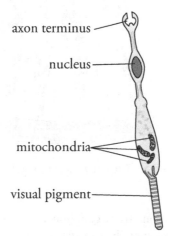

Figure 17 Rod Cell Structure

Defects in Visual Acuity

Normal vision is termed **emmetropia**. Too much or too little curvature of the cornea or lens results in visual defects. Too much curvature causes light to be bent too much and to be focused in front of the retina. The result is **myopia**, or nearsightedness. Myopia can be corrected by a concave (diverging) lens, which will cause the light rays to diverge slightly before they reach the cornea. **Hyperopia**, farsightedness, results from the focusing of light behind the retina. Hyperopia can be corrected by a convex (converging) lens, which causes light rays to converge before reaching the cornea. **Presbyopia** is an inability to **accommodate** (focus). It results from loss of flexibility of the lens, which occurs with aging.

---

[36] Remember: *Cones—Color—aCuity.*

[37] Each type of cone makes a particular pigment protein which is specialized to change conformation when light of the appropriate frequency strikes it.

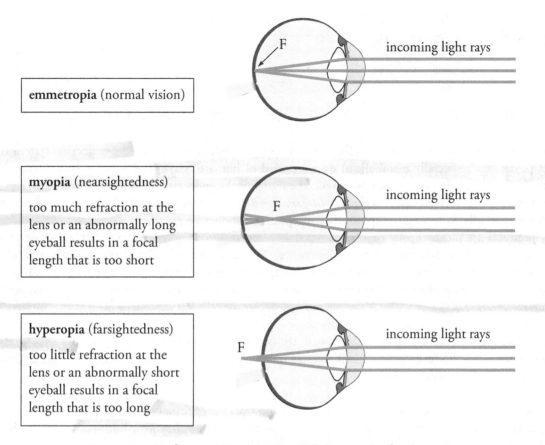

emmetropia (normal vision)

incoming light rays

F

myopia (nearsightedness)

too much refraction at the lens or an abnormally long eyeball results in a focal length that is too short

incoming light rays

F

hyperopia (farsightedness)

too little refraction at the lens or an abnormally short eyeball results in a focal length that is too long

incoming light rays

F

Figure 18   Defects in Visual Acuity ("F" denotes the focal point)

Modality	Receptor	Receptor type	Organ	Stimulus
Vision	• rods and cones	• electromagnetic	• retina	• light
Hearing	• auditory hair cells	• mechanoreceptor	• organ of Corti	• vibration
Olfaction	• olfactory nerve endings	• chemoreceptor	• individual neurons	• airborne chemicals
Taste	• taste cells	• chemoreceptor	• taste bud	• food chemicals
Touch (a few examples)	• Pacinian corpuscles • free nerve endings • temperature receptors	• mechanoreceptor • nociceptor • thermoreceptor	skin	• pressure • pain • temperature
Interoception (two examples)	• aortic arch baroreceptors • pH receptors	• baroreceptor • chemoreceptor	• aortic arch • aortic arch / medulla oblongata	• blood pressure • pH

Table 4   Summary of Sensation

7.6   THE ENDOCRINE SYSTEM

Hormone Types: Transport and Mechanisms of Action

While the nervous system regulates cellular function from instant to instant, the endocrine system regulates physiology (especially metabolism) over a period of hours to days. The nervous system communicates via the extremely rapid action potential. The signal of the endocrine system is the **hormone**, defined as a molecule which is *secreted into the bloodstream* by an endocrine gland, and which has its effects upon *distant* target cells possessing the appropriate receptor. An **endocrine gland** is a *ductless* gland whose secretory products are picked up by capillaries supplying blood to the region. (In contrast, **exocrine glands** secrete their products into the external environment by way of ducts, which empty into the gastrointestinal lumen or the external world.) A **hormone receptor** is a polypeptide that possesses a ligand-specific binding site. Binding of ligand (hormone) to the site causes the receptor to modify target cell activity. *Tissue-specificity of hormone action is determined by whether the cells of a tissue have the appropriate receptor.*

Some signaling molecules modify the activity of the cell which secreted them; this is an **autocrine** activity (*auto-* means self). For example, a T cell secretes interleukin 2, which binds to receptors on the same T cell to stimulate increased activity.

Hormones can be grouped into one of two classes. *Hydrophilic* hormones, such as **peptides** and **amino-acid derivatives**, must bind to receptors on the cell surface, while *hydrophobic* hormones, such as the **steroid hormones**, bind to receptors in the cellular interior.

Peptide Hormones

Peptide hormones are synthesized into the rough ER and modified in the Golgi. Then they are stored in vesicles until needed, when they are released by exocytosis. In the bloodstream they dissolve in the plasma, since they are hydrophilic. Their hydrophilicity also means they cannot cross biological membranes and thus are required to communicate with the interior of the target cell by way of a ___,[38] discussed in Chapter 5. To briefly review, the peptide hormone is a first messenger which must bind to a cell-surface receptor. The receptor is a polypeptide with a domain on the inner surface of the plasma membrane that contains the ability to catalytically activate a second messenger. The end result of second messenger activation is that the function of proteins in the cytoplasm is changed. A key feature of second messenger cascades is signal amplification, which allows a few activated receptors to change the activity of many enzymes in the cytoplasm.

Because peptide hormones modify the activity of existing enzymes in the cytoplasm, their effects are exerted rapidly, minutes to hours from the time of secretion. Also, the duration of their effects is brief.

There are two subgroups within the peptide hormone category: polypeptides and amino acid derivatives. An example of a polypeptide hormone is insulin, which has a complex tertiary structure involving disulfide bridges. It is secreted by the β cells of the pancreatic islets of Langerhans in response to elevated blood glucose and binds to a cell-surface receptor with a cytoplasmic domain possessing protein kinase

---

[38] second messenger cascade

activity. Amino acid derivatives, as their name implies, are derived from single amino acids and contain no peptide bonds. For example, tyrosine is the parent amino acid for the catecholamines (which include epinephrine) and the thyroid hormones. Despite the fact that these two classes are derived from the same precursor molecule, they have different properties. The catecholamines act like peptide hormones, while the thyroid hormones behave more like steroid hormones. Epinephrine is a small cyclic molecule secreted by the adrenal medulla upon activation of the sympathetic nervous system. It binds to cell-surface receptors to trigger a cascade of events that produces the second messenger cyclic adenosine monophosphate (cAMP) and activates protein kinases in the cytoplasm. Thyroid hormones incorporate iodine into their structure. They enter cells, bind to DNA, and activate transcription of genes involved in energy mobilization.

Steroid Hormones

Steroids are hydrophobic molecules synthesized from cholesterol in the smooth endoplasmic reticulum. Due to their hydrophobicity, steroids can freely diffuse through biological membranes. Thus they are not stored but rather diffuse into the bloodstream as soon as they are made. If a steroid hormone is not needed, it will not be made. Steroids' hydrophobicity also means they cannot be dissolved in the plasma. Instead they journey through the bloodstream stuck to proteins in the plasma, such as albumin. [What holds the steroid bound to a plasma protein?[39]] The small, hydrophobic steroid hormone exerts its effects upon target cells by *diffusing through the plasma membrane to bind with a receptor in the cytoplasm*. Once it has bound its ligand, the steroid hormone-receptor complex is transported into the nucleus, where it acts as a sequence-specific regulator of transcription. Because steroid hormones must modify transcription to change the *amount* and/or type of proteins in the cell, their effects are exerted slowly, over a period of days, and persist for days to weeks.

Steroids regulating sexuality, reproduction, and development are secreted by the testes, ovaries, and placenta. Steroids regulating water balance and other processes are secreted by the adrenal cortex. All other endocrine glands secrete peptide hormones. (Note that although thyroid hormone is derived from an amino acid, its mechanism of action more closely resembles that of the steroid hormones.)

	Peptides	Steroids
Structure	hydrophilic, large (polypeptides) or small (amino acid derivatives)	hydrophobic, small
Site of synthesis	rough ER	smooth ER
Regulation of release	stored in vesicles until a signal for secretion is received	synthesized only when needed and then used immediately, not stored
Transport in bloodstream	free	stuck to protein carrier
Specificity	only target cells have appropriate surface receptors (exception: thyroxine = cytoplasmic)	only target cells have appropriate cytoplasmic receptors
Mechanism of effect	bind to receptors that generate second messengers which result in modification of *enzyme activity*	bind to receptors that alter *gene expression* by regulating DNA transcription
Timing of effect	rapid, short-lived	slow, long-lasting

Table 5 Peptide vs. Steroid Hormones

---

[39] No bond—just hydrophobic interactions

Organization and Regulation of the Human Endocrine System

The endocrine system has many different roles. Hormones are essential for gamete synthesis, ovulation, pregnancy, growth, sexual development, and overall level of metabolic activity. Despite this diversity of function, endocrine activity is harmoniously orchestrated. Maintenance of order in such a complex system might seem impossible to accomplish in a preplanned manner. Regulation of the endocrine system is not preplanned or rigidly structured, but is instead generally automatic. Hormone levels rise and fall as dictated by physiological needs. The endocrine system is ordered yet dynamic. This flexible, automatic orderliness is attributable to feedback regulation. The amount of a hormone secreted is controlled not by a preformulated plan but rather by changes in the variable the hormone is responsible for controlling. Continuous circulation of blood exposes target cells to regulatory hormones and also exposes endocrine glands to serum concentrations of physiological variables that they regulate. Thus *regulator* and that which *is regulated* are in continuous communication. Concentration of a species X in the aqueous portion of the bloodstream is denoted "serum [X]."

An example of feedback regulation is the interaction between the hormone calcitonin and serum $[Ca^{2+}]$. The function of calcitonin is to prevent serum $[Ca^{2+}]$ from peaking above normal levels, and the amount of calcitonin secreted is directly proportional to increases in serum $[Ca^{2+}]$ above normal. When serum $[Ca^{2+}]$ becomes elevated, calcitonin is secreted. Then when serum $[Ca^{2+}]$ levels fall, calcitonin secretion stops. The falling serum $[Ca^{2+}]$ level (*that which is regulated*) feeds back to the cells which secrete calcitonin (*regulators*). The serum $[Ca^{2+}]$ level is a **physiological endpoint** which must be maintained at constant levels. This demonstrates the role of the endocrine system in maintaining **homeostasis**, or physiological consistency.

An advantage of the endocrine system and its feedback regulation is that very complex arrays of variables can be controlled automatically. It's as if the variables controlled themselves. However, some integration (a central control mechanism) is necessary. Superimposed upon the hormonal regulation of physiological endpoints is another layer of regulation: hormones that regulate hormones. Such meta-regulators are known as **tropic hormones**.

For example, adrenocorticotropic hormone (ACTH) is secreted by the anterior pituitary. The role of ACTH is to stimulate increased activity of the portion of the adrenal gland called the **cortex**, which is responsible for secreting cortisol (among other steroid hormones). ACTH is a tropic hormone because it does not directly affect physiological endpoints, but merely regulates another regulator (cortisol). Cortisol regulates physiological endpoints, including cellular responses to stress and serum [glucose]. Feedback regulation applies to tropic hormones as well as to direct regulators of physiological endpoints; the level of ACTH is influenced by the level of cortisol. When cortisol is needed, ACTH is secreted, and when the serum [cortisol] increases sufficiently, ACTH secretion slows.

You may have noticed that in both of our examples the effect of feedback was *inhibitory*: The result of hormone secretion inhibits further secretion. Inhibitory feedback is called **negative feedback** or **feedback inhibition**. Most feedback in the endocrine system (and if you remember, most biochemical feedback) is negative. There are few exceptions (examples of positive feedback), which we will not emphasize here. A key example will be discussed in Chapter 12 with the reproductive systems.

There is yet another layer of control. Many of the functions of the endocrine system depend on instructions from the brain. The portion of the brain which controls much of the endocrine system is the **hypothalamus**, located at the center of the brain. The hypothalamus controls the endocrine system by releasing tropic hormones that regulate other tropic hormones, called **releasing and inhibiting factors** or **releasing and inhibiting hormones**.

For example (Figure 19), the hypothalamus secretes corticotropin releasing hormone (CRH, also known as CRF, where "F" stands for factor). The role of CRH is to cause increased secretion of ACTH. Just as ACTH secretion is regulated by feedback inhibition from cortisol, CRH secretion, too, is inhibited by cortisol. You begin to see that regulatory pathways in the endocrine system can get pretty complex.

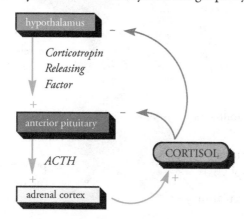

Figure 19   Feedback Regulation of Cortisol Secretion

Understanding that the hypothalamus controls the anterior pituitary and that the anterior pituitary controls most of the endocrine system is important. Damage to the connection between the hypothalamus and the pituitary is fatal, unless daily hormone replacement therapy is given. This endocrine control center is given a special name: **hypothalamic-pituitary** control axis (Figure 20). The hypothalamus exerts its control of the pituitary by secreting its hormones into the bloodstream, just like any other endocrine gland; what's unique is that a special miniature circulatory system is provided for efficient transport of hypothalamic releasing and inhibiting factors to the anterior pituitary. This blood supply is known as the **hypothalamic-pituitary portal system**. You will also hear the term *hypothalamic-hypophysial portal system*. **Hypophysis** is another name for the pituitary gland.

A Note on Portal Systems: As a general rule, blood leaving the heart moves through only one capillary bed before returning to the heart, since the pressure drops substantially in capillaries. A portal system, however, consists of two capillary beds in sequence, allowing for direct communication between nearby structures. The two portal systems you need to understand are: the hypothalamic-pituitary portal system and the hepatic portal system (from the gastrointestinal tract to the liver (Chapter 9).

One more bit of background information is necessary before we can delve into specific hormones. The pituitary gland has two halves: front (*anterior*) and back (*posterior*); see Figure 20. The **anterior pituitary** is also called the **adenohypophysis** and the **posterior pituitary** is also known as the **neurohypophysis**. It is important to understand the difference. The anterior pituitary is a normal endocrine gland, and it is controlled by hypothalamic releasing and inhibiting factors (essentially tropic hormones). The posterior pituitary is composed of axons which descend from the hypothalamus. These hypothalamic neurons that send axons down to the posterior pituitary are an example of **neuroendocrine cells**, neurons which secrete hormones into the bloodstream. The hormones of the posterior pituitary are ADH (antidiuretic hormone or vasopressin), which causes the kidney to retain water during times of thirst, and oxytocin, which causes milk let-down for nursing as well as uterine contractions during labor. [Are these hormones made by axon termini in the posterior pituitary or by somas in the hypothalamus?[40]]

---

[40] All hypothalamic and pituitary hormones are peptides, and there is no protein synthesis at axon termini. Hence, ADH and oxytocin must be made in nerve cell bodies in the hypothalamus and transported down the axons to the posterior pituitary.

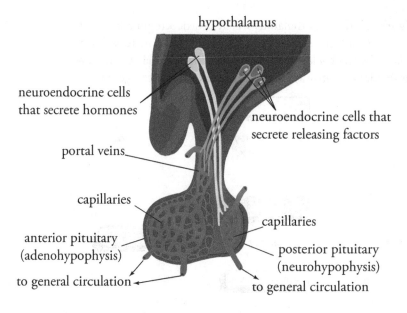

Figure 20   The Hypothalamic-Pituitary Control Axis

Major Glands and Their Hormones

The major hormones and glands of the endocrine system are listed in Table 6. Many of these hormones will be discussed in detail in later chapters. Insulin and glucagon will be discussed in the chapter on digestion and energy metabolism (Chapter 9). Testosterone, estrogen, progesterone, FSH and LH will be presented in the chapter on reproductive biology (Chapter 12). The function of epinephrine has already been presented as part of the sympathetic nervous system response. In general, the hormones are involved in development of the body and in maintenance of constant conditions, homeostasis, in the adult. [Is epinephrine secreted by a duct into the bloodstream?[41]]

Thyroid hormone and **cortisol** have broad effects on metabolism and energy usage. Thyroid hormone is produced from the amino acid tyrosine in the thyroid gland and comes in two forms, with three or four iodine atoms per molecule. The production of thyroid hormone is increased by thyroid stimulating hormone (TSH) from the anterior pituitary, which is regulated by the hypothalamus and the central nervous system in turn. The mechanism of action of thyroid hormone is to bind to a receptor in the cytoplasm of cells that then regulates transcription in the nucleus. The effect of this regulation is to increase the overall metabolic rate and body temperature, and, in children, to stimulate growth. Exposure to cold can increase the production of thyroid hormone. Cortisol is secreted by the adrenal cortex in response to ACTH from the pituitary. In general, the effects of cortisol tend to help the body deal with stress. Cortisol helps to mobilize glycogen and fat stores to provide energy during stress and also increases the consumption of proteins for energy. These effects are essential, since removal of the adrenal cortex can result in the death of animals exposed to even a small stress. Long-term high levels of cortisol tend to have negative effects, however, including suppression of the immune system.

---

[41] No. Endocrine hormones are not secreted through ducts.

7.6

- Would an inhibitor of protein synthesis block the action of thyroid hormone?[42]
- Would the production of ATP by mitochondria be stimulated or repressed by thyroid hormone?[43]
- Would thyroid hormone affect isolated mitochondria directly?[44]

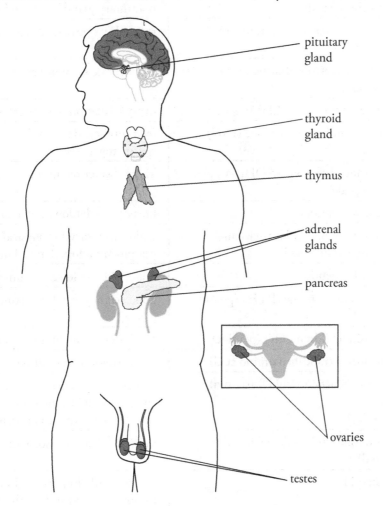

pituitary gland

thyroid gland

thymus

adrenal glands

pancreas

ovaries

testes

Figure 21   The Major Endocrine Glands

---

[42] Yes. Thyroid hormone binds to a receptor that regulates transcription. The mRNA stimulated by thyroid hormone receptor in the nucleus must be processed and translated before the effects of thyroid hormone can become evident.

[43] Thyroid hormone stimulates the basal metabolic rate throughout the body. More ATP will be consumed, so the mitochondria are stimulated to make more ATP.

[44] No. Thyroid hormone affects mitochondria *indirectly*, through the regulation of nuclear genes.

Gland	Hormone [class]	Target/effect
Hypothalamus	releasing and inhibiting factors (peptides)	anterior pituitary/modify activity
Anterior pituitary	growth hormone (GH) (peptide)	↑ bone & muscle growth, ↑ cell turnover rate
	prolactin (peptide)	mammary gland/milk production
tropic	thyroid stimulating hormone (TSH) (peptide)	thyroid/↑ synthesis & release of TH
	adrenocorticotropic hormone (ACTH) (peptide)	↑ growth & secretory activity of adrenal ctx
gonadotropic	luteinizing hormone (LH) (peptide)	ovary/ovulation, testes/testosterone synth.
	follicle stimulating hormone (FSH) (peptide)	ovary/follicle development, testes/ spermatogenesis
Posterior pituitary	antidiuretic hormone (ADH, vasopressin) (peptide)	kidney/water retention
	oxytocin (peptide)	breast/milk letdown, uterus/contraction
Thyroid	thyroid hormone (TH, thyroxine) (modified amino acid)	child: necessary for physical & mental development; adult: ↑ metabolic rate & temp.
thyroid C cells	calcitonin (peptide)	bone, kidney; lowers serum [Ca^{2+}]
Parathyroids	parathyroid hormone (PTH) (peptide)	bone, kidney, small intestine/raises serum [Ca^{2+}]
Thymus	thymosin (children only) (peptide)	T cell development during childhood
Adrenal medulla	epinephrine (modified amino acid)	sympathetic stress response (rapid)
Adrenal cortex	cortisol ("glucocorticoid") (steroid)	longer-term stress response; ↑ blood [glucose]; ↑ protein catabolism; ↓ inflammation & immunity; many other
	aldosterone ("mineralocorticoid") (steroid)	kidney/↑ Na+ reabsorption to ↑ b.p.
	sex steroids	not normally important, but an adrenal tumor can overproduce these, causing masculinization or feminization
Endocrine pancreas (islets of Langerhans)	insulin (β cells secrete) (peptide) —absent or ineffective in diabetes mellitus	↓ blood [glucose]/↑ glycogen & fat storage
	glucagon (α cells secrete) (peptide)	↑ blood [glucose]/↓ glycogen & fat storage
	somatostatin (SS—δ cells secrete) (peptide)	inhibits many digestive processes
Testes	testosterone (steroid)	male characteristics, spermatogenesis
Ovaries/placenta	estrogen (steroid)	female characteristics, endometrial growth
	progesterone (steroid)	endometrial secretion, pregnancy
Heart	atrial natriuretic factor (ANF) (peptide)	kidney/↑ urination to ↓ blood pressure
Kidney	erythropoietin (peptide)	bone marrow/↑ RBC synthesis

Table 6 Summary of the Hormones of the Endocrine System

7.6

Summary

- The neuron is the basic structural and functional unit of the nervous system. It has several specialized structures that allow it to transmit action potentials.

- Neurons receive incoming information via dendrites. Signals are summed by the axon hillock, and if the signal is greater than the threshold, an action potential is initiated.

- The action potential is an all-or-none signal that includes depolarization (via voltage-gated sodium channels) and repolarization (via voltage-gated potassium channels); it begins and ends at the cell's resting potential of –70 mV.

- Since action potentials are all-or-none events, intensity is coded by the frequency of the action potential.

- Neurons communicate with other neurons, organs, and glands at synapses. Most synapses are chemical in nature; an action potential causes the release of neurotransmitter into the synaptic cleft, and binding of the neurotransmitter to receptors on the postsynaptic cell triggers a change, either stimulatory or inhibitory, in that cell.

- The central nervous system includes the spinal cord and the brain; specialized areas control specific aspects of human behavior, movement, intelligence, emotion, and reflexes.

- The peripheral nervous system includes the somatic (voluntary) and autonomic (involuntary) subdivisions.

- The sympathetic branch of the autonomic system controls our fight-or-flight response; norepinephrine is the primary neurotransmitter of this system, and it is augmented by epinephrine from the adrenal medulla.

- The parasympathetic branch of the autonomic system controls our resting and digesting state; acetylcholine is the primary neurotransmitter of this system.

- Humans have several types of receptors (mechanoreceptors, chemoreceptors, nociceptors, thermoreceptors, electromagnetic receptors, and proprioceptors) that allow us to detect a variety of stimuli.

- Humans have several types of receptors (mechanoreceptors, chemoreceptors, nociceptors, thermoreceptors, electromagnetic receptors, and proprioceptors) that allow us to detect a variety of stimuli.

- The endocrine system controls our overall physiology and homeostasis by hormones that travel through the bloodstream. Hormones are released from endocrine glands, travel to distant target tissues via the blood, bind to receptors on target tissues, and exert effects on target cells.

- Peptide hormones are made from amino acids, bind to receptors on the cell surface, and typically affect target cells via second messenger pathways. Effects tend to be rapid and temporary.

- Steroid hormones are derived from cholesterol, bind to receptors in the cytoplasm or nucleus, and bind to DNA to alter transcription. Effects tend to occur more slowly and are more permanent.

CHAPTER 7 FREESTANDING PRACTICE QUESTIONS

1. In humans, vision is due to stimulation of what type of receptor?

   A) Electromagnetic receptors
   B) Mechanoreceptors
   C) Gustatory receptors
   D) Nociceptors

2. Which of the following is the correct order of events during synaptic transmission?

   A) Depolarization of presynaptic membrane → Voltage-gated calcium channels open → Neurotransmitter binds to ligand-gated ion channels → Membrane depolarization of postsynaptic cell → Neurotransmitters cross the synaptic cleft
   B) An action potential reaches the end of an axon at the synaptic knob → Depolarization of presynaptic membrane → Voltage-gated sodium channels open → Neurotransmitter binds to ligand-gated ion channels → Membrane depolarization of postsynaptic cell
   C) Depolarization of presynaptic membrane → Neurotransmitter binds to ligand-gated ion channels → Neurotransmitter in the synaptic cleft is degraded and/or removed → An action potential reaches the end of an axon
   D) An action potential reaches the end of an axon → Voltage-gated calcium channels open → Neurotransmitter binds to ligand-gated ion channels → Neurotransmitter in the synaptic cleft is degraded and/or removed

3. People who suffer from severe epilepsy are sometimes treated with a "split brain" procedure that prevents most communication between the left and right hemispheres of the brain. The structure that is most likely cut in this operation is the:

   A) corpus callosum.
   B) medulla.
   C) thalamus.
   D) pons.

4. Myasthenia gravis, an autoimmune disorder, results from the production of antibodies against acetylcholine receptors in the body. Which of the following statements is FALSE?

   A) A patient may have difficulty opening his/her eyes.
   B) Repeated injection of human acetylcholine receptor into an animal model will produce clinical symptoms in that animal.
   C) The disease does not directly affect the release of neurotransmitter.
   D) This disease only impacts the neuromuscular junction.

5. Which of the following hormones has its receptor located on the cell surface?

   A) Renin
   B) Thyroid hormone
   C) Oxytocin
   D) Aldosterone

6. Parathyroid adenomas are tumors that can lead to hyperparathyroidism. Which of the following can occur in a patient with a parathyroid adenoma?

    I.   Increased frequency of bone fractures
    II.   Decreased reabsorption of calcium by the kidneys
    III.   Increased serum calcium levels

A) I only
B) II only
C) I and II
D) I and III

7. Of the following, which would alter gene expression by regulating DNA transcription?

A) Glucagon
B) Insulin
C) Pepsin
D) Cortisol

8. High blood pressure could be rectified through:

    I.   an increase in ADH.
    II.   an decrease in aldosterone.
    III.   ACE inhibitors.

A) I only
B) I and II only
C) III only
D) II and III only

CHAPTER 7 PRACTICE PASSAGE

Long-term potentiation (LTP) involves communication between two neurons and is a major cellular mechanism underlying learning and memory processes. During LTP, a presynaptic neuron releases the neurotransmitter glutamate, which binds to receptors on the postsynaptic neuron. This leads to an influx of sodium, and ultimately calcium, followed by activation of various genes (see Figure 1). The initial receptor activated by glutamate is the AMPA receptor; the NMDA receptor is blocked by extracellular Mg^{2+} that must be displaced by a sufficient change in membrane potential before that channel will fully open.

LTP has been shown to be disrupted in neurodegenerative disorders, such as Alzheimer's disease, leading to memory deficits. In brains of Alzheimer's patients, loss of vital neurons occurs in the hippocampus (a region of the brain involved in memory acquisition). Several mechanisms are hypothesized to lead to this neurodegeneration. One involves calcium-mediated toxicity and occurs due to excessive glutamate-induced neuronal excitation.

Another potential contributing factor to this cell loss is exposure to chronic stress, which results in elevated levels of corticosteroids that can influence neuronal activity in the brain. This has led to the formation of the "Glucocorticoid Hypothesis of Aging." The intact hippocampus has an inhibitory effect on the stress axis (hypothalamic-pituitary-adrenal axis) that is responsible for inducing release of cortisol from the adrenal gland during times of stress. Thus, if the hippocampal region is compromised, it could lead to lack of inhibition of the stress axis and further release of cortisol, causing a feed-forward cycle of excessive release of steroids with each stressful event.

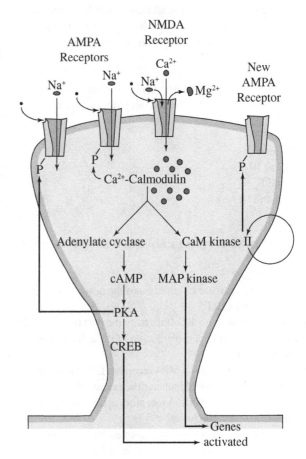

Figure 1 Synaptic Transmission During LTP

1. In which region of the brain is the hippocampus located?

A) Cerebellum
B) Occipital lobe
C) Temporal lobe
D) Hypothalamus

2. One treatment for Alzheimer's disease involves a drug that blocks NMDA receptors. This treatment could lead to all of the following EXCEPT:

A) a suppression of LTP.
B) a suppression of gene expression.
C) a significant decrease in intracellular sodium.
D) a significant decrease in intracellular calcium.

3. A researcher removes the adrenal glands from a rat and then supplements the rat with baseline levels of steroids for the remainder of its lifespan. Which of the following would be expected?

 I.   Blunted sympathetic nervous system response
 II.   Slowing of age-related neurodegeneration
 III. Enhancement of LTP

A) II only
B) II and III
C) I and II
D) I, II and III

4. Which of the following statements is LEAST likely to be true?

A) Drugs that increase Cl^- influx into the postsynaptic cell could disrupt LTP.
B) Drugs that increase K^+ efflux from the postsynaptic cell would result in hyperpolarization of the cell and would increase LTP.
C) The insertion of new AMPA receptors in the postsynaptic cell membrane would increase the rate at which Mg^{2+} is displaced from NMDA receptors upon subsequent stimulation by glutamate.
D) The influx of Na^+ upon initial stimulation by glutamate depolarizes the postsynaptic cell in order to displace Mg^{2+}.

5. AMPA receptors are found throughout the central nervous system and are comprised of four different subunits. Not all AMPA receptors have all the subunits. If a knockout mouse was made deficient for the gene for one of the AMPA receptor subunits, what would be the expected outcome?

A) An observed deficit only in LTP and the mouse's ability to learn.
B) Altered function in any region containing an AMPA receptor.
C) No change in LTP function due to the NMDA receptor still being present and functional.
D) Altered function and/or compensatory expression of other AMPA receptor subunits in regions with AMPA receptors that lack the affected subunit.

6. Based on Figure 1, what is a logical function of CREB?

A) Interact with the genomic DNA to enhance transcription
B) Interact with RNA to enhance translation
C) Bind ribosomes to enhance transcription
D) Bind RNA polymerase to enhance replication

7. Excessive calcium influx into the cell has been shown to result in neuronal injury in many CNS disorders. However, calcium is integral to many neuronal functions, so cells must balance levels of intracellular calcium carefully. Normal calcium functions in the cell include all of the following EXCEPT:

A) memory acquisition and storage.
B) release of synaptic vesicles from the cytoskeleton at the axon terminal.
C) release from the sarcoplasmic reticulum to aid in muscle contraction.
D) simple diffusion across the cell membrane in heart muscle to sustain depolarization.

SOLUTIONS TO CHAPTER 7 FREESTANDING PRACTICE QUESTIONS

1. **A**   Electromagnetic receptors, as the name suggests, detect electromagnetic radiation. Remember that electromagnetic radiation is a spectrum that spans radio waves (longest wavelength), microwaves, infrared, visible light, ultraviolet, X-rays, and gamma rays (shortest wavelength). In humans, the only electromagnetic receptors are the eye's photoreceptors that detect the visible light region of the electromagnetic spectrum. Stimulation of photoreceptors (also known as rods and cones) allows vision to occur (choice A is correct). Mechanoreceptors, such as the hair cells of the ear, are stimulated by mechanical disturbances (choice B is wrong). Gustatory receptors are chemoreceptors that respond to taste (choice C is wrong). Nociceptors respond to pain (choice D is wrong). Even without knowing that photoreceptors are electromagnetic receptors, you should know how the other receptors are stimulated and can reach the correct answer by process of elimination.

2. **D**   The correct order of events is: 1) an action potential reaches the end of an axon at the synaptic knob, 2) depolarization of presynaptic membrane, 3) voltage-gated calcium channels open, 4) neurotransmitter is released from the presynaptic cell, 5) neurotransmitter crosses the synaptic cleft, 6) neurotransmitter binds to ligand-gated ion channels on the postsynaptic membrane, 7) membrane depolarization of postsynaptic cell, 8) voltage-gated sodium channels open, 9) an action potential is initiated, and 10) neurotransmitter in the synaptic cleft is degraded and/or removed (choices A, B, and C are wrong).

3. **A**   The corpus callosum is a bundle of axons that connects the left and right hemispheres of the brain and is responsible for the vast majority of the communication between the two hemispheres. Cutting this structure in half prevents the rapid cross-hemispheric communication that is observed during seizures in patients with severe epilepsy. The medulla and pons are part of the hindbrain and play roles in basic autonomic processes (choices B and D are wrong), and the thalamus is a relay station for somatic sensory stimuli located in the diencephalon (choice C is wrong).

4. **D**   Acetylcholine is a neurotransmitter in several areas in the body including the neuromuscular junction, pre- and postganglionic parasympathetic neurons, and preganglionic sympathetic neurons (choice D is the false statement and the correct answer choice). As acetylcholine receptors become nonfunctional with the binding of antibody, patients have difficulty with muscle contraction, and opening of the eyes may be one possible symptom of this (choice A is a true statement and can be eliminated). Repeated injection of acetylcholine receptor into an animal model will result in an immune response and subsequent attack of the endogenous acetylcholine receptors, producing myasthenia gravis symptoms (choice B is a true statement and can be eliminated). The antibodies attack the postsynaptic neuron receptors and do not result in a direct change in neurotransmitter release (choice C is a true statement and can be eliminated).

5. **C**   Oxytocin is a peptide hormone, and as such its receptor would be expected to be found on the surface of target cells (choice C is correct). Renin is an *enzyme* (not a hormone) released by juxtaglomerular (JG) cells in the kidney (choice A is wrong). Thyroid hormone is a tyrosine-derived hormone that behaves like a steroid hormone; the thyroid hormone receptor is found within cells, not on their surface (choice B is wrong). Aldosterone is a steroid hormone; its receptor would be found within target cells, not on their surface (choice D is wrong).

6. **D**   Hyperparathyroidism means having an abnormally high level of parathyroid hormone. The functions of parathyroid hormone include 1) enhancing the breakdown of bone by osteoclasts and the release of calcium into the bloodstream, 2) enhancing the reabsorption of calcium in the nephrons of the kidneys, and 3) enhancing the absorption of calcium in the small intestine. Item I is true: High PTH levels cause calcium to leave the bone and enter the bloodstream, resulting in weak bones that can fracture easily (choice B can be eliminated). Item II is false: PTH leads to increased reabsorption of calcium to increase serum calcium levels (choice C can be eliminated). Item III is true: High PTH levels cause serum calcium levels to rise since it is being removed from the bone, reabsorbed by the kidneys, and absorbed by the small intestines (choice A can be eliminated). The correct answer is choice D.

7. **D**   Hormones can be classified as either steroids or peptides. Steroid hormones diffuse into a cell, bind to receptors in the cytosol, and then the steroid-receptor complex binds to DNA to regulate gene transcription. Peptide hormones bind to cell surface receptors and modify (via second messenger systems) enzymatic activity within the cell. This question is just asking you to identify the steroid hormone. Glucagon and insulin are peptide hormones (choices A and B can be eliminated), and pepsin is not a hormone at all (choice C can be eliminated). Cortisol is a steroid (choice D is correct) and would act to modify transcription.

8. **D**   Item I is false: An increase in ADH would lead to increased retention of water, increased blood volume, and increased blood pressure (choices A and B can be eliminated). Since both remaining answer choices include Item III, Item III must be true. Thus we only need to evaluate Item II to get the correct answer. Item II is true. Aldosterone causes increased sodium reabsorption at the distal tubule; not only does water passively follow the salt as it is reabsorbed, but the resulting increase in blood osmolarity triggers the release of ADH, leading to additional water retention. This increases blood volume and pressure. Therefore a decrease in aldosterone would cause opposite effects and a reduction in blood pressure (choice C can be eliminated). Note that Item III is true: ACE (angiotensin converting enzyme) is the enzyme that converts angiotensin I into angiotensin II, a very powerful vasoconstrictor and stimulator of aldosterone release. ACE is part of the pathway to increase blood pressure; inhibiting it would thus decrease blood pressure.

SOLUTIONS TO CHAPTER 7 PRACTICE PASSAGE

1. **C** The passage states that the hippocampus is involved in memory acquisition; thus, it is likely to be located in the temporal lobe of the cerebrum. The cerebellum is involved in balance and coordination, not memory (choice A is wrong), the occipital lobe is responsible for vision (choice B is wrong), and the hypothalamus is involved in maintaining homeostasis and hormonal regulation (choice D is wrong).

2. **C** If NMDA receptor activation is necessary for LTP, then blocking this receptor would likely suppress LTP (choice A could occur and can be eliminated). Based on Figure 1, activation of the NMDA receptor triggers an influx of intracellular calcium and a cascade of events resulting in activation of gene expression; thus, blocking this receptor could lead to both a significant decrease in intracellular calcium and a suppression of gene expression (choices B and D could occur and can be eliminated). Since the NMDA receptor allows an influx of sodium, some reduction in intracellular sodium could be expected; however, this is unlikely to be significant since the AMPA receptor would still be functional and is the main source of Na^+ influx (choice C would not occur and is the correct answer choice).

3. **C** Item I is true: The adrenal glands secrete both steroid hormones (from the adrenal cortex) and epinephrine (from the adrenal medulla). If the researcher only replaces the steroids, then the sympathetic response (which relies on epinephrine) could be blunted (choices A and B can be eliminated). Since both remaining answer choices include Item II, then Item II must be true and we only need to evaluate Item III. Item III is false: Based on Figure 1, corticosteroids do not seem to play an integral role in LTP. In addition, the passage only discusses their possible involvement in neuronal cell death at high concentrations. Keeping baseline levels may not lead to cell death, but would not necessarily enhance LTP (choice D can be eliminated and choice C is correct). Note that Item II is in fact true: Based on information in the passage (the Glucocorticoid Aging Hypothesis), stress levels of corticosteroids could lead to age-related neurodegeneration. Thus, if the levels of these hormones are kept at baseline throughout the life of the animal, it is possible to attenuate age-related neurodegeneration.

4. **B** The passage states that the NMDA receptor is blocked by extracellular Mg^{2+} that must be displaced by a sufficient change in membrane potential. It is fair to assume that this change must be a depolarization, since the initial receptor activated is the AMPA receptor, and according to the figure, that receptor allows an influx of Na^+ (choice D is likely to be true and can be eliminated). Additional AMPA receptors would increase the rate of depolarization and thus the rate of Mg^{2+} displacement. This is in fact the basis for LTP; the first stimulation leads to the effects shown in the figure, including new receptors in the membrane, thus the effect of subsequent stimulation is enhanced (choice C is likely to be true and can be eliminated). Anything that would lead to a hyperpolarization of the cell would not displace Mg^{2+} and would disrupt the calcium influx and all associated events, including LTP. An increase of Cl^- influx would hyperpolarize the cell and disrupt LTP (choice A is likely to be true and can be eliminated), but an increase in K^+ efflux, while it would hyperpolarize the cell, would not increase LTP (choice B is unlikely to be true and is the correct answer choice).

5. **D**   The question states essentially that AMPA receptors can be varied (have variable subunits) and are found throughout the CNS. Certainly if the gene for one of the subunits was deficient, we would expect some deficit to be present. However, because of the widespread location of these receptors, we would not expect the deficit to be limited to only the region of the brain responsible for LTP (choice A is wrong), nor would we expect the deficit to be found in ANY region with receptors, because some regions may have AMPA receptors that do not have the knocked out subunit (choice B is wrong). According to the diagram, function of both AMPA and NMDA receptors are required during LTP, so if one of the receptors was compromised we might expect some alteration in LTP function (choice C is wrong). The most likely outcome is that there would be altered function or potentially compensatory expression of other AMPA receptor subunits in those regions of the CNS that contain an affected AMPA receptor (choice D is correct).

6. **A**   In the diagram, CREB is located immediately before gene activation, which would suggest it has something to do with transcription (choices B and D are wrong). Ribosomes do not have anything to do with transcription (choice C is wrong and choice A is correct). CREB stands for cAMP Response Element Binding and is a transcription factor; thus, it interacts with DNA to enhance transcription.

7. **D**   Based on Figure 1, calcium plays an integral role in the cellular processes for LTP, and LTP is necessary for learning and memory (choice A is a normal function of calcium and can be eliminated). Calcium influx at the axon terminal breaks the synapsin bond between neurotransmitter vesicles and the cytoskeleton so that the vesicles can dock at the plasma membrane and release neurotransmitter into the synaptic cleft (choice B is a calcium function and can be eliminated). Calcium is stored in the sarcoplasmic reticulum of muscle cells and then released after depolarization of the cell; this exposes myosin binding sites on action to allow actin-myosin interaction and muscle contraction (choice C is a function of calcium and can be eliminated). Since calcium is an ion, it cannot readily cross the cell membrane via simple diffusion; it must cross through a channel via facilitated diffusion, or in some cases it is actively transported across the membrane. Calcium does function to sustain depolarization in heart muscle, but it enters via calcium channels and is passed from cell to cell via gap junctions; it does not participate in simple diffusion (choice D is wrong).

Chapter 8
The Circulatory, Lymphatic, and Immune Systems

8.1 OVERVIEW OF THE CIRCULATORY SYSTEM

The cells of a multicellular organism have the same basic requirements as unicellular organisms. Living so close to billions of other cells has many advantages, but there are drawbacks too. Each cell must compete with its neighbors for nutrients and oxygen and must also cope with the waste products that are inevitable in so dense a civilization. Other requirements of community living are efficient communication and homeostasis. The circulatory system addresses these problems by accomplishing the following goals:

1) Distribute nutrients from the digestive tract, liver, and adipose (fat) tissue.
2) Transport oxygen from the lungs to the entire body and carbon dioxide from the tissues to the lungs.
3) Transport metabolic waste products from tissues to the excretory system (i.e., the kidneys).
4) Transport hormones from endocrine glands to targets and provide feedback.
5) Maintain homeostasis of body temperature.
6) *Hemostasis* (blood clotting). This does not address a need of a multicellular organism *per se*, but rather is necessitated by the presence of the circulatory system itself.

The flow of blood through a tissue is known as **perfusion**. Inadequate blood flow, known as **ischemia**, results in tissue damage due to shortages of O_2 and nutrients, and buildup of metabolic wastes. When adequate circulation is present but the supply of oxygen is reduced, a tissue is said to suffer from **hypoxia**. [What's the difference between ischemia and hypoxia?[1]]

In the following sections we will study the components of the circulatory system. We will not delve into its thermoregulatory role, which will be covered in Chapter 11 (The Respiratory System and the Skin).

Components of the Circulatory System

The functions of the circulatory system involve transport of blood throughout the body and exchange of material between the blood and tissues. The **heart** is a muscular pump that forces blood through a branching series of vessels to the lungs and the rest of the body. Vessels that carry blood away from the heart at high pressure are **arteries**, and vessels that carry blood back toward the heart at low pressure are **veins**. As arteries pass farther from the heart, the pressure of blood decreases, and they branch into increasingly smaller arteries called **arterioles**. The arterioles then pass into the **capillaries**, very small vessels, often just wide enough for a single blood cell to pass. Arterioles have smooth muscle in their walls that can act as a control valve to restrict or increase the flow of blood into the capillaries of tissues. The capillaries have thin walls made of a single layer of cells, and are designed to allow the exchange of material between the blood and tissues. After passing through capillaries, blood collects in small veins called **venules**, and then into the veins leading back to the heart. From the heart, the blood can be pumped out once again through the arteries to the capillaries in the tissues.

- If the arterioles constrict in a tissue, will material diffuse through the wall of the arterioles into the tissue?[2]

---

[1] In hypoxia, wastes are adequately removed, but in ischemia they build up. Ischemia is worse.

[2] No. All exchange of material between the blood and tissues must occur in capillaries. The walls of arterioles are too thick and muscular for exchange to occur.

To achieve both efficient oxygenation of blood in the lungs and transport of oxygenated blood to the tissues, the heart has evolved in humans to have two sides separated by a thick wall to pump blood in two separate circuits. The right side of the heart pumps blood to the lungs, and the left side of the heart pumps blood to the rest of the body. The flow of blood from the heart to the lungs and back to the heart is the **pulmonary circulation**, and the flow of blood from the heart to the rest of the body and back again is the **systemic circulation** (Figure 1).

- In fish, blood passes from the heart to the gills and then to the rest of the body. Why have mammals evolved a separate circulation for the lungs?[3]

By having two separate circulations, most blood passes through only one set of capillaries before returning to the heart. There are exceptions to this, however: **portal systems**. In the hepatic portal system, blood passes first through capillaries in the intestine, then collects in veins to travel to the liver, where the vessels branch and the blood passes again through capillaries (Chapter 9). Another example is the hypothalamic-hypophysial portal system, in which blood passes through capillaries in the hypothalamus to the portal veins, then to capillaries in the pituitary (Chapter 7). The portal systems evolved as direct transport systems, to transport nutrients directly from the intestine to the liver or hormones from the hypothalamus to the pituitary, without passing through the whole body.

- If the hypothalamic-hypophysial portal circulation is severed, how does this affect the function of the pituitary?[4]

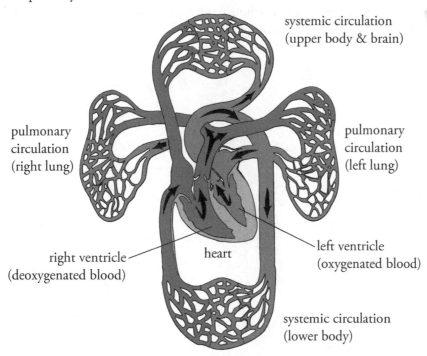

Figure 1   Pulmonary and Systemic Circuits

---

[3]   Blood is pumped away from the heart at high pressure in arteries to pass through the capillaries. If the blood is to pass through one bed of capillaries, and then through another bed of capillaries, the pressure must be very high in the first set of capillaries or blood will not have enough pressure to pass through the second set of capillaries. Having two separate circulations solves this problem.

[4]   Normally, the pituitary receives hormones directly from the hypothalamus. If the portal system is severed, hormones must take a longer route and will be diluted and degraded before they reach the pituitary. As a result, secretion by the pituitary will not be effectively regulated by the hypothalamus.

8.2 THE HEART

The heart has two kinds of chambers involved in pumping blood, the **atria** and the **ventricles** (Figure 2). The atria are reservoirs or "waiting rooms" where blood can collect from the veins before getting pumped into the ventricles. The muscular ventricles pump blood out of the heart at high pressures into the arteries. The systemic circulation and the pulmonary circulation are separated within the heart, so the right and left sides of the heart each have one atrium and one ventricle. The right atrium receives deoxygenated blood from the systemic circulation (from the large veins: the **inferior vena cava** and the **superior vena cava**) and pumps it into the right ventricle. From the right ventricle blood passes through the pulmonary artery to the lungs. Oxygenated blood from the lungs returns through the pulmonary veins to the left atrium and is pumped into the left ventricle before being pumped out of the heart in a single large artery, the **aorta**, to the systemic circulation.

- Do all of the arteries of the body carry oxygenated blood?[5]

- Based on the above, you can conclude that blood flows:[6]
    A. from the lungs into the right atrium, since the right side of the heart deals with deoxygenated blood.
    B. from the right ventricle to the right atrium, since the atrium is a low-pressure chamber.
    C. from the right atrium to the left ventricle, since the right side of the heart deals with deoxygenated blood and the left side must pump blood to the body.
    D. from the lungs into the left atrium and from there to the left ventricle, since the left side of the heart deals with oxygenated blood.

---

[5] No. The pulmonary artery carries deoxygenated blood from the heart to the lungs.

[6] Oxygenated blood flows from the lungs to the left atrium (choice A is wrong), then to the left ventricle (choice **D** is right and choice C is wrong). The atrium is a low pressure chamber, however blood flow from the ventricles to the atria is prevented by the atrioventricular valves (choice B is wrong).

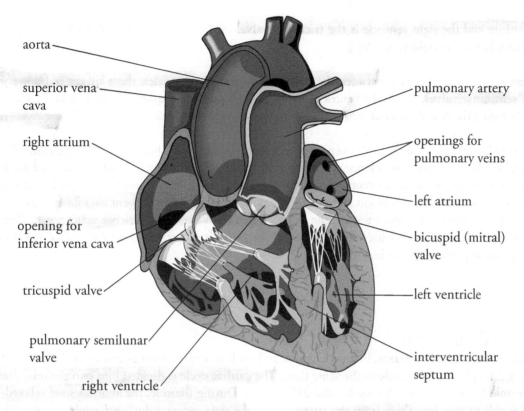

aorta

superior vena
cava

right atrium

opening for
inferior vena cava

tricuspid valve

pulmonary semilunar
valve

right ventricle

pulmonary artery

openings for
pulmonary veins

left atrium

bicuspid (mitral)
valve

left ventricle

interventricular
septum

Figure 2   The Heart

The heart is a large muscular organ which requires a blood supply of its own. The very first branches from
the aorta are **coronary arteries** which branch to supply blood to the wall of the heart. They are called "coronary" because they encircle the heart forming a crown shape. Deoxygenated blood from the heart collects
in **coronary veins**, which merge to form the **coronary sinus**, located beneath a layer of fat on the outer wall
of the heart. (A sinus is an open space; in the case of the cardiovascular system, it is a pool of low-pressure
blood.) Blood in the coronary sinus is the only deoxygenated blood which does not end up in the inferior
vena cava or superior vena cava. Instead, the coronary sinus drains directly into the right atrium.

Valves

Valves are necessary to ensure one-way flow through the circulatory system. Valves in the heart are especially important, since the pressure differentials there are so extreme. In particular, ventricular pressure is
very high and atrial pressure is lower. Hence, an **atrioventricular valve** (**AV valve**) between each ventricle
and its atrium is necessary to prevent backflow.

The AV valve between the left atrium and the left ventricle is the **bicuspid** (or **mitral**) **valve**. [The mitral
valve must withstand enormous pressures. What would happen if it ruptured?[7]] The AV valve between the

---

[7] The left ventricle would pump blood in both directions; out the aorta and back into the left atrium. The result will be elevated pulmonary
blood pressure and pulmonary edema.

right atrium and the right ventricle is the **tricuspid valve.** [What valve prevents blood flow between the left ventricle and the right ventricle?[8]]

Another set of valves is needed between the large arteries and the ventricles; these are the **pulmonary** and **aortic semilunar valves.** [Since the ventricles are ultra-high pressure chambers, why is it necessary to put valves between them and the arteries?[9]] Together these two valves are known simply as the *semilunar valves.*

There are also valves throughout the venous system. This is necessary because in passing through capillaries, blood loses its pressure. Hence there is not much of a driving force pushing it toward the heart. Contraction of skeletal muscle becomes important, because normal body movements push and squeeze the veins, pressurizing venous blood and pushing it along. Venous valves prevent backflow; as long as the valves hold up, the blood moves toward the heart. When the valves fail, **varicose veins** result. Pregnant women often suffer from varicose veins because the growing fetus presses against the inferior vena cava, causing venous pressure in the legs to rise.

The Cardiac Cycle

The heart contracts, then relaxes, in a cycle which ends only in death. The left and right sides of the heart proceed through the same cycle at the same time. The cardiac cycle is divided into two periods, **diastole** and **systole** (pronounced dy-AS-toe-lee and SIS-toe-lee). During diastole, the ventricles are relaxed, and blood is able to flow into them from the atria. In fact, the atria contract during diastole, to propel blood into the ventricles more rapidly. [How strong is atrial compared to ventricular contraction?[10]] At the end of diastole, the ventricles contract, initiating systole. The ensuing buildup of pressure causes the AV valves to slam shut. Over the next few milliseconds, the pressure in the ventricles increases rapidly, until the semilunar valves fly open and blood rushes into the aorta and pulmonary artery. Systole is the period of time during which the ventricles are contracting, beginning at the "lub" sound and ending at the "dup." At the end of systole, the ventricles are nearly empty[11] and stop contracting. As a result, the pressure inside falls rapidly, and blood begins to flow backward, from the pulmonary artery into the right ventricle, and from the aorta into the left ventricle. But very little backflow actually occurs, because the semilunar valves slam shut when the pressure in the ventricles becomes lower than the pressure in the great arteries. At this point, the heart has completed a full cardiac cycle and is back in diastole.

---

[8] None! The two ventricles are separated by a thick muscular wall. Remember: the left and right halves are separate.

[9] The ventricles are only pressurized while contracting. When they are not contracting, they must have a very low pressure so that blood can flow into them from the atria.

[10] Much weaker. The atria really only contract to ensure that most of the blood they contain passes into the ventricles. In contrast, the ventricles must propel blood through arteries, capillary beds, and veins. Hence, the muscular walls of the atria are much thinner than those of the ventricles.

[11] Actually, only about 2/3 of the blood is normally ejected from the ventricle; this is the **ejection fraction.**

- Which one of the following is true during systole?[12]
  - A. The bicuspid valve is open.
  - B. Blood does not flow through the aortic valve.
  - C. Both semilunar valves are closed.
  - D. Pressure in the atria is low, and thus the atria fill with blood from the vena cava and pulmonary veins.

Heart Sounds, Heart Rate, and Cardiac Output

The "lub-dup" of the heartbeat is produced by valves slamming shut. The "lub" results from the closure of the AV valves at the beginning of systole, and the "dup" is the sound of the semilunar valves closing at the end of systole. [Based on this, which is longer: systole or diastole?[13]]

The **heart rate** (HR) or **pulse** is the number of times the "lub-dup" cardiac cycle is repeated per minute. The normal pulse rate is about one beat per second, ranging from 45 beats per minute (b.p.m.) in athletes to 80 or more beats per minute in the elderly and in children. The explanation for this variation is that a stronger heart pumps more blood each time it contracts, and thus may beat fewer times per minute and still provide adequate circulation. Athletes have strong hearts, while children and the elderly have weaker hearts. The amount of blood pumped with each systole is known as the **stroke volume** (SV). The total amount of blood pumped per minute is termed the **cardiac output** (CO), defined by the equation

$$\text{cardiac output (L/min)} = \text{stroke volume (L/beat)} \times \text{heart rate (beats/min)}$$
$$CO = SV \times HR$$

- An overweight child weighing 110 pounds, a female athlete weighing 110 pounds, and an elderly man weighing 110 pounds all require a cardiac output of about 5 L/min. But the child and the old man have a stroke volume of 1/16 L, while the athlete's stroke volume is 1/9 L. How can the child and the old man supply enough blood to their bodies?[14]
- Which is larger: the cardiac output of the right ventricle or of the left ventricle?[15]

---

[12] During systole the ventricles are contracting. The bicuspid valve separates the left atrium from the left ventricle, and must be closed to prevent backflow into the left atrium (choice A is wrong). The high pressures generated during systole force blood out of the ventricles through the aortic and pulmonary semilunar valves (choices B and C are wrong). While the ventricles are contracting, the atria are resting, and blood can flow into them from the vena cava and pulmonary veins. This flow would be prevented if there were any pressure in the atria (choice **D** is correct). Note that closure of the AV valves ensures that the super-high ventricular pressure does not spread to the atria.

[13] Diastole is longer, since it occupies the space between *lub-dup* and *lub-dup*. Systole is shorter, since it occupies the space between *lub* and *dup*.

[14] The athlete's heart can provide the necessary cardiac output by pumping at a leisurely rate of 45 beats per minute. But the hearts of the child and old man will have to work hard to pump enough blood; their pulses will be 80 beats per minute.

[15] Neither, they are equal. The same amount of blood must pass through both sides of the heart or blood would back up in either the pulmonary or systemic circulatory system.

The Frank-Starling Mechanism and Venous Return

There are several ways to increase cardiac output. One is increasing heart rate, as we saw above. Also, a stronger heart has a larger stroke volume and is capable of a greater cardiac output. Another mechanism of increased stroke volume is termed the **Frank-Starling mechanism**. If the heart muscle is stretched, it will contract more forcefully. How can the heart muscle be stretched? By filling it with more blood, of course. The return of blood to the heart by the vena cava is termed **venous return**. If venous return is increased, the heart fills more. As a result, its muscle fibers are stretched, and they respond by contracting more forcefully. The result is that a larger volume of blood enters the heart *and* the heart contracts better. The stroke volume can be increased significantly in this manner. The control of cardiac output in this manner is largely automatic: The more blood the heart receives from the tissues, the more it pumps out to the tissues.

There are two principal ways to increase venous return: 1) Increase the total volume of blood in the circulatory system. The body does this by retaining water (by urinating less). 2) Contraction of large veins can propel blood toward the heart. The presence of valves throughout the venous system is essential here; without valves, contraction of the veins would cause blood to flow backwards, through the venules to the capillaries. [If the arterioles in a large part of the systemic circulation dilate, how will this affect cardiac output?[16]]

Cardiac Muscle

The force of contraction in the ventricles and atria is generated by the cardiac muscle cells that form the muscular walls of the chambers of the heart. The nature of the force generation in contractile cells and the differences between skeletal muscle, cardiac muscle and smooth muscle will be presented in Chapter 10, but it is necessary to present some aspects of cardiac muscle to understand the heart. All muscle cells, including those of cardiac muscle, share with neurons the ability to propagate an action potential across their surface. The action potential in all muscle cells, as in neurons, is a wave of depolarization of the plasma membrane. [Do ligand-gated ion channels propagate action potentials in cardiac muscle?[17]]

A difference between neurons and cardiac muscle cells is that cardiac muscle is a **functional syncytium**. A syncytium is a tissue in which the cytoplasm of different cells can communicate via gap junctions. In cardiac muscle, the gap junctions are found in the **intercalated disks**, the connections between cardiac muscle cells. The depolarization of a cardiac muscle cell can be communicated directly through the cytoplasm to neighboring cardiac muscle cells through these gap junctions. (Recall that this is an example of an electrical synapse; there are no chemical synapses between cardiac muscle cells.) As a result, once an action potential starts, it spreads in a wave of depolarization throughout the cardiac muscle tissue in the atria or the ventricles. The atria and the ventricles are separate syncytia. The action potential in the heart is transmitted from the atrial syncytium to the ventricles by the **cardiac conduction system**. Transmission of the action potential is delayed slightly as it passes through the part of the conduction system known

---

[16] If the arterioles open, more blood will flow through the tissues. The more blood that flows through the tissues, the greater the venous return and the greater the cardiac output.

[17] No. Ligand-gated ion channels may help to create the threshold depolarization required to trigger an action potential but do not play a role in propagating an action potential. Propagation of action potentials requires *voltage*-gated ion channels.

as the A-V node (Figure 5). [Why?[18] What would happen if gap junctions in the heart were blocked, but voltage-gated ion channels remained functional?[19]]

Voltage-gated sodium channels, also called **fast sodium channels**, play an important role in cardiac muscle, as in neurons, but, in addition, another type of voltage-gated channel, the **slow calcium channel**, is involved in the cardiac muscle action potential. Like all voltage-gated channels, these channels open in response to a change in membrane potential to a specific voltage (the threshold voltage) and, when open, allow the passage of calcium down its gradient. These channels also stay open longer than the fast sodium channels do, causing the membrane depolarization to last longer in cardiac muscle than in neurons, producing a plateau phase (Figure 4).

The nature of the action potential in cardiac muscle affects the function of this tissue. Cardiac cells, like all cells with an excitable membrane, have a period during and just after the action potential during which they are refractory to new action potentials. Another result of the long depolarization in cardiac muscle is that the contraction of muscle lasts a long time, strengthening the force with which blood is expelled. To maximize the entry of calcium in the cell, cardiac muscle has involutions of the membrane called T tubules. The action potentials travel down along T tubules, allow the entry of calcium from the extracellular environment, and also induce the sarcoplasmic reticulum to release calcium. The combination of intracellular and extracellular calcium causes the contraction of actin-myosin fibers (Chapter 10). [Will the absolute refractory period, during which a cell will not fire an action potential, be longer in cardiac or neuronal cells?[20] Will the strength of contraction by cardiac muscle be affected by the extracellular concentration of calcium ions?[21]]

Rhythmic Excitation of the Heart

Once an action potential is initiated, it will spread throughout the cardiac muscle of the heart. Interestingly, the heart is *not* stimulated to contract by neuronal or hormonal influences, although these can change the rate and strength of contraction (the **contractility** of the heart). Isolated cardiac muscle cells will in some circumstances continue contracting on their own, free of any external influences. So, what initiates the action potential in heart tissue? The initiation of each action potential that starts each cardiac cycle occurs automatically from within the heart itself, in a special region of the right atrium called the **sinoatrial (SA) node**. Under normal circumstances, the cells of the SA node act as the **pacemaker of the heart**. The SA node exhibits automaticity and its action potential is commonly divided into 3 separate phases; Phase 0, Phase 3 and Phase 4. (*Note:* Other cardiac myocytes (muscle cells) additionally have Phases 1 and 2, but the SA node does *not;* see Figure 3 below.)

---

[18] In order for the heart to function normally, the atria must contract first (during diastole) to completely fill the ventricles with blood before they begin contracting during systole. Thus, the action potential must be propagated through the atrial syncytium before being propagated through the ventricular syncytium.

[19] The gap junctions between cells are necessary for the propagation of action potentials in cardiac muscle. A cell with blocked gap junctions could have an action potential on its own membrane in this circumstance if it reached threshold depolarization, but it would be unable to transmit the action potential to neighboring cells.

[20] The absolute refractory period is the period during the action potential in which a new action potential cannot be induced. If the membrane is still depolarized as part of an action potential, it will be refractory to new action potentials. Cardiac muscle action potentials last much longer than neuronal (or skeletal muscle) action potentials, and will therefore have a longer absolute refractory period.

[21] Yes. A significant portion of the calcium that stimulates contraction comes from the extracellular pool, entering the cell as part of the action potential.

The SA node is unique in that it has an *unstable resting potential* (not really resting, huh?). This is **Phase 4** (automatic slow depolarization) and is caused by special **sodium leak channels** that are responsible for its rhythmic, automatic excitation. This inward sodium leak brings the cell potential to the threshold for voltage-gated calcium channels; when they open they cause **Phase 0**, the upstroke of the pacemaker potential. It is caused mainly by an inward flow of Ca^{2+}. (*Note*: Skeletal muscle cells and other myocytes depolarize because of a *Na^+* influx, not *Ca^{2+}* like the SA node.) This Ca^{2+} drives the membrane potential of the SA nodal cells toward the positive Ca^{2+} equilibrium potential. Note also that the Ca^{2+} channels operate more slowly than the Na^+ channels, leading to a more gradual upsweep in the action potential.

Phase 3 is repolarization. It is caused by closure of the Ca^{2+} channels and opening of the K^+ channels, leading to an outward flow of K^+ from the cell. This loss of positively charged K^+ ions drives the membrane potential back down toward the negative K^+ equilibrium potential.

The SA node cells transmit their action potential through intercalated discs to the rest of the conduction cells in the heart (as well as to the atrial myocytes), repolarize, then start the process over again, repeated once per heartbeat for the life of the individual (Figure 3).

- Why don't potassium leak channels cause spontaneous action potentials in neurons or muscle cells?[22]

Note that while several regions of the heart can spontaneously depolarize (e.g., the AV node, Purkinje fibers), the SA node has the most Na^+ leak channels of all of the conduction system. Thus, it reaches threshold before any other region of the heart does, and sets the rate of heart contraction (that's why it's called the "**pacemaker**" of the heart). When the SA nodal cells are injured or the pathway of atrial depolarization is blocked, these other regions of the heart will take over the pacemaking responsibility, but pace the heart at a slower rate.

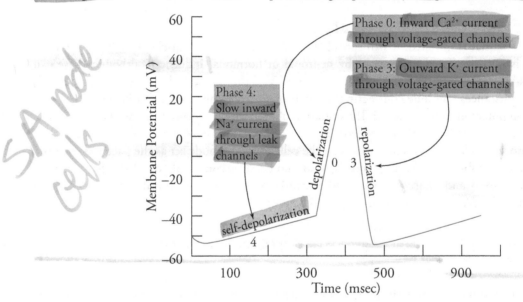

Figure 3 The Pacemaker Potential of the SA Node

---

[22] Potassium leak channels allow potassium to leave the cell, down a gradient, polarizing the membrane; the *opposite* effect of sodium leak channels. Sodium is at a higher concentration outside of the cell, so sodium leak channels allow sodium to enter the cell and depolarize the membrane.

The cardiac muscle cells of the heart have an action potential that differs from the SA node and the other conduction system cells. These muscle cells have a resting membrane potential of about −90mV (very close to the K⁺ equilibrium potential). The action potentials here have a long duration, up to 300 milliseconds normally. The phases of the action potential in these cells are Phases 0–4 (see Figure 4 below).

Phase 0 (depolarization) is again the upstroke of the action potential and is caused by the transient increase is Na⁺ conductance (just like in neurons). Action potentials propagating through the intercalated discs stimulate myocytes to reach threshold for voltage-gated Na⁺ channels. Once threshold is reached, the Na⁺ channels open and Na⁺ rushes into the cell.

In **Phase 1** (initial repolarization) the Na⁺ channels inactivate and K⁺ channels open. This leads to an efflux of K⁺ and a slight drop in cell potential. Furthermore, the increased potential due to the initial Na⁺ influx causes the opening of voltage-gated Ca²⁺ channels; this leads to **Phase 2**, the **plateau** phase. During the plateau, the influx of Ca²⁺ ions balance the K⁺ efflux from phase one, leading to a transient equilibrium in cell potential.

Phase 3 (repolarization) occurs when the Ca²⁺ channels close and the K⁺ channels continue to allow K⁺ to leave the cell (again, this is just like in neurons). **Phase 4** (the resting membrane potential) is the period during which inward and outward current are equal. Remember, this is dictated by action of the Na⁺/K⁺ ATPase and slow K⁺ leak channels.

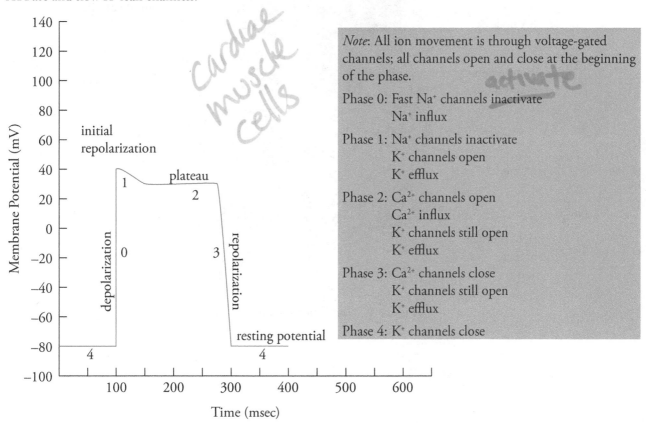

Figure 4   Phases of the Membrane Potential in a Cardiac Muscle Cell

Thus, each heartbeat begins as an action potential in the **sinoatrial (SA) node** then spreads throughout the atria, causing them to contract and fill the ventricles with blood. The action potential also spreads down the special conduction pathway which transmits action potentials very rapidly without contracting. The pathway connects the SA node to the **atrioventricular (AV) node**. Since this pathway connects the two nodes, it is referred to as the **internodal tract**. Note that while the impulse travels to the AV node almost instantaneously, it spreads through the atria more slowly, because contracting heart muscle cells pass the impulse more slowly than specialized conduction fibers. At the AV node, the impulse is delayed slightly, then passes from the node to the ventricles via the conduction pathway again. This part of the conduction pathway is known as the **AV bundle (bundle of His)**. The AV bundle divides into the **right** and **left bundle branches**, and then into the **Purkinje fibers**, which allow the impulse to spread rapidly and evenly over both ventricles. Note that the Purkinje fibers spread over the inferior portion of the ventricles (paradoxically called the "apex" of the heart). The result is that this region of the ventricles contracts first, and blood is pushed toward the superior region of the heart (paradoxically called the "base"), where the valves and arteries are (Figure 5).

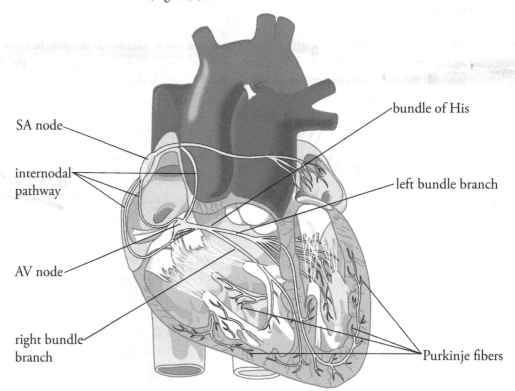

Figure 5   The Cardiac Conduction System

Regulation of the Heart by the Autonomic Nervous System

The autonomic nervous system does not initiate action potentials in the heart, but it does regulate the rate of contraction. The intrinsic firing rate of the SA node is about 120 beats per minute. The reason the normal heart rate is only about 60–80 beats/minute is that the parasympathetic nervous system continually inhibits depolarization of the SA node. In particular, the **vagus nerve** (a cranial nerve) contains preganglionic axons which synapse in ganglia near the SA node. The postganglionic neurons innervate the SA node, releasing acetylcholine (ACh). The ACh inhibits depolarization by binding to receptors on the cells of the SA node. The constant level of inhibition provided by the vagus nerve is known as **vagal tone.** [Does ACh always inhibit postsynaptic cells? If not, how can different responses be elicited by the same neurotransmitter?[23]] In summary, the role of the *parasympathetic* system in controlling the heart is to modulate the rate by *inhibiting rapid automaticity.*

The sympathetic system can also influence the heart. At rest, however, most nervous input is from the vagus. The sympathetic system kicks in when increased cardiac output is needed during a "fight or flight" response. The sympathetic system affects the heart in two ways: First, sympathetic postganglionic neurons directly innervate the heart, releasing norepinephrine. Second, epinephrine secreted by the adrenal medulla binds to receptors on cardiac muscle cells. The effect of sympathetic activation is stimulatory. The heart rate increases, and so does the force of contraction.

The heart rate and blood pressure are tightly regulated. In any regulatory system, three components are required: input (afferent information), integration (the function of the central nervous system), and output (efferent information, discussed in the above two paragraphs). The input in this regulatory system is complex, but we can highlight one key element: In the aortic arch and in the carotid arteries there are special receptors known as **baroreceptors**, which monitor pressure (like a *baro*meter). When they notify the central nervous system that the pressure is too high, the CNS sends out information to correct the problem: increased vagal tone and decreased sympathetic input. When the pressure is too low, the opposite happens. People with high blood pressure have a poorly functioning regulatory system and must take medications designed to keep things under control.

8.3 HEMODYNAMICS

Resistance

Hemodynamics is the study of blood flow. The driving force for blood flow is a difference in pressure from arteries to veins. The force opposing flow is friction, which results when blood squeezes through many tiny branching vessels. The technical term for this opposing force is **resistance**. Ohm's law summarizes the relationship between these variables: $\Delta P = Q \times R$. Here, ΔP is the pressure gradient (in mm Hg) from the arterial system to the venous system, Q stands for blood flow (in L/min), and R denotes resistance. The usefulness of this simple equation is this: it shows us that if we want to change blood flow,

---

[23] ACh is the neurotransmitter released by all autonomic preganglionic neurons, all parasympathetic postganglionic neurons, and all somatic motor neurons. In most cases it is stimulatory, i.e., causes an action potential to occur, causes an effect in an organ. Whether a neurotransmitter is stimulatory or inhibitory depends only on the nature of its receptor on the postsynaptic cell.

we can only change it by changing either the pressure or the resistance; those are the only independent variables in the equation.

We know that pressure can be varied by increasing the *force* or *rate* of cardiac contraction. What about resistance? The principal determinant of resistance is the degree of constriction of arteriolar smooth muscle, also known as **precapillary sphincters**. If arteriolar smooth muscles contract, it becomes more difficult for blood to flow from arteries into capillaries; that is, the resistance goes up. The resistance of the entire systemic circuit is easily calculated using the above equation in the form $R = \Delta P/Q$. We can measure ΔP and Q, then solve for R. This quantity is known as the **peripheral resistance**.

The sympathetic nervous system controls the peripheral resistance. A certain amount of pressure in the arterial system is always desirable; otherwise not all tissues would be perfused. This basal level of pressure is provided by a constant level of norepinephrine released by millions of sympathetic postganglionic axons innervating precapillary sphincters. This constant nervous input is known as **adrenergic tone**. (Adrenergic means sympathetic; the word comes from adrenaline, which is another name for epinephrine.) [Why might tense, stressed out people tend to have high blood pressure?[24]]

The sympathetic system can increase the overall peripheral resistance, thus increasing blood pressure. It can also specifically divert blood away from one tissue so that another is preferentially perfused. In particular, sympathetic activation causes precapillary sphincters in the gut to contract, while arterioles supplying skeletal muscle are allowed to relax. The result is that blood flow is diverted from the gut to skeletal muscle, which facilitates the fight or flight response.

Blood Pressure

When physicians measure blood pressure, what they are actually measuring is **systemic arterial pressure**. This is the force per unit area exerted by blood upon the walls of arteries. You may recall that a typical blood pressure reading looks like this: 120/80, pronounced "120 over 80." What do the two numbers mean? 120 mm Hg is the **systolic pressure**, and 80 mm Hg is the **diastolic pressure**. In other words, 120 mm Hg is the highest pressure that ever occurs in the circulatory system of this particular patient during the time the blood pressure is being measured. This level is attained as the ventricles contract (that is, during systole). 80 mm Hg is as low as the pressure gets between heartbeats (that is, during diastole) during the measurement. The **pulse pressure** is the difference between systolic and diastolic pressures.

The measurement is taken using a **sphygmomanometer**, or "blood pressure cuff." This is an inflatable bag attached to a manometer (pressure-measuring device). The physician wraps the cuff around the upper arm and places a stethoscope at a point below the cuff where the pulse can be heard. Then she inflates the cuff until no blood flows into the arm (silence is heard in the stethoscope). Then she gradually reduces the cuff pressure, until a pulse first becomes audible. The significance of this point is that systolic arterial pressure is just greater than the pressure of the cuff. Hence, this pressure level is written down as the systolic pressure (120 in our example above). The pulse is very loud; this sound comes from blood slamming into arteries (which are constricted by the cuff) each time the heart beats. Then the physician continues to release pressure from the cuff. At a certain level, the pulse becomes much more quiet (usually inaudible). The significance of this is that now the cuff is loose enough so that blood flows smoothly through

---

[24] Tension and stress are similar to fear. Both involve activation of the sympathetic nervous system.

arteries and does not create the pounding noise described above. The point at which the pulse becomes inaudible is written down as the diastolic pressure. This is the lowest arterial pressure occurring at any time during the cardiac cycle.

It is important to emphasize the last sentence: this is the lowest *arterial* pressure occurring at any time during the cardiac cycle. You must realize that throughout the cardiac cycle, the pressure in the vena cava is about *zero* mm Hg. The highest pressures in the circulatory system are achieved in the left ventricle, aorta, and other large arteries. (That's what we measured with the cuff.) But every large artery branches, giving rise to many arterioles, and every arteriole gives rise to many capillaries. The result of all this branching is that the pressure generated by the heart is dissipated (Figure 6). By the time blood reaches the vena cava, it depends on valves to prevent backflow because the driving pressure is negligible.

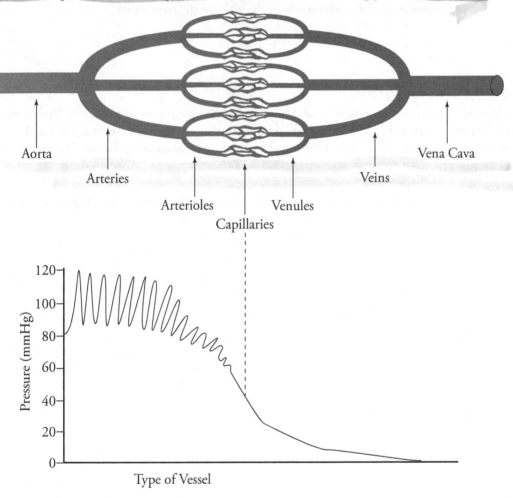

Figure 6   Pressures Throughout the Circulatory System

8.3

Why is the diastolic arterial pressure as high as it is? In other words, between heartbeats, why does the arterial pressure remain elevated? Without the heart contracting, wouldn't you expect the pressure to fall rapidly? This is the reason arteries are highly elastic and muscular. When the heart contracts, the arteries distend like balloons. During diastole, the arteries exert pressure on the blood, just as an inflated balloon exerts pressure on the air it contains. This maintains diastolic pressure, which is important because it provides a continued driving force for blood.

- Which one of the following will increase cardiac output?[25]
  - A. Blocking sodium leak channels in the sinoatrial node
  - B. Stimulation of the heart by the parasympathetic nervous system
  - C. Significant dehydration due to prolonged exercise in the heat
  - D. Contraction of smooth muscle in the walls of the large veins

Local Autoregulation

The nervous system does not control blood flow to every single region of the body. The amount of feedback information this would require would be huge. Instead, tissues in need of extra blood flow are able to requisition it themselves. This phenomenon is known as **local autoregulation**. The mechanism is simple: Certain metabolic wastes have a direct effect on arteriolar smooth muscle, causing it to relax. Hence, when a tissue is underperfused, wastes build up, and vasodilation occurs automatically. Autoregulation is the principal determinant of coronary blood flow (blood supply to the heart); it generally overrides nervous input.

---

[25] Blocking the sodium leak channels will slow the spontaneous firing of action potentials by the sinoatrial node and slow the heart rate. Slowing the heart rate will decrease, not increase the cardiac output (choice A is wrong). The parasympathetic nervous system slows the heart rate and therefore decreases the cardiac output (choice B is wrong). Dehydration will reduce venous return and reduce the stroke volume of the heart, leading to a reduction in cardiac output (choice C is wrong). However, the large veins do have smooth muscle, although less than arteries, and can constrict in response to sympathetic stimulation. This would increase the filling pressure (the pressure gradient) driving blood into the right atrium, thus increasing venous return, stroke volume, and cardiac output (choice D is correct). Note that this is a difficult and complex question because we do not normally think of the veins as having smooth muscle, and furthermore, we tend to think of blood flow *reduction* when a vessel constricts. The MCAT also has difficult and complex questions. The key to answering this question correctly is to have confidence in the elimination of choices A, B, and C. Thus choice D, however improbable it may seem, must be the correct answer.

8.4   COMPONENTS OF BLOOD

Blood has a liquid portion called **plasma**, and a portion which is composed of cells. The cellular elements of blood are known as **formed elements**. Plasma accounts for 55 percent of the volume of blood, and consists of the following items dissolved in water: electrolytes, buffers, sugars, blood proteins, lipoproteins, CO_2, O_2, and metabolic waste products. **Electrolytes** refer to Na^+, K^+, Cl^-, Ca^{2+}, and Mg^{2+} ions. **Buffers** in the blood maintain a constant pH of 7.4; the principal blood buffer is bicarbonate (HCO_3^-).

- During exercise, a significant amount of lactic acid is produced by fermentation in muscles that are not receiving adequate oxygen. Despite this increase in lactic acid, the pH of the blood does not change dramatically. Why not?[26]

The principal sugar in the blood is glucose. A constant concentration must be maintained so that all the cells of the body receive adequate nutrition. The blood proteins, most of which are made by the liver, include albumin, immunoglobulins (antibodies), fibrinogen, and lipoproteins. **Albumin** is essential for maintenance of **oncotic pressure** (osmotic pressure in the capillaries due only to plasma proteins). The **immunoglobulins** are a key part of the immune system (Section 8.7). **Fibrinogen** is essential for blood clotting (hemostasis). **Lipoproteins** are large particles consisting of fats, cholesterol, and carrier proteins. Their role is to transport lipids in the bloodstream. CO_2 and O_2 are involved in respiration, of course. However, CO_2 is also important for its role in buffering the blood (see the reaction in Footnote 26). The principal *metabolic waste product* is **urea**, a breakdown product of amino acids. Urea is basically a carrier of excess nitrogen. There are other important waste products too, such as **bilirubin**, a breakdown product of heme (the oxygen-binding moiety of hemoglobin, discussed below).

By centrifuging whole blood, one can separate the plasma from the formed elements, as shown below. The volume of blood occupied by the red blood cells (**erythrocytes**) is known as the **hematocrit** (Figure 7). The normal hematocrit in adult males is 40–45 percent; in females it is lower, approximately 35–40 percent. White blood cells (**leukocytes**) and platelets account for a small volume (about 1 percent). All the formed elements of the blood develop from special cells in the bone marrow, known as **bone marrow stem cells**.

If whole blood is allowed to clot, one is left with a solid clot plus a clear fluid known as **serum**. Hence, serum is similar to plasma except that it lacks all the proteins involved in clotting.

---

[26] The HCO_3^- buffer system prevents pH changes via the reaction $CO_2 + H_2O \rightleftharpoons H_2CO_3 \rightleftharpoons HCO_3^- + H^+$.

8.4

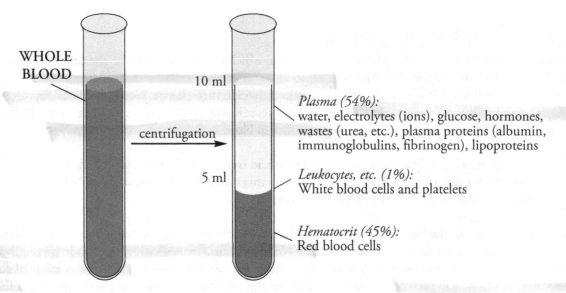

WHOLE
BLOOD

10 ml

centrifugation

5 ml

Plasma (54%):
water, electrolytes (ions), glucose, hormones,
wastes (urea, etc.), plasma proteins (albumin,
immunoglobulins, fibrinogen), lipoproteins

Leukocytes, etc. (1%):
White blood cells and platelets

Hematocrit (45%):
Red blood cells

Figure 7 The Hematocrit and the Components of Blood

Erythrocytes (Red Blood Cells—RBCs)

The hormone **erythropoeitin** (made in the kidney) stimulates RBC production in the bone marrow. Aged RBCs are eaten by phagocytes in the spleen and liver.

The erythrocyte is a cell, but it has no nucleus or other organelles such as mitochondria. However, it does require the energy of ATP for processes such as ion pumping and basic maintenance of cell structure during its 120-day lifetime in the bloodstream. Lacking mitochondria, the RBC relies on glycolysis for ATP synthesis. The purpose of the RBC is to transport O_2 to the tissues from the lungs and CO_2 from the tissues to the lungs. Hence it requires a large surface area for gas exchange. A high surface-to-volume ratio is achieved by the RBC's flat, biconcave shape (like a deflated basketball or a throat lozenge, see Figure 8). The RBC is able to carry oxygen because it contains millions of molecules of **hemoglobin** (more on hemoglobin below).

Figure 8 Red Blood Cells (Erythrocytes)

Blood Typing

Blood typing is the classification of a person's blood based on the presence or absence of certain surface antigens on their red blood cells. The two most important blood group antigens are the **ABO blood group** and the **Rh blood group.** The ABO blood group consists of glycoproteins that are coded for by three different alleles: I^A, I^B, and i. These alleles and their genotypes and phenotypes were discussed in more detail in Chapter 6 (Genetics and Evolution).

8.4

The other main antigen used in blood typing is the Rh (rhesus) factor. The expression of this antigen follows a classically dominant pattern: RR and Rr genotypes lead to the expression of the protein on the surface of the red blood cell (Rh positive), and the rr genotype leads to the absence of the protein (Rh negative). The combinations of the ABO alleles and the Rh alleles (and the respective antigens they code for) determine the overall blood type of an individual. Table 1 summarizes these blood types.

	$I^A I^A$ or $I^A i$	$I^B I^B$ or $I^B i$	$I^A I^B$	ii
RR or Rr	type A+	type B+	type AB+	type O+
rr	type A-	type B-	type AB-	type O-

Table 1   Blood Group Genotypes and Phenotypes

Determining blood type is critical when performing blood transfusions. Antibodies to the A and B antigens are produced early in infancy and can cause clumping and destruction of red blood cells bearing the incorrect antigen (called a **transfusion reaction**). For example, a person with A+ blood produces anti-B antibodies; if transfused with type B blood, these antibodies will clump and destroy the donated type B cells, possibly leading to the death of the recipient.

Antibodies to the Rh antigen do not develop unless a person with Rh– blood is exposed to Rh+ blood, an event called "sensitization." Subsequent exposure to Rh+ blood can then result in a transfusion reaction. This is particularly dangerous in the case of an Rh– mother carrying an Rh+ baby. Typically, if it is the first baby there are no complications (unless the mother had been previously sensitized); the mother's blood and the baby's blood do not mix during pregnancy. However, on delivery, some Rh+ cells from the child can mix with the mother's Rh– blood and lead to her sensitization. Future Rh+ babies are then at risk, since the anti-Rh antibodies can cross the placental barrier to clump and/or destroy the Rh+ baby's red blood cells. This is known as **hemolytic disease of the newborn** or *erythroblastosis fetalis*, and can be fatal. Injection of the mother at the time of birth with anti-Rh antibodies can clump and lead to the destruction of any stray Rh+ cells from the baby; this can prevent sensitization of the mother and protect any future unborn Rh+ children.

Two special blood types are AB+ and O–. Type AB+ individuals do not make antibodies to any of the blood group antigens, since their red blood cells possess all three of the antigens. Thus, type AB+ individuals are known as **"universal recipients"** because they can receive any of the other blood types without complication. Type O– individuals do not possess any of the surface antigens that could trigger a reaction in an individual with a different blood type. Thus, O– individuals are known as "universal donors" because they can donate blood to any of the other blood types, typically without complication. (Note that type O– individuals do make anti-A and anti-B antibodies, and these can sometimes cause issues in recipients. It is always best to match blood types between donors and recipients when possible.)

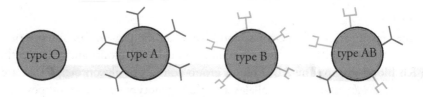

Figure 9   RBC Surface Antigens

Leukocytes

The white blood cell's role is to fight infection and dispose of debris. All white blood cells are large complex cells with all the normal eukaryotic cell structures (nucleus, mitochondria, etc.). Some white blood cells (**macrophages** and **neutrophils**) move by amoeboid motility (crawling). This is important because they are able to squeeze out of capillary intercellular junctions (spaces between capillary endothelial cells) and can therefore roam free in the tissues, hunting for foreign particles and pathogens. Some white blood cells exhibit **chemotaxis**, which means movement directed by chemical stimuli. The chemical stimuli can be toxins and waste products released by pathogens, or can be chemical signals released from other white blood cells. There are six types of white blood cells (Table 2).

Cell	Role
monocytes:	
macrophage	phagocytose debris and microorganisms; amoeboid motility; chemotaxis
lymphocytes:	
B cell	mature into *plasma cell* and produce antibodies
T cell	kill virus-infected cells, tumor cells, and reject tissue grafts; also control immune response
granulocytes:	
neutrophil	phagocytose bacteria resulting in pus; amoeboid motility; chemotaxis
eosinophil	destroy parasites; allergic reactions
basophil	store and release histamine; allergic reactions

Table 2   Roles of the Six Types of Leukocytes

Platelets and Hemostasis

Like red blood cells, platelets have no nuclei and a limited lifespan. They are derived from the fragmentation of large bone marrow cells called **megakaryocytes**, which are derived from the same stem cells that give rise to red blood cells and white blood cells. The function of platelets is to aggregate at the site of damage to a blood vessel wall, forming a **platelet plug**. This immediately helps stop bleeding. **Hemostasis** is a term for the body's mechanism of preventing bleeding.

The other component of the hemostatic response is **fibrin**. This is a threadlike protein which forms a mesh that holds the platelet plug together. When the fibrin mesh dries, it becomes a scab, which seals and protects the wound. The plasma protein **fibrinogen** is converted into fibrin by a protein called **thrombin** when bleeding occurs. A blood clot, or **thrombus**, is a scab circulating in the bloodstream. Calcium as well as many accessory proteins are necessary for the activation of thrombin and fibrinogen. Several of the proteins depend on vitamin K for their function. Defects in these proteins result in **hemophilia** ("loving to bleed"), an X-linked recessive group of diseases involving excessive bleeding.

hemophilia ⇒ X-linked recessive

8.5

8.5 TRANSPORT OF GASES

Oxygen

Oxygen is too hydrophobic to dissolve in the plasma in significant quantities. Hence, RBCs are used to bind and carry O_2. RBCs are able to carry oxygen because they contain millions of molecules of **hemoglobin** (Hb). This is a complex protein composed of four polypeptide subunits. Each subunit contains one molecule of **heme**, which is a large multi-ring structure that has a single iron atom bound at its center. The role of heme with its iron atom is to bind O_2. Since each hemoglobin has four subunits and each subunit has one heme, each molecule of hemoglobin can carry four molecules of oxygen. Hemoglobin has some important properties which make it an excellent oxygen carrier.

The four subunits of hemoglobin do not bind oxygen independently of each other. When none of the subunits have oxygen bound, all four subunits assume a **tense** conformation that has a relatively low affinity for oxygen. (A *conformation* is a specific three-dimensional structure of a protein.) When one of the subunits binds oxygen, its conformation changes from a tense to a **relaxed** state that has a higher affinity for oxygen. The change in the three-dimensional structure of the subunit with oxygen bound is then communicated to the other subunits through contacts between the polypeptides to alter their conformation and increase their affinity for oxygen as well. Thus, hemoglobin is said to bind oxygen **cooperatively**.

- Myoglobin is a molecule with a structure very similar to hemoglobin, but with a single subunit that has one binding site. Does myoglobin display cooperativity in oxygen binding?[27]
- If binding of oxygen is cooperative, is it saturable?[28]
- Does hemoglobin have higher affinity for oxygen in the tissues or in the lungs?[29]

This has monumental significance for the ability of the blood to transport oxygen efficiently. The level of O_2 in active tissues is very low, because they use it in oxidative phosphorylation. Hence, in the tissues, hemoglobin has low affinity for oxygen and tends to release any oxygen which it carries. The level of O_2 in the lungs is of course very high. Hence, when a red blood cell is passing through a capillary in the lungs, the hemoglobin it contains will have higher affinity due to cooperative binding and will tend to

---

[27] Cooperativity requires more than one binding site in a protein so that one binding site can alter the affinity of another. Myoglobin cannot be cooperative in oxygen binding since it has only one binding site.

[28] There are a limited number of binding sites, even if they are cooperative, so binding will be saturated at a high concentration (partial pressure) of oxygen. There is a limit to the oxygen carrying capacity of the blood.

[29] At higher partial pressure of oxygen, more of the hemoglobin protein will have at least one of the subunits occupied with oxygen. Since binding is cooperative, the more oxygen that is bound, the higher the affinity for oxygen. The partial pressure of oxygen is higher in the lungs than in the tissues, so hemoglobin will have higher affinity for oxygen in the lungs.

bind oxygen very strongly. The result is that a lot of oxygen is picked up by RBCs in the lungs, and most of it is released as they pass through active tissues that need oxygen. This is an amazing example of how structural biochemistry determines physiology (or vice versa).

There is even more complexity to the hemoglobin story. It turns out that certain factors stabilize the tense configuration (which has a low O_2 affinity). These factors are:

1) decreased pH,
2) increased P_{CO_2} (level of CO_2 in the blood), and
3) increased temperature.

The fact that these factors stabilize tense hemoglobin and thus reduce its oxygen affinity is known as the **Bohr effect**. This system is truly incredible when you realize that these three factors perfectly characterize the environment within active tissues. [What is the significance of this?[30]]

The affinity of hemoglobin for oxygen can be quantified by measurement of the fraction of O_2-binding sites which have bound O_2. If hemoglobin is in the relaxed configuration, then as more oxygen becomes available, much more of it will be bound up. But if it is in the tense configuration, the tendency to bind oxygen is reduced, and less will be bound. This can be described mathematically using the notion of **percent saturation (% sat.)**:

% sat. = (# of O_2 molecules bound) ÷ (# of O_2 binding sites) × 100%

- At a given P_{O_2}, which has a higher % sat.: tense or relaxed hemoglobin?[31]

This information can be depicted graphically, using an **O_2-Hemoglobin Dissociation Curve**, which plots % sat. vs. P_{O_2} (Figure 10). The sigmoidal shape of the curve resembles the behavior of cooperative enzymes (Chapter 2).

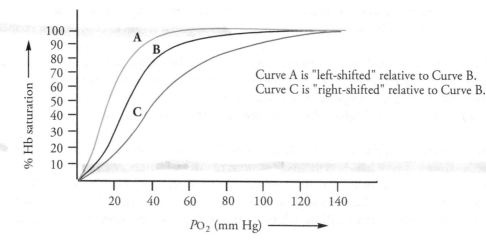

Curve A is "left-shifted" relative to Curve B.
Curve C is "right-shifted" relative to Curve B.

Figure 10 O_2-Hemoglobin Dissociation Curves

---

[30] When a tissue is active, its cells metabolize a lot of glucose and this results in an elevated P_{CO_2}. Soon the cells run low on oxygen and begin to perform lactic acid fermentation. The result is a drop in pH. Finally, whenever there is a lot of metabolic activity, the temperature increases. So, due to the Bohr effect, hemoglobin is most ready to release its load of oxygen in regions of the body where oxygen is most needed!

[31] Relaxed, since it has a higher affinity. This just means that at any O_2 level, relaxed hemoglobin will bind more O_2 than tense hemoglobin will.

Answer all of the following questions about Figure 10 before looking at the footnote.[32]

- Curve ____ represents Hb with the highest affinity of all.
- Curve C could be the result of ____.
- Curve A would most likely be seen in what region of the body?
- Why do all the curves level off?
- It is interesting to note that fetal hemoglobin is a bit different from adult hemoglobin. The fetus must be able to "steal" oxygen away from the mother's blood. Hence, the O_2 dissociation curve for fetal hemoglobin is ____-shifted relative to the curve for adult hemoglobin.

Carbon Dioxide

Carbon dioxide is transported in the blood in three ways:

1) 73% of CO_2 transport is accomplished by the conversion of CO_2 to **carbonic acid**, which can dissociate into **bicarbonate** and a **proton** according to this reaction: $CO_2 + H_2O \rightleftharpoons H_2CO_3 \rightleftharpoons HCO_3^- + H^+$. These compounds are extremely water-soluble and are thus easily carried in the blood. The conversion of CO_2 into carbonic acid is catalyzed by an RBC enzyme called **carbonic anhydrase**. Remember that this reaction is also important as the principal plasma pH buffer.
2) Some CO_2 (~ 20%) is transported by simply being stuck onto hemoglobin. It does *not* bind to the oxygen-binding sites, but rather to other sites on the protein. Binding of CO_2 to hemoglobin is important in the Bohr effect because it stabilizes tense Hb.
3) CO_2 is somewhat more water-soluble than O_2, so a fair amount (~ 7%) can be dissolved in the blood and carried from the tissues to the lungs. Virtually no oxygen can be dissolved in the blood.

Exchange of Substances Across the Capillary Wall

The capillaries are the site of exchange between the blood and tissues. To facilitate exchange, capillaries have walls of only a single layer of flattened endothelial cells, and there are spaces (**intercellular clefts**) between the endothelial cells which make up the capillary wall. Three types of substances must be able to pass through the clefts: nutrients, wastes, and white blood cells. We will discuss each of these in turn. [Is it necessary for O_2 and CO_2 to pass through the clefts?[33]]

There are three main types of nutrients: amino acids, glucose, and lipids. Amino acids and glucose are absorbed from the digestive tract and carried by a special vein called the **hepatic portal vein** to the liver. It is called a *portal vein* because it connects two capillary beds: the one in the intestinal wall and the one inside the liver. The liver stores amino acids and glucose, and releases them into the bloodstream as

---

[32] Curve A is farthest to the left and thus represents the highest affinity. Curve C could be the result of the Bohr effect. At a given O_2 level, the hemoglobin studied in Curve C has less of a tendency to bind oxygen (a lower affinity). Curve A would most likely be seen in the lungs, where there is plenty of oxygen and relaxed hemoglobin predominates. All the curves level off because 100% is the maximum degree of saturation; all the hemoglobin molecules become completely saturated. Fetal Hb has a left-shifted curve (higher affinity).

[33] No, they can pass straight through any cell by simple diffusion.

needed. From the bloodstream they can pass through capillary clefts into the tissues. The journey of lipids through the bloodstream is different. Fats are absorbed from the intestine and packaged into **chylomicrons**, which are a type of lipoprotein. The chylomicrons enter tiny lymphatic vessels in the intestinal wall called **lacteals**. The lacteals empty into larger lymphatics, which eventually drain into a large vein near the neck. Hence, dietary fats bypass the hepatic vein. The result is that after eating a fatty meal, a person's blood will appear milky. (The term for this is **lipemia**, which means "lipids flowing in the blood.") The chylomicrons are taken up by the liver and converted into another type of lipoprotein, which is released into the bloodstream. This lipoprotein carries fats to **adipocytes** (fat cells) for storage. When fats are to be used for energy, adipocyte triglycerides are hydrolyzed, and free fatty acids are released into the bloodstream. They pass easily through capillary pores and thus can be picked up by cells of various tissues.

Many wastes are produced during cellular metabolism. They diffuse through the capillary walls into the bloodstream. The liver removes many wastes and converts them into forms which can be excreted in the feces. Such compounds are passed into the gut as **bile**. Other wastes are excreted directly by the kidneys.

White blood cells must be able to pass out of capillaries in order to patrol the tissues for invading microorganisms. Two of the six types of white blood cell can squeeze through the clefts: the _____ and the _____. These are large cells which depend on _____ in order to fit through the clefts, which are too small to allow RBCs to pass.[34]

It is also important to realize that water has a great tendency to flow out of capillaries, through the clefts. There are two reasons: 1) the hydrostatic pressure (fluid pressure) created by the heart simply tends to squeeze water out of the capillaries, and 2) the high osmolarity of the tissues tends to draw water out of the bloodstream. The circulatory system deals with this problem by giving the plasma a high osmolarity. [Would dissolving NaCl in the plasma accomplish this?[35]] Plasma osmolarity is provided by high concentrations of large plasma proteins, mainly albumin. Albumin is too large and rigid to pass through the clefts, so it remains in the capillaries and keeps water there too. The osmotic pressure provided by plasma proteins is given a special name: **oncotic pressure**. However, some water does leak out, resulting in an interesting cycle.

1) At the beginning of the capillary, the hydrostatic pressure is high. The result is that water squeezes out into the tissues.
2) As water continues to leave the capillary, the relative concentration of plasma proteins increases.
3) At the end of the capillary the hydrostatic pressure is quite low, but since the blood is now very concentrated, the oncotic pressure is very high. As a result, water flows back into the capillary from the tissues.

Thus, some water is lost into the tissues, but due to the oncotic pressure of the plasma proteins, the net loss is normally low. Occasionally the system breaks down and a significant amount of water is lost into the tissues. For example, during **inflammation**, capillaries dilate, increasing the size of the intercellular clefts. This allows more space for white blood cells to migrate into the tissues. The unfortunate side-effect is that plasma proteins and a lot of water are lost into the tissues. The result is water in the tissues, or swelling, termed **edema**. Small amounts of fluid loss into the tissues are normal; even some protein is normally lost. Fluid, proteins, and white blood cells in the tissues are returned to the bloodstream via the lymphatic system.

---

[34] Macrophages and neutrophils can squeeze through the clefts, even though they are larger than RBCs, because they are capable of *amoeboid motility*, as noted in Table 2. RBCs are not capable of independent motility.

[35] No, because salts can freely pass out of the capillaries.

- What would occur if capillaries throughout the circulatory system were made more permeable?[36]
- Albumin is made in the liver. Alcoholics with diseased livers make insufficient amounts of albumin, and thus have insufficient plasma oncotic pressure. What result would you predict?[37]

8.6 THE LYMPHATIC SYSTEM

The lymphatic system (Figure 11) is a one-way flow system which begins with tiny lymphatic capillaries in all the tissues of the body that merge to form larger lymphatic vessels. These merge to form large lymphatic ducts. Lymphatic vessels have valves, and the larger lymphatic ducts have smooth muscles in their walls. As a result, the lymphatic system acts like a suction pump to retrieve water, proteins, and white blood cells from the tissues. The fluid in lymphatic vessels is called **lymph**. The lymph is filtered by numerous **lymph nodes**. The lymph nodes are an important part of the immune system because they contain millions of white blood cells that can initiate an immune response against anything foreign that may have been picked up in the lymph. The large lymphatic ducts merge to form the **thoracic duct**, which is the largest lymphatic vessel, located in the chest. The thoracic duct empties into a large vein near the neck. Also, lymphatic vessels from the intestines dump dietary fats in the form of chylomicrons into the thoracic duct.

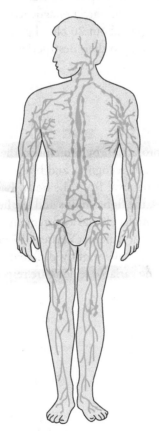

Figure 11 The Lymphatic System: Vessels and Lymph Nodes

---

[36] A significant volume of fluid will be lost from the plasma into tissues, decreasing the blood volume and cardiac output. Circulatory shock can result.

[37] The result is edema of the entire body, including the limbs, abdomen, and lungs.

8.7 THE IMMUNE SYSTEM

The interior of the body provides a warm, protective, nourishing environment where micro-organisms can flourish. We could not survive without a versatile and efficient immune system to destroy invaders without destroying the body itself. There are three types of immunity: innate, humoral, and cell-mediated.

Innate Immunity

Innate immunity refers to the general, non-specific protection the body provides against various invaders. The simplest example of innate immunity is the barrier to the outside world known as **skin**. The skin prevents many types of pathogens from infecting us. Here is a list of the principal components of innate immunity:

1) The skin is an excellent barrier against the entry of microorganisms.
2) Tears, saliva, and blood contain **lysozyme**, an enzyme that kills some bacteria by destroying their cell walls.
3) The **extreme acidity of the stomach** destroys many pathogens which are ingested with food or swallowed after being passed out of the respiratory tract.
4) Macrophages and neutrophils indiscriminately phagocytize microorganisms.[38]
5) The **complement system** is a group of about 20 blood proteins that can nonspecifically bind to the surface of foreign cells, leading to their destruction.

Humoral Immunity, Antibodies, and B Cells

Humoral immunity refers to specific protection by proteins in the plasma called **antibodies (Ab)** or **immunoglobulins (Ig)**. Antibodies specifically recognize and bind to microorganisms (or other foreign particles), leading to their destruction and removal from the body. Each antibody molecule is composed of two copies of two different polypeptides, the **light chains** and the **heavy chains**, joined by disulfide bonds (Figure 12). In addition, each antibody molecule has two regions, the **constant region** and the **variable (antigen binding) region**. There are several different classes of immunoglobulins: IgG, IgA, IgM, IgD, and IgE. The classes of immunoglobulins have slightly different functions, with most of the antibody circulating in plasma in the IgG class. The variable regions are responsible for the specificity of antibodies in recognizing foreign particles.

---

[38] Do not confuse this portion of innate immunity with cell-mediated immunity. You are correct to notice that cells are involved, but this activity is placed in the "innate" category because we are referring to non-specific phagocytosis. Humoral and cell-mediated immunity are highly specific. One other subtlety: When a macrophage eats an antigen which has been coated with specific antibodies, we are dealing with humoral immunity; this is different from the indiscriminate, nonspecific pathogen phagocytosis discussed above.

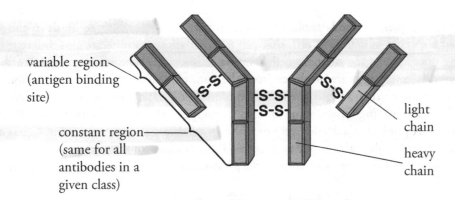

variable region
(antigen binding
site)

constant region
(same for all
antibodies in a
given class)

light
chain

heavy
chain

Figure 12   Antibody Structure

Each antibody forms a unique variable region that has a different binding specificity. The molecule that an antibody binds to is known as the **antigen** (**Ag**). Examples of antigens are viral capsid proteins, bacterial surface proteins, and toxins in the bloodstream (such as tetanus toxin). [Would an antibody against a cytoplasmic bacterial protein help the immune system to remove the bacteria?[39]] The specificity of antigen binding is determined by the fit of antigen in a small three-dimensional cleft formed by the variable region of the antibody molecule (Figure 12). [If the antigen binding site is small, can antibodies recognize large proteins as antigens?[40] Why might an antibody that binds tightly to a small region of a protein, five amino acids out of 200, have very low affinity for the same five amino acids of the protein when presented as an isolated peptide?[41]] Antigens are often large molecules which have many different recognition sites for different antibodies. The small site that an antibody recognizes within a larger molecule is called an **epitope**. Very small molecules often do not elicit the production of antibodies on their own but will when bound to an antigenic large molecule like a protein. The protein in this case is called a **carrier**, and the small molecule that becomes antigenic is known as a **hapten**. When antibody binds to an antigen, the following can contribute to removal of the antigen from the body:

1) Binding of antibody may directly inactivate the antigen. For example, binding of antibody to a viral coat protein may prevent the virus from binding to cells.
2) Binding of antibody can induce phagocytosis of a particle by macrophages and neutrophils.
3) The presence of antibodies on the surface of a cell can activate the complement system to form holes in the cell membrane and lyse the cell.

Antibodies are produced by a type of lymphocyte called **B cells**. Antibodies produced by an individual B cell can recognize only one specific antigen, but B cells in general produce antibodies that recognize an immense array of antigens. How do B cells produce such a broad array of antibodies? Does the genome encode a gene for every possible antibody molecule, a million genes for a million different potential antibodies? No. Immature B cells are derived from precursor stem cells in the bone marrow. The genes that encode antibody proteins are assembled by recombination from many small segments during B cell development. Thus, there are many different B cell clones, each with a different variable region. The

---

[39] No. Antibodies are soluble in the plasma, so they can only recognize antigens on surfaces that are accessible to them. A protein in the cytoplasm of a bacteria would never be accessible to antibodies in the plasma and therefore could not be recognized.

[40] Yes. Antibodies often recognize proteins as antigens, but they do not recognize the whole protein. Usually antibodies recognize a small part of a protein as an antigen.

[41] In the intact protein the five amino acids assume a specific three-dimensional conformation that is recognized well by the antibody. The five amino acids as a small peptide, however, will not fold the same way and probably would not be as well recognized by the antibody.

immature B cells express antibody molecules on their surface. When antigen binds to the antibody on the surface of a specific immature B cell, that cell is stimulated to proliferate and differentiate into two kinds of cells: **plasma cells** and **memory cells**. Plasma cells actively produce and secrete antibody protein into the plasma. Memory cells are produced from the same clone and have the same variable regions, but do not secrete antibody; they are like pre-activated, dormant B-cells. The memory cells remain dormant, sometimes for years, waiting for the same antigen to reappear. If it does, the memory cells *then* become activated, and start producing antibody very quickly; so quickly that no symptoms of illness appear. This method of selecting B cells with specific antigen binding is called **clonal selection**. [In general, every cell of the body is said to possess the same copy of the genome. Is this true in the immune system?[42]]

- Which one of the following best describes the mechanism by which production of specific antibody is achieved in response to antigen exposure?[43]
  A. Immature B cell clones expressing several different antibody genes select for one gene and turn off expression of the others.
  B. Antigen stimulates proliferation of a specific B cell clone expressing a single antibody protein that recognizes that antigen.
  C. The variable regions of antibody proteins on an immature B cell clone form a pocket around the antigen, and the antibody genes are recombined to fit the bound antigen.
  D. Antibody light and heavy chains are mixed on each B cell's surface in different combinations to produce different antigen recognition.

The first time a person encounters an antigen during an infection, it can take a week or more for B cells to proliferate and secrete significant levels of antibody. This is known as the **primary immune response** and is too slow to prevent symptoms of the infection from occurring. The immune response to the same antigen the second time a person is exposed, the **secondary immune response**, is much swifter and stronger, so much so that symptoms never develop, and the person is said to "be immune." This immunity can last for years and is due to the presence of the memory cells produced during the first infection. **Vaccination** is used to improve the response to infection by exposing the immune system to an antigen associated with a virus or bacterium, thus building up the secondary immune response if the live pathogen is encountered in the future. [Vaccination against some viruses is ineffective in preventing future infection, while it is highly effective against other viruses. Does the failure of vaccination to protect against some viruses indicate a failure in the ability to produce memory cells?[44]]

Cell-Mediated Immunity and the T Cell

There are two types of **T cells**: **T helpers** ("CD4 cells") and **T killers** (cytotoxic T cells, "CD8 cells").[45] The role of the T helper is to activate B cells, T killer cells, and other cells of the immune system. Hence, the T helper is the central controller of the whole immune response. It communicates with other cells by

---

[42] No. Recombination during development of B cells and T cells makes these an exception to the generalization that every cell contains the whole genome.

[43] **B is correct.** The two key features of clonal selection in B cells are 1) recombination during development to produce many clones, each with a single antigen recognition specificity, and 2) selection of a clone out of the many clones based on specific recognition of antigen by preexisting antibody genes.

[44] No. It is probably the result of mutation by the virus. Vaccination against one form of virus and production of memory cells will not protect against a virus if the viral antigen mutates so that it is no longer recognized by the immune system.

[45] "CD" stands for "Cell Differentiation marker."

releasing special hormones called **lymphokines** and **interleukins**.[46] The T helper cell is the host of HIV, the virus which causes AIDS.

The role of the T killer cell is to *destroy abnormal host cells*, namely:
1) Virus-infected host cells
2) Cancer cells
3) Foreign cells such as the cells of a skin graft given by an incompatible donor

The "T" in "T cell" stands for **thymus**. T cells are named after this gland because this is where they develop during childhood. Trillions of different T cells are produced in the bone marrow during childhood. Each of these is specific for a particular antigen, just as with B cells. [If a T cell is specific for an antigen, does that mean it releases antibodies that bind to the antigen?[47]] The protein on the T-cell surface that can bind antigen is the **T-cell receptor**.

The production of these trillions of different T cells with different T-cell receptors is random. As a result, many of them will be specific for normal molecules found in the human body, or *self* antigens. It is very important to get rid of all T cells specific for self antigen, because such T cells can cause an **autoimmune reaction**, in which the immune system attacks the host. The role of the thymus in T-cell development is to destroy all self-specific T cells. The result of this is that billions of T cells survive, but billions of others do not. The ones that survive go on to proliferate if stimulated by antigen in the proper context, each producing a group of identical T cells, all specific for a particular antigen. Such a group is known as a **T cell clone**. Clonal selection in response to antigen recognition is similar in B and T cells.

The function of T cells is exceedingly complex. As a brief introduction, the way a T cell recognizes a bad cell is by "examining" (binding to) proteins on its surface. One important group of cell-surface proteins is known as the **major histocompatibility complex (MHC)**. Our cells are all programmed to have MHC proteins on their surfaces so that the immune system can keep an eye on what is going on inside every cell. There are two kinds of MHCs, known as MHC class I and MHC class II, or simply **MHC I** and **MHC II**. MHC I proteins are found on the surface of every nucleated cell in the body. Their role is to randomly pick up peptides from the inside of the cell and display them on the cell surface. This allows T cells to monitor cellular contents. For example, if a cell is infected with a virus, one of its class I MHC complexes will display a piece of a virus-specific protein. When a T killer cell detects the viral protein (by binding to it) displayed on the cell's MHC I, it becomes activated and will proliferate.

The role of MHC II is more complex. Only certain special cells have MHC II. These cells are known as **antigen-presenting cells (APCs)**. The antigen-presenting cells include macrophages and B cells. Their role is to phagocytize particles or cells, chop them up, and display fragments using the MHC II display system, which T helpers then recognize (bind to). After a T helper is activated by antigen displayed in MHC II, it will activate B cells (and stimulate proliferation of T killer cells) that are specific for that antigen. The activated B cells mature into plasma cells and secrete antibodies specific for the antigen. The complexity of this process helps explain why the primary immune response takes a week or more.

- Can a T helper cell become activated after encountering a foreign particle floating in the blood? If so, how? If not, why not, and what else is required?[48]

---

[46] *Lympho-* is short for lymphocytes, and *-kine* means move or activate. *Inter-* means between, and *-leukin* is for leukocytes or white blood cells.

[47] No, only B cells make antibodies. If a T helper is specific for an antigen, it will activate B cells or T killers to destroy it.

[48] No, T helpers are only activated by antigen presented on MHC II. For a foreign particle to activate a helper T cell, the particle must first be displayed by an antigen-presenting cell (macrophage or B cell). The antigen-presenting cell must phagocytize the particle, hydrolyze it into fragments in a lysosome, and allow it to bind to an MHC II which will be displayed on the cell surface.

8.7

Other Tissues Involved in the Immune Response

The **bone marrow** is the site of synthesis of all the cells of the blood from a common progenitor. The cell which gives rise to all the various blood cells is called the bone marrow stem cell. **Lymph nodes** were discussed earlier in this chapter. The **spleen** filters the blood and is a site of immune cell interactions, just like lymph nodes. The spleen also destroys aged RBCs. The **thymus** is the site of T cell maturation. The thymus shrinks in size in adults since the maturation of the immune system and T cells is most active in children. The **tonsils** are masses of lymphatic tissue in the back of the throat that help "catch" pathogens which enter the body through respiration or ingestion. The **appendix** is very similar to the tonsils, both in structure and function, and is found near the beginning of the large intestine. Neither the appendix nor the tonsils are required for survival and are often removed if they become infected.

8.7

Summary

- The circulatory and lymphatic systems transport materials (O_2, CO_2, nutrients, wastes, hormones, etc.) around the body. The lymphatic system helps to filter and return tissue fluid (lymph) to the circulatory system.

- Deoxygenated blood returning from the body enters the heart at the right atrium, and is pumped to the lungs by the right ventricle. The oxyenated blood returns to the heart at the left atrium, and is pumped to the body by the left ventricle.

- AV valves (tricuspid on the right and bicuspid, or mitral, on the left) separate the atria and ventricles. Semilunar valves (pulmonary on the right and aortic on the left) separate the ventricles and the arteries.

- Veins always return blood to the heart. Most veins carry deoxygenated blood; an exception are the pulmonary veins, which return blood from the lungs to the heart.

- Arteries always carry blood away from the heart. Most arteries carry oxygenated blood; an exception are the pulmonary arteries, which carry blood from the heart to the lungs.

- The cardiac muscle cell action potential is prolonged by the opening of voltage-gated calcium channels. The influx of calcium causes a long plateau in the action potential.

- Cardiac muscle is a functional syncytium; cells are connected by intercalated disks, which contain gap junctions. The gap junctions are electrical synapses that easily allow the transmission of the action potential, and thus contraction, to spread from cell to cell.

- The SA node is the "pacemaker" of the heart. It has an unstable resting potential that rises until threshold is reached and an action potential is fired. This action potential (and subsequent contraction) is then transmitted throughout the heart.

- Systemic blood pressure is directly proportional to cardiac output (the volume of blood pumped per minute) and to peripheral resistance (the force opposing blood flow through the vessels).

- Cardiac output is directly proportional to stroke volume and heart rate, while peripheral resistance is inversely related to vessel diameter.

- Blood is approximately 55 percent plasma, 40 to 45 percent erythrocytes (red blood cells), and 1 percent leukocytes (white blood cells) and platelets.

- ABO and Rh antigens on the surface of erythrocytes determine blood type; type AB+ is the universal recipient and type O– is the universal donor.

- Oxygen is transported in the blood bound to hemoglobin, a protein in red blood cells. Carbon dioxide is transported in the blood primarily as bicarbonate ion; some also binds to hemoglobin.

- Innate immunity is nonspecific and includes things like the skin, lysozyme, stomach acid, phagocytes, and the complement system.

- Humoral immunity is the production of antibodies by B-cells that are highly specific for particular antigens (foreign molecules).

- Cell-mediated immunity is handled by T cells. Killer (cytotoxic) T cells destroy "self" cells that are displaying abnormal antigen on MHC I. Helper T cells are activated by antigen displayed on MHC II, and secrete chemicals to help activate and stimulate the proliferation of killer T cells and B cells.

CHAPTER 8 FREESTANDING PRACTICE QUESTIONS

1. The cardiac cycle is divided into systole and diastole, during which the ventricles contract and relax, respectively. During systole, blood is ejected from the ventricles and is pumped into either the aorta or pulmonary artery. The pressure in the ventricles rapidly increases; however, the volume of blood in the ventricles initially remains unchanged. This is referred to as *isovolumetric contraction*. Which of the following is the most likely reason for isovolumetric contraction?

A) Decreased ventricular contractility due to over-stretching of cardiac sarcomeres.
B) The pressure in the aorta is initially greater that of the left ventricle.
C) The pressure within the pulmonary vein is initially lower than that of the right ventricle.
D) The action potential that propagates through the bundle of His and Purkinje fibers has not yet depolarized all of the ventricles.

2. The ductus arteriosus is a shunt in the fetal circulation that diverts a portion of the blood from the pulmonary circulation into the aorta. Failure of the ductus arteriosus to close shortly after birth results in a condition referred to as a *patent ductus arteriosus* and, in severe cases, the generation of a left-to-right shunt. A left-to-right shunt would result in all of the following EXCEPT:

A) increased mixing of oxygenated blood with deoxygenated blood.
B) decreased blood flow into the systemic circulation.
C) increased blood flow into the pulmonary circulation.
D) decreased vascular pressure in the pulmonary circulation.

3. Blood pressure is directly proportional to cardiac output and peripheral resistance. Which of the following will raise blood pressure?

A) Consumption of a large meal, because it increases the heart rate.
B) Exercise, because it increases cardiac output.
C) Sizable blood loss, because it increases epinephrine levels due to the fear response.
D) A localized allergic reaction, because it causes fluid loss to the tissue at the site.

4. What are the names of the two portal systems in the body?

A) The pancreatic and the hypothalamic-hypophyseal
B) The pancreatic and the renal-urinary
C) The hepatic and the hypothalamic-hypophyseal
D) The hepatic and the renal-urinary

5. T-cell antigen receptors are different from antibodies because:

A) T-cell receptors must interact with antigen uniquely presented by other cells but not with free antigen.
B) T-cell receptors bind various cytokines.
C) T-cell receptors bind complement proteins to lyse cells.
D) T-cell receptors are mediators of allergic reactions.

6. Hepatitis B is an inflammatory disease of the liver. While the virus itself is relatively benign, the body's attempt to eradicate it causes unwanted liver inflammation. Which of the following blood test results could be from an individual who has been vaccinated against Hepatitis B and does not have an active infection?

A) Negative for anti-Hepatitis B antibodies and negative for Hepatitis B antigen
B) Negative for anti-Hepatitis B antibodies and positive for Hepatitis B antigen
C) Positive for anti-Hepatitis B antibodies and positive for Hepatitis B antigen
D) Positive for anti-Hepatitis B antibodies and negative for Hepatitis B antigen

7. Individuals affected with DiGeorge syndrome have a T-cell deficiency due to congenital lack, or incomplete development, of the thymus. Based on this statement, individuals affected with this syndrome will:

A) have normal humoral immunity.
B) have normal cell mediated immunity.
C) be susceptible to infection.
D) be resistant to infection.

8. Which of the following statements about antibodies is true?

   I.   Antibodies are produced by B cells.
   II. Antibodies only recognize peptide antigens.
   III. Antibodies can mark an antigen for destruction by killer T cells.

A) I only
B) II only
C) I and II
D) I and III

CHAPTER 8 PRACTICE PASSAGE

Atherosclerosis is one of the leading causes of death in North America. The disease is characterized by the development of plaques within large and medium-sized arteries, resulting in the restriction of blood flow to tissues and organs. Although many of the complex interactions that lead to the pathogenesis of the disease are not very well understood, it has been demonstrated that macrophages infiltrate between the endothelium and smooth muscle tissue surrounding vessels (called the *intima*) where they ingest cholesterol and become *foam cells*. Smooth muscle cells are recruited and migrate to the intima as well; they become fibroblast-like and begin to deposit collagen and lipids extracellularly. Atherosclerotic plaques build up slowly over time, often without noticeable clinical manifestations.

Cardiac muscle has a high metabolic demand, necessitating a rich supply of blood. As a result, formation of an advanced atherosclerotic plaque within a coronary artery can have severe consequences. An initial warning sign is *angina pectoris* (chest pain) noticed during exercise. This exertional ischemic pain (resulting from inadequate blood supply to the heart) is temporary and resolves itself once the activity is ceased and blood supply catches up to the demand. However, should the blood flow to a particular segment of heart tissue be restricted for an extended period, a *myocardial infarction* (death of heart muscle tissue) may occur. Often, these events are the result of a coronary *thrombus* (blood clot) further compromising the flow of blood through atherosclerotic vessels. Essentially, the thrombus is the "straw that breaks the camel's back" when it comes to meeting blood supply demands for myocardial tissue.

Thrombolytic drugs are often utilized in myocardial infarction cases in order to dissolve the thrombus and restore blood flow. However, because of the anti-coagulative effects of these medications there is a risk of internal bleeding and hemorrhagic stroke.

1. Which of the following statements concerning atherosclerosis is true?

A) People develop atherosclerosis only during excessive exercise.
B) Plaques often build up in veins, preventing the flow of blood returning to the heart.
C) It is difficult to diagnose the disease in its early stages.
D) Thrombolytic drugs can be used to reverse atherosclerosis.

2. Chronic ischemia can lead to the death of large regions of cardiac muscle tissue, leading to an insufficient force of contraction to propel blood through the circulatory system. If blood pressure in the aorta was low, but blood pressure in pulmonary circulation was normal, which region of the heart has likely been affected?

A) Sinoatrial node
B) Left ventricle
C) Right ventricle
D) Left atrium

3. One would expect cardiac output to increase the most with:

A) increased levels of antidiuretic hormone and stimulation of the vagus nerve.
B) increased levels of antidiuretic hormone and inhibition of the vagus nerve.
C) decreased levels of antidiuretic hormone and stimulation of the vagus nerve.
D) decreased levels of antidiuretic hormone and inhibition of the vagus nerve.

4. Which of the following ions are correctly paired with their function/phase during a cardiac muscle cell's action potential?

    I. K^+ : repolarization
   II. Ca^{2+} : plateau phase
  III. K^+ : plateau phase

A) I only
B) III only
C) I and II only
D) I, II and III

5. Thrombolytic drugs would NOT be indicated in a patient who has:

A) a coronary thrombus.
B) a myocardial infarction.
C) hemophilia.
D) elevated levels of platelets.

6. In the interventricular septum, the conduction pathway in the heart splits into a left and right bundle while traveling to the apex of the heart. Which of the following best describes the action potential transmission and muscle contraction of the heart in a patient with a left bundle branch block?

A) SA node → ventricular contraction → AV node → atrial contraction

B) SA node → atrial contraction → AV node → ventricles

C) Atrial contraction → AV node → right ventricular contraction → left ventricular contraction

D) SA node → atrial contraction → AV node → right ventricular contraction → left ventricular contraction

7. Atherosclerosis can affect the vasculature of many different organs and tissues other than the heart. Ischemic necrosis of peripheral arteries can lead to the death of the tissues supplied by these vessels. This condition, termed *gangrene*, is most similar to:

A) myocardial infarction.
B) formation of foam cells.
C) coronary thrombus.
D) angina pectoris.

SOLUTIONS TO CHAPTER 8 FREESTANDING PRACTICE QUESTIONS

1. **B** At the start of systole the semilunar valves are closed, and although the ventricles are contracting, no blood is ejected. The semilunar valves will remain closed until the pressure within the ventricle exceeds that of the aorta or pulmonary artery (choice B is correct), at which point the semilunar valves open and blood is ejected from the ventricles. While overstretching of the cardiac sarcomeres could lead to decreased contractility (because of less overlap between actin and myosin filaments), this would not explain why the contraction is isovolumetric (choice A is wrong). It is true that the pulmonary vein has very low pressure and would be at a lower pressure than the right ventricle, but this does not explain why contraction (which pumps blood into the pulmonary artery rather than into the pulmonary *vein*) would be isovolumetric (choice C is wrong). Ventricular depolarization, initiated by the atrioventricular node, propagates through the bundle of His and Purkinje fibers and depolarizes all of the ventricles in about 120 to 200 ms. The approximate duration of ventricular contraction is 300 to 450 ms; in other words, depolarization of the ventricles is very rapid, and all of the myocytes of the ventricles have been depolarized well before the pressure within the ventricles begins to change (choice D is wrong).

2. **D** Since the left side of the heart deals with oxygenated blood and the right side of the heart deals with deoxygenated blood, a left-to-right shunt would cause increased mixing of oxygenated and deoxygenated blood (choice A would occur and can be eliminated). A left-to-right shunt, particularly one connecting the aorta and pulmonary artery, would result in blood flow from the high-pressure aorta into the lower-pressure pulmonary artery (both choices B and C would occur and can be eliminated). This additional flow into the pulmonary artery would result in an increased blood volume in the pulmonary circulation and a subsequent increase (not decrease) in pulmonary vascular pressure (choice D would not occur and is the correct answer choice).

3. **B** Exercise will cause muscle contraction, which pushes blood along the veins, increasing venous return to the heart. According to the Frank-Starling mechanism, the increase in venous return will increase stroke volume, increasing cardiac output and therefore blood pressure. Further, the increased heart rate due to exercise will also increase cardiac output and blood pressure. Consumption of a large meal will activate the parasympathetic nervous system (rest and digest), so the vagus nerve will be stimulated and the heart rate will decrease. This will decrease the cardiac output and decrease blood pressure (choice B is wrong). Blood loss will decrease blood volume and thus blood pressure. If the blood loss is sizable, the decrease in pressure will be larger than the increase in heart rate from the epinephrine produced by the fear response (choice C is wrong). The loss of fluid to the tissues will decrease blood volume, and thus also blood pressure (choice D is wrong).

4. **C** A portal system consists of two capillary beds connected by a vein. The hepatic portal system connects the small intestine's nutrient absorption to the detoxification systems of the liver, and the hypothalamic-hypophyseal portal system provides a short connection for the hormones of the hypothalamus to control the hormones of the anterior pituitary. The renal system (kidney) and the urinary system (bladder) are connected by the ureter (which carries urine, not blood). Also, do not get confused by the connection of the glomerular capillaries to the peritubular capillaries (the vasa recta); these are connected by an artery (the efferent arteriole), not a vein (choices B and D can be eliminated). The pancreas has an exocrine duct system and a single capillary bed (choice A can be eliminated).

5. **A** T-cell receptors must bind antigen that is presented by MHC proteins on the surface of other cells. They are unable to bind free antigen. Cytokines have their own family of receptors and are not bound by T-cell receptors or antibodies (choice B is wrong). T-cell receptors do not bind complement proteins; the complement system is a set of proteins that can be activated, sometimes by antibodies, to cause nonspecific cell lysis (choice C is wrong). IgE and some other antibodies are involved with allergic reactions, but T-cell receptors are not (choice D is wrong).

6. **D** Vaccination involves the introduction of non-pathogenic antigen into the body in order to trigger the production of antibodies and memory lymphocytes. Individuals who have been vaccinated against Hepatitis B would test positive for anti-Hepatitis B antibodies (choices A and B can be eliminated). Individuals who do not have an active Hepatitis B infection would test negative for Hepatitis B antigens (choice C can be eliminated and choice D is correct).

7. **C** DiGeorge syndrome is also known as *thymic aplasia*. The T cells (or cell-mediated arm) of the immune system are affected and there is an increased susceptibility to infection (choice D is wrong), both from the lack of killer T cells (choice B is wrong), and from the lack of helper T cells and the subsequent effect on the humoral branch of the immune system (choice A is wrong).

8. **A** Item I is true: Antibodies are produced by the B cells of the immune system (choice B can be eliminated). Item II is false: Antibodies can recognize a great diversity of antigens which include, but are not limited to, peptides (choice C can be eliminated). Item III is false: Antibodies can mark an antigen for destruction by macrophages and other phagocytes. Killer T cells do not directly destroy antigens; rather, they kill cells that are producing antigens (such as cells infected by a virus). Further, the mechanism of cell destruction by killer T cells does not involve antibodies (choice D can be eliminated and choice A is correct).

SOLUTIONS TO CHAPTER 8 PRACTICE PASSAGE

1. **C** The passage describes atherosclerotic plaques as building up "slowly over time, often without noticeable clinical manifestations." This would be consistent with the assertion that the disease is difficult to diagnose, particularly early in its progression (choice C is true). The passage says that the initial warning sign of atherosclerosis (chest pain) may be initially noticed during bouts of exercise, but it does not say that exercise contributes to the development of atherosclerosis (choice A is false; note also that this answer option is too extreme because of the word "only"). The first paragraph says plaques develop in arteries (not veins), and obstruct the flow of blood to tissues and organs (not the return to the heart; choice B is false). Although thrombolytic drugs are discussed in the passage, they are described as a treatment for blood clots in coronary arteries that have been rendered vulnerable due to atherosclerotic plaques. They are not used to treat atherosclerosis itself (choice D is false).

2. **B** Low blood pressure in the aorta (the major artery leading to the systemic circulation) indicates that blood flow has been compromised. Since the left ventricle is responsible for pumping blood into the aorta, this is most likely the affected region (choice B is correct). The sinoatrial node is responsible for the rhythm of the heart, but has nothing to do with pressure generation beyond affecting heart rate, and in any case, if the SA node were affected, the pressure in both the aorta and the pulmonary circulation would be low (choice A is wrong). If blood travelling through pulmonary circulation (i.e., to the lungs) is normal, then the right ventricle (which pumps blood to the lungs) is probably not affected (choice C is wrong). The left atrium receives blood returning from the pulmonary circulation. It is not responsible for the large pressures generated to pump blood through the aorta and the systemic circulation (choice D is wrong).

3. **B** This is a two-by-two question, where two decisions must be made to get to the right answer. ADH acts at the kidneys to increase water retention. This results in an increase in total blood volume, an increase in stroke volume (due to the Frank-Starling mechanism), and an increase in cardiac output (CO = SV × HR, choices C and D can be eliminated). The vagus nerve decreases both the heart rate and the force of contraction; thus, to increase cardiac output, the vagus nerve must be inhibited (choice B is correct and choice A is wrong).

4. **D** Item I is true: The efflux of K^+ near the end of the action potential repolarizes the cell (choice B can be eliminated). Items II and III are true: The plateau phase is due to an influx of Ca^{2+} and an efflux of K^+ (choices A and C can be eliminated, and choice D is correct).

5. **C** A patient with hemophilia already has difficulty clotting their blood; treating such a patient with thrombolytic drugs would not be helpful in any way, and could be seriously detrimental to the patient (thrombolytics would not be indicated in choice C, and this is the correct answer). The passage describes the use of thrombolytics in the treatment of myocardial infarction, typically caused by a coronary thrombus (choices A and B could be treated via thrombolytics and can be eliminated). Platelets are an important mediator in the clotting process; elevated platelet levels could lead to more frequent and/or severe blood clots. Thrombolytic drugs could be utilized in order to prevent development of these potentially life-threatening clots (choice D could be treated with thrombolytics and can be eliminated).

6. **D**   Action potentials in the heart are generated at the SA node (choice C is wrong), then transmitted through the atria (causing their contraction; choice A is wrong) before being delayed at the AV node and finally traveling to the ventricles and causing their contraction. The action potential must travel via the left and right bundles in the interventricular septum in order to reach the ventricular muscle. With a left bundle branch block, conduction to the left ventricle is diminished, resulting in delayed left ventricular contraction (choice D is better than choice A).

7. **A**   The question describes a condition in which blood flow is restricted, resulting in an inability of oxygen supply to meet oxygen demand (ischemia) and tissue death. This is what occurs in the case of a myocardial infarction, as described in the passage; blood flow is restricted to cardiac muscle tissue, resulting in tissue death (choice A is correct). The formation of foam cells is the beginning of atherosclerosis, and does not involve tissue death (choice B is wrong). A coronary thrombus can cause myocardial infarction, but is only a clot, not actual tissue death (choice C is wrong), and angina pectoris is a symptom of atherosclerosis and possible myocardial infarction, but again, is not itself tissue death (choice D is wrong).

Chapter 9
The Excretory and
Digestive Systems

9.1 THE EXCRETORY SYSTEM OVERVIEW

Excretion is the disposal of waste products. "The excretory system" generally refers to the kidneys, even though the liver, large intestine, and skin are involved in excretion, too. Let's begin by summarizing the excretory roles of these organs, to see where the kidneys fit into the picture.

Liver

The **liver** is responsible for excreting many wastes by chemically modifying them and releasing them into bile (discussed later in this chapter). In particular, the liver deals with hydrophobic or large waste products, which cannot be filtered out by the kidney. (The kidney can only eliminate small hydrophils dissolved in plasma.) For example: In the liver, old heme units are broken down into bilirubin which is then tagged with a molecule called glucuronate; the resulting bilirubin glucuronate is excreted with bile.

The liver is also very important in excretion because it synthesizes **urea** (Figure 1) and releases it into the bloodstream. Urea is a carrier of excess nitrogen resulting from protein breakdown. Excess nitrogen must be converted to urea because free ammonia is toxic. Urea derives its name from the fact that it is excreted in urine.

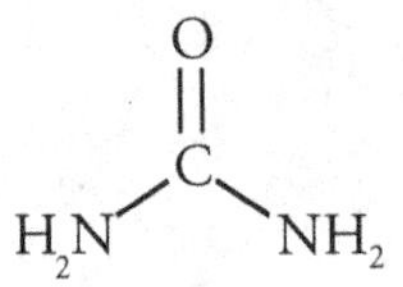

$$H_2N \overset{\overset{\textstyle O}{\|}}{\underset{}{C}} NH_2$$

Figure 1   Urea

Colon

The **large intestine** reabsorbs water and ions (sodium, calcium, etc.) from feces. In this sense it doesn't really excrete anything, but merely processes wastes already destined for excretion. However, the colon is also capable of excreting excess ions (e.g., sodium, chloride, calcium) into the feces, using active transport.

Skin

The skin produces sweat, which contains water, ions, and urea. In other words, sweat is similar to urine. In this sense, the skin is an excretory organ. However, sweating is not primarily controlled by the amount of waste that needs to be excreted, but rather by temperature and level of sympathetic nervous system activity. Therefore, the excretory role of the skin is secondary.

Kidneys

The final responsibility for excretion of hydrophilic wastes lies with the kidneys. Substances which must be excreted in the urine include urea, sodium, bicarbonate, and water. "But wait," you say, "sodium, bicarbonate, and water aren't waste products!" Actually, they sometimes are wastes, when they are present at abnormally high concentrations. You begin to see that the kidney is not like the colon, a passive container for wastes waiting to be excreted. It is a sensitive regulator that must keep concentrations at *optimum levels*, as opposed to simply dumping things.

This is the homeostatic role of the kidneys. **Homeostasis** refers to the constancy of physiological variables. For example, the normal serum Na^+ concentration is 142 mEq/L. Variations in this level greater than 15 percent are fatal due to dysfunction of neurons, cardiac muscle cells, and other cell types. There are other components to homeostasis which the kidney does not control (e.g., temperature maintenance).

Excretory and Homeostatic Roles of the Kidney

1) Excretion of hydrophilic wastes
2) Maintenance of constant solute concentration and constant pH
3) Maintenance of constant fluid volume (important for blood pressure and cardiac output)

As a simplification, we can say that these goals are accomplished via three processes:

- The first process is **filtration**. This entails the passage of pressurized blood over a filter (like a coffee filter). Cells and proteins remain in the blood (like coffee grinds), while water and small molecules are squeezed out into the **renal tubule** (like java). During filtration, water, waste products, and also useful small molecules such as glucose are filtered into the renal tubule. The fluid in the tubule is called **filtrate**, and it will eventually be made into urine.
- The second process is **selective reabsorption**. Here we take back useful items (glucose, water, amino acids), while leaving wastes and some water in the tubule.
- The third process is **secretion**. This involves the addition of substances to the filtrate. Secretion can increase the rate at which substances are eliminated from the blood; because not only are the substance filtered out, more of them are added to the filtrate *after* filtration.

The last step in urine formation is **concentration and dilution**. This involves the selective reabsorption of water, and is where we decide whether to make dilute urine or concentrated urine. After this step, whatever remains in the renal tubule gets excreted as urine.

9.2 ANATOMY AND FUNCTION OF THE URINARY SYSTEM

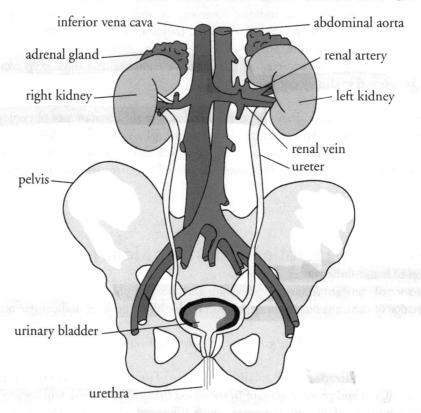

Figure 2 Gross Anatomy of the Urinary System

Each kidney is a filtration system that removes unwanted materials from the blood and passes them to the bladder for storage and eventual elimination. Blood enters the kidney from a large **renal artery**, which is a direct branch of the lower portion of the aorta (the abdominal aorta). Purified blood is returned to the circulatory system by the large **renal vein**, which empties into the inferior vena cava. Urine leaves each kidney in a **ureter**, which empties into the **urinary bladder.** The bladder is a muscular organ which stretches as it fills with urine. When it becomes full, signals of urgency are sent to the brain. There are two sphincters controlling release of urine from the bladder: an **internal sphincter** made of smooth (involuntary) muscle and an **external sphincter** made of skeletal (voluntary) muscle. The internal sphincter relaxes reflexively (and the bladder contracts) when the bladder wall is stretched. If a person decides the time is appropriate, they can relax the external sphincter, allowing urine to flow from the bladder into the urethra and out of the body.

A frontal section (separating front from back) through the kidney demonstrates its internal anatomy. The outer region is known as the **cortex**, and the inner region is the **medulla**. The **medullary pyramids** are pyramid-shaped striations within the medulla. This appearance is due to the presence of many **collecting ducts** (Figure 3). Urine empties from the collecting ducts and leaves the medulla at the tip of a pyramid, known as a **papilla** (plural: **papillae**). Each papilla empties into a space called a **calyx** (plural: **calyces**). The calyces converge to form the **renal pelvis**, which is a large space where urine collects. The renal pelvis empties into the ureter.

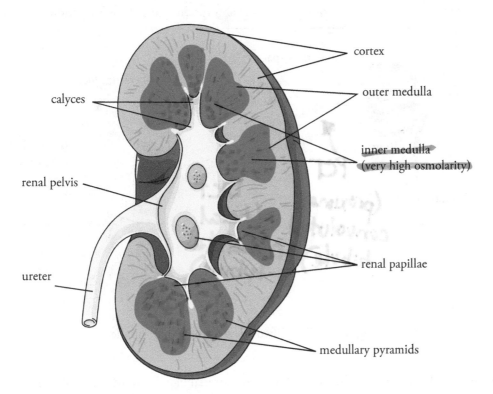

Figure 3   Internal Anatomy of the Kidney

Simplified Microscopic Anatomy and Function

The functional unit of the kidney is the **nephron**. It consists of two components:

1) A rounded region surrounding the capillaries where filtration takes place, known as the **capsule**, and

2) a coiled tube known as the **renal tubule** (Figure 4). The tubule receives filtrate from the capillaries in the capsule at one end and empties into a **collecting duct** at the other end. The collecting duct dumps urine into the renal pelvis.

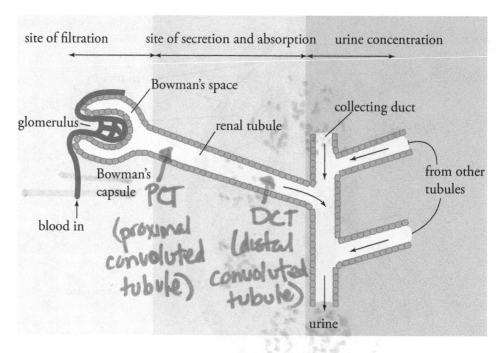

Figure 4   Simplified View of the Renal Tubule

Many blood vessels surround the nephron. They carry arterial blood toward the capillaries of the capsule for filtration, then surround the tubule to carry filtered blood and reabsorbed substances away from the tubule (Figure 5).

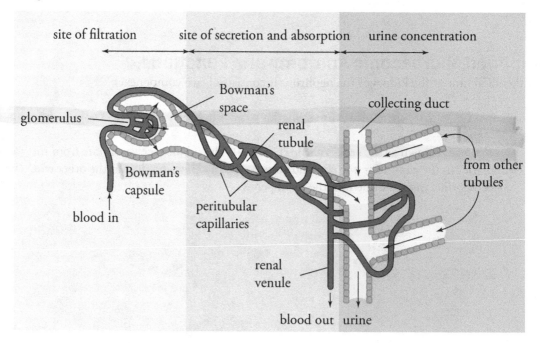

Figure 5   Simplified View of the Renal Tubule Plus Blood Vessels

The pictures above depict most of the structures responsible for the three processes involved in urine formation. Let's go through the steps again, but this time in more detail.

Filtration

Blood from the renal artery flows into an **afferent arteriole**, which branches into a ball of capillaries known as the **glomerulus**. From there the blood flows into an **efferent arteriole**. Constriction of the efferent arteriole results in high pressure in the glomerulus, which causes fluid (essentially blood plasma) to leak out of the glomerular capillaries. The fluid passes through a filter known as the **glomerular basement membrane** and enters **Bowman's capsule**. As you can see from the figures, the lumen of Bowman's capsule is continuous with the lumen of the rest of the tubule. Substances which are too large to pass through the glomerular basement membrane are not filtered; they remain in the blood in the glomerular capillaries and drain into the efferent arteriole.[1] Examples are blood cells and plasma proteins.

- Which of the following are present in the filtrate in Bowman's capsule in concentrations similar to those seen in blood?[2]
  - I. Albumin (a plasma protein)
  - II. Glucose
  - III. Sodium

  - A. I and II only
  - B. II only
  - C. I and III only
  - D. II and III only

Selective Reabsorption

The filtrate in the tubule consists of water and small hydrophilic molecules such as sugars, amino acids, and urea. Some of these substances must be returned to the bloodstream. They are extracted from the tubule, often via active transport, and picked up by **peritubular capillaries**, which drain into venules that lead to the renal vein. For example, glucose is actively transported out of the filtrate and returned to the bloodstream by a cotransporter identical to the one involved in glucose absorption in the small intestine. A lot (most) of the reabsorption occurs in the part of the tubule nearest to Bowman's capsule, called the **proximal convoluted tubule (PCT)**. All solute movement in the PCT is accompanied by water movement. As a result, a lot of water reabsorption occurs in this region also; roughly 70 percent of the volume of the filtrate is reabsorbed here. The amount (final volume) of urine we make is determined by much smaller fluxes taking place in the distal nephron. This makes sense if you think about it: about 5 percent of our circulating blood is continuously being filtered out of the glomerulus; most of this must be taken back. Note that reabsorption in the PCT is selective in that it chooses what to reabsorb, but it is not overly regulated, since it reabsorbs "as much as possible," not a certain amount.

---

[1] The glomerular basement membrane is actually a layer lining *each capillary* of the glomerulus.

[2] Item I: False. Plasma proteins are too large to pass through the filter. **Item II: True.** Glucose passes through into the filtrate and must be reclaimed during selective reabsorption. **Item III: True.** Sodium also passes into the filtrate. It will be reclaimed or left in the filtrate to be urinated out, depending on physiological needs. The answer is **D**.

Selective reabsorption takes place further along the nephron as well, in the **distal convoluted tubule** (**DCT**). Reabsorption in this location is more regulated than in the PCT, usually via hormones (see below, under "Concentration and Dilution").

- Which one of the following best describes selective reabsorption?[3]
    A. In normal individuals, only a small portion of the serum glucose is filtered into the tubule. Of this amount, about 50% is reabsorbed by the epithelial cells of the tubule.
    B. In normal individuals, the concentration of glucose which is filtered into the tubule is identical to the serum [glucose]. Of the filtered glucose, 100% is reabsorbed by the epithelial cells of the tubule.
    C. Epithelial cells of the renal tubule actively transport glucose into the filtrate.
    D. Glucose is kept in the bloodstream by the filtering action of the glomerular basement membrane.

Secretion

Secretion is the movement of substances into the filtrate (usually via active transport) thus increasing the rate at which they are removed from the plasma. Not everything that needs to be removed from the blood gets filtered out at the glomerulus; secretion is a "back-up" method that ensures what needs to be eliminated, gets eliminated. As with reabsorption, secretion occurs all along the tubule; however unlike reabsorption, most secretion takes place in the DCT and the collecting duct. Note also that this is the primary way that many drugs and toxins are deposited in the urine.

Concentration and Dilution

Before filtrate is discarded into the ureter as urine, adjustments are made so that the urine volume and osmolarity are appropriate. This occurs in the last part of the tubule, known as the **distal nephron** (meaning the most distant part of the tubule), which includes the **DCT** and the **collecting duct**. It is controlled by two hormones: **ADH** and **aldosterone**.

1) *ADH:* When you are dehydrated, the *volume of fluid* in the bloodstream is low and the *solute concentration* in the blood is high. Hence, you need to make small amounts of highly concentrated urine. Under these conditions (low blood volume and high blood osmolarity) **antidiuretic hormone** (**ADH** or **vasopressin**) is released by the posterior pituitary. This prevents **diuresis** (water loss in the urine) by increasing water reabsorption in the distal nephron. This is accomplished by making the distal nephron permeable to water. (Without ADH, the distal tubule is impermeable to water. Note that this is the first time we have encountered a layer in the body which is impermeable to water.) As a result, water flows out of the filtrate into the

---

[3] As stated in the section on filtration, glucose is small enough that all of it freely passes through the glomerular basement membrane (choice D is wrong), as are ions, amino acids, and water. However, even though glucose is filtered into the tubule, it must be reclaimed into the bloodstream or we would constantly lose glucose into the urine. 100 percent of filtered glucose is normally reclaimed (choice **B** is correct and choice A is wrong), and in no instance is glucose ever transported *into* the filtrate (choice C is wrong). Note that in diabetes, the blood glucose level is so high that the cotransporters responsible for glucose reabsorption become saturated, and large amounts of glucose are left in the urine.

tissue of the kidney, where it is picked up by the peritubular capillaries. [Why would water tend to flow out of the tubule into the tissue of the kidney?] A drop in blood pressure can also trigger ADH release (renal regulation of blood pressure will be discussed below).

After drinking a lot of water, the plasma volume is too high, and a large volume of dilute urine is necessary. In this case, no ADH is secreted. The result is that the distal tubule is not permeable to water. This means that any water in the filtrate remains in the tubule and is lost in the urine, or *diuresed.* The reason alcohol causes people to diurese is that it inhibits ADH secretion by the posterior pituitary.

2) *Aldosterone:* When the blood *pressure* is low, **aldosterone** is released by the adrenal cortex. It causes increased reabsorption of Na$^+$ by the distal nephron. The result is increased plasma osmolarity, which leads to increased thirst and water retention, which raises the blood pressure. (The fact that increased serum [Na$^+$] increases blood pressure is the reason people with high blood pressure have to avoid salty foods.) When the blood pressure is high, aldosterone is not released. As a result, sodium is lost in the urine. Plasma osmolarity (and eventually blood pressure) fall. Other triggers for the release of aldosterone are low blood osmolarity, and low blood volume, and **angiotensin II** (discussed below).

ADH and aldosterone work together to increase blood pressure. First, aldosterone causes sodium reabsorption, which results in increased plasma osmolarity. This causes ADH to be secreted, which results in increased water reabsorption and thus increased plasma volume.

Actual Microscopic Anatomy and Function

Up to this point we have presented a conceptual outline of kidney function, and we have referred to a simplified nephron, depicted as a straight tube. But the nephron is more complex than that (Figure 6). Bowman's capsule empties into the first part of the tubule, known as the proximal convoluted tubule (PCT). Again, proximal means "near" (near the glomerulus), and convoluted just means twisting and turning. Both Bowman's capsule and the PCT are located in the **renal cortex**, the outer layer of the kidney. The PCT empties into the next region of the nephron, known as the **loop of Henle**. This is a long loop that dips down into the **renal medulla**, the inner part of the kidney. The part that heads into the medulla is called the **descending limb of the loop of Henle**, and the part that heads back out toward the cortex is the **ascending limb**. The descending limb is thin walled, but part of the ascending limb is thin and the other part is thick. These are referred to simply as the *thin ascending limb* and the *thick ascending limb* of the loop of Henle. [What might be the structural difference between a thick portion of the tubule and a thin portion?] As we continue down the tubule, the loop of Henle becomes the distal convoluted tubule (DCT). The DCT dumps into a **collecting duct**. Many collecting ducts merge to form larger tributaries which empty into renal calyces. Figure 6 shows the actual anatomy and function of the nephron. You should familiarize yourself with the information in the picture, but this level of detail is too advanced to warrant extensive discussion. The conceptual material presented above is more typical of MCAT questions.

---

4   Because the renal medulla has a very high osmolarity, which causes water to exit the tubule by osmosis.

5   The two portions are composed of different types of epithelial cells. Thin portions of the tubule are composed of *squamous* (flat) epithelial cells, which are not very metabolically active. Thick portions are composed of *cuboidal* epithelial cells, which are large thick cells busily performing active transport.

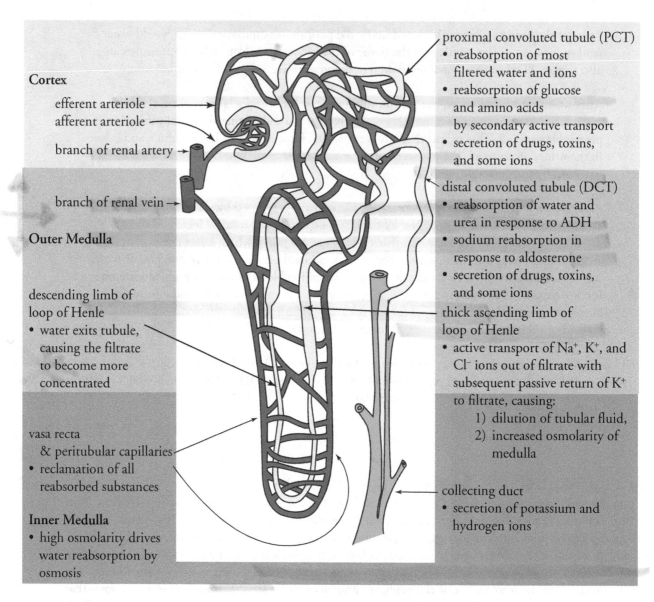

Cortex

efferent arteriole

afferent arteriole

branch of renal artery →

branch of renal vein →

Outer Medulla

descending limb of loop of Henle
- water exits tubule, causing the filtrate to become more concentrated

vasa recta
& peritubular capillaries
- reclamation of all reabsorbed substances

Inner Medulla
- high osmolarity drives water reabsorption by osmosis

proximal convoluted tubule (PCT)
- reabsorption of most filtered water and ions
- reabsorption of glucose and amino acids by secondary active transport
- secretion of drugs, toxins, and some ions

distal convoluted tubule (DCT)
- reabsorption of water and urea in response to ADH
- sodium reabsorption in response to aldosterone
- secretion of drugs, toxins, and some ions

thick ascending limb of loop of Henle
- active transport of Na^+, K^+, and Cl^- ions out of filtrate with subsequent passive return of K^+ to filtrate, causing:
  1) dilution of tubular fluid,
  2) increased osmolarity of medulla

collecting duct
- secretion of potassium and hydrogen ions

Figure 6   Regions and Functions of the Nephron

The Loop of Henle Is a Countercurrent Multiplier

Although we do not intend to go into too much detail on renal physiology, one concept is important to mention: the notion of a **countercurrent multiplier**. The significance of the loop of Henle is that the ascending and descending limbs go in opposite directions and have different permeabilities. The descending limb is permeable to water, but not to ions. Hence, water exits the descending limb, flowing by diffusion into the high-osmolarity medullary interstitium.[6] Thus, the filtrate becomes concentrated. The thin ascending limb is *not* permeable to water, but passively loses ions from the high-osmolarity filtrate into the renal medullary interstitium. Additionally, the thick ascending limb actively transports salt out of the filtrate into the medullary interstitium, and the medullary interstitium becomes *very* salty. This is important

---

[6]   *Interstitium* is a generic word for "tissue." It literally means "an in-between region"; in this case it means tissue in-between renal tubules.

because the medulla will suck water out of the collecting duct by osmosis whenever the collecting duct is permeable to water (e.g., in the presence of ADH).

Don't spend too much time pondering over this now (you will in medical school). Just remember that *the loop of Henle is a countercurrent multiplier that makes the medulla very salty, and that this facilitates water reabsorption from the collecting duct. This is how the kidney is capable of making urine with a much higher osmolarity than plasma.*

Other biological systems use countercurrent multiplication. For example, oxygen and blood flow in opposite directions in fish gills. This allows the most oxygenated blood to take oxygen from the freshest water. Therefore, as much oxygen is absorbed as possible.

The Vasa Recta Are Countercurrent Exchangers

Like the loop of Henle, the **vasa recta** form a loop that helps to maintain the high concentration of salt in the medulla. In short, the ascending portions of the vasa recta are near the descending limb of the loop of Henle and thus carry off the water that leaves the descending limb. Also, the vasa recta are branches of efferent arterioles. The vasa recta are "eager" to reabsorb water because the blood they contain is like coffee grinds which have been drained. The important thing to remember is that the vasa recta return to the bloodstream any water that is reabsorbed from the filtrate.

9.3   RENAL REGULATION OF BLOOD PRESSURE AND PH

Since the **glomerular filtration rate** (**GFR**) depends directly on pressure, the kidney has built-in mechanisms to help regulate systemic and local (glomerular) blood pressure. The **juxtaglomerular apparatus** (**JGA**) is a specialized contact point between the afferent arteriole and the distal tubule. At this contact point, the cells in the afferent arteriole are called **juxtaglomerular** (**JG**) **cells**, and those in the distal tubule are known as the **macula densa.** The JG cells are baroreceptors that monitor systemic blood pressure. When there is a decrease in blood pressure, the JG cells secrete an enzyme called **renin** into the bloodstream. Renin catalyzes the conversion of **angiotensinogen** (a plasma protein made by the liver) into **angiotensin I,** which is further converted to **angiotensin II** by **angiotensin-converting enzyme** (**ACE**) in the lungs. Angiotensin II is a powerful vasoconstrictor that immediately raises the blood pressure. It also stimulates the release of aldosterone, which (as discussed previously) helps raise the blood pressure by increasing sodium (and, indirectly, water) retention.

The cells of the macula densa are chemoreceptors, and monitor filtrate osmolarity in the distal tubule. When filtrate osmolarity decreases (indicating a reduced filtration rate), the cells of the macula densa stimulate the JG cells to release renin. The macula densa also causes a direct dilation of the afferent arteriole, increasing blood flow to (and thus blood pressure and filtration rate in) the glomerulus.

filtrate osmolarity ↓
↓
macula densa stimulates JG cells to release renin
↓
direct dilation of afferent arterioles → increased blood flow
↑

1) decrease in BP → JG cells secrete renin

2) angiotensinogen —renin→ angiotensin I
angiotensin I —ACE→ angiotensin II ⟹ vaso-constrictor

3) angiotensin II immediately raises BP

4) further increases BP

stimulates release of aldosterone ↑

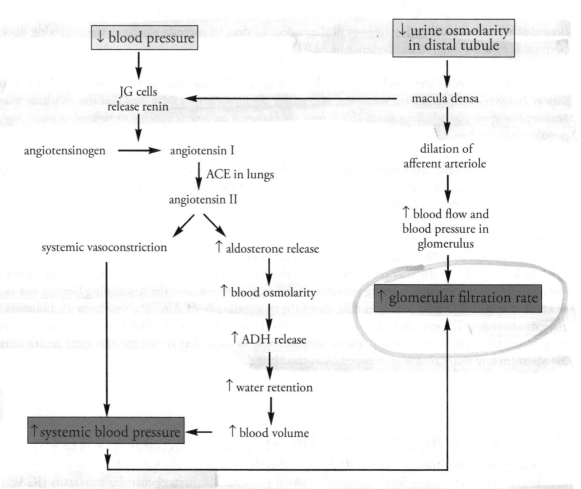

Figure 7   Regulation of Blood Pressure and GFR by the Kidney

Renal Regulation of pH

The kidney is essential for maintenance of constant blood pH. It accomplishes this by a very simple and direct mechanism: when the plasma pH is too high, HCO_3^- is excreted in the urine; when the plasma pH is too low, H^+ is excreted. We will not go into the details. Just be aware that the enzyme **carbonic anhydrase** is involved. It is found in epithelial cells throughout the nephron, except the flat (squamous) cells of the thin parts of the loop of Henle. Carbonic anhydrase catalyzes the conversion of CO_2 into carbonic acid (H_2CO_3), which dissociates into bicarbonate plus a proton. Once this reaction has taken place, the kidney can reabsorb or secrete bicarbonate or protons as needed. (Recall that carbonic anhydrase was discussed in Chapter 8, because it is found in RBCs.) Generally speaking, protons are secreted and bicarbonate is reabsorbed; the amounts are adjusted to adjust pH.

Renal pH adjustments are slow, requiring several days to return plasma pH to normal after a disturbance. The other organ important for pH regulation is the lung. By exhaling excess CO_2, the lung removes an acid (H_2CO_3) from the blood, thus raising the pH. Hence, *hyperventilation* (deep, rapid breathing) raises plasma pH. Respiratory adjustments to the plasma pH are rapid, taking effect in just minutes.

9.4 ENDOCRINE ROLE OF THE KIDNEY

Several hormones affect the kidney, and the kidney makes one as well. All are peptides except aldosterone, which is a steroid. The one made by the kidney is **erythropoietin** (**EPO**). You should know the basic role and source of each of the following hormones. You're unlikely to see very detailed memory-oriented questions on the MCAT, but as a doctor you will know this stuff like the back of your hand.

Hormone	Source	Target and effect
aldosterone	adrenal cortex	Causes sodium reabsorption and potassium secretion by increasing the synthesis of basolateral Na^+/K^+ ATPases in the distal nephron. End result: increased serum $[Na^+]$, increased blood volume (through the action of ADH), and thus increased blood pressure.
ADH	posterior pituitary	ADH is secreted when plasma volume is too low, blood pressure is too low, or plasma osmolarity is too high. It causes water reabsorption by causing epithelial cells of the distal nephron to become permeable to water, which allows water to flow out of the filtrate into the medullary interstitium. Vasa recta return this water to the bloodstream. The result is more concentrated urine, and more dilute blood. ADH and aldosterone work together to increase blood pressure: first, aldosterone causes sodium reabsorption, which results in increased plasma osmolarity; this causes ADH to be secreted, which results in increased water reabsorption and thus increased plasma volume.
calcitonin	C cells	C cells are located in the thyroid gland but do not secrete thyroid hormone. They secrete calcitonin when the serum $[Ca^{2+}]$ is too high. Calcitonin causes $[Ca^{2+}]$ to be removed from the blood by 1) deposition in bone, 2) reduced absorption by the gut, and 3) excretion in urine.
para-thormone	para-thyroid	There are four parathyroid glands, found embedded in the thyroid gland. The function of parathormone (PTH) is opposite that of calcitonin.
EPO	kidney	Erythropoietin (EPO) causes increased synthesis of red blood cells in the bone marrow. It is released when blood oxygen content falls.

Table 1 Hormones Affecting or Secreted by Kidney

9.5   THE DIGESTIVE SYSTEM—AN OVERVIEW

Food contains molecules that are substrates in **catabolic reactions** (reactions that break down molecules to supply energy) and **anabolic reactions** (synthesis of macromolecules). Digestion is the breakdown of polymers (polypeptides, fats, starch) into their building blocks. This breakdown is accomplished by **enzymatic hydrolysis** (Figure 8). Food also contains vitamins, which are not substrates, but rather serve a catalytic role as enzyme cofactors or prosthetic groups. Digestion and absorption of foodstuffs is the primary function of the digestive system. A secondary function, which we will touch on only briefly, is protection from disease.

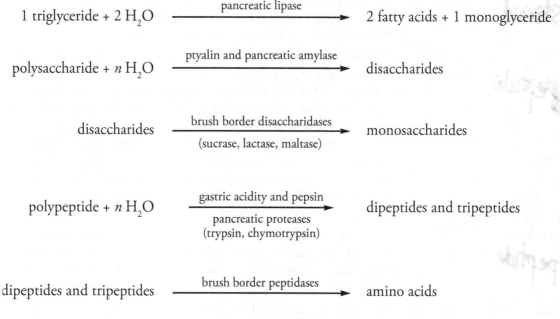

Figure 8   Enzymatic Hydrolysis of Biological Macromolecules

Digestion is accomplished along the **gastrointestinal** *(GI)* **tract**, also known as the **digestive tract**, the **alimentary canal**, or simply the **gut**. The GI tract is a long, muscular tube extending from the mouth to the anus. This tube is derived from the cavity produced by **gastrulation** during embryogenesis; the anus is derived from the **blastopore** (discussed in Chapter 12). The inside of the gut is the **GI lumen**. The lumen is continuous with the space outside the body. (Food could go from the plate into the lumen and from there into the toilet bowl without ever contacting the bloodstream, the muscles, the bones, etc.) The GI lumen is a compartment where the usable components of foodstuffs are extracted, while wastes are left to be excreted as feces. The entire GI tract is composed of specific tissue layers which surround the lumen (Figure 9).

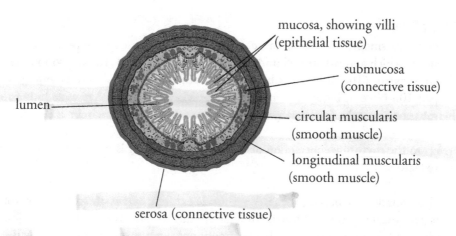

Figure 9 Layers of the GI Tract

GI Epithelium

Because it is exposed to substances from the outside world, the innermost lining of the lumen is composed of the same type of cells that line the outer surface of the body and the inner surface of the respiratory tract: epithelial cells. By definition, epithelial cells are attached to a **basement membrane.**[7] The surface of the epithelial cell which faces into the lumen is the **apical surface** (apex means top; avpical is the adjective). In the small intestine, the apical surfaces of these cells have outward folds of their plasma membrane called **microvilli** to increase their surface area. The apical surface is separated from the remainder of the cell surface by **tight junctions**, which are bands running all the way around the sides of epithelial cells, creating a barrier that separates body fluids from the extracellular environment (see Chapter 5). The sides and bottom of an epithelial cell form the surface opposite the lumen, known as the **basolateral** surface (Figure 10). As discussed below, specialized epithelial cells are responsible for most of the secretory activity of the GI tract.

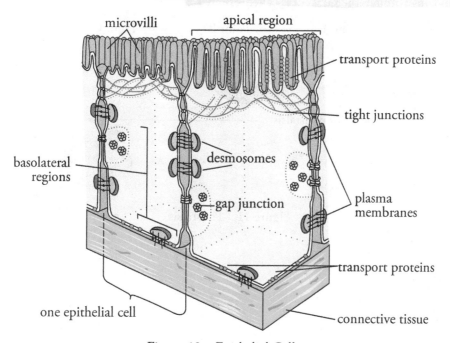

Figure 10 Epithelial Cells

---

[7] *Epi-* means "upon", and *-thelial* refers to the bumpy microscopic appearance of the basement membrane (it means "nippley").

GI Smooth Muscle

GI muscle is known as **smooth muscle** because of its smooth microscopic appearance. This contrasts with **striated muscle**, which appears striped under magnification. Skeletal (voluntary) muscle and cardiac (heart) muscle are striated. (The differences between smooth, skeletal, and cardiac muscle cells will be covered in Chapter 10.) Note in Figure 9 that there are two layers of smooth muscle lining the gut. The **longitudinal layer** runs along the gut lengthwise, while the **circular layer** encircles it.

GI motility refers to the rhythmic contraction of GI smooth muscle. It is determined by a complex interplay between five factors:

1) Like cardiac muscle (Chapter 8), GI smooth muscle exhibits *automaticity*. In other words, it contracts periodically without external stimulation, due to spontaneous depolarization.
2) Like cardiac muscle, GI smooth muscle is a **functional syncytium**, meaning that when one cell has an action potential and contracts, the impulse spreads to neighboring cells.
3) The GI tract contains its own massive nervous system, known as the **enteric nervous system**. The enteric nervous system plays a major role in controlling GI motility.
4) GI motility may be increased or decreased by hormonal input.
5) The parasympathetic nervous system stimulates motility and causes sphincters to relax (allowing the passage of food through the gut), while sympathetic stimulation does the opposite.

GI motility serves two purposes: mixing of food and movement of food down the gut. Mixing is accomplished by disordered contractions of GI smooth muscle, which result in churning motions. Movement of food down the GI tract is accomplished by an orderly form of contraction known as **peristalsis** (Figure 11). During peristalsis, contraction of circular smooth muscle at point A prevents food located at point B from moving backward. Then longitudinal muscles at point B contract, with the result being shortening of the gut so that it is pulled up over the food like a sock. As a result, the food moves toward point C. Then circular smooth muscles at point B contract to prevent the food from moving backward, and longitudinal muscles at point C contract, with the result being movement of food past point C, and so on. A ball of food moving through the GI tract is called a **bolus**.

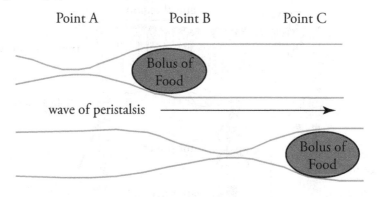

Figure 11 Peristalsis

GI Secretions

Generally speaking, GI secretion (release of enzymes, acid, bile, etc.) is stimulated by food in the gut and by the parasympathetic nervous system, and is inhibited by sympathetic stimulation. There are two types of secretion: **endocrine** and **exocrine**. [What's the difference?[8]] Exocrine glands are composed of specialized epithelial cells, organized into sacs called **acini** (singular: **acinus**). Acinar cells secrete products which pass into ducts. It is important to keep the contrast between endocrine and exocrine in mind. Figure 12 shows the microscopic structure of an exocrine gland.

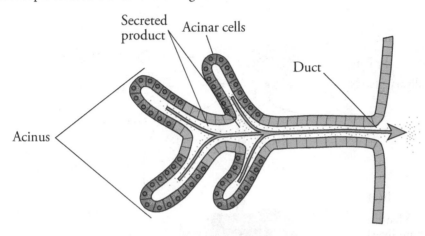

Figure 12   Exocrine Gland Structure

Most exocrine secretion in the GI tract is performed by exocrine glands within special digestive organs. These glands release enzymes into ducts (see Figure 12) that ultimately empty into the GI lumen. The digestive organs primarily involved in exocrine secretion include the liver, gallbladder, and pancreas. However, some exocrine secretion is performed by specialized individual epithelial cells in the wall of the gut itself. These cells are miniature exocrine glands, releasing secretions directly into the gut lumen. Important examples are the cells of the **gastric glands** in the stomach and specialized mucus-secreting cells called **goblet cells**. The gastric glands secrete acid and pepsinogen (a protease zymogen discussed below). Goblet cells are found along the entire GI tract. Mucus is a slimy liquid which protects and lubricates the gut; any body surface covered with mucus is known as a **mucus membrane**. One last secretion must be mentioned: water. Whenever a meal is to be digested it must be dissolved in water. Hence, each day, gallons of water are secreted into the GI lumen. Most of it is reabsorbed in the small intestine, and the colon is responsible for reclaiming whatever water is left.

Endocrine secretion is also accomplished by both specialized organs (the pancreas) and by cells in the wall of the gut. Remember that endocrine secretions (hormones) do not empty into ducts but instead are picked up by nearby capillaries. In other words, you should realize that when the same organ has both endocrine and exocrine activities, these functions are accomplished by separate cells, which are usually grouped in such a way as to be microscopically distinguishable. For example, the two principal cell types in the pancreas are: 1) exocrine cells, referred to simply as **pancreatic acinar cells**, which are organized into acini that drain into ducts, and 2) endocrine cells clumped together in groups known as **islets of Langerhans**, which are supplied with capillaries.

---

[8]   *Exocrine* glands secrete their products (digestive enzymes, etc.) into *ducts* that drain into the GI lumen. *Endocrine* glands are ductless glands; their secretions (hormones) are picked up by capillaries and thus enter the bloodstream.

9.6 THE GASTROINTESTINAL TRACT

Although the GI tract is a continuous tube, each portion is seen as a separate organ: mouth, pharynx, esophagus, etc. Here we will summarize the major structures and functions of each GI organ. The liver, gallbladder, and pancreas, known as **accessory organs**, are covered in Section 9.7. Section 9.8 details the absorptive process.

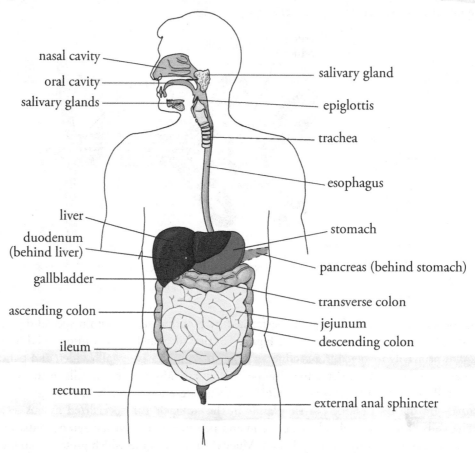

Figure 13   Organs of the Digestive System

Mouth

The mouth has three roles in the digestion of foodstuffs:

1) fragmentation,
2) lubrication, and
3) some enzymatic digestion.

[handwritten annotations: chewing; saliva; amylase, lipase, lysozyme]

Fragmentation is accomplished by **mastication** (**chewing**). The **incisors** (front teeth) are for cutting, the **cuspids** (canine teeth) are for tearing, and the **molars** are for grinding.

Lubrication and some digestion are accomplished by **saliva**, a viscous fluid secreted by salivary glands. Saliva contains **salivary amylase (ptyalin)**, which hydrolyzes starch, breaking it into fragments. The smallest fragment yielded by salivary amylase is the disaccharide; digestion to monosaccharides occurs only at the intestinal brush border (discussed below). Saliva also contains a small amount of **lingual lipase** for fat digestion. No digestion of proteins occurs in the mouth. Lastly, saliva also contains **lysozyme**, which attacks ____.[9] Hence the mouth also participates in innate immunity.

The muscles of the mouth and the muscular tongue are important for compacting chewed food into a smooth lump which can be swallowed, a **bolus**.

- When carbohydrates are broken down by ptyalin, can they be absorbed in the mouth?[10]

Pharynx and Esophagus

The **pharynx** is what we commonly call the throat. [Key trivia: The floppy thing that hangs down at the back of the throat is called the ____.[11]] The pharynx contains the openings to two tubes: the **trachea** and the **esophagus**. The trachea is a cartilage-lined tube at the front of the neck which conveys air to and from the lungs. The esophagus is a muscular tube behind the trachea which conveys food and drink from the pharynx to the stomach. During swallowing, solids and liquids are excluded from the trachea by a flat cartilaginous flap, the **epiglottis**. A bolus of food passes through the pharynx, over the epiglottis, and into the esophagus, where it is conveyed to the stomach by peristalsis. Two muscular rings regulate movement of food through the esophagus. The **upper esophageal sphincter** is near the top of the esophagus, and the **lower esophageal sphincter** (also known as the **cardiac sphincter** since it is found near the heart) is at the end of the esophagus, at the entrance to the stomach (Figure 13). [Does the lower esophageal sphincter regulate movement of substances into or out of the esophagus?[12]]

Stomach

The stomach is a large hollow muscular organ which serves three purposes: partial digestion of food, regulated release of food into the small intestine, and destruction of microorganisms. The following list highlights some of the attributes and secretions that allow the stomach to accomplish these goals. **Gastric** is an adjective meaning "related to the stomach."

---

[9] bacterial cell walls. Remember, lytic phages make lysozyme too.

[10] No. Sugars are not broken down into monosaccharides until they reach the intestinal brush border. Only monosaccharides can be absorbed into the body. Absorption requires special transmembrane transporters located on the intestinal brush border; each transporter is specific for a particular monosaccharide.

[11] uvula

[12] It is there to prevent reflux from the stomach into the esophagus. There is no reason to regulate movement of substances out of the esophagus into the stomach, since nothing is stored in the esophagus; it's just a conduit.

Acidity

Gastric pH is about 2, due to the secretion of HCl by parietal cells, located in the gastric mucosa. Effects: 1) destruction of microorganisms, 2) acid-catalyzed hydrolysis of many dietary proteins, and 3) conversion of pepsinogen to pepsin.

Pepsin

This is an enzyme secreted by **chief cells** in the stomach wall. It catalyzes proteolysis (protein breakdown). Pepsin is secreted as **pepsinogen**, which is an inactive precursor that must be converted to the active form (pepsin). As noted above, this conversion is catalyzed by gastric acidity. The secretion of an inactive precursor is a common theme in the GI tract; the inactive form is known as a **zymogen**. Most zymogens are activated by proteolysis (cleavage of the protein at a specific site that activates it). Pepsinogen is unique because it is activated by_____ instead of____.[13]

acidic proteolysis → *proteolytic cleavage by another enzyme*

Motility

The stomach constantly churns food. Like chewing, this breaks up food particles so that they are exposed to gastric acidity and enzymes. Food mixed with gastric secretions is known as **chyme.**

Sphincters

The lower esophageal sphincter prevents reflux of chyme into the esophagus. The **pyloric sphincter** prevents the passage of food from the stomach into the duodenum. Opening of the pyloric sphincter (stomach emptying) is inhibited when the small intestine already has a large load of chyme. More specifically, stretching or excess acidity in the duodenum inhibits further stomach emptying, by causing the pyloric sphincter to contract. This effect is mediated both by nerves connecting the duodenum and stomach, and by hormones. The main hormone responsible is **cholecystokinin**, secreted by epithelial cells in the wall of the duodenum. [Is this hormone secreted into the lumen of the duodenum or into the lumen of the stomach?[14]]

neither! secreted into bloodstream

Gastrin

This is a hormone secreted by cells in the stomach wall known as **G cells**. It stimulates acid and pepsin secretion and gastric motility. Gastrin secretion is stimulated by food in the stomach and by parasympathetic stimulation. The small molecule **histamine** (which is secreted in response both to stomach stretching and to gastrin) binds to parietal cells to stimulate acid release. The ulcer-healing drugs cimetidine (Tagamet) and ranitidine (Zantac) function by blocking the binding of histamine to its receptor (the "H_2 receptor") on parietal cells. This results in less gastric acidity, which allows ulcers to heal.

Small Intestine

Food leaving the stomach enters the small intestine, a tube which is about an inch wide and 10 feet long. (After death, it measures about 25 feet due to relaxation of longitudinal muscles.) The small intestine is

---

[13] Pepsinogen is unusual in that it is activated to pepsin by acidic proteolysis (autocleavage) instead of proteolytic cleavage by another enzyme.

[14] Neither! It's a hormone; by definition, it is secreted into the bloodstream.

divided into three segments: the **duodenum**, **jejunum**, and **ileum**. Digestion begins in the mouth (ptyalin), continues in the stomach, and is completed in the duodenum and jejunum. Absorption begins in the duodenum and continues throughout the small intestine. The anatomy and function of the small intestine are described below. In Section 9.8 we will detail the specific mechanisms of digestion and absorption of carbohydrates, proteins, and fats.

Surface Area

The key feature that allows the small intestine to accomplish absorption is its large surface area; this results from 1) length, 2) villi, and 3) microvilli. **Villi** (singular: **villus**) are macroscopic (multicellular) projections in the wall of the small intestine. **Microvilli** are microscopic foldings of the cell membranes of individual intestinal epithelial cells. The lumenal surface of the small intestine is known as the **brush border** due to the brush-like appearance of microvilli.

The Intestinal Villus

The villus is a finger-like projection of the wall of the gut into the lumen. It has three very important structures:

1) The villus contains capillaries, which absorb dietary monosaccharides and amino acids. The capillaries merge to form veins, which merge to form the large **hepatic portal vein**, which transports blood containing amino acid and carbohydrate nutrients from the gut to the liver.
2) The villus also contains small lymphatic vessels called **lacteals**, which absorb dietary fats. The lacteals merge to form large lymphatic vessels, which transport dietary fats to the thoracic duct, which empties into the bloodstream.
3) **Peyer's patches** are part of the immune system. They are collections of lymphocytes dotting the villi that monitor GI contents and thus confer immunity to gut pathogens and toxins.

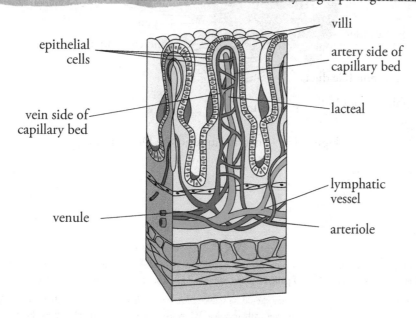

Figure 14   An Intestinal Villus

Bile and Pancreatic Secretions in the Duodenum

A key anatomical feature of the duodenum is that two ducts empty into it (Figure 15). One is the **pancreatic duct**, which delivers the exocrine secretions of the pancreas (digestive enzymes and bicarbonate). The other is the **common bile duct**, which delivers **bile**. This is a green fluid containing **bile acids**, which are made from cholesterol in the liver and are normally absorbed and recycled. Bile is stored in the **gallbladder** until it is needed. Bile has two functions: It is a vehicle for the disposal (excretion) of waste products by the liver, and it is essential for the digestion of fats, as discussed below. The bile duct and the pancreatic duct empty into the duodenum via the same orifice, known as the **sphincter of Oddi** (Figure 15).

9.6

- If a gallstone became lodged in the sphincter of Oddi, what would happen?[15]
- Bile acids secreted into the duodenum are normally reabsorbed in the ileum. Bile acid sequestrants are drugs which bind bile acids in the small intestine, causing them to remain in the GI lumen and eventually be excreted as feces. Each of the following is most likely true about such drugs EXCEPT that:[16]
    - A. they are stable at low pH levels.
    - B. they result in a decrease in the level of cholesterol in the bloodstream.
    - C. it would be reasonable to be concerned that they might disrupt fat absorption.
    - D. they would be administered intravenously (injected into a vein).

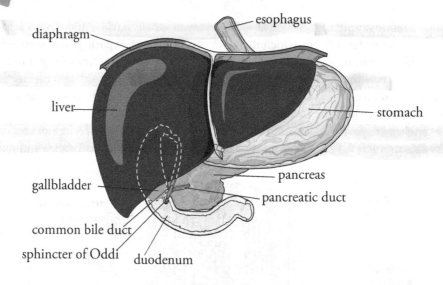

Figure 15 Anatomy around the Duodenum

---

[15] Both the bile and the pancreatic ducts would be blocked, and digestion would be severely impaired (especially fat digestion, but also protein and carbohydrate digestion due to failure of pancreatic zymogens and amylase to reach the intestinal lumen).

[16] Since the drugs must pass through the stomach they should be stable at low pH levels (choice A is true and can be eliminated). The text states that bile acids are made from cholesterol and normally recycled. It is reasonable to assume that blocking this recycling would require the conversion of more cholesterol into bile acids, which would lower the serum cholesterol level. This is in fact what bile acid sequestrants are used for (choice B is true and can be eliminated). It would be reasonable to be concerned about fat absorption, based on the fact that bile acids are necessary for this absorption, as stated in the text (choice C is true and can be eliminated). However, the drugs would have to be *swallowed* to end up within the GI lumen, not injected (choice **D** is false and is the correct answer choice).

Duodenal Enzymes

Some duodenal epithelial cells secrete enzymes. Duodenal **enterokinase** activates the pancreatic zymogen **trypsinogen** to trypsin (Section 9.7). Other duodenal enzymes are peculiar in that they are not truly secreted, but rather do their work inside or on the surface of the brush border epithelial cell. These duodenal enzymes are called **brush border enzymes**. Their role is to hydrolyze the smallest carbohydrates and proteins (like disaccharides and dipeptides) into monosaccharides and amino acids (Section 9.8).

Duodenal Hormones

Other duodenal epithelial cells secrete hormones. The three main duodenal hormones are **cholecystokinin (CCK)**, **secretin**, and **enterogastrone**. CCK is secreted in response to fats in the duodenum. It causes the pancreas to secrete digestive enzymes, stimulates gallbladder contraction (bile release), and decreases gastric motility. Note that all these processes cooperate to deal with fats in the duodenum, by digesting them and preventing further stomach emptying. Secretin is released in response to acid in the duodenum. It causes the pancreas to release large amounts of a high-pH aqueous buffer, namely HCO_3^- in water. This neutralizes HCl released by the stomach. Duodenal pH must be kept neutral or even slightly basic for pancreatic digestive enzymes to function. Enterogastrone decreases stomach emptying.

Jejunum and Ileum

Substances not absorbed in the duodenum must be absorbed in these lower segments of the small intestine. The lower small intestine performs special absorptive processes. For example, absorption of vitamin B_{12} occurs only in the ileum (and only when vitamin B_{12} is complexed with **intrinsic factor**, a glycoprotein secreted by the parietal cells of the stomach). A valve called the **ileocecal valve** separates the ileum from the cecum, which is the first part of the large intestine.

- True or false? When a pancreatic exocrine cell secretes an alkaline fluid into the duodenum, a corresponding decrease in pH must occur in that cell's cytoplasm.[17]

Colon (Large Intestine)

Like the rest of the intestine, the colon is a muscular tube. It is 3 or 4 feet long and several inches wide. Its role is to absorb water and minerals, and to form and store feces until the time of defecation. Abnormalities of colon function result in poor fluid absorption and diarrhea, which can cause dehydration and death. The first part of the colon is the **cecum**. Entrance of chyme into the cecum is controlled by the ileocecal valve. The **appendix** is a finger-like appendage of the cecum. It is composed primarily of lymphatic tissue and was mentioned in the preceding chapter. The last portion of the colon is called the **rectum**. Exit of feces (**defecation**) from the rectum occurs through the **anus**. Defecation is controlled by the **anal sphincter**, which has an internal portion and an external portion. The internal anal sphincter consists of smooth muscle, which is under autonomic control. The external anal sphincter consists of skeletal muscle and is under voluntary control. (Note that this is the same arrangement as seen in the urinary sphincters.) Most of the wastes from a meal are defecated about a day after it is eaten. However, the wastes from a

---

[17] True. In the pancreas, CO_2 is converted to carbonic acid by carbonic anhydrase. Carbonic acid dissociates into bicarbonate (HCO_3^-) plus a proton. If the bicarbonate is secreted into the gut, the proton is left behind. Thus the pH falls. Severe diarrhea may involve the loss of large amounts of bicarbonate from the gut, and this may cause a significant decrease in the plasma pH level.

meal are first present in stool after just a few hours and some residue of a meal is typically still present in the colon after several days.

The colon contains billions of bacteria of various species. Many are facultative or obligate anaerobes. Undigested materials are metabolized by colonic bacteria. This often results in gas, which is given off as a waste product of bacterial metabolism. **Colonic bacteria** are important for two reasons: 1) the presence of large numbers of normal bacteria helps keep dangerous bacteria from proliferating, due to competition for space and nutrients, and 2) colonic bacteria supply us with **vitamin K**, which is essential for blood clotting.

9.7 THE GI ACCESSORY ORGANS

The GI accessory organs are those that play a role in digestion, but are not actually part of the alimentary canal. They include the **pancreas, liver, gallbladder**, and the large **salivary glands** found outside the mouth. We have already discussed saliva, so the salivary glands will not be discussed further here. The pancreas and liver are essential for GI function. The gallbladder is not essential, but can become infected, obstructed, or cancerous, and is thus medically important.

Exocrine Pancreas

Pancreatic enzymes released into the duodenum are essential for digestion. **Pancreatic amylase** hydrolyzes polysaccharides to disaccharides. **Pancreatic lipase** hydrolyzes triglycerides at the surface of a micelle (Section 9.7). **Nucleases** hydrolyze dietary DNA and RNA. Several different **pancreatic proteases** are responsible for hydrolyzing polypeptides to di- and tripeptides. Pancreatic proteases are secreted in their inactive **zymogen** forms. [Why do you suppose digestive enzymes are stored and released in an inactive form?[18]] Zymogens must be activated by removal of a portion of the polypeptide chain. **Trypsinogen** is a zymogen which is converted to the active form, **trypsin**, by **enterokinase**, an intestinal enzyme. Other pancreatic enzymes are then activated by trypsin. These include **chymotrypsinogen** (active form: **chymotrypsin**), **procarboxypeptidase** (active form: **carboxypeptidase**), and **procollagenase** (active form: **collagenase**).

Control of the Exocrine Pancreas

Two hormones discussed previously help to control pancreatic secretion. **Cholecystokinin** (CCK) secreted into the bloodstream by the duodenum causes the pancreas to secrete enzymes. **Secretin**, also released by the duodenum, causes the pancreas to secrete water and bicarbonate (high pH). Parasympathetic nervous system activation increases pancreatic secretion; sympathetic activation reduces it.

---

[18] It is a safety mechanism. Active digestive enzymes could be dangerous to the pancreatic cells themselves.

Endocrine Pancreas

The endocrine pancreas consists of small regions within the pancreas known as islets of Langerhans. There are three types of cells in the islets, and each secretes a particular hormone into the bloodstream.

1) α cells secrete **glucagon** in response to low blood sugar. Glucagon functions to mobilize stored fuels by stimulating the liver to hydrolyze glycogen and release glucose into the bloodstream, and by stimulating adipocytes (fat cells) to release fats into the bloodstream.

2) β cells secrete **insulin** in response to elevated blood sugar (e.g., after a meal). Its effects are opposite those of glucagon: insulin stimulates the removal of glucose from the blood for storage as glycogen and fat.

3) δ cells secrete **somatostatin**. It inhibits many digestive processes.

Focus on Blood Glucose

1) **Lowering blood glucose:** Insulin is essential for life because it causes sugar to be removed from the bloodstream and stored. Diabetics lack insulin or have dysfunctional insulin receptors. Their blood sugar levels are extraordinarily high. The excess glucose directly destroys many physiological systems at the cellular level, including neurons, blood vessels, and the kidneys.

2) **Raising blood glucose:** Three hormones can raise the blood glucose level: glucagon (a polypeptide hormone from the pancreas), epinephrine (an amino acid derivative from the adrenal medulla), and cortisol (a steroid or glucocorticoid from the adrenal cortex). Note that of these three hormones, one is a steroid, one is a polypeptide, and one is an amino acid derivative. Also note that there is only one hormone that can lower blood glucose, while three different hormones can raise blood glucose. It makes sense to have many ways to raise blood glucose, and for it to be less easy to lower blood glucose, since low blood glucose levels are immediately fatal, while elevated blood glucose is harmless in the short term. (Over several years, however, it is harmful.)

- Which one of the following statements is true?[19]
  - A. Insulin stimulates the release of glucose into the blood and also stimulates peristalsis in the small intestine.
  - B. Gastrin stimulates stomach emptying and inhibits secretion of gastric acid.
  - C. Cholecystokinin stimulates peristalsis in the intestine and inhibits stomach emptying.
  - D. Glucagon stimulates the storage of glucose and stimulates small intestinal peristalsis.

Liver and Gallbladder

The exocrine secretory activity of the liver is simple: it secretes bile. The liver actually produces about 1 liter of bile a day. The principal ingredients of bile include bile acids (known as **bile salts** in the deprotonated—anionic—form), cholesterol, and bilirubin (from RBC breakdown). Bile emulsifies large fat particles in the duodenum, creating smaller clusters of fat particles called **micelles**. The smaller particles

---

[19] Insulin stimulates the *removal* of glucose from the blood (choice A is false), gastrin *causes* acid secretion (choice B is false), and glucagon functions to *raise* blood glucose (choice D is false). Choice **C** is a true statement.

9.7

have a greater collective surface area than the large particles, and thus are more easily digested by hydrophilic lipases (from the pancreas). Also, bile helps fatty particles to diffuse across the intestinal mucosal membrane.

Bile made in the liver can go to one of two places: it is either directly secreted into the duodenum or it is stored for later use in the **gallbladder**. Bile stored in the gallbladder is concentrated, and released when a fatty meal is eaten. A **gallstone** is a large crystal formed from bile made with ingredients in incorrect proportions.

The gallbladder itself has no secretory activity. Bile release from this organ is dictated by both the endocrine system and the nervous system. Both CCK (released by the duodenal cells) and the parasympathetic nervous system stimulate contraction of the gallbladder wall.

9.7

The liver plays a more complicated role in the *processing* of absorbed nutrients than it does in digestion (breakdown). In order to understand this process, it helps to consider the **hepatic portal system**. The liver receives blood from two places. First, it receives oxygenated blood from the hepatic arteries. Second, it receives venous blood draining the stomach and intestines through the **hepatic portal vein**. (Hepatic means "relating to the liver.") As this blood percolates through the liver, nutrients are extracted by hepatocytes (liver cells). The hepatocytes monitor the blood and make changes to the body's physiology based on what is and is not present (much as the hypothalamus does in the hypothalamic-pituitary portal system). For example, if blood glucose is low, the liver will initiate a cascade that leads to glycogen breakdown as well as new glucose production (gluconeogenesis). The free glucose can be released to raise blood glucose levels.

Both the liver and the skeletal muscles are capable of storing glucose as glycogen and subsequently breaking glycogen down when glucose is needed. However only the liver is able to release free glucose to the bloodstream. The product of glycogen breakdown is glucose-6-phosphate; in order to move into the bloodstream, this product must be dephosphorylated, and only the liver contains the enzyme needed to accomplish this (glucose-6-phosphatase).

The waste products from protein catabolism (breakdown) are also regulated through the liver. When proteins are broken down into amino acids, and amino acids are broken down even further (e.g., to enter the Krebs cycle to generate ATP during starvation), nitrogenous by-products are released in the form of NH_3 (ammonia). Ammonia in high levels is toxic to the body, so it is transported to the liver where it is converted into urea. Urea is then absorbed into the bloodstream and excreted by the kidney in urine.

Lipid metabolism is assisted by the liver as well. Lipids exit the intestine and enter the lymphatic system in molecules called **chylomicrons**. Chylomicrons are degraded by lipases into triglycerides, glycerol, and cholesterol rich **chylomicron remnant**s. These remnants are taken up by hepatocytes and combined with proteins to make lipoproteins (HDL, LDL, VLDL, etc.). These lipoproteins then re-enter the blood and are the source of cholesterol and triglycerides for the other tissues of the body.

Many important plasma proteins (such as albumin, globulins, fibrinogens, and other clotting factors necessary to stop bleeding) are made in the liver and secreted into the plasma. People with liver disease often have problems with sealing wounds due to a lack of clotting factors. They also have a tendency to swell up; the lack of albumin allows fluid to leave the bloodstream and enter the tissues.

Finally, the liver is the major center for drug and toxin detoxification in the body. The smooth ER in hepatocytes contains enzyme pathways that break down drugs and toxins into forms that are less toxic and more readily excreted by the renal and gastrointestinal systems. Interestingly, sometimes these same enzyme pathways in hepatocytes are used to convert some drugs into their active forms. Therefore, people with liver disease must have drug levels in their blood monitored closely when they are on medications that are affected by the detoxification system of the liver.

9.8 A DAY IN THE LIFE OF FOOD

In order to draw the above information together, let's trace the path of each of the three main types of dietary nutrients: carbohydrates, proteins, and fats.

Carbohydrates

You purchase a sourdough baguette and tear off a hunk. Chewing increases the bread's surface area, allowing it to soak up more saliva. Ptyalin hydrolyzes starch into fragments, while the tongue and cheeks form a bolus. As you swallow, the upper esophageal sphincter relaxes. Peristalsis carries the bolus to the stomach; the lower esophageal relaxes to let it pass. In the stomach, strong acid destroys most of the microorganisms which were present in the bread, while further hydrolyzing some polysaccharides. The stomach thoroughly churns the bread, forming acidic chyme, which is gradually released into the duodenum. In the duodenum, pancreatic amylase chops the polysaccharides into disaccharides, which diffuse to the intestinal brush border. Here the disaccharides are hydrolyzed to monosaccharides. Digestion is complete. Up to this point, none of the sugar composing the bread has entered your body; it remains on the lumenal side of GI epithelial tight junctions.

Since they are bulky and hydrophilic, monosaccharides must be taken up into the intestinal epithelial cell by active transport. An apical symport transports one sugar into the cell while allowing sodium to flow in, down its large concentration gradient (Figure 16). [Is this primary or secondary active transport?[20]] The large sodium concentration gradient is created by constant activity of Na^+/K^+ ATPases on the basolateral surface of the cell, pumping Na^+ out. As secondary active transport continues to pack the epithelial cell with monosaccharides, their concentration gets quite high. Hence, there is now a concentration gradient driving them out of the cell into nearby capillaries. This movement occurs by facilitated diffusion (uniports) at the basolateral surface of the cell. In the bloodstream, sugars dissolve into the plasma as it flows into the hepatic portal vein toward the liver.

---

[20] Secondary, since transport is powered by a pre-existing gradient, not directly by ATP hydrolysis.

9.8

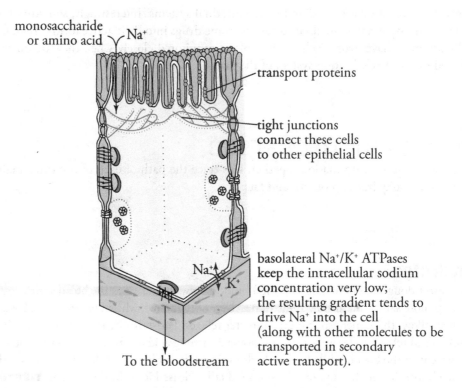

Figure 16 Absorption of Hydrophilic Food Monomers

The liver takes up some of the sugars and begins to store them or use their energy. Nonetheless, the blood sugar level increases rather suddenly. When the pancreas is exposed to elevated blood glucose levels, the β cells of the islets of Langerhans secrete insulin. The insulin causes many different cells (liver, muscle, nerve, and fat cells) to take up, utilize, and store glucose. Soon the blood sugar level returns to normal, and you're ready for dessert.

Proteins

The next day, you're well rested from an iron-pumping session and are ready for a nice can of albacore in spring water. You buy generic because it's the same quality but cheaper (and check to make sure it's dolphin-safe).

In your mouth, the tuna is ground and mixed with saliva. No digestion of protein occurs in the mouth. A bolus is formed, and you swallow. Churning of the stomach mixes the tuna with acid, mucus, and enzymes. The low pH kills microorganisms and causes many peptide bonds to hydrolyze. Activated pepsin attacks polypeptides, breaking them into fragments. Chyme is gradually released into the duodenum.

Chyme in the duodenum causes duodenal epithelial cells to secrete CCK and secretin. As a result, the gallbladder releases concentrated bile and the pancreas secretes a basic (high pH) solution of bicarbonate plus digestive zymogens. In the gut, trypsinogen is activated to trypsin by enterokinase. Trypsin then activates other zymogens. The activated proteases go to work on polypeptides from the tuna until all that's left are dipeptides and tripeptides. These are hydrolyzed by brush border peptidases.

Amino acid absorption is similar to monosaccharide absorption: A secondary active transporter (symport) specific to each amino acid couples the uptake of an amino acid to the entrance of sodium into the cell, and a uniporter facilitates movement out of the intestinal epithelial cell into the interstitium. Just as with carbohydrates, the amino acid ends up in the liver, where it is catabolized for energy or used in synthesis (anabolism).

Fats

"Enough of sourdough and tuna fish!" you declare, as you enter an ice cream shop. The almost-pure triglycerides melt in your mouth and are swallowed. The stomach's churning mixes the triglycerides with acid and mucus to some extent, but because they are extremely hydrophobic, they end up just floating in a layer above the aqueous contents of the stomach. Eventually they are emptied into the duodenum where they stimulate CCK release into the bloodstream. Then the pancreas sends enzymes into the gut, via the sphincter of Oddi. But there is a problem: pancreatic lipase cannot digest the fats if they are organized into huge hydrophobic droplets.

Fortunately, CCK in the bloodstream also stimulates gallbladder contraction. This sends bile down the bile duct into the duodenum. Bile acids emulsify the lipids from the ice cream, forming tiny micelles. Then pancreatic lipase can go to work. It hydrolyzes triglycerides to monoglycerides plus free fatty acids, as shown below. These move into intestinal epithelial cells by simple diffusion, which they are able to do thanks to their greasy hydrophobicity and small size. Once inside, they are converted back to triglycerides, which are packaged into **chylomicrons**. These are large particles composed of fats and proteins which are designed to transport fats in the bloodstream (Figure 17).

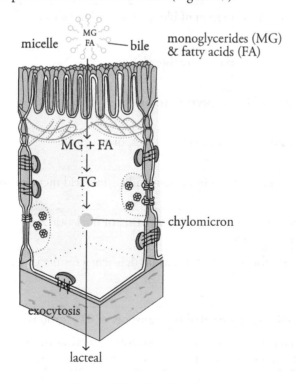

Figure 17 Fat Absorption

The chylomicrons do not enter intestinal blood capillaries. Instead, they enter tiny lymphatic capillaries known as **lacteals**. These merge to form larger lymphatic vessels, which eventually empty into the thoracic duct. This empties into a large vein near the heart. A few minutes after your sundae, huge amounts of fat are released from the thoracic duct directly into the bloodstream. Your plasma attains a milky yellow color which is easily noticeable when a blood sample is taken. The term for milky plasma is **lipemia**, meaning "fat in the blood."

The chylomicrons circulate throughout the body and are gradually whittled away by removal of fat. In particular, adipose and liver tissues contain the enzyme **lipoprotein lipase**, which hydrolyzes chylomicron triglycerides into monoglycerides and free fatty acids. These diffuse into adipocytes and liver cells, are remade into triglycerides, and then stored.

9.9 VITAMINS

Vitamins are nutrients which must be included in the diet because they cannot be synthesized in the body. They are divided into **fat-soluble** and **water-soluble** categories. Fat-soluble vitamins require bile acids for solubilization and absorption. Excess fat-soluble vitamins are stored in adipose tissue. Excess water-soluble vitamins are excreted in urine by the kidneys.

Vitamin	Function
fat-soluble	
A (retinol)	A visual pigment which changes conformation in response to light
D	Stimulates Ca^{2+} absorption from the gut; helps control Ca^{2+} deposition in bones
E	Prevents oxidation of unsaturated fats
K	Necessary for formation of blood coagulation factors
water-soluble	
B_1 (thiamine)	Needed for enzymatic decarboxylations
B_2 (riboflavin)	Made into FAD, an electron transporter
B_3 (niacin)	Made into NAD^+, an electron transporter
B_6 (pyridoxine)	A coenzyme involved in protein and amino acid metabolism
B_{12} (cobalamin)	A coenzyme involved in the reduction of nucleotides to deoxynucleotides
C (ascorbic acid)	Necessary for collagen formation; deficiency results in scurvy
Biotin	Prosthetic group essential for transport of CO_2 groups
Folate	Enzyme cofactor used in the transport of methylene groups; synthesis of purines and thymine; required for normal fetal nervous system development

Table 2 Vitamins

Summary

- The kidneys filter the blood to remove hydrophilic wastes. They also play a major role in homeostasis by regulating blood pressure, pH, ion balance, and water balance.

- Urine is produced by first filtering the blood, then by modifying the filtrate via reabsorption (moving substances from the filtrate to the blood) and secretion (moving substances from the blood to the filtrate), and finally by concentrating the filtrate to conserve body water.

- Filtration occurs at the glomerulus, most reabsorption and secretion occurs in the PCT, selective reabsorption and secretion occur in the DCT, and concentration occurs in the collecting duct.

- The Loop of Henle establishes a concentration gradient in the medulla; this gradient is critical to the reabsorption of water and the creation of a concentrated urine.

- ADH increases the water permeability of the collecting duct to allow reabsorption of water, and aldosterone increases Na^+ reabsorption at the distal tubule. Both hormones work together to help regulate blood pressure.

- When systemic blood pressure falls, the kidneys release renin. Renin is an enzyme that converts the blood protein angiotensinogen into angiotensin I, which is further converted to angiotensin II. Angiotensin II is a potent vasoconstrictor, and also increases the release of aldosterone; the ultimate goal is to increase blood pressure.

- The digestive system organs are divided into two categories: the alimentary canal and the accessory organs. The alimentary canal is the long muscular tube consisting of the mouth, esophagus, stomach, small intestine, and large intestine. The accessory organs have a digestive role, but are not part of the tube. They include the salivary glands, the liver, the gallbladder, and the pancreas.

- The mouth breaks down food mechanically by chewing, and also begins starch digestion via salivary amylase.

- The stomach is primarily a storage tank for food. Mechanical digestion occurs through churning of the food, acid hydrolysis begins chemical digestion, and protein digestion is begun via pepsin.

- Almost all chemical digestion and nutrient absorption takes place in the small intestine. The large intestine primarily reabsorbs water and stores feces; no digestion takes place in the large intestine.

- The liver produces bile (secreted into the small intestine), which emulsifies fat to increase the efficiency of fat digestion. The gallbladder stores and concentrations bile.

- The pancreas secretes the majority of the digestive enzymes used in the small intestine, along with bicarbonate to help neutralize the acid entering the small intestine from the stomach. The pancreas is also a major endocrine organ, secreting insulin and glucagon to regulate blood glucose.

CHAPTER 9 FREESTANDING PRACTICE QUESTIONS

1. The loop of Henle uses a countercurrent multiplier system to create an area of high ion concentration in the renal medulla. Which of the following statements about the loop of Henle is true?

   A) The descending limb is permeable to ions and water.
   B) The descending limb is permeable to water but not to ions.
   C) The ascending limb is permeable to ions and water.
   D) The ascending limb is permeable to water but not to ions.

2. All of the following would increase glomerular filtration rate EXCEPT:

   A) constriction of efferent arterioles in the kidney.
   B) increased circulatory volume.
   C) dilation of afferent arterioles in the kidney.
   D) increased filtrate osmolarity.

3. The kidneys play a role in all of the following processes EXCEPT:

   A) erythropoeisis.
   B) increased absorption of calcium in the intestine.
   C) vasoconstriction.
   D) stimulation of the sympathetic nervous system.

4. Which of the following statements about angiotensin II is true?

   I. Angiotensin II is a vasodilator.
   II. Angiotensin II is a substrate for ACE.
   III. Angiotensin II stimulates aldosterone release from the adrenal cortex.

   A) I only
   B) II only
   C) III only
   D) II and III

5. Which of the following is *not* an effect of gastrin?

   A) Promote parietal cell atrophy
   B) Decrease stomach pH
   C) Activate chief cells
   D) Indirectly stimulate protein degradation

6. A defect in pancreatic amylase would prevent digestion of which of the following nutrients?

   A) Starch
   B) Maltose
   C) Fructose
   D) Proteins

7. Hydrochloric acid is present in the stomach, resulting in an approximate pH of 2. Which of the following is NOT a correct statement about HCl?

   A) It destroys microorganisms in the stomach.
   B) It is secreted by G cells.
   C) It converts pepsinogen to pepsin.
   D) It participates in the acid hydrolysis of proteins.

8. The hepatic portal vein carries deoxygenated blood from the alimentary canal into the liver, where it is filtered before continuing to the heart via the hepatic vein and inferior vena cava. Blood from which of the following organs does NOT drain into the hepatic portal vein?

   A) Stomach
   B) Small intestine
   C) Colon
   D) Kidneys

CHAPTER 9 PRACTICE PASSAGE

The kidneys are critical in regulating and maintaining fluid balance and blood pressure; fulfilling this role requires a particular microanatomy. The nephron is a tubule that starts at the glomerulus, enters the cortex, loops into the medulla, turns around, and returns to the cortex. These tubules empty into collecting ducts, which empty into the renal calyces and then into the ureter. Since the kidneys are so crucial in maintaining fluid balance, they receive 20 percent of the cardiac output. Aldosterone and vasopressin are two main hormones that affect renal function.

Aldosterone is the primary effector hormone in the *renin-angiotensin-aldosterone system* (RAAS) and is one of the most potent mineralocorticoid hormones. It is secreted in response to low blood pressure, low plasma sodium levels, and high plasma potassium levels. The macula densa cells within the kidneys secrete renin in response to a decrease in mean arterial pressure, decreased sodium levels in the filtrate, or increased sympathetic activity. Renin is an enzyme that converts angiotensinogen into angiotensin I, which is then converted into angiotensin II by angiotensin converting enzyme (ACE). ACE is located in the lungs as well as within peripheral blood vessels and is a major target for antihypertensive drugs. Angiotensin II is a powerful vasoconstrictor and acts to increase blood pressure; further, angiotensin II is a powerful stimulator of aldosterone. Aldosterone receptors are located in the cells of the distal nephron and, when stimulated, act to increase sodium resorption, thereby increasing water retention and thus, total blood volume and pressure. Additionally, aldosterone acts to increase bicarbonate levels in the blood by increasing the secretion of hydrogen ions into the collecting duct.

Vasopressin is a peptide hormone and is secreted by the posterior pituitary. The main effect of vasopressin is an increase in the permeability of the collecting duct to water (these are normally impermeable to water). The hormone achieves this by stimulating the insertion of *aquaporins* into the apical membranes of the epithelial cells of these ducts. The aquaporins allow free passage of water, which escapes out of the nephron and into the hyperosmotic kidney interstitium; this reclaimed water ultimately redistributes to the systemic circulation. Vasopressin can also stimulate increased reabsorption of sodium in the thick ascending loop of Henle, and may act as a dipsogen (an agent that causes thirst). Vasopressin release is stimulated by a decreased plasma volume, by pressure receptors, and by an increased plasma osmotic pressure via osmoreceptors in the hypothalamus.

Other hormones acting on or produced by the kidneys include atrial natriuretic peptide (ANP) and erythropoietin (EPO). Although EPO does not act on the kidneys, it is released by the kidneys and stimulates red blood cell production. ANP, on the other hand, is released by atrial myocytes in response to excess atrial stretch. ANP acts as a vasodilator, and increases glomerular filtration rate; this hormone also inhibits renin secretion and reduces aldosterone secretion.

1. Which of the following could be the result of a hormone-secreting tumor of the kidneys?

A) Increased sodium retention
B) Elevated hemoglobin
C) Concentrated urine
D) Increased thirst

2. Which of the following will occur directly after increased consumption of table salt?

    I.   Aldosterone release
    II. Renin release
    III. Vasopressin release

A) I only
B) II only
C) III only
D) I and II only

3. Which of the following statements is correct?

A) Glomeruli are circular in shape, and contain a capillary system, which separates two arterioles.
B) Vasa recta can be found accompanying the loop of Henle in the adrenal cortex.
C) The distal tubules empty into the minor calyx via the renal papilla.
D) Aldosterone acts to increase potassium reabsorption.

4. Alcohol acts as a diuretic; consumption of alcohol produces large quantities of dilute urine. Which of the following statements is NOT a possible explanation for this observation?

A) Alcohol decreases the action of ACE, thereby inhibiting the release of aldosterone from the adrenal gland and decreasing water reabsorption by the collecting duct.
B) Alcohol acts to stimulate renin release.
C) Alcohol inhibits the secretion of vasopressin, therefore diminishing the kidneys' ability to concentrate urine.
D) Alcohol stimulates the release of ANP from the atria.

5. Where is the site of release of aldosterone?

A) Adrenal cortex
B) Adrenal medulla
C) Renal cortex
D) Renal medulla

6. Compared with vasopressin, aldosterone:

A) has a receptor in a similar location within the cell.
B) stimulates the formation of second messengers inside the cell.
C) is more hydrophilic than vasopressin.
D) has a different mechanism of action, but achieves a similar end result.

7. Which of the following statements comparing ANP and angiotensin is correct?

A) ANP increases blood pressure and urine volume, whereas angiotensin II decreases blood pressure and urine volume.
B) ANP decreases blood pressure and increases urine volume, whereas angiotensin II increases blood pressure and decreases urine volume.
C) ANP decreases blood pressure and urine volume, whereas angiotensin II increases blood pressure and urine volume.
D) ANP increases blood pressure and decreases urine volume, whereas angiotensin II decreases blood pressure and increases urine volume.

SOLUTIONS TO CHAPTER 9 FREESTANDING PRACTICE QUESTIONS

1. **B**   The descending limb of the loop of Henle is permeable to water but not to ions (choice B is correct and choice A is wrong); water leaves the filtrate, thereby concentrating it. The ascending limb is permeable to ions but not to water (choices C and D can be eliminated). Na^+, K^+, and Cl^- are actively transported out of the filtrate, and K^+ is passively transported, concentrating the renal medulla.

2. **D**   Constricting efferent arterioles would restrict flow out of the glomerulus, and dilating afferent arterioles increase flow into the glomerulus; in either case, pressure at the glomerulus would rise and filtration rate would increase (choices A and C can be eliminated). An increase in circulatory volume will increase blood pressure and further enhance this effect on a systemic level (choice B can be eliminated). However, if the filtrate osmolarity is high, the macula densa will not send signals to stimulate the juxtaglomerular cells and the GFR will not be increased (choice D would not increase GFR and is the correct answer choice).

3. **D**   Erythropoietin is released by the kidneys and stimulates red blood cell production in bone marrow (the kidneys play a role in choice A so it can be eliminated). Calcitriol (vitamin D) is activated in the kidneys and promotes the uptake of calcium in the intestines (the kidneys play a role in choice B so it can be eliminated). Renin is released by the kidneys and triggers the production of angiotensin II, which causes vasoconstriction (the kidneys play a role in choice C so it can be eliminated). However, sympathetic nervous system stimulation comes from the products of the adrenal glands, not the kidneys (the kidneys do not play a role in choice D, so it is the best answer choice).

4. **C**   Item I is false: Angiotensin II acts as a vasoconstrictor to increase blood pressure (choice A can be eliminated). Item II is false: Angiotensin I is the substrate for ACE, which converts angiotensin I into angiotensin II (choices B and D can be eliminated and choice C is correct.) Item III is true: Angiotensin II stimulates the release of ADH from the posterior pituitary gland and aldosterone from the adrenal cortex, thereby increasing blood pressure.

5. **A**   Gastrin acts on parietal cells in a stimulatory manner, causing them to release HCl (choice B is an effect and can be eliminated). Parietal cell atrophy occurs in the *absence* of gastrin (choice A is not an effect of gastrin and is the correct answer choice). Additionally, gastrin activates chief cells to release pepsinogen (choice C is an effect and can be eliminated). The combination of pepsinogen from the chief cells and acid from the parietal cells stimulates the cleavage and activation of pepsinogen to pepsin, with subsequent degradation of proteins (choice D is an effect and can be eliminated).

6. **A**   Amylase hydrolyzes starch into maltose, which is further broken down into individual glucose molecules by brush border enzymes in the small intestine (choice A is correct and choice B is wrong). Fructose is already a monosaccharide and can be absorbed without further digestion (choice C is wrong), and proteins are digested by proteases like trypsin or pepsin (choice D is wrong).

7. **B** Answer choices A, C, and D are all consistent with the function of HCl in the stomach. Choice B is incorrect because HCl is secreted by parietal cells, not G cells. G cells secrete gastrin, a hormone.

8. **D** The stomach, small intestine, and colon (large intestine) are part of the alimentary canal, and their blood supplies drain into the hepatic portal vein to be filtered by the liver (choices A, B, and C can be eliminated). Blood that passes through the kidneys drains directly into the inferior vena cava via the renal veins (choice C is correct).

SOLUTIONS TO CHAPTER 9 PRACTICE PASSAGE

1. **B** EPO is the only hormone secreted by the kidneys. It will act to increase red blood cell production, thus increasing hemoglobin. Don't confuse renin with a hormone! Renin is an enzyme that acts on an existing blood protein (angiotensinogen) to convert it to an active form (angiotensin). It does not bind to receptors anywhere and does not have a direct role on cellular function (as do hormones). Certainly if the secretion of renin were increased, then all other answer choices would also occur. There would be an increase in aldosterone and a subsequent increase in sodium retention. The increased sodium retention would increase vasopressin release and the urine would be concentrated. Both the increased sodium and vasopressin would act to increase thirst, but since renin is not a hormone and this question specifically asks about a "hormone-secreting tumor of the kidney," choices A, C, and D are wrong.

2. **C** Item I is false: Aldosterone causes the reabsorption of Na^+ when blood osmolarity is low. If table salt (NaCl) has just been consumed, blood osmolarity is likely high (choices A and D can be eliminated). Item II is false: The passage states that decreased (not increased) sodium levels stimulate renin release (choice B can be eliminated and choice C is correct). Item III is in fact true: Since vasopressin release is stimulated by increased plasma osmolarity, increased sodium intake will stimulate vasopressin release.

3. **A** The glomeruli are small knots of capillaries, supplied with blood by the afferent arterioles and drained of blood by the efferent arterioles. Although the vasa recta do surround the loop of Henle, they are found in the medulla, not the cortex (choice B is wrong). The distal tubules empty into the collecting ducts (which then empty into the minor calyces; choice C is wrong). Aldosterone acts to increase sodium reabsorption (not potassium), and in any case, the passage states that the release of aldosterone can be triggered by high plasma potassium. If its release is triggered by high plasma potassium, aldosterone is unlikely to stimulate the reabsorption of potassium, driving the levels up even higher (choice D is wrong).

4. **B**   Decreased water reabsorption means increased water elimination; in other words, the production of large quantities of dilute urine (choice A could explain the observation and can be eliminated). Similarly, since the passage describes the action of vasopressin in reclaiming water from the nephron, an inhibition of vasopressin secretion would lead to decreased water reclamation (reabsorption) and the production of dilute urine (choice C could explain the observation and can be eliminated). The passage states that ANP acts to increase glomerular filtration rate (increase urine production) and to decrease renin and aldosterone secretion; both of these would decrease water reabsorption and lead to the production of dilute urine (choice D could explain the observation and can be eliminated). However, if alcohol were to stimulate renin release, more aldosterone would be secreted, leading to the reabsorption of more water and the production of a concentrated urine (choice B does not explain the observation and is the correct answer choice). Note that the actual action of alcohol is to inhibit vasopressin, but the question only asks which of the answer choices was a *possible* explanation.

5. **A**   Aldosterone is released by the adrenal glands (choices C and D are wrong), and specifically from the adrenal cortex (choice B is wrong). The adrenal medulla releases epinephrine and norepinephrine.

6. **D**   The passage states that vasopressin is a peptide hormone and that aldosterone is a steroid hormone. Therefore, aldosterone is more hydrophobic than vasopressin (choice C can be eliminated), and it crosses the cell membrane to bind to an intracellular receptor (vasopressin would bind to a cell-surface receptor; choice A can be eliminated). After binding its receptor, aldosterone acts as a transcription factor rather than stimulate the production of second messengers (choice B can be eliminated). However, even though vasopressin and aldosterone have different direct molecular responses and are stimulated by different mechanisms, both act to decrease urine output and increase blood volume (choice D is correct).

7. **B**   Both ANP and angiotensin II act on arteries but in opposite ways. The passage states that ANP acts as a vasodilator and thus would decrease blood pressure, but angiotensin II is a vasoconstrictor and would increase blood pressure (choices A and D can be eliminated). Angiotensin II would decrease urine volume by stimulating aldosterone (and indirectly vasopressin); the passage states that ANP reduces aldosterone secretion, and thus it would increase urine volume (choice C can be eliminated and choice B is correct).

Chapter 10
The Muscular and Skeletal Systems

10.1 OVERVIEW OF MUSCLE TISSUE

There are three types of muscle which differ in cellular physiology, anatomy, and function. The type we are all familiar with is **skeletal muscle** (Section 10.2), which is also known as *voluntary* muscle, because its role is to contract in response to conscious intent. The next muscle type is called **cardiac muscle** because it is found only in the wall of the heart. Skeletal and cardiac muscle are said to be **striated** because of their microscopic appearance. The third type of muscle is **smooth muscle**, which is found in the walls of all hollow organs such as the GI tract, the urinary system, the uterus, etc. It is responsible for GI motility, constriction of blood vessels, uterine contractions, and so on. We have no conscious control over cardiac or smooth muscle because they are innervated only by the autonomic nervous system. The three types of muscle share some characteristics and differ in others. In Sections 10.3 and 10.4 we characterize cardiac and smooth muscle by comparison with skeletal muscle.

10.2 SKELETAL MUSCLE

Movement of Joints

Skeletal muscle provides voluntary movement of the body in response to stimulation by somatic motor neurons, but skeletal muscle alone cannot move the body. Skeletal muscle requires the framework of the bones of the skeleton for movement to occur. Skeletal muscles are attached at each end to two different bones. Muscles are often attached to bones by **tendons**, strong connective tissue formed primarily of collagen. By contracting, skeletal muscle can draw the points of attachment on the two bones closer together. [What effect does expansion of skeletal muscle have on the two bones the muscle is connected to?[1]] Skeletal muscles can move a joint by **flexing** (reducing the angle of the joint), **extending** (increasing the angle of the joint), by **abducting** (moving away from the body's midline) or **adducting** (moving toward the body's midline), as well as many other types of movement. [Which of these movements involve contraction of skeletal muscle?[2] Does flexing the elbow bring the hand closer to or farther from the shoulder?[3]] One of the two bones joined by a skeletal muscle is generally closer to the center of the body and tends to stay in place when the muscle contracts. The point on this bone where the muscle attaches is called the **origin** of that skeletal muscle, and the point where the muscle attaches on the bone more distant from the center of the body is referred to as the muscle's **insertion**. When a muscle contracts, its insertion point is brought closer to its origin.

An example of a skeletal muscle and its action is the flexion of the elbow joint by the biceps brachii (Figure 1). The origin of this muscle lies in the shoulder joint, and the insertion lies in the bones of the forearm. Contraction of the biceps brachii brings its insertion (the forearm) closer to its origin (the shoulder). Since muscles can only *contract* to move a joint, different muscles are necessary for flexion and extension (opposite movements) of a joint. For the elbow, the *triceps* brachii (the muscle on the back of the upper arm) is

---

[1] None. Muscle cannot expand with force. Muscle can only contract (get shorter) to cause force on bones and movement.

[2] All of them. It is the only way to move bones and joints: by contracting skeletal muscles.

[3] Flexing decreases the angle of a joint. If the elbow is flexed, the hand will be closer to the shoulder.

responsible for extension. [Where is the origin of the triceps brachii?[4]] The origin and the insertion for the triceps brachii are on the opposite side of the arm as for the biceps brachii, so that contraction of the triceps has the opposite effect on the lower arm as contraction of the biceps. [Do both the biceps brachii and the triceps brachii contract vigorously simultaneously to cause movement?[5]] Muscles that are responsible for movement in opposite directions are termed **antagonistic**, while muscles that move a joint in the same direction are **synergistic**. Usually, the contraction of antagonistic muscles is coordinated by the nervous system so that one muscle relaxes while the other contracts. [Do antagonistic muscles receive stimulation by neurons that release different neurotransmitters?[6]]

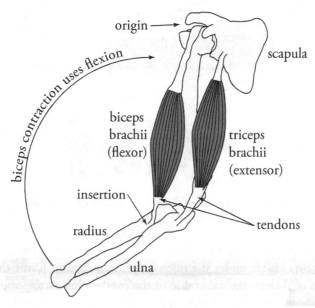

Figure 1   Skeletal Muscle

Structure of Skeletal Muscle

Each skeletal muscle is composed not only of muscle tissue, but also of connective tissue that holds the contractile tissue together in bundles called **fascicles** to allow flexibility within the muscle (Figure 2). Looking within each bundle, it is possible to see many fine **muscle fibers** (also called **myofibers**). Each muscle fiber is a single skeletal muscle cell. Skeletal muscle cells are **multinucleate syncytia** formed by the fusion of individual cells during development. They are innervated by a single nerve ending, and stretch the entire length of the muscle. The myofiber has a cell membrane, called the **sarcolemma**, that is made of the plasma membrane and an additional layer of polysaccharide and collagen. This additional

---

[4]   The origin of the triceps is the point of attachment nearer the center of the body, or the shoulder, on the opposite side of the biceps attachment.

[5]   Usually, no. Muscles that oppose each other's action are usually regulated by the nervous system in the opposite manner, so that one relaxes while the other contracts.

[6]   No. All skeletal muscle is innervated by somatic motor neurons which release acetylcholine at the neuromuscular junction. The difference in regulation is not the *form* of the signal (i.e., the *type* of neurotransmitter) that is sent to the muscle, but the *timing* of the signal (i.e., the *frequency* of stimulation, and thus the *amount* of neurotransmitter released).

layer helps the cell to fuse with tendon fibers. Within each skeletal muscle cell (myofiber) there are many smaller units called **myofibrils**. The myofibril in the muscle cell is like a specialized organelle; it is responsible for the striated appearance of skeletal muscle and generates the contractile force of skeletal muscle.

thin → actin
thick → myosin

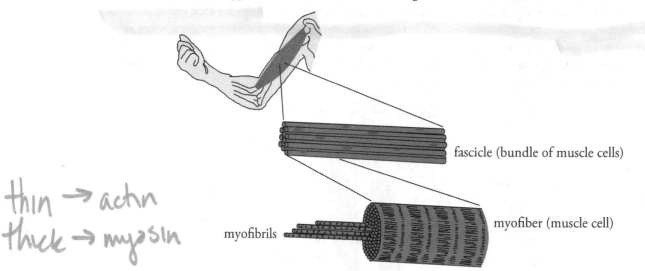

fascicle (bundle of muscle cells)

myofiber (muscle cell)

myofibrils

Figure 2 Levels of Skeletal Muscle Organization

The proteins in the myofibril that generate contraction are polymerized **actin** and **myosin**. Actin polymerizes to form **thin filaments** visible under the microscope, and myosin forms **thick filaments** (Figure 3). The striated appearance of skeletal muscle is due to the overlapping arrangement of bands of thick and thin filaments in **sarcomeres**. A myofibril is composed of many sarcomeres aligned end-to-end. Each sarcomere is bound by two **Z lines**. Thin filaments (actin) attach to each Z line and overlap with thick filaments (myosin) in the middle of each sarcomere; the thick filaments are not attached to the Z lines. The regions of the sarcomere composed only of thin filaments are referred to as the **I bands**. The full length of the thick filament represents the **A band** within each sarcomere; this includes both the overlapping regions of thick and thin filaments (where contraction is generated), as well as the region composed of only thick filaments (this is seen in resting sarcomeres only and is referred to as the **H zone**). See Figure 3.

I-bands ⇒ only thin filaments
A band ⇒ length of thick filaments
(including overlap w/ thin filaments)

H zone ⇒ only thick filaments in the middle of the A band

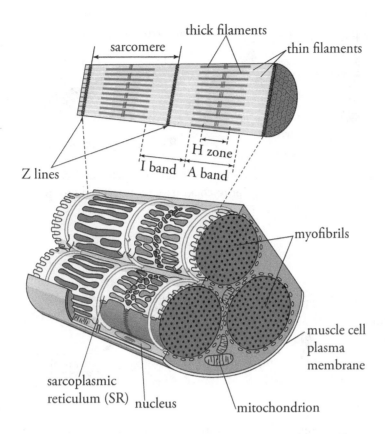

Figure 3 The Sarcomere and a Cross-Section of a Myofiber

The Sliding Filament Model of Muscle Contraction

Within each sarcomere, actin and myosin filaments overlap with each other (Figures 3 and 4). Contraction occurs when the thin and thick filaments slide across each other, drawing the Z lines of each sarcomere closer together and shortening the length of the muscle cell. [During muscle contraction, do the thin and thick filaments shorten?[7]] Filament sliding is powered by ATP hydrolysis. Myosin is an enzyme which uses the energy of ATP to create movement. (You will hear the term "myosin ATPase.") Each myosin monomer contains a **head** and a **tail**. The head attaches to a specific site on an actin molecule (the **myosin binding site**). When it is attached, myosin and actin are said to be connected by a **cross bridge**. Contraction occurs when the angle between the head and tail decreases. Filament sliding occurs in four steps. It is important to remember which step requires a new ATP molecule.

Steps of the contractile cycle:
1) Binding of the myosin head to a myosin binding site on actin, also known as **cross bridge formation**. At this stage, myosin has ADP and P_i bound.
2) The **power stroke**, in which the myosin head moves to a low-energy conformation, and pulls the actin chain towards the center of the sarcomere. ADP is released.
3) Binding of a new ATP molecule is necessary for *release* of actin by the myosin head (key!).
4) ATP hydrolysis occurs immediately and the myosin head is *cocked* (set in a high-energy conformation, like the hammer of a gun). Another cycle begins when the myosin head binds to a new binding site on the thin filament.

---

[7] No. The thin and thick filaments slide across each other to shorten the sarcomere without themselves changing in length.

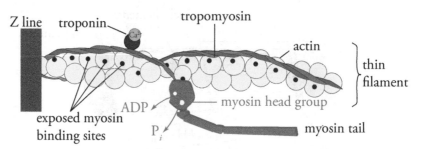

a) original position of filaments and Z line
prior to cocking of myosin head group

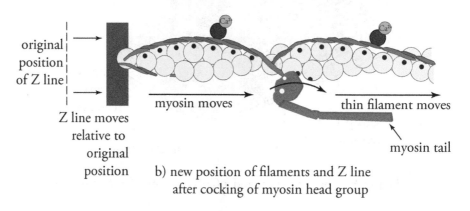

b) new position of filaments and Z line
after cocking of myosin head group

Figure 4 Filament Sliding

Excitation-Contraction Coupling in Skeletal Muscle

The above four steps in the contractile cycle occur spontaneously. In other words, if you put actin and myosin into a beaker and add ATP and Mg^{2+} (necessary for all reactions involving ATP), ATP will be hydrolyzed and the filaments will slide past one another. But in the myofiber, contraction occurs only when the cytoplasmic $[Ca^{2+}]$ increases. This is because in addition to polymerized actin, the thin filament contains the **troponin-tropomyosin complex** (Figure 5) that prevents contraction when Ca^{2+} is not present. **Tropomyosin** is a long fibrous protein that winds around the actin polymer, blocking all the myosin-binding sites. **Troponin** is a globular protein bound to the tropomyosin that can bind Ca^{2+}. When troponin binds Ca^{2+}, troponin undergoes a conformational change that moves tropomyosin out of the way, so that myosin heads can attach to actin and filament sliding can occur.

Tropomyosin blocks myosin binding spots on actin filament
Troponin is attached to tropomyosin and binds Ca^{2+}

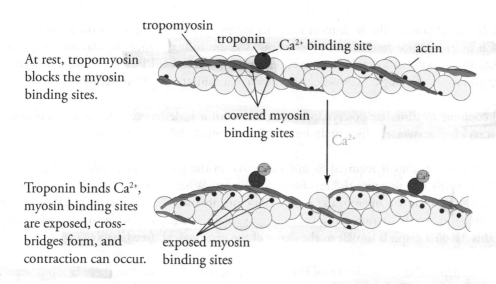

At rest, tropomyosin blocks the myosin binding sites.

Troponin binds Ca²⁺, myosin binding sites are exposed, cross-bridges form, and contraction can occur.

Figure 5 The Troponin/Tropomyosin Complex

- What protein is responsible for ATP hydrolysis during muscle contraction?[8] *myosin*
- In the absence of actin, which step in ATP hydrolysis by myosin is prevented, the hydrolysis of ATP or the release of ADP?[9] *release of ADP*
- If troponin-tropomyosin is added to myosin and actin filaments in a test tube along with ATP, which one of the following will be true?[10]
    A. The hydrolysis of ATP will become insensitive to the concentration of calcium.
    B. The hydrolysis of ATP will become sensitive to the concentration of calcium.
    C. ATP will be hydrolyzed when actin binds myosin.
    D. ATP will be hydrolyzed during the power stroke.

The Neuromuscular Junction and Impulse Transmission

The **neuromuscular junction** (NMJ) is the synapse between an axon terminus (synaptic knob) and a myofiber. The NMJ is not a single point, but rather a long trough or invagination (infolding) of the cell membrane; the axon terminus is elongated to fill the long synaptic cleft. The purpose of this arrangement is to allow the neuron to depolarize a large region of the postsynaptic membrane at once. The postsynaptic membrane (the myofiber cell membrane) is known as the **motor end plate**. ACh is the neurotransmitter at the NMJ.

Impulse transmission at the NMJ is typical of chemical synaptic transmission: An action potential arrives at the axon terminus, triggering the opening of *Ve Ca²⁺* channels; the resulting increase in *Ca²⁺* triggers the *release* of acetylcholine.[11] The postsynaptic membrane contains ACh receptors, which are

---

[8] Myosin is the protein with the ATPase activity.

[9] In the absence of actin, myosin can still hydrolyze ATP, but it cannot release ADP after hydrolysis.

[10] **B is correct.** Without troponin-tropomyosin, ATP hydrolysis will begin as soon as ATP, actin and myosin are mixed. In the presence of troponin-tropomyosin, myosin cannot bind actin, but if calcium is added, the troponin-tropomyosin complex allows binding and ATP hydrolysis can occur once again.

[11] An action potential arrives at the axon terminus, triggering the opening of **voltage-gated Ca²⁺** channels; the resulting increase in **intracellular Ca²⁺** triggers the **release of vesicles** of acetylcholine.

ligand-gated Na⁺ channels. The ACh must reach its receptor by diffusing across the synaptic cleft. Binding of ACh to its receptor results in a postsynaptic sodium influx, which depolarizes the postsynaptic membrane. This depolarization is known as an **end plate potential** (EPP). The smallest measurable EPP, caused by exocytosis of a single ACh vesicle, is known as a **miniature EPP** (MEPP).

ACh will continue to stimulate postsynaptic receptors until it is destroyed. This is accomplished by the enzyme **acetylcholinesterase**, which hydrolyzes ACh to choline plus an acetyl unit.

As in neurons, summation is required to initiate an AP in the postsynaptic cell. In other words, a single MEPP is insufficient to cause the myofiber to contract. When a sufficient EPP occurs, threshold is reached, and ____ channels open in the postsynaptic membrane.[12] This initiates an AP in the myofiber. The AP is propagated as in neurons, by a continuing wave of voltage-gated sodium channel opening. The shape of this AP on a graph is similar to the shape of the neuronal AP (see Chapter 7).

This AP must depolarize the entire myofiber if contraction is to occur. But there is a problem: Action potentials occur only at the cell surface, because they are by nature a depolarization of the cell membrane. The myofiber is so thick that an AP on its surface will not depolarize its interior. The solution is to have deep invaginations of the cell membrane, which allow the AP to travel into the thick cell. These deep infoldings are called **transverse tubules** (T-tubules).

Another specialized membrane in the myofiber is the **sarcoplasmic reticulum** (SR). This is a huge, specialized smooth endoplasmic reticulum, which enfolds each myofibril in the cell (Figure 3). The SR is specialized to sequester and release Ca²⁺. Active transporters in the SR rapidly remove calcium from the *sarcoplasm* (myofiber cytoplasm). Then, when an AP travels down the T-tubular network, it depolarizes the cell, and with it, the SR. The SR contains voltage-gated Ca²⁺ channels, which allow Ca²⁺ to rush out of the SR into the sarcoplasm upon depolarization. The increase in sarcoplasmic [Ca²⁺] causes troponin-tropomyosin to change conformation, allowing myosin to bind actin. Actin and myosin fibers slide across each other, and the muscle fiber contracts. When the cell repolarizes, calcium is actively sequestered by the SR, and contraction is ended.

Mechanics of Contraction

The smallest measurable muscle contraction is known as a muscle **twitch**. The nervous system can increase the force of contraction in two ways.

1) **Motor unit recruitment.** A motor unit is a group of myofibers innervated by the branches of a single motor neuron's axon. A muscle twitch results from the activation of one motor neuron, and a larger twitch can be obtained by activating ("recruiting") more motor neurons (and thus more myofibers).

---

[12] voltage-gated sodium channels

2) **Frequency summation**. Each contraction ends when the SR returns the $[Ca^{2+}]$ to low resting levels. If a second contraction occurs rapidly enough, however, there is insufficient time for the Ca^{2+} to be sequestered by the SR, and the second contraction builds on the first. The force of contraction increases. A rapidly repeating series of stimulations results in the strongest possible contraction, known as tetanus. This is a normal occurrence which the nervous system uses to obtain strong contractions.[13]

A note of clarification: The skeletal muscle action potential has a refractory period as does the neural AP. For frequency summation to occur, the amount of time between successive stimulations must be greater than the duration of the refractory period, but brief enough so that the sarcoplasmic $[Ca^{2+}]$ has not been returned to its low resting level.

One topic of muscle physiology which is less likely to appear on the MCAT, but worth mentioning, is the **length-tension relationship**. A muscle contracts most forcefully at an optimum length. This corresponds to a sarcomere length of 2.2 microns. The explanation is that at this length, a maximum degree of overlap between thick and thin filaments occurs. A greater sarcomere length makes the overlap smaller with fewer myosin heads able to bind to actin. A shorter length causes filaments to obstruct each other's movement by bumping together.

- The central nervous system can increase the strength of skeletal muscle contraction by:[14]
  - A. increasing the size of action potentials in somatic motor neurons that innervate the muscle.
  - B. increasing the number of neurons that innervate each skeletal muscle cell.
  - C. increasing the number of motor neurons leading to a muscle that are firing action potentials.
  - D. decreasing firing by inhibitory neurons that innervate the skeletal muscle.

Energy Storage in the Myofiber

ATP provides the energy for contraction, and supplies must be regenerated by glucose catabolism. However, glycolysis and the TCA cycle are not fast enough to keep pace with the rapid ATP utilization during extended contraction. There is a need for an *intermediate-term* energy storage molecule. **Creatine phosphate** is that molecule. During contraction, its hydrolysis drives the regeneration of ATP from $ADP + P_i$.

Muscle is highly aerobic tissue, with abundant mitochondria. **Myoglobin** is a globular protein and is similar to one of the four subunits of hemoglobin. The role of myoglobin is to provide an oxygen reserve by taking O_2 from hemoglobin and then releasing it as needed.

---

[13] Do not confuse this with the disease tetanus, caused by *tetanospasmin*, a bacterial toxin. The disease is an exaggerated, uncontrolled example of the normal process.

[14] Each muscle cell is innervated by a single neuron (choice B is wrong), and the more neurons that fire, the more muscle cells that will contract; the more muscle cells that contract, the greater the total force of contraction (choice C is correct). Action potentials are all-or-none events; the depolarization is the same size in a given neuron (choice A is wrong), and there are no inhibitory neurons that innervate the neuromuscular junction. Only acetylcholine, which is excitatory to muscle cells, is released at these synapses (choice D is wrong). (All motor neurons release a constant, small, baseline amount of ACh onto the muscle cell; this provides a baseline level of contraction that we commonly call "muscle tone". To inhibit a muscle, the amount of baseline ACh is reduced.)

Nonetheless, during prolonged contraction, the supply of oxygen runs low, and metabolism becomes anaerobic. Lactic acid is produced and moves into the bloodstream, causing a drop in pH. The liver picks up this lactate and converts it into pyruvate, which can be used in various pathways.

Cramps may result from exhaustion of energy supplies (temporary lack of ATP) in muscle cells. **Rigor mortis** is rigidity of skeletal muscles which occurs soon after death. It results from complete ATP exhaustion; without ATP, myosin heads cannot release actin, and the muscle can neither contract nor relax.

10.3   CARDIAC MUSCLE COMPARED TO SKELETAL MUSCLE

Cardiac muscle is similar to skeletal muscle in the following ways:

1) Thick and thin filaments are organized into sarcomeres. Hence, both cardiac and skeletal muscle are microscopically striated (striped).
2) T-tubules are present and serve the same function (transmission of APs into the interior of the large, thick cell).
3) Troponin-tropomyosin regulates contraction in the same way.
4) The length-tension relationship works the same way and is more significant in cardiac muscle. Skeletal muscle is fixed at a certain maximum length due to its attachments to bones, but cardiac muscle has no such limitations. Increasing the amount of blood that returns to the heart (e.g., through vigorous skeletal muscle contraction during exercise) can stretch cardiac muscle to optimize the length-tension relationship and maximize cardiac output, however *excess* stretch on cardiac muscle (e.g., dilation and enlargement of the heart, which can occur in heart failure) can lead to a *decrease* in contraction strength and a *decrease* in the ejection fraction (the fraction of blood the left ventricle ejects with each contraction). If the ejection fraction drops too low, death results.

Cardiac muscle is *different* from skeletal muscle in some important ways:

1) Cardiac muscle cells are not structurally syncytial (they each have only one nucleus), while skeletal muscle cells are syncytial. But all the muscle cells of the heart are interconnected by gap junctions known as **intercalated disks**, which allow action potentials to propagate throughout the entire heart without allowing nuclei and cytoplasmic contents to be shared; only small items like ions can pass. Heart muscle is thus called a *functional* syncytium because it acts like a syncytium (but isn't really).
2) Cardiac muscle cells are each connected to several neighbors by intercalated disks.
3) Cardiac muscle contraction does *not* depend on stimulation by motor neurons. In fact, the most important nerve releasing ACh at chemical synapses with the heart is inhibitory! This is the vagus nerve, a parasympathetic nerve. It synapses with the sinoatrial node, where it releases ACh to inhibit spontaneous depolarization (discussed below), with the result being a slower heart rate. Contrast this with skeletal muscle innervation, in which neurons release ACh to stimulate contraction. [If neurons don't trigger cardiac contraction, what does?[15]]

---

[15]   Pacing by the sinoatrial node, as discussed in Chapter 8

4) The AP in cardiac muscle depends not only on voltage-gated sodium channels (**fast sodium channels**, as in skeletal muscle), but also on voltage-gated calcium channels. These are called **slow channels** because they respond more slowly to threshold depolarization, opening later than the fast channels and taking longer to close. The voltage-gated calcium channels cause the cardiac AP to have the distinctive plateau shown in Figure 6.

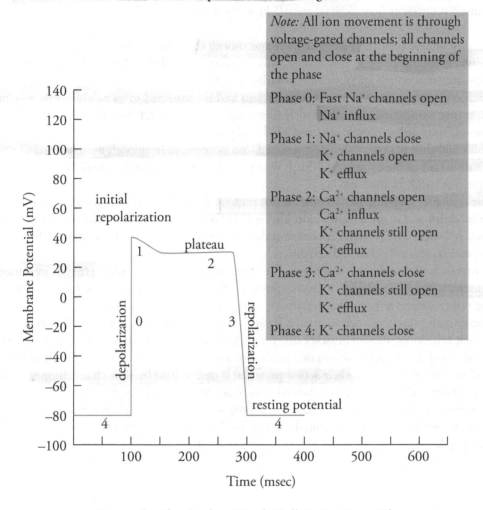

Note: All ion movement is through voltage-gated channels; all channels open and close at the beginning of the phase

Phase 0: Fast Na⁺ channels open
   Na⁺ influx

Phase 1: Na⁺ channels close
   K⁺ channels open
   K⁺ efflux

Phase 2: Ca²⁺ channels open
   Ca²⁺ influx
   K⁺ channels still open
   K⁺ efflux

Phase 3: Ca²⁺ channels close
   K⁺ channels still open
   K⁺ efflux

Phase 4: K⁺ channels close

Figure 6 The Cardiac Muscle Cell Action Potential

The significance of the plateau phase is twofold: 1) a longer duration of contraction facilitates ventricular emptying (better ejection fraction), and 2) a longer refractory period helps prevent disorganized transmission of impulses throughout the heart, and makes summation and tetanus impossible. This is advantageous because the heart must relax after each contraction. So remember: Skeletal muscle cells and neurons have the same steeply-spiking AP, while cardiac muscle cells have a spike and a plateau. Figure 6 shows the phases of the cardiac action potential. This was discussed in more detail in Chapter 8.

10.4   SMOOTH MUSCLE COMPARED TO SKELETAL MUSCLE

Smooth muscle is like skeletal muscle in that contraction is accomplished by sliding of actin and myosin filaments; the four-step contractile cycle is the same. Another similarity is that contraction is triggered by an increase in cytoplasmic [Ca^{2+}]. Like skeletal muscle cells, smooth muscle cells do not branch. However, smooth muscle is different from skeletal muscle in many ways:

1) Smooth muscle cells are much narrower and shorter than skeletal muscle cells.

2) T-tubules are *not* present. The smooth muscle cell is so small that they are unnecessary; a depolarization on the surface can depolarize the entire cell.

3) Each smooth muscle cell has only one nucleus and is connected to its neighbors by gap junctions (like cardiac muscle cells) which allow impulses to spread from cell to cell. Hence, both smooth and cardiac muscle are functional syncytia.

4) Thick and thin filaments are not organized into sarcomeres in smooth muscle. Instead they are dispersed in the cytoplasm. This is why the cell appears smooth instead of striated (no regular A band, H zone, etc.).

5) The troponin–tropomyosin complex is not present. Instead, contraction is regulated by **calmodulin** and **myosin light-chain kinase** (**MLCK**). In brief, calmodulin binds Ca^{2+} and then activates MLCK. MLCK phosphorylates a portion of the myosin molecule, thus activating its enzymatic/mechanical activity.

6) While skeletal muscles rely heavily on Ca^{2+} from sarcoplasmic reticulum, the SR in smooth muscles is poorly developed. It stores some Ca^{2+} that can be released upon depolarization, but the cell also relies heavily on extracellular stores of Ca^{2+} for contraction

7) The smooth muscle cell action potential varies depending on the location of the smooth muscle cell. Most smooth muscle cells can elicit action potentials (also called **spike potentials**) similar to skeletal muscle action potentials, but since smooth muscle cells have almost no sodium fast channels and their action potential is determined by slow channels only, it takes ten to twenty times as long as a skeletal muscle action potential (Figure 7).

8) Some smooth muscle that must sustain prolonged contractions (such as the uterus or vascular smooth muscle) has action potentials similar to those of cardiac muscle, although with a less-sharp spike.

9) Smooth muscles have a constantly fluctuating resting potential. Ions pass through the gap junctions between neighboring cells, causing the changes in resting potential to propagate like waves through the connected smooth muscle cells. These fluctuations in resting potential are called "slow waves." Slow waves are NOT spike potentials and do NOT elicit muscle contractions, but they are necessary to help *coordinate* the action potentials. In response to local stimuli (e.g., stretching of smooth muscle in the gut wall due to a food bolus), neurotransmitter from parasympathetic neurons is released. The neurotransmitter binds to receptors on smooth muscle cells and primes them for an action potential by pushing their electrical potential closer to threshold. Slow waves then pass through these "primed" smooth muscle cells, they reach threshold and undergo an action (spike) potential (Figure 7). The amplitude of these slow waves is increased by ACh and decreased by NE (e.g., stimulating the gut during a parasympathetic response, and slowing it down during a sympathetic one).

10) Like skeletal muscle, smooth muscles are innervated by motor neurons, but in the case of smooth muscle they are *autonomic* motor neurons instead of somatic motor neurons. Individual neurons do activate smooth muscle cells (as in skeletal muscle), but, as mentioned previously, the action potential then spreads from cell to cell. (Recall that in skeletal muscle, each action potential is limited to one large myofiber, while the heart is one large functional syncytium in which each action potential spreads to every cell. Hence, regarding innervation and the spread of impulses, smooth muscle shares features of both skeletal and cardiac muscle.)

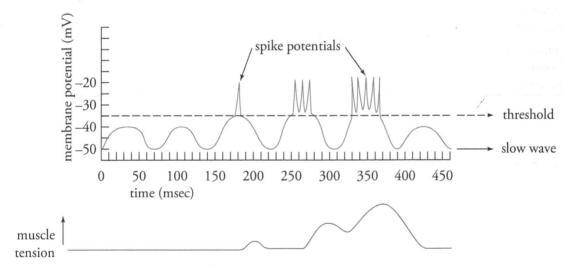

Acetylcholine increases amplitude of slow wave.
Norepinephrine decreases amplitude of slow wave.

Figure 7 The Smooth Muscle Cell Spike Potential and Slow Waves

Feature	Skeletal Muscle	Cardiac Muscle	Smooth Muscle
Appearance	Striated	Striated	No striations
Upstroke of action potential	Inward Na^+ current	Inward Ca^{2+} (SA node) Inward Na^+ (atria, ventricles, Purkinje)	Inward Na^+
Plateau	No	Yes (except for SA node)	No
Duration of AP	2-3 msec	150 msec (SA node) 300 msec (other cells)	20 msec
Calcium from	AP opens voltage-gated Ca^{2+} channels in SR, Ca^{2+} released from SR	AP opens voltage-gated Ca^{2+} channels, inward Ca^{2+} current during plateau Ca^{2+}-induced-Ca^{2+} release from SR	AP opens Ca^{2+} channels in cell membrane, inward Ca^{2+} current
Molecular basis for contraction	Ca^{2+} troponin binding	Ca^{2+} troponin binding	Ca^{2+} calmodulin binding, myosin light-chain kinase activation
Functional syncytium	No	Yes	Yes
Contraction dependent on extracellular Ca^{2+}	No	Partially	Yes

Table 1   Comparison of Skeletal, Cardiac and Smooth Muscle

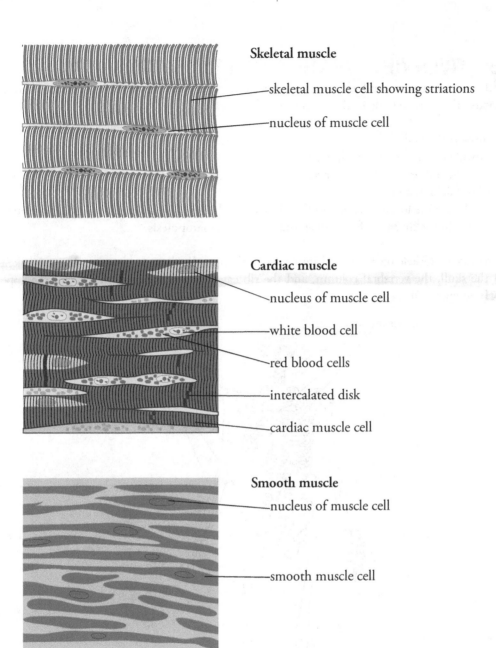

Skeletal muscle

—skeletal muscle cell showing striations

—nucleus of muscle cell

Cardiac muscle

—nucleus of muscle cell

—white blood cell

—red blood cells

—intercalated disk

—cardiac muscle cell

Smooth muscle

—nucleus of muscle cell

—smooth muscle cell

Figure 8   Three Types of Muscle Tissue

10.5   OVERVIEW OF THE SKELETAL SYSTEM

As vertebrates, we have an **endoskeleton** made of bone. This contrasts with the chitinous exoskeleton of arthropods. The vertebrate skeletal system serves five roles:

1) support the body,
2) provide the framework for movement,
3) protect vital organs (brain, heart, etc.),
4) store calcium, and
5) synthesize the formed elements of the blood (red blood cells, white blood cells, platelets). This occurs in the marrow of flat bones and is called **hematopoiesis.**

The vertebrate endoskeleton is divided into **axial** and **appendicular** components. The axial skeleton consists of the skull, the vertebral column, and the rib cage. All other bones are part of the appendicular skeleton (see Figure 9).

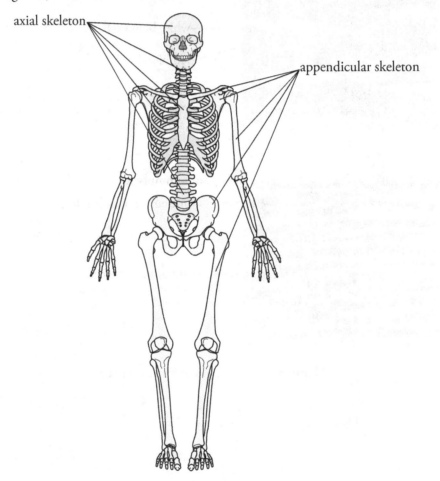

Figure 9   Axial and Appendicular Skeletons

10.6 CONNECTIVE TISSUE

Bone is an example of **connective tissue**. Connective tissue consists of cells and the materials they secrete. All connective tissue cells are derived from a single progenitor, the **fibroblast**. This name derives from its ability to secrete fibrous material such as **collagen**, a strong fibrous protein. Another important fibrous extracellular protein is **elastin**, which gives tissue the ability to stretch and regain its shape. Fibroblast-derived cells include **adipocytes** (fat cells), **chondrocytes** (cartilage cells), and **osteocytes** (bone cells).

There are two types of connective tissue: loose and dense. **Loose connective tissue** includes adipose (fat) tissue and material located between cells throughout the body, known as the **extracellular matrix**. The main ingredients of the extracellular matrix are **proteoglycans**, which are large macropolymers consisting of a protein core with many attached carbohydrate chains. The carbohydrate chains are called **glycosaminoglycans (GAGs)**. Like all carbohydrates, they are very hydrophilic. Hence, in the body, they are always surrounded by a large amount of water ("water of solvation"). This gives tissues their characteristic thickness and firmness. Dehydration results in saggy skin because of decreased hydration of the extracellular matrix. Another important example of loose connective tissue is the **basement membrane**, which is a sheet of collagen that supports cell layers (as discussed in the description of epithelial cells in Chapter 9). **Dense connective tissue** refers to tissues that contain large amounts of collagen, such as bones, cartilage, tendons, and ligaments.

10.7 BONE STRUCTURE

Macroscopic

There are two primary bone shapes: **flat** and **long**. Flat bones, such as the scapula, the ribs, and the bones of the skull, are the location of hematopoiesis and are important for protection of organs. The bones of the limbs are long bones, important for support and movement. The main shaft of a long bone is called the **diaphysis**. The flared end is called the **epiphysis**.

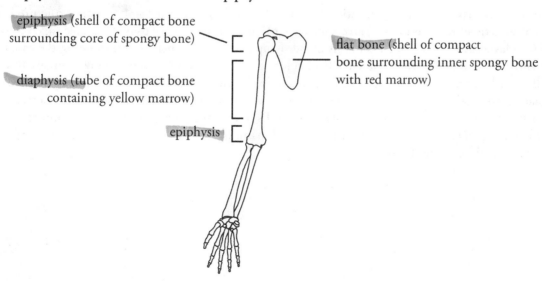

epiphysis (shell of compact bone surrounding core of spongy bone)

flat bone (shell of compact bone surrounding inner spongy bone with red marrow)

diaphysis (tube of compact bone containing yellow marrow)

epiphysis

Figure 10 Gross Anatomy of Bone

The general structure of bone may be either **compact** or **spongy**. As the names imply, compact bone is hard and dense while spongy bone is porous. Spongy bone is always surrounded by a layer of compact bone. The diaphysis of long bones is a tube composed only of compact bone.

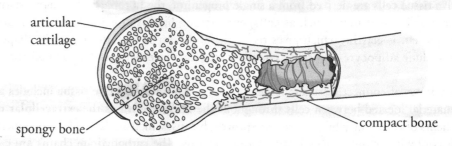

articular cartilage

spongy bone

compact bone

Figure 11   Compact and Spongy Bone

Bone marrow is non-bony material found in the shafts of long bones and in the pores of spongy bones. **Red marrow**, found in spongy bone within flat bones, is the site of hematopoiesis. Its activity increases in response to erythropoietin, a hormone made by the kidney. **Yellow marrow**, found in the shafts of long bones, is filled with fat and is inactive.

Microscopic

Bone is composed of two principal ingredients: collagen and **hydroxyapatite**, which is a solid material consisting of calcium phosphate crystals. During bone synthesis, collagen is laid down in a highly ordered structure. Then, hydroxyapatite crystals form around the collagen framework, giving bone its characteristic strength and inflexibility.

Spongy bone under the microscope looks like a sponge. It has a disorganized structure in which many spikes of bone surround marrow-containing cavities. The spikes of bone in spongy bone are called **spicules** or **trabeculae**.

Compact bone has a specific organization (Figure 12). The basic unit of compact bone structure is the **osteon** (sometimes referred to as a **Haversian system**). In the center of the osteon is a hole called the **central** (or **Haversian**) **canal**, which contains blood, lymph vessels, and nerves. Surrounding the canal are concentric rings of bone termed **lamellae** (which just means "sheets" or "layers"). Tiny channels, or **canaliculi**, branch out from the central canal to spaces called **lacunae** ("lakes"). In each lacuna is an **osteocyte**, or mature bone cell. Osteocytes have long processes which extend down the canaliculi to contact other osteocytes through gap junctions. This allows the cells to exchange nutrients and waste through an otherwise impermeable membrane. **Perforating** (or **Volkmann's**) **canals** are channels that run perpendicular to central canals to connect osteons.

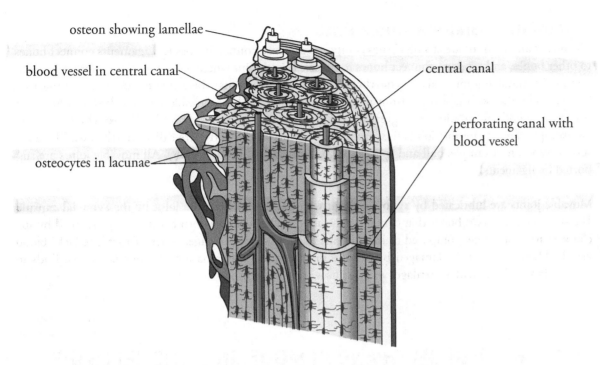

osteon showing lamellae

blood vessel in central canal

central canal

perforating canal with blood vessel

osteocytes in lacunae

Figure 12 Microscopic Structure of Compact Bone

10.8 TISSUES FOUND AT JOINTS

Cartilage

Cartilage is a strong but very flexible extracellular tissue secreted by cells called **chondrocytes**. There are three types of cartilage: hyaline, elastic, and fibrous. **Hyaline cartilage** is strong and somewhat flexible. The larynx and trachea are reinforced by hyaline cartilage, and joints are lined by hyaline cartilage known as **articular cartilage**, as shown in Figure 11. **Elastic cartilage** is found in structures (such as the outer ear and the epiglottis) that require support and more flexibility than hyaline cartilage can provide; it contains elastin. **Fibrous cartilage** is very rigid and is found in places where very strong support is needed, such as the pubic symphysis (the anterior connection of the pelvis) and the intervertebral disks of the spinal column. Cartilage is not innervated and does not contain blood vessels (it is **avascular**). It receives nutrition and immune protection from the surrounding fluid. [Why do cartilage injuries take a long time to heal?[16]]

---

[16] Cells in cartilage are not directly supplied by blood and have a low rate of metabolism. Thus, they are slow to repair damage. Often the damaged cartilage is simply removed or repaired surgically.

Ligaments, Tendons, and Joints

Ligaments and tendons are strong tissues composed of dense connective tissue. **Ligaments** connect bones to other bones, and **tendons** connect bones to muscles. The point where one bone meets another is called a **joint**. Immovable joints, called **synarthroses**, are basically points where two bones are fused together. For example, the skull is formed from many fused bones. Slightly movable joints, called **amphiarthroses**, provide both movability and a great deal of support (*amphi-* means "both"). The vertebral joints are an example. Freely movable joints (i.e., most of the joints in the body) are called **diarthroses**. There are several types, for example, ball and socket (hip, shoulder), and hinge (elbow). All movable joints are supported by ligaments.

Movable joints are lubricated by **synovial fluid**, which is kept within the joint by the **synovial capsule**. The surfaces of the two bones that contact each other are perfectly smooth because they are lined by special **articular cartilage** (composed of hyaline cartilage). Like all cartilage, articular cartilage lacks blood vessels. Hence, it is easily damaged by overuse or infection. Inflammation of joints (**arthritis**) leads to destruction of the articular cartilage, which causes pain and stiffness.

10.9 BONE GROWTH AND REMODELING; THE CELLS OF BONE

Most bone growth occurs by **endochondral ossification**, in which hyaline cartilage is produced and then replaced by bone. **Intramembranous ossification** refers to the synthesis of bone from an embryonic tissue called **mesenchyme**. This tissue is found in layers, thus intramembranous ossification results in flat bones (such as the bones of the skull).

Growth of long bones proceeds as follows: During childhood, a structure called the **epiphyseal plate** is seen between the diaphysis and the epiphysis. The epiphyseal plate is a disk of hyaline cartilage that is actively being produced by chondrocytes. As the chondrocytes divide, the epiphysis and diaphysis are forced apart. Then the cartilage is replaced by bone (ossified). This process is stimulated by growth hormone, and the rate of ossification is slightly faster than the rate of chondrocyte cell division (cartilage growth). Thus, at about the age of 18, the diaphysis and epiphyses meet and fuse together, and lengthening can no longer occur. This "fusion of the epiphyses" is easily observed in X-rays and can be used to notify adolescents when they have stopped growing taller. In adults, the fusion point is referred to as the **epiphyseal line**.

During adulthood, bones do not elongate. However, bone is continually degraded and remade in a process termed **remodeling**. The cells which make bone by laying down collagen and hydroxyapatite are called **osteoblasts**. The osteoblast synthesizes bone until it is surrounded by bone. The space it is left in is now called a lacuna, and the osteoblast is now called an **osteocyte**. Cells called **osteoclasts** continually destroy bone by dissolving the hydroxyapatite crystals. The osteoclast is a large phagocytic cousin of the macrophage. Bone destroyed by osteoclasts must be replaced by osteoblasts.

An increased ratio of osteoclast to osteoblast activity results in the liberation of calcium and phosphate into the bloodstream (and a decreased ratio has the opposite effect). Hence, activity of these cells is important not only for bone structure, but also for maintenance of proper blood levels of calcium and phosphate. The hormones **PTH** (**parathyroid hormone**), **calcitonin**, and **calcitriol** (derived by the kidney from vitamin D) regulate their activity and thus blood calcium levels. PTH and calcitriol increase blood calcium, and calcitonin reduces it. The specific effects of these hormones are listed in Table 2.

Hormone	Effect on bones	Effect on kidneys	Effect on intestines
PTH	stimulates osteoclast activity	increases reabsorption of calcium, stimulates conversion of vitamin D into calcitriol	indirectly (via calcitriol) increases intestinal calcium absorption
calcitriol	may stimulate osteoclast activity, but minor effect	increases reabsorption of phosphorus	increases intestinal absorption of calcium
calcitonin	inhibits osteoclast activity	decreases reabsorption of calcium	n/a

Table 2 Hormonal Control of Calcium Homeostasis

10.9

Summary

- There are three types of muscle tissue: skeletal, cardiac, and smooth.

- Skeletal muscles are voluntary, striated, multinucleate, and attached to the bones. They are individually innervated.

- The group of skeletal muscle cells controlled by a single neuron is called a motor unit, and each muscle is made of several motor units. All the cells in a motor unit contract together; to increase the strength of a contraction, additional motor units are recruited.

- Skeletal muscles are bundled into fascicles of many myofibers (cells), which are composed of myofibrils (strings of sarcomeres).

- Actin and myosin are organized into sarcomeres, which are the contractile units of the skeletal muscle cell. The arrangement of actin and myosin produces a characteristic banding pattern (striations): A band, I band, A band, I band, etc. Overlap of actin and myosin during the sliding filament theory produces sarcomere shortening.

- The four steps of the sliding filament theory involve the binding of myosin to actin (crossbridge formation), the pulling of actin toward the center of the sarcomere (power stroke), the release of actin (ATP binding), and resetting myosin to a high-energy conformation (ATP hydrolysis).

- Depolarization of the muscle cell triggers the release of calcium into the cytosol from the sarcoplasmic reticulum. Calcium binds to troponin, changing its shape, and subsequently changing the position of the tropomyosin to which the troponin is bound. This exposes the myosin binding sites on actin and allows contraction to occur. This is known as excitation-contraction coupling.

- Cardiac muscle is also striated, meaning that it, too, is organized into sarcomeres. Sliding filaments and excitation-contraction occur as in skeletal muscle. However, cardiac muscle is involuntary and autorhythmic. The cells are uninuclear and connected by gap junctions to form a functional syncytium.

- Cardiac muscle cells have an action potential that includes a long plateau phase. The plateau is the result of the opening of voltage-gated Ca^{2+} channels.

- Smooth muscle lacks striations and sarcomeres; however, calcium is still needed for smooth muscle cells to contract. They are involuntary.

- Bone is a dense connective tissue that functions primarily in body support and protection. Bones also play a role in mineral storage; resorption and deposition of bone is regulated by parathyroid hormone and calcitonin, respectively, to regulate blood calcium levels.

- Compact bone is organized into osteons, long cylinders of hard, dense bone. Compact bone forms the outer shell of all bones, and the shaft (diaphysis) of long bones.

- Spongy bone contains much more space than compact bone and is filled with red bone marrow; this is where blood cell formation takes place. Spongy bone forms the core of flat bones, and is found at the ends (epiphyses) of long bones.

CHAPTER 10 FREESTANDING PRACTICE QUESTIONS

1. Which of the following is NOT true regarding smooth muscle cells?

   A) They are uninucleate and relatively small in size compared to skeletal muscle.
   B) Gap junctions may exist between adjacent smooth muscle cells.
   C) Ca^{2+} influx and binding to troponin results in actin and myosin binding and contraction.
   D) They lack striations due to nonlinear alignment of the sarcomeres.

2. Rigor mortis, the stiffening of body limbs after death, is due to:

   A) the inability of the myosin head to detach from actin due to loss of ATP.
   B) the inability of the myosin head to attach to actin due to the loss of ATP.
   C) the inability of the myosin head to detach from actin due to loss of ADP.
   D) the inability of the myosin head to attach to actin due to the loss of ADP.

3. The neurotransmitter released at somatic axon synapses is:

   A) dopamine.
   B) norepinephrine.
   C) acetylcholine.
   D) epinephrine.

4. Lambert-Eaton syndrome is characterized by the formation of antibodies to voltage-gated calcium channels, rendering them inactive. Which of the following processes involved in generating a muscle contraction would be directly affected?

   A) Saltatory conduction
   B) Release of neurotransmitter at the synaptic cleft
   C) Binding of neurotransmitter at the muscle end plate
   D) Release of calcium from the sarcoplasmic reticulum

5. Which of the following is a possible way to distinguish between muscle types?

   A) Skeletal muscle can contract via peristalsis, while smooth muscle cannot.
   B) Skeletal muscle contraction depends on motor neuron stimulation, while cardiac muscle does not.
   C) Cardiac muscle cells are syncytial, while smooth muscle cells are not.
   D) Cardiac muscle contractions are regulated by influxes of calcium, while smooth muscle is not.

6. A young patient is found to have signs and symptoms of osteoporosis, or decreased bone density. The patient undergoes a variety of studies and is found to have a tumor secreting excessive levels of a particular hormone. What hormone could this tumor be secreting?

   A) Parathyroid hormone
   B) Calcitonin
   C) Vitamin D
   D) Thyroxine

7. Bisphosphonates are drugs that prevent the loss of bone mass and are used to treat osteoporosis and similar diseases. Which of the following is the most likely mechanism of action for this drug class?

   A) Osteoblast inhibition
   B) Osteoclast inhibition
   C) Stimulation of PTH
   D) Calcitonin inhibition

8. Synovial fluid is an essential lubricant for highly movable joints. Which of the following joints does not have synovial fluid?

   A) Shoulder
   B) Hip
   C) Finger
   D) Cranium (frontal-parietal)

CHAPTER 10 PRACTICE PASSAGE

The mammalian plasma membrane is a dynamic barrier that maintains a specific milieu of biomolecules within the cell. The intracellular compartment contains enzymes and ions with proportions drastically different from the interstitium and blood. Various concentration gradients across the plasma membrane require enormous amounts of energy to establish, but they are critical to normal cellular physiology. Dissipation of these gradients, either as a result of malfunctioning integral membrane proteins or of physical disruption of the lipid bilayer, disturbs cellular processes. Changes in ion concentrations, for example, may lead to virtually instantaneous changes in resting membrane potential, muscular contraction, and secretion. Over time, an abnormal distribution of molecules across the membrane leads to cell death. When very large numbers of cells die at once, the released cell contents mix with the extracellular environment and can alter the concentrations of proteins and ions within the blood. This may lead to systemic imbalances and, if not corrected, the death of the organism.

Traumatic crush injuries of the body destroy muscle tissue. If the injury is extensive, breakdown of myocytes (specifically, skeletal muscle cells) manifests as a group of clinical symptoms referred to as *rhabdomyolysis*. Sequestration of plasma within affected myocytes occurs and may lead to noticeable swelling. In severe cases, the redistribution of fluid from the blood into the muscular compartment causes symptomatic hypovolemia. In addition, the excess fluid increases the pressure within the muscular compartment; this eventually compromises local blood flow, leading to ischemic damage to the muscle and neurological dysfunction. As a result, patients often experience pain and weakness. Injured myocytes release phosphates and sulfates into the blood (which decreases pH), as well as several proteins. If the proteins are small (usually, less than 70,000 daltons), they may filter across the renal glomerular membrane and into Bowman's capsule. In a healthy individual, about 75 percent of myoglobin (16,700 daltons) present in the blood is freely filtered into Bowman's capsule; however, myoglobin concentrations in the blood are normally negligible. Large amounts of this protein will precipitate within the nephron tubules and lead to their damage. Signs of kidney failure may occur within days of the initial insult.

Measuring the levels of intracellular enzymes in the blood is frequently used to detect and monitor the course of disruptive cellular traumas, including rhabdomyolysis. Concentrations of creatine kinase (CK), glutamic-oxaloacetate transaminase, and skeletal muscle-specific aldolase transiently rise and fall following a traumatic event. Rhabdomyolysis produces CK levels that are elevated above the normal range in 100 percent of cases, often to values five to ten times greater than normal. Different isoforms of CK exist, and more sensitive laboratory techniques can distinguish between CK originating primarily from skeletal muscle, brain, or cardiac muscle.

While trauma is the most common cause of rhabdomyolysis, any process that compromises the integrity of the myocyte plasma membrane may lead to this phenomenon. Inherited myopathies like Duchene muscular dystrophy and malignant hyperthermia, electrocution, seizure activity, hypothermia, certain viral or bacterial infections, cocaine use, and many prescription drugs may result in this disorder.

1. Which of the following most accurately reflects the status of the renin-angiotensin system in a patient following extensive disruptive myocyte injury?

A) The renin-angiotensin system is activated because of increased blood volume.
B) The renin-angiotensin system is activated because of decreased blood volume.
C) The renin-angiotensin system is suppressed because of increased blood volume.
D) The renin-angiotensin system is suppressed because of decreased blood volume.

2. Which of the following statements is true regarding myoglobin?

A) Plasma myoglobin levels increase when red blood cells leak intracellular contents.
B) Myoglobin's quaternary structure allows maximal oxygen delivery to myocytes.
C) Myoglobin may damage renal tubule cells.
D) Actively contracting muscles causes a right shift in the myoglobin-oxygen dissociation curve.

3. Which of the following is LEAST likely to occur after extensive disruptive myocyte injury?

A) Decreased blood flow within the affected muscle tissue
B) Irregular heart rhythm resulting from increased blood potassium levels
C) Increased serum levels of lactate dehydrogenase
D) Decreased ventilation rate due to acid-base disturbances

4. Which of the following features is/are shared among skeletal, smooth, and cardiac muscle cells?

   I.   Myofibrils are arranged into sarcomeres.
   II.   Calcium plays a regulatory role in contraction.
   III.   Acetylcholine binding to muscle plasma membrane receptors is excitatory.

A) I and II only
B) II only
C) II and III only
D) III only

5. According to information provided in the passage, which of the following assumption should NOT be made regarding the use of blood CK levels as a tool for diagnosing rhabdomyolysis?

A) 100 percent of patients with elevated CK levels have some degree of disruptive skeletal muscle injury.
B) CK will be elevated to some degree in 100 percent of patients with disruptive skeletal muscle injury.
C) Patients with non-elevated CK levels do not have extensive disruptive skeletal muscle injury.
D) Patients with elevated CK levels may not have disruptive skeletal muscle injury.

6. Urine from a patient suffering from severe 3rd degree burns (burns that affect the skin and underlying muscle tissue) appears dark brown; analysis reveals the presence of large amounts of a heme-containing protein. Which of the following statements is the most likely rationale for this patient's abnormally colored urine?

A) Myoglobin is normally too large to filter into Bowman's capsule, but high myoglobin concentrations in this patient's blood have damaged the renal tubules, causing them to become leaky and to allow myoglobin access to the urine.
B) Myoglobin is small enough to filter into Bowman's capsule and is normally found in large quantities in the urine; the patient's urine is dark because of large amounts of hemoglobin.
C) Myoglobin is small enough to filter into Bowman's capsule; the patient's urine is dark because there is an abnormally high amount of myoglobin in the blood.
D) Myoglobin is normally too large to filter into Bowman's capsule; the patient's urine is dark because large amounts of hemoglobin (which is much smaller than myoglobin) has been released from destroyed red blood cells.

7. Skeletal muscle is derived from which embryological germ layer?

A) Endoderm
B) Mesoderm
C) Ectoderm
D) Neuroectoderm

SOLUTIONS TO CHAPTER 10 FREESTANDING PRACTICE QUESTIONS

1. **C** It is important to remember that smooth muscle is activated very differently from cardiac or skeletal muscle. Smooth muscle lacks troponin and tropomyosin and utilizes other regulatory enzymes including MLCK, or myosin light-chain kinase. All the other statements are true regarding smooth muscle (choices A, B, and D can be eliminated).

2. **A** During muscle contraction, the binding of ATP to the myosin head group is required to detach myosin from the actin filament. If there is no detachment (myosin and actin remain connected), the muscles remain stiff and immovable (choices B and D are wrong). Because ATP formation is an active process that requires living cells, levels of ATP decline rapidly after death, and ADP levels rise correspondingly. Thus it is the lack of ATP after death that leads to rigor mortis (choice A is correct and choice C is wrong). Note that this is a two-by-two question: a single piece of information can be used to eliminate two answer choices.

3. **C** Somatic axons stimulate skeletal muscle, so the synapse under discussion is the motor end plate, and acetylcholine is always released at the motor end plate. Dopamine is a neurotransmitter used in the brain (choice A is wrong), norepinephrine is the neurotransmitter secreted by sympathetic neurons (choice B is wrong), and epinephrine is a hormone (choice D is wrong).

4. **B** Release of neurotransmitter from the axon terminal is dependant upon calcium influx from voltage-gated channels, and is greatly impaired in Lambert-Eaton syndrome (choice B is correct). Saltatory conduction is primarily dependent on sodium channels, not calcium (choice A is wrong), binding of neurotransmitter at the motor end plate does not depend on calcium (choice C is wrong), and although the calcium channels of the sarcoplasmic reticulum are voltage-gated, they are intracellular and are not likely to encounter antibodies (choice D is wrong).

5. **B** It is true that skeletal muscle contraction depends on motor neuron stimulation; remember that skeletal muscles are voluntary. However, cardiac muscle is not voluntary; contraction is controlled by the sinoatrial node. This is a possible way to distinguish between these muscle types (choice B is correct). Smooth muscle, not skeletal muscle, contracts using peristalsis, such as in the digestive tract (choice A is wrong). Cardiac muscle cells form a functional syncytium; the cells are connected by gap junctions and function as unit. Smooth muscle also functions in this manner (choice C is wrong). All muscle contractions are regulated by influxes of calcium (choice D is wrong).

6. **A** The patient is described as having signs and symptoms of decreased bone density. This could be the result of either excessive bone resorption or poor bone formation. Of the hormones listed, parathyroid is known to cause bone resorption by stimulating osteoclasts. Calcitonin functions to inhibit osteoclasts, preventing bone resorption (choice B is wrong). Excessive levels of vitamin D would result in increased calcium absorption in the small intestine and, more likely, subsequent bone formation (choice C is wrong). Thyroxine is not involved in calcium regulation (choice D is wrong).

7. **B** Osteoporosis is a disease where bone mineral density is reduced due to increased bone re-sorption. The cells that are responsible for resorbing bone matrix are osteoclasts; these are stimulated by PTH and inhibited by calcitonin. In contrast, osteoblasts build bone and are stimulated by calcitonin. If bisphosphonates help prevent bone loss, they must either in-hibit bone resorption or stimulate bone building. Inhibiting osteoclasts would reduce bone resorption and could be a mechanism of action of bisphosphonates (choice B is correct). In-hibiting osteoblasts is the opposite effect and would not help build bone (choice A is wrong); an increase of PTH stimulates osteoclasts and would increase bone resorption (choice C is wrong). Calcitonin reduces osteoclast activity and stimulates osteoblasts, so inhibiting calci-tonin would not help bone loss (choice D is wrong).

8. **D** Synovial fluid lubricates movable joints. Of the joints listed, the only stationary one is the frontal-parietal joint or the frontal-parietal suture (choices A, B, and C wrong).

SOLUTIONS TO CHAPTER 10 PRACTICE PASSAGE

1. **B** The passage states that as injured myocytes swell, fluid is redistributed from blood into the muscular compartment, causing hypovolemia. This decreased blood volume (choices A and C are wrong) will cause a drop in blood pressure that will activate the renin-angiotensin system (choice B is correct and choice D is wrong).

2. **C** According to the passage, myoglobin released from injured myocytes precipitates in renal nephrons, damaging them and causing kidney failure (choice C is true). Red blood cells contain hemoglobin, not myoglobin (choice A is wrong), and unlike hemoglobin, which is made up of four globular protein subunits, myoglobin consists of a single protein subunit. As a result, myoglobin has no quaternary structure (choice B is wrong) and it cannot partici-pate in cooperative binding (choice D is wrong).

3. **D** According to the passage, injured myocytes swell with fluid, sometimes increasing pressures to the point where blood flow is compromised (choice A is likely and can be eliminated). Intracellular potassium concentrations are normally much higher than extracellular levels. When large numbers of myocytes lyse, they release enough potassium to alter total blood potassium levels. This may lead to life-threatening changes in heart rhythm (choice B is likely and can be eliminated). Lactate dehydrogenase is an intracellular enzyme found in the cytoplasm of muscle cells. It helps to convert pyruvate to lactic acid when the muscle must function in anaerobic conditions. Just like other enzymes mentioned in the passage, lactate dehydrogenase levels will increase when myocytes are disrupted (choice C is likely and can be eliminated). The passage states that the release of certain phosphates and sulfates decreases blood pH. This would trigger an increase in ventilation rate in order to help in-crease blood pH back to normal (choice D is unlikely and is the correct answer choice).

4. **B** Item I is false: Cardiac and skeletal muscle cells are described as *striated* because the regular arrangement of their protein filaments into sarcomeres produces a regular banding pattern along the cell. Smooth muscle lacks this feature; remember that myosin and actin need not be organized into sarcomeres for physical interaction to occur (choice A can be eliminated). Item II is true: In all types of muscle, calcium binds to tissue-specific regulatory molecules (choice D can be eliminated). Item III is false: Acetylcholine is released from all neurons in-nervating skeletal muscle, and the binding of ACh to skeletal muscle receptors is excitatory (leads to contraction). However, ACh is also released from parasympathetic effector neurons, and is not always excitatory in those cases. ACh released by parasympathetic neurons onto cardiac muscle tissue is also inhibitory, reducing both the rate and force of contraction (choice C can be eliminated and choice B is correct).

5. **A** According to the passage, "rhabdomyolysis produces CK levels that are elevated above the normal range in 100 percent of cases" (choices B and C are fair assumptions and can be eliminated). The passage also states that multiple isoforms of CK exist. Thus, a patient with cardiac muscle injury or brain injury will also present with elevated CK levels, even though they have undergone NO skeletal muscle injury (choice D is a fair assumption and can be eliminated). In other words, not all patients with elevated CK have skeletal muscle injury (choice A should not be assumed and is the correct answer choice).

6. **C** The passage states that proteins < 70,000 daltons are small enough to be freely filtered into Bowman's capsule; thus, myoglobin, at 16,700 daltons, can enter the capsule (choices A and D are wrong). The passage further states that under normal conditions (e.g., no injury), myoglobin concentrations in the blood are negligible (choice B is wrong). Only when large numbers of cells become damaged (as in a burn victim) can myoglobin proteins access the circulation and, subsequently, the urine. In particular, this patient is described as having severe burns that affect the skin and underlying muscle tissue (choice C is correct).

7. **B** You should memorize the basic tissues and structures that are derived from each of the three germ layers. The mesoderm forms not only muscle tissue, but also bone, blood vessels, and nongland organs. The endoderm forms the inner linings of the digestive system, the urinary system, and the respiratory system, as well as glandular organs such as the liver and pancreas. The ectoderm forms the skin, hair, and fingernails, as well as all nervous system structures (note that "neuroectoderm" is not an embryonic germ layer).

Chapter 11
The Respiratory
System and the Skin

11.1 FUNCTIONS OF THE RESPIRATORY SYSTEM

Single-cell eukaryotes that require oxygen to perform oxidative phosphorylation can acquire it by simple diffusion of oxygen from the surrounding medium. Even simple multicellular organisms such as coelenterates (jellyfish and hydra) can still receive sufficient oxygen by diffusion between cells and the environment. Larger organisms, such as the vertebrates, evolved a respiratory system to exchange O_2 and CO_2 between the atmosphere and the blood and a circulatory system to transport those gases between the respiratory system and the rest of the tissues of the body. [What parts of glucose metabolism produce CO_2, and what point in glucose metabolism utilizes oxygen?[1]]

The simple movement of air into and out of the lungs is properly called **ventilation**, whereas the actual exchange of gases (between either the lungs and the blood or the blood and the other tissues of the body) is called **respiration**.[2] The parts of the respiratory system that participate *only* in ventilation are referred to as the **conduction zone**, and the parts that participate in actual gas exchange are referred to as the **respiratory zone**. Additional tasks performed by the respiratory system include the following:

1) *pH regulation.* In the blood, CO_2 is converted to carbonic acid by the RBC enzyme carbonic anhydrase (Chapter 8). When CO_2 is exhaled by the lungs, the amount of carbonic acid in the blood is decreased, and as a result the pH of the blood increases (becomes more alkaline). Hence, minute-to-minute variations in respiration affect blood pH. *Hyper*ventilation (too much breathing) causes alkalinization of the blood, known as **respiratory alkalosis**. *Hypoventilation* (too little breathing) causes acidification of the blood, or **respiratory acidosis**. [Which organ regulates pH over a period of hours to days?[3]]
2) *Thermoregulation.* Breathing results in significant heat loss. Dogs depend on panting for dissipation of excess heat, because they cannot sweat.
3) *Protection from disease and particulate matter.* The lungs provide a large moist surface where chemicals and pathogens can do harm. The **mucociliary escalator** and alveolar macrophages, discussed below, protect us from harmful inhaled particles.

11.2 ANATOMY OF THE RESPIRATORY SYSTEM

The Conduction Zone

As mentioned previously, the part of the respiratory system designed only to allow gases to enter and exit the system is called the conduction zone (Figure 1). Inhaled air follows this pathway: **nose → nasal cavity → pharynx → larynx → trachea → bronchi → terminal bronchioles → respiratory bronchioles → alveolar ducts → alveoli** (the respiratory bronchioles, alveolar ducts, and alveoli are parts of the respiratory zone and will be discussed later). The nose is important for warming, humidifying, and filtering

---

[1] Pyruvate dehydrogenase and the Krebs cycle produce CO_2 during oxidative respiration, and oxygen is reduced to water by the last electron carrier in electron transport, cytochrome *c* oxidase.

[2] Sometimes these terms are used interchangeably. For example, we refer to "respiratory rate" when we really mean "ventilation rate."

[3] The kidney

inhaled air; nasal hairs and sticky mucus act as filters. The nasal cavity is an open space within the nose. The pharynx is the throat (a common pathway for air and food) at the bottom of which is the larynx. The larynx has three functions: 1) it is made entirely of cartilage and thus keeps the airway open, 2) it contains the **epiglottis**, which seals the trachea during swallowing to prevent the entry of food, and 3) it contains the **vocal cords**, which are folds of tissue positioned to partially block the flow of air and vibrate, thereby producing sound. The **trachea** is a passageway which must remain open to permit air flow. Rings of cartilage prevent its collapse. The trachea branches into two **primary bronchi**, each of which supplies one lung. Each bronchus branches repeatedly to supply the entire lung. Collapse of bronchi is prevented by small plates of cartilage. Very small bronchi are called **bronchioles**. They are about 1 mm wide and contain no cartilage. Their walls are made of smooth muscle, which allows their diameters to be regulated to adjust airflow into the system. The smallest (and final) branches of the conduction zone are aptly called the **terminal bronchioles**.

The smooth muscle of the walls of the terminal bronchioles is too thick to allow adequate diffusion of gases; this is why no gas exchange occurs in this region. The conduction zone is strictly for ventilation.

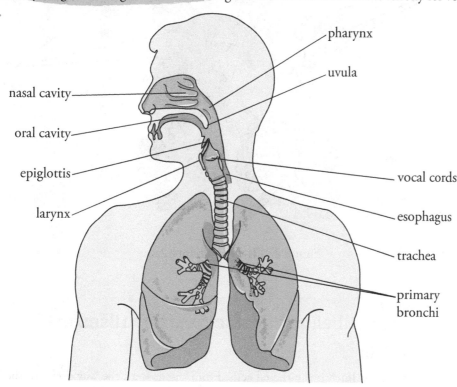

Figure 1 The Conduction Zone

The Respiratory Zone

The region of the system where gas exchange occurs is the respiratory zone (Figure 2). The actual structure across which gases diffuse is called the **alveolus** (plural: **alveoli**). Alveoli are tiny sacs with very thin walls (they're so thin that they're transparent!). The wall of the alveolus is only one cell thick, except where capillaries pass across its outer surface. The duct leading to the alveoli is called an **alveolar duct**, and its walls are entirely made of alveoli. The alveolar duct branches off a **respiratory bronchiole**. This is a tube made of smooth muscle, just like the terminal bronchioles, but with one important difference: the respiratory bronchiole has a few alveoli scattered in its walls. This allows it to perform gas exchange, so it is part of the respiratory zone.

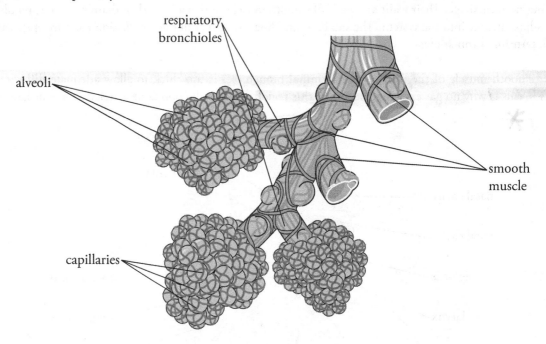

Figure 2   The Respiratory Zone

The Respiratory Epithelium: Protection from Disease and Particulate Matter

The entire respiratory tract is lined by epithelial cells. From the nose all the way down to the bronchioles, the epithelial cells are tall **columnar** (column-shaped) cells. They are too thick to assist in gas exchange; they merely provide a conduit for air. Some of these cells are specialized to secrete a layer of sticky mucus and are called **goblet cells** (just like in the gastrointestinal tract) . The columnar epithelial cells of the upper respiratory tract have cilia on their apical surfaces which constantly sweep the layer of mucus toward the pharynx, where mucus containing pathogens and inhaled particles can be swallowed or coughed out. This system is known as the **mucociliary escalator**. [What would be the advantage of swallowing pathogens and particles?[4]]

---

4   Gastric acidity destroys many pathogens. Also, particles which would likely harm the delicate alveoli are unlikely to harm the tough lining of the GI tract.

The alveoli, alveolar ducts, and the smallest bronchioles (respiratory bronchioles) are involved in gas exchange. Oxygen and CO_2 must be able to diffuse across the layer of epithelial cells in order to pass freely between the bloodstream and the air in the lungs. Tall columnar cells with cilia would be too large to permit rapid diffusion. Hence, gas-exchanging surfaces are lined with a single layer of thin, delicate squamous epithelial cells. (Squamous means flat.) A single layer of squamous epithelial cells is called *simple squamous epithelium*. It would also be unacceptable to have a layer of mucus covering the gas exchange surface, so another method of protection from disease and inhaled particles is necessary. Alveolar macrophages fill this role by patrolling the alveoli, engulfing foreign particles.

Surfactant

Imagine a bee hive made of tissue paper. If you put it in a steamy bathroom, what would happen? Would all the small air spaces remain filled with air? No, the hive would collapse into a wet ball, because the mutual attraction of water molecules would overcome the flimsy support structure provided by the fine paper fibers. The tendency of water molecules to clump together creates **surface tension**, which is the force that causes wet hydrophilic surfaces (e.g., the tissue paper) to stick together in the presence of air. Think of it this way: air is hydrophobic, so hydrophilic substances in the presence of air tend to clump together. Now imagine a bee hive made of thin wax paper. If you put it into a steamy room, does it collapse? No, because the wax on the surface of the paper prevents adjacent pieces of paper from being strongly attracted. In other words, the wax destroys the surface tension.

The alveoli are as fine and delicate as tissue paper, and they too tend to collapse due to surface tension. This problem is solved by a soapy substance called **surfactant** (*surf*ace *acti*ve substance), which coats the alveoli (Figure 3). Just like the wax in our example above, surfactant reduces surface tension. Surfactant is a complex mixture of phospholipids, proteins, and ions secreted by cells in the alveolar wall. [Is it likely that these are the principal lining cells of the alveolar wall?[5]]

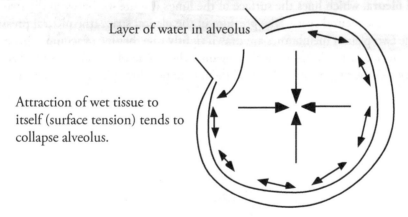

Layer of water in alveolus

Attraction of wet tissue to itself (surface tension) tends to collapse alveolus.

Figure 3   Surface Tension in an Alveolus

---

[5]   No, the principal cells of the alveolar wall are thin squamous cells designed to allow diffusion of gases. Cells which actively secrete substances (i.e., surfactant) are large, metabolically active cells with many mitochondria. The basic alveolar lining cells (simple squamous epithelium) are called Type 1 alveolar cells. The fat (cuboidal) epithelial cells that secrete surfactant are called Type 2 alveolar cells.

- There is not sufficient surfactant within a fetus' lungs until about the eighth month of gestation, so some premature infants lack the protective effects of surfactant when they are born. Which of the following statements best describes resulting effects upon respiration in "preemies" (babies born prematurely)?[6]
    - A. Surface tension would be abnormally low.
    - B. The alveoli would collapse.
    - C. Oxygen would be unable to diffuse through water.
    - D. Respiration is unnecessary, since the infant is dependent on the mother.

11.3 PULMONARY VENTILATION

Pulmonary ventilation is the circulation of air into and out of the lungs to continually replace the gases in the alveoli with those in the atmosphere. The drawing of air into the lungs is termed **inspiration**, and the movement of air out of the lungs is termed **expiration**. Inspiration is an active process driven by the contraction of the diaphragm, which enlarges the chest cavity (and the lungs along with the chest cavity) drawing air in. Passive expiration is driven by the elastic recoil of the lungs and does not require active muscle contraction. These processes will be described in more detail below.

The Pleural Space and Lung Elasticity

The lungs are large elastic bags that tend to collapse in upon themselves if removed from the chest cavity. The structures of the chest prevent this collapse however, and allow the lungs to remain inflated during inspiration and expiration. The lungs are not directly connected to the chest wall, however. Each lung is surrounded by two membranes, or **pleura**: the **parietal pleura**, which lines the inside of the chest cavity, and the **visceral pleura**, which lines the surface of the lungs (Figure 4). Between the two pleura is a very narrow space called the **pleural space**. The pressure in the pleural space (the **pleural pressure**) is negative, meaning that the two pleural membranes are drawn tightly together by a vacuum. This negative pressure keeps the outer surface of the lungs drawn up against the inside of the chest wall. Additionally, a thin layer of fluid between the two pleura helps hold them together through surface tension.

---

[6]   In the absence of surfactant, surface tension would be high (choice A is wrong), and the alveoli would collapse on every exhalation like tissue-paper beehives (choice B is correct). It would take an enormous exertion to reopen the collapsed alveoli to get any air (oxygen) into them; the result is poor oxygen delivery to the alveoli and thus to the blood (for this reason, preemies are typically kept on ventilators until their surfactant levels are higher and they are stronger in general). Note that oxygen has some ability to diffuse through water, but choice C is wrong mostly due to irrelevance. It's not as though in the absence of surfactant the lungs suddenly fill with water. Respiration is always necessary once a baby is born; this question specifically refers to infants born prematurely (choice D is wrong).

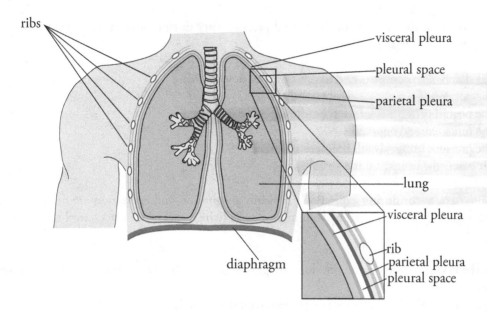

Figure 4 The Lungs and Pleura

- If the pleural space is punctured, opening it to the external atmosphere, which one of the following will occur?[7]
    - A. Fluid will leak out of the pleural space.
    - B. Air will leak out of the pleural space.
    - C. Air will leak into the pleural space.
    - D. Since the pressure within the pleural space is equal to atmospheric pressure during expiration, nothing will happen.

Inspiration is caused by muscular expansion of the chest wall, which draws the lungs outward (expands them), and causes air to enter the system. The lungs expand along with the chest due to the negative pressure in the pleural space. The expansion of the chest during inspiration is driven primarily by contraction of the **diaphragm**, a large skeletal muscle that is stretched below the ribs between the abdomen and the chest cavity. When resting, the diaphragm is shaped like a dome, bulging upward into the chest cavity. When it contracts, the diaphragm flattens and draws the chest cavity downward, forcing it and the lungs (which are stuck to the inside wall of the chest cavity) to expand. The external **intercostal muscles** between the ribs also contract during inspiration, pulling the ribs upward and further expanding the chest cavity. Inspiration is an *active* process, requiring contraction of muscles to occur.

Resting expiration, by contrast, is a *passive* process (no muscle contraction required). When the diaphragm and rib muscles relax, the elastic recoil of the lungs draws the chest cavity inward, reducing the volume of the lungs and pushing air out of the system into the atmosphere. During exertion (or at other times when a more forcible exhalation is required), contraction of abdominal muscles helps the expiration process by pressing upward on the diaphragm, further shrinking the size of the lungs and forcing more air out. This is called a **forced expiration** and is an active process.

---

[7] The pleural space is always at negative pressure, or the lung would collapse. If the pleural pressure is negative, and an opening to the atmosphere is made, then air will rush into the pleural space and the lungs will collapse. The correct answer is **C**. (Note that choice A will probably also occur, but the amount of fluid is so minimal as to be insignificant. C is the better choice.)

11.3

The pressure of air in the alveoli and the pleural pressure vary during inspiration and expiration. During inspiration, the following steps occur:

1) The diaphragm contracts and flattens (moves downward).
2) The volume of the chest cavity expands.
3) The pleural pressure decreases, becoming more negative.
4) The lungs expand outward.
5) The pressure in the alveoli becomes negative.
6) Air enters the lungs and the alveoli.

The opposite steps occur during expiration. Typically inspiration and expiration are not consciously controlled although they are mediated by voluntary muscle (which means we *can* control the processes if we want to!).

- At the beginning of inspiration, does the pleural pressure increase, decrease, or remain the same?[8]
- When is the alveolar pressure exactly zero (equal to atmospheric)?[9]
- What would be the result of a hole in the lung that allowed inhaled air to flow into the pleural cavity?[10]

Pulmonary Ventilation: Volumes and Capacities

Spirometry is the measurement of the volume of air entering or exiting the lungs at the various stages of ventilation.[11] A **spirometer** is a device used for these measurements. Data can be plotted on a **spirometric graph** (Figure 5). The volumes and capacities defined below should be familiar to you but do *not* need to be memorized.

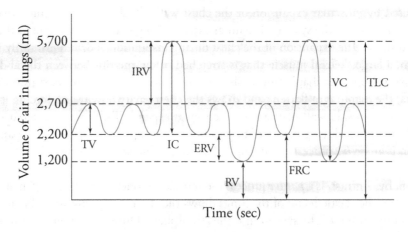

Figure 5 Lung Volumes and Capacities

---

[8] At the beginning of inspiration, pleural pressure decreases (becomes more negative), sucking the lungs open.

[9] At the end of a resting expiration, air tends to neither enter nor leave the lungs, until another inspiration begins. This is when alveolar pressure is zero. Also, just after inspiration, before expiration begins, there is an instant of zero pressure.

[10] A hole in the lung would allow air to flow into the pleural cavity, just like a hole from the pleural space to the exterior. This would cause the lung to collapse, because negative pleural pressure is the only significant force opposing lung collapse. Inspiration would be impossible.

[11] *Spir-* is from re*spir*ation.

The **tidal volume** (TV) is the amount of air that moves in and out of the lungs with normal light breathing and is equal to about 10 percent of the total volume of the lungs (0.5 liters out of 5–6 liters). The **expiratory reserve volume** (ERV) is the volume of air that can be expired after a passive resting expiration. The **inspiratory reserve volume** (IRV) is the volume of air that can be inspired after a relaxed inspiration. The **functional residual capacity** (FRC) is the volume of air left in the lungs after a resting expiration. The **inspiratory capacity** (IC) is the maximal volume of air which can be inhaled after a resting expiration. The **residual volume** (RV) is the amount of air that remains in the lungs after the strongest possible expiration. The **vital capacity** (VC) is the maximum amount of air that can be forced out of the lungs after first taking the deepest possible breath. The **total lung capacity** (TLC) is the vital capacity plus the residual volume (TLC = VC + RV).

- Is the total volume of the lungs exchanged with each breath?[12]

 In emphysema, lung elasticity is greatly reduced. Each of the following occurs EXCEPT:[13]
  - A. Residual volume increases.
  - B. Total lung capacity increases.
  - C. Resting expiration becomes active instead of passive.
  - D. Pleural pressure becomes more negative.

11.4 GAS EXCHANGE

The Pulmonary Circulation

Deoxygenated blood is carried toward the lungs by the pulmonary artery, which has left and right branches. These large arteries branch many times, eventually giving rise to a huge network of **pulmonary capillaries**, also called **alveolar capillaries**. Each alveolus is surrounded by a few tiny capillaries, which are just wide enough to permit the passage of RBCs, and have extremely thin walls to permit diffusion of gases between blood and alveolus. The capillaries drain into venules, which drain into the pulmonary veins. The lungs are supplied with lymphatic vessels as well.

Small increases in left atrial pressure have very little effect on the pulmonary circulation because pulmonary veins can dilate, accommodating excess blood. However, if the pressure in the left atrium increases above a certain level, the pressure will increase in pulmonary capillaries, and fluid (essentially blood plasma) will be forced out of the capillaries and into the surrounding lung tissue. Fluid in the lungs resulting

---

[12] No, some air always remains in the lungs; the FRC during relaxed breathing or the RV during deep breathing.

[13] Typically, when the lungs are stretched on inspiration, elastic recoil draws them inward and leads to expiration. The loss of elasticity means that the lungs do not want to recoil as strongly (or at all) and remain in their stretched position (choice B would occur and can be eliminated). Thus, expiration is not as efficient and more air remains in the lungs after expiration than normal (choice A would occur and can be eliminated). In order to make expiration more efficient, contraction of internal intercostal and abdominal muscles must be used to compress the chest cavity and push air out (choice C would occur and can be eliminated). Even at rest, alveoli are typically stretched somewhat and elastic recoil tends to draw them inward; this helps creates the negative pleural pressure. However if lung elasticity is reduced, there is less of a force drawing them inward, and the pleural pressure would be less negative, not more (choice **D** would not occur and is the correct answer choice).

from increased blood pressure is known as **pulmonary edema**. Normally, the lymphatic system prevents pulmonary edema from developing by carrying interstitial fluid out of the lungs.

- Which of the following may result from increased pulmonary capillary hydrostatic pressure?[14]
    I. Accumulation of interstitial fluid in the lungs
    II. Fluid accumulation in the alveoli
    III. Decreased oxygenation of the blood due to excess fluid slowing O_2 diffusion

    A. I and II only
    B. I and III only
    C. II and III only
    D. I, II, and III

The lungs are "designed" to expose a large amount of blood to a large amount of air. Hence the primary property of the lung is its enormous surface area, close to that of a tennis court. The goal is to allow O_2 from the atmosphere to diffuse into pulmonary capillaries, where it is bound by hemoglobin in RBCs. Simultaneously, CO_2 diffuses from the blood to the alveolar gas. [To review, how is CO_2 carried in the blood?[15]]

Air is a complex mixture of many gases, with nitrogen and oxygen as its primary components and other gases such as water vapor and carbon dioxide forming small percentages of the total (Table 1). In cities, poisons such as carbon monoxide may attain significant concentrations (partial pressures).

Gas	% of atmosphere
N_2	80%
O_2	20%
H_2O	0.5%
CO_2	0.04%

Table 1 Approximate Atmospheric Gas Compositions

Each gas that is part of a mixture contributes to the total pressure of the mixture in proportion to its abundance. The contribution of each individual gas to the total pressure is termed the **partial pressure**. The partial pressure of Gas X is abbreviated Px. For example, P_{O_2} designates the partial pressure of oxygen. [If the total atmospheric pressure is 760 torr, what is the partial pressure of oxygen (P_{O_2}) in the atmosphere?[16]] The total pressure is the sum of all partial pressures.

Gases in the air equilibrate with gases in liquids. If you place a beaker of water in a room, after a time the gases in the room will diffuse into the water. Hence, partial pressures are also used to describe the amount of gases carried in the bloodstream.

---

[14] If the hydrostatic pressure is high enough, all of these will result (choice D).

[15] Most is transported as $HCO_3^- + H^+$ (carbonic anhydrase is the key enzyme); some is bound non-specifically to Hb; a little can dissolve in plasma.

[16] Oxygen forms 20% of the atmosphere (Table 1). The partial pressure of oxygen in the atmosphere is 20% of 760 torr, or about 150 torr.

In the lungs, oxygen and carbon dioxide diffuse between the alveolar air and blood in the alveolar capillaries (Figure 6). The driving force for the exchange of gases in the lungs is the difference in partial pressures between the alveolar air and the blood. For diffusion to occur (from the air to the blood) gases must first pass across the alveolar epithelium, then through the interstitial liquid, and finally across the capillary endothelium. These three barriers to diffusion together form the **respiratory membrane** (the pathway is obviously reversed for diffusion from the blood to the air). [Do the lipid membranes of the alveolar and capillary cells act as barriers to the diffusion of oxygen and carbon dioxide?[17]]

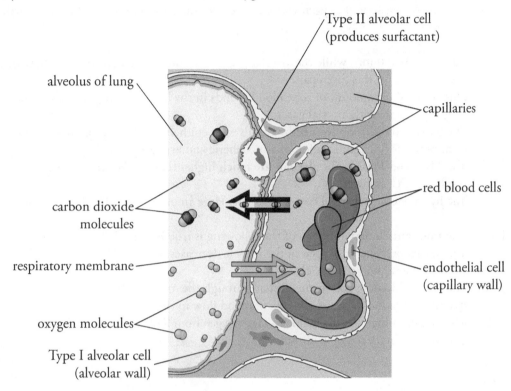

Figure 6 Diffusion of Gases Between an Alveolus and a Capillary

As blood passes through the alveolar capillaries, the oxygen pressure gradient between the alveolar air and the blood drives the net diffusion of oxygen into the blood. The arterial P_{O_2} is denoted P_aO_2.

- Is the P_{O_2} at the arterial end of pulmonary capillaries greater than, less than, or equal to the P_{O_2} in the venous end?[18]

---

[17] No, lipid bilayers do not act as barriers to the diffusion of such small hydrophobic molecules.

[18] Less than. Deoxygenated blood (P_{O_2} = 40 torr) enters the pulmonary system in the pulmonary artery. As the deoxygenated blood passes through the capillaries, it becomes increasingly oxygenated until it emerges at the venous end equilibrated with the alveolar oxygen pressure (P_{O_2} = 100 torr).

- Although the partial pressures of oxygen and nitrogen in the atmosphere are relatively constant, the partial pressure of water vapor can vary considerably. If water vapor in the atmosphere increases, which one of the following will occur?[19]
    - A. The total atmospheric pressure will increase.
    - B. The partial pressures of oxygen and nitrogen will decrease.
    - C. The partial pressure of oxygen will decrease, and the partial pressure of nitrogen will increase.
    - D. The partial pressure of oxygen will increase, and the partial pressure of nitrogen will decrease.

- Atmospheric P_{O_2} is 150 torr, while the arterial P_{O_2} is 100 torr. Which one of the following is the best explanation for this discrepancy?[20]
    - A. Due to the short amount of time blood spends in the lungs, atmospheric gases do not fully equilibrate with arterial gases.
    - B. The barrier to diffusion formed by the alveolar epithelium plus the capillary endothelium prevents full equilibration of atmospheric and arterial gases.
    - C. The P_{H_2O} and P_{CO_2} in the alveolus are much higher than in the atmosphere; as a result, the P_{O_2} is lower.
    - D. The hydrophobic nature of oxygen prevents large amounts from dissolving in blood.

- During vigorous muscle activity, each of the following is true EXCEPT:[21]
    - A. The partial pressure of oxygen in the muscle decreases; as a result, oxygen diffuses from the blood into the muscle.
    - B. The flow of blood in the venous system through the muscle is reduced.
    - C. Arteriolar dilation increases the rate of blood flow to the muscle.
    - D. Myoglobin in muscle cells is able to take oxygen from RBC hemoglobin because myoglobin has a higher oxygen affinity.

---

[19] Total atmospheric pressure is defined as the force exerted against a surface due to the weight of the air above that surface, thus it is determined primarily by gravitational forces and changes very little (choice A is wrong). Partial pressure however, is defined as the portion of total pressure due to a particular gas, thus if the partial pressure of water increases (and since the total pressure remains the same), the relative partial pressures of oxygen and nitrogen would have to decrease (choice **B** is correct and choices C and D are wrong).

[20] The alveolar P_{O_2} is only 100 torr because water and CO_2 take up a greater proportion of gases in the alveolus than in the atmosphere. The gases in the alveolus do not have the same composition as the atmosphere since they are not fully exchanged with each breath (choice **C** is correct). While it is true that blood spends only a short amount of time in the lungs, the barrier (respiratory membrane) is extremely thin, allowing for rapid and complete equilibration of gases under normal circumstances (choices A and B are wrong). Choice D is true but irrelevant; most oxygen in the blood is carried on hemoglobin.

[21] During vigorous exertion, blood flow to the muscle through arterioles is increased (choice C is true and can be eliminated), thus flow from the muscles through veins and venules must also increase; blood does not pool in the muscles during activity (choice **B** is false and the correct answer choice). As O_2 is used to make ATP, P_{O_2} in the muscle decreases and the resulting increased O_2 gradient from blood to muscle tissue allows oxygen to diffuse into the muscle cells (choice A is true and can be eliminated). This effect is enhanced by the fact that myoglobin has a higher affinity for oxygen than hemoglobin (choice D is true and can be eliminated).

11.5 REGULATION OF VENTILATION RATE

Proper regulation of the rate and depth of breathing is essential. Although breathing can be voluntarily controlled for short periods of time, it is normally an involuntary process directed by the **respiratory control center** in the medulla of the brain stem. The stimuli that affect ventilation rate are both mechanical and chemical (Table 2).

The principal chemical stimuli that affect ventilation rate are increased P_{CO_2}, decreased pH, and decreased P_{O_2} (with CO_2 and pH being the primary regulators and O_2 secondary). These variables are monitored by special autonomic sensory receptors. **Peripheral chemoreceptors** are located in the aorta and the carotid arteries and monitor the P_{CO_2}, pH, and P_{O_2} of the blood, while **central chemoreceptors** are found in the medullary respiratory control center, and monitor P_{CO_2} and pH of the cerebrospinal fluid (CSF). Recall that pH and P_{CO_2} are connected through the carbonic acid buffer system of the blood (discussed briefly in Chapters 8 and 9).

$$CO_2 + H_2O \rightleftharpoons H_2CO_3 \rightleftharpoons H^+ + HCO_3^-$$

Respiration eliminates CO_2 from the body. Thus, changes in ventilation rate can have rapid effects on pH due to the decrease or increase in P_{CO_2} and the resulting shift to maintain the above equilibrium. For example, a person hyperventilating during an anxiety attack can have an elevated pH. [Why do we give these folks a paper bag to breath into?[22]] A person whose ventilation rate has been reduced due to extreme alcohol intoxication can become acidotic. Similarly, changes in pH can be compensated for by increasing or decreasing ventilation rate. For example, diabetics who are acidotic due to the metabolism of proteins and fats instead of glucose will have an increased ventilation rate to remove CO_2 and increase pH.

Mechanical stimuli that affect ventilation rate include physical stretching of the lungs and irritants. The mechanical stretching of lung tissue stimulates stretch receptors that inhibit further excitatory signals from the respiratory center to the muscles involved in inspiration. The walls of bronchi and larger bronchioles contain smooth muscle. Contraction of this smooth muscle is known as **bronchoconstriction**. Irritation of the inner lining of the lung stimulates irritant receptors, and reflexive contraction of bronchial smooth muscle prevents irritants from continuing to enter the passageways. This contractile response is determined by parasympathetic nerves that release ACh. During an allergy attack, mast cells release histamine, which also causes bronchoconstriction. Epinephrine opposes this; it increases ventilation by causing airway smooth muscles to relax (this is **bronchodilation**). [Asthma is caused by spasm of airway smooth muscles. Patients with asthma carry "inhalers," which are small aerosol cans whose contents they spray into their lungs during an asthma attack. Based on the above, what might inhalers contain?[23]]

There are also **irritant receptors** in the lung that trigger coughing and/or bronchoconstriction when an irritating chemical (such as smoke) is detected.

---

[22] Breathing into a paper bag forces them to rebreathe their exhaled CO_2. This pushes the equilibrium of the equation to the right and brings pH back down to normal.

[23] They contain epinephrine, antihistamines (drugs that block histamine receptors on smooth muscle cells), and anticholinergics (drugs that block acetylcholine receptors on smooth muscle cells).

11.5

Stimulus	Receptor	Effect
stretch of lung	stretch receptor in lung	inhibits inspiration
$\uparrow P_{CO_2}$	peripheral chemoreceptors and medullary respiratory center	increased P_{CO_2} causes $\downarrow$pH via carbonic anhydrase; the $\downarrow$pH is what is actually sensed (see below)
$\downarrow$pH	as above	increases respiratory rate
$\downarrow P_{O_2}$	peripheral chemoreceptors	increases respiratory rate
chemical irritation	irritant receptor in lung	coughing and/or bronchoconstriction

Table 2 Factors that Regulate Ventilation Rate

11.6 STRUCTURE AND LAYERS OF THE SKIN

The skin is the largest organ in the body, by size and by weight (Figure 7). Its role is to protect us from pathogens, to prevent excessive evaporation of water, and to regulate body temperature (Section 11.7). The outermost layer of the skin is called the **epidermis**; it lies upon the deeper **dermis**, which rests on **subcutaneous tissue** or **hypodermis**. The hypodermis is a protective, insulating layer of fat (adipose tissue).

The epidermis is composed of stratified (many layers of) squamous epithelial cells. These cells are constantly sloughed off and then replenished by mitosis of cells at the deepest part of the epidermis, the **stratum basale**. A cell in this layer divides, and one of the resulting daughter cells moves outward. Soon this cell will die and be pushed farther and farther outward by continued mitosis below, until it flakes away from the surface of the body. The significance of many layers of epithelial cells is that they provide a strong protective structure.

Another important facet of the stratified squamous cells of the epidermis is that they are **keratinized**. This means that as they die, they become filled with a thick coating of the tough, hydrophobic protein **keratin**. Keratin helps make the skin waterproof.

Epidermal epithelial cells also contain **melanin**. This is a brown pigment, produced by specialized cells in the epidermis termed *melanocytes*, that helps absorb the ultraviolet light of the sun to prevent damage to underlying tissues.

Beneath the epidermis lies the **dermis**. The dermis consists of various cell-types embedded in a connective tissue matrix. It contains blood vessels that nourish both the dermis and the epidermis (the epidermis has no blood vessels of its own). The dermis also contains **sensory receptors**, which convey information about touch, pressure, pain, and temperature to the central nervous system. Also found in the dermis are **sudoriferous** (sweat) glands, **sebaceous** (oil) glands, and **hair follicles**. Hairs consist of dead epithelial cells bound tightly together. Some specialized regions of skin contain **ceruminous** (wax) glands (e.g., the external ear canal).

The sudoriferous gland is composed of a tube-like structure that originates in the dermis and leads through the epidermis to a pore on the surface of the skin. The purpose of sweat is to allow loss of excess heat by evaporation. Sweat contains water, electrolytes, and urea. Sweat glands are responsive to aldosterone. People living in hot climates must sweat a lot. In order to conserve sodium, they have a high level of aldosterone, and thus their sweat does not waste salt.

11.6

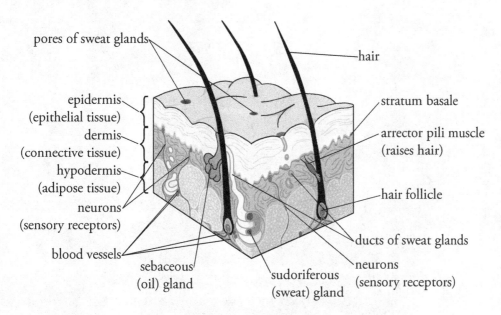

Figure 7   Skin Layers

11.7   TEMPERATURE REGULATION BY THE SKIN

Humans are **homeotherms**, meaning their body temperature is relatively constant. Heat is generated by metabolic processes and muscle contraction. Some homeotherms (e.g., bears) can increase their temperature by burning special fat called **brown adipose tissue**; this process is called **chemical thermogenesis** or **non-shivering thermogenesis**. But this is *not* an important mechanism of temperature regulation in adult humans. Also, while it is true that an increased level of thyroid hormone can increase the metabolic rate and thus increase body temperature, this mechanism takes several weeks to kick in and is not thought to be important in day-to-day temperature regulation. So, practically, only four strategies are available to cope with cold weather:

1)   Contraction of skeletal muscles produces heat, whether it is involuntary (shivering) or voluntary (jumping up and down).

2)   The skin insulates us so that we conserve heat generated by metabolism. Subcutaneous (beneath the skin) tissue contains a layer of insulating fat, which helps.

3)   Heat loss by conduction is minimized by constriction of blood vessels in the dermis (**cutaneous vasoconstriction**). Cutaneous vasoconstriction occurs in response to cold weather or upon activation of the sympathetic nervous system. This is why the skin becomes cold and pale when one is frightened.

4)   Obviously, contrivances such as clothing and blankets help us conserve heat.

A mechanism for dissipation of excess heat is also necessary. This is accomplished by two mechanisms in the skin:

1)   Sweating, which allows heat loss by evaporation.

2)   Dilation of blood vessels in the dermis (**cutaneous vasodilation**) results in heat loss by conduction.

Summary

- The primary functions of the respiratory system are gas exchange and pH regulation. pH regulation by the respiratory system is very fast.

- The organs of the respiratory system are divided into the conduction zone and the respiratory zone.

- The conduction zone is for ventilation only and includes the nose and nasal cavity, the pharynx, the larynx, the trachea, and the respiratory tree from the primary bronchi to the terminal bronchioles.

- The larynx is made entirely of cartilage, and includes the epiglottis (which separates food and air) and the vocal cords (for sound production).

- The respiratory zone is for gas exchange and includes the respiratory bronchioles, the alveolar ducts, and the alveoli.

- Surfactant reduces the surface tension inside the alveoli and makes it easier to inflate them.

- Inspiration is an active process and requires the contraction of the diaphragm to expand the chest cavity. An increase in the size of the chest cavity (and lungs) reduces their pressure, and air flows in.

- Expiration is primarily a passive process; the diaphragm relaxes and lung elastic recoil helps return them to their resting state. Forced expiration requires the contraction of the abdominal muscles to forcibly reduce the size of the chest cavity. In either case, the reduction in the size of the chest cavity increases their pressure and pushes the air out.

- Ventilation rate is determined primarily by P_{CO_2} and the need to regulate pH, according to the following equilibrium: $CO_2 + H_2O \rightleftharpoons H_2CO_3 \rightleftharpoons H^+ \rightleftharpoons + HCO_3^-$. As CO_2 levels increase, pH falls, and ventilation rate increases (the reverse is also true).

- The skin is made of three main layers: the epidermis (epithelial tissue), the dermis (connective tissue), and the hypodermis (adipose tissue).

- The epidermis provides a barrier to infection and water loss.

- The dermis is where sweat glands, nerves, blood vessels, and sensory receptors are found.

- The hypodermis is a layer of fat for protection and insulation.

- Thermoregulation is primarily a function of the dermis. When temperatures rise, blood vessels in the dermis dilate to release heat, and sweat glands are activated. When temperature falls, blood vessels constrict to retain heat. Also, involuntary skeletal muscle contractions occur (shivering) to produce heat.

CHAPTER 11 FREESTANDING PRACTICE QUESTIONS

1. Patients injected with agents that paralyze muscles during surgeries must be artificially ventilated until they recover. These drugs interfere with which neurotransmitter?

    A) Acetylcholine
    B) Norepinephrine
    C) Dopamine
    D) GABA

2. A patient presents to the emergency room in diabetic ketoacidosis (DKA), a life-threatening complication of diabetes, which results in metabolic acidosis, as well as very high serum glucose levels. Which of the following vital signs would be expected in this patient, as compared to baseline?

    A) Increased blood pressure
    B) Increased respiratory rate
    C) Decreased heart rate
    D) Decreased respiratory rate

3. Patients can often alleviate symptoms of an asthma attack by using drugs called *sympathomimetics* that mimic the effects of norepinephrine. Based on this information, which is the most likely explanation for why patients with asthma have difficulty breathing?

    A) Constriction of bronchial smooth muscle leads to diminished air flow.
    B) Dilation of bronchial smooth muscle leads to diminished air flow.
    C) Constriction of smooth muscle surrounding blood vessels leads to decreased blood flow to the lungs.
    D) Interference with skeletal muscle neurons leads to decreased force of contraction of the diaphragm.

4. A middle-aged man is in a coma after a motor vehicle accident. His respiratory rate has significantly decreased due to trauma to the medulla. All of the following are true EXCEPT:

    A) there will be a decrease in the $[H^+]$ of his blood.
    B) normal regulation of ventilation rate has been disrupted.
    C) there will be an increase in P_{CO_2} of his blood.
    D) there will be a decrease in P_{O_2} of his blood.

5. All of the following are functions of the respiratory system EXCEPT:

A) regulation of pH.
B) protection from particulate matter.
C) removal of nitrogenous waste.
D) regulation of body temperature.

6. Which of the following homeostatic responses maximizes the dissipation of excess heat through the skin?

A) Increased release and evaporation of sudoriferous gland secretions and constriction of dermal blood vessels
B) Increased release and evaporation of sudoriferous gland secretions and dilation of dermal blood vessels
C) Decreased release and evaporation of sudoriferous gland secretions and constriction of dermal blood vessels
D) Decreased release and evaporation of sudoriferous gland secretions and dilation of dermal blood vessels

7. A cancer of the skin is more likely to involve which population of cells?

A) Cells in the outer (most superficial) layer of the epidermis that have uncontrolled mitosis
B) Cells in the outer (most superficial) layer of the epidermis that have uncontrolled meiosis
C) Cells in the deepest layer of the epidermis that have uncontrolled mitosis
D) Cells in the deepest layer of the epidermis that have uncontrolled meiosis

CHAPTER 11 PRACTICE PASSAGE

Occupational and environmental lung diseases are estimated to affect more than 20 million individuals in the United States alone. These disease are generally caused by inhalation of toxic dusts and fumes and include silicosis, asbestosis, coal worker's pneumoconiosis (black lung disease), and berryliosis, as well as several diseases caused by the inhalation of dust and spores associated with agricultural businesses. Exposure to mineral dusts often leads to restrictive lung diseases (where the total lung capacity is reduced), while exposure to chemical agents leads to occupational asthma and other obstructive diseases (where air flow through the bronchial tubes is restricted).

Coal worker's pneumoconiosis (CWP) is a restrictive lung disease caused by long-term exposure to and inhalation of coal dust. Once inhaled, coal dust cannot be destroyed or removed, and consequently is simply engulfed by resident alveolar macrophages. These macrophages tend to aggregate and can be visualized microscopically as granular black areas that give the disease its common name. The aggregations lead to inflammation, damage to the lung tissue, fibrosis, and the formation of nodules throughout the lungs.

CWP is generally divided into simple and complicated classes. Simple CWP can develop early on from chronic exposure to coal dust; chest x-ray reveals nodules between 5 mm and 1 cm in diameter. Symptoms are similar to those experienced with cigarette smoking (cough, excess mucus, etc.). Upon continued, long-term exposure to coal dust (>10-15 years), simple CWP can progress to complicated CWP, which is characterized by lung nodules anywhere from 1 cm in diameter to the size of an entire lung lobe, significant reduction in lung volume and gas diffusion capacity, and premature mortality. Alveolar hypoxia can lead to pulmonary vasoconstriction; thus, complicated CWP can also be associated with right-side heart failure (*cor pulmonare*).

Lung function can be assessed by measurement of flow volumes during inspiration and expiration. Obstructive diseases tend to have increased total lung capacity and residual volume along with reduced flow. Restrictive diseases caused by damage to lung tissue tend to have reduced lung capacity and residual volumes, but normal flow. Restrictive diseases caused by damage to the inspiratory muscles or chest wall have reduced lung capacity, increased residual volume, and reduced flow. Figure 1 shows the expiratory flow-volume curves for four different patients.

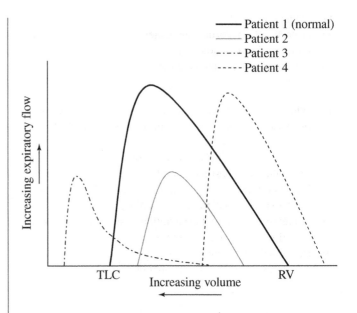

Figure 1 Expiratory flow-volume curves. Total lung capacity (TLC) and residual volume (RV) are indicated on the normal curve.

1. Agonistic drugs increase a particular response while antagonistic drugs reduce a response. Which of the following drugs would be the best choice to treat occupational asthma?

A) Parasympathetic agonist
B) Parasympathetic antagonist
C) Sympathetic agonist
D) Sympathetic antagonist

2. The FEV_1 is a measurement of the total amount of air that can be forcibly expired in 1 second after a complete inhalation. In which of the following conditions would a reduced FEV_1 be expected?

   I. CWP
   II. Occupational asthma
   III. Chronic obstructive pulmonary disease (COPD)

A) I only
B) II only
C) II and III only
D) I, II, and III

3. Which of the following would be NOT associated with complicated CWP?

A) Lung nodules 2–3 cm in diameter
B) Decreased pressure in the pulmonary vasculature
C) Right ventricular hypertrophy
D) Granular blackened areas in the lungs

4. In which of the following vessels would hemoglobin be the LEAST saturated with oxygen?

A) Aorta
B) Pulmonary veins
C) Coronary arteries
D) Pulmonary arteries

5. Botulism is a type of food poisoning in which a toxin released by the bacteria *Clostridium botulinum* inhibits the release of acetylcholine from motor neurons. In severe cases, this can lead to paralysis of the diaphragm. Which of the following would be expected in an individual suffering from severe botulism?

A) Decreased total lung capacity, decreased residual volume, and normal flow
B) Decreased total lung capacity, increased residual volume, and decreased flow
C) Increased total lung capacity, decreased residual volume, and normal flow
D) Increased total lung capacity, increased residual volume, and decreased flow

6. Which of the following statements about the respiratory system is true?

A) The ratio of cartilage to smooth muscle decreases as the bronchial tubes branch smaller and smaller.
B) The respiratory zone participates in gas exchange only, while the conduction zone participates in both ventilation and gas exchange.
C) Contraction of the diaphragm is mediated entirely by the autonomic nervous system.
D) An increase in carbon dioxide leads to an accumulation of carbonic acid, a decrease in blood pH, and a decrease in ventilation rate.

7. Which of the patients in Figure 1 is most likely suffering from CWP?

A) Patient 1
B) Patient 2
C) Patient 3
D) Patient 4

SOLUTIONS TO CHAPTER 11 FREESTANDING PRACTICE QUESTIONS

1. **A** The diaphragm is the primary ventilatory muscle; it is a skeletal muscle, and acetylcholine is the neurotransmitter that mediates nerve transmission to skeletal muscle (choice A is correct). Norepinephrine is the neurotransmitter used at postsynaptic synapses in the sympathetic nervous system; although interference with this neurotransmitter could affect the smooth muscle surrounding the bronchi, it would not affect the diaphragm and ventilation (choice B is incorrect). Dopamine and GABA are neurotransmitters that are only found in the central nervous system; paralysis in these patients is produced at the level of the muscle itself, not the central nervous system (choices C and D are incorrect).

2. **B** The metabolic acidosis (decreased blood pH) would lead to hyperventilation (increased respiratory rate) in an attempt to compensate for the low pH by reducing the amount of CO_2 (thus raising the pH; choice B is correct and choice D is wrong). It is important to remember the equation: $CO_2 + H_2O \rightleftharpoons H_2CO_3 \rightleftharpoons H^+ + HCO_3^-$. This is enough to answer the question; however, it is also true that patients in DKA have very high levels of serum glucose, which overwhelm the glucose reabsorption mechanisms of the kidney, leading to glucose in the urine. This glucose has an osmotic pressure effect and leads to severe water loss in the urine (diuresis). This in turn leads to potentially severe dehydration, which would ultimately result in lower blood pressure (choice A is incorrect), and elevated heart rates (choice C is incorrect).

3. **A** In asthma, constriction of bronchial smooth muscle decreases the diameter of the bronchi, leading to diminished air flow. Sympathomimetics stimulate the adrenergic receptors on smooth muscle, causing the muscle to dilate and improving air flow through the bronchi (choice A is correct). Dilation of bronchial smooth muscle would improve air flow, rather than diminish it, as flow is proportional to diameter (choice B is incorrect). Norepinephrine causes constriction of smooth muscle around blood vessels, not dilation, which would lead to less blood flow to the lungs. In any case, asthma is primarily a problem of ventilation (moving air in and out), not perfusion (the flow of blood to the lungs; choice C is incorrect). Acetylcholine, not norepinephrine, is the neurotransmitter that mediates contraction of skeletal muscle (choice D is incorrect).

4. **A** The centers that regulate respiratory rate are found in the medulla. Since the question text states his respiratory rate has significantly decreased due to trauma in this region, the normal feedback mechanisms (such as pH and P) will not be effective in restoring normal ventilatory patterns (choice B is true and can be eliminated). The reduced rate of respiration will lead to an accumulation of CO_2 and a drop in O_2 in his blood (choices C and D are true and can be eliminated). The excess CO_2 will shift the equilibrium of $CO_2 + H_2O \rightleftharpoons H_2CO_3 \rightleftharpoons H^+ + HCO_3^-$ to the right, leading to an increase in $[H^+]$ and a drop in pH (choice A is false and is the correct answer choice).

5.   C   The respiratory system participates in pH regulation via changes in the ventilation rate. An increase in ventilation (hyperventilation) will lead to rapid removal of CO_2 and, due to the carbonic anhydrase buffer system, an increase in the pH ($CO_2 + H_2O \rightleftharpoons H_2CO_3 \rightleftharpoons H^+ + HCO_3^-$). A decrease in ventilation (hypoventilation) will lead to a decrease in pH (choice A is a function of the respiratory system and can be eliminated). The mucociliary escalator protects the body from particulate matter by either swallowing or coughing out the mucus-coated particle (choice B is a function of the respiratory system and can be eliminated). Hyperventilation also leads to heat loss; in order to dissipate excess heat, dogs depend on panting (choice D is a function of the respiratory system and can be eliminated). However, the respiratory system is not involved in the removal of nitrogenous waste; that is, a function of the renal excretory system (choice C is not a function of the respiratory system and is the correct answer choice).

6.   B   Sudoriferous (sweat) glands are exocrine glands found within the skin that secrete water and electrolytes. As water evaporates from the skin surface, heat is dissipated. Thus, the hotter you are, the more you sweat (choices C and D are wrong). Dilating dermal blood vessels will increase blood flow to the skin and increase conductive heat loss (choice B is the correct and choice A is wrong).

7.   C   Meiosis only occurs in sperm and ova (choices B and D are wrong). Stem cells (basal cells) located in the deepest layer of the epidermis undergo mitosis throughout an individual's life. With each mitotic event, daughter cells arise, move outward (superficially), and differentiate as they do so; eventually, they die and are sloughed off. The daughter cells that differentiate lose their ability to divide, thus it is more likely that the stem cells (which retain their ability to divide) could develop into a cancer (choice C is a better answer than choice A).

SOLUTIONS TO CHAPTER 11 PRACTICE PASSAGE

1.   C   The passage states that occupational asthma is characterized by restricted air flow through bronchial tubes. Activation of the sympathetic nervous system leads to dilation of these tubes, thus a sympathetic agonist would be the best choice in this case (choice C is correct and choice D is wrong). Activation of the parasympathetic system would worsen the air flow, since it leads to bronchial constriction (choice A is wrong). While a parasympathetic antagonist might help, a sympathetic agonist would have a faster and stronger response (choice C is better than choice B).

2.   C   Reduced FE_{V1} measurements are typically seen in conditions where air flow is reduced. Item I is false: Coal worker's pneumoconiosis is described in the passages as a restrictive disease caused by lung-tissue damage, thus total lung capacity would be reduced but flow would be normal (choices A and D can be eliminated). Since both remaining answer choices include Item II, Item II must be true and you can focus on Item III. Item III is true: The passages states that obstructive diseases are characterized by reduced air flow (choice B can be eliminated and choice C is correct). Note that Item II is in fact true: Occupational asthma is classified in the passage as an obstructive disease. FYI, in Figure 1, the curve for Patient 3 is what would be expected for an obstructive disease; the drop to residual volume is gradual, indicating a reduced flow rate.

3. **B**   The passage states that "alveolar hypoxia can lead to pulmonary vasoconstriction," which would increase pulmonary pressures, not decrease them (choice B would not be associated with complicated CWP and is the correct answer choice). The increased pulmonary pressure could lead to a hypertrophy (increase in size) of the right ventricle, in order to generate a stronger force with which to move the blood against the higher pressure (choice C could be associated and can be eliminated). Complicated CWP is associated with lung nodules greater than 1 cm in diameter (choice A can be eliminated) and both simple and complicated CWP would have granular blackened areas in the lungs (choice D can be eliminated).

4. **D**   This is a free-standing question. Hemoglobin is the oxygen-carrying protein found in red blood cells. It is most saturated in areas where oxygen content is high (such as the lungs) and least saturated in areas where oxygen content is low. Pulmonary arteries carry blood from the heart toward the lungs, thus they contain blood with low oxygen levels, and the hemoglobin in these vessels would be the least saturated (choice D is correct). The other vessels all carry oxygen-rich blood, and the hemoglobin would be more saturated with oxygen. The aorta carries blood from the heart to the rest of the body (choice A is wrong), the pulmonary veins carry blood from the lungs to the left chambers of the heart (choice B is wrong), and the coronary arteries are the first branches off the aorta; they deliver oxygen-rich blood directly to the heart muscle (choice C is wrong).

5. **B**   This is a two-by-two question, in which two decisions determine the correct answer choice. The passage states that damage to the inspiratory muscles (of which the diaphragm is the primary muscle) can lead to restrictive lung disease characterized by reduced total lung capacity (choices C and D can be eliminated), increased residual volume (choice A can be eliminated), and decreased flow.

6. **A**   Most of the cartilage is found near the top of the bronchial tree. After the tertiary bronchial tubes, the cartilage disappears altogether and the tubes are formed out of smooth muscle (choice A is true and the correct answer choice). The conduction zone only participates in ventilation, not gas exchange (choice B is false and can be eliminated). The diaphragm is skeletal muscle and its contraction is predominantly mediated by somatic neurons (and is under voluntary control; choice C is false and can be eliminated). It is true that increased CO_2 would lead to an accumulation of carbonic acid and a decrease in blood pH, but that would cause an increase in ventilation rate in order to remove the excess CO_2 (choice D is false and can be eliminated).

7. **D**   Patient 1 is listed on the figure legend as "normal," so choice A can be eliminated first. CWP is a restrictive lung disease caused by damage to the lung tissue, due to chronic inhalation of coal dust. As described in the final paragraph, a patient suffering from this disease would have a reduced total lung capacity (choice C, Patient 3, has an increased total lung capacity and can be eliminated), and a reduced residual volume (choice B, Patient 2, has an increased residual volume and can be eliminated).

Chapter 12
The Reproductive Systems

12.1 THE MALE REPRODUCTIVE SYSTEM

Anatomy

The principal male reproductive structures that are visible on the outside of the body are the scrotum and the penis. The scrotum is essentially a bag of skin containing the male gonads, which are known as **testes** (testicles). [Does the scrotum have any active role, or is it merely a container?[1]] The testes have two roles: 1) synthesis of sperm (**spermatogenesis**), and 2) secretion of male sex hormones (**androgens**, e.g., testosterone) into the bloodstream. More detail on these topics is given later. Here we will trace the path of a sperm from its origination to its final destination.

The sites of spermatogenesis within the testes are the **seminiferous tubules**. The walls of the seminiferous tubules are formed by cells called **sustenacular cells** (also known as *Sertoli cells*). Sustenacular cells protect and nurture the developing sperm, both physically and chemically; their role will be discussed in more detail below. The tissue between the seminiferous tubules is simply referred to as testicular interstitium.[2] Important cells found in the testicular interstitium are the **interstitial cells** (also known as Leydig cells). They are responsible for androgen (testosterone) synthesis.

The seminiferous tubules empty into the **epididymis**, a long coiled tube located on the posterior (back) of each testicle (Figure 1). The epididymis from each testicle empties into a **ductus deferens** (also call the *vas deferens*), which in turn leads to the **urethra** (the tube inside the penis). To get to the urethra, the ductus deferens leaves the scrotum and follows a peculiar path: It enters the **inguinal canal**, a tunnel that travels along the body wall toward the crest of the hip bone. (There are two inguinal canals, left and right.) From the inguinal canal, the ductus deferens enters the pelvic cavity. Near the back of the urinary bladder, it joins the duct of the seminal vesicle (discussed below) to form the **ejaculatory duct**. The ejaculatory ducts from both sides of the body then join the urethra.

A pair of glands known as **seminal vesicles** is located on the posterior surface of the bladder. They secrete about 60 percent of the total volume of the **semen** into the ejaculatory duct. Semen is a highly nourishing fluid for sperm and is produced by three separate glands: the seminal vesicles, the **prostate**, and the **bulbourethral glands**. These are collectively referred to as the **accessory glands** (see Table 1). The ejaculatory duct empties into the **urethra** as it passes through the prostate gland. One final set of glands, the bulbourethral glands, contributes to the semen near the beginning of the urethra.

---

[1] The scrotum is important for temperature regulation. Sperm synthesis in the testes must occur at a few degrees below normal body temperature. This is why the testes are located outside the body. Relaxation of the scrotum facilitates cooling of the testes. When the environment is cold, the scrotum contracts, pulling the testes up against the body, warming them.

[2] *Interstitium* is a term used to describe a thing or a region which is "between" other structures.

Gland and secretions	Function of secretions	% of total ejaculate volume
Seminal vesicles—mostly fructose	Nourishment of sperm	60%
Prostate gland—fructose and a coagulant	Nourishment, allows semen to coagulate after ejaculation	35%
Bulbourethral glands—thick, alkaline mucus	Lubricate urethra, neutralize acids in male urethra and in female vagina	3%
Testes—sperm	Male gamete	2%

Table 1   The Accessory Glands

The urethra exits the body via the penis. Penile erection facilitates deposition of semen near the opening of the uterus during intercourse. Specialized **erectile tissue** in the penis allows erection. It is composed of modified veins and capillaries surrounded by a connective tissue sheath. Erection occurs when blood accumulates at high pressure in the erectile tissue. Three compartments contain erectile tissue: the **corpora cavernosa** (there are two of these) and the **corpus spongiosum** (only one).

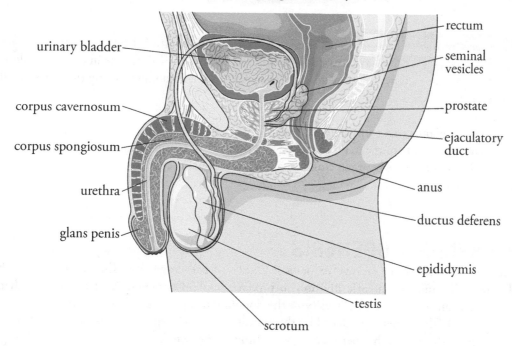

Figure 1   The Male Reproductive System

The Male Sexual Act

The three stages of the male sexual act are: arousal, orgasm, and resolution. These events are controlled by an integrating center in the spinal cord, which responds to physical stimulation and input from the brain. The cerebral cortex can activate this integrating center (as in sexual arousal during sleep) or inhibit it (anxiety interferes with sexual function).

Arousal is dependent upon parasympathetic nervous input and can be subdivided into two stages: erection and lubrication. **Erection** involves dilation of arteries supplying the erectile tissue. This causes swelling, which in turn obstructs venous outflow. This causes the erectile tissue to become pressurized with blood. **Lubrication** is also a function of the parasympathetic system. The bulbourethral glands secrete a viscous mucous which serves as a lubricant.

Stimulation by the sympathetic nervous system is required for **orgasm**, which can also be divided into two stages: emission and ejaculation. **Emission** refers to the propulsion of sperm (from the ductus deferens) and semen (from the accessory glands) into the urethra by contractions of the smooth muscle surrounding these organs. Emission is followed by **ejaculation**, in which semen is propelled out of the urethra by rhythmic contractions of muscles surrounding the base of the penis. Ejaculation is actually a reflex reaction caused by the presence of semen in the urethra. Emission and ejaculation together constitute the male orgasm.

Resolution, or a return to a normal, unstimulated state, is also controlled by the sympathetic nervous system. It is caused primarily by a constriction of the erectile arteries. This results in decreased blood flow to the erectile tissue and allows the veins to carry away the trapped blood, returning the penis to a flaccid state. This typically takes 2–3 minutes.

- Name four glands that contribute to semen.[3]
- Which components of the male sexual act can occur if all sympathetic activity is blocked?[4]
- What is the difference between emission and ejaculation?[5]

12.2 SPERMATOGENESIS

What processes in a human being involve meiosis? Only one: **gametogenesis**. This is the process whereby **diploid germ cells** undergo **meiotic division** to produce **haploid gametes**. As discussed in Chapter 6, meiotic cell division fosters genetic diversity in the population (by independent assortment of genes and by recombination). The gametes produced by the male are known as **spermatozoa**, or *sperm*; females produce **ova**, or *eggs*. The role of the sperm is to swim through the female genital tract to reach the egg and fuse with it. This fusion is known as **syngamy**, and it results in a **zygote**. The gametes produced by males and females differ dramatically in structure but contribute equally to the genome of the zygote (except in the special case of the two different sex chromosomes, X and Y, given to male offspring). Although both gametes contribute equally to the genome, the egg provides *every other part of the zygote*, since the only

[3] Seminal vesicles, prostate, testes, and bulbourethral glands

[4] Erection and lubrication (arousal only)

[5] Emission is the movement of sperm and semen components into the urethra; ejaculation is the movement of semen from the urethra out of the body.

part of the sperm which enters the egg is a haploid genome. The term for this is **maternal inheritance**. For instance, mitochondria are inherited maternally.

Sperm synthesis is called **spermatogenesis** (Figure 2). It begins at puberty and occurs in the testes throughout adult life. [Do females also make gametes throughout adult life?[6]] The seminiferous tubule is the site of spermatogenesis. The entire process of spermatogenesis occurs with the aid of the specialized sustenacular cells found in the wall of the seminiferous tubule. Immature sperm precursors are found in the outer wall of the tubule, and nearly-mature spermatozoa are deposited into the lumen; from there they are transported to the epididymis. The cells that give rise to spermatogonia (and to their female counterparts, oogonia) are known as **germ cells**; under the right conditions, they germinate, and give rise to a complete organism.

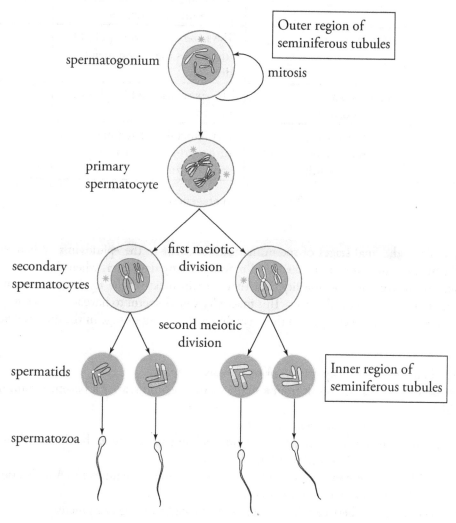

spermatogonium

Outer region of seminiferous tubules

mitosis

primary spermatocyte

first meiotic division

secondary spermatocytes

second meiotic division

spermatids

Inner region of seminiferous tubules

spermatozoa

Figure 2 Spermatogenesis

---

[6] No. This is discussed below.

Table 2 below gives the names of the sperm precursors, along with the meiotic role of each stage, and some mnemonic comments. Fill in the female version when you read that section.

Stage	Jobs	Mnemonic	Female version
spermatogonium	1. Mitotically reproduce prior to meiosis 2. Replicate DNA in S phase of meiosis	The spermatoGONium is GONNA become a sperm.	
primary spermatocyte	Meiosis I	Any gamete precursor (male or female) with "cyte" undergoes a meiotic division.	
secondary spermatocyte	Meiosis II	The *secondary* spermatoCYTE undergoes the *second* meiotic division.	
spermatid	Turn into a spermatozoan	The spermatid's a kid, almost mature	
spermatozoan	Finish maturing: 1. in seminiferous tubule, 2. in epididymis.	Just remember that a mature sperm is called a spermatozoan.	

Table 2 Gametogenesis

As noted in Table 2, the final stages of sperm maturation occur in the epididymis. When they first enter the epididymis, spermatozoa are incapable of motility. Many days later, when they reach the ductus deferens, they are fully capable of motility. But they remain inactive due to the presence of inhibitory substances secreted by the ductus deferens. This inactivity causes sperm to have a very low metabolic rate, which allows them to conserve energy and thus remain fertile during storage in the ductus deferens for as long as a month.

- Do spermatogonia divide by mitosis or by meiosis?[7]
- How many mature sperm result from a single spermatogonium after it becomes committed to meiosis?[8]
- Which of the following statements is/are true?[9]
  - I.   During gametogenesis, sister chromatids remain paired with each other until anaphase of the second meiotic cell division.
  - II. A difference between mitosis and meiosis is that mitosis requires DNA replication prior to cell division but meiosis does not.
  - III. Recombination between sister chromatids during gametogenesis increases the genetic diversity of offspring.

---

[7]   Mitosis. Spermatogonia undergo the meiotic S phase (replicate the genome), but the stages which undergo the actual meiotic *divisions* are called spermatocytes. All gamete precursors with "cyte" in their name undergo a meiotic division.

[8]   Four haploid cells result from the reductive division (meiosis) of one diploid spermatogonium. Compare this to oogenesis.

[9]   **Item I: True.** Meiosis I involves the pairing, recombination, and separation of homologous chromosomes. Meiosis II is like mitosis, where sister chromatids separate. Item II: False. Both require DNA replication in a preceding S phase. Item III: False. Sister chromatids don't recombine, homologous chromosomes do. (Even if sister chromatids did recombine, it would make no difference since they are identical.)

Spermatids develop into spermatozoa in the seminiferous tubules with the aid of sustenacular cells. The DNA condenses, the cytoplasm shrinks, and the cell shape changes so that there is a **head**, containing the haploid nucleus and the acrosome, and a flagellum which forms the **tail**. There is also a **neck** region at the base of the tail, which contains many mitochondria. [Where do these mitochondria get their energy?[10]] The **acrosome** is a compartment on the head of the sperm that contains hydrolytic enzymes required for penetration of the ovum's protective layers. **Bindin** is a protein on the sperm's surface that attaches to receptors on the zona pellucida surrounding the ovum (discussed below).

- Concerning spermatogenesis, which of the following is/are true?[11]
  - I. Spermatocytes possess a flagellum.
  - II. Flagellar movement of sperm involves rotation of a basal structure embedded in the sperm membrane.
  - III. Spermatids possess a haploid genome.

Hormonal Control of Spermatogenesis

Testosterone plays the essential role of stimulating division of spermatogonia. **Luteinizing hormone (LH)** stimulates the interstitial cells to secrete testosterone. **Follicle stimulating hormone (FSH)** stimulates the sustenacular cells. The hormone **inhibin** is secreted by sustenacular cells; its role is to inhibit FSH release. [From where, and why?[12]]

- Which of the following is/are true?[13]
  - I. Luteinizing hormone reaches its target tissue through the hypothalamic-hypophysial portal system.
  - II. The absence of luteinizing hormone does not affect spermatogenesis.
  - III. Increased testosterone levels in the blood decrease the production of follicle stimulating hormone.

---

[10] From the fructose which the seminal vesicles contribute to the semen and from vaginal secretions.

[11] Item I: False. The flagellum does not begin to form until the spermatid stage. Item II: False. This describes prokaryotic flagella. **Item III: True.** Meiosis is complete by the spermatid stage. Remember, the spermatid's a kid. It's just like a sperm, only immature.

[12] FSH and LH are gonadotropins secreted by the anterior pituitary. The reason this occurs is to provide negative feedback.

[13] Item I: False. LH is secreted by the anterior pituitary and reaches its targets via the systemic circulation. GnRH reaches its target via the portal system. Item II: False. LH is necessary because it stimulates the interstitial cells to secrete testosterone, which is necessary for germ cell stimulation. **Item III: True.** Testosterone, estrogen, progesterone, and inhibin are all hormones which exert feedback inhibition upon the anterior pituitary and hypothalamus.

12.3 DEVELOPMENT OF THE MALE REPRODUCTIVE SYSTEM

The gender of a developing embryo is determined by its sex chromosomes, either XX in females or XY in males. During the early weeks of development, however, male and female embryos are indistinguishable. Early embryos, whether male or female, have undifferentiated gonads, and possess both **Wolffian ducts** that can develop into male internal genitalia (epididymis, seminal vesicles, and ductus deferens) and **Müllerian ducts** that can develop into female internal genitalia (uterine tubes, uterus and vagina). In the absence of a Y chromosome, Müllerian duct development occurs by default, and female internal genitalia result. Female *external* genitalia (labia, clitoris) are also the default; note that the external genitalia are not derived from the Müllerian ducts. Genetic information on the Y chromosome of XY embryos leads to the development of testes, which cause male internal and external genitalia to develop by producing testosterone and **Müllerian inhibiting factor** (MIF).

MIF is produced by the testes and causes regression of the Müllerian ducts; this prevents the development of female internal genitalia. Testosterone secretion by cells which will later give rise to the testes begins around week 7 of gestation. By week 9, testes are formed, and their interstitial cells supply testosterone. The testosterone that is responsible for the development of male external genitalia enters the systemic circulation and must be converted to **dihydrotestosterone** in target tissues in order to exert its effect (Figure 3).

- If an XY genotype embryo fails to secrete testosterone, will it have testes or ovaries?[14]

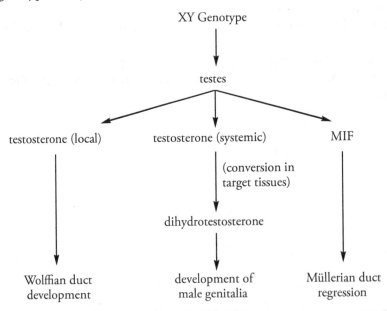

Figure 3   Control of Development of the Male Reproductive System

---

[14] Testosterone is *produced by* the embryonic testes. Their development does not depend on testosterone. Hence, an XY embryo which didn't secrete testosterone would most likely have testes nonetheless.

- Which one of the following would best characterize an embryo with an XY genotype that lacks the receptor for testosterone?[15]
  - A. Testes, ductus deferens, and seminal vesicles are present; external genitalia are female.
  - B. Ovaries, uterine tubes, and uterus are present; external genitalia are female.
  - C   Testes are present; external genitalia are female; neither Müllerian nor Wolffian ducts develop.
  - D. Testes and male external genitalia are present.

The development of the male and female reproductive systems is closely related. As described above, the three main fetal precursors of the reproductive organs are the Wolffian ducts, the Müllerian ducts, and the gonads. While the Wolffian ducts are the precursors of internal male genitalia, they essentially disappear in the female reproductive system. For the Müllerian ducts, this process is reversed; they essentially disappear in the male reproductive system and form the internal genitalia of the female system. Structures arising from these ducts tend to have the same function (e.g., ductus deferens in males and the uterine tubes in females both carry gametes), but because they arise from different precursors, they are considered to be **analogous structures**.

In both sexes, the gonads go on to form either the testes or the ovaries; because they are derived from the same undeveloped structure, testes and ovaries are considered homologous organs. There are a number of other homologous structures in males and females due to their common origins within the fetus (see Table 3).

Male Organ	Female Organ	Function
Testis	Ovary	Gamete and hormone reproduction
Penis	Clitoris	Erectile tissue, sensation
Bulbourethral glands	Greater vestibular glands	Lubrication
Scrotum	Labia majora	External skin folds

Table 3 Homologous Reproductive Structures

12.4   ANDROGENS AND ESTROGENS

All hormones involved in the development and maintenance of male characteristics are termed **androgens**, while those involved in development and maintenance of female characteristics are termed **estrogens**. The primary androgen produced in the testes is testosterone. It is converted into dihydrotestosterone within the cells of target tissues. The primary estrogen produced in the ovaries is estradiol.

Testosterone is required in the testes for spermatogenesis (Section 12.2). The role of testosterone in the embryonic development of the male internal and external genitalia has already been discussed. After birth the level of testosterone falls to negligible levels until puberty, at which time it increases and remains high for the remainder of adult life. Elevated levels of testosterone are responsible for the development

---

[15] The XY genotype would lead to the development of testes (choice B is wrong), and the testes would produce MIF and testosterone. MIF would cause the degeneration of the Müllerian ducts, and no female internal genitalia would develop. However, the inability to respond to testosterone (because of the missing receptor) would prevent the development of the Wolffian ducts (choice A is wrong) as well as the male external genitalia (choice D is wrong). The external genitalia would default to female (choice C is correct).

and maintenance of male **secondary sexual characteristics** (maturation of the genitalia, male distribution of facial and body hair, deepening of the voice, and increased muscle mass). The pubertal growth spurt and fusion of the epiphyses (see Chapter 10) also result.

The role of estrogen in the female is analogous to the role of testosterone in the male. Beginning at puberty, estrogen is required to regulate the uterine cycle and for the development and maintenance of female secondary sexual characteristics (maturation of the genitalia, breast development, wider hips, and pubic hair). Estrogen causes the fusion of the epiphyses in females.

- Why are tumors derived from interstitial cells more easily diagnosed in boys than in grown men?[16]
- If testosterone levels are abnormally elevated during childhood, how will the height of the individual be affected?[17]
- How do androgens reach the cytoplasm to bind to cytoplasmic receptors?[18]
- How would an RNA polymerase II inhibitor alter the effects of dihydrotestosterone in target cells?[19]
- Which is the more abundant androgen in the blood: testosterone or dihydrotestosterone?[20]

During puberty and adult life, sex steroid production is controlled by the hypothalamus and the anterior pituitary. **Gonadotropin releasing hormone (GnRH)** from the hypothalamus stimulates the pituitary to release the gonadotropins: follicle-stimulating hormone (FSH) and luteinizing hormone (LH). In men, LH acts on interstitial cells to stimulate testosterone production, and FSH stimulates the sustenacular cells. In women FSH stimulates the granulosa cells to secrete estrogen, and LH simulates the formation of the corpus luteum and progesterone secretion. Feedback inhibition by the steroids inhibits the production of GnRH and LH and FSH. Inhibin, produced by sustenacular cells and the granulosa cells, provides further feedback regulation of FSH production (Figure 4).

---

[16] Interstitial cells secrete testosterone. Levels of testosterone are normally very low in boys. An abnormal increase will lead to puberty at an abnormally young age ("precocious puberty"). The results would be less obvious in an adult male.

[17] The child will undergo precocious puberty, involving an early growth spurt, so the child will be unusually tall. But then early fusion of the epiphyses will result in a shorter adult height than expected.

[18] These highly hydrophobic molecules can diffuse through the cell membrane and bind to cytoplasmic receptors.

[19] Once its ligand is bound, the steroid receptor activates transcription of specific mRNA. Messenger RNA is transcribed by RNA pol II. Hence, we would expect inhibition of pol II to prevent the effects of all steroid hormones.

[20] The concentration of testosterone is higher. Dihydrotestosterone is produced from testosterone inside target cells. It is present in the blood in much lower concentrations than testosterone.

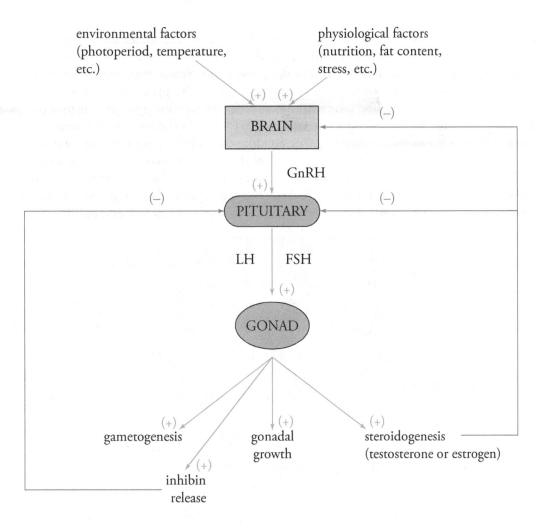

Figure 4   Regulation of Sex Steroid Production

12.5   FEMALE REPRODUCTIVE SYSTEM

Anatomy and Development

We mentioned in Section 12.3 that male and female genitalia are derived from a common undifferentiated precursor. Because of this, the structures of the female external genitalia are homologous to those of the male. In the female, the XX genotype leads to the formation of ovaries capable of secreting the female sex hormones (estrogens) instead of testes that secrete androgens. In the male, testosterone causes a pair of skin folds known as **labioscrotal swellings** to grow and fuse, forming the scrotum. In the female, without the influence of testosterone, the labioscrotal swellings form the **labia majora** of the vagina (labia = lips, majora = larger). The structure that gave rise to the penis in the male embryo becomes the **clitoris** in the female, located within the labia majora in the uppermost part of the vulva. Just beneath the clitoris is the **urethral opening**, where urine exits the body. Surrounding the urethral opening is another pair of skin folds called the **labia minora**.

The opening of the **vagina** is also found between the labia minora. The female internal genitalia (vagina, uterine tubes, uterus) are derived from the Müllerian ducts, so there are no homologous structures in the male. The vagina is a tube which would end in the pelvic cavity, except that another hollow organ, the **uterus**, opens into its upper portion. The part of the uterus which opens into the vagina is called the **cervix** ("neck," as in "cervical"). The innermost lining of the uterus (closest to the lumen) is the **endometrium**. It is responsible for nourishing a developing embryo, and in the absence of pregnancy it is shed each month, producing menstrual bleeding. Surrounding the endometrium is the **myometrium**, which is a thick layer of smooth muscle comprising the wall of the uterus. The uterus ends in two **uterine tubes** (also called *fallopian tubes*), which extend into the pelvis on either side. Each uterine tube ends in a bunch of finger-like structures called **fimbriae**. The fimbriae brush up against the **ovary**, which is the female gonad. [At the time of ovulation, where does the oocyte come from and where does it go?[21]]

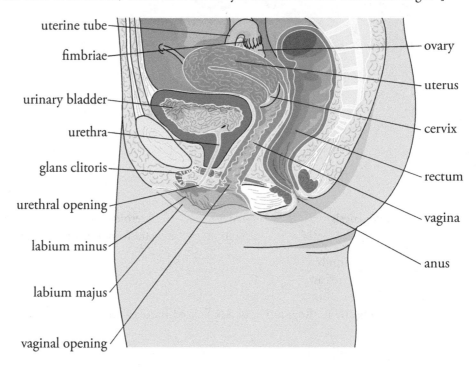

Figure 5 The Female Reproductive System

- What is the fate of the Wolffian ducts and their derivatives in the female?[22]
- Is estrogen production by the ovaries required for the development of the uterine tubes and uterus?[23]

---

[21] It emerges from the ovary (sometimes causing pain in the middle of the menstrual cycle) and must be swept into the uterine tube by a constant flow of fluid into the uterine tube caused by cilia.

[22] In the absence of testosterone, they atrophy.

[23] No, the Müllerian ducts develop into vagina, uterus, and uterine tubes by default as long as MIF is absent.

12.5

The Female Sexual Act

The stages are the same as in the male: **arousal**, **orgasm**, and **resolution**. The arousal stage, as in the male, is subdivided into erection and lubrication and is controlled by the parasympathetic nervous system. The clitoris and labia minora contain erectile tissue and become engorged with blood, just as in the male. Lubrication is provided by mucus secreted by **greater vestibular glands** and by the vaginal epithelium. Orgasm in the female is controlled by the sympathetic nervous system and involves muscle contractions, just as in the male, in addition to a widening of the cervix. (These events are thought to facilitate the movement of sperm into the uterus.) The female does not experience ejaculation. Resolution is also the same as in the male, controlled by the sympathetic system, but can take up to 20–30 minutes (compared to 2–3 minutes in the male).

12.6   OOGENESIS AND OVULATION

Oogenesis begins prenatally. In the ovary of a female fetus, germ cells divide mitotically to produce large numbers of **oogonia**. [How is this different from the male scenario?[24]] Oogonia not only undergo mitosis *in utero*, but they also enter the first phase of meiosis and are arrested in prophase I (as primary oocytes). The number of oogonia peaks at about 7 million at mid-gestation (20 weeks into the fetal life). At this time mitosis ceases, conversion to primary oocytes begins, and there is a progressive loss of cells so that at birth there are only about 2 million primary oocytes. By puberty this number is further reduced to only about 400,000. Only about 400 oocytes are ever actually **ovulated** (released) in the average woman, and the remaining 99.9 percent will simply degenerate.

The primary oocytes formed in a female fetus can be frozen in prophase I of meiosis for decades, until they re-enter the meiotic cycle. Beginning at puberty and continuing on a monthly basis, hormonal changes in the woman's body stimulate completion of the first meiotic division and ovulation. This meiotic division yields a large secondary oocyte (containing all of the cytoplasm and organelles) and a small **polar body** (containing half the DNA, but no cytoplasm or organelles). The polar body (called the *first* polar body) remains in close proximity to the oocyte. The second meiotic division (i.e., completion of oogenesis) occurs *only if* the secondary oocyte is fertilized by a sperm; this division is also unequal, producing a large ovum and the second polar body. Note that if fertilization does occur, the nuclei from the sperm and egg do not fuse immediately. They must wait for the secondary oocyte to release the second polar body and finish maturing to an ootid and then an ovum. Finally, the two nuclei fuse, and a diploid (2n) zygote is formed.

- Is the secondary oocyte haploid?[25]
- When an oogonium undergoes meiosis, three cells result. How many of these are eggs, and why do only three cells result? (Meiosis results in four cells in the male.)[26]

Before we move on to a discussion of the menstrual cycle, you will need more background information on oogenesis. The primary oocyte is not an isolated cell. It is found in a clump of supporting cells called

---

[24] It only happens in *adult* males. Here, we're talking about events in the ovaries of a female while she's still in her mother's womb.

[25] Yes. After the first meiotic division, the cell is haploid; the homologous chromosomes have been separated. (They are, however, still replicated, hence the reason for meiosis II.)

[26] Only one egg results. The three cells which result are two polar bodies plus one ovum. There are only three because the first polar body does not divide. (In meiosis in the male, both cells derived from the first meiotic division go on to divide.)

granulosa cells, and the entire structure (oocyte plus granulosa cells) is known as a **follicle**. The granulosa cells assist in maturation. [What is the male counterpart of the granulosa cell?[27]] An immature primary oocyte is surrounded by a single layer of granulosa cells, forming a **primordial follicle**.

As the primordial follicle matures, the granulosa cells proliferate to form several layers around the oocyte, and the oocyte itself forms a protective layer of mucopolysaccharides termed the **zona pellucida**. There may be several follicles in the ovary; they are surrounded and separated by cells termed **thecal cells**. [What is the male counterpart of the thecal cells, and to which hormone do they respond?[28]] Of the several maturing follicles, only one progresses to the point of ovulation each month; all others degenerate. The mature follicle is known as a **Graafian follicle**. During ovulation, the Graafian follicle bursts, releasing the secondary oocyte with its zona pellucida and protective granulosa cells into the fallopian tube. At this point the layer of granulosa cells surrounding the ovum is known as the **corona radiata**. The follicular cells remaining in the ovary after ovulation form a new structure called the **corpus luteum** (Figure 6).

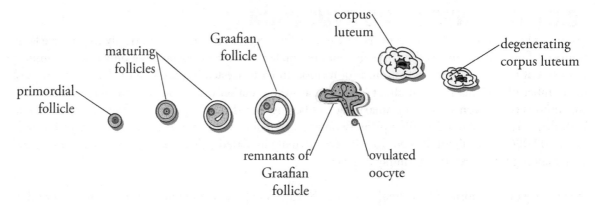

Figure 6   The Fate of a Follicle

Estrogen is made and secreted by the granulosa cells (with help from the thecal cells) during the first half of the menstrual cycle. Both estrogen and progesterone are secreted by the corpus luteum during the second half of the cycle. Estrogen is a steroid hormone that plays an important role in the development of female secondary sexual characteristics, in the menstrual cycle, and during pregnancy. [How does estrogen exert its effect on a cell?[29]] Progesterone is also a steroid hormone involved in the hormonal regulation of the menstrual cycle and pregnancy, but with different effects than estrogen.

---

[27] The cells that support and nurture developing spermatocytes are the sustenacular cells.

[28] They are analogous to the testicular interstitial cells. Both interstitial and thecal cells are stimulated by LH.

[29] A cytoplasmic receptor binds estrogen and binds to specific DNA elements in promoters and enhancers to regulate transcription.

12.7 THE MENSTRUAL CYCLE

The menstrual cycle is (on average) a 28-day cycle that includes events occurring in the ovary (discussed above and referred to as the **ovarian cycle**), as well as events occurring in the uterus (the shedding of the old endometrium and preparation of a new endometrium for potential pregnancy), referred to as the **uterine cycle**.

The Ovarian Cycle

The ovarian cycle can be subdivided into three phases (Figure 7):

1) During the **follicular phase**, a primary follicle matures and secretes estrogen. Maturation of the follicle is under the control of follicle stimulating hormone (FSH) from the anterior pituitary. The follicular phase lasts about 13 days.

2) In the **ovulatory phase**, a secondary oocyte is released from the ovary. This is triggered by a surge of luteinizing hormone (LH) from the anterior pituitary. The surge also causes the remnants of the follicle to become the corpus luteum. Ovulation typically occurs on day 14 of the cycle.

3) The **luteal phase** begins with full formation of the corpus luteum in the ovary. This structure secretes both estrogen and progesterone, and has a life span of about two weeks. The average length of the luteal phase is about 14 days.

The hormones secreted from the ovary during the ovarian cycle direct the uterine cycle.

The Uterine Cycle

The uterine cycle covers the same 28 days that were discussed above, but the focus is on the preparation of the endometrium for potential implantation of a fertilized egg. The uterine cycle can also be subdivided into three phases (Figure 7):

1) The first phase is **menstruation**, triggered by the degeneration of the corpus luteum and subsequent drop in estrogen and progesterone levels. The sharp decrease in these hormones causes the previous cycle's endometrial lining to slough out of the uterus, producing the bleeding associated with this time period. Menstruation typically lasts about 5 days.

2) During the **proliferative phase** of the menstrual cycle, estrogen produced by the follicle induces the proliferation of a new endometrium. This phase lasts about 9 days.

3) After ovulation the **secretory phase** occurs, in which estrogen and progesterone produced by the corpus luteum further increase development of the endometrium, including secretion of glycogen, lipids, and other material. If pregnancy does not occur, the death of the corpus luteum and decline in the secretion of estrogen and progesterone trigger menstruation once again. The secretory phase typically lasts about 14 days.

12.7

The menstrual cycle repeats every 28 days from puberty until menopause (at about age 50–60).

- At what stage of development is the endometrium when ovulation occurs?[30]
- Where is the secondary oocyte during the secretory phase?[31]
- If estrogen and progesterone were given to a woman without cyclic variation, how would this affect menstruation?[32]

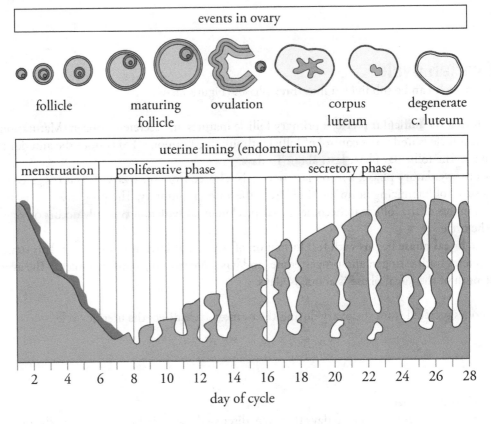

Figure 7   The Ovarian and Uterine Cycles

---

[30] The endometrium is at the proliferative phase, under the influence of ovarian estrogen.

[31] The secondary oocyte is traveling down the uterine tube toward the uterus. If it fails to implant in the uterus, the secretory phase ends and menstruation begins.

[32] Menstruation occurs because the estrogen and progesterone secreted by the corpus luteum decrease suddenly when the corpus luteum degenerates. If estrogen and progesterone are kept at high levels, such as with a pill (or pregnancy), then menstruation will not occur.

Focus on the Hormones

The anterior pituitary and the hypothalamus play a role in the menstrual cycle by regulating the secretion of estrogen and progesterone from the ovary (Figure 8). Estrogen and progesterone then regulate the events in the uterus. The following is a summary:

1) GnRH from the hypothalamus stimulates the release of FSH and LH from the anterior pituitary.

2) Under the influence of FSH, the granulosa and thecal cells develop during the follicular phase and secrete estrogen. Secretion of GnRH, FSH, and LH is initially inhibited by estrogen; however, estrogen, which increases throughout the follicular stage, reaches a threshold near the end of this phase and has a positive effect on LH secretion.

3) This sudden surge in LH causes ovulation. After ovulation, LH induces the follicle to become the corpus luteum and to secrete estrogen and progesterone (this marks the beginning of the secretory phase). If pregnancy does not occur, the combined high levels of estrogen and progesterone feedback to strongly inhibit secretion of GnRH, FSH, and LH. When LH secretion drops, the corpus luteum regresses, no longer secretes estrogen or progesterone, and menstruation occurs.

- If LH levels remained high, how would this affect the secretion of estrogen and progesterone?[33]
- What would happen if the estrogen and progesterone levels in a woman's blood were kept artificially high for the entire month?[34]
- What would happen if the artificial hormones were suddenly taken away?[35]

12.7

---

[33] If LH levels remained high, the corpus luteum would not regress, and estrogen and progesterone would also remain high, thus maintaining the endometrium so that menstruation would not occur. This is in effect what happens if an embryo is fertilized and implants, except the hormone in this case is not LH but hCG, human chorionic gonadotropin, an LH-like hormone (see the next section).

[34] The woman would not ovulate. That's what (most) birth control pills are: estrogen and progesterone.

[35] The endometrium would slough off, and the woman would menstruate. (This is why there are 21 pills of one color and 7 pills of another color. The 7 pills contain no hormones; they are either placebos or sometimes iron supplements. If a woman took the hormone pill every day and never took the 7 placebos, she would never menstruate. Also, the placebos are actually unnecessary; these 7 pills are only present in order to help establish the habit of taking a pill every day.)

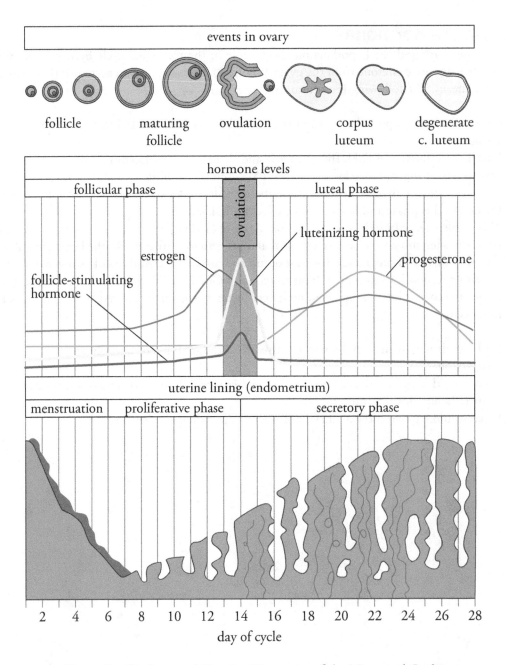

Figure 8 Pituitary and Ovarian Hormones of the Menstrual Cycle

12.8 HORMONAL CHANGES DURING PREGNANCY

There are still a couple of points we have not made completely clear: How can pregnancy occur if the uterine lining is lost each month, and why does the body discard the endometrium?

Recall that the physiological reason for endometrial shedding is a decrease in estrogen and progesterone levels, which occurs as the corpus luteum degenerates. Why does the corpus luteum degenerate? Due to a decrease in luteinizing hormone. Why does LH decrease? Due to feedback inhibition from the high levels of estrogen and progesterone secreted by the corpus luteum.

Let's begin with why LH levels decrease. During pregnancy, ovulation should be prevented. The way ovulation is prevented is for the constant high levels of estrogen and progesterone seen during pregnancy to inhibit secretion of LH by the pituitary; no LH surge, no ovulation. Constant high levels of estrogen inhibit LH release. The result is pregnancy without continued ovulation. The *secondary* result is the one we were trying to explain: When the corpus luteum secretes a lot of estrogen and progesterone during the menstrual cycle, LH levels drop, causing the corpus luteum to degenerate. The point is that the corpus luteum degenerates unless fertilization has occurred.

So how can pregnancy occur? If pregnancy is to occur, the endometrium must be maintained, because it is the site of gestation (i.e., where the embryo lives and is nourished). If fertilization takes place, within a few days a developing embryo becomes **implanted** in the endometrium, and a **placenta** begins to develop. The **chorion** is the portion of the placenta that is derived from the zygote. It secretes **human chorionic gonadotropin**, or **hCG**, which can take the place of LH in maintaining the corpus luteum. In the presence of hCG, the corpus luteum does not degenerate, the estrogen and progesterone levels stay elevated, and menstruation does not occur. This answers the question of *how* pregnancy can occur. hCG is the hormone tested for in pregnancy tests because its presence absolutely confirms the presence of an embryo.

- Which of the following occur(s) during the menstrual cycle immediately prior to ovulation?[36]
  - I. A surge in luteinizing hormone release from the anterior pituitary
  - II. Completion of the second meiotic cell division by the oocyte
  - III. Shedding of the endometrium

- As a woman ages, the number of follicles remaining in the ovaries decreases until ovulation ceases. At this point, termed **menopause**, the menstrual cycle no longer occurs. Which of the following occur(s) during menopause?[37]
  - I. FSH levels drop dramatically and stay low.
  - II. Estrogen levels are abnormally high.
  - III. LH levels are very high and stay high.

---

[36] **Item I: True.** The LH surge *causes* ovulation. Item II: False. Meiosis I is completed prior to ovulation. Meiosis II isn't completed until after fertilization. Item III: False. Ovulation occurs around day 14 of the cycle. Menstruation begins at day 1.

[37] In the absence of estrogen and progesterone secretion by follicles, there is no feedback inhibition of LH and FSH, so their levels are very high in postmenopausal women. Hence, only item III is true.

- Which of the following statements concerning the menstrual cycle is/are true?[38]
  - I. The proliferative phase of the endometrium coincides with the maturation of ovarian follicles.
  - II. The secretory phase of the endometrial cycle is dependent on the secretion of estrogen from cells surrounding secondary oocytes.
  - III. Luteinizing hormone levels are highest during the menstrual phase of the endometrial cycle.

12.9   FERTILIZATION AND CLEAVAGE

A secondary oocyte is ovulated and enters the uterine tube. It is surrounded by the **corona radiata** (a protective layer of granulosa cells) and the **zona pellucida** (located just outside the egg cell membrane). The oocyte will remain fertile for about a day. If intercourse occurs, sperm are deposited near the cervix, and are activated, or **capacitated**. Sperm capacitation involves the dilution of inhibitory substances present in semen. The activated sperm will survive for two or three days. They swim through the uterus toward the secondary oocyte.

Fertilization is the fusion of a spermatozoan with the secondary oocyte (Figure 9). It normally occurs in the uterine tube. In order for fertilization to occur, a sperm must penetrate the corona radiata and bind to and penetrate the zona pellucida. It accomplishes this using the **acrosome reaction**. The **acrosome** is a large vesicle in the sperm head containing hydrolytic enzymes which are released by exocytosis. After the corona radiata has been penetrated, an **acrosomal process** containing actin elongates toward the zona pellucida. The acrosomal process has **bindin**, a species-specific protein which binds to receptors in the zona pellucida. Finally, the sperm and egg plasma membranes fuse, and the sperm nucleus enters the secondary oocyte. In about twenty minutes, the secondary oocyte completes meiosis II, giving rise to an ootid and the second polar body. The ootid matures rapidly, becoming an **ovum**. Then the sperm and egg nuclei fuse, and the new diploid cell is known as a **zygote**.

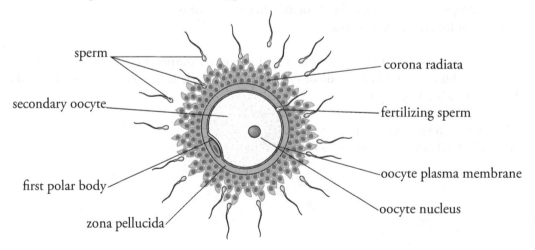

Figure 9   Fertilization

---

[38] **Item I: True.** This is explained in the text. Item II: False. It is secretion of estrogen and progesterone *by the corpus luteum* that drives the secretory phase. The corpus luteum is in the ovary, while the secondary oocyte is out in the uterine tube. Item III: False. The luteinizing hormone level peaks during the proliferative phase, since this is when ovulation occurs.

12.9

Penetration of an ovum by more than one sperm is known as **polyspermy**. It is normally prevented by the **fast block to polyspermy** and the **slow block to polyspermy**, which occur upon penetration of the egg by a spermatozoan. The fast block consists of a depolarization of the egg plasma membrane. This depolarization prevents other spermatozoa from fusing with the egg cell membrane. The slow block results from a Ca^{2+} influx caused by the initial depolarization. The slow block is also known as the **cortical reaction**. It has two components: swelling of the space between the zona pellucida and the plasma membrane, and hardening of the zona pellucida. The Ca^{2+} influx has one other noteworthy effect. It causes increased metabolism and protein synthesis, referred to as **egg activation**.

- Because of a particular disease, a man produces sperm without acrosomes. His spermatozoa are abnormal in that they:[39]
  - A. are immotile.
  - B. cannot undergo capacitation.
  - C. are incapable of fertilizing the egg.
  - D. can fertilize the eggs of many species.

- Which one of the following would NOT cause or indicate infertility?[40]
  - A. A lack of progesterone secretion during the latter half of the menstrual cycle
  - B. Failure of mitosis to occur after the male pronucleus fuses with the nucleus of the ovum
  - C. Excessively acidic pH of the vaginal secretions
  - D. A decrease in the concentration of LH after ovulation

12.9

Cleavage

The process of **embryogenesis** begins within hours of fertilization, but proceeds slowly in humans. The first stage is **cleavage**, in which the zygote undergoes many cell divisions to produce a ball of cells known as the **morula**. The first cell division occurs about 36 hours after fertilization. [The morula is the same size as the zygote, which indicates that the dividing cells spend most of their time in what phases of the cell cycle?[41] During cleavage of the zygote, do homologous chromosomes physically interact with each other?[42]]

---

[39] Acrosomal enzymes are necessary for penetration of the corona radiata, and the acrosomal process is necessary for binding to an penetration of the zona pellucida. Sperm that lack an acrosome would be unable to complete these processes, which are necessary for fertilization (choice **C** is correct and choice D is wrong). The acrosome has nothing to do with motility (motility is the flagella's job; choice A is wrong), and capacitation is the activation of sperm in the female reproductive tract. It has nothing to do with the acrosome (choice B is wrong).

[40] Progesterone is secreted from the corpus luteum, which is formed from the remnants of the Graafian follicle after ovulation. A lack of progesterone might indicate that the corpus luteum did not form, and thus ovulation did not occur (choice A could indicate infertility and can be eliminated). The male pronucleus is just the haploid sperm nucleus. After this fuses with the ovum nucleus, the now diploid zygote must undergo cleavage (rapid mitosis) to form an embryo. If mitosis fails to occur, no embryo would develop (choice B would cause infertility and can be eliminated). Excessively acidic pH in the vagina could be harmful to sperm, which prefer a more alkaline environment. Sperm damaged by acids may not be motile, or may not be able to successfully fertilize an egg (choice C could lead to infertility and can be eliminated). However, LH normally decreases after ovulation. This is expected and not an indicator of infertility (choice **D** is the correct answer choice).

[41] They must spend most of their time during the S (synthesis) and M (mitotic) phases, skipping the G_1 and G_2 (gap or growth) phases.

[42] No. Pairing of homologous chromosomes only takes place during meiosis, which only occurs during gametogenesis.

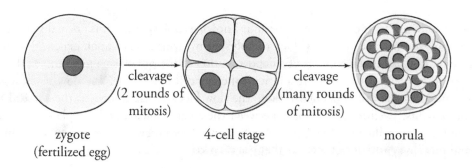

Figure 10   Cleavage

As cell divisions continue, the morula is transformed into a **blastocyst** (Figure 11). This process is known as **blastulation**. The blastocyst consists of a ring of cells called the **trophoblast** surrounding a cavity, and an **inner cell mass** adhering to the inside of the trophoblast at one end of the cavity. The **trophoblast** will give rise to the **chorion** (the zygote's contribution to the placenta). The inner cell mass will become the **embryo.**

- If two inner cell masses form in the blastula, what will the result be?[43]

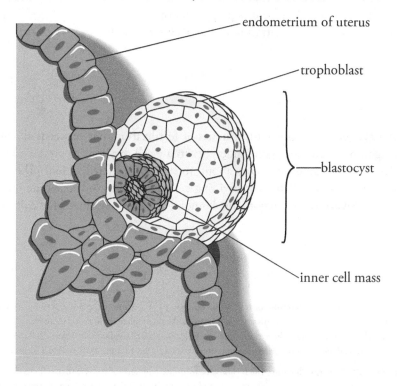

Figure 11   The Blastocyst at the Beginning of Implantation

---

[43] The inner cell mass becomes the embryo. Two inner cell masses derived from a single zygote and enclosed by the same trophoblast will result in a pair of identical twins sharing the same placenta.

12.10 IMPLANTATION AND THE PLACENTA

The developing blastocyst reaches the uterus and burrows into the endometrium, or **implants**, about a week after fertilization (Figure 11). The trophoblast secretes proteases that lyse endometrial cells. The blastocyst then sinks into the endometrium and is surrounded by it, absorbing nutrients through the trophoblast into the inner cell mass. The embryo receives a large part of its nutrition in this manner for the first few weeks of pregnancy. This is why the secretory phase of the endometrial cycle occurs: endometrial cells store glycogen, lipids, and other nutrients so that the early embryo may derive nourishment directly from the endometrium. Later, an organ develops which is specialized to facilitate exchange of nutrients, gases, and even antibodies between the maternal and embryonic bloodstreams: the **placenta**. Because it takes about three months for the placenta to develop, it is during the first trimester (three months) of pregnancy that hCG is essential for maintenance of the endometrium (Section 12.8).

- What happens if the corpus luteum is removed during the first trimester?[44]

During the last six months of pregnancy, the corpus luteum is no longer needed because the placenta itself secretes sufficient estrogen and progesterone for maintenance of the endometrium.

The development of the placenta involves the formation of **placental villi**. These are chorionic projections extending into the endometrium, into which fetal capillaries will grow. Surrounding the villi are sinuses (open spaces) filled with maternal blood. [Does oxygen-containing blood pass from the mother into the developing fetus?[45]]

The embryo is not the only important structure derived from the inner cell mass. There are three others: amnion, yolk sac, and allantois. The **amnion** surrounds a fluid-filled cavity which contains the developing embryo. Amniotic fluid is the "water" which "breaks" (is expelled) before birth. The **yolk sac** is important in reptiles and birds because it contains the nourishing yolk. Mammals do not store yolk. Our yolk sac is important because it is the first site of red blood cell synthesis in the embryo. Finally, the **allantois** develops from the embryonic gut and forms the blood vessels of the umbilical cord, which transport blood between embryo and placenta.

- Each of the following has the same genome EXCEPT:[46]
  - A. Chorion
  - B. Amnion
  - C. Yolk sac
  - D. Endometrium

---

[44] The woman menstruates, and the embryo is lost. Remember, the role of hCG is to substitute for LH in stimulating the corpus luteum. The role of the corpus luteum is to make estrogen and progesterone, which maintain the endometrium.

[45] No. The placenta is like a lung in that it facilitates exchange of substances between the two bloodstreams without allowing actual mixing.

[46] The chorion, amnion, and yolk sac are all derived from the inner cell mass of the blastula, and therefore must have the same genome (choices A, B, and C can be eliminated). However, the endometrium is derived from the mother (it is the inner lining of the uterus), and would have a different genome than the embryo (choice **D** is correct).

12.11 POST-IMPLANTATION DEVELOPMENT

We have examined embryogenesis from fertilization through blastulation. The next phase is **gastrulation**. Gastrulation is when the three **primary germ layers** (the **ectoderm**, the **mesoderm**, and the **endoderm**) become distinct.

In primitive organisms, the **blastula** (equivalent to blastocyst) is a hollow ball of cells, and gastrulation involves the **invagination** (involution) of these cells to form layers. Imagine pushing your fist into a big soft round balloon to create an inner layer (contacting your fist) and an outer layer (contacting the air). The inner layer is the endoderm, and the outer layer is the ectoderm. The mesoderm (middle layer) develops from the endoderm. The cavity (where your fist is) is primitive gut, or **archenteron**. The opening (where your wrist is) is the **blastopore**, and will give rise to the anus. The whole structure is the **gastrula**. (Don't be confused: The *gastr*ula has a *blast*opore; the *blast*ula has no opening.)

In humans, things are a little different. The gastrula develops from a double layer of cells called the **embryonic disk**, instead of from a spherical blastula. But the end result is the same: three layers. You need to know what parts of the human body are derived from each layer.

Ectoderm	Mesoderm	Endoderm
• Entire nervous system • Pituitary gland (both lobes), adrenal medulla • Cornea and lens • Epidermis of skin and derivatives (hair, nails, sweat glands, sensory receptors) • Nasal, oral, anal epithelium	• All muscle, bone, and connective tissue • Entire cardiovascular and lymphatic system, including blood • Urogenital organs (kidneys, ureters, gonads, reproductive ducts) • Dermis of skin	• GI tract epithelium (except mouth and anus) • GI glands (liver, pancreas, etc.) • Respiratory epithelium • Epithelial lining of urogenital organs and ducts • Urinary bladder

Table 4 Fates of the Primary Germ Layers

Pay attention to what *types* of thing are derived from each layer, and you'll see that it's relatively easy to memorize. One key thing to note is that **ectoderm** and *epithelium* are not synonymous. Epithelium outside the body (epidermis) is derived from ectoderm, but epithelium inside the body (gut lining) comes from endoderm.

- Which of the following statements is/are true?[47]
    I. Oxygen must diffuse across the chorionic membrane to reach the fetus from the mother.
    II. Transplantation of cells from the trophoblast of one embryo to the trophoblast of another embryo will result in an infant with a mixed genetic composition.
    III. All of the cells of the blastocyst are functionally equivalent.

The next step after gastrulation is **neurulation**, the formation of the nervous system. It proceeds by the invagination and pinching off of a layer of ectoderm along the dorsum (back) of the embryo to form the

---

[47] **Item I: True.** The chorion is part of the placenta. Item II: False. The trophoblast is derived from the outer cell mass and gives rise only to the chorion. The embryo is derived entirely from the inner cell mass. Item III: False. The trophoblast and the inner cell mass are both components of the blastocyst, and they have very different roles.

dorsal neural groove. This gives rise to the **neural tube**, which gives rise to the brain and spinal cord. The formation of the neural tube is induced by instructions from the underlying notochord, which is mesodermal in origin. It gives rise to the vertebral column. Other ectodermal cells migrate through the body to form peripheral nervous system ganglia.

Neurulation is one component of **organogenesis**, the development of organ systems. By the eighth week of gestation, all major organ systems are present, and the **embryo** is now called a **fetus**. Even though the developmental process has attained staggering complexity, by the end of the first trimester the fetus is still only 5 cm long. [During which trimester is the developing human most sensitive to toxins such as drugs and radiation?[48]]

- A radioactive dye is detected only in the cells of placental villi. Weeks earlier, it must have been injected into the:[49]
  A. inner cell mass.
  B. trophoblast.
  C. endometrium.
  D. zygote.

- During gastrulation, do tissues derived from the trophoblast move inward to form the lining of the primitive gut?[50]

---

[48] During the first trimester, when the organs are being formed.

[49] The placenta is derived from the chorion, which is derived from the cells of the trophoblast, thus injecting a dye into the trophoblast would lead to its detection in the placental villi (choice **B** is correct). The inner cell mass ultimately becomes the embryo, thus dye injected into the inner cells mass would be detected in the embryo, not the placenta (choice A is wrong). The endometrium is derived from the mother and is only the site of implantation and placental development. It does not actually contribute to the placenta, thus dye injected into the endometrium would not be detected in the placenta (choice C is wrong). The zygote is the precursor to all embryonic and extraembryonic structures. Injecting a dye into the zygote would lead to its detection not only in the placenta, but also in the amnion, chorion, and embryo itself (choice D is wrong).

[50] No. Gastrulation involves only cells derived from the inner cell mass.

12.12   DIFFERENTIATION

The specialization of cell types during development is termed **differentiation** because as cells specialize they become different from their parent cells and from each other. By specializing, a cell becomes better able to perform a particular task, while becoming less adept at other tasks. For example, a sensory neuron is the best vehicle for the transmission of a nerve impulse over great distances, but is quite incapable of obtaining nourishment on its own, or even of reproducing itself.

Primitive (stem) cells in an early embryo have the potential to become any cell type. They are known as **totipotent** cells. There is a certain point in the development of a cell at which the cell fate becomes fixed; at this point the cell is said to be **determined**. Determination precedes differentiation. This means a cell is determined before it is visibly differentiated. Determination can be **induced** by a cell's environment, such as exposure to diffusible factors or neighboring cells, or it can be preprogrammed.

- During early embryonic development, cells near the developing notochord undergo an irreversible developmental choice to become skeletal muscle later in development, although they do not immediately change their appearance. This is an example of which of the following?[51]
  - A. Determination
  - B. Differentiation
  - C. Totipotency
  - D. Induction

There is such a thing as **dedifferentiation**. This is the process whereby a specialized cell *un*specializes and may become totipotent. If a dedifferentiated cell proliferates in an uncontrolled manner, the result can be cancer. The most important lesson you can learn from the notion of dedifferentiation is that every cell has the same genome. The specialization of cell types is a function of things in the cytoplasm and maybe proteins and RNA in the nucleus, but no genetic changes normally take place during development and differentiation.

- Can you think of two exceptions to this rule, where a particular cell type normally has a unique genome?[52]

---

[51] A cell whose fate is fixed is said to be determined, however if it has not yet undergone a change in appearance, it has not yet been differentiated (choice **A** is correct and choice B is wrong). Since the cell is destined to become muscle, it is no longer totipotent (choice C is wrong). Although the cells are found near the notochord, there is no reason to assume the location is the reason for their determination. They could be cytoplasmically determined (choice D is wrong).

[52] One exception is B cells and T cells of the immune system. They undergo gene (DNA!) rearrangements in the process of attaining antigen specificity. The other exception is gametes. They have unique genomes because of 1) reductive division with independent assortment, and 2) recombination.

12.13   BIRTH AND LACTATION

The technical term for birth is **parturition**. It is dependent on contraction of muscles in the uterine wall. The very high levels of progesterone secreted throughout pregnancy help to repress contractions in uterine muscle, but near the end of pregnancy uterine excitability increases. This increased excitability is likely to be a result of several factors, including a change in the ratio of estrogen to progesterone, the presence of the hormone **oxytocin** secreted by the posterior pituitary, and mechanical stretching of the uterus and cervix.

Weak contractions of the uterus occur throughout pregnancy. As pregnancy reaches full term, however, rhythmic **labor contractions** begin. It is thought that the onset of labor contractions is the result of a positive feedback reflex: The increased pressure on the cervix crosses a threshold that causes the posterior pituitary to increase the secretion of oxytocin. Oxytocin causes the uterine contractions to increase in intensity, creating greater pressure on the cervix that stimulates still more oxytocin release and even stronger contractions.

The first stage of labor is dilation of the cervix. The second stage is the actual birth, involving movement of the baby through the cervix and birth canal, pushed by contraction of uterine (smooth) and abdominal (skeletal) muscle. The third stage is the expulsion of the placenta, after it separates from the wall of the uterus. Contractions of the uterus after birth help to minimize blood loss.

During pregnancy, milk production and secretion would be a waste of energy, but after parturition it is necessary. During puberty, estrogen stimulates the development of breasts in women. The increased levels of estrogen and progesterone secreted by the placenta during pregnancy cause the further development of glandular and adipose breast tissue. But while these hormones stimulate breast development, they inhibit the release of **prolactin** and thus the production of milk. After parturition, the levels of estrogen and progesterone fall and milk production begins. Every time suckling occurs, the pituitary gland is stimulated by the hypothalamus to release a large surge of prolactin, prolonging the ability of the breasts to secrete milk. If the mother stops breast-feeding the infant, prolactin levels fall and milk secretion ceases. The converse is also true: Milk secretion can continue for years, as long as nursing continues. The breasts do not leak large amounts of milk when the infant is not nursing. This is because the posterior pituitary hormone **oxytocin** is necessary for **milk let-down** (release). Oxytocin is also released when suckling occurs.

12.13

Summary

- The primary sex organs produce gametes and hormones. The testes are the male primary sex organ and the ovaries are the female primary sex organ.

- Male internal genitalia are formed from Wolffian ducts and female internal genitalia are formed from Müllerian ducts.

- Spermatogenesis takes place in the seminiferous tubules and results in four haploid sperm from a single spermatogonium. It begins at puberty and continues on a daily basis for the life of the male. FSH stimulates spermatogenesis and LH stimulates testosterone production.

- Sperm travel from the seminiferous tubules to the epididymis, then to the ductus deferens, then to the urethra. Semen is a supportive fluid for sperm, produced by the seminal vesicles, the prostate, and the bulbourethral glands.

- Oogenesis begins prenatally, producing primary oocytes. It occurs again on a monthly basis, beginning at puberty and ending at menopause; this produces one secondary oocyte (which is ovulated) and the first polar body. Oogenesis is only completed if the secondary oocyte is fertilized, in which case an ovum and the second polar body will be produced.

- FSH stimulates follicle development and estrogen secretion during the first half of the menstrual cycle. LH stimulates ovulation and the formation of the corpus luteum, as well as progesterone and estrogen secretion, during the second half of the menstrual cycle.

- Estrogen stimulates growth of the endometrium during the first half of the menstrual cycle; progesterone and estrogen maintain and enhance the endometrium during the second half of the menstrual cycle. If no fertilization takes place, estrogen and progesterone levels fall, and the endometrium is sloughed off.

- Arousal is mediated by the parasympathetic nervous system, while orgasm and resolution are mediated by the sympathetic nervous system.

- Fertilization takes place in the uterine tubes, and cleavage begins 24–36 hours later. The zygote becomes a morula, the morula becomes a blatstula, and the blastula implants in the endometrium.

- The trophoblast becomes the placenta and the inner cell mass becomes the embryo.

- The first eight weeks of development are the embryonic stage, during which gastrulation (formation of the three primary germ layers), neurulation (formation of the nervous system), and organogenesis occur.

- The fetal stage begins at the eighth week of development and ends at the birth of the baby.

- Labor is a positive feedback cycle triggered by mild (initially) uterine contractions that push the baby's head on the cervix. This stimulates the release of oxytocin, which causes a stronger uterine contraction, and a bigger stretch of the cervix. This positive feedback loop will continue until the birth of the baby.

- Prolactin stimulates milk production and oxytocin stimulates milk ejection in a baby-driven cycle.

CHAPTER 12 FREESTANDING PRACTICE QUESTIONS

1. Which of the following structures undergoes mitosis?

   A) Spermatid
   B) Spermatogonium
   C) Primary spermatocyte
   D) Secondary spermatocyte

2. Which of the following statements regarding childbirth is true?

   A) Release of oxytocin from the anterior pituitary, combined with increased mechanical pressure of the fetal head on the cervix, creates a positive feedback loop that increases uterine contractions.
   B) Release of progesterone from the placenta, combined with increased mechanical pressure of the fetal head on the cervix, creates a positive feedback loop that increases uterine contractions.
   C) Release of progesterone from the posterior pituitary, combined with increased mechanical pressure of the fetal head on the cervix, creates a negative feedback loop that increases uterine contractions.
   D) Release of oxytocin from the posterior pituitary, combined with mechanical pressure of the fetal head on the cervix, creates a positive feedback loop that increases uterine contractions.

3. Which of the following is NOT a difference between spermatogenesis and oogenesis?

   A) Spermatogenesis in a male begins at puberty whereas oogenesis in a female begins when the female is an embryo.
   B) Spermatogenesis produces four sperm whereas oogenesis produces one ovum.
   C) Spermatogenesis produces primary spermatocytes for a male's entire life, whereas oogenesis ceases to produce primary oocytes when a female reaches menopause.
   D) Spermatogenesis occurs in the testes whereas oogenesis occurs in the ovaries.

4. Which of the following hormones is NOT elevated during the first trimester of pregnancy?

   A) Estrogen
   B) Progesterone
   C) GnRH
   D) hCG

5. Ovulation usually occurs on the 14th day of the ovarian cycle. All of the following occurs during ovulation and the days immediately following ovulation EXCEPT:

   A) the ovary releases a secondary oocyte.
   B) a surge of FSH from the anterior pituitary causes the follicle to become the corpus luteum.
   C) the follicle secretes progesterone once it becomes the corpus luteum.
   D) a surge of LH can be detected.

6. Ectopic pregnancy, where implantation of the embryo occurs in the fallopian tube rather than the uterus, is possible because:

   A) though fertilization takes place in the uterus, implantation does not occur immediately and thus the embryo could migrate back up into the fallopian tubes.
   B) fertilization occurs in the fallopian tubes and the embryo may fail to migrate to the uterus.
   C) the fimbriae may hold the embryo in the fallopian tube rather than pushing it towards the uterus.
   D) fertilization may have occurred in the ovary with subsequent implantation in the fallopian tube.

7. Postpartum women often experience mild to moderate uterine contractions when nursing. These contractions are triggered by the release of:

   A) estrogen.
   B) oxytocin.
   C) progesterone.
   D) prolactin.

8. The greater vestibular glands in the female (Bartholin's glands) have a similar function as which of the following male reproductive glands?

   A) Bulbourethral glands (Cowper's glands)
   B) Seminal vesicles
   C) Prostate
   D) Testes

CHAPTER 12 PRACTICE PASSAGES

Passage I

The uterus is a complex reproductive sex organ common to most mammals. In addition to providing structural support to the pelvic and abdominal viscera, it plays a critical role in several aspects of sexual reproduction and development. Anatomically speaking, the human uterus is bordered inferiorly by the cervix (which extends into the vagina), and superolaterally by each of the paired uterine tubes (which lead to the ovaries.) A simplified representation of the thickness of the endometrial lining and its associated arteries is depicted below in Figure 1.

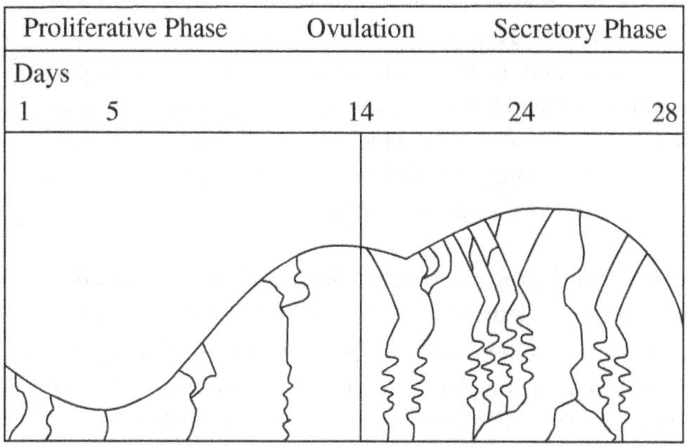

Figure 1 Endometrial Histology

The organ itself is divided into several layers, each of which has a structure well-suited to carrying out its function. The innermost layer, known as the *endometrium*, is an excellent example of this interplay between structure and function. It consists of two different zones: an outer layer adjacent to the muscular myometrium called the *basal layer*, and a variable inner layer in direct contact with the uterine cavity called the *functional layer*. Throughout the female menstrual cycle, the basal layer serves as a source of progenitor cells for the functional layer, which undergoes many changes during the cycle. These changes, which correspond to changes in circulating levels of particular hormones, can be divided into three main uterine phases: menstrual, proliferative, and secretory.

The different uterine phases are directly influenced by a series of hormones released during the menstrual cycle. These hormones are under the influence of the hypothalamic-pituitary-ovarian axis. When the hypothalamus releases gonadotropin releasing hormone (GnRH), it binds to receptors on cells in the anterior pituitary to induce the release of follicle stimulating hormone (FSH) and luteinizing hormone (LH). LH acts on the thecal cells of the ovarian follicle to cause androgen production; the androgens then diffuse into the granulosa cells of the

follicle, where FSH induces their conversion into estrogen. Estrogen is the main sex hormone seen during the proliferative phase of uterine development, and is responsible for rebuilding the endometrial lining after menstruation. Its levels peak just before ovulation, which occurs at about Day 14 in a typical cycle. After ovulation, the oocyte enters the fallopian tubes, while the ruptured follicle left behind transforms into the corpus luteum. This structure begins secreting progesterone, which, along with slightly lowered levels of estrogen, is the dominant hormone of the secretory phase of the uterine cycle. Progesterone serves to further build up the endometrial lining of the uterus and increase its glandular secretions, which prepare it for implantation. Progesterone is responsible for maintaining a robust endometrium. If fertilization and implantation occur, then the corpus luteum is sustained by human chorionic gonadotropin (hCG) for 2–3 months, at which time the corpus luteum regresses and progesterone production is taken over by the placenta. If fertilization and implantation does not occur, the corpus luteum regresses within 2 weeks (approximately Day 28 of the cycle), and menstruation occurs.

1. Endometriosis is a condition in which retrograde menstruation occurs into the peritoneal cavity, leading to deposition of endometrial tissue throughout different areas of the body. Which of the following would NOT be a possible symptom of this condition?

A) Infertility
B) Increased diameter of the uterine tube lumen
C) Pelvic pain
D) Partial or complete adhesion of the fimbriae to one other

2. Which of the following is most directly responsible for the sloughing off of tissue from the uterine lining during Days 1–4 of the menstrual cycle?

A) Increased estrogen levels
B) Increased progesterone levels
C) Decreased estrogen levels
D) Decreased progesterone levels

3. A tumor affecting the posterior pituitary of a 32-year-old woman would be LEAST likely to directly produce which of the following consequences?

A) An increase in the production of breastmilk
B) A decrease in urine volume
C) An activation of several feedback mechanisms in the hypothalamic-pituitary axis
D) An increase in circulating levels of vasopressin

4. In which of the following meiotic phases is the female gamete arrested immediately after being released into the oviduct?

A) Metaphase II
B) Metaphase I
C) Prophase II
D) Prophase I

5. All of the following will be elevated at one point or another over the course of a regular monthly menstrual cycle in a nonpregnant woman EXCEPT which one of the following?

A) Estrogen
B) hCG
C) FSH
D) LH

6. During which phase is the basal layer most responsive to ovarian hormones?

A) During the menstrual phase
B) During the proliferative phase
C) During the secretory phase
D) The basal layer remains unresponsive throughout the cycle.

7. Which of the following statements regarding the uterus and ovaries is false?

A) A patient with a tumor creating abnormally high levels of estrogen and progesterone is expected to have decreased levels of LH.
B) High levels of estrogen and progesterone are seen at different times during the course of the menstrual cycle.
C) The uterine lining's histological changes are directly regulated by FSH and LH.
D) During menstruation, estrogen and progesterone levels are at their lowest.

Passage II

Multiple-birth pregnancies, often seen as birth of twins, occur via several mechanisms in which a single or several ova become fertilized and result in the birth of two or more children. Historically, twinning occurred in 1 out of 80 pregnancies, but the frequency in the United States as of 2002 has risen to 1 in 32 live births. In part, this change originates from increased use of assisted reproductive therapy, but several iatrogenic causes, resulting in increased ovum transport time, also plays a role.

Dizygotic, or fraternal, twins originate from the release and fertilization of two ova in a single ovulatory cycle. Following implantation, this forms a dichorionic and diamnionic pregnancy with a single fused or two separate placentas. *Monozygotic*, or identical, twins originate from the release and fertilization of a single ovum in an ovulatory cycle. Division of the fertilized ovum then results in a number of outcomes depending upon the development of the zygote. The supportive structures formed before the division of the zygote (with the exception of the placenta, which develops similarly as with a dizygotic pregnancy) are shared between the two zygotes, and those structures formed after the division are separate.

Multiple birth pregnancies carry increased risks to both the mother and the fetuses. Intrauterine growth restriction can result due to a monochorial twin pregnancy developing an arteriovenous shunt. The twin on the arterial side of the shunt donates blood to the twin on the venous side, resulting in increased growth of the recipient twin. This size difference can result in severe growth restriction of the donor twin and possibly death. Other complications include premature delivery, polyhydramnios (excess amniotic fluid), premature rupture of membranes, and pregnancy-induced hypertension.

1. Which of the following is the most likely result following the division of a zygote immediately after chorion formation?

A) A monozygotic, diamnionic, dichorionic pregnancy
B) A monozygotic, diamnionic, monochorionic pregnancy
C) A monozygotic, monoamnionic, dichorionic pregnancy
D) A monozygotic, monoamnionic, monochorionic pregnancy

2. Elevated plasma concentrations of follicle stimulating hormone, luteinizing hormone, and estradiol are detectable in patients with a history of dizygotic multiple births. If similar laboratory values were detected in a patient with a history of only singleton births, what would be a likely response?

A) Decreased release of pituitary GnRH
B) Ovarian atrophy
C) Increased anterior pituitary hormone release
D) Decreased GnRH in the hypophyseal portal system

3. A pregnant patient presents in the emergency room with severe abdominal pain. Following ultrasound, the physician diagnoses severe intrauterine growth restriction of the two 33-week-old fetuses and recommends to the mother that labor be induced. Which of the following would result in labor induction?

A) Sympathetic nervous system agonists
B) Calcium channel blockers
C) Pitocin (synthetic oxytocin)
D) Progestin (synthetic progesterone)

4. Fetal development can be heavily impacted by both prescription and illicit drug use. Which of the following factors LEAST affects drug permeability across the placenta?

A) Hydrophobicity
B) Molecular weight
C) Plasma protein binding
D) Maternal age

5. An expectant mother undergoes amniocentesis early in her pregnancy and discovers that the karyotype obtained contains a third copy of chromosome 21. She carries the baby to term but the child displays none of the expected symptoms of Down syndrome. She has him karyotyped but this time it comes back normal. What is a possible explanation for this?

A) The extra chromosome was eliminated in subsequent divisions.
B) The sampled tissue was maternal in origin.
C) The second karyotype should be repeated because Down syndrome presents later in life.
D) The mother experienced a miscarriage.

6. Recent research discovered a link between contraceptive use around the time of pregnancy and multiple birth pregnancies. What is the most likely reason for this observation?

A) Decreased fallopian tube ciliary beating
B) Increased luteal phase of the menstrual cycle
C) Increased secretory phase of the menstrual cycle
D) Suppression of ovulation

7. Monozygotic twins, while commonly referred to as identical, can vary significantly in several ways. Which of the following would be the most likely cause of monozygotic twins being born with significantly different birth weights?

A) Maternal diabetes
B) A placenta with poor implantation
C) Elevated maternal growth hormone
D) Difference due to paternal meiosis

SOLUTIONS TO CHAPTER 12 FREESTANDING PRACTICE QUESTIONS

1. **B**   The spermatogonia in the testes periodically undergo mitosis to produce both more spermatogonia and primary spermatocytes, ensuring a continual supply of primary spermatocytes for gametogenesis throughout the male reproductive lifespan. Primary spermatocytes, which are diploid, undergo meiosis I to become haploid secondary spermatocytes, which then undergo meiosis II to become (haploid) spermatids (choices C and D are wrong). Spermatids do not undergo mitosis or meiosis, but develop into mature spermatozoa (choice A is wrong).

2. **D**   Labor and delivery is one example of a positive feedback loop, in which the release of oxytocin from the posterior pituitary combined with mechanical pressure of the fetal head work together to increase uterine contractility in an effort to expel the baby from the uterus (choice D is correct and choice A is wrong). Progesterone, released early in pregnancy from the corpus luteum and later in pregnancy from the placenta itself, decreases uterine contractility (choices B and C are wrong). Levels of progesterone are high early in pregnancy in order to keep the developing fetus inside the uterus, but levels diminish later in pregnancy in anticipation of the upcoming delivery of the baby. Note that this question is a two-by-two elimination; the role of oxytocin in delivery allows the elimination of two answer choices and determining its regulatory mechanism differentiates between the remaining two.

3. **C**   Spermatogenesis only begins once a male reaches puberty, and then continues for the rest of his life (choice C is not a difference and is the correct answer choice). Oogenesis begins when a female is an embryo, and the cells are arrested at the primary oocyte phase when she is a fetus (choice A is a difference and can be eliminated). Spermatogenesis produces four sperm from each spermatogonia, whereas oogenesis produces one ovum and two polar bodies per oogonia (choice B is a difference and can be eliminated). The testes are the male gonads and the site of spermatogenesis; the ovaries are the female gonads and the site of oogenesis (choice D is a difference and can be eliminated).

4. **C**   The corpus luteum secretes estrogen and progesterone, which help maintain pregnancy (these hormones are elevated in the first trimester; choices A and B can be eliminated). Estrogen and progesterone feedback and inhibit the secretion of GnRH from the hypothalamus (choice C would not be elevated and is the correct answer choice). hCG is a hormone secreted by the embryo that helps to maintain the corpus luteum during the first trimester until the placenta is formed (choice D would be elevated and can be eliminated).

5. **B**   During ovulation, the ovary releases a secondary oocyte (choice A is true and can be eliminated). A surge of LH, not FSH from the anterior pituitary, causes the follicle to become the corpus luteum (choice D is true and can be eliminated, and choice B is false and the correct answer choice). Once the follicle becomes the corpus luteum, it produces and secretes progesterone that stabilizes and enhances the endometrium (choice C is true and can be eliminated).

6. **B** Fertilization occurs in the fallopian tube after an egg has been released from the ovary (choices A and D are wrong). The fimbriae sweep the egg from the ovary into the fallopian tube (not the uterus) once it has been ovulated (choice C is wrong). Choice B describes the process accurately, including the correct location of fertilization and the failure to migrate prior to implantation.

7. **B** When suckling occurs, oxytocin is released from the posterior pituitary to trigger milk ejection from the glands towards the nipple. As this hormone is also responsible for stimulating uterine contractions during delivery, it can have a similar but less intense effect when nursing. Prolactin is involved in nursing, but is responsible for stimulating the production of milk and does not have an effect on the uterus (choice D is wrong). Estrogen and progesterone do not play a role in this situation (choices A and C are wrong).

8. **A** The greater vestibular glands are located at the posterior of the vaginal opening, are stimulated on arousal, and secrete an alkaline mucus. This helps neutralize the acidity of the vagina to make it a more hospitable environment for sperm, which can be damaged by acids. The bulbourethral glands in the male are stimulated on arousal and secrete an alkaline mucus into the urethra. This helps neutralize any traces of acid that might remain from earlier passage of urine through that duct, and makes the urethra a more hospitable environment for sperm. The seminal vesicles and the prostate produce semen (a supportive fluid for sperm), and are stimulated at orgasm (choices B and C are wrong), and the testes are the male primary sex organs; they produce sperm and testosterone (choice D is wrong).

SOLUTIONS TO CHAPTER 12 PRACTICE PASSAGE I

1. **B** "Retrograde" means "opposite to normal," thus retrograde menstruation must mean the flow of menstrual fluid opposite to its normal course. The question text states that the flow is into the peritoneal (abdominal) cavity, and the only entrance from the uterus to this cavity is via the uterine tubes. This could lead to deposition of endometrial tissue in the uterine tube, reducing the diameter of its lumen (choice B is not a symptom and is the correct answer choice). If the tube narrows too much or closes completely, infertility could be the result; oocytes would not be able to migrate toward the uterus and sperm would not be able to migrate toward the ovary (recall that fertilization occurs in the uterine tube, choice A is a possible symptom and can be eliminated). Deposition of endometrial tissue in the peritoneal cavity near the pelvis can cause inflammation and pain in that region (choice C is a possible symptom and can be eliminated). Deposition of endometrial tissue on the fimbriae could cause them to stick together (note that this could also cause infertility if the oocyte cannot enter after ovulation; choice D is a possible symptom and can be eliminated).

2.   **D**   The passage states that progesterone, made by the corpus luteum, is responsible for maintaining the endometrium after ovulation. It also states that the corpus luteum will regress and disappear if pregnancy does not occur, and when this occurs, menstruation follows immediately after. Thus, the presence of the progesterone made by the corpus luteum is what keeps the endometrium thickened. Without the corpus luteum, progesterone levels fall and the endometrial lining degenerates and sloughs off (menstruation; choice D is correct and choice B is wrong). Increased estrogen is seen mainly during the follicular phase and is responsible for rebuilding the endometrium after menstruation (choice A is wrong). Lastly, decreased estrogen, although occurring before menstruation, is not the main trigger for menstruation (choice D is better than choice C).

3.   **A**   A tumor in the posterior pituitary could lead to an increase in the hormones normally released from it, namely, vasopressin (ADH) and oxytocin (choice D is likely and can be eliminated). An increase in vasopressin would cause the kidneys to retain water, thus decreasing urine volume (choice B is likely and can be eliminated). Increased levels of vasopressin and oxytocin would feedback to the hypothalamus and pituitary, thus initiating compensatory activity (choice C is likely and can be eliminated). However, lactogenesis (milk production) is under the control of prolactin, a hormone of the anterior pituitary. It would not be affected by a tumor in the posterior pituitary (choice A is unlikely and is the correct answer choice).

4.   **A**   This is a straightforward memory (freestanding) question. The oocyte, just before it is released from a Graafian follicle during ovulation, is arrested at metaphase II, and remains in metaphase II after ovulation unless it gets fertilized, at which point it finishes meiosis.

5.   **B**   The passages states that "if fertilization and implantation occur" (i.e., pregnancy), "the corpus luteum is sustained by human chorionic gonadotropin." This suggests that hCG is present only when pregnancy occurs (choice B is not found in nonpregnant women and is the correct answer choice). The passage discusses the importance of the hypothalamic-pituitary-ovarian axis in controlling the monthly menstrual cycle and describes the effects of the hormones on that cycle. Estrogen is elevated during the cycle as it is necessary to stimulate the rebuilding of the endometrium during the proliferative phase of the uterine cycle (choice A would be elevated in nonpregnant women and can be eliminated). The hypothalamus releases GnRH, which stimulates the release of both FSH and LH; both of these hormones are needed to stimulate development of the ovarian follicle (including estrogen release; choices C and D would be elevated in nonpregnant women and can be eliminated).

6.   **D**   The passage states that the basal layer serves as the source of progenitor cells for the functional layer. In other words, it is the layer responsible for adding cells to the functional layer during the proliferative and secretory phases. This layer would thus have to remain unaffected by ovarian hormones so that it could continuously serve as a "stem cell-like" layer of undifferentiated cells. If the basal layer was equally influenced by these hormones, it too could be thickened and sloughed off, and if this were to occur, then there would be no progenitors to restart the next cycle. Only the differentiated cells, which are in the functional layer, can be influenced by ovarian hormones.

7. **C** The changes in the uterine lining that occur during the menstrual cycle are controlled directly by estrogen and progesterone, which are controlled by FSH and LH. Thus, the uterus is only indirectly controlled by FSH and LH (choice C is a false statement and the correct answer choice). The hypothalamic-pituitary-ovarian axis is controlled by a negative feedback mechanism, wherein high levels of target hormone (estrogen and progesterone) will feed back on the hypothalamus and pituitary to control the release of the tropic hormones FSH and LH. Thus, high levels of estrogen and progesterone would be expected to decrease LH (choice A is true and can be eliminated). The passage states that estrogen is elevated during the proliferative and secretory phases of the cycle, while progesterone is elevated during the secretory phase of the cycle (choice B is true and can be eliminated). Menstruation is the body's response to low levels of progesterone and estrogen; these hormones are what build up the uterine endometrium in the first place, thus withdrawal of this influence causes the endometrium to collapse and slough off (choice D is true and can be eliminated).

SOLUTIONS TO CHAPTER 12 PRACTICE PASSAGE II

1. **B** According to the passage, supportive structures formed before the division of the zygote are shared and structures formed after the division are separate. Given that the division occurred after chorion formation, there will be a single, shared chorion (monochorionic, choices A and C can be eliminated). The amnion is formed after the chorion (and in this case after the division), so there will be two, separate amnions (diamnionic; choice D can be eliminated and choice B is correct).

2. **D** Elevated levels of FSH, LH would result in feedback inhibition of GnRH at the hypothalamus. Transport of GnRH between the hypothalamus and anterior pituitary occurs via the hypophyseal portal system and decreased levels of GnRH would likely occur (choice D is correct). The hypothalamus produces GnRH (not the pituitary, choice A is wrong), and the decrease in GnRH would decrease FSH and LH release from the anterior pituitary (choice C is wrong). Ovarian atrophy is unlikely given the fact that FSH and LH are elevated, and these act in a stimulatory fashion directly on the ovary (choice B is wrong).

3. **C** Natural oxytocin stimulates the strong uterine contractions seen during labor, thus it is logical to assume that synthetic oxytocin would trigger these contractions and induce labor (choice C is correct). The sympathetic nervous system causes uterine relaxation (choice A is wrong) and calcium channel blockers would inhibit muscle contraction (and hence relax the uterus; choice B is wrong). High progesterone levels during pregnancy tend to keep the uterus quiet and relaxed. It is the drop in progesterone near the end of pregnancy that helps to trigger labor, so progestin would not result in labor induction (choice D is wrong).

4. **D** The permeability of a drug across the placenta is dictated by hydrophobicity or hydrophilicity, molecular weight, and plasma protein binding. Increased hydrophobicity increases permeability, decreased molecular weight increases permeability, and increased plasma protein binding decreases permeability (choices A, B, and C affect permeability and can be eliminated). There is no evidence linking maternal age to placental drug permeability (choice D does not affect permeability and is the correct answer choice).

5. **D** Amniocentesis can obtain a sample of fluid from any fetus present at the time of testing. In this instance, it's possible that the mother could have been carrying twins (one with Down syndrome and the other without). The affected twin was not carried to term, thus the surviving child would have a normal karyotype (choice D is correct). Chromosome elimination (i.e., nondisjunction in mitosis) is incredibly rare and it would be even more unlikely to have the same chromosome be eliminated in all cells (choice A is wrong). Since the mother is not described as having Down syndrome, maternal tissue would not possess that karyotype (choice B is wrong) and Down syndrome presents at birth (choice C is wrong). Note that choice D may not be immediately obvious as the correct answer, but since all other answer choices are wrong, it is the only remaining possibility.

6. **A** According to the passage, increased ovum transport time is associated with multiple birth pregnancies. Ciliary beating is responsible for propelling the ovum toward the uterus, thus a decrease in ciliary beating could delay ovum transport and increase the chance of a multiple birth pregnancy (choice A is correct). The luteal and secretory phases of the menstrual cycle occur at the same time, but refer to the follicle and uterus, respectively (choices B and C cannot both be correct and are not the answer). Note also that changes in the length of the luteal or secretory phase would not affect ovum transport. Suppression of ovulation would result in no ovum release and no pregnancy (choice D is wrong).

7. **B** Discordance in size can occur as a result of poor nutrient delivery. This could be caused by poor placental development in one fetus but normal development in the other (choice B is correct). Maternal diabetes and elevated maternal growth hormone are systemic problems and would likely have an equal impact on both of the twins (choices A and C are wrong). Monozygotic twins originate from a single ovum and sperm; differences in the twins could not be due to paternal meiosis, which accounts for differences between sperm (choice D is not correct).

Appendix
Some Molecular
Biology Techniques

The material in this section is not *strictly* MCAT material, thus it is presented in this appendix as a reference source; in other words, you don't need to memorize it. But read it for practice. The MCAT is a test of your ability to deal with new material like this, presented on the exam in passage form.

A.1 ENZYME-LINKED IMMUNO-SORBENT ASSAY (ELISA)

As the name suggests, an ELISA is a biochemical technique that utilizes antigen-antibody interactions ("immuno-sorbency") to determine the presence of either

- antigens (like proteins or cytokines), or
- specific immunoglobulins (antibodies)

in a sample (such as cells recovered from a tumor biopsy or a patient's serum). Figure 1 illustrates the basic protocol when testing for the presence of a specific antigen.

Step 1: The experimental wells are coated with antibodies that are specific for the target antigen.

Step 2: A sample of serum or cell extract is added to the wells.

Step 3: The antibodies immobilize the antigen by binding to it (if it is present in the sample).

Step 4: Any unbound proteins remaining in the sample are washed away.

Step 5: An enzyme-linked antibody that also recognizes the target protein is added to the wells.

Step 6: The wells are filled with a solution that changes color in the presence of the detection enzyme (the one linked to the antibody added in Step 5). A color change indicates the target protein was present in the sample; no color change means the protein was absent.

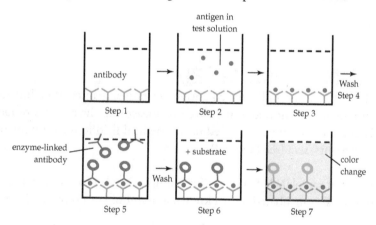

Figure 1 Testing for the Presence of Antigen

When testing for the presence of a specific antibody in a sample, the *antigen* (for which the antibody is specific) is first allowed to adhere directly to the wells. The sample is added as above, and then mixed with enzyme-linked antibodies (see Figure 2).

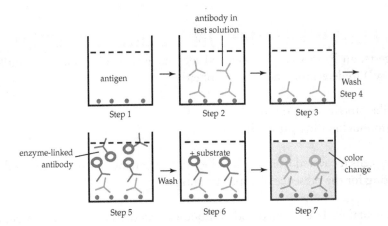

Figure 2 Testing for the Presence of Antibody

ELISA can be used to screen patients for viral infections. For example, serum from a patient suspected to be infected with HIV is loaded into wells that are coated with HIV coat proteins. If the serum contains anti-HIV antibodies (indicating infection), the antibodies will adhere to the proteins on the wells, bind enzyme-linked antibodies, and effect a color change.

A.2   RADIOIMMUNOASSAY (RIA)

RIAs are similar to ELISAs but use radiolabeled antibodies rather than enzyme-linked antibodies. Thus, the presence of target proteins or antibodies is assayed by measuring the amount of radioactivity instead of a color change. RIAs are more extensively used in the medical field to measure the relative amounts of hormones or drugs in patients' sera (see Figure 3).

Step 1: A known amount of radiolabeled antigen (for example, insulin that was synthesized with ^{125}I-labeled tyrosines) is incubated with a known amount of antibody that is specific to the antigen.

Step 2: The insulin:antibody complexes are isolated.

Step 3: The total amount of radioactivity is measured.

Step 4: Unlabeled insulin (also called *cold insulin*) is mixed into the solution in increasing amounts. The cold insulin competes with the labeled insulin (*hot insulin*) for the antibody. As more cold insulin is added, less total radioactivity is recovered and measured. This competition assay helps formulate a standard curve (see Figure 4).

Step 5: Steps 1–3 are repeated using patient serum instead of the cold insulin. The standard curve is used to extrapolate the amount of insulin that is circulating in a patient's serum.

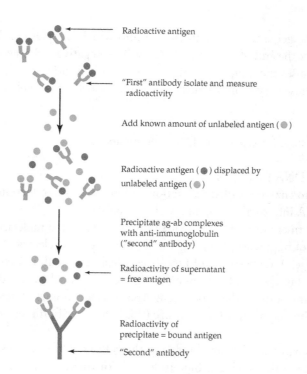

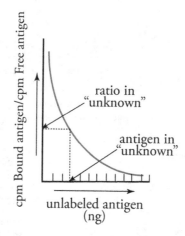

Figure 3   Radioimmunoassay (RIA)

Figure 4   Standard Curve

A.3   ELECTROPHORESIS

Electrophoresis is a means of separating things by size (for example, nucleic acids or proteins) or by charge (for example, proteins). A "gel" is made out of either acrylamide or agarose, by solubilizing the acrylamide or agarose, pouring it into a rectangular mold, and then allowing it to cool and solidify. Acrylamide and agarose form "nets" as they solidify; the more acrylamide or agarose used in the initial solution, the smaller the pores in the nets.

The mold used to pour the gel creates wells in the gel into which samples can be loaded. An electrical current is applied such that the end of the gel with the wells is negatively charged and the opposite end is positively charged. This causes the samples to migrate toward the positive pole, according to size; smaller things migrate faster (because they fit more easily through the pores of the gel) and larger things migrate more slowly.

For example, here are the steps for separating DNA fragments by size:

Step 1: Isolate the sample DNA from cells.
Step 2: Expose the DNA to enzymes called **restriction endonucleases** (see section A.5), which cleave the strands of DNA into smaller fragments of varying size.
Step 3: Denature the assortment of DNA fragments into single-stranded molecules.
Step 4: Load the mixture of fragments into the gel wells, and apply the electrical current (this is called "running a gel"). Each strand of DNA (negatively charged!) migrates toward the positive end of the gel, but the smaller fragments migrate more quickly, and thus are found farther from the wells at any point in the experiment. You run the samples alongside a "standard" lane, which contains fragments of known size (this help identify the size of the unknowns).

Once the fragments are separated, you can simply use the gel to determine sizes, or you can transfer the fragments to a nitrocellulose filter and continue to work with them. This is called "blotting" and is described below (see Figure 5).

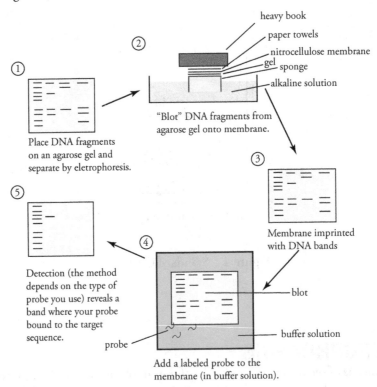

Figure 5 Blotting

A.4 BLOTTING

Simply put, blotting is the transfer of DNA or proteins from an electrophoresis gel to a nitrocellulose filter. Once they are transferred, further experiments can be run to isolate or detect a particular DNA fragment or protein (called "probing"). Blotting is classified by the type of molecule being probed.

Southern Blotting

Southern blotting allows you detect the presence of specific sequences within a heterogeneous sample of DNA. This process also allows you to isolate and purify target sequences of DNA for further study.

Step 1: Separate the DNA fragments on an electrophoresis gel.

Step 2: Transfer the fragments to a nitrocellulose filter.

Step 3: The filter is "probed" for the target DNA sequence. Hybridization probes are short, single-stranded sequences of nucleic acid (usually DNA) that have two important features:

- they are complementary to (and thus will base-pair with) a portion of the target DNA sequence, and
- they are constructed with radiolabeled nucleotides, which allows the visualization of the target sequence with special film.

Probes are often engineered to complement mutations or certain gene rearrangements, making Southern blotting a useful diagnostic tool.

Northern Blotting

Northern blotting is almost identical to Southern blotting, except that mRNAs are separated via gel electrophoresis (instead of DNA). The rest of the process is the same; once the mRNAs have been separated on the gel, they are transferred to a nitrocellulose filter, and detected via radiolabeled DNA (or RNA) probes. This technique allows you to determine whether specific gene products (normal or pathologic) are being expressed (if their mRNA is present in a cell, they are probably being translated to protein).

Western Blotting

Western blotting allows you to detect the presence of certain proteins within a sample and also serves as a diagnostic tool. You are able to determine, for example, whether cancer cells express certain tumor-promoting growth receptors on their surface. Here are the steps:

Step 1: Cancer cells are collected and solubilized in detergent to release their cytoplasmic contents.

Step 2: The cell contents, which contain hundreds of different denatured proteins (proteins that have lost their secondary and tertiary structures), are loaded onto a gel. Because of the detergent used, the proteins are all negatively charged.

Step 3: An electric current is applied. The proteins migrate toward the positive pole, with the smaller proteins migrating the farthest from the wells.

Step 4: The separated proteins from the gel are transferred to a nitrocellulose filter.

Step 5: The filter is probed for the target protein. Probing for proteins in western blotting differs from probing in Southern or northern blotting in that antibodies are used as the probes rather than nucleic acids. This is similar to the technique in ELISA; a primary antibody is used first, which will recognize only the target protein via its antigen-binding portions. Then, an enzyme-linked secondary antibody is used that recognizes the constant region of the primary antibody. The enzyme on the secondary antibody will fluoresce when a detection substrate is added, and this light can be photographed with special film. The target protein will show up as a band with an intensity that is proportional to the abundance of the protein in the sample (see Figure 6).

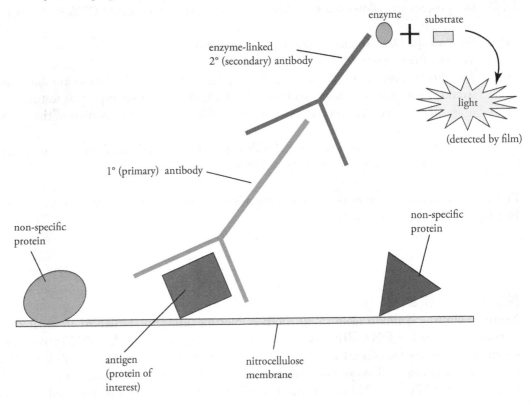

Figure 6   Western Blotting Detection

You're probably wondering if eastern blots exist. While some have tried to coin the phrase to refer to screening for phospholipids, the term is not widely accepted by the scientific community, and it will *not* be on the MCAT!

A.5 RECOMBINANT DNA

In the past twenty years, a major change has occurred in biology that has allowed it to not only describe the mechanisms of life, but also to manipulate living organisms. The cloning and sequencing of genes, production of recombinant DNA, and the subsequent production of recombinant proteins for use as therapeutic agents in medicine have now become commonplace procedures. A **recombinant protein** is one which has been obtained by transcribing and translating a novel combination of DNA (**recombinant DNA**) from different organisms. For example, the gene for human insulin can be placed in a bacterial **plasmid** (described below). Bacteria with the plasmid will then produce insulin that can be used to treat diabetes. To a large extent these advances are due to the development of new technologies for the handling of DNA, such as the discovery of restriction endonucleases that cleave particular DNA sequences.

Restriction endonucleases are bacterial enzymes which recognize specific sequences of DNA and cut the double-stranded molecule in two pieces. A **nuclease** is an enzyme which cuts nucleic acids. An *endo-nuclease* cuts in the middle of a DNA chain (contrast with *exonucleases*, which nibble nucleotides from the ends of DNA chains). They are isolated from bacteria and used in the lab. Their natural role in the bacterium is to destroy viral DNA which gets injected into the cell; thus, they *restrict* the reproduction of hostile viruses.

Restriction enzymes have found great use in molecular biology, where they have permitted manipulation of genes to create recombinant DNA. For example, in Figure 7 below, the cutting-specificity of a restriction enzyme known as *Eco*RI is shown (other restriction enzymes cut at different sequences). The free ends of the DNA molecule that were complementary are known as **sticky ends** since they are able to base pair with other DNA molecules with similar sequences. Some restriction enzymes leave DNAs with **blunt ends** rather than sticky ends. That is, the 3' and 5' ends at the cut site are even, with no overhanging bases.

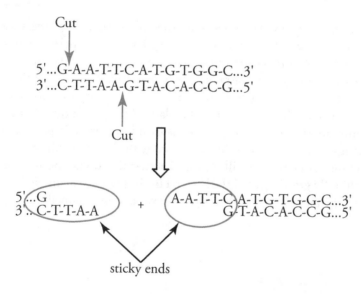

Figure 7   Restriction Digestion of DNA by *Eco*RI

A.5

Study the sequence shown in Figure 7. Notice anything in particular? If you read the top strand from left to right (5' to 3'), it begins GAATTC. Now read the bottom strand from right to left (still 5' to 3'), but only read the six nucleotides on the *left* side of the chain. It says GAATTC (same as above)! Just looking at these six nucleotides, we see that the chain possesses **two-fold rotational symmetry**. The six 5' nucleotides of the top chain are the same as the six 3' nucleotides of the bottom one. Sequences with two-fold rotational symmetry are known as **palindromes**. Many restriction enzymes recognize palindromic sequences.

When a fragment of double-stranded DNA is created by cutting with a restriction endonuclease, it can be inserted into DNA from any source that was also digested by the same restriction endonuclease. For example, *Eco*RI-generated DNA fragments from a human can be isolated, mixed with *Eco*RI-digested DNA from a bacterial plasmid, then joined by the enzyme DNA ligase. Hybrid DNA produced in this fashion is referred to as recombinant DNA, and is commonly propagated as parts of plasmids.

Plasmids

Plasmids are small circular ds-DNA molecules found in bacteria that are capable of autonomous replication (replication that is independent of chromosome replication). This can result in plasmid copy numbers in excess of 100 in a single bacterial cell. The presence of a large number of copies is convenient, since it allows for the isolation of a large amount of plasmid DNA with the identical sequence. Plasmids have been manipulated by recombinant techniques to propagate and express foreign genes in bacteria. The presence of restriction enzyme sites in plasmid DNA permits any desired sequence with complementary sticky ends to be inserted into the plasmid. The plasmid can then be reintroduced into the bacterial cell.

The plasmids used in recombination experiments are specially designed. At the very least, they usually have multiple restriction sites (sites that are sensitive to restriction endonucleases) an origin of replication (this will allow the bacterial DNA replication machinery to forge duplicate copies of the plasmid), and a drug resistance gene (such as ampicillin resistance). They may have other useful sites, such as a promoter (to allow the expression of the inserted gene). They may have a eukaryotic promoter and a poly-adenylation signal as well (this would allow you to use the plasmid for gene expression in eukaryotes as well as prokaryotes). The drug-resistance gene helps when isolating the bacteria possessing the plasmid from other bacteria. For example, bacteria containing a plasmid with the ampicillin-resistance gene are able to grow in the presence of the antibiotic ampicillin, while bacteria that do not possess the plasmid will die in the presence of ampicillin. By growing all of the bacteria in the presence of ampicillin, only those bacteria that possess and express the plasmid can be selectively grown and maintained.

Uses of Recombinant DNA

One use of recombinant DNA technology is the production of eukaryotic proteins by laboratory bacteria (Figure 8). There are many other examples (which will not be discussed here).

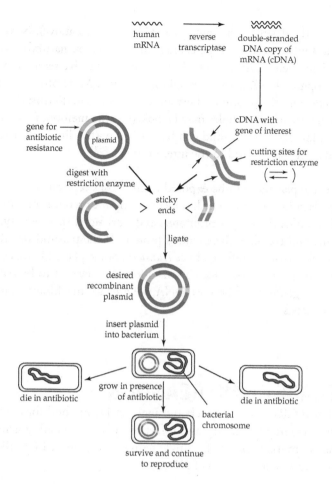

Figure 8   Expression of a Human Gene in Bacteria

This is conceptually simple: All you have to do is get eukaryotic DNA into a plasmid and get the plasmid into a bacterium (called **transformation**, see below), and the bacterium should express the genes. However, you can't insert a eukaryotic gene into a plasmid and expect to get the correct gene product from a bacterium because prokaryotes lack the equipment necessary for splicing out the introns. The solution is to insert **complementary DNA (cDNA)** into a plasmid. Complementary DNA is DNA copied from fully spliced eukaryotic mRNA (this is accomplished by a special enzyme you have encountered before: reverse transcriptase). Once the cDNA is ligated into a bacterial plasmid and bacteria are transformed with this plasmid, they can produce the protein encoded by the cDNA. The cells can then be lysed to release the protein.

More About Bacterial Transformation

Transformation is a method of genetically engineering bacteria, by introducing and expressing novel genes (recombinant DNA, discussed above). (*Note*: **Transfection** refers to an analogous procedure, using mammalian cells as the recipient of new genes.) Generally, the genes introduced are ones that you would like to manufacture in bulk and investigate.

The first step is to integrate the desired gene into a plasmid (described above). Next, the plasmid must be inserted into the bacteria. Only a very small percentage of bacteria are naturally willing to accept pieces of DNA floating around in their environment. These "competent" bacteria express special machinery that translocates the hydrophilic DNA across the lipid membrane. More often, the bacteria (or other cell types) must be coaxed to take up the plasmid. There are several ways to do this; the cells may be cooled in calcium chloride and then heat shocked, holes may be poked in the membrane with the application of an electric field ("electroporation"), or the plasmid can be masked within lipid vesicles, which will fuse with the cell membrane and deliver the plasmid to the interior of the cell.

Once inside the bacteria, the plasmid will be exposed to the host's replication and transcription machinery, which replicates the plasmid (remember, it has its own origin of replication) and transcribes its genes (remember, the plasmid contains the proper promoters and start signals). Newly synthesized mRNA can then access host ribosomes and translate the encoded protein. If the plasmid remains within the cytosol of the bacterium, the transformation is referred to as *transient*. Some plasmids are constructed to integrate within the host's genome; these stable transformations allow the plasmid to be replicated each time the bacterium replicates its own genome, while host DNA polymerase machinery constitutively transcribes and translates the plasmid genes.

A.6 POLYMERASE CHAIN REACTION

Polymerase chain reaction (PCR) is a very quick and inexpensive method for detecting and amplifying specific DNA sequences, screening hereditary and infectious diseases, cloning genes, and fingerprinting DNA. Designed to generate myriad copies of a single template sequence, PCR allows the amplification and subsequent analysis of very small samples of DNA.

Let's say that PCR is to be used to determine whether a certain viral gene has been integrated within a bacterial host genome. A nuclear extract of the bacteria is obtained. Then primers are carefully constructed that will help locate the viral gene (if it is present within the host). Primers are engineered DNA oligonucleotides (~15 bases of single stranded DNA) that will recognize and base pair with specific DNA sequences; in this case, the primers will each recognize a 15-base stretch of the viral gene. Two primers, which will flank a total of ~10 kb of DNA, are used. The "forward primer" will recognize a 15-base stretch at the 3' end of the sense strand, and the "reverse primer" will recognize a 15-base stretch at the 3' end of the antisense strand. When base-paired to their respective gene sequences, the primers will bookend (on opposite sides) the intervening target gene segment (see Figure 9).

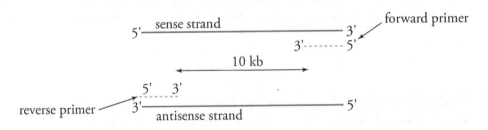

Figure 9   PCR Primers

The primers have free 3' hydroxyl groups, to which dNTPs can be added in a 5' to 3' direction. This will allow the elongation of complementary strands of DNA. The bacterial DNA is mixed with multiple copies of the forward and reverse primers, lots of dNTP bases, a heat-sensitive DNA polymerase, and ions into a buffer. The mixture is then placed into a PCR machine, which will carry out three basic steps (see Figure 10):

Step 1: <u>Initialization</u>. The sample is heated to ~95°C. Heating the sample "melts" the hydrogen bonds that hold the ds-DNA together and, thus, creates single-stranded DNA.

Step 2: <u>Annealing</u>. The sample is cooled to ~55°C. At this temperature, the primers base-pair with the template strands.

Step 3: <u>Elongation</u>. The sample is heated to ~72°C. Using the primers as starting points, the heat-sensitive DNA polymerase (usually *Taq* polymerase isolated from algae that thrive in hot springs) elongates strands of DNA that are complementary to each of the template strands. Each strand is polymerized in the 5' to 3' direction. Any mismatched primers will dissociate from the template strands and will not be extended (this helps ensure the purity of the PCR product).

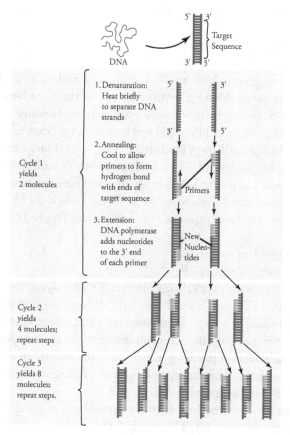

Figure 10 PCR Steps

The cycle repeats every 17 seconds. Because two new complementary strands are synthesized for each template strand in the sample, the PCR product grows at an exponential rate, yielding over a billion copies in just 30 cycles. The sample of DNA is separated via electrophoresis and stained to visualize the products, including the amplified viral gene segment (if present).

Reverse Transcriptase-Polymerase Chain Reaction (RT-PCR)

This is an extension of classic PCR and is used to detect the relative expression of specific gene products. While RT-PCR does not measure the actual expression or abundance of proteins, the technique provides a gauge of gene transcription by measuring the relative amount of target mRNAs. To conduct an RT-PCR experiment, all of the mRNAs from within a cell population are first isolated, then converted into complementary DNA (cDNA) using the enzyme reverse transcriptase. This "library" of cDNAs is then subjected to PCR, using primers specific for a certain gene of interest. If the gene was actively transcribed at the time of harvest, its mRNA will have yielded a cDNA, which will be amplified by the PCR reaction and visualized on a gel.

A.7 DNA SEQUENCING

DNA sequencing is a method by which scientists can determine gene sequences. This provides the basis for investigating the genetics of health and disease. Knowing gene sequences is also a critical component of other experimental techniques, for example, when constructing primers for PCR reactions.

The most widely used DNA sequencing method (the Sanger technique) hinges on a simple yet important structural characteristic of DNA molecules. The ringed ribose of a dNTP has various substituents attached to its carbons: a nitrogenous base at the 1' carbon, a hydrogen at the 2' carbon (recall that a hydroxyl group occupies this site in RNA), a hydroxyl group at the 3' carbon, and a string of three phosphates at the 5' carbon. The 3' carbon hydroxyl group serves as the binding site for another dNTP. Without a free 3' carbon hydroxyl group, dNTPs could not be linked together, and DNA synthesis would not be possible. The Sanger technique utilizes a modified dNTP, which lacks the 3' carbon hydroxyl group. These dideoxynucleotide triphosphates (ddNTPs) maintain their 5' carbon triphosphate moiety and can be incorporated normally into a growing DNA molecule, however, because they lacking the 3' carbon hydroxyl group no further bases can be added to them. Thus, these ddNTPs terminate stand elongation at the point of their insertion. The basic protocol is as follows (see Figure 11):

Step 1: Obtain a sample of DNA to sequence.

Step 2: Denature the DNA into single strands.

Step 3: Mix the sample of DNA with radiolabeled primers, DNA polymerase, and a mixture of dCTP, dTTP, dGTP, dATP, and ddATP (with the dideoxy form making up 1 percent of the adenine base population). This step of the assay will yield a population of newly synthesized DNA fragments, varying in length, each complimentary to the template strand and covalently bonded to a radiolabeled primer at the 5' end (this will aid in the detection of the newly synthesized fragments later). The variety in length of the fragments results from the random insertion of a ddATP into the growing chain.

Step 4: Conduct three more separate reactions as in the previous step, using each of the three other bases in dideoxy form (ddCTP, ddGTP, and ddTTP).

Step 5: Separate the fragments via gel electrophoresis, running each reaction from Steps 3 and 4 in a separate lane.

Step 6: Transfer the fragments to a membrane, and visualize them with radio-sensitive film.

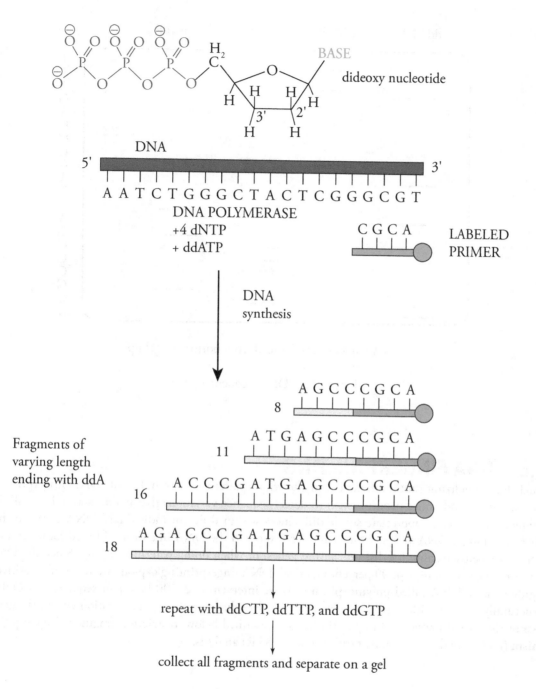

dideoxy nucleotide

Figure 11   DNA Sequencing Reactions

The smallest fragment (i.e., the fragment that migrates the farthest from the well) is a primer with only a single ddNTP attached to it. The lane it ran in corresponds to the first base incorporated into the strand and, thus, the first base of the sequence of the complimentary strand. The second smallest fragment is a primer with two bases attached; this fragment ran in the lane corresponding to the base at the second position in the complimentary strand (see Figure 12). Reading the membrane from bottom (farthest from the wells) to top (closest to the wells) indicates the sequence (in the 5' to 3' direction) of the complimentary strand. Remembering the simple rules of base-pairing (A:T and C:G), you can easily extrapolate the sequence of the template strand.

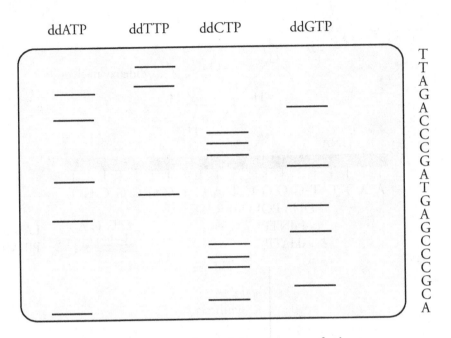

DNA sequence can be read from bottom of gel up

Figure 12 DNA Sequencing Gel

A.8 DNA FINGERPRINTING

Much like visualizing subtle differences in the whorl pattern of a thumbprint, DNA fingerprinting allows scientists (and police departments!) to detect sequence variations that make each individual's DNA unique. The ability to appreciate subtle differences within different individuals' DNA comes in handy when matching a DNA sample from a murder suspect to the DNA in a drop of blood found at a crime scene, or when screening for disease-causing genes, or when doing paternity testing. Since the DNA of any two people is more than 99 percent identical, DNA fingerprinting exploits stretches of repetitive and highly variable DNA called **polymorphisms**. These intervening 2–100 base-pair sequences of DNA are structurally variable with respect to their sequence, length, multiplicity, and location within the genome. Two of the several methods of fingerprinting are described below, **restriction fragment length polymorphism** (RFLP) analysis and **short tandem repeat** (STR) analysis.

Restriction Fragment Length Polymorphism (RFLP) Analysis

Step 1: This method uses restriction endonucleases to cut 10–100 base-pair stretches of polymorphic DNA (called minisatellites) into small fragments. Because of the size variations inherent in this DNA, the resulting DNA fragments (now referred to as RFLPs) also vary in size, and are unique to an individual.

A.8

Step 2: The RFLPs are separated via gel electrophoresis and transferred to a membrane. Southern blotting techniques are used to analyze the sample. The membrane is probed with radiolabeled DNA oligonucleotides that base-pair with specific RFLP sequences, and the membrane is visualized with special film. Polymorphic DNA, even though recovered from the same chromosomal region, will yield unique band distributions for each person. When RFLPs are recovered from DNA sequences within genes, mutations can be detected. For example, sickle cell disease is caused by a single base substitution in the beta chain of hemoglobin. The substituted valine at the sixth position (normally, glutamic acid is present) will introduce a novel restriction site within the gene. When cut with restriction endonucleases, the point mutation generates a different sized RFLP (when compared to the normal gene cut with the same enzymes) and will yield an anomalous banding pattern.

Short Tandem Repeat (STR) Analysis

Step 1: This method uses PCR to amplify 5–10 base-pair stretches of highly polymorphic and repetitive DNA located within noncoding (introns) regions of the genome. These STRs vary with respect to the sequence and number of repeats found at each locus. To profile an individual, a sample of DNA is obtained and the polymorphic DNA is amplified with PCR.

Step 2: The amplified STRs are separated via electrophoresis and analyzed with Southern blotting (see Figure 13).

A.8

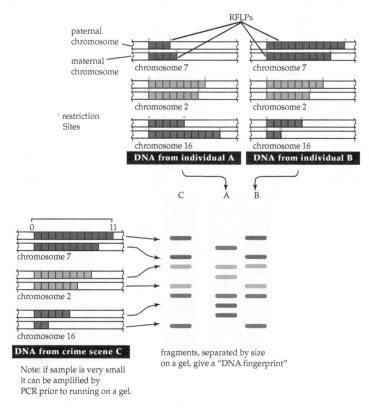

Figure 13   RFLP Analysis

Biology Glossary

After each entry, the section number in the *MCAT Biology* text where the term is discussed is given.

5' cap [Section 3.4]

A methylated guanine nucleotide added to the 5' end of eukaryotic mRNA. The cap is necessary to initiate translation of the mRNA.

A band [Section 10.2]

The band of the sarcomere that extends the full length of the thick filament. The A band includes regions of thick and thin filament overlap, as well as a region of thick filament only. A bands alternate with I bands to give skeletal and cardiac muscle tissue a striated appearance. The A band does not shorten during muscle contraction.

absolute refractory period [Section 7.1]

A period of time following an action potential during which no additional action potential can be evoked regardless of the level of stimulation.

accessory glands [Section 12.1]

The three glands in the male reproductive system that produce semen: the seminal vesicles, the prostate, and the bulbourethral glands.

accessory organs [Section 9.7 and Chapter 12]

1. In the GI tract, organs that play a role in digestion, but are not directly part of the alimentary canal. These include the liver, the gallbladder, the pancreas, and the salivary glands.

2. In the reproductive systems, any organ involved in reproduction that is not a gonad (testis or ovary).

acetylcholine (ACh) [Section 7.2]

The neurotransmitter used throughout the parasympathetic nervous system as well as at the neuromuscular junction.

acetylcholinesterase (AChE) [Section 7.2]

The enzyme that breaks down acetylcholine in the synaptic cleft.

acetyl-CoA [Section 2.6]

The first substrate in the Krebs cycle, produced primarily from the oxidation of pyruvate by the pyruvate dehydrogenase complex, however acetyl-CoA is also produced during fatty acid oxidation and protein catabolism.

acid hydrolases [Section 5.2]

Enzymes that degrade various macromolecules and that require an acidic pH to function properly. Acid hydrolases are found within the lysosomes of cells.

acinar cells [Section 9.5]

Cells that make up exocrine glands, and that secrete their products into ducts. For example, in the pancreas, acinar cells secrete digestive enzymes; in the salivary glands, acinar cells secrete saliva.

acrosome [Section 12.2]

A region at the head of a sperm cell that contains digestive enzymes which, when released during the acrosome reaction, can facilitate penetration of the corona radiata of the oocyte and fertilization.

actin [Section 10.2]

A contractile protein. In skeletal and cardiac muscle, actin polymerizes (along with other proteins) to form the thin filaments. Actin is involved in many contractile activities, such as cytokinesis, pseudopod formation, and muscle contraction.

action potential [Section 7.1]

A localized change in a neuron's or muscle cell's membrane potential that can propagate itself away from its point of origin. Action potentials are an all-or-none process mediated by the opening of voltage-gated Na^+ and K^+ channels when the membrane is brought to the threshold potential; opening of the Na^+ channels causes a characteristic depolarization, while opening of the K^+ channels repolarizes the membrane.

activation energy (E_a) [Section 2.2]
The amount of energy required to produce the transition state of a chemical reaction. If the activation energy for a reaction is very high, the reaction occurs very slowly. Enzymes (and other catalysts) increase reaction rates by reducing activation energy.

active site [Section 2.3]
The three-dimensional site on an enzyme where substrates (reactants) bind and a chemical reaction is facilitated.

active transport [Section 5.3]
The movement of molecules through the plasma membrane against their concentration gradients. Active transport requires input of cellular energy, often in the form of ATP. An example is the Na^+/K^+-ATPase in the plasma membranes of all cells.

adenine [Section 3.1]
One of the four aromatic bases found in DNA and RNA; also a component of ATP, NADH, and $FADH_2$. Adenine is a purine; it pairs with thymine (in DNA) and with uracil (in RNA).

adenohypophysis [Section 7.6]
See "anterior pituitary gland."

adipocyte [Section 8.5]
Fat cell.

adrenal medulla [Section 7.4]
The inner region of the adrenal gland. The adrenal medulla is part of the sympathetic nervous system, and releases epinephrine (adrenaline) and norepinephrine into the blood when stimulated. These hormones augment and prolong the effects of sympathetic stimulation in the body.

adrenergic tone [Section 8.3]
A constant nervous input to the arteries that keeps them somewhat constricted to maintain a basal level of blood pressure.

adrenocorticotropic hormone (ACTH) [Section 7.6]
A tropic hormone produced by the anterior pituitary gland that targets the adrenal cortex, stimulating it to release cortisol and aldosterone.

afferent arteriole [Section 9.2]
The small artery that carries blood toward the capillaries of the glomerulus.

afferent neuron [Section 7.3]
A neuron that carries information (action potentials) to the central nervous system; a sensory neuron.

albumin [Section 8.4]
A blood protein produced by the liver. Albumin helps to maintain blood osmotic pressure (oncotic pressure).

aldosterone [Section 7.6]
The principal mineralocorticoid secreted by the adrenal cortex. This steroid hormone targets the kidney tubules and increases renal reabsorption of sodium.

alimentary canal [Section 9.5]
Also known as the *gastrointestinal* (GI) *tract* or the *digestive tract*, the alimentary canal is the long muscular "tube" that includes the mouth, esophagus, stomach, small intestine, and large intestine.

allele [Section 6.1]
A version of a gene. For example, the gene may be for eye color, and the alleles include those for brown eyes, those for blue eyes, those for green eyes, etc. At most, diploid organisms can possess only two alleles for a given gene, one on each of the two homologous chromosomes.

allosteric regulation [Section 2.4]
The modification of enzyme activity through interaction of molecules with specific sites on the enzyme other than the active site (called allosteric sites).

alveoli [Section 11.2]
(Singular: *alveolus*) Tiny sacs, with walls only a single cell thick, found at the end of the respiratory bronchiole tree. Alveoli are the sites of gas exchange in the respiratory system.

amino acid acceptor site [Section 3.5]
The 3' end of a tRNA molecule that binds an amino acid. The nucleotide sequence at this end is CCA.

amino acid activation [Section 3.5]
See "tRNA loading."

aminoacyl tRNA [Section 3.5]
A tRNA with an amino acid attached. This is made by an aminoacyl-tRNA synthetase, an enzyme that is specific to the amino acid being attached.

amnion [Section 12.10]
A sac filled with fluid (amniotic fluid) that surrounds and protects a developing embryo.

amylase [Section 9.6]
An enzyme that digests starch into disaccharides. Amylase is secreted by salivary glands and by the pancreas.

anabolism [Section 2.6]
The process of building complex structures out of simpler precursors (e.g., synthesizing proteins from amino acids).

analogous structures [Section 6.8]
Physical structures in two different organisms that have functional similarity due to their evolution in a common environment, but that have different underlying structure. Analogous structures arise from convergent evolution.

anal sphincter [Section 9.6]
The valve that controls the release of feces from the rectum. It has an internal part made of smooth muscle (thus involuntary) and an external part made of skeletal muscle (thus voluntary).

anaphase [Section 5.5]
The third phase of mitosis. During anaphase, replicated chromosomes are split apart at their centromeres (the sister chromatids are separated from each other) and moved to opposite sides of the cell.

anaphase I [Section 6.2]
The third phase of meiosis I. During anaphase I the replicated homologous chromosomes are separated (the tetrad is split apart) and pulled to opposite sides of the cell.

anaphase II [Section 6.2]
The third phase of meiosis II. During anaphase II the sister chromatids are finally separated at their centromeres and pulled to opposite sides of the cell. Note that anaphase II is identical to mitotic anaphase, except that the number of chromosomes was reduced by half during meiosis I.

androgens [Section 12.4]
Male sex hormones. Testosterone is the primary androgen.

angiotensinogen [Section 9.3]
A normal blood protein produced by the liver, angiotensinogen is converted to angiotensin I by renin (secreted by the kidney when blood pressure falls). Angiotensin I is further converted to angiotensin II by ACE (angiotensin converting enzyme). Angiotensin II is a powerful systemic vasoconstrictor and stimulator of aldosterone release, both of which result in an increase in blood pressure.

antagonist [Section 10.2]
Something that acts to oppose the action of something else. For example, muscles that move a joint in opposite directions are said to be *antagonists*.

anterior pituitary gland [Section 7.6]
Also known as the *adenohypophysis*, the anterior pituitary is made of glandular tissue. It makes and secretes six different hormones: FSH, LH, ACTH, TSH, prolactin and growth hormone. The anterior pituitary is controlled by releasing and inhibiting factors from the hypothalamus.

antibody (Ab) [Section 8.7]
Also called *immunoglobulins*, antibodies are proteins secreted by activated B-cells (plasma cells) that bind in a highly specific manner to foreign proteins (such as those found on the surface of pathogens or transplanted tissues). The foreign proteins are called *antigens*. Antibodies generally do not destroy antigens directly, rather, they mark them for destruction through other methods, and can inactivate antigens by clumping them together or by covering necessary active sites.

anticodon [Section 3.5]
A sequence of three nucleotides (found in the anticodon loop of tRNA) that is complementary to a specific codon in mRNA. The codon to which the anticodon is complementary specifies the amino acid that is carried by that tRNA.

antidiuretic hormone (ADH) [Section 7.6]
Also called *vasopressin*, this hormone is produced in the hypothalamus and secreted by the posterior pituitary gland. It targets the kidney tubules, increasing their permeability to water, and thus increasing water retention by the body.

antigen (Ag) [Section 8.7]
A molecule (usually a protein) capable of initiating an immune response (antibody production).

antigen presenting cell [Section 8.7]
Cells that possess MHC II (B cells and macrophages), and are able to display bits of ingested antigen on their surface in order to activate T cells. (See also "MHC.")

antiparallel orientation [Section 3.1]
The normal configuration of double-stranded DNA in which the 5' end of one strand is paired with the 3' end of the other.

antiport [Section 5.3]
A carrier protein that transports two molecules across the plasma membrane in opposite directions.

aorta [Section 8.2]
The largest artery in the body; the aorta carries oxygenated blood away from the left ventricle of the heart.

appendix [Section 9.6]
A mass of lymphatic tissue at the beginning of the large intestine that helps trap ingested pathogens.

aqueous humor [Section 7.5]
A thin, watery fluid found in the anterior segment of the eye (between the lens and the cornea). The aqueous humor is constantly produced and drained, and helps to bring nutrients to the lens and cornea, as well as to remove metabolic wastes.

arousal [Section 12.1]
A function in the reproductive system, controlled by the parasympathetic nervous system, that includes erection (via dilation of erectile arteries) and lubrication.

artery [Section 8.1]
A blood vessel that carries blood away from the heart chambers. Arteries have muscular walls to regulate blood flow and are typically high-pressure vessels.

A site [Section 3.5]
Aminoacyl-tRNA site; the site on a ribosome where a new amino acid is added to a growing peptide.

ATP synthase [Section 2.6]
A protein complex found in the inner membrane of the mitochondria. It is essentially a channel that allows H^+ ions to flow from the intermembrane space to the matrix (down the gradient produced by the enzyme complexes of the electron transport chain); as the H^+ ions flow through the channel, ATP is synthesized from ADP and P_i.

atrioventricular (AV) bundle [Section 8.2]
Also known as the *bundle of His*, this is the first portion of the cardiac conduction system after the AV node.

atrioventricular (AV) node [Section 8.2]
The second major node of the cardiac conduction system (after the SA node). The cardiac impulse is delayed slightly at the AV node, allowing the ventricles to contract just after the atria contract.

atrioventricular valves [Section 8.2]
The valves in the heart that separate the atria from the ventricles. The *tricuspid* valve separates the right atrium from the right ventricle, and the *bicuspid* (or *mitral*) valve separates the left atrium from the left ventricle. These valves close at the beginning of systole, preventing the backflow of blood from ventricles to atria, and producing the first heart sound.

atrium [Section 8.2]
One of two small chambers in the heart that receive blood and pass it on to the ventricles. The right atrium receives deoxygenated blood from the body through the superior and inferior vena cavae, and the left atrium receives oxygenated blood from the lungs through the pulmonary veins.

attachment [Section 4.1]
The first step in viral infection. Attachment of a virus to its host is very specific and is also known as *adsorption*.

auditory tube [Section 7.5]
The tube that connects the middle ear cavity with the pharynx; also known as the *Eustachian tube*. Its function is to equalize middle ear pressure with atmospheric pressure so that pressure is equal on both sides of the tympanic membrane.

autoimmune reaction [Section 8.7]
An immune reaction directed against normal (necessary) cells. For example, type I diabetes mellitus is an autoimmune reaction directed against the β cells of the pancreas (destroying them and preventing insulin secretion), and against insulin itself.

autonomic nervous system (ANS) [Section 7.4]
The division of the peripheral nervous system that innervates and controls the visceral organs (everything but the skeletal muscles). It is also known as the *involuntary nervous system* and can be subdivided into the sympathetic and parasympathetic divisions.

autotroph [Section 4.2]
An organism that can makes its own food, typically using CO_2 as a carbon source.

auxotroph [Section 4.2]
A bacterium that cannot survive on minimal medium (glucose alone) because it lacks the ability to synthesize a molecule it needs to live (typically an amino acid). Auxotrophs must have the needed substance (the *aux*iliary *troph*ic substance) added to their medium in order to survive. The are typically denoted by the substance they require followed by a "−" sign in superscript. For example, a bacterium that cannot synthesize leucine would be a leucine auxotroph, and would be indicated as Leu⁻.

avascular [Section 10.8]
Lacking a blood supply, e.g., cartilage.

axon [Section 7.1]
A long projection off the cell body of a neuron down which an action potential can be propagated.

bacillus [Section 4.2]
A bacterium having a rod-like shape (plural = bacilli).

bacteriophage [Section 4.1]
A virus that infects a bacterium.

baroreceptor [Section 7.5]

A sensory receptor that responds to changes in pressure; for example, there are baroreceptors in the carotid arteries and the aortic arch that monitor blood pressure.

Bartholin's glands [Section 12.5]

See "vestibular glands."

basement membrane [Section 10.6]

A layer of collagen fibers that separates epithelial tissue from connective tissue.

basilar membrane [Section 7.5]

The flexible membrane in the cochlea that supports the organ of Corti (the structure that contains the hearing receptors). The fibers of the basilar membrane are short and stiff near the oval window and long and flexible near the apex of the cochlea. This difference in structure allows the basilar membrane to help transduce pitch.

B cell [Section 8.7]

A type of lymphocyte that can recognize (bind to) an antigen and secrete an antibody specific for that antigen. When activated by binding an antigen, B cells mature into *plasma cells* (that secrete antibody) and *memory cells* (that patrol the body for future encounters with that antigen).

bicarbonate [Section 8.5]

HCO_3^-. This ion results from the dissociation of carbonic acid and, together with carbonic acid, forms the major blood buffer system. Bicarbonate is also secreted by the pancreas to neutralize stomach acid in the intestines.

bicuspid valve [Section 8.2]

See "atrioventricular valve."

bile [Section 9.7]

A green fluid made from cholesterol and secreted by the liver. It is stored and concentrated in the gallbladder. Bile is an amphipathic molecule that is secreted into the small intestine when fats are present, and serves to emulsify the fats for better digestion by lipases.

binary fission [Section 4.2]

An asexual method of bacterial reproduction that serves only to increase the size of the population; there is no introduction of genetic diversity. The bacterium simply grows in size until it has doubled its cellular components, then it replicates its genome and splits into two.

bipolar neuron [Section 7.1]

A neuron with a single axon and a single dendrite, often projecting from opposite sides of the cell body. Bipolar neurons are typically associated with sensory organs; an example is the bipolar neurons in the retina of the eye.

blastocyst [Section 12.9]

A fluid-filled sphere formed about 5 days after fertilization of an ovum that is made up of an outer ring of cells and an inner cell mass. This is the structure that implants in the endometrium of the uterus.

blotting [Section A.4]

The transfer of DNA or proteins from an electrophoresis gel to a nitrocellulose filter.

Bohr effect [Section 8.5]

The tendency of certain factors to stabilize hemoglobin in the tense conformation, thus reducing its affinity for oxygen and enhancing the release of oxygen to the tissues. The factors include increased P_{CO_2}, increased temperature, increased bisphosphoglycerate (BPG), and decreased pH. Note that the Bohr effect shifts the oxy-hemoglobin saturation curve to the right.

bone marrow [Section 10.7]

A non-bony material that fills the hollow spaces inside bones. Red bone marrow is found in regions of spongy bone and is the site of blood cell production. Yellow bone marrow is found in the diaphysis (shaft) of long bones, is mostly fat, and is inactive.

Bowman's capsule [Section 9.2]

The region of the nephron that surrounds the glomerulus. The capsule collects the plasma that is filtered from the capillaries in the glomerulus.

bronchioles [Section 11.2]
Very small air tubes in the respiratory system (diameter 0.5–1.0 mm). The walls of the bronchioles are made of smooth muscle to help regulate air flow.

brush border enzymes [Section 9.6]
Enzymes secreted by the mucosal cells lining the intestine. The brush border enzymes are disaccharidases and dipeptidases that digest the smallest carbohydrates and peptides into their respective monomers.

bulbourethral glands [Section 12.1]
Small, paired glands found inferior to the prostate in males and at the posterior end of the penile urethra. They secrete an alkaline mucus on sexual arousal that lubricates the urethra and helps to neutralize any traces of acidic urine in the urethra that might be harmful to sperm.

Bundle of His [Section 8.2]
See "atrioventricular (AV) bundle."

calcitonin [Sections 7.6 and 10.9]
A hormone produced by the C-cells of the thyroid gland that decreases serum calcium levels. It targets the bones (stimulates osteoblasts) and the kidneys (reduces calcium reabsorption.

calcitriol [Section 10.9]
A hormone produced from vitamin D that acts to increase serum calcium levels.

calmodulin [Section 10.4]
A cytoplasmic Ca^{2+}-binding protein. Calmodulin is particularly important in smooth muscle cells, where binding of Ca^{2+} allows calmodulin to activate myosin light-chain kinase, the first step in smooth muscle cell contraction.

canaliculus [Section 10.7]
Very small tube or channel, such as is found between lacunae (connecting them together) in compact bone.

capacitation [Section 12.9]
An increase in the fragility of the membranes of sperm cells when exposed to the female reproductive tract. Capacitation is required so that the acrosomal enzymes can be released to facilitate fertilization.

capillary [Section 8.5]
The smallest of all blood vessels, typically having a diameter just large enough for blood cells to pass through in single file. Capillaries have extremely thin walls to facilitate the exchange of material between the blood and the tissues.

capsid [Section 4.1]
The outer protein coat of a virus.

carbonic anhydrase [Section 8.5]
An enzyme present in erythrocytes (as well as in other places) that catalyzes the conversion of CO_2 and H_2O into carbonic acid.

cardiac conduction system [Section 8.2]
The specialized cells of the heart that spontaneously initiate action potentials and transmit them to the cardiac muscle cells. The cells of the conduction system are essentially cardiac muscle cells, but lack the contractile fibers of the muscle cells, thus they are able to transmit impulses (action potentials) more quickly and efficiently than cardiac muscle tissue. The cardiac conduction system includes the SA node, the internodal tract, the AV node, the AV bundle, the right and left bundle branches, and the Purkinje fibers.

cardiac muscle [Sections 8.2 and 10.3]
The muscle tissue of the heart. Cardiac muscle is striated, uninucleate, and under involuntary control (controlled by the autonomic nervous system). Note also that cardiac muscle is self-stimulatory, and autonomic control serves only to modify the intrinsic rate of contraction.

cardiac output [Section 8.2]

The volume of blood pumped out of the heart in one minute (vol/min); the product of the stroke volume (vol/beat) and the heart rate (beat/min). Cardiac output is directly proportional to blood pressure.

cardiac sphincter [Section 9.6]

See "lower esophageal sphincter."

carrier protein [Section 5.3]

An integral membrane protein that undergoes a conformational change to move a molecule from one side of the membrane to another. See also "uniporter," "antiporter," and "symporter."

cartilage [Section 10.6]

A strong connective tissue with varying degrees of flexibility. Elastic cartilage is the most flexible, forming structures that require support but also need to bend, such as the epiglottis and outer ear. Hyaline cartilage is more rigid than elastic cartilage, and forms the cartilages of the ribs, the respiratory tract, and all joints. Fibrocartilage is the least flexible of them all, and forms very strong connections, such as the pubic symphysis and the intervertebral disks.

catabolism [Section 2.6]

The process of breaking down large molecules into smaller precursors, e.g. digestion of starch into glucose.

catalase [Section 5.2]

The primary enzyme in peroxisomes; catalase catalyzes the hydrolysis of hydrogen peroxide (H_2O_2) into water and oxygen.

catalyst [Section 2.2]

Something that increases the rate of a chemical reaction by reducing the activation energy for that reaction. The ΔG of the reaction remains unchanged.

cAMP [Section 5.4]

See "cyclic AMP."

cDNA [Section A.5]

Complementary DNA. DNA produced synthetically by reverse transcribing mRNA. Because of eukaryotic mRNA splicing, cDNA contains no introns.

cecum [Section 9.6]

The first part of the large intestine.

cell surface receptor [Section 5.4]

An integral membrane protein that binds extracellular signaling molecules, such as hormones and peptides.

central canal [Section 10.7]

The hollow center of an osteon, also known as a *Haversian canal*. The central canal contains blood vessels, lymphatic vessels, and nerves. Bone is laid down around the central canal in concentric rings called *lamellae*.

central chemoreceptors [Section 11.5]

Receptors in the central nervous system that monitor the pH of cerebrospinal fluid to help regulate ventilation rate.

central nervous system [Section 7.4]

The subdivision of the nervous system consisting of the brain and spinal cord.

centriole [Section 5.4]

A structure composed of a ring of nine microtubule triplets, found in pairs at the MTOC (microtubule organizing center) of a cell. The centrioles duplicate during cell division, and serve as the organizing center for the mitotic spindle.

centromere [Section 5.2]

A structure near the middle of eukaryotic chromosomes to which the fibers of the mitotic spindle attach during cell division.

cerebellum [Section 7.4]

The region of the brain that coordinates and smoothes skeletal muscle activity.

cerebral cortex [Section 7.4]
A thin (4 mm) layer of gray matter on the surface of the cerebral hemispheres. The cerebral cortex is the conscious mind, and is functionally divided into four pairs of lobes: the frontal lobes, the parietal lobes, the temporal lobes, and the occipital lobes.

cerebrospinal fluid (CSF) [Section 7.4]
A clear fluid that circulates around and through the brain and spinal cord. CSF helps to physically support the brain and acts as a shock absorber. It also exchanges nutrients and wastes with the brain and spinal cord.

ceruminous gland [Section 11.6]
A gland that secretes a waxy product, found in the external ear canal.

cervix [Section 12.5]
The opening to the uterus. The cervix is typically plugged with a sticky acidic mucus during non-fertile times (to form a barrier against the entry of pathogens), however during ovulation the mucus becomes more watery and alkaline to facilitate sperm entry.

channel protein [Section 5.3]
An integral membrane protein that selectively allows molecules across the plasma membrane. See also entries under "ion channel," "voltage-gated channel," and "ligand-gated channel."

chemical synapse [Section 7.2]
A type of synapse at which a chemical (a neurotransmitter) is released from the axon of a neuron into the synaptic cleft where it binds to receptors on the next structure in sequence, either another neuron or an organ.

chemoreceptor [Section 7.5]
A sensory receptor that responds to specific chemicals. Some examples are gustatory (taste) receptors, olfactory (smell) receptors, and central chemoreceptors (respond to pH changes in the cerebrospinal fluid).

chemotaxis [Section 4.2]
Movement that is directed by chemical gradients, such as nutrients or toxins.

chemotroph [Section 4.2]
An organism that relies on a chemical source of energy (such as ATP) instead of using light to make ATP (like phototrophs do).

chief cells [Section 9.6]
Pepsinogen-secreting cells found at the bottom of the gastric glands of the stomach.

chitin [Section 4.3]
A polysaccharide found in the cell walls of fungi and in the exoskeletons of insects.

cholecystokinin (CCK) [Section 9.6]
A hormone secreted by the small intestine (duodenum) in response to the presences of fats. It promotes release of bile from the gallbladder and pancreatic juice from the pancreas, and reduces stomach motility.

cholesterol [Section 5.3]
A large, ring-shaped lipid found in cell membranes. Cholesterol is the precursor for steroid hormones, and is used to manufacture bile salts.

chondrocyte [Section 10.8]
A mature cartilage cell.

chorion [Section 12.8]
The portion of the placenta derived from the zygote. The chorionic villi secrete hCG to help maintain the endometrium during the first trimester of a pregnancy.

choroid [Section 7.5]
The darkly pigmented middle layer of the eyeball, found between the sclera (outer layer) and the retina (inner layer).

chromatin [Section 3.1]
DNA that is densely packed around histone proteins. The genes in heterochromatin are generally inaccessible to enzymes and are turned off.

chromosome [Section 3.1]
A single piece of double-stranded DNA; part of the genome of an organism. Prokaryotes have circular chromosomes and eukaryotes have linear chromosomes.

chylomicrons [Sections 8.5 and 9.8]
A type of lipoprotein; the form in which absorbed fats from the intestines are transported to the circulatory system.

chyme [Section 9.6]
Partially digested, semiliquid food mixed with digestive enzymes and acids in the stomach.

chymotrypsin [Section 9.7]
One of the main pancreatic proteases; it is activated (from chymotrypsinogen) by trypsin.

cilia [Section 5.4]
A hair-like structure on the cell surface composed of microtubules in a "9 + 2" arrangement (nine pairs of microtubules surrounding 2 single microtubules in the center). The microtubules are connected with a contractile protein called *dynein*. Cilia beat in a repetitive sweeping motion, which helps to move substances along the surface of the cell. They are particularly important in the respiratory system, where they sweep mucus out of the trachea and up to the mouth and nose.

ciliary muscles [Section 7.5]
Muscles that help focus light on the retina by controlling the curvature of the lens of the eye.

circular smooth muscle [Section 9.5]
The inner layer of smooth muscle in the wall of the digestive tract. When the circular muscle contracts, the tube diameter is reduced. Certain areas of the circular muscle are thickened to act as valves (sphincters).

citric acid cycle [Section 2.6]
See "Krebs cycle."

clathrin [5.3]
A fibrous protein found on the intracellular side of the plasma membrane (also found associated with the Golgi complex) that helps to invaginate the membrane. Typically cell surface receptors are associated with clathrin-coated pits at the plasma membrane, and binding of the ligand to the receptor triggers invagination.

cleavage [Section 12.9]
The rapid mitotic divisions of a zygote that begin within 24–36 hours after fertilization.

coccus [Section 4.2]
A bacterium having a round shape (plural = cocci).

cochlea [Section 7.5]
The curled structure in the inner ear that contains the membranes and hair cells used to transduce sound waves into action potentials.

codominance [Section 6.1]
A situation in which a heterozygote displays the phenotype associated with each of the alleles, e.g., human blood type AB.

codon [Section 3.2]
A group of three nucleotides that is specific for a particular amino acid, or that specifies "stop translating."

coenzyme [Section 2.6]
An organic molecule that associates non-covalently with an enzyme, and that is required for the proper functioning of the enzyme.

co-factor [Section 2.6]
An inorganic molecule that associates non-covalently with an enzyme, and that is required for the proper functioning of the enzyme.

collagen [Section 10.6]

A protein fiber with a unique triple-helix structure that gives it great strength. Tissues with a lot of collagen fibers are typically very strong, e.g., bone, tendons, ligaments, etc.

collecting duct [Section 9.2]

The portion of the nephron where water reabsorption is regulated via antidiuretic hormone (ADH). Several nephrons empty into each collecting duct, and this is the final region through which urine must pass on its way to the ureter.

colon [Section 9.6]

See "large intestine."

common bile duct [Section 9.6]

The duct that carries bile from the gallbladder and liver to the small intestine (duodenum).

compact bone [Section 10.7]

A dense, hard type of bone constructed from osteons (at the microscopic level). Compact bone forms the diaphysis of the long bones, and the outer shell of the epiphyses and all other bones.

competitive inhibitor [Section 2.5]

An enzyme inhibitor that competes with substrate for binding at the active site of the enzyme. When the inhibitor is bound, no product can be made.

complement system [Section 8.7]

A group of blood proteins that bind non-specifically to the surface proteins of foreign cells (such as bacteria), ultimately leading to the destruction of the foreign cell.

cones [Section 7.5]

Photoreceptors in the retina of the eye that respond to bright light and provide color vision.

conjugation [Section 4.2]

A form of genetic recombination in bacteria in which plasmid and/or genomic DNA is transferred from one bacterium to the other through a conjugation bridge.

connective tissue [Section 10.6]

One of the four basic tissue types in the body (epithelial, connective, muscle, and nervous). Connective tissue is a supportive tissue consisting of relatively few cells scattered among a great deal of extracellular material (matrix), and includes adipose tissue (fat), bone, cartilage, the dermis of the skin, tendons, ligaments, and blood.

convergent evolution [Section 6.8]

A form of evolution in which different organisms are placed into the same environment and exposed to the same selection pressures. This causes the organisms to evolve along similar lines. As a result, they may share functional, but not structural similarity (because they possessed different starting materials). Convergent evolution produces *analogous structures*.

cooperativity [Section 2.5]

A type of substrate binding to a multi-active site enzyme, in which the binding of one substrate molecule facilitates the binding of subsequent substrate molecules. A graph of reaction rate vs. substrate concentration appears sigmoidal. Note that cooperativity can be found in other situations as well, for example, hemoglobin binds oxygen cooperatively.

cornea [Section 7.5]

The clear portion of the tough outer layer of the eyeball, found over the iris and pupil.

corona radiata [Section 12.6]

The layer of granulosa cells that surround an oocyte after it has been ovulated.

coronary vessels [Section 8.2]

The blood vessels that carry blood to and from cardiac muscle. The coronary arteries branch off the aorta and carry oxygenated blood to the cardiac tissue. The coronary veins collect deoxygenated blood from the cardiac tissue, merge to form the coronary sinus, and drain into the right atrium.

corpus callosum [Section 7.4]
The largest bundle of white matter (axons) connecting the two cerebral hemispheres.

corpus luteum [Section 12.6]
"Yellow body." The remnants of an ovarian follicle after ovulation has occurred. The cells enlarge and begin secreting progesterone, the dominant female hormone during the second half of the menstrual cycle. Some estrogen is also secreted.

cortex [Section 9.2]
The outer layer of an organ, e.g., the renal cortex, the ovarian cortex, the adrenal cortex, etc.

cortical reaction [Section 12.9]
See "slow block to polyspermy."

corticosteroids [Section 7.6]
Steroid hormones secreted from the adrenal cortex. The two major classes are the *mineralocorticoids* and *glucocorticoids*. Aldosterone is the principal mineralocorticoid, and cortisol is the principal glucocorticoid.

cortisol [Section 7.6]
The principal glucocorticoid secreted from the adrenal cortex. This steroid hormone is released during stress, causing increased blood glucose levels and reducing inflammation. The latter effect has led to a clinical use of cortisol as an anti-inflammatory agent.

creatine phosphate [Section 10.2]
An energy storage molecule used by muscle tissue. The phosphate from creatine phosphate can be removed and attached to an ADP to generate ATP quickly.

cristae [Sections 2.6 and 5.2]
The folds of the inner membrane of a mitochondrion.

cross bridge [Section 10.2]
The connection of a myosin head group to an actin filament during muscle contraction (the sliding filament theory).

crossing over [Section 6.2]
The exchange of DNA between paired homologous chromosomes (tetrads) during prophase I of meiosis.

cyclic AMP (cAMP) [Section 5.4]
A cyclic version of adenosine monophosphate, where the phosphate is esterified to both the 5' and the 3' carbons, forming a ring. Cyclic AMP is an important intracellular signaling molecule, often called the "second messenger." It serves to activate cAMP-dependent kinases, which regulate the activity of other enzymes in the cell. Levels of cAMP are in part regulated by adenylyl cyclase, the enzyme that makes cAMP, and the activity of adenylyl cyclase is ultimately controlled by the binding of various ligands to cell surface receptors.

cytokinesis [Section 5.5]
The phase of mitosis during which the cell physically splits into two daughter cells. Cytokinesis begins near the end of anaphase, and is completed during telophase.

cytosine [Section 3.1]
One of the four aromatic bases found in DNA and RNA. Cytosine is a pyrimidine; it pairs with guanine.

dendrite [Section 7.1]
A projection off the cell body of a neuron that receives a nerve impulse from a different neuron and sends the impulse to the cell body. Neurons can have one or several dendrites.

dense connective tissue [Section 10.8]
Connective tissue with large amounts of either collagen fibers or elastic fibers, or both. Dense tissues are typically strong (e.g., bone, cartilage, tendons, etc.).

depolarization [Section 7.1]
The movement of the membrane potential of a cell away from rest potential in a more positive direction.

dermis [Section 11.6]

A layer of connective tissue underneath the epidermis of the skin. The dermis contains blood vessels, lymphatic vessels, nerves, sensory receptors, and glands.

desmosome [Section 5.4]

A general cell junction, used primarily for adhesion.

determination [Section 12.12]

The point during cellular development at which a cell becomes committed to a particular fate. Note that the cell is not differentiated at this point; determination comes before differentiation. Determination can be due to cytoplasmic effects or to induction by neighboring cells.

diaphragm [Section 11.3]

The primary muscle of inspiration. The diaphragm is stimulated to contract at regular intervals by the respiratory center in the medulla oblongata (via the phrenic nerve). Although it is made of skeletal muscle (and can therefore be voluntarily controlled), these stimulations occur autonomously.

diaphysis [Section 10.7]

The shaft of a long bone. The diaphysis is hollow and is made entirely from compact bone.

diastole [Section 8.2]

The period of time during which the ventricles of the heart are relaxed.

diastolic pressure [Section 8.3]

The pressure measured in the arteries while the ventricles are relaxed (during diastole).

diencephalon [Section 7.4]

The portion of the forebrain that includes the thalamus and hypothalamus.

differentiation [Section 12.12]

The specialization of cell types, especially during embryonic and fetal development.

diffusion [Section 5.3]

The movement of a particle (the solute) from its region of high concentration to its region of low concentration (or *down its concentration gradient*).

diploid organism [Section 6.1]

An organism that has two copies of its genome in each cell. The paired genomes are said to be homologous.

distal convoluted tubule [Section 9.2]

The portion of the nephron tubule after the loop of Henle, but before the collecting duct. Selective reabsorption and secretion occur here; most notably regulated reabsorption of water and sodium.

divergent evolution [Section 6.8]

A form of evolution in which the same organism is placed into different environments with different selection pressures. This causes the organisms to evolve differently; to diverge from their common ancestor. The resulting (new) species may share structural (but not necessarily functional) similarity; divergent evolution produces *homologous structures*.

DNA ligase [Section 3.3]

See "ligase."

DNA polymerase [Section 3.3]

Also called DNA pol, this is the enzyme that replicates DNA. Eukaryotes have a single version of the enzyme, simply called DNA pol; prokaryotes have three versions, called DNA pol I, DNA pol II, and DNA pol III.

dominant [Section 6.1]

1. The allele in a heterozygous genotype that is expressed.

2. The phenotype resulting from either a heterozygous genotype or a homozygous dominant genotype.

dorsal root ganglion [Section 7.4]
A group of sensory neuron cell bodies found just posterior to the spinal cord on either side. A pair of root ganglia exists for each spinal nerve that extends from the spinal cord. The ganglia are part of the peripheral nervous system (PNS).

downstream [Section 3.4]
Toward the 3' end of an RNA transcript (the 3' end of the DNA coding strand). Stop codons and (in eukaryotes) the poly-A tail are found "downstream."

ductus deferens [Section 12.1]
A thick, muscular tube that connects the epididymis of the testes to the urethra. Muscular contractions of the vas deferens during ejaculation help propel the sperm outward. Severing of the vas deferens (vasectomy) results in sterility of the male.

duodenum [Section 9.6]
The first part (approximately 5 percent) of the small intestine.

dynein [Section 5.4]
A contractile protein connecting microtubules in the "9 + 2" arrangement of cilia and eukaryotic flagella. The contraction of dynein produces the characteristic movements of these structures.

ectoderm [Section 12.11]
One of the three primary (embryonic) germ layers formed during gastrulation. Ectoderm ultimately forms external structures such as the skin, hair, nails, and inner linings of the mouth and anus, as well as the entire nervous system.

edema [Section 8.5]
Swelling.

effector organ [Section 7.3]
The organ that carries out the command sent along a particular motor neuron.

efferent arteriole [Section 9.2]
The small artery that carries blood away from the capillaries of the glomerulus.

efferent neuron [Section 7.3]
A neuron that carries information (action potentials) away from the central nervous system; a motor neuron.

ejaculation [Section 12.1]
A subphase of male orgasm, a reflex reaction triggered by the presence of semen in the urethra. Ejaculation is a series of rhythmic contractions of muscles near the base of the penis that increase pressure in the urethra, forcing the semen out.

ejection fraction [Section 10.3]
The fraction of the end-diastolic volume ejected from the ventricles in a single contraction of the heart. The ejection fraction is normally around 60 percent of the end-diastolic volume.

elastin [Section 10.6]
A fibrous, connective-tissue protein that has the ability to recoil to its original shape after being stretched. Elastin is found in great amounts in lung tissue, arterial tissue, skin, and the epiglottis.

electrical synapse [Section 7.2]
A type of synapse in which the cells are connected by gap junctions, allowing ions (and therefore an action potential) to spread easily from cell to cell.

electron transport chain [Section 2.6]
A series of enzyme complexes found along the inner mitochondrial membrane. NADH and $FADH_2$ are oxidized by these enzymes; the electrons are shuttled down the chain and are ultimately passed to oxygen to produce water. The electron energy is used to pump H^+ out of the mitochondrial matrix; the resulting H^+ gradient is subsequently used to drive the production of ATP.

electrophoresis [Section A.3]
A means of separating things by size (for example, nucleic acids or proteins) or by charge (for example, proteins).

ELISA [Section A.1]
A biochemical technique that utilizes antigen-antibody interactions to determine the presence of either antigens (like proteins or cytokines), or specific immunoglobulins (antibodies) in a sample (such as cells recovered from a tumor biopsy or a patient's serum).

embryonic stage [Section 12.10]
The period of human development from implantation through eight weeks of gestation. Gastrulation, neurulation, and organogenesis occur during this time period. The developing baby is known as an *embryo* during this time period.

emission [Section 12.1]
A subphase of male orgasm. Emission is the movement of sperm (via the ductus deferens) and semen (via the accessory glands) into the urethra in preparation for ejaculation.

endocrine gland [Section 7.6]
A ductless gland that secretes a hormone into the blood.

endocrine system [Section 7.6]
A system of ductless glands that secrete chemical messengers (hormones) into the blood.

endocytosis [Section 5.3]
The uptake of material into a cell, usually by invagination. See also "phagocytosis," "pinocytosis," and "receptor-mediated endocytosis."

endoderm [Section 12.11]
One of the three primary (embryonic) germ layers formed during gastrulation. Endoderm ultimately forms internal structures, such as the inner lining of the GI tract and some glandular organs.

endometrial cycle [Section 12.7]
The 28 days of the menstrual cycle as they apply to the events in the uterus. The endometrial cycle is also known as the *uterine cycle*, and has three subphases: menstruation, the proliferative phase, and the secretory phase.

endometrium [Section 12.7]
The inner epithelial lining of the uterus that thickens and develops during the menstrual cycle, into which a fertilized ovum can implant, and which sloughs off during menstruation if a pregnancy does not occur.

endospore [Section 4.2]
A bacterial structure formed in unfavorable growth conditions. Endospores have very tough outer shells made of peptidoglycan and can survive harsh conditions. The bacterium inside the endospore is essentially dormant and can become active (called germination) when conditions again become favorable.

endosymbiotic theory [Section 5.2]
The theory that mitochondria and chloroplasts originated as independent unicellular organisms living in symbiosis with larger cells.

endotoxin [Section 4.2]
A normal component of the outer membrane of Gram-negative bacteria. Endotoxins produce extreme immune reactions (septic shock), particularly when many of them enter the circulation at once.

end plate potential [Section 10.2]
The depolarization of the motor end plate on a muscle cell.

enteric nervous system [Section 9.5]
The nervous system of the gastrointestinal tract. It controls secretion and motility within the GI tract, and is linked to the central nervous system.

enterogastrone [Section 9.6]
A hormone secreted by the small intestine (duodenum) in response to the presence of food. It decreases the rate at which chyme leaves the stomach and enters the small intestine.

enterokinase [Section 9.6]
A duodenal enzyme that activates trypsinogen (from the pancreas) to trypsin.

envelope [Section 4.1]

A lipid bilayer that surrounds the capsid of an animal virus. The envelope is acquired as the virus buds out through the plasma membrane of its host cell. Not all animal viruses possess an envelope.

enzyme [Section 2.2]

A physiological catalyst. Enzymes are usually proteins, although some RNAs have catalytic activity.

epidermis [Section 11.6]

The outermost layer of the skin. The epidermis is made of epithelial tissue that is constantly dividing at the bottom; the cells migrate to the surface (dying along the way) to be sloughed off at the surface.

epididymis [Section 12.1]

A long, coiled duct on the outside of the testis in which sperm mature.

epiglottis [Section 11.2]

A flexible piece of cartilage in the larynx that flips downward to seal the trachea during swallowing.

epinephrine [Section 7.4]

A hormone produced and secreted by the adrenal medulla that prolongs and increases the effects of the sympathetic nervous system.

epiphyseal plate [Section 10.9]

A band of cartilage (hyaline) found between the diaphysis and the epiphyses of long bones during childhood and adolescence. Cell proliferation in the middle of the epiphyseal plate essentially forces the diaphysis and epiphyses further apart, while the older cartilage at the edges of the plate is replaced with bone. This is what allows bone growth during childhood. The epiphyseal plate gets thinner and thinner the older a person gets, until finally it fuses (the diaphysis and epiphyses connect) in late adolescence, preventing further elongation of the bones.

epiphysis [Section 10.7]

One of the two ends of a long bone (pl: epiphyses). The epiphyses have an outer shell made of compact bone and an inner core of spongy bone. The spongy bone is filled with red bone marrow, the site of blood cell formation.

epistasis [Section 6.1]

A situation in which the expression of one gene prevents expression of all allelic forms of another gene, e.g., the gene for male pattern baldness is epistatic to the hair color gene.

epithelial tissue [Section 9.5]

One of the four basic tissue types in the body (epithelial, connective, muscle, and nervous). Epithelial tissue is a lining and covering tissue (e.g. skin, the lining of the stomach and intestines, the lining of the urinary tract, etc.) or a glandular tissue (e.g. the liver, the pancreas, the ovaries, etc.).

epitope [Section 8.7]

The specific site on an antigenic molecule that binds to a T-cell receptor or to an antibody.

EPSP [Section 7.2]

Excitatory postsynaptic potential; a slight depolarization of a postsynaptic cell, bringing the membrane potential of that cell closer to the threshold for an action potential.

erectile tissue [Section 12.1]

Specialized tissue with a lot of space that can fill with blood upon proper stimulation, causing the tissue to become firm. Erectile tissue is found in the penis, the clitoris, the labia, and the nipples.

erythrocyte [Section 8.4]

A red blood cell; they are filled with hemoglobin, and the function of the erythrocytes is to carry oxygen in the blood.

erythropoietin [Section 7.6]

A hormone produced and released by the kidney that stimulates the production of red blood cells by the bone marrow.

estrogen [Section 7.6]

The primary female sex hormone. Estrogen stimulates the development of female secondary sex characteristics during puberty, maintains those characteristics during adulthood, stimulates the development of a new uterine lining after menstruation, and stimulates mammary gland development during pregnancy.

euchromatin [Section 3.1]

DNA that is loosely packed around histones. This DNA is more accessible to enzymes and the genes in euchromatin can be activated if needed.

eukaryotic [Section 5.1]

A cell characterized by the presence of a nucleus and other membrane-bound organelles. Eukaryotes can be unicellular (protists) or multicellular (fungi, plants, and animals).

excision [Section 4.1]

The removal (and usually the activation) of a viral genome from its host's genome.

excitation-contraction coupling
       [Section 10.2]

The mechanism that ensures that skeletal muscle contraction does not occur without neural stimulation (excitation). At rest, cytosolic $[Ca^{2+}]$ is low, and the troponin-tropomyosin complex covers the myosin-binding sites on actin. When the muscle is stimulated by a neuron, Ca^{2+} is released from the sarcoplasmic reticulum into the cytosol of the muscle cell. Ca^{2+} binds to troponin, causing a conformation change in the troponin-tropomyosin complex that shifts it away from the myosin-binding sites. This allows myosin and actin to interact according to the sliding filament theory.

excretion [Section 9.1]

The elimination of waste products from the body.

exocrine gland [Section 7.6]

A gland that secretes its product into a duct, which ultimately carries the product to the surface of the body or into a body cavity. Some examples of exocrine glands and their products are sweat glands (sweat), gastric glands (acid, mucus, protease), the liver (bile), sebaceous glands (oil), and lacrimal glands (tears).

exocytosis [Section 5.3]

The secretion of a cellular product to the extracellular medium through a secretory vesicle.

exon [Section 3.4]

A nucleotide sequence in RNA that contains protein-coding information. Exons are typically separated by introns (intervening sequences) that are spliced out prior to translation.

exotoxin [Section 4.2]

A toxin secreted by a bacterium into its surrounding medium that help the bacterium compete with other species. Some exotoxins cause serious diseases in humans (botulism, tetanus, diphtheria, toxic shock syndrome).

expiration [Section 11.3]

The movement of air out of the respiratory tract. Expiration can be passive (caused by relaxation of the diaphragm and elastic recoil of the lungs) or active (caused by contraction of the abdominal muscles, which increases intraabdominal pressure and forces the diaphragm up past its normal relaxed position).

facilitated diffusion [Section 5.3]

Movement of a hydrophilic molecule across the plasma membrane of a cell, down its concentration gradient, through a channel, pore, or carrier molecule in the membrane. Because of the hydrophilic nature of the molecule, it requires a special path through the lipid bilayer.

facultative anaerobe [Section 4.2]

An organism that will use oxygen to produce energy (aerobic metabolism) if it is available, and that can ferment (anaerobic metabolism) if it is not.

FADH$_2$ [Section 2.6]
The reduced form (carries electrons) of FAD (flavin adenine dinucleotide). This is the other main electron carrier in cellular respiration (NADH is the most common).

fallopian tubes [Section 12.5]
See "uterine tubes."

fascicle [Section 10.2]
A bundle of skeletal muscle cells. Fascicles group together to form skeletal muscles.

fast block to polyspermy [Section 12.9]
The depolarization of the egg plasma membrane upon fertilization, designed to prevent the entry of more than one sperm into the egg.

feedback inhibition [Section 2.4]
Also called *negative feedback*, the inhibition of an early step in a series of events by the product of a later step in the series. This has the effect of stopping the series of events when the products are plentiful and the series is unnecessary. Feedback inhibition is the most common form of regulation in the body, controlling such things as enzyme reactions, hormone levels, blood pressure, body temperature, etc.

fermentation [Section 2.6]
The reduction of pyruvate to either ethanol or lactate in order to regenerate NAD$^+$ from NADH. Fermentation occurs in the absence of oxygen, and allows glycolysis to continue under those conditions.

fertilization [Section 12.9]
The fusion of a sperm with an ovum during sexual reproduction. In humans, fertilization typically occurs in the uterine tubes and requires capacitation of the sperm and release of the acrosomal enzymes. Fertilization is a species-specific process, requiring binding of a sperm protein to an egg receptor.

F (fertility) factor [Section 4.2]
A bacterial plasmid that allows the bacterium to initiate conjugation. Bacteria that possess the F factor are known as F$^+$ "males."

fetal stage [Section 12.11]
The period of human development beginning at eight weeks of gestation and lasting until birth (38–42 weeks of gestation). During this stage the organs formed in the embryonic stage grow and mature. The developing baby is known as a *fetus* during this time period.

fibrinogen [Section 8.4]
A blood protein essential to blood clotting. The conversion of fibrinogen to its active form (fibrin) is among the final steps in clot formation, and is triggered by thrombin.

fibroblast [Section 10.6]
A generic connective tissue cell that produces fibers; the progenitor of all other connective tissue cell types.

filtration [Section 9.2]
The movement of a substance across a membrane via pressure. In the kidney, filtration refers specifically to the movement of plasma across the capillary walls of the glomerulus, into the capsule and tubule of the nephron. Filtration at the glomerulus is driven by blood pressure.

fimbriae [Section 12.5]
Fingerlike projections of the uterine (fallopian) tubes that drape over the ovary.

first law of thermodynamics [Section 2.1]
The law of conservation of energy; the energy of the universe is constant, thus if the energy of a system increases, the energy of its surroundings must decrease, and vice versa.

flagella [Section 4.2]
A long, whip-like filament that helps in cell motility. Many bacteria are flagellated, and sperm are flagellated.

fluid mosaic model [Section 5.3]
The current understanding of membrane structure, in which the membrane is composed of a mix of lipids and proteins (a mosaic) that are free to move fluidly among themselves.

follicle [Section 12.6]

A developing oocyte and all of its surrounding (supporting) cells.

follicle stimulating hormone (FSH) [Section 7.6]

A tropic hormone produced by the anterior pituitary gland that targets the gonads. In females, FSH stimulates the ovaries to develop follicles (oogenesis) and secrete estrogen; in males, FSH stimulates spermatogenesis.

follicular phase [Section 12.7]

The first phase of the ovarian cycle, during which a follicle (an oocyte and its surrounding cells) enlarges and matures. This phase is under the control of FSH from the anterior pituitary, and typically lasts from day 1 to day 14 of the menstrual cycle. The follicle secretes estrogen during this time period.

F_1 generation [Section 6.3]

The first generation of offspring from a given genetic cross.

formed elements [Section 8.4]

The cellular elements of blood; erythrocytes, leukocytes, and platelets.

formylmethionine (fMet) [Section 3.5]

A modified methionine used as the first amino acid in all prokaryotic proteins.

frameshift mutation [Section 3.2]

A mutation caused by an insertion or deletion of base pairs in a gene sequence in DNA such that the reading frame of the gene (and thus the amino acid sequence of the protein) is altered.

Frank-Starling mechanism [Section 8.2]

A mechanism by which the stroke volume of the heart is increased by increasing the venous return to the heart (thus stretching the ventricular muscle).

functional syncytium [8.2]

A tissue in which the cytoplasms of the cells are connected by gap junctions, allowing the cells to function as a unit. Cardiac and smooth muscle tissues are examples of functional syncytiums.

gallbladder [Section 9.7]

A digestive accessory organ near the liver. The gallbladder stores and concentrates bile produced by the liver, and is stimulated to contract by cholecystokinin (CCK).

gametogenesis [Section 12.2]

The formation of haploid gametes (sperm or ova) via meiosis.

ganglion [Section 7.4]

A clump of gray matter (unmyelinated neuron cell bodies) found in the peripheral nervous system.

gap junction [Sections 5.4 and 8.2]

A junction formed between cells, consisting of a protein channel called a *connexon* on each of the two cells, that connect to form a single channel between the cytoplasms of both cells. Gap junctions allow small molecules to flow between the cells, and are important in cell-to-cell communication, for example, in relaying the action potential between cardiac muscle cells, and relaying nutrients between osteocytes.

gap phase [Section 5.5]

A phase in the cycle between mitosis and S phase (G_1) or between S phase and mitosis (G_2). During gap phases the cell undergoes normal activity and growth; G_1 may include preparation for DNA replication and G_2 includes preparation for mitosis. Note that non-dividing cells remain permanently in G_1, known as G_0 for these cells.

gastrin [Section 9.6]

A hormone released by the G cells of the stomach in the presence of food. Gastrin promotes muscular activity of the stomach as well as secretion of hydrochloric acid, pepsinogen, and mucus.

gastrulation [Section 12.11]
The division of the inner cell mass of a blastocyst (developing embryo) into the three primary germ layers. Gastrulation occurs during weeks 2-4 of gestation.

gene [Sections 3.2 and 6.1]
A portion of DNA that codes for some product, usually a protein, including all regulatory sequences. Some genes code for rRNA and tRNA, which are not translated.

gene pool [Section 6.6]
The sum of all genetic information in a population.

genetic code [Section 3.2]
The "language" of molecular biology that specifies which amino acid corresponds to which three-nucleotide group (a codon).

genome [Section 3.1]
All the genetic information in an organism; all of an organism's chromosomes.

genotype [Section 6.1]
The combination of alleles an organism carries. In a homozygous genotype, both alleles are the same, whereas in a heterozygous genotype the alleles are different.

Gibbs free energy [Section 2.1]
The energy in a system that can be used to drive chemical reactions. If the change in free energy of a reaction (ΔG, the free energy of the products minus the free energy of the reactants) is negative, the reaction will occur spontaneously.

glomerulus [Section 9.2]
The ball of capillaries at the beginning of the nephron where blood filtration takes place.

glucagon [Section 7.6]
A peptide hormone produced and secreted by the α cells of the pancreas. It targets primarily the liver, stimulating the breakdown of glycogen, thus increasing blood glucose levels.

glycogenolysis [Section 2.6]
A term for glycogen breakdown.

glycolipid [Section 5.3]
A membrane lipid consisting of a glycerol molecule esterified to two fatty acid chains and a sugar molecule.

glycolysis [Section 2.6]
The anaerobic splitting of a glucose molecule into 2 pyruvic acid molecules, producing two net ATP molecules and two NADH molecules. This is the first step in cellular respiration.

goblet cells [Section 9.5]
Unicellular exocrine glands found along the respiratory and digestive tracts that secrete mucus.

Golgi apparatus [Section 5.2]
A stack of membranes found near the rough ER in eukaryotic cells that is involved in the secretory pathway. The Golgi apparatus is involved in protein glycosylation (and other protein modification) as well as sorting and packaging proteins.

gonadotropin releasing hormone (GnRH) [Section 12.4]
A hormone released from the hypothalamus that triggers the anterior pituitary to secrete FSH and LH.

gonadotropins [Section 7.6]
Anterior pituitary tropic hormones FSH (follicle stimulating hormone) and LH (luteinizing hormone) that stimulate the gonads (testes and ovaries) to produce gametes and to secrete sex steroids.

G-protein-linked receptor [Section 5.4]
A cell surface receptor associated with an intracellular protein that binds and hydrolyzes GTP. When GTP is bound, the protein is active, and can regulate the activity of adenylyl cyclase; this modifies the intracellular levels of the second messenger cAMP. When the GTP is hydrolyzed to GDP, the protein becomes inactive again.

Graafian follicle [Section 12.6]
A large, mature, ovarian follicle with a well-developed antrum and a secondary oocyte. Ovulation of the oocyte occurs from this type of follicle.

Gram-negative bacteria [Section 4.2]
Bacteria that have a thin peptidoglycan cell wall covered by an outer plasma membrane. They stain very lightly (pink) in Gram stain. Gram-negative bacteria are typically more resistant to antibiotics than Gram-positive bacteria.

Gram-positive bacteria [Section 4.2]
Bacteria that have a thick peptidoglycan cell wall, and no outer membrane. They stain very darkly (purple) in Gram stain.

granulosa cells [Section 12.6]
The majority of the cells surrounding an oocyte in a follicle. Granulosa cells secrete estrogen during the follicular phase of the ovarian cycle.

gray matter [Section 7.4]
Unmyelinated neuron cell bodies and short unmyelinated axons.

growth hormone [Section 7.6]
A hormone released by the anterior pituitary that targets all cells in the body. Growth hormone stimulates whole body growth in children and adolescents, and increases cell turnover rate in adults.

guanine [Section 3.1]
One of the four aromatic bases found in DNA and RNA. Guanine is a purine; it pairs with cytosine.

gustatory receptors [Section 7.5]
Chemoreceptors on the tongue that respond to chemicals in food.

gyrase (DNA gyrase) [Section 3.1]
A prokaryotic enzyme used to twist the single circular chromosome of prokaryotes upon itself to form supercoils. Supercoiling helps to compact prokaryotic DNA and make it sturdier.

hair cells [Section 7.5]
Sensory receptors found in the inner ear. Cochlear hair cells respond to vibrations in the cochlea caused by sound waves and vestibular hair cells respond to changes in position and acceleration (used for balance).

haploid organism [Section 6.1]
An organism that has only a single copy of its genome in each of its cells. Haploid organisms possess no homologous chromosomes.

Hardy-Weinberg law [Section 6.6]
A law of population genetics that states that the frequencies of alleles in a given gene pool do not change over time. There are five assumptions required for this law to hold true: there must be no mutation, there must be no natural selection, there must be no migration, there must be random mating between individuals in the population, and the population must be large. A population meeting all of these conditions, in which the allele frequency is not changing, is said to be in *Hardy-Weinberg equilibrium*.

Haversian canal [Section 10.7]
See "central canal."

Haversian system [Section 10.7]
See "osteon."

hCG [Section 12.8]
Human chorionic gonadotropin; a hormone secreted by the trophoblast cells of a blastocyst (i.e., a developing embryo) that prolongs the life of the corpus luteum, and thus increases the duration and amount of secreted progesterone. This helps to maintain the uterine lining so that menstruation does not occur. The presence of hCG in the blood or urine of a woman is used as a positive indicator of pregnancy.

helicase [Section 3.3]
An enzyme that unwinds the double helix of DNA and separates the DNA strands in preparation for DNA replication.

hematocrit [Section 8.4]
The percentage of whole blood made up of erythrocytes. The typical hematocrit value is between 40–45 percent.

hematopoiesis [Section 10.5]
The synthesis of blood cells (occurs in the red bone marrow).

hemizygous gene [Section 6.5]
A gene appearing in a single copy in diploid organisms, e.g., X-linked genes in human males.

hemoglobin [Section 8.5]
A four-subunit protein found in red blood cells that binds oxygen. Each subunit contains a heme group, a large multi-ring molecule with an iron atom at its center. One hemoglobin molecule can bind four oxygen molecules in a cooperative manner.

hemophilia [Section 8.4]
A group of X-linked recessive disorders in which blood fails to clot properly, leading to excessive bleeding if injured.

hemostasis [Section 8.4]
The stoppage of bleeding; blood clotting.

hepatic portal vein [Section 8.5]
A vein connecting the capillary bed of the intestines with the capillary bed of the liver. This allows amino acids and glucose absorbed from the intestines to be delivered first to the liver for processing before being transported throughout the circulatory system.

heterotroph [Section 4.2]
An organism that cannot make its own food, and thus must ingest other organisms.

heterozygous [Section 6.1]
A genotype in which two different alleles are possessed for a given gene.

hexokinase [Section 2.6]
The enzyme that catalyzes the phosphorylation of glucose to form glucose-6-phosphate in the first step of glycolysis. This is one of the main regulatory steps of this pathway. Hexokinase is feedback-inhibited by glucose-6-P.

Hfr bacterium [Section 4.2]
High frequency of recombination bacterium. An F^+ bacterium that has the fertility factor integrated into its chromosome. When conjugation takes place, it is able to transfer not only the F factor, but also its genomic DNA.

histones [Section 3.1]
Globular proteins that assist in DNA packaging in eukaryotes. Histones form octamers around which DNA is wound to form a nucleosome.

hnRNA [Section 3.4]
Heterogeneous nuclear RNA; the primary transcript made in eukaryotes before splicing.

homeostasis [Section 9.1]
The maintenance of relatively constant internal conditions (such as temperature, pressure, ion balance, pH, etc) regardless of external conditions.

homologous chromosomes [Section 5.5]
A pair of similar chromosomes that have the same genes in the same order, but may have different versions (alleles) of those genes. One of the pair of chromosomes came from Mom in an ovum, and the other came from Dad in a sperm. Humans have 23 pairs of homologous chromosomes.

homologous structures [Section 6.8]
Physical structures in two different organisms that have structural similarity due to a common ancestor, but may have different functions. Homologous structures arise from divergent evolution.

homozygous [Section 6.1]
A genotype in which two identical alleles are possessed for a given gene. The alleles can both be dominant (homozygous dominant) or both be recessive (homozygous recessive).

humoral immunity [Section 8.7]
Specific defense of the body by antibodies, secreted into the blood by B cells.

hydroxyapatite [Section 10.7]
Hard crystals consisting of calcium and phosphate that form the bone matrix.

hyperpolarization [Section 7.2]
The movement of the membrane potential of a cell away from rest potential in a more negative direction.

hypodermis [Section 11.6]
Also called subcutaneous layer, this is a layer of fat located under the dermis of the skin. The hypodermis helps to insulate the body and protects underlying muscles and other structures.

hypophysis [Section 7.6]
The pituitary gland.

hypothalamic-pituitary portal system [Section 7.6]
A set of veins that connect a capillary bed in the hypothalamus (the primary capillary plexus) with a capillary bed in the anterior pituitary gland (the secondary capillary plexus). Releasing and inhibiting factors from the hypothalamus travel along the veins to directly affect cells in the anterior pituitary.

hypothalamus [Section 7.6]
The portion of the diencephalon involved in maintaining body homeostasis. The hypothalamus also controls the release of hormones from the pituitary gland.

H zone [Section 10.2]
The region at the center of an A band of a sarcomere that is made up of myosin only. The H zone gets shorter (and may disappear) during muscle contraction.

I band [Section 10.2]
The region of a sarcomere made up only of thin filaments. The I band is bisected by a Z line. I bands alternate with A bands to give skeletal and cardiac muscle a striated appearance. I bands get shorter (and may disappear completely) during muscle contraction.

ileocecal valve [Section 9.6]
The sphincter that separates the final part of the small intestine (the ileum) from the first part of the large intestine (the cecum). It is typically kept contracted (closed) so that chyme can remain in the small intestine as long as possible. The ileocecal valve is stimulated to relax by the presence of food in the stomach.

ileum [Section 9.6]
The final (approximately 55 percent) of the small intestine.

immunoglobulins [Section 8.7]
See "antibody."

implantation [Section 12.10]
The burrowing of a blastocyst (a developing embryo) into the endometrium of the uterus, typically occurring about a week after fertilization.

incomplete dominance [Section 6.1]
A situation in which a heterozygote displays a blended version of the phenotypes associated with each allele, e.g., pure-breeding white-flowered plants crossed with pure-breeding red-flowered plants produces heterozygous offspring plants with pink flowers.

inducible enzyme [Section 3.4]
An enzyme whose transcription can be stimulated by an abundance of its substrate.

induction [Section 12.12]
The process by which neighboring cells can influence the determination (and subsequent differentiation) of a cell.

inflammation [Section 8.5]
An irritation of a tissue caused by infection or injury. Inflammation is characterized by four cardinal symptoms: redness (rubor), swelling (tumor), heat (calor), and pain (dolor).

inhibin [Section 12.2]
A protein hormone secreted by the sustenacular cells of the testes or the granulosa cells of the ovaries that acts to inhibit the release of FSH from the anterior pituitary.

innate immunity [Section 8.7]
General, non-specific protection to the body, including the skin (barrier), gastric acid, phagocytes, lysozyme, and complement.

inner cell mass [Section 12.9]
The mass of cells in the blastocyst that ultimately give rise to the embryo and other embryonic structures (the amnion, the umbilical vessels, etc.).

inspiration [Section 11.3]
The movement of air into the respiratory tract. Inspiration is an active process, requiring contraction of the diaphragm.

insulin [Section 7.6]
A peptide hormone produced and secreted by the β cells of the pancreas. Insulin targets all cells in the body, especially the liver and muscle, and allows them to take glucose out of the blood (thus lowering blood glucose levels).

integral membrane protein [Section 5.3]
A protein embedded in the lipid bilayer of a cell. These are typically cell surface receptors, channels, or pumps.

intercalated discs [Section 8.2]
The divisions between neighboring cardiac muscle cells. Intercalated disks include gap junctions, which allow the cells to function as a unit.

intercostal muscles [Section 11.3]
Muscles located in between the ribs that play a role in ventilation.

interleukin [Section 8.7]
A chemical secreted by a T cell (usually the helper Ts) that stimulates activation and proliferation of other immune system cells.

intermediate filaments [Section 5.4]
Cytoskeletal filaments with a diameter in between that of the microtubule and the microfilament. Intermediate filaments are composed of many different proteins and tend to play structural roles in cells.

interneuron [Section 7.3]
A neuron found completely within the central nervous system. Interneurons typically connect sensory and motor neurons, especially in reflex arcs.

internodal tract [Section 8.2]
The portion of the cardiac conduction system between the SA node and the AV node.

interphase [Section 5.5]
All of the cell cycle except for mitosis. Interphase includes G_1, S phase, and G_2.

interstitial cell [Section 12.1]
Also called *Leydig cells*, these are cells within the testes that produce and secrete testosterone. They are stimulated by luteinizing hormone (LH).

intron [Section 3.4]
A nucleotide sequence that intervenes between protein-coding sequences. In DNA, these intervening sequences typically contain regulatory sequences, however in RNA they are simple spliced out to form the mature (translated) transcript.

ion channel [Section 5.3]
A protein channel in a cell plasma membrane that is specific for a particular ion, such as Na^+ or K^+. Ion channels may be constitutively open (leak channels), or regulated (voltage-gated or ligand-gated).

IPSP [Section 7.2]
Inhibitory postsynaptic potential; a slight hyperpolarization of a postsynaptic cell, moving the membrane potential of that cell further from threshold.

iris [Section 7.5]
A pigmented membrane found just in front of the lens of the eye. In the center of the iris is the *pupil*, a hole through which light enters the eyeball. The iris regulates the diameter of the pupil in response to the brightness of the light.

islets of Langerhans [Section 9.7]
Also called simply "islet cells," these are the endocrine cells in the pancreas. Different cell types within the islets secrete insulin, glucagon, and somatostatin.

jejenum [Section 9.6]
The middle (approximately 40 percent) of the small intestine.

juxtaglomerular apparatus (JGA) [Section 9.3]
A contact point between the afferent arteriole of the glomerulus and the distal convoluted tubule of the nephron. It is involved in regulating blood pressure.

juxtaglomerular cells [Section 9.3]
The cells of the afferent arteriole at the juxtaglomerular apparatus. They are baroreceptors that secrete renin upon sensing a decrease in blood pressure.

keratin [Section 11.6]
A protein-based substance secreted by cells of the epidermis as they migrate outward. The keratin makes the cells tougher (better able to withstand abrasion) and helps make the skin waterproof.

kinase [Section 2.4 and 5.4]
An enzyme that transfers a phosphoryl group from ATP to other compounds. Kinases are frequently used in regulatory pathways, phosphorylating other enzymes.

K_m [Section 2.5]
The substrate concentration required to reach $1/2\ V_{max}$; a measure of an enzyme's affinity for its substrate.

Krebs cycle [Section 2.6]
The third stage of cellular respiration, in which acetyl-CoA is combined with oxaloacetate to form citric acid. The citric acid is then decarboxylated twice and isomerized to recreate oxaloacetate. In the process, 3 molecules of NADH, 1 molecule of $FADH_2$, and 1 molecule of GTP are formed.

labia [Section 12.5]
The folds of skin that enclose the vaginal and urethral openings in females.

labor contractions [Section 12.13]
Strong contractions of the uterus (stimulated by oxytocin) that force a baby out of the mother's body during childbirth. Labor contractions are part of a positive feedback cycle, during which the baby's head stretches the cervix, that stimulates stretch receptors that activate the hypothalamus, that stimulates the posterior pituitary to release oxytocin, that stimulates strong uterine contractions (labor contractions) that cause the baby's head to stretch the cervix. The cycle is broken once the baby is delivered.

lacteals [Section 9.6]
Specialized lymphatic capillaries in the intestines that take up lipids as well as lymph.

lactic acid [Section 2.6]
Produced in muscle cells from the reduction of pyruvate (under anaerobic conditions) to regenerate NAD^+ so that glycolysis can continue. A rise in lactic acid levels usually accompanies an increase in physical activity.

lacunae [Section 10.7]
Small cavities in bone or cartilage that hold individual bone or cartilage cells.

lagging strand [Section 3.3]
The newly forming daughter strand of DNA that is replicated in a discontinuous fashion, via Okazaki fragments that will ultimately be ligated together; the daughter strand that is replicated in the opposite direction that the parental DNA is unwinding.

lag phase [Section 4.2]
A short period of time prior to exponential growth of a bacterial population during which no, or very limited, cell division occurs.

large intestine [Section 9.6]
The final part of the digestive tract, also called the colon. The primary function of the large intestine is to reabsorb water and to store feces.

larynx [Section 11.2]
A rigid structure at the top of the trachea made completely out of cartilage. The larynx has three main functions: (1) its rigidness ensures that the trachea is held open (provides an open airway), (2) the epiglottis folds down to seal the trachea during swallowing, thus directing food to the esophagus, and (3) this is where the vocal cords are found (voice production).

lawn [Section 4.2]
A dense growth of bacteria that covers the surface of a Petri dish.

Law of independent assortment [Section 6.3]
Mendel's second law. The Law of Independent Assortment states that genes found on different chromosomes, or genes found very far apart on the same chromosome (i.e., unlinked genes) sort independently of one another during gamete formation (meiosis).

Law of Segregation [Section 6.3]
Mendel's first law, also called the *Principle of Segregation*, states that the two alleles of a given gene will be separated from one another during gamete formation (meiosis).

leading strand [Section 3.3]
The newly forming daughter strand of DNA that is replicated in a continuous fashion; the daughter strand that is replicated in the same direction that the parental DNA is unwinding.

leak channel [Section 5.3]
An ion channel that is constitutively open, allowing the movement of the ion across the plasma membrane according to its concentration gradient.

length-tension relationship [Section 10.2]
The relationship of muscle length to its ability to generate strong contractions. Maximum tension (contraction strength) is achieved at sarcomere lengths between 2.0 and 2.2 microns. Tension decreases outside of this range.

leukocyte [Section 8.4]
A white blood cell; leukocytes are involved in disease defense.

Leydig cell [Section 12.1]
See "interstitial cell."

ligament [Section 10.8]
A strong band of connective tissue that connects bones to one another.

ligand [Section 5.3]
The specific molecule that binds to a receptor.

ligand-gated ion channel [Section 5.3]
An ion channel that is opened or closed based on the binding of a specific ligand to the channel. Once opened, the channel allows the ion to cross the plasma membrane according to its concentration gradient. An example is the acetylcholine receptor at the neuromuscular junction, which, when ACh binds, opens a cation channel in the muscle cell membrane.

ligase [Section 3.3]
An enzyme that connects two fragments of DNA to make a single fragment; also called *DNA ligase*. This enzyme is used during DNA replication and is also used in recombinant DNA research.

lipoproteins [Section 8.4]
Large conglomerations of protein, fats, and cholesterol that transport lipids in the bloodstream.

linkage [Section 6.4]
The failure of two separate genes to obey the Law of Independent Assortment, as might occur if the genes were found close together on the same chromosome.

lipid [Section 4.3]
A hydrophobic molecule, usually formed from long hydrocarbon chains. The most common forms in which lipids are found in the body are as triglycerides (energy storage), phospholipids (cell membranes), and cholesterol (cell membranes and steroid synthesis).

liver [Section 8.7]
The largest organ in the abdominal cavity. The liver has many roles, including processing of carbohydrates and fats, synthesis of urea, production of blood proteins, production of bile, recycling of heme, and storage of vitamins.

local autoregulation [Section 8.3]
The ability of tissues to regulate their own blood flow in the absence of neural stimulation. This is generally accomplished via metabolic wastes (such as CO_2) that act as vasodilators.

log phase [Section 4.2]
The period of exponential growth of a bacterial population.

long bone [Section 10.7]
The most common class of bone in the body, long bones have a well-defined shaft (the diaphysis) and two well-defined ends (the epiphyses).

longitudinal muscle [Section 9.5]
The outer layer of smooth muscle in the wall of the digestive tract. When the longitudinal muscle contracts, the tube shortens.

loop of Henle [Section 9.2]
The loop of the nephron tubule that dips downward into the renal medulla. The loop of Henle sets up a concentration gradient in the kidney, so that from the cortex to the renal pelvis osmolarity increases. The descending limb of the loop of Henle is permeable to water, but not to sodium, whereas the ascending limb is permeable to sodium, but not to water (and in fact, actively transports sodium out of the filtrate).

loose connective tissue [Section 10.6]
Connective tissue that lacks great amount of collagen or elastic fibers, e.g., adipose tissue and areolar (general connective) tissue.

lower esophageal sphincter [Section 9.6]
Formerly called the *cardiac sphincter*, this sphincter marks the entrance to the stomach. Its function is to prevent reflux of acidic stomach contents into the esophagus; note that it does not regulate entry into the stomach.

lumen [Section 9.5]
The inside of a hollow organ (e.g., the stomach, intestines, bladder, etc.) or a tube (e.g., blood vessels, ureters, etc.).

luteal phase [Section 12.7]
The third phase of the ovarian cycle, during which a corpus luteum is formed from the remnants of the follicle that has ovulated its oocyte. The corpus luteum secretes progesterone and estrogen during this time period, which typically lasts from day 15 to day 28 of the menstrual cycle. Formation of the corpus luteum is triggered by the same LH surge that triggers ovulation, however in the absence of LH (levels quickly decline after the surge), the corpus luteum begins to degenerate.

luteinizing hormone (LH) [Section 7.6]
A tropic hormone produced by the anterior pituitary gland that targets the gonads. In females LH triggers ovulation and the development of a corpus luteum during the menstrual cycle; in males, LH stimulates the production and release of testosterone.

lymphatic system [Section 8.6]
A set of vessels in the body that runs alongside the vessels of the circulatory system. It is a one-way system, with lymphatic capillaries beginning at the tissues and ultimately emptying into the large veins near the heart. It serves to return excess tissue fluid (lymph) to the circulatory system, and filters that fluid through millions of white blood cells on its way back to the heart.

lymph node [Section 8.6]
A concentrated region of white blood cells found along the vessels of the lymphatic system.

lymphocyte [Sections 8.4 and 8.7]
The second most common of the five classes of leukocytes. Lymphocytes are involved in specific immunity and include two cell types, B cells and T cells. B cells produce and secrete antibodies and T cells are involved in cellular immunity.

lymphokine [Section 8.7]
A chemical secreted by a T cell (usually the helper Ts) that stimulates activation and proliferation of other immune system cells.

lysogenic cycle [Section 4.1]
A viral life cycle in which the viral genome is incorporated into the host genome where it can remain dormant for an unspecified period of time. Upon activation, the viral genome is excised from the host genome and typically enters the lytic cycle.

lysosome [Section 5.2]
A eukaryotic organelle filled with digestive enzymes (acid hydrolases) that is involved in digestion of macromolecules such as worn organelles or material ingested by phagocytosis.

lysozyme [Section 4.1]
An enzyme that lyses bacteria by creating holes in their cell walls. Lysozyme is produced in the end stages of the lytic cycle so that new viral particles can escape their host; it is also found in human tears and human saliva.

lytic cycle [Section 4.1]
A viral life cycle in which the host is turned into a "virus factory" and ultimately lysed to release the new viral particles.

macrophage [Section 8.4]
A large, non-specific, phagocytic cell of the immune system. Macrophages frequently leave the bloodstream to crawl around in the tissues and perform "clean up" duties, such as ingesting dead cells or cellular debris at an injury site, or pathogens.

macula densa [Section 9.3]
The cells of the distal tubule at the juxtaglomerular apparatus. They are receptors that monitor filtrate osmolarity as a means of regulating filtration rate. If a drop is osmolarity is sensed, the macula densa dilates the afferent arteriole (to increase blood pressure in the glomerulus and thus increase filtration) and stimulates the juxtaglomerular cells to secrete renin (to raise systemic blood pressure).

maternal inheritance [Section 5.2]
Genes that are inherited only from the mother, such as mitochondrial genes (all of a zygote's organelles come only from the ovum).

matrix [Sections 2.6 and 5.2]
The interior of a mitochondrion (the region bounded by the inner membrane). The matrix is the site of action of the pyruvate dehydrogenase complex and the Krebs cycle.

mechanoreceptor [Section 7.5]
A sensory receptor that responds to mechanical disturbances, such as shape changes (being squashed, bent, pulled, etc.). Mechanoreceptors include touch receptors in the skin, hair cells in the ear, muscle spindles, and others.

medium [Section 4.2]
The environment in which or upon which bacteria grow. It typically contains a sugar source and any other nutrients that bacteria may require. "Minimal medium" contains nothing but glucose.

medulla [Section 9.2]
The inner region of an organ, e.g., the renal medulla, the ovarian, medulla, the adrenal medulla, etc.

medulla oblongata [Section 7.4]
The portion of the hindbrain that controls respiratory rate and blood pressure, and specialized digestive and respiratory functions such as vomiting, sneezing, and coughing.

meiosis [Section 6.2]
A type of cell division (in diploid cells) that reduces the number of chromosomes by half. Meiosis usually produces haploid gametes in organisms that undergo sexual reproduction. It consists of a single interphase (G_1, S, and G_2) followed by two sets of chromosomal divisions, meiosis I and meiosis II. Meiosis I and II can both be subdivided into four phases similar to those in mitosis.

melanin [Section 11.6]
A pigment produced by melanocytes in the bottom cell layer of the epidermis. Melanin production is increased on exposure to UV radiation (commonly called "tanning" and helps prevent cellular damage due to UV radiation.

memory cell [Section 8.7]
A cell produced when a B cell is activated by antigen. Memory cells do not actively fight the current infection, but patrol the body in case of future infection with the same antigen. If the antigen should appear again in the future, memory cells are like "preactivated" B cells, and can initiate a much faster immune response (the secondary immune response).

meninges [Section 7.4]
The protective, connective tissue wrappings of the central nervous system (the dura mater, arachnoid mater, and pia mater).

menopause [Section 12.8]
The period of time in a woman's life when ovulation and menstruation cease. Menopause typically begins in the late 40s.

menstruation [Section 12.7]
The first phase of the uterine (endometrial) cycle, during which the unused endometrium from the previous cycle is shed off. Estrogen and progesterone levels are low during this time period. Menstruation typically lasts from day 1 to day 5 of the cycle.

mesoderm [Section 12.11]
One of the three primary (embryonic) germ layers formed during gastrulation. Mesoderm ultimately forms "middle" structures such as the bones, muscles, blood vessels, heart, kidneys, etc.

metaphase [Section 5.5]
The second phase of mitosis. During metaphase, replicated chromosomes align at the center of the cell (the metaphase plate).

metaphase I [Section 6.2]
The second phase of meiosis I. During metaphase I the paired homologous chromosomes (tetrads) align at the center of the cell (the metaphase plate).

metaphase II [Section 6.2]
The second phase of meiosis II. Metaphase II is identical to mitotic metaphase, except that the number of chromosomes was reduced by half during meiosis I.

MHC [Section 8.7]
Major histocompatibility complex, a set of proteins found on the plasma membranes of cells that help display antigen to T cells. MHC I is found on all cells and displays bits of proteins from within the cell; this allows T cells to monitor cell contents and if abnormal peptides are displayed on the surface, the cell is destroyed by killer T cells. MHC II is found only on macrophages and B cells. This class of MHC allows these cells (known as antigen presenting cells) to display bits of "eaten" (phagocytosed or internalized) proteins on their surface, allowing the activation of helper Ts.

microfilament [Section 5.4]
The cytoskeleton filaments with the smallest diameter. Microfilaments are composed of the contractile protein actin. They are dynamic filaments, constantly being made and broken down as needed, and are responsible for events such as pseudopod formation and cytokinesis during mitosis.

microtubule [Section 5.4]
The largest of the cytoplasmic filaments. Microtubules are composed of two types of protein, α tubulin and β tubulin. They are dynamic fibers, constantly being built up and broken down, according to cellular needs. Microtubules form the mitotic spindle during cell division, form the base of cilia and flagella, and are used for intracellular structure and transport.

microvilli [Section 9.5]
Microscopic outward folds of the cells lining the small intestine; microvilli serve to increase the surface area of the small intestine for absorption.

midbrain [Section 7.4]
The portion of the brain responsible for visual and auditory startle reflexes.

milk let-down [Section 12.13]
The release of milk from the mammary glands via contraction of ducts within the glands. Contraction is stimulated by oxytocin, which is released from the posterior pituitary when the baby begins nursing.

missense mutation [Section 3.2]
A point mutation in which a codon that specifies an amino acid is mutated into a codon that specifies a different amino acid.

mitochondrion [Section 5.2]
An organelle surrounded by a double-membrane (two lipid bilayers) where ATP production takes place. The interior (matrix) is where PDC and the Krebs cycle occur, and the inner membrane contains the enzymes of the electron transport chain and ATP synthase.

mitosis [Section 5.5]
The phase of the cell cycle during which the replicated genome is divided. Mitosis has four phases (prophase, metaphase, anaphase, telophase) and includes cytokinesis (the physical splitting of the cell into two new cells).

mitral valve [Section 8.2]
See "atrioventricular valve."

monocistronic mRNA [Section 3.4]
mRNA that codes for a single type of protein, such as is found in eukaryotic cells.

morula [Section 12.9]
A solid clump of cells resulting from cleavage in the early embryo. Because there is very little growth of these cells during cleavage, the morula is only about as large as the original zygote.

motor end plate [Section 10.2]
The portion of the muscle cell membrane at the neuromuscular junction; essentially the postsynaptic membrane at this synapse.

motor unit [Section 10.2]
A motor neuron and all the skeletal muscle cells it innervates. Large motor units are typically found in large muscles (e.g., the thighs and buttocks) and produce gross movements. Small motor units are found in smaller muscles (e.g., the rectus muscles that control movements of the eyeball, the fingers) and produce more precise movements.

motor unit recruitment [Section 10.2]
A mechanism for increasing tension (contractile strength) in a muscle by activating more motor units.

mRNA [Section 3.4]
Messenger RNA; the type of RNA that is read by a ribosome to synthesize protein.

mucociliary escalator [Section 11.2]
The layer of ciliated, mucus-covered cells in the respiratory tract. The cilia continually beat, sweeping contaminated mucus upward toward the pharynx.

mucosa [Section 9.6]
The layer of epithelial tissue that lines body cavities in contact with the outside environment (respiratory, digestive, urinary, and reproductive tracts).

Müllerian ducts [Section 12.3]
Early embryonic ducts that can develop into female internal genitalia in the absence of testosterone.

Müllerian inhibiting factor (MIF) [Section 12.3]
A substance secreted by embryonic testes that causes the regression of the Müllerian ducts.

multipolar neuron [Section 7.1]
A neuron with a single axon and multiple dendrites; the most common type of neuron in the nervous system.

mutualism [Section 4.3]
A form of symbiosis in which both organisms involved benefit from the association.

myelin [Section 7.1]
An insulating layer of membranes wrapped around the axons of almost all neurons in the body. Myelin is essentially the plasma membranes of specialized cells; *Schwann cells* in the peripheral nervous system, and *oligodendrocytes* in the central nervous system.

myofiber [Section 10.2]
A skeletal muscle cell, also known as a muscle fiber. Skeletal muscle cells are formed from the fusion of many smaller cells (during development), consequently they are very long and are multinucleate.

myofibril [Section 10.2]
A string of sarcomeres within a skeletal muscle cell. Each muscle cell contains hundreds of myofibrils.

myoglobin [Section 10.2]
A globular protein found in muscle tissue that has the ability to bind oxygen. Myoglobin helps to store oxygen in the muscle for use in aerobic respiration. Muscles that participate in endurance activities (including cardiac muscle) have abundant supplies of myoglobin.

myometrium [Section 12.5]
The muscular layer of the uterus. The myometrium is made of smooth muscle that retains its ability to divide in order to accommodate the massive size increases that occur during pregnancy. The myometrium is stimulated to contract during labor by the hormone oxytocin.

myosin [Section 10.2]
One of the contractile proteins in muscle tissue. In skeletal and cardiac muscle, myosin forms the thick filaments. Myosin has intrinsic ATPase activity and can exist in two conformations, either high energy or low energy.

myosin light-chain kinase (MLCK) [Section 10.4]
A kinase in smooth muscle cells activated by calmodulin in the presence of Ca^{2+}. As its name implies, this kinase phosphorylates myosin, activating it so that muscle contraction can occur.

NADH [Section 2.6]
The reduced form (carries electrons) of NAD^+ (nicotinamide adenine dinucleotide). This is the most common electron carrier in cellular respiration.

Na^+/K^+ ATPase [Section 5.3]
A protein found in the plasma membranes of all cells in the body that uses the energy of an ATP (hydrolyzes ATP) to move three Na^+ ions out of the cell and two K^+ ions into the cell, thus establishing concentration gradients for these ions across the cell membrane.

natural selection [Section 6.7]
The mechanism described by Charles Darwin that drives evolution. Through mutation, some organisms possess genes that make them better adapted to their environment. These organisms survive and reproduce more than those that do not possess the beneficial genes, thus these genes are passed on to offspring, making the offspring better adapted. Over time, these genes (and the organisms that possess them) become more abundant, and the less beneficial genes (and the organisms that possess them) become less abundant.

negative feedback [Section 2.4]
See "feedback inhibition."

nephron [Section 9.2]
The functional unit of the kidney. Each kidney has about a million nephrons; this is where blood filtration and subsequent modification of the filtrate occurs. The nephron empties into collecting ducts, which empty into the ureter.

neurohypophysis [Section 7.6]
See "posterior pituitary gland."

neuron [Section 7.1]
The basic functional and structural unit of the nervous system. The neuron is a highly specialized cell, designed to transmit action potentials.

neuromuscular junction (NMJ) [Section 10.2]
The synapse between a motor neuron and a muscle cell. At the NMJ, the muscle cell membrane is invaginated and the axon terminus is elongated so that a greater area of membrane can be depolarized at one time.

neurotransmitter [Section 7.2]
A chemical released by the axon of a neuron in response to an action potential that binds to receptors on a postsynaptic cell and causes that cell to either depolarize slightly (EPSP) or hyperpolarize slightly (IPSP). Examples are acetylcholine, norepinephrine, GABA, dopamine, and others.

neurulation [Section 12.11]
The formation of the nervous system during weeks 5-8 of gestation. Neurulation begins when a section of the ectoderm invaginates and pinches off to form the neural groove, which ultimately forms the neural tube, from which the brain and spinal cord develop.

nociceptors [Section 7.5]
Pain receptors. Nociceptors are found everywhere in the body except for the brain.

nodes of Ranvier [Section 7.1]
Gaps in the myelin sheath of the axons of peripheral neurons. Action potentials can "jump" from node to node, thus increasing the speed of conduction (saltatory conduction).

noncompetitive inhibitor [Section 2.5]
An enzyme inhibitor that binds at a site other than the active site of an enzyme (i.e., binds at an *allosteric site*). This changes the three-dimensional shape of the enzyme such that it can no longer catalyze the reaction.

nondisjunction [Section 6.2]
The failure of homologous chromosomes or sister chromatids to separate properly during cell division. This could occur during anaphase I of meiosis (homologous chromosomes), or during anaphase II of meiosis or anaphase of mitosis (sister chromatids).

nonsense mutation [Section 3.2]
A point mutation in which a codon that specifies an amino acid is mutated into a stop (nonsense) codon.

norepinephrine (NE) [Section 7.4]
The neurotransmitter used by the sympathetic division of the ANS at the postganglionic (organ-level) synapse.

nuclear envelope [Section 5.2]
The double lipid bilayer that surrounds the DNA in eukaryotic cells.

nuclear localization sequence [Section 5.2]
A sequence of amino acids that directs a protein to the nuclear envelope, where it is imported by a specific transport mechanism.

nuclear pore [Section 5.2]
A protein channel in the nuclear envelope that allows the free passage of molecules smaller than 60 kD.

nucleolus [Section 5.2]
A region within the nucleus where rRNA is transcribed and ribosomes are partially assembled.

nucleoside [Section 3.1]
A structure composed of a ribose molecule linked to one of the aromatic bases. In a deoxynucleoside, the ribose is replaced with deoxyribose.

nucleosome [Section 3.1]
A structure composed of two coils of DNA wrapped around an octet of histone proteins. The nucleosome is the primary form of packaging of eukaryotic DNA.

nucleotide [Section 3.1]
A nucleoside with one or more phosphate groups attached. Nucleoside triphosphates (NTPs) are the building blocks of RNA and are also used as energy molecules, especially ATP. Deoxynucleoside triphosphates (dNTPs) are the building blocks of DNA; in these molecules, the ribose is replaced with deoxyribose.

nucleus [Section 5.2]
An organelle bounded by a double membrane (double lipid bilayer) called the nuclear envelope. The nucleus contains the genome and is the site of replication and transcription.

obligate aerobe [Section 4.2]
An organism that requires oxygen to survive (aerobic metabolism only).

obligate anaerobe [Section 4.2]
An organism that can only survive in the absence of oxygen (anaerobic metabolism); oxygen is toxic to obligate anaerobes.

Okazaki fragments [Section 3.3]
Small fragments of DNA produced on the lagging strand during DNA replication, joined later by DNA ligase to form a complete strand.

olfactory receptors [Section 7.5]
Chemoreceptors in the upper nasal cavity that respond to odor chemicals.

oncotic pressure [Section 8.4]
The osmotic pressure in the blood vessels due only to plasma proteins (primarily albumin).

oogonium [Section 12.6]
A precursor cell that undergoes mitosis during fetal development to produce more oogonium. These cells are the activated to produce primary oocytes, which remain dormant until stimulated to undergo meiosis I during some future menstrual cycle.

operator [Section 3.4]
A specific DNA nucleotide sequence where transcriptional regulatory proteins can bind.

operon [Section 3.4]
A nucleotide sequence on DNA that contains three elements: a coding sequence for one or more enzymes, a coding sequence for a regulatory protein, and upstream regulatory sequences where the regulatory protein can bind. An example is the lac operon found in prokaryotes.

optic disk [Section 7.5]
The "blind spot" of the eye, this is where the axons of the ganglion cells exit the retina to form the optic nerve. There are no photoreceptors in the optic disk.

optic nerve [Section 7.5]
The nerve extending from the back of the eyeball to the brain that carries visual information. The optic nerve is made up of the axons of the ganglion cells of the retina.

organ of Corti [Section 7.5]
The structure in the cochlea of the inner ear made up of the basilar membrane, the auditory hair cells, and the tectorial membrane. The organ of Corti is the site where auditory sensation is detected and transduced to action potentials.

organogenesis [Section 12.11]
The stage of human development during which the organs are formed. Organogenesis begins after gastrulation and is completed by the 8th week of gestation.

orgasm [Section 12.1]
A function of the reproductive system controlled by the sympathetic nervous system. In males, orgasm includes emission and ejaculation; in females it is mainly a series of rhythmic contractions of the pelvic floor muscles and the uterus.

origin of replication [Section 3.3]
The specific location on a DNA strand where replication begins. Prokaryotes typically have a single origin of replication, while eukaryotes have several per chromosome.

osmosis [Section 5.3]
The movement of water (the solvent) from its region of high concentration to its region of low concentration. Note that the water concentration gradient is opposite to the solute concentration gradient, since where solutes are concentrated, water is scarce.

osmotic pressure [Section 5.3]
The force required to resist the movement of water by osmosis. Osmotic pressure is essentially a measure of the concentration of a solution. A solution that is highly concentrated has a strong tendency to draw water into itself, so the pressure required to resist that movement would be high. Thus, highly concentrated solutions are said to have high osmotic pressures.

ossicles [Section 7.5]
The three small bones found in the middle ear (the *malleus*, the *incus*, and the *stapes*) that help to amplify the vibrations from sound waves. The malleus is attached to the tympanic membrane and the stapes is attached to the oval window of the cochlea.

osteoblast [Section 10.9]
A cell that produces bone.

osteoclast [Section 10.9]
A phagocytic-like bone cell that breaks down bone matrix to release calcium and phosphate into the bloodstream.

osteocyte [Section 10.6]
A mature, dormant osteoblast.

osteon [Section 10.7]
The unit of compact bone, formerly called a *Haversian system*. Osteons are essentially long cylinders of bone; the hollow center is called the *central canal*, and is where blood vessels, nerves, and lymphatic vessels are found. Compact bone is laid down around the central canal in rings (lamellae).

outer ear [Section 7.5]
The portion of the ear consisting of the pinna and the external auditory canal. The outer ear is separated from the middle ear by the tympanic membrane (the eardrum).

oval window [Section 7.5]
The membrane that separates the middle ear from the inner ear.

ovarian cycle [Section 12.7]
The 28 days of the menstrual cycle as they apply to events in the ovary. The ovarian cycle has three subphases: the follicular phase, ovulation, and the luteal phase.

ovary [Section 12.5]
The female primary sex organ. The ovary produces female gametes (ova) and secretes estrogen and progesterone.

ovulation [Section 12.6]
The release of a secondary oocyte (along with some granulosa cells) from the ovary at the approximate midpoint of the menstrual cycle (typically around day 14). Ovulation is triggered by a surge in LH.

oxaloacetate [Section 2.6]
A four-carbon molecule that binds with the two-carbon acetyl unit of acetyl-CoA to form citric acid in the first step of the Krebs cycle.

oxidation [Section 2.6]
To attach oxygen, to remove hydrogen, or to remove electrons from a molecule.

oxidative phosphorylation [Section 2.6]
The oxidation of high-energy electron carriers (NADH and $FADH_2$) coupled to the phosphorylation of ADP, producing ATP. In eukaryotes, oxidative phosphorylation occurs in the mitochondria.

oxytocin [Sections 7.6 and 12.13]
A hormone released by the posterior pituitary that stimulates uterine contractions during childbirth and milk ejection during breastfeeding.

pacemaker potential [Section 8.2]
A self-initiating action potential that occurs in the conduction system of the heart and triggers action potentials (and thus contraction) in the cardiac muscle cells. The pacemaker potential is triggered by the regular, spontaneous depolarization of the cells of the conduction system, due to a slow inward leak of positive ions (Na^+ and Ca^{2+}). Because the SA node has the fastest leak, it typically reaches the threshold for the pacemaker potential before any other region of the conduction system, and thus sets the pace of the heart.

pancreas [Section 9.7]
An organ in the abdominal cavity with two roles. The first is an exocrine role: to produce digestive enzymes and bicarbonate, which are delivered to the small intestine via the pancreatic duct. The second is an endocrine role: to secrete insulin and glucagon into the bloodstream to help regulate blood glucose levels.

pancreatic duct [Section 9.7]
The main duct of the pancreas. The pancreatic duct carries the exocrine secretions of the pancreas (enzymes and bicarbonate) to the small intestine (duodenum).

parasite [Section 4.1]
An organism that requires the aid of a host organism to survive, and that harms the host in the process.

parasympathetic nervous system
                [Section 7.4]
The division of the autonomic nervous system known as the "resting and digesting" system. It causes a general decrease in body activities such as heart rate, respiratory rate, and blood pressure, an increase in blood flow to the GI tract, and an increase in digestive function. Because the preganglionic neurons all originate from either the brain or the sacrum, it is also known as the *craniosacral* system.

parathyroid hormone (PTH) [Section 7.6]
A hormone produced and secreted by the parathyroid glands that increases serum calcium levels. It targets the bones (stimulates osteoclasts), the kidneys (increases calcium reabsorption), and the small intestine (increases calcium absorption).

parietal cells [Section 9.6]
Cells found in gastric glands that secrete hydrochloric acid (for hydrolysis of ingested food) and gastric intrinsic factor (for absorption of vitamin B_{12}).

partial pressure [Section 11.4]
The contribution of an individual gas to the total pressure of a mixture of gases. Partial pressures are used to describe the amounts of the various gases carried in the bloodstream.

passive transport [Section 5.3]
Movement across the membrane of a cell that does not require energy input from the cell. Passive transport relies on concentration gradients to provide the driving force for movement, and includes both simple and facilitated diffusion.

polymerase chain reaction (PCR)
[Section A.6]
A very quick and inexpensive method for detecting and amplifying specific DNA sequences.

penetrance [Section 6.1]
The percentage of individuals with a particular genotype that actually display the phenotype associated with that genotype.

penetration [Section 4.1]
The second step in viral infection, the injection of the viral genome into the host cell.

pepsin [Section 9.6]
A protein-digesting enzyme secreted by the chief cells of the gastric glands. Pepsin is secreted in its inactive form (pepsinogen) and is activated by gastric acid. It is unusual in that its pH optimum is around 1–2; most of the enzymes in the body function best at neutral pHs.

peptide hormone [Section 7.6]
A hormone made of amino acids (in some cases just a single, modified amino acid). Peptide hormones are generally hydrophilic and cannot cross the plasma membranes of cells, thus receptors for peptide hormones must be found on the cell surface. An exception is *thyroxine*, which is hydrophobic enough to enter the cells easily. Binding of a peptide hormone to its receptor usually triggers a second messenger system within the cell.

peptidoglycan [Section 4.2]
A complex polymer of sugars and amino acids; the substance from which bacterial cell walls are made.

peptidyl transferase [Section 3.5]
The enzymatic activity of the ribosome that catalyzes the formation of a peptide bond between amino acids. It is thought that the rRNA of the ribosome possesses the peptidyl transferase activity.

perfusion [Section 8.1]
The flow of blood through a tissue.

peripheral chemoreceptors [Section 11.3]
Receptors in the carotid arteries and the aorta that monitor blood pH to help regulate ventilation rate.

peripheral membrane protein [Section 5.3]
A protein that is associated with the plasma membrane of a cell, but that is not embedded in the lipid bilayer. Peripheral proteins typically associate with embedded proteins through hydrogen bonding or electrostatic interactions.

peripheral nervous system [Section 7.4]
All parts of the nervous system except for the brain and spinal cord.

peripheral resistance [Section 8.3]
The resistance to blood flow in the systemic circulation. Peripheral resistance increases if arteries constrict (diameter decreases), and an increase in peripheral resistance leads to an increase in blood pressure.

periplasmic space [Section 4.2]
The space between the inner and outer cell membranes in Gram-negative bacteria. The peptidoglycan cell wall is found in the periplasmic space, and this space sometimes contains enzymes to degrade antibiotics.

peristalsis [Section 9.5]
A wave of contraction that sweeps along a muscular tube, pushing substances along the tube (e.g., food through the digestive tract, urine through the ureters, etc.).

peroxisome [Section 5.2]
Small organelles that contain hydrogen peroxide produced as a byproduct of lipid metabolism. Peroxisomes convert hydrogen peroxide to water and oxygen by way of the enzyme catalase.

phagocytosis [Section 5.3]
The non-specific uptake of solid material by a cell accomplished by engulfing the particle with plasma membrane and drawing it into the cell.

pharynx [Section 11.2]
A passageway leading from behind the nasal cavity to the trachea. The pharynx is divided into three regions, named for their location. The *nasopharynx* is behind the nasal cavity, the *oropharynx* is behind the oral cavity, and the *laryngopharynx* is behind the larynx. The nasopharynx is a passageway for air only, but the oropharynx and laryngopharynx are passageways for both air and food; consequently they are lined with a much thicker layer of cells to resist damage due to abrasion.

phenotype [Section 6.1]
The physical characteristics resulting from the genotype. Phenotypes are usually described as dominant or recessive.

phosphatase [Section 2.4]
An enzyme that dephosphorylates (or removes a phosphoryl group) from a compound.

phosphofructokinase (PFK) [Section 2.6]
The enzyme that catalyzes the phosphorylation of fructose-6-phosphate to form fructose-1-6-bisphosphate in the third step of glycolysis. This is the main regulatory step of glycolysis. PFK is feedback-inhibited by ATP.

phospholipid [Section 5.3]
The primary membrane lipid. Phospholipids consist of a glycerol molecule esterified to two fatty acid chains and a phosphate molecule. Additional, highly hydrophilic groups are attached to the phosphate, making this molecule extremely amphipathic.

phosphorylase [Section 2.4]
An enzyme that transfers a free-floating inorganic phosphate to another molecule.

photoreceptor [Section 7.5]
A receptor that responds to light.

phototroph [Section 4.2]
An organism that utilizes light as its primary energy source.

pilus [Section 4.2]
A long projection on a bacterial surface involved in attachment, e.g., the sex pilus attaches F^+ and F^- bacteria during conjugation.

pinocytosis [Section 5.3]
The non-specific uptake of liquid particles into a cell by invagination of the plasma membrane and subsequent "pinching off" of a small bit of the extracellular fluid.

placenta [Section 12.10]
An organ that develops during pregnancy, derived in part from the mother and in part from the zygote. The placenta is the site of exchange of nutrients and gases between the mother's blood and the fetus' blood. The placenta is formed during the first three months of pregnancy.

placental villi [Section 12.10]
Zygote-derived projections that extend into the endometrium of the uterus during pregnancy. Fetal capillaries grow into the placental villi, which are surrounded by a pool of maternal blood. This facilitates nutrient and gas exchange between the mother and the fetus, without actually allowing the bloods to mix.

plaque [Section 4.2]
A clear area in a lawn of bacteria. Plaques represent an area where bacteria are lysing (dying) and a usually caused by lytic viruses.

plasma [Section 8.4]
The liquid portion of blood; plasma contains water, ions, buffers, sugars, proteins, etc. Anything that dissolves in blood dissolves in the plasma portion.

plasma cell [Section 8.7]
An activated B cell that is secreting antibody.

plasmid [Section 4.2]
A small, extrachromosomal (outside the genome), circular DNA molecule found in prokaryotes.

platelets [Section 8.4]
Extremely small pseudo-cells in the blood, important for clotting. They are not true cells, but are broken-off bits of a larger cell (a megakaryocyte).

pleiotropic gene [Section 6.1]
A gene that has effects on several different characteristics.

pleura [Section 11.3]
The membranes that line the surface of the lungs (visceral pleura) and the inside wall of the chest cavity (parietal pleura).

pleural pressure [Section 11.3]
The pressure in the (theoretical) space between the lung surface and the inner wall of the chest cavity. Pleural pressure is negative with respect to atmospheric pressure; this keeps the lungs stuck to the chest cavity wall.

point mutation [Section 3.2]
A type of mutation in DNA where a single base is substituted for another.

polar body [Section 12.6]
A small cell with extremely little cytoplasm that results from the unequal cytoplasmic division of the primary (produces the first polar body) and secondary (produces the second polar body) oocytes during meiosis (oogenesis). The polar bodies degenerate.

poly-A tail [Section 3.4]
A string of several hundred adenine nucleotides added to the 3' end of eukaryotic mRNA.

polycistronic mRNA [Section 3.4]
mRNA that codes for several different proteins by utilizing different reading frames, nested genes, etc. Polycistronic mRNA is a characteristic of prokaryotes.

polyspermy [Section 12.9]
The fertilization of an oocyte by more than one sperm. This occurs in some animals, but in humans, blocks to polyspermy exist (the fast block and the slow block) so that only a single sperm can penetrate the oocyte.

population [Section 6.6]
A subset of a species consisting of members that mate and reproduce with one another.

pore [Section 5.3]
A pathway through a plasma membrane that restricts passage based only on the size of the molecule. Pores are made from porin proteins.

portal system [Section 8.1]
A system of blood vessels where the blood passes from arteries to capillaries to veins, then through a second set of capillaries, and then through a final set of veins. There are two portal systems in the body, the hepatic portal system and the hypothalamic portal system.

posterior pituitary gland [Section 7.6]
Also known as the *neurohypophysis*, the posterior pituitary is made of nervous tissue (i.e., neurons) and stores and secretes two hormones made by the hypothalamus: oxytocin and ADH. The posterior pituitary is controlled by action potentials from the hypothalamus.

postganglionic neuron [Section 7.4]
In the autonomic division of the PNS, a neuron that has its cell body located in an autonomic ganglion (where a preganglionic neuron synapses with it), and whose axon synapses with the target organ.

potassium leak channel [Section 5.3]
An ion channel specific for potassium found in the plasma membrane of all cells in the body. Leak channels are constitutively open and allow their specific ion to move across the membrane according to its gradient. Potassium leak channels allow potassium to leave the cell.

power stroke [Section 10.2]
The step in the sliding filament theory during which myosin undergoes a conformational change to its low energy state, in the process dragging the thin filaments (and the attached Z lines) toward the center of the sarcomere. Note that the power stroke requires ATP only indirectly: to set the myosin molecule in its high-energy conformation during a different step of the sliding filament theory.

preganglionic neuron [Section 7.4]
In the autonomic division of the PNS, a neuron that has its cell body located in the CNS, and whose axon extends into the PNS to synapse with a second neuron at an autonomic ganglion. (The second neuron's axon synapses with the target organ.)

primary active transport [Section 5.3]
Active transport that relies directly on the hydrolysis of ATP.

primary bronchi [Section 11.2]
The first branches off the trachea. There are two primary bronchi, one for each lung.

primary immune response [Section 8.7]
The first encounter with an antigen, resulting in activated B cells (for antibody secretion) and T cells (for cellular lysis and lymphocyte proliferation). The primary immune response takes approximately ten days, which is long enough for symptoms of the infection to appear.

primary oocytes [Section 12.6]
Diploid cells resulting from the activation of an oogonium; primary oocytes are ready to enter meiosis I.

primary spermatocytes [Section 12.2]
Diploid cells resulting from the activation of a spermatogonium; primary spermatocytes are ready to enter meiosis I.

primase [Section 3.3]
An RNA polymerase that creates a primer (made of RNA) to initiate DNA replication. DNA pol binds to the primer and elongates it.

productive cycle [Section 4.1]
A life cycle of animal viruses in which the mature viral particles bud from the host cell, acquiring an envelope (a coating of lipid bilayer) in the process.

progesterone [Section 7.6]
A steroid hormone produced by the corpus luteum in the ovary during the second half of the menstrual cycle. Progesterone maintains and enhances the uterine lining for the possible implantation of a fertilized ovum. It is the primary hormone secreted during pregnancy.

prokaryote [Section 4.2]
An organism that lacks a nucleus or any other membrane-bound organelles. All prokaryotes belong to either Domain Bacteria or Domain Archea (formerly Kingdom Monera).

prolactin [Section 7.6]
A hormone secreted by the anterior pituitary that targets the mammary glands, stimulating them to produce breast milk.

proliferative phase [Section 12.7]
The second phase of the uterine (endometrial) cycle, during which the endometrium (shed off during menstruation) is rebuilt. This phase of the cycle is under the control of estrogen, secreted from the follicle developing in the ovary during this time period. The proliferative phase typically lasts from day 6 to day 14 of the menstrual cycle.

promoter [Section 3.4]
The sequence of nucleotides on a chromosome that activates RNA polymerase so that transcription can take place. The promoter is found upstream of the *start site*, the location where transcription actually begins.

prophase [Section 5.5]
The first phase of mitosis. During prophase the replicated chromosomes condense, the spindle is formed, and the nuclear envelope breaks apart into vesicles.

prophase I [Section 6.2]
The first phase of meiosis I. During prophase I the replicated chromosomes condense, homologous chromosomes pair up, crossing over occurs between homologous chromosomes, the spindle is formed, and the nuclear envelope breaks apart into vesicles. Prophase I is the longest phase of meiosis.

prophase II [Section 6.2]
The first phase of meiosis II. Prophase II is identical to mitotic prophase, except that the number of chromosomes was reduced by half during meiosis I.

proprioceptor [Section 7.5]
A receptor that responds to changes in body position, such as stretch on a tendon, or contraction of a muscle. These receptors allow us to be consciously aware of the position of our body parts.

prostate [Section 12.1]
A small gland encircling the male urethra just inferior to the bladder. Its secretions contain nutrients and enzymes and account for approximately 35 percent of the ejaculate volume.

prosthetic group [Sections 2.5 and 2.6]
A non-protein, but organic, molecule (such as a vitamin) that is covalently bound to an enzyme as part of the active site.

proximal convoluted tubule [Section 9.2]
The first portion of the nephron tubule after the glomerulus. The PCT is the site of most reabsorption; all filtered nutrients are reabsorbed here as well as most of the filtered water.

P site [Section 3.5]
Peptidyl-tRNA site; the site on a ribosome where the growing peptide (attached to a tRNA) is found during translation.

ptyalin [Section 9.6]
Salivary amylase (see "amylase").

pulmonary artery [Section 8.2]
The blood vessel that carries deoxygenated blood from the right ventricle of the heart to the lungs.

pulmonary circulation [Section 8.1]
The flow of blood from the heart, through the lungs, and back to the heart.

pulmonary edema [Section 11.4]
A collection of fluid in the alveoli of the lungs, particularly dangerous because it impedes gas exchange. Common causes of pulmonary edema are increased pulmonary blood pressure or infection in the respiratory system.

pulmonary vein [Section 8.2]
One of several vessels that carry oxygenated blood from the lungs to the left atrium of the heart.

pupil [Section 7.5]
A hole in the center of the iris of the eye that allows light to enter the eyeball. The diameter of the pupil is controlled by the iris in response to the brightness of the light.

purine bases [Section 3.1]
Aromatic bases found in DNA and RNA that are derived from purine. They have a double-ring structure and include adenine and guanine.

Purkinje fibers [Section 8.2]
The smallest (and final) fibers in the cardiac conduction system. The Purkinje fibers transmit the cardiac impulse to the ventricular muscle.

pyloric sphincter [Section 9.6]
The valve that regulates the passage of chyme from the stomach into the small intestine.

pyrimidine bases [Section 3.1]
Aromatic bases found in DNA and RNA that have a single-ring structure. They include cytosine, thymine, and uracil.

pyruvate dehydrogenase complex [Section 2.6]
A group of three enzymes that decarboxylates pyruvate, creating an acetyl group and carbon dioxide. The acetyl group is then attached to coenzyme A to produce acetyl-CoA, a substrate in the Krebs cycle. In the process, NAD^+ is reduced to NADH. The pyruvate dehydrogenase complex is the second stage of cellular respiration.

pyruvic acid [Section 2.6]
The product of glycolysis; 2 pyruvic acid (pyruvate) molecules are produced from a single glucose molecule. In the absence of oxygen, pyruvic acid undergoes fermentation and is reduced to either lactic acid or ethanol; in the presence of oxygen, pyruvic acid is oxidized to produce acetyl-CoA, which can enter the Krebs cycle.

radioimmunoassay (RIA) [Section A.2]
RIAs are similar to ELISAs but use radio-labeled antibodies rather than enzyme-linked antibodies. Thus, the presence of target proteins or antibodies is assayed by measuring the amount of radioactivity instead of a color change.

receptor-mediated endocytosis [Section 5.3]
A highly specific cellular uptake mechanism. The molecule to be taken up must bind to a cell surface receptor found in a clathrin-coated pit.

recessive [Section 6.1]
The allele in a heterozygous genotype that is not expressed; the phenotype resulting from possession of two recessive alleles (homozygous recessive).

recombination frequency (RF) [Section 6.4]
The RF value; the percentage of recombinant offspring resulting from a given genetic cross. The recombination frequency is proportional to the physical distance between two genes on the same chromosome. If the recombination frequency is low, the genes under consideration may be linked.

rectum [Section 9.6]
The final portion of the large intestine.

reduction [Section 2.6]
To remove oxygen, to add hydrogen, or to add electrons to a molecule.

reflex arc [Section 7.3]
A relatively direct connection between a sensory neuron and a motor neuron that allows an extremely rapid response to a stimulus, often without conscious brain involvement.

relative refractory period [Section 7.2]
The period of time following an action potential when it is possible, but difficult, for the neuron to fire a second action potential, due to the fact that the membrane is further from threshold potential (hyperpolarized).

release factor [Section 3.5]
A cytoplasmic protein that binds to a stop codon when it appears in the A-site of the ribosome. Release factors modify the peptidyl transferase activity of the ribosome, such that a water molecule is added to the end of the completed protein. This releases the finished protein from the final tRNA, and allows the ribosome subunits and mRNA to dissociate.

renal reabsorption [Section 9.2]
The movement of a substance from the filtrate (in the renal tubule) back into the bloodstream. Reabsorption reduces the amount of a substance in the urine.

renal tubule [Section 9.2]
The portion of the nephron after the glomerulus and capsule; the region of the nephron where the filtrate is modified along its path to becoming urine.

renin [Section 9.3]
An enzyme secreted by the juxtaglomerular cells when blood pressure decreases. Renin converts angiotensinogen to angiotensin I.

replication [Section 3.3]
The duplication of DNA.

replication fork(s) [Section 3.3]
The site(s) where the parental DNA double helix unwinds during replication.

replication bubbles [Section 3.3]
Multiple sites of replication found on large, linear eukaryotic chromosomes.

repolarization [Section 7.1]
The return of membrane potential to normal resting values after a depolarization or hyperpolarization.

repressible enzyme [Section 3.4]
An enzyme whose transcription can be stopped by an abundance of its product.

repressor [Section 3.4]
A regulatory protein that binds DNA at a specific nucleotide sequence (sometimes known as the operator) to prevent transcription of downstream genes.

residual volume [Section 11.3]
The volume of air remaining in the lungs after a maximal forced exhalation, typically about 1200 mL.

resolution [Section 12.1]
A function of the reproductive system (controlled by the sympathetic nervous system) that returns the body to its normal resting state after sexual arousal and orgasm.

respiratory acidosis [Section 11.1]
A drop in blood pH due to hypoventilation (too little breathing) and a resulting accumulation of CO_2.

respiratory alkalosis [Section 11.1]
A rise in blood pH due to hyperventilation (excessive breathing) and a resulting decrease in CO_2.

resting membrane potential [Section 5.3]
An electrical potential established across the plasma membrane of all cells by the Na^+/K^+-ATPase and the K^+ leak channels. In most cells, the resting membrane potential is approximately -70 mV with respect to the outside of the cell.

restriction endonuclease [Section A.5]
A bacterial enzyme that recognizes a specific DNA nucleotide sequence and that cuts the double helix at a specific site within that sequence.

retina [Section 7.5]
The innermost layer of the eyeball. The retina is made up of a layer of photoreceptors, a layer of bipolar cells, and a layer of ganglion cells.

retinal [Section 7.5]
A chemical derived from vitamin A found in the pigment proteins of the rod photoreceptors of the retina. Retinal changes conformation when it absorbs light, triggering a series of reactions that ultimately result in an action potential being sent to the brain.

retrovirus [Section 4.1]
A virus with an RNA genome (e.g., HIV) that undergoes a lysogenic life cycle in a host with a double-stranded DNA genome. In order to integrate its genome with the host cell genome, the virus must first reverse-transcribe its RNA genome to DNA.

reverse transcriptase [Section 4.1]
An enzyme that polymerizes a strand of DNA by reading an RNA template (an RNA dependent DNA polymerase); used by retroviruses in order to integrate their genome with the host cell genome.

ribosome [Section 3.5]
A structure made of two protein subunits and rRNA; this is the site of protein synthesis (translation) in a cell. Prokaryotic ribosomes (also known as 70S ribosomes) are smaller than eukaryotic ribosomes (80S ribosomes). The S value refers to the sedimentation rate during centrifugation.

RNA dependent RNA polymerase [Section 4.1]
A viral enzyme that makes a strand of RNA by reading a strand of RNA. All prokaryotic and eukaryotic RNA polymerases are DNA dependent; they make a strand of RNA by reading a strand of DNA.

RNA polymerase [Section 3.4]
An enzyme that transcribes RNA. Prokaryotes have a single RNA pol, while eukaryotes have three; in eukaryotes, RNA pol I transcribes rRNA, RNA pol II transcribes mRNA, and RNA pol III transcribes tRNA.

rods [Section 7.5]
Photoreceptors in the retina of the eye that respond to dim light and provide us with black and white vision.

rough endoplasmic reticulum [Section 5.2]
A large system of folded membranes within a eukaryotic cell that has ribosomes bound to it, giving it a rough appearance. These ribosomes synthesize proteins that will ultimately be secreted from the cell, incorporated into the plasma membrane, or transported to the Golgi apparatus or lysosomes.

rRNA [Section 3.5]
Ribosomal RNA; the type of RNA that associates with ribosomal proteins to make a functional ribosome. It is thought that the rRNA has the peptidyl transferase activity.

rule of addition [Section 6.3]
A statistical rule stating that the probability of either of two independent (and mutually exclusive) events occurring is the *sum* of their individual probabilities.

rule of multiplication [Section 6.3]
A statistical rule stating that the probability of two independent events occurring together is the *product* of their individual probabilities.

saltatory conduction [Section 7.1]
A rapid form of action potential conduction along the axon of a neuron in which the action potential appears to jump from node of Ranvier to node of Ranvier.

saprophyte [Section 4.3]
An organism (such as a fungus) that feeds off dead plants and animals.

sarcolemma [Section 10.2]
The plasma membrane of a muscle cell.

sarcomere [Section 10.2]
The unit of muscle contraction. Sarcomeres are bounded by Z lines, to which thin filaments attach. Thick filaments are found in the center of the sarcomere, overlapped by thin filaments. Sliding of the filaments over one another during contraction reduces the distance between Z lines, shortening the sarcomere.

sarcoplasmic reticulum (SR) [Section 10.2]
The smooth ER of a muscle cell, enlarged and specialized to act as a Ca^{2+} reservoir. The SR winds around each myofibril in the muscle cell.

Schwann cell [Section 7.1]
One of the two peripheral nervous system supporting (glial) cells. Schwann cells form the myelin sheath on axons of peripheral neurons.

sclera [Section 7.5]
The white portion of the tough outer layer of the eyeball.

sebaceous glands [Section 11.6]
Oil-forming glands found all over the body, especially on the face and neck. The product (sebum) is released to the skin surface through hair follicles.

secondary active transport [Section 5.3]
Active transport that relies on an established concentration gradient, typically set up by a primary active transporter. Secondary active transport relies on ATP indirectly.

secondary immune response [Section 8.7]
A subsequent immune response to previously-encountered antigen that results in antibody production and T cell activation. The secondary immune response is mediated by memory cells (produced during the primary immune response) and is much faster and stronger than the primary response, typically taking only a day or less. This is not long enough for the infection to become established; symptoms do not appear, thus the person is said to be "immune" to that particular antigen.

secondary oocyte [Section 12.6]
A haploid cell resulting from the first meiotic division of oogenesis. Note that the cytoplasmic division in this case is unequal, producing one large cell with almost all of the cytoplasm (the secondary oocyte) and one smaller cell with virtually no cytoplasm (the first polar body). The secondary oocyte, along with some follicular cells, is released from the ovary during ovulation.

secondary spermatocytes [Section 12.2]
Haploid cells resulting from the first meiotic division of spermatogenesis. Secondary spermatocytes are ready to enter meiosis II.

secondary sex characteristics [Section 12.4]
The set of adult characteristics that develop during puberty under the control of the sex steroids. In males the secondary sex characteristics include enlargement and maturation of the genitalia, growth of facial, body, and pubic hair, increased muscle mass, and lowering of the voice. In females, the characteristics include the onset of menstruation and the menstrual cycle, enlargement of the breasts, widening of the pelvis, and growth of pubic hair.

second law of thermodynamics [Section 2.1]
The entropy (disorder) of the universe (or system) tends to increase.

second messenger [Section 5.4]
An intracellular chemical signal (such as cAMP) that relays instructions from the cell surface to enzymes in the cytosol.

secretin [Section 9.6]
A hormone secreted by the small intestine (duodenum) in response to low pH (e.g., from stomach acid). It promotes the release of bicarbonate from the pancreas to act as a buffer.

secretion [Sections 9.5 and 9.2]

1. The secretion of useful substances from a cell, either into the blood (endocrine secretion) or into a cavity or onto the body surface (exocrine secretion).

2. In the nephron, the movement of substances from the blood to the filtrate along the tubule. Secretion increases the rate at which substances can be removed from the body.

secretory phase [Section 12.7]
The third phase of the uterine (endometrial) cycle, during which the rebuilt endometrium is enhanced with glycogen and lipid stores. The secretory phase is primarily under the control of progesterone and estrogen (secreted from the corpus luteum during this time period), and typically lasts from day 15 to day 28 of the menstrual cycle.

semen [Section 12.1]
An alkaline, fructose-rich fluid produced by three different glands in the male reproductive tract and released during ejaculation. Semen is very nourishing for sperm.

semicircular canals [Section 7.5]
Three loop-like structures in the inner ear that contain sensory receptors to monitor balance.

semiconservative replication [Section 3.3]
DNA replication. Each of the parental strands is read to make a complementary daughter strand, thus each new DNA molecule is composed of half the parental molecule paired with a newly synthesized strand.

semilunar valves [Section 8.2]
The valves in the heart that separate the ventricles from the arteries. The pulmonary semilunar valve separates the right ventricle from the pulmonary artery, and the aortic semilunar valve separates the left ventricle from the aorta. These valves close at the end of systole, preventing the backflow of blood from arteries to ventricles, and producing the second heart sound.

seminal vesicles [Section 12.1]
Paired glands found on the posterior external wall of the bladder in males. Their secretions contain an alkaline mucus and fructose, among other things, and make up approximately 60 percent of the ejaculate volume.

seminiferous tubules [Section 12.1]
Small convoluted tubules in the testes where spermatogenesis takes place.

Sertoli cells [Section 12.1]
See "sustenacular cells."

serum [Section 8.4]
Plasma with the clotting factors removed. Serum is often used in diagnostic tests since it does not clot.

sex-linked trait [Section 6.5]
A trait determined by a gene on either the X or the Y chromosomes (the sex chromosomes).

Shine-Dalgarno sequence [Section 3.5]
The prokaryotic ribosome-binding site on mRNA, found 10 nucleotides 5' to the start codon.

signal recognition particle (SRP) [Section 5.2]
A cytoplasmic protein that recognizes the signal sequences of proteins destined to be translated at the rough ER. It binds first to the ribosome translating the protein with the signal sequence, then to an SRP receptor on the rough ER.

signal sequence [Section 5.2]
A short sequence of amino acids, usually found at the N-terminus of a protein being translated, that directs the ribosome and its associated mRNA to the membranes of the rough ER where translation will be completed. Signal sequences are found on membrane-bound proteins, secreted proteins, and proteins destined for other organelles.

signal transduction [Section 5.4]
The intracellular process triggered by the binding of a ligand to its receptor on the cell surface. Typically this activates second messenger pathways.

silent mutation [Section 3.2]
A point mutation in which a codon that specifies an amino acid is mutated into a new codon that specifies the same amino acid.

simple diffusion [Section 5.3]
The movement of a hydrophobic molecule across the plasma membrane of cell, down its concentration gradient. Since the molecule can easily interact with the lipid bilayer, no additional help (such as a channel or pore) is required.

single strand binding proteins [Section 3.3]
Proteins that bind to and stabilize the single strands of DNA exposed when helicase unwinds the double helix in preparation for replication.

sinoatrial (SA) node [Section 8.2]
A region of specialized cardiac muscle cells in the right atrium of the heart that initiate the impulse for heart contraction; for this reason the SA node is known as the "pacemaker" of the heart.

sister chromatid [Section 5.5]
Identical copies of a chromosome, produced during DNA replication and held together at the centromere. Sister chromatids are separated during anaphase of mitosis.

skeletal muscle [Section 10.1]
Muscle tissue that is attached to the bones. Skeletal muscle is striated, multinucleate, and under voluntary control.

sliding filament theory [Section 10.2]
The mechanism of contraction in skeletal and cardiac muscle cells. It is a series of four repeated steps: (1) myosin binds actin, (2) myosin pulls actin toward the center of the sarcomere, (3) myosin releases actin, and (4) myosin resets to its high-energy conformation.

slow block to polyspermy [Section 12.9]
Also known as the *cortical reaction*, the slow block occurs after a sperm penetrates an oocyte (fertilization). It involves an increase in intracellular $[Ca^{2+}]$ in the egg, which causes the release of cortical granules near the egg plasma membrane. This results in the hardening of the zona pellucida and its separation from the surface of the egg, preventing the further entry of more sperm into the egg.

small intestine [Section 9.6]
The region of the digestive tract where virtually all digestion and absorption occur. It is subdivided into three regions: the duodenum, the jejunum, and the ileum.

smooth endoplasmic reticulum [Section 5.2]
A network of membranes inside eukaryotic cells involved in lipid synthesis (steroids in gonads), detoxification (in liver cells), and/or Ca^{2+} storage (muscle cells).

smooth muscle [Section 10.4]
Muscle tissue found in the walls of hollow organs, e.g., blood vessels, the digestive tract, the uterus, etc. Smooth muscle is non-striated, uninucleate, and under involuntary control (controlled by the autonomic nervous system).

soma [Section 7.1]
The cell body of a neuron.

somatic nervous system [Section 7.4]
The division of the peripheral nervous system that innervates and controls the skeletal muscles; also known as the *voluntary nervous system*.

spatial summation [Section 7.2]
Integration by a postsynaptic neuron of inputs (EPSPs and IPSPs) from multiple sources.

spermatid [Section 12.2]
A haploid but immature cell resulting from the second meiotic division of spermatogenesis. Spermatids undergo significant physical changes to become mature sperm (spermatozoa).

spermatogenesis [Section 12.2]
Sperm production; occurs in human males
on a daily basis from puberty until death.
Spermatogenesis results in the production of
four mature gametes (sperm) from a single
precursor cell (spermatogonium). For maximum
sperm viability, spermatogenesis requires cooler
temperatures and adequate testosterone.

spermatogonium [Section 12.2]
A diploid cell that can undergo mitosis to form
more spermatogonium, and can also be triggered
to undergo meiosis to form sperm.

S phase [Section 5.5]
The phase of the cell cycle during which the
genome is replicated.

sphincter of Oddi [Section 9.6]
The valve controlling release of bile and pancreatic
juice into the duodenum.

sphygmomanometer [Section 8.3]
A blood pressure cuff.

spirochete [Section 4.2]
A bacterium having a spiral shape (plural =
spirochetes).

spleen [Section 8.7]
An abdominal organ that is considered part of the
immune system. The spleen has four functions:
(1) it filters antigen from the blood, (2) it is the
site of B cell maturation, (3) it stores blood, and
(4) it destroys old red blood cells.

splicing [Section 3.4]
One type of eukaryotic mRNA processing in
which introns are removed from the primary
transcript and exons are ligated together. Splicing
of transcripts can be different in different tissues.

spongy bone [Section 10.7]
A looser, more porous type of bone tissue found
at the inner core of the epiphyses in long bones
and all other bone types. Spongy bone is filled
with red bone marrow, important in blood cell
formation.

start site [Section 3.4]
The location on a chromosome where
transcription begins.

steroid hormone [Section 7.6]
A hormone derived from cholesterol. Steroids are
generally hydrophobic and can easily cross the
plasma membranes of cells, thus receptors for
steroids are found intracellularly. Once the steroid
binds to its receptor, the receptor-steroid complex
acts to regulate transcription in the nucleus.

stomach [Section 9.6]
The portion of the digestive tract that stores
and grinds food. Limited digestion occurs in
the stomach, and it has the lowest pH in the
body (pH 1–2).

stop codon [Section 3.5]
A group of three nucleotides that does not specify
a particular amino acid, but instead serves
to notify the ribosome that the protein being
translated is complete. The stop codons are UAA,
UGA, and UAG. They are also known as *nonsense
codons*.

striated muscle [Section 10.1]
See "skeletal muscle."

stroke volume [Section 8.2]
The volume of blood pumped out of the heart in a
single beat (contraction).

submucosa [Section 9.5]
The layer of connective tissue directly under the
mucosa of an open body cavity.

substrate(s) [Section 2.3]
The reactants in an enzyme-catalyzed reaction.
Substrate binds at the active site of an enzyme.

sudoriferous gland [Section 11.6]
A sweat gland located in the dermis of the skin.
Sweat consists of water and ions (including Na^+
and urea) and is secreted when temperatures rise.

summation [Sections 7.2 and 10.2]
1. The integration of input (EPSPs and IPSPs) from many presynaptic neurons by a single postsynaptic neuron, either temporally or spatially. Summation of all input can either stimulate the postsynaptic neuron and possibly lead to an action potential, or it can inhibit the neuron, reducing the likelihood of an action potential.

2. The integration of single muscle twitches into a sustained contraction (tetany).

supercoiling [Section 3.1]
A method of DNA protection utilized by prokaryotes, in which their large circular chromosome is coiled upon itself.

surfactant [Section 11.2]
An amphipathic molecule secreted by cells in the alveoli (type 2 alveolar cells) that reduces surface tension on the inside of the alveolar walls. This prevents the alveoli from collapsing upon exhale and sticking together, thus reducing the effort required for inspiration.

sustenacular cells [Section 12.1]
Cells that form the walls of the seminiferous tubules and help in spermatogenesis. Sustenacular cells are also called *Sertoli cells*, and respond to FSH.

sympathetic nervous system [Section 7.4]
The division of the autonomic nervous system known as the "fight or flight" system. It causes a general increase in body activities such as heart rate, respiratory rate, and blood pressure, and an increase in blood flow to skeletal muscle. It causes a general decrease in digestive activity. Because all of its preganglionic neurons originate from the thoracic or lumbar regions of the spinal cord, it is also known as the *thoracolumbar* system.

symport [Section 5.3]
A carrier protein that transports two molecules across the plasma membrane in the same direction. For example, the Na^+-glucose cotransporter in intestinal cells is a symporter.

synapse [Section 7.2]
A neuron-to-neuron, neuron-to-organ, or muscle cell-to-muscle cell junction.

synapsis [Section 6.2]
Pairing of homologous chromosomes in a diploid cell, as occurs during prophase I of meiosis.

synaptic cleft [Section 7.2]
A microscopic space between the axon of one neuron and the cell body or dendrites of a second neuron, or between the axon of a neuron and an organ.

syncytium [Section 10.2]
A large multinucleate cell, typically formed by the fusion of many smaller cells during development (e.g., a skeletal muscle cell), or formed by nuclear division in the absence of cellular division.

synergist [Section 10.2]
Something that works together with another thing to augment the second thing's activity. For example, a muscle that assists another muscle is said to be a synergist. An enzyme that helps another enzyme is a synergist.

synovial fluid [Section 10.8]
A lubricating, nourishing fluid found in joint capsules.

systemic circulation [Section 8.1]
The flow of blood from the heart, through the body (not including the lungs), and back to the heart.

systole [Section 8.2]
The period of time during which the ventricles of the heart are contracted.

systolic pressure [Section 8.3]
The pressure measured in the arteries during contraction of the ventricles (during systole).

T cell [Sections 8.4 and 8.7]

A type of lymphocyte. The major subtypes of T cells are the helper T cells (CD4) and the killer T cells (CD8, or cytotoxic T cells). Helper T cells secrete chemicals that help killer Ts and B cells proliferate. Killer T cells destroy abnormal self-cells (e.g., cancer cells) or infected cells.

telencephalon [Section 7.4]

The cerebral hemispheres.

telomere [Section 5.2]

A specialized region at the ends of eukaryotic chromosomes that contains several repeats of a particular DNA sequence. These ends are maintained (in some cells) with the help of a special DNA polymerase called *telomerase*. In cells that lack telomerase, the telomeres slowly degrade with each round of DNA replication; this is thought to contribute to the eventual death of the cell.

telophase [Section 5.5]

The fourth (and final) phase of mitosis. During telophase the nuclear envelope reforms, chromosomes decondense, and the mitotic spindle is disassembled.

telophase I [Section 6.2]

The fourth phase of meiosis I. Telophase I is identical to mitotic telophase, except that the number of chromosomes is now reduced by half. After this phase the cell is considered to be haploid. Note however, that the chromosomes are still replicated, and the sister chromatids must still be separated during meiosis II.

telophase II [Section 6.2]

The fourth and final phase of meiosis II. Telophase II is identical to mitotic telophase, except that the number of chromosomes was reduced by half during meiosis I.

temporal summation [Section 7.2]

Summation by a postsynaptic cell of input (EPSPs or IPSPs) from a single source over time.

tendon [Section 10.2]

Strong bands of connective tissue that connect skeletal muscle to bone.

testcross [Section 6.3]

A genetic cross between an organism displaying a recessive phenotype (homozygous recessive) and an organism displaying a dominant phenotype (for which the genotype is unknown), done to determine the unknown genotype.

testes [Section 12.1]

The primary male sex organ. The testes are suspended outside the body cavity in the scrotum and have two functions: (1) produce sperm, and (2) secrete testosterone.

testosterone [Section 12.4]

The primary androgen (male sex steroid). Testosterone is a steroid hormone produced and secreted by the interstitial cells of the testes. It triggers the development of secondary male sex characteristics during puberty (including spermatogenesis) and maintains those characteristics during adulthood.

tetanus [Section 10.2]

A smooth sustained muscle contraction, such as occurs in skeletal muscle when stimulation frequency is high enough (this is the normal type of contraction exhibited by skeletal muscle).

tetrad [Section 6.2]

A pair of replicated homologous chromosomes. Tetrads form during prophase I of meiosis so that homologous chromosomes can exchange DNA in a process known as "crossing over."

thalamus [Section 7.4]

The central structure of the diencephalon of the brain. The thalamus acts as a relay station and major integrating area for sensory impulses.

thecal cells [Section 12.6]

A layer of cells surrounding the granulosa cells of the follicles in an ovary. Thecal cells help produce the estrogen secreted from the follicle during the first phase of the ovarian cycle.

thermoreceptor [Section 7.5]
A receptor that responds to changes in temperature.

theta replication [Section 3.3]
DNA replication in prokaryotes, so named because as replication proceeds around the single, circular chromosome, it takes on the appearance of the Greek letter theta.

thick filament [Section 10.2]
In skeletal and cardiac muscle tissue, a filament composed of bundles of myosin molecules. The myosin head groups attach to the thin filaments during muscle contraction and pull them toward the center of the sarcomere.

thin filament [Section 10.2]
In skeletal and cardiac muscle tissue, a filament composed of actin, tropomyosin, and troponin. Thin filaments are attached to the Z lines of the sarcomeres and slide over thick filaments during muscle contraction.

thrombus [Section 8.4]
A blood clot that forms in an unbroken blood vessel. Thrombi are dangerous because they can break free and begin traveling in the bloodstream (become an *embolus*). Emboli ultimately become stuck in a small vessel and prevent adequate blood delivery to tissues beyond the sticking point, leading to tissue death. A brain embolism can lead to stroke, a heart embolism to a heart attack, and a pulmonary embolism to respiratory failure.

thymine [Section 3.1]
One of the four aromatic bases found in DNA. Thymine is a pyrimidine; it pairs with adenine.

thymus [Section 8.7]
An immune organ located near the heart. The thymus is the site of T cell maturation and is larger in children and adolescents.

thyroid stimulating hormone (TSH) [Section 7.6]
A tropic hormone produced by the anterior pituitary gland that targets the thyroid gland, stimulating it to produce and release thyroid hormone.

thyroxine [Section 7.6]
Also called *thyroid hormone*, thyroxine is produced and secreted by follicle cells in the thyroid gland. It targets all cells in the body and increases overall body metabolism.

tidal volume [Section 11.3]
The volume of air inhaled and exhaled in a normal, resting breath, typically about 500 mL.

tight junction [Section 5.4]
Also called *occluding junctions*, tight junctions form a seal between cells that prevents the movement of substances across the cell layer, except by diffusion through the cell membranes themselves. Tight junctions are found between the epithelial cells lining the intestines and between the cells forming the capillaries in the brain (the blood-brain barrier).

tolerant anaerobe [Section 4.2]
An organism that can survive in the presence of oxygen (oxygen is not toxic), but that does not use oxygen during metabolism (anaerobic metabolism only).

tonsils [Section 8.7]
Paired masses of lymphatic tissue near the back of the throat that help trap inhaled or swallowed pathogens.

topoisomerase [Section 3.3]
An enzyme that cuts one or both strands of DNA to relieve the excess tension caused by the unwinding of the helix by helicase during replication.

total lung capacity [Section 11.3]
The maximum volume of air that the lungs can contain. Total lung capacity is the sum of the vital capacity and the residual volume, and is typically about 6000 mL (6 L).

totipotent [Section 12.12]
Having the ability to become anything, e.g., a zygote is totipotent.

trachea [Section 11.2]
The main air tube leading into the respiratory system. The trachea is made of alternating rings of cartilage and connective tissue.

transcription [Sections 3.2 and 3.4]
The enzymatic process of reading a strand of DNA to produce a complementary strand of RNA.

transduction [Section 4.1]
The transfer by a lysogenic virus of a portion of a host cell genome to a new host.

transition mutation [Section 3.2]
A point mutation in which a pyrimidine is substituted for a pyrimidine, or a purine is substituted for a purine.

translation [Sections 3.3 and 3.4]
The process of reading a strand of mRNA to synthesize protein. Protein translation takes place on a ribosome.

transmembrane domain [Section 5.3]
The portion of an integral membrane protein that passes through the lipid bilayer.

transverse tubule [Section 10.2]
See "T tubules."

transversion mutation [Section 3.2]
A point mutation in which a pyrimidine is substituted for a purine, or vice versa.

tricarboxylic acid (TCA) cycle [Section 2.6]
See "Krebs cycle."

tricuspid valve [Section 8.2]
See "atrioventricular valve."

tRNA [Section 3.5]
Transfer RNA; the type of RNA that carries an amino acid from the cytoplasm to the ribosome for incorporation into a growing protein.

tRNA loading [Section 3.5]
The attachment of an amino acid to a tRNA (note that this is a specific interaction). tRNA loading requires two high-energy phosphate bonds.

trophoblast [Section 12.9]
The outer ring of cells of a blastocyst. The trophoblast takes part in formation of a placenta.

tropic hormone [Section 7.6]
A hormone that controls the release of another hormone.

tropomyosin [Section 10.2]
A helical protein that winds around actin helices in skeletal and cardiac muscle cells to form the thin filament of the sarcomere. In the absence of Ca^{2+}, tropomyosin covers the myosin-binding sites on actin and prevents muscle contraction. When calcium is present, a conformational change in tropomyosin occurs so that the myosin-binding sites are exposed and muscle contraction can occur.

troponin [Section 10.2]
A globular protein that associates with tropomyosin as part of the thin filament of the sarcomere. Troponin is the protein that binds Ca^{2+}, which causes the conformational change in tropomyosin required to expose the myosin-binding sites on actin and initiate muscle contraction.

trypsin [Section 9.7]
The main protease secreted by the pancreas; trypsin is activated (from trypsinogen) by enterokinase, and subsequently activates the other pancreatic enzymes.

T-tubules [Section 10.2]
Also called *transverse tubules*, these are deep invaginations of the plasma membrane found in skeletal and cardiac muscle cells. These invaginations allow depolarization of the membrane to quickly penetrate to the interior of the cell.

tympanic membrane [Section 7.5]
The membrane that separates the outer ear from the middle ear. The tympanic membrane is also known as the *eardrum*.

umbilical cord [Section 12.10]
The cord that connects the embryo of a developing mammal to the placenta in the uterus of the mother. The umbilical cord contains fetal arteries (carry blood toward the placenta) and veins (carry blood away from the placenta). The umbilical vessels derive from the *allantois*, a structure that develops from the embryonic gut.

uniport [Section 5.3]
A carrier protein that transports a single molecule across the plasma membrane.

universal acceptor (recipient) [Section 8.4]
A person with blood type AB⁺. Because this person's red blood cells possess all of the typical blood surface proteins, they will not display an immune reaction if transfused with any of the other blood types.

universal donor [Section 8.4]
A person with blood type O⁻. Because this person's red blood cells possess none of the typical blood surface proteins, they cannot initiate an immune reaction in a recipient.

upstream [Section 3.4]
Toward the 5' end of an RNA transcript (the 5' end of the DNA coding strand). The promoter and start sites are "upstream."

uracil [Section 3.4]
One of four aromatic bases found in RNA. Uracil is pyrimidine; it pairs with adenine.

urea [Section 9.1]
A waste product of protein breakdown, produced by the liver and released into the bloodstream to be eliminated by the kidney.

ureters [Section 9.2]
The tubes that carry urine from the kidneys to the bladder.

urethra [Section 12.1]
The tube that carries urine from the bladder to the outside of the body. In males it also carries semen and sperm during ejaculation.

urinary sphincter [Section 9.2]
The valve that controls the release of urine from the bladder. It has an internal part made of smooth muscle (thus involuntary) and an external part made of skeletal muscle (thus voluntary).

uterine cycle [Section 12.7]
The shedding of the old endometrium and preparation of a new endometrium for potential pregnancy.

uterine tubes [Section 12.5]
Also called *fallopian tubes*, these tubes extend laterally from either side of the uterus and serve as a passageway for the oocyte to travel from the ovary to the uterus. This is also the normal site of fertilization. Severing of the uterine tubes (tubal ligation) results in sterility of the female.

uterus [Section 12.5]
The muscular female organ in which a baby develops during pregnancy.

vaccination [Section 8.7]
The deliberate exposure of a person to an antigen in order to provoke the primary immune response and memory cell production. Typically the antigens are those normally associated with pathogens, thus if the live pathogen is encountered in the future, the secondary immune response can be initiated, preventing infection and symptoms.

vagal tone [Section 8.2]

The constant inhibition provided to the heart by the vagus nerve. Vagal tone reduces the intrinsic firing rate of the SA node from 120 beats/minute to around 80 beats/minute.

vagina [Section 12.5]

The birth canal; the stretchy, muscular passageway through which a baby exits the uterus during childbirth.

vagus nerves [Section 7.4]

Cranial nerve pair X. The vagus nerves are very large mixed nerves (they carry both sensory input and motor output) that innervate virtually every visceral organ. They are especially important in transmitting parasympathetic input to the heart and digestive smooth muscle.

vasa recta [Section 9.3]

The capillaries that surround the tubules of the nephron. The vasa recta reclaims reabsorbed substances, such as water and sodium ions.

vas deferens [Section 12.1]

See "ductus deferens."

vein [Section 8.1]

A blood vessel that carries blood toward the heart chambers. Veins do not have muscular walls, have valves to ensure that blood flows in one direction only, and are typically low-pressure vessels.

vena cava [Section 8.2]

One of two large vessels (superior and inferior) that return deoxygenated blood to the right atrium of the heart.

venous return [Section 8.2]

The amount of blood returned to the heart by the vena cavae.

ventricle [Section 8.2]

One of two large chambers in the heart. The ventricles receive blood from the atria and pump it out of the heart. The right ventricle has thin walls and pumps deoxygenated blood to the lungs through the pulmonary artery. The left ventricle has thick walls and pumps oxygenated blood to the body through the aorta.

vestibular glands [Section 12.5]

Paired glands near the posterior of the vaginal opening that secrete an alkaline mucus upon sexual arousal. The mucus helps to reduce the acidity of the vagina (which could be harmful to sperm) and lubricates the vagina to facilitate penetration.

villi [Section 9.6]

(Singular: *villus.*) Folds of the intestinal mucosa that project into the lumen of the intestine; villi serve to increase the surface area of the intestine for absorption.

virus [Section 4.1]

A nonliving, intracellular parasite. Viruses are typically just pieces of nucleic acid surrounded by a protein coat.

vital capacity [Section 11.3]

The maximum amount of air that can be forcibly exhaled from the lungs after filling them to their maximum level, typically about 4500 mL.

vitamin [Section 9.9]

One of several different nutrients that must be consumed in the diet, and generally not synthesized in the body. Vitamins can be hydrophobic (fat-soluble) or hydrophilic (water-soluble).

vitreous humor [Section 7.5]

A thick, gelatinous fluid found in the posterior segment of the eye (between the lens and the retina). The vitreous humor is only produced during fetal development and helps maintain intraocular pressure (the pressure inside the eyeball).

voltage-gated ion channel [Section 5.3]
An ion channel that is opened or closed based on the electrical potential across the plasma membrane. Once opened, the channel allows ions to cross the membrane according to their concentration gradients. Examples are the Na^+ and K^+ voltage-gated channels involved in the action potential of neurons.

white matter [Section 7.4]
Myelinated axons.

Wolffian ducts [Section 12.3]
Early embryonic ducts that can develop into male internal genitalia under the proper stimulation (testosterone).

yolk sac [Section 12.10]
An embryonic structure particularly important in egg-laying animals because it contains the yolk, the only source of nutrients for the embryo developing inside the egg. In humans, the yolk sac is very small (since mammals get their nutrients via the placenta) and is the site of synthesis of the first red blood cells.

Z lines [Section 10.2]
The ends of a sarcomere.

zona pellucida [Section 12.6]
A thick, transparent coating rich in glycoproteins that surrounds an oocyte.

zygote [Section 12.9]
A diploid cell formed by the fusion of two gametes during sexual reproduction.

zymogen [Section 9.5]
An inactive precursor of an enzyme, activated by various methods (acid hydrolysis, cleavage by another enzyme, etc.).

NOTES

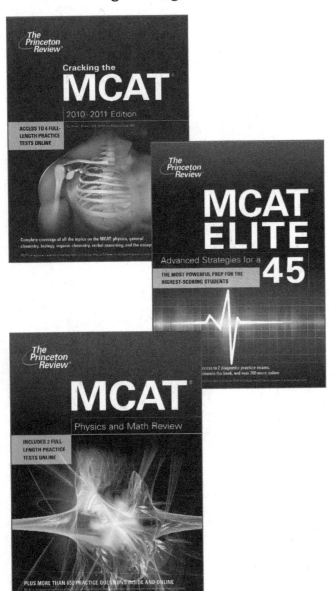